DATE DUE

JE 11 '03			

DEMCO 38-296

« « » »

The Russian Far East

The Russian Far East

« « A HISTORY » »

John J. Stephan

Stanford University Press
Stanford, California

Stanford University Press, Stanford, California
© 1994 by the Board of Trustees of the
Leland Stanford Junior University
Printed in the United States of America

Original printing 1994
Last figure below indicates year of this printing:
04   03   02   01   00   99   98   97   96

CIP data appear at the end of the book

Stanford University Press publications are distributed
exclusively by Stanford University Press within the
United States, Canada, and Mexico; they are distributed
exclusively by Cambridge University Press throughout
the rest of the world.

To
John Albert White

« « » »

Preface

This volume is an outgrowth of an interest kindled in 1964 by Professor John Albert White, who in a University of Hawaii course entitled "Siberia and the Pacific" led me to question the conventional insularity of Russian and Asian studies and to realize that Russian relations with Pacific Asia are inseparable from developments within the Russian Far East. Knowledge about the region is plentiful but fragmented. Geographers and economists have produced studies of resources, industry, trade, transport, and settlement. Anthropologists have examined aboriginal cultures. Strategists have tabulated divisions, ships, and missiles. Historians have written about exploration, revolution, foreign policy, collectivization, and labor camps. Biographers, diarists, novelists, and poets have personalized the past with varying doses of memory and imagination. Collectively these works fill several yards of shelf space, yet readers would be hard put to find anything that contemplates the Far Eastern experience holistically. As E. M. Forster once said, we know so much but connect so little.

Since the early 1970s a general history of the area has been in preparation at the Institute of History, Archaeology, and Ethnography of Peoples of the Far East in Vladivostok, until 1991 directed by Andrei Krushanov. Called by a colleague "the founder of a Far Eastern school of historiography," Krushanov was well qualified to oversee such an enterprise. For over three decades he managed a cottage industry of books, articles, and dissertations interpreting Far Eastern history in accordance with the most recent Party decree. To prepare what was envisioned as a four-volume *History of the Far East USSR*, Krushanov mobilized seventeen senior editors and over 250 specialists. Once launched, the bureaucratic supertanker moved sluggishly but gathered an inexorable momentum. The first two volumes came out well after the advent of perestroika, achieving instant historiographical obsolescence. Since then Krushanov, the Party, and the Soviet Union have passed from the scene, leaving the supertanker adrift.

While Krushanov's heirs pondered what to salvage and what to scrap, minds unencumbered by ideological ballast darted ahead into uncharted seas. Yuzhno-Sakhalinsk archivists and museum workers set up their own historical society and journal to address hitherto taboo issues about Sakhalin and the Kurile Islands. The president of the Society for Study of the Amur Region unlocked a row of skeleton-filled closets with archival keys. History buffs celebrated what they saw as the color, vigor, and piety of prerevolutionary Khabarovsk, Vladivostok, Blagoveshchensk, and Nikolaevsk. Journalists publicized names of victims and perpetrators of Stalinist terror. As the economy collapsed, however, commercial forces increasingly impinged upon habits of composition, impelling some to write for the market and forcing others to put their works "in the drawer."

This attempt at a comprehensive history of the Far East, the first in any language, represents the culmination of a quarter-century of research focusing at first on Sakhalin and the Kurile Islands and gradually widened to embrace the Priamur, the Primorye, and the Northeast (Kamchatka and Magadan districts). The sources are largely Russian, supplemented by Western, Japanese, Chinese, and Korean materials. Regional periodicals, newspapers, and interviews conducted since 1966 fill some of the lacunae in the secondary literature. The study draws from American, British, German, and Japanese archives for documentation relating to international trade, foreign communities, the Russo-Japanese War, the civil war, Allied intervention, Stalinism, frontier problems, the Second World War, and the Korean War. I did not have access to Soviet archives when the manuscript was in preparation; however, some wayward KGB files provided useful insights on the fates of Far Eastern intellectuals in the 1930s, and private archives illuminated the vicissitudes of individuals and families under tsarist and Soviet rule. The growing accessibility of repositories in Tomsk (where Far Eastern archives for 1844–1939 were relocated in 1942), Khabarovsk,

Vladivostok, Blagoveshchensk, Magadan, and Yuzhno-Sakhalinsk should enable historians to write monographs that will form the basis of a more refined synthesis. In the meantime this volume offers a preliminary and perforce rudimentary sketch of the historical architecture of a region where Europe, Asia, and America come together.

Research for this volume was greatly assisted by archivists and librarians. I am indebted to Lori Emadi, Matsui Masato, and Patricia Polansky of the University of Hawaii Library; Ron Bulatoff, Elena Danielson, Galina Dotsenko, Joseph Dwyer, Hilja Kukk, Carol Leadenheam, Molly Molloy, and Linda Wheeler of the Hoover Institution Library and Archives, Stanford, California; Wojciech Zalewski of the Stanford University Library; Laurence Miller, Dmytro Shtohryn, and Helen Sullivan of the Slavic and East European Library, University of Illinois, Urbana; Ellen Scaruffi of the Bakhmeteff Archive and Evgeny Beshenkovsky of the Harriman Institute Library at Columbia University; Edward Kasinec of the New York Public Library Slavonic Collection; Albert E. Graham, Matsumoto Hisao, and Fumi Norcia of the Library of Congress; Edward J. Boone, Jr., of the MacArthur Memorial Archives, Norfolk, Virginia; Dean C. Allard, Director of the Naval Historical Center, Washington, D.C.; Oksana Procyk of Widener Library, Harvard University; Hartmut Walravens of the Staatsbibliothek Preussischer Kulturbesitz, Berlin; Dr. Maria Keipart of the German Foreign Ministry Archives, Bonn; Akizuki Takako and Akizuki Toshiyuki of Hokkaido University Library; Robert Kvasnicka, Kathy Nicastro, John Taylor, and John Van Dereedt of the National Archives and Records Service, Washington, D.C.; Aleksandr Bukhreyev and Alla Milyenina of the Khabarovsk Regional Library; Nina Ivantsova and Tatyana Matveyeva of the Primorye Regional Library, Vladivostok; Lyudmila Kazarinova of the State Scientific and Technical Library, Novosibirsk; and Zoya Sorokina of the Lenin Library, Moscow.

The following people generously gave their time and expertise: Jan Albers, George Akita, Terence Armstrong, Olga Bakich, the late Pyotr Balakshin, Edward Beauchamp, Nikolai Bolkhovitinov, Cyril Bryner, the late O. Edmund Clubb, David Collins, the late Violet Conolly, Alvin D. Coox, Alexander Dallin, Basil Dmytryshyn, the late Paul Dotsenko, Terence Emmons, Robert Fahs, Victor Fischer, James Forsyth, Grover C. Furr, J. Arch Getty, James R. Gibson, Paul A. Goble, Bruce Grant, Hara Teruyuki, Hasegawa Tsuyoshi, Jonathan Haslam, Hata Ikuhiko, Hora Tomio, Juha Janhunen, John M. Jennings, Katō Kyūzō, Kimura Hiroshi, Gunnar

Knapp, the late George A. Lensen, G. Patrick March, Steven G. Marks, Martha Mautner, Elisa Miller, Victor L. Mote, John Curtis Perry, Richard A. Pierce, E. Bruce Reynolds, Boris Z. Rumer, John Charles Schencking, Ulrich Schweinfurth, the late Theodore Shabad, Canfield F. Smith, Judith Thornton, John Tichotsky, Toda Yasushi, Donald W. Treadgold, Elizabeth Vaughan, Thomas Vaughan, Allen S. Whiting, Ella Wiswell, David Wolff, and Xu Jingxue. I am grateful to Ban Byung-yool, Kim Ki-hoon, and Suh Dae-sook, who pointed out and translated Korean sources; to Tao Tienyi, who translated passages from a Qing travel diary; and to Jane Eckelman, who prepared the maps. I should also like to thank those who have critiqued all or part of the manuscript: Mark Bassin, Robert Conquest, John Erickson, Amir Khisamutdinov, Robert Valliant, Robert E. Weinberg, and two anonymous readers for Stanford University Press, where Muriel Bell, Peter J. Kahn, and Barbara Mnookin provided valuable editorial guidance.

Visits to Russia since 1959, and to the Far East since 1966, have left a legacy of indebtedness to the late Boris Alyonkin, Evgeniya Alyonkina, Aleksandr Bechtold, Vera Belashko, Natasha Bezruchko, the late Nikolai Bilim, the late Yury Borshchevsky, Kirill Cherevko, Valery Chichkanov, Elena Chukovskaya, Elena Demidova, Georgy Derzhavin, the Derzhavin family (Igor, now deceased, Tatiana, Sergei, and Lena), Galina Dudarets, Evdokiya Gayer, Viktor Goncharenko, Vladimir Ivanov, Andrei Kalachinsky, the Kharlamov family (Viktor, Valentina, Svetlana, and Lena), Vladimir Khokhlov, Yuri Kochanovsky, Aleksandr Kostanov, Yury Kosygin, Evgeny Kovrigin, Vladislav Latyshev, Ilya Lerman, Igor Litvinenko, Aleksandr Lopachev, the late Aleksandr Makarov, the late Mikhail Masiuk, Aleksandra Maslova, Pavel Minakir, Anatoly Mizyun, Natasha Nazarenko, Valery Pereslavtsev, Dmitry Petrov, Boris Polevoi, Nikolai Romanovsky, Sergei Saktaganov, Valery Simakov, Boris Slavinsky, Valery Slyusarev, Mikhail Svetachev, the late Innokenty Tuezov, Mikhail Vysokov, Lidiya Zhukova, Irina Zhulpa, and Klara Zilova.

My wife Barbara and family have been more supportive than words can convey.

Research was assisted by the International Research and Exchanges Board (IREX), the U.S. National Academy of Sciences, the Kennan Institute for Advanced Russian Studies, the Japan Foundation, the Far Eastern Division of the Soviet (now Russian) Academy of Sciences, and the North Pacific Program of the Fletcher School of Law and Diplomacy, Tufts University.

Russian words are transliterated by the Library of Congress system in the Notes and Select Bibliography. In the text apostrophes denoting hard and soft signs are omitted; *g* is represented by *v* in "evo" and "ovo"; *ii, ia, io, iu,* and *e* are written *y, ya, yo, yu,* and *ye*. Japanese words are romanized by the modified Hepburn system of *Kenkyusha's New Japanese-English Dictionary* (Tokyo: Kenkyūsha, 1954). Chinese words are represented in *pinyin*, except for authors who have published under the Wade-Giles rendering. Chinese, Japanese, and Korean surnames precede given names. For well-known names and words (G. F. Müller, N. N. Muraviev, V. K. Blücher, Chiang Kai-shek, Kwantung Army, Politburo, etc.) I have used the conventional spelling. Brief biographies of selected figures in the text are given in Appendix D. Dates follow the Gregorian calendar.

Although many have contributed to this volume, the author bears responsibility for any shortcomings.

J. J. S.

Honolulu
July 1993

« « » »

Contents

PART III «» THE SOVIET FAR EAST

Appendixes

14 pages of photographs follow p. 50
10 pages of photographs follow p. 156

« « » »

Maps and Illustrations

Maps

Illustrations following p. 50

1. Tortoise and stelae in front of Khabarovsk Museum, ca. 1918
2. Tortoise with stelae removed, 1972
3. Gennady Nevelskoi
4. Nikolai Muraviev-Amursky
5. Monument to Muraviev-Amursky, Khabarovsk, ca. 1910
6. Lenin on Muraviev's pedestal, Khabarovsk, 1972
7. Orochen Youth with Ussuri tiger trophies

Illustrations following p. 156

Sources of Illustrations

1, 8, 9, 10, 11, 13, 14, Wladimir Arsenjew, *Russen und Chinesen in Ostsibirien* (Berlin, 1926); **3,** A. I. Alekseev, *Amurskaia ekspeditsiia* (Moscow, 1974); **4,** Richard Maak, *Puteshestvie na Amur* (St. Petersburg, 1859); **5, 7, 12, 18,** *Aziatskaia Rossiia* (St. Petersburg, 1914); **15,** courtesy of Valery Slyusarev; **16,** W. P. Hammon Collection, Hoover Institution Archives; **17,** Siberian calendar (1897); **19, 24, 25, 26, 32,** Rodney Sprigg Collection, Hoover Institution Archives; **20,** *Krasnoznamennyi Tikhookeanskii flot* (Moscow, 1981); **21,** V. N. Jernakov, *Nikolai Apollonovich Baikov* (Melbourne, 1968), courtesy of Nina Christesen; **22,** V. K. Arsen'ev, *Skvoz taigu* (Moscow, 1949); **23,** Henry Kittredge Norton, *The Far Eastern Republic* (New York, 1927); **27, 34, 35,** Walter Grayson Collection, Hoover Institution Archives; **28, 30,** Isadore Yelsky Collection, Hoover Institution Archives; **29, 47,** National Archives; **31,** American Red Cross, courtesy Sarah Mathews, Hoover Institution Archives; **33,** George Montandon, *Deux ans chez Koltchak et chez les Bolcheviques* (Paris, 1923); **36,** E. G. Vishnevskii, *Argonavtsy beloi mechty* (Harbin, 1933); **37,** *Pervopokhodnik*, no. 17 (February 1974); **38,** *Sibirskaia sovetskaia entsiklopediia*, 2 (Novosibirsk, 1930); **39, 49, 50** *Dal'nevostochnyi pogranichnyi* (Khabarovsk, 1983); **40,**

Forpost geroev (Khabarovsk, 1976); **41,** *Narody Azii i Afriki* (Moscow, 1971); **42,** *Sovety Severo-Vostoka SSSR* (Magadan, 1979); **43,** *Stalin* (Moscow, 1939); **44,** courtesy of Asahi Shimbunsha; **45,** N. M. Pegov, *Dalekoe i blizkoe* (Moscow, 1982); **46,** *Sovietland,* 1939, no. 2; **48,** courtesy of Boris Slavinsky; **51,** E. A. Kandala, *Stoiat na Amure russkie sela* (Khabarovsk, 1986); **52,** courtesy of John Tichotsky.

« « » »

Text Abbreviations and Acronyms

The following abbreviations and acronyms are used throughout (for other abbreviations used in the back matter see Notes p. 355 and Select Bibliography p. 415):

AKO	Kamchatka Company (1924–36)
BAM	Baikal-Amur Mainline
CC	Central Committee
CER	Chinese Eastern Railway
Cheka	State security organ (20 Dec. 1917–6 Feb. 1922)
CHON	Special purpose units (1920–24)
CPSU	Communist Party of the Soviet Union (1952–91)
Dalbank	Far Eastern State Bank (1923–31)
Dalbiuro	Far Eastern Bureau of the RKP(b) (1920–25)
Dalintorg	Far Eastern Trade Organization (1965–)
Dalkrai	Far Eastern region (1926–38)
Dalkraiispolkom	Far Eastern Executive Committee (1926–38)
Dalkraikom	Far Eastern Regional Committee of the VKP(b) (1926–38)

Dalrevkom	Far Eastern Revolutionary Committee (1920–25)
Dalsovnarkom	People's Commissariat of Far Eastern Soviets (1917–18)
Dalstroi	Far Eastern Construction Trust (1931–57)
DOSAAF	All-Union Volunteer Society for Assistance to the Army, Aviation and Fleet (1951–91)
DVGU	Far Eastern State University (1920–39, 1956–)
FER	Far Eastern Republic (1920–22)
FESCO	Far Eastern Steamship Company (1957–)
GPO	Far Eastern branch of the Cheka/GPU (1920–22)
GPU	State security organ (6 Feb. 1922–1 Nov. 1923)
IKOR	American Association for Jewish Colonization in the Soviet Union
kraikom	Regional Party committee
kraiispolkom	Regional executive committee
KSP	Ploughed frontier perimeter ("control tracking strip")
MGB	Ministry of State Security (26 Feb. 1946–June 1953)
MVD	Ministry of Internal Affairs (26 Feb. 1946–)
NEP	New Economic Policy (1921–28)
NKVD	State Security organ (10 July 1934–25 Feb. 1946)
NRA	People's Revolutionary Army (1920–22)
obkom	District Party committee
OGPU	State security organ (2 Nov. 1923–10 July 1934)
OKDVA	Special Red-Bannered Far Eastern Army (1930–38)
RKP(b)	Russian Communist Party (of Bolsheviks) (1918–25)
RSDRP	Russian Social Democratic Workers' Party (1898–1917)
RSDRP(b)	Russian Social Democratic Workers' Party (of Bolsheviks) (Apr. 1917–Mar. 1918)
RSFSR	Russian Soviet Federated Socialist Republic
Sevvostlag	Colloquial appellation for USVITL
Sibbiuro	Siberian Bureau of the RKP(b) (1918–24)
SR	Socialist Revolutionary

Tsentrosibir	Central Executive Committee of Siberian Soviets (1917–18)
USVITL	Northeast Corrective Labor Camp Administration (1932–53)
VKP(b)	All-Union Communist Party (of Bolsheviks) (1925–52)

« « » »

The Russian Far East

« « » »

Introduction

Wedged between China, Korea, Japan, and the United States, the Russian Far East has emerged as a volatile arena where forces that tore apart the former Soviet Union interact with dynamics energizing Pacific Asia. A once supine appanage of the Center (Moscow, St. Petersburg, Petrograd, as the case may be) is redefining itself in both Russian and Northeast Asian contexts under the banners of capitalism and regionalism. As closed frontiers give way to entrepreneurial enclaves, some Far Easterners are articulating autonomist aspirations. Such assertiveness endows the Far East with a robust topicality that in turn nurtures our susceptibility to what Russian wits call the "illusion of stormy activity."

Visualizing the Far East requires a tolerance for ambiguity. Located at the interstices of conventionally defined regions, it awkwardly straddles parts of the Russian Republic, Northeast Asia, and the North Pacific. Moreover, it lacks a clearly defined periphery. At once within and distinct from Siberia, at once connected with and separate from China, Japan, and Korea, the Far East is a matrix of overlapping borderlands. To contemplate the Far East exclusively through either Eurocentric or Asiacentric prisms is to don blinkers. Just as we need to use both eyes for three-dimensional vision, so we need both Asian and Russian perspectives to behold the Far East in all its manifold identities.

Distinctions between domestic and foreign policy break down when applied to the Far East. Seen from metropolitan Russia, the Far East was variously a distant periphery, a colony, and a strategic base. Yet for those who lived there, the Far East had its own political, economic, and social dynamics. Local officials implemented and at times took initiatives toward Asia-Pacific neighbors. One governor-general negotiated an international treaty that altered Russia's frontiers. The Far East's relations with China, Japan, and Korea were not altogether unlike those between Texas and Mexico.

Ironically, the Far East's cosmopolitan past bequeathed a parochial historiography. Linguistic barriers, intellectual conventions, and political agendas have insulated Russian, Soviet, Chinese, Japanese, and Western writing about the region. Post-Soviet authors have yet to free themselves from the habit of retrospectively russifying the record of Far Eastern discovery, colonization, and development. Nor are Chinese and Japanese works entirely free of national pretensions and irredentist subtexts. For their part, Western slavicists trained in a Eurocentric tradition tend to marginalize the Far East or to lose sight of it in Siberia.

The Far East has been a meeting ground for diverse peoples and cultures for many centuries. Long before the dawn of recorded history, Northeast Asia served as a bridge for migrations between Inner Asia and North America. Neolithic communities in the Priamur and the Primorye shared affinities with counterparts in China, Korea, Japan, Siberia, and North America. A millennium of Chinese suzerainty and some 300 years of Russian rule added new hues to a kaleidoscopic demography. Infusions of Mongols, Chinese, Koreans, and Japanese formed layers over a Paleosiberian and Tungusic aboriginal base. Immigrants from Europe and Asia created a mosaic of Chinese, Korean, Japanese, Russian, Ukrainian, Cossack, Polish, German, Finnish, and Estonian communities.

Cultural diversity did not prevent the Far East from acquiring a coherent regional identity after the creation of a unified administration in 1884. Russian penetration of northeastern China after 1896 sensitized Far Eastern merchants, professional people, journalists, and even military officers to divergences between imperial and regional interests. This awareness found scope for expression as metropolitan power collapsed during two revolutions, civil war, and foreign intervention, culminating in the creation of the Far Eastern Republic (FER) in 1920. Although the FER was absorbed into Soviet Russia in 1922, outlying areas retained their autonomy for two or more years. Meanwhile, a cohort of former partisans, Party underground workers, and FER officials formed regional networks. The failure of the central Party apparatus to control these networks converged with Japanese continental expansion after 1931 to invoke the specter of Far Eastern secession in conjunction with "traitors" (Trotskyists, Rightists, Red Army commanders). Stalin and his entourage exorcised the specter by balkanizing the regional administration, gelding the regional economy, and annihilating regional elites.

What went wrong in the Far East? Why did it not develop like British Columbia or Hokkaido? How did such a rich land and littoral, settled by such talented and hard-working people, and bordering on such dynamic economies present a spectacle redolent of a Third World basket case? Geography, demography, and economics provide partial answers. Beneath unfulfilled potentials runs an undercurrent of tragedy that cannot be ascribed to any ideology, party, or regime. The tragedy has a Russian-Soviet mother and an Asian-American father. Both parents wrought havoc on the region with the best of intentions: oppression in the name of progress, militarization in the name of security, homicide in the name of race or class, ecocide in the name of growth. These destructive forces welled up from below as much as they descended from above. Thousands of ordinary people betrayed the land and one another out of idealism, envy, spite, greed, or fear. The Far East's sociocultural chemistry and geostrategic environment gave it a special place within Russia's tragedy.

Far Eastern history casts in sharp relief human resilience in the face of adversity. Adversity on Russia's eastern periphery has commonly been defined in terms of climate, isolation, and coercion. But adversity also took the form of exposure to the magnetic field of politically prescribed collective action. From the Primorye to Chukotka, individuals of different backgrounds kept their consciences intact in a political culture that turned the masses into accomplices. Although their behavior was not always consistent and their motives not always unambiguous, these people left accounts of what they saw, heard, and endured. From beneath the rubble of Marxism-Leninism and socialist realism is emerging testimony of compelling authenticity and power. Diaries, memoirs, letters, and family chronicles suggest how different were individual experiences of settlement, revolution, war, foreign intervention, collectivization, terror, stagnation, and perestroika. By rescuing such diversity from oblivion, this testimony opens the vaults of memory and holds up a mirror of self-knowledge.

PART I

Northeast Asian Ecumene

1

« « » »

Geography and Prehistory

Don't let them scare you about land ending here. Sakhalin
is out there, and our planet's a sphere.
— Vladimir Vysotsky (1963)

Our imagination does not readily vi-
sualize the Russian Far East in ei-
ther Asia or Europe, although history if not geography suggests that it is part
of both.[1] Simultaneously comprising the northern periphery of East Asia
and the eastern periphery of the Russian Republic, it has an elasticity inher-
ent in the Russian term *Dalny Vostok*, which can refer to anything from a
province to half the world. Russia's Far Eastern realm expanded and contracted over the course of over 350 years, leaving a legacy of intermittently
contentious frontiers with indigenous Northeast Asian polities (China,
Korea, Japan) and with a relative newcomer to the region — the United
States. A Russian presence in Manchuria during 1896–1954 amounted to an
extension of the Far East into China. Administrative vagaries have obscured
the Far East's internal contours by including or excluding Yakutia and Transbaikalia.* In some contexts the entire Far East vanishes into Siberia's ca-
pacious embrace.

This study focuses on the Far Eastern core, an area of 1,201,400 square
miles embracing the Priamur, the Primorye, the Okhotsk seaboard, Kamchatka, Chukotka, Sakhalin, and the Kurile Islands (see Map 1). Yakutia,
Transbaikalia, Russian America, and Manchuria receive attention to the
extent that events transpiring in these areas have impinged on the core,

*Transbaikalia and parts of Yakutia were periodically administered as part of the Far East
before the Second World War. Since 1963, Yakutia has been in the Far Eastern Economic
Region. Transbaikalia is in the Far Eastern Military District.

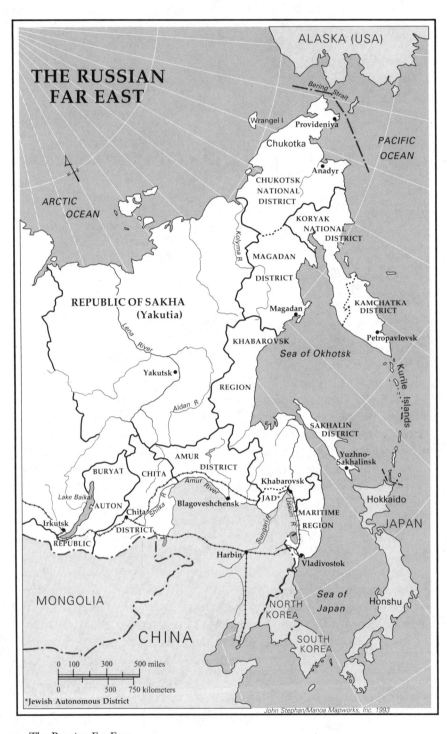

THE RUSSIAN FAR EAST

ALASKA (USA)

Bering Strait

ARCTIC
OCEAN

PACIFIC
OCEAN

Wrangel I.   Provideniya

Chukotka

Anadyr

CHUKOTSK
NATIONAL
DISTRICT

KORYAK
NATIONAL
DISTRICT

Kolyma R.

MAGADAN

DISTRICT

REPUBLIC OF SAKHA
(Yakutia)

Magadan

KAMCHATKA
DISTRICT

KHABAROVSK

Sea of Okhotsk

Petropavlovsk

Lena River

Yakutsk

REGION

Aldan R.

Kurile Islands

SAKHALIN
DISTRICT

AMUR   DISTRICT

Yuzhno-
Sakhalinsk

BURYAT   CHITA

Amur River

Khabarovsk

Lake Baikal   AUTON

Shilka R.

Chita

Blagoveshchensk

JAD*

Hokkaido

Irkutsk

DISTRICT

Sungari R.

Ussuri R.

MARITIME
REGION

JAPAN

REPUBLIC

Harbin

Vladivostok

MONGOLIA

NORTH
KOREA

*Sea of
Japan*

Honshu

CHINA

SOUTH
KOREA

0 100   300   500 miles

0   500   750 kilometers

*Jewish Autonomous District

John Stephan/Manoa Mapworks, Inc. 1993

1. The Russian Far East

which formed a single administrative unit for all but eighteen months from 1884 until 1938.

Environments

Extending roughly 3,000 miles from north to south and 2,000 miles from east to west, the Far East has a wide variety of environments. The Sea of Japan, the Sea of Okhotsk, the Arctic Ocean, and the Pacific give the Far East's 16,000-mile littoral a range of maritime climates shaped by latitude, winds, and currents. Chukotka's stark scenery recalls that of northwestern Alaska, and the Primorye's green coastal hills are not unlike those of northern California. The warm *kuroshio* current combines with geothermally heated beaches to produce a "Kurile Riviera" on Kunashir Island. The southern Primorye is generally credited with the most liveable climate. Vladivostok has comparatively mild winters, and residents are fond of saying that their town has more sunny days than the Black Sea resort of Sochi. True enough, but its summer humidity rivals that of Calcutta.

The Far Eastern interior, separated from the Pacific rim by mountains of 3,000 to 5,000 feet, has a continental climate, with hotter summers, colder winters, and less rain and snow than the littoral. Seasonal temperatures go to extremes. Yakutia holds the world record for cold outside of Antarctica. When the mercury there falls below minus 50 degrees Fahrenheit, alcohol thickens, steel cracks like glass, and exhaled breath turns to ice. Conversely, the August sun in Transbaikalia has been known to carbonize roof shingles.

The Sikhote Alin Range ("Far Eastern Urals") divides the Primorye into two ecological zones (see Map 2), each shaped by Asian monsoon winds blowing alternately from Siberia (October to May) and the Sea of Japan (June to September). The eastern, maritime slopes of the Sikhote Alin are favored with warmer winters, more flowers, and fewer mosquitoes than the western (continental) slopes. Climatic differentiations occur among the hills of Vladivostok, which like San Francisco has its own microclimates. Fog may shroud the Golden Horn, the city's main harbor, when Amur Bay beaches across town are bathed in sunshine.

The Ussuri taiga sustains a rich flora and fauna. Siberian conifers and birch are joined by oak, maple, walnut, and Korean cedar. Ginseng and tigers thrive in the Sikhote Alin Range. The former attracted people; the latter ate them, if one is to believe lore about peasants being pulled through izba windows and soldiers being snatched from marching columns.[2] In

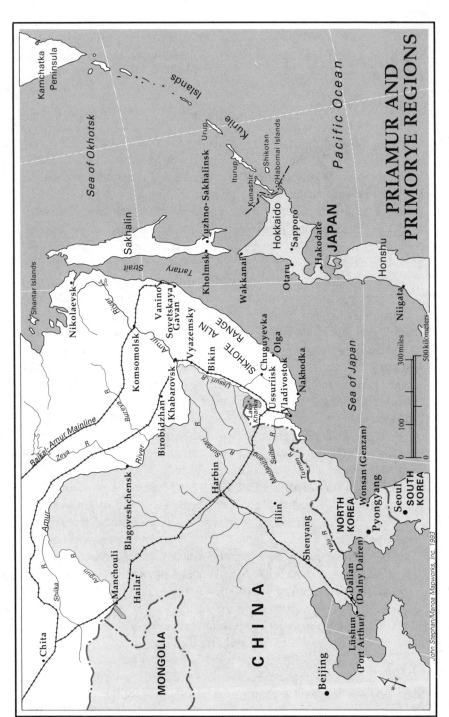

2. Priamur and Primorye Regions

point of fact, tigers disconcerted rather than devoured nineteenth-century settlers. Unaccustomed to sharing space with humans, they prowled around farms and occasionally made themselves at home in outdoor privies and bathhouses. Although buttons and a butterfly net were all that was left of an unlucky German lepidopterist in 1914,[3] fang-toothed felines were more partial to puppies. Dogs vanished from the streets of Vladivostok in the 1860s, guaranteeing a niche for their predators in municipal nomenclature (Tiger Street, Tiger Hill, etc.). Hunted to the verge of extinction by the 1950s, Ussuri tigers rebounded as a protected species, confirmed by paw prints and telltale canine remains in Vladivostok as late as 1986. In the early 1990s, however, their numbers again fell as poachers catered to the Chinese market for tiger skins.[4]

Nature has richly endowed the Far East with boons and banes to man. Timber, minerals, fish, and pests abound. Ubiquitous lakes and swamps offer ideal breeding grounds for vexatious insects. In Yakutia, mosquitoes (locally nicknamed "fascists") are said to suffocate reindeer by swarming up their nostrils. Clouds of *gnus* ("vile"), a collective sobriquet for winged piranha (gnats, midges, horseflies), have halted construction projects in the taiga.

Nature in the Far East destroys on a spectacular scale. Unlike Siberian rivers, the Amur does not flow into the Arctic Ocean. Benefits accruing from this circumstance are periodically negated when, swollen by melting snow and monsoon rains, the "Russian Mississippi"[5] turns into an inland sea and inundates thousands of square miles. Far Easterners respect *Amur batyushka* ("Father Amur") and watch its moods, especially in August when they follow water-level bulletins with the avidity of stock market brokers. When not flooded, the taiga can burn. In the summer of 1987 a conflagration along the upper Amur devastated an area four times the size of Austria. Kamchatka and the Kuriles regularly experience volcanic eruptions, earthquakes, and tidal waves. In 1952 a fifty-foot tsunami demolished a town on Paramushir Island in the Kuriles.

Permafrost covers 70 percent of the Far East, leaving a deep imprint on local lifestyles and severely restricting development. Within the zone the earth is frozen to a depth of anywhere from three feet to a mile below the surface. To deal with the "active layer" (the upper six to ten feet, which melts and refreezes seasonally), structures must be kept off the ground by pylons, and streets must have special roadbeds. Permafrost does have advantages. Water can be transported without pipes simply by drilling passages in the frozen ground, and in rain-scarce Yakutia permafrost retains groundwater essential to vegetation.

Nature has determined patterns of human settlement. In the Far East, as in Canada, people have traditionally clustered on arable lands along the southern fringe. As a result most Far Easterners have lived close to the frontiers of China, Korea, and Japan, a circumstance that has accentuated both cosmopolitan and xenophobic sensibilities.

Prehistory

The Far East could be the oldest part of Asia. Crystalline rock in northern Yakutia has been identified as the nucleus around which the continent formed nearly four billion years ago.[6] Two to three million years ago, magmatic activity at the juncture of continent and ocean formed Kamchatka and the Kurile Islands.

A million years ago, Northeast Asia had a temperate climate. Grass covered Chukotka, and conifers and chestnut trees grew on Kamchatka.[7] Starting about 500,000 years ago, a series of ice ages turned arctic grasslands into tundra and left the Priamur and the Primorye as taiga supporting mammoths, bears, tigers, and elk. By absorbing water, glaciers lowered the sea level so that land bridges formed from Korea along the Japanese archipelago and Chukotka to North America.[8]

Humans are thought to have lived in the Far East 300,000 years ago.[9] The exact provenance of these people is still unclear, but they appear to have entered the Amur Basin from Mongolia and Manchuria during warm intervals between ice ages when the Priamur and the Primorye shared analogous vegetation and climatic conditions with what is now northeastern China, Korea, and Japan. Such conditions partly explain the commonalities of Paleolithic artifacts excavated in the Priamur, the Primorye, North China, Korea, and Japan. Land bridges made possible migrations between Asia and America. About ten millennia ago, with land bridges submerged by rising sea levels, the Paleolithic ecumene gave way to several Neolithic variants, including a reindeer culture around Lake Baikal, a hunting culture along the Amur, and a maritime culture along the Northwest Pacific littoral. Neolithic pottery from the Priamur and the Primorye has affinities with that of Korea and Japan. Similarities in the cosmic serpents and dragons on Amur petroglyphs and aboriginal art of North America, Indonesia, and Polynesia suggest the possibility of more far-flung links.[10]

In the first and second centuries A.D., the Priamur, the Primorye, Manchuria, Korea, and Japan formed a single cultural entity on the threshold of exposure to complex influences emanating from China. Chinese and Korean settlers brought bronze implements to the Tumen and Suifen rivers in the third century. During the fourth and fifth centuries, majestic burial mounds similar to those in Korea and Japan were built as far north as the Ussuri. When the Korean-Tungusic state of Koguryŏ pushed into the Khanka Plain from the southwest during the sixth century, sinitic cultural forms conveyed overtones of suzerainty, heralding a Chinese millennium.[11]

2

« « » »

The Chinese Millennium

Siberia is the oldest home of the Chinese people.
— Li Ji (1972)

Chinese were aware of Northeast Asian aborigines long before extending suzerainty over the Priamur and the Primorye. References to Amur natives can be found in the chronicles of the Eastern Zhou (770 B.C.–256 B.C.).[1] Han dynasty (202 B.C.–A.D. 220) records mention "fishskin" tribes (Nanai), "hairy people" (possibly Ainu), and Yi-lou who washed themselves with urine, as did the Chukchi in the seventeenth century.[2]

Energies released by the reunification of China under the Sui and Tang dynasties propelled Chinese imperial power into the region during the seventh century (see Map 3). Shortly after 630, Tang forces descended on the Sungari, established an outpost on the Amur, and collected tribute from native chiefs, who in turn had their local authority legitimized by the Son of Heaven. Tributary delegations came from as far as Sakhalin (Kuyedao).[3] Expanding at the expense of Koguryŏ, Tang units crossed the Khanka Plain and built a fortified base at Sucheng (Suchan) around 660.

The demise of Koguryŏ in 668 sent Korean refugees northward across the Tumen, where in 698 they joined with Tungusic tribes to form the kingdom of Bohai; its capital, Mudanjiang, lay 150 miles northwest of what is today Vladivostok. Korean colonists settled the southern Primorye and eastern Manchuria as far north as the Sungari River.[4] Bohai's administration in the southern Primorye was based at Shuaibinfu, whose thirty-foot-thick walls are still visible outside of Ussuriisk. Smaller forts were built in the Sikhote Alin. While maintaining tributary relations with the Tang emperors, Bohai sent envoys to the Japanese imperial court at Nara, where Bokkai (Bohai) became a synonym for China.[5]

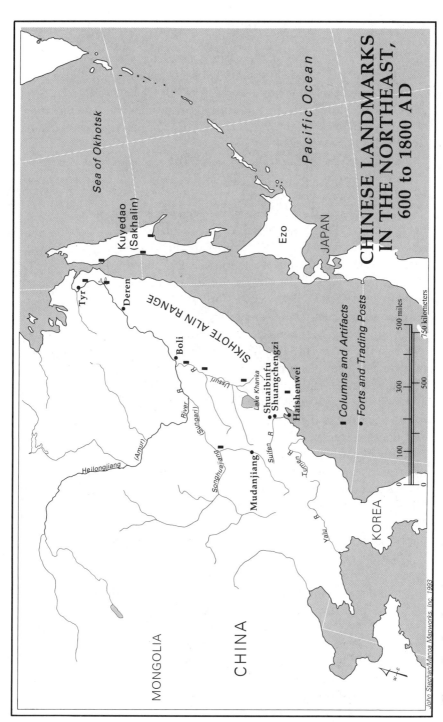

3. Chinese Landmarks in the Northeast, A.D. 600 to 1800

Bohai did not long survive the collapse of the Tang in 907, being overrun in 926 by Mongol-speaking people called Khitans, who under the dynastic name Liao went on to conquer most of North China by 947. The Liao administration extended farther north and east than Bohai had, embracing all of the Sikhote Alin, as well as the right bank of the Amur upstream of Boli (today's Khabarovsk).[6]

Liao in turn fell victim to Tungusic-speaking peoples called Jurchens, who established the Jin ("Gold") dynasty in 1115 and created an administration for Xubin Province (the Primorye) at Shuangchengzi (Ussuri-isk).[7] The process of sinicization went further in Jin than it had in Liao, judging from the large numbers of Chinese artifacts (coins, Buddhist figurines, roof tiles, and giant stone tortoises and stone columns inscribed with Chinese texts) excavated in the Primorye.[8] By the thirteenth century the Suifen Valley and Khanka Plain were well-populated agricultural oases, crisscrossed by roads, defended by forts, and governed by a Confucian bureaucracy of largely Han Chinese.[9]

In 1213 Khitan-Mongol tribes under Temuchin (better known as Genghis Khan) attacked the Primorye from Manchuria. The invaders devastated the Jurchen-Chinese population, whose survivors fled into the taiga.[10] After the Mongols had conquered China and established the Yuan dynasty in 1264, they consolidated their hold over the Northeast. Forts, settlements, and roads in the Primorye were rebuilt. Korean peasants were resettled along the Suifen River as a buffer against possible Japanese attacks. Enlisting Han Chinese, the Mongols built and garrisoned posts along the Amur and Ussuri rivers, establishing an administrative center at Tyr on the lower Amur. Crossing the Tatar Strait to Sakhalin, they subdued the Gilyaks (Nivkh) and Ainu in 1308 after a forty-year struggle. Around 1320 the Mongols abandoned Sakhalin and the Priamur but continued to garrison the Primorye until the collapse of the Yuan dynasty in 1368.[11]

Ming dynasty (1368–1644) energies that took the form of maritime expeditions to India, Arabia, and East Africa in the early fifteenth century also found expression in the Northeast. The tribute system was revived along the Amur and Ussuri, and tribal chiefs were brought to Beijing for investiture. In 1409 the military governorship of Nurgan was created, embracing the Primorye, the lower Amur, and Sakhalin.[12] Annoyed by raids on Tyr, the Yong-le emperor in 1412 ordered one of his court eunuchs Yi Shiha to mount an expedition down the Sungari-Amur. He embarked in 1413 on twenty-five vessels carrying 1,000 soldiers, architects, scribes, sculptors, carpenters, masons, and tile-makers. On a bluff overlooking the Amur at Tyr, Yi built a Temple of Eternal Harmony and left inscriptions in Chinese, Tibetan, Mongol, and Jurchen describing the expedition, praising the Yong-le emperor, and celebrating Ming beneficence.[13] To underline imperial benevolence and authority, Yi distributed beads, utensils, and Buddhist figurines, and invested tribal leaders with brocade, banners, writing seals, and paper money.[14] When word reached Beijing that shamans had instigated the destruction of Buddhist images, Yi found himself leading expeditions to Tyr in 1428 and 1433, during which additional monuments were constructed.[15]

Toward the end of the sixteenth century, Jurchen tribes in Manchuria had come under the leadership of a chief named Nurhachi. By 1616 Nurhachi had captured Ming posts along the Ussuri and Suifen rivers, gaining control of the Sikhote Alin. With income from Sikhote Alin ginseng and support from Chinese collaborators, he built a formidable military machine. After Nurhachi's death in 1626, his successors, calling themselves Manchus, drove the Ming out of Beijing. There they founded the Qing Dynasty in 1644, the same year that Russians appeared on the Amur.

Genesis of a "Blank Spot"

Scholars have long acknowledged the cardinal importance of early Chinese ties with the Priamur and the Primorye. Nikita Bichurin, head of the Russian Orthodox Mission in Beijing from 1807 to 1821, showed that dynastic chronicles provided insights into Far Eastern developments from the third to the seventeenth centuries. The celebrated nineteenth-century explorers Richard Maak, Nikolai Przhevalsky, and Mikhail Venyukov testified to an enduring Chinese heritage along the Amur and Ussuri rivers. After conducting research during 1898–99 on the lower Amur and Sakhalin, the ethnographer and orientalist Berthold Laufer became convinced of the "dependence of art of the Amur tribes on the Chinese."[16] "Chinese appeared in the Ussuri region long before Russians," remarked a Russian visitor in 1901.[17] Viktor Panov, a prominent Vladivostok journalist and writer, substantiated this statement by chronicling a thousand-year Chinese presence in the Primorye.[18]

Chinese associations figured prominently in the work of the internationally celebrated ethnographer Vladimir Arseniev, director of the Regional Studies Museum in Khabarovsk before and after the October Revolution.[19] Excavations on the Khanka Plain and surveys in the Sikhote Alin convinced Arseniev that China had left an indelible imprint on the prehistory of the Primorye. He noted, moreover, that some local aborigines still regarded the Son of Heaven as their overlord. To educate the public about this ancient link, Arseniev placed at the front of the Khabarovsk Museum a Jin Dynasty granite tortoise bracketed by stelae inscribed in Chinese characters.[20]

In the Soviet era, treatment of early Chinese associations with the Far East varied in accordance with political vicissitudes. Relations between Moscow and Beijing could hardly have been better when Aleksei Okladnikov began excavating sites in the southern Primorye in 1953.[21] In this fraternal atmosphere, Okladnikov lamented that Chinese statues along the Amur, Ussuri, and Suifen rivers had been defaced, that Russian settlers had used Buddhist figurines for house props, and that all that remained of the Temple of Eternal Harmony at Tyr was a pile of bricks.[22] Other scholars at this time chorused that Chinese sources were essential to reconstruct the prehistory of the Priamur, the Primorye, and Sakhalin.[23] However, as Sino-Soviet fraternity faded in the late 1950s, the Chinese contribution to Far Eastern prehistory began to shrink. Bohai, Liao, and Jin gradually lost their Chinese identity. References to Ming expeditions along the Amur contracted into cryptic footnotes.[24]

The deterioration of Sino-Soviet relations fueled irredentist rhetoric in both Beijing and Taibei during the 1960s. Mao Zedong declared in 1964 that Russia had "taken too much land," citing among other areas the Priamur and the Primorye.[25] A map published in Taibei that year depicted the entire Soviet Far East within China's "historical frontiers."[26] After border clashes along the Ussuri River in 1969, Beijing openly called the Priamur and the Primorye "historically Chinese possessions."[27] Not to be outdone, a Taiwan historian claimed that "Siberia" etymologically derived from "Xiboliya," a group of tribes that paid tribute to China 2,000 years ago.[28] Taking a similar tack, the Xinhua news agency in 1977 announced the discovery of "close connections" between North China and the Amur Basin some 2,700 years ago that confirmed that the latter had been "an integral part of our great motherland since ancient times."[29] The following year the Institute of Modern History of the Chinese Academy of Social Sciences published the first of a three-volume philippic against Russian encroachment on the Priamur, the Primorye, and Sakhalin.[30] By 1981 the Arctic Ocean was being called China's northern frontier in the thirteenth century.[31]

Moscow reacted to the irredentist challenge by mounting a propaganda counteroffensive. *Pravda* lambasted "Maoists" for coveting Soviet territory, and the Academy of Sciences mobilized researchers for combat against "Great Han chauvinism" on the historiographical front.[32] Galvanized by the confluence of patriotic instincts and Party directives, archaeologists and historians set out to minimize the Chinese presence in Northeast Asia before the seventeenth century. China found no place in the archaeology of the Soviet Far East.[33] Beijing's claims to ancient Middle Kingdom-Priamur links were dismissed as "outright falsifications," and Bohai, Liao, Jin, Yuan, and Qing were relabeled Tungus-Korean, Khitan, Jurchen, Mongol, and Manchu respectively.[34] Denigration eventually escalated into denial. Soviet readers in the 1980s learned that no Chinese had even set foot in the Primorye until the nineteenth century.[35]

Toponymy was inducted to serve on the historiographical front. Following a directive from the Party Central Committee, the KGB in 1972 prepared a hit list of 1,200 place-names to be changed, including many of Chinese origin. In 1973 the Academy of Sciences announced new names for towns, villages, rivers, mountains, plains, and bays. The Ussuri River tributaries Iman, Waku, and Li Fuzin became Bolshaya Ussurka, Malinovka, and Rudny respectively. Suchan became Partizansk, Iman Dalnerechensk, and Tetyukhe Dalnegorsk.[36] Zealous historians employed the new names in old contexts, as if Peter the Great had founded Leningrad.[37] Beijing retaliated by pointedly referring to Khabarovsk as Boli and Vladivostok as Haishenwei.

The Chinese "blank spot" remained impervious to glasnost. Attuned to patriotic sensibilities, perestroikist pundits exhibited their editorial fearlessness elsewhere. At the Institute of History in Vladivostok, Academician Andrei Krushanov fortified the perimeters of silence. To avoid mentioning Ming expeditions on the Amur, the editor of *History of the Far East USSR* contrived to leap from Mongol conquest to Russian entrée as if nothing had transpired in the intervening 400 years.[38] Meanwhile in Khabarovsk, a granite tortoise still greets visitors to the Regional Studies Museum, but the stelae with Chinese inscriptions are nowhere to be seen.

3

《 《 》 》

Russian Entrée

Only the Russians went to the Pacific Ocean not to conquer but to bring peace, protection, and a higher spiritual
and material culture than the small peoples of the North
and the Priamur had at that time.
— Vladimir Klipel (1976)

When Vasco Nuñez de Balboa glimpsed the Pacific through Pan-
amanian foliage in 1513, the Grand Duchy of Muscovy had yet to extend its
control over the Volga. Yet by the mid-seventeenth century, barely sixty years
after crossing the Urals, Russians had reached the Sea of Okhotsk, descended the Amur River, and passed through the straits separating Asia and
America. This dynamic has been characterized variously as conquest, assimi-
lation, infiltration, infestation, and an "urge to the sea."[1] As a result, Russia
acquired a permanent outlet on the Pacific before it did on the Baltic or the
Black Sea.

A variety of forces propelled eastward expansion. Foremost among these
was the lure of "soft gold": pelts of squirrels, otters, martens, beavers,
ermine, mink, arctic foxes, and sables. Furs served as a commodity of exchange and a major export, accounting for a third of state treasury receipts
in 1660. An insatiable demand for pelts soon depleted supplies in the Urals
and Western Siberia, prompting movement into unexploited regions farther east. Undemarcated space itself beckoned, holding out prospects of
livelihood and security. Peasants were attracted by visions of free land.
Fugitives and religious sectarians sought refuge in the taiga's commodious
embrace. Strategists searched for defensible frontiers. Located on a vast
Eurasian plain, Russian principalities had proved vulnerable to invaders
from the East as late as 1571, when Tatar raiders burned Moscow.

Russia's eastward trajectory followed a network of Siberian rivers, natural arteries for shallow-draft boats. Fortified wooden stockades (*ostrogs*) built at junctions and portages served as milestones: Tyumen (1586), Tobolsk (1587), Salekhard (1595), Narym (1596), Tomsk (1604), Turukhansk (1607), Yeniseisk (1618), Krasnoyarsk (1628), Yakutsk (1632), and Okhotsk (1647). Spearheading the movement were Cossacks, who at this time included peasants, hunters, exiles, vagabonds, and river pirates such as Yermak, engaged by the Stroganov merchants in 1581 to remove the khan of Sibir from the eastern slopes of the Urals. Under the rubric "Lithuanians" came recycled prisoners-of-war, immigrants, and foreign mercenaries of Lithuanian, Polish, White Russian, Ukrainian, Swedish, German, and Danish extraction. Carpenters, blacksmiths, and agriculturists, "Lithuanians," *streltsy* (literally "shooters" who carried harquebuses), and Cossacks together formed a category called "serving men" as distinct from those who came to Siberia illegally or without official functions, such as *promyshlenniki*, private hunters and trappers who discovered that they could do better by trading bread, salt, tobacco, ironware, beads, and alcohol to the aboriginal peoples for furs.

During the seventeenth and eighteenth centuries, Siberia drew peasants primarily from the White Sea coastal area and Perm region. Some crossed the Urals under state sponsorship. Others came on their own to escape serfdom. Moscow set up checkpoints in the Urals to net runaway serfs, but the quarry usually eluded these obstacles, although sometimes at the cost of abandoning families and possessions. Peasants adapted by subsisting on the West Siberian plain, joining the Cossacks, or apprenticing themselves as carpenters, blacksmiths, and boatmen. A few wound up as serfs on monastery estates, but binding a peasant to the land proved more difficult in Siberia than in European Russia.[2]

Moscow tried to impose a measure of control in Siberia by dividing it into intendancies, each based in a major ostrog and commanded by a military officer called a *voevoda*. Voevodas were drawn from noblemen whose names had been submitted to the tsar by the Military Affairs Office. Each voevoda was assisted by senior clerks and at times a military commander drawn from the sons of boyars and the serving nobility. Mobility between serving men and higher officers was nonexistent.[3] Each voevoda reported to the Office of Siberian Affairs, which monitored the collection, tallying, and transportation of furs. Moscow experimented with giving one voevoda supervisory powers over others but eventually settled on a fragmented rather than a unified Siberian administration. Jurisdictional boundaries in

Siberia were left vague, so that local conflicts not infrequently arose over undemarcated lands. In the 1630s, the Tobolsk and Tomsk voevodas both claimed the Lena Basin, leading to skirmishes between their serving men. Moscow resolved this conflict by establishing a *voevodstvo* at Yakutsk in 1638.[4] Strategically located on the middle course of the Lena, Yakutsk emerged as a fulcrum for Russian expansion toward the Sea of Okhotsk, Kamchatka, Chukotka, and the Amur.

Encounters with the Aborigines

Rather than hunting fur-bearing animals, serving men hunted the natives, adopting a Mongol-Tatar practice called *yasak* (fur tribute from able-bodied males). In addition to providing the state with revenue, yasak expanded state frontiers. Lands from which yasak was collected, together with the people living on those lands, were regarded as belonging to the tsar. In order to ensure compliance, serving men kept aboriginal hostages in each ostrog, periodically displaying them to reassure and intimidate relatives.

Aborigines reacted variously to the appearance of yasak-collectors. In western Siberia, the Khanty and the Mansi welcomed Russians as deliverers from Muslim heirs to the Mongol Empire.[5] Farther east, the Evenki willingly served as guides, interpreters, and agents of influence.[6] Encounters with the Yakuts were less harmonious. Once inhabiting the environs of Lake Baikal, the Yakuts had been driven northward by Mongols into the Lena Basin, where by the seventeenth century they had evolved a reindeer-raising economy and a hierarchical tribal society. Each tribe consisted of 1,000 to 2,000 members led by a chief. The Yakuts fought with the Evenki, the Yukagirs, and among themselves, kidnapping women and engaging in blood feuds, yet nothing prepared them for the Russians, as the following Yakut legend suggests.[7]

Chief Tyngyn had many servants and workers. Among the workers, two newcomers differed from the rest. They had deep-set blue eyes, high sharp noses, hirsute faces, and tight-fitting clothes. Unable to speak coherently, they gesticulated. Tyngyn's wife had a presentiment of evil and urged her husband to kill them, but Tyngyn saw nothing dangerous. After two years the mysterious workers asked Tyngyn for a pair of ox hides as payment. Taking the skins, they indicated with gestures that they wanted whatever land the skins could cover. Tyngyn saw nothing wrong with such a curious request and readily agreed. The two workers thereupon sliced the skins into long, thin strips and enclosed a large field, marking the boundaries with wooden stakes. Tyngyn watched them with bewilderment. The strange men then departed to the south. Next spring they returned, bringing with them many others with the same features and clothing. Around the marked-off land, they built a wall. Frightened, the Yakuts took counsel and decided to beat off the intruders. They shot arrows at the wall. Loud noises were heard from within the enclosure, and after each noise a Yakut fell. Many Yakuts died that day, including Tyngyn and all his sons.

Adult Yakut males who submitted to the Russians found themselves subject to yasak. Official pelt quotas were often supplemented by an extra, personal levy by individual collectors. Refusal invited the execution of hostages and burning of villages. The Yakutsk voevoda, Pyotr Golovin, managed to collect over 100,000 sable pelts between 1638 and 1642 by hanging recalcitrants from meat hooks.[8]

Brutality galvanized resistance. Setting aside tribal animosities, Yakuts and Tungusic-speaking tribes along the Lena rebelled in 1642. Golovin responded with a campaign of terror during which a henchman named Poyarkov tortured and butchered hundreds of men, women, and children.[9] Some Yakuts withdrew northward, but their respite proved short-lived, for Cossacks pursued them to the Kolyma Basin, the Okhotsk seaboard, and Chukotka, appropriating property and torching settlements.[10] Between 1642 and 1682 the Yakut population is estimated to have fallen by 70 percent.[11]

To resuscitate declining fur deliveries, Moscow took steps in the late seventeenth century to protect Siberian natives. Limits were imposed on the magnitude and frequency of yasak collections. Administrative boundaries were demarcated to spare aborigines from double yasak liability. Promyshlenniki came under state supervision. Codes were drawn up forbidding executions without Moscow's consent.[12] Although cooperative chiefs were granted gifts and tokens of authority, they were still forced to hand over relatives as hostages, to be displayed when the yasak was delivered.[13]

Conquerors tend to seek sexual gratification unceremoniously in any case, but voevodas attempted to introduce an element of order into an unruly market by adopting the Yakut practice of collecting *yasyr* ("woman tribute").[14] Aboriginal entrepreneurs promptly commercialized yasyr, offering women and children for sale to promyshlenniki, who in turn sold them for pelts to serving men. Insofar as this traffic siphoned off yasak proceeds, Moscow tried to eradicate it. Prohibiting the sale of women to serving men turned out to be as unenforceable as prohibiting the sale of alcohol to natives.[15]

Conquest of the Northeast

From the Lena Basin Russians pushed along the Okhotsk and arctic seaboards toward Kamchatka and Chukotka, collecting pelts and tusks (mammoth, walrus) from Eskimos, Aleuts, Chukchi, Kamchadals, and Koryaks. As in Yakutia, the newcomers used native allies (Yukagirs) against refractory aborigines (Chukchi).[16]

Native resistance in the Northeast took several decades to overcome. Koryaks made travel between Yakutsk and the Pacific littoral hazardous until a sea link was opened between Okhotsk and Kamchatka in 1716.[17] One Russian historian called the pacification of Kamchatka a "fifty-year war," adding that "nowhere did Russian conquest and administration show such cruelty and rapacity."[18] During 1697–99 Vladimir Atlasov and a hundred serving men cut their way through 12,000 Chukchi, 8,000 Koryaks, and 8,000 Kamchadals, qualifying the Anadyrsk voevoda as the Pizarro of Kamchatka.[19]

Kamchatka's aborigines reacted with an admixture of defiance and despair. Slaughtered whenever they revolted, they began killing themselves. Suicide epidemics prompted Moscow to take the unusual step of ordering local authorities to restrain natives from taking their own lives. Kamchatka fell silent around 1750, but Chukotka continued to be a hot spot, with the Anadyrsk ostrog ultimately going up in flames in 1770. Although the peninsula was declared pacified in 1789, the Chukchi stubbornly rejected the Russian Orthodox faith and occasionally roughed up Russian officials well into the nineteenth century.[20]

Adjustments and Accommodation

The Russians' treatment of Siberian natives improved during the eighteenth century. Mindful of the strategic advantage of winning over the Buryat Mongols, authorities became more sensitive to the feelings of the Yakuts.[21] Upon the abolition of the Yakutsk voevodstvo in 1708, the Northeast was incorporated into Irkutsk Province, whose governors had little inclination to get involved in aboriginal affairs and delegated tax, judicial, and police authority to native chiefs. As the fur trade declined, Empress

Catherine abolished the hostage system and terminated quotas for pelts, retaining yasak to fill a ceremonial function.[22] The Orthodox Church dispensed charity and set up schools for native Siberians at Yakutsk in the 1730s and on Kamchatka around 1750.[23] Although rebuffed by the Buryat Mongols and the Chukchi, the Church baptized and gave Russian names to thousands of Yakuts, Evenki, Yukagirs, and Ainu. Practical considerations expedited professions of faith, for native converts enjoyed exemption from yasak.

State servants as well as aborigines took advantage of material opportunities. Following the time-honored Russian custom of "feeding" (*kormlenie*), officeholders remunerated themselves with bribes and extortion without fear of punishment as long as pelts accrued to the state in sufficient quantities.[24] The throne's tolerance did not extend to the private retention of choice pelts, but temptation proved hard to resist. Most voevodas who survived their terms ended up in a court of justice.[25]

Occupational hazards at this time outpaced perquisites. Between 1677 and 1697, the voevodas of Yakutsk, Albazin, Nerchinsk, and Irkutsk were murdered by subordinates.[26] On Kamchatka ad hoc homicide chronically substituted for the time-consuming formal administration of justice. When it came to killing, Russians treated natives no worse than they did each other. Atlasov harvested lives without regard to ethnicity. Golovin used meat hooks on Yakuts, but he did not shrink from employing hot coals, pliers, and the knout on his own men and their wives.[27]

The absence of racial prejudice expressed itself socially and culturally in relations between Russians and aborigines, called variously *inorodtsy* ("people of different birth") and *inovertsy* ("people of another belief").[28] The barrier posed by religion could be removed by baptism. Baptized native males served with Cossacks and streltsy. Baptized females had the Church's blessing to wed Russians and often did so.[29] As mixed marriages proliferated, native cultures held their own and in some cases prevailed. On Kamchatka offspring of Russian-Kamchadal couples were Orthodox in religion but Kamchadal in speech, clothing, and diet.[30] In Yakutia the lifestyles of Russian settlers underwent "yakutization."[31] Although decimated, Chief Tyngyn's descendents wielded metaphorical ox hides to stake out and claim the cultural ground.

4

« « » »

Amur Setback

When the Russians first arrived on the Amur, the natives
cultivated fields and kept cattle. Ten years afterwards these
fields had become deserts; and a country that formerly
exported grain could not even support its own reduced
population.   — E. G. Ravenstein (1861)

In 1600 the Priamur's approximately
32,000 inhabitants fell into three
groups corresponding roughly to the upper, middle, and lower reaches of
the Amur.[1] From the confluence of the Shilka and the Argun to the Zeya
lived Mongol-speaking agriculturists whom the Russians called Daurians
(see Map 4). The middle Amur was inhabited by Tungusic-speaking tribes
known as Diuchers. The lower Amur and northern Sakhalin were populated by ancestors of the Nanai (Goldy), Ulchi, and Nivkhi (Gilyaks).
These peoples recognized Chinese suzerainty in the fifteenth century, but
Ming dynastic decline during the sixteenth century created a new political
dynamic in the Northeast. The Manchus subdued the Daurians and
Diuchers in the 1630s and relocated some of them to the Sungari and
Nonni river valleys, ironically depleting the Amur region of potential defenders on the eve of Russian penetration.[2]

Penetration and Expansion, 1644–58

Russian expansion across Siberia moved in two prongs, sometimes parallel, sometimes converging, along and between river systems. The northern prong met little resistance until it reached Yakutia. Its southern counterpart had to cope with remnants of the Mongol Empire along the fringes of

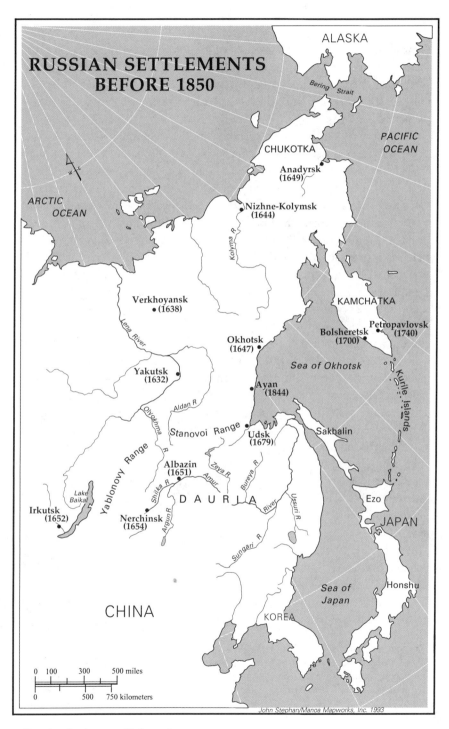

4. Russian Settlements Before 1850

Central Asia and the northern slopes of the Altai and Sayan ranges. By the 1640s Yakutsk had emerged as a fulcrum for Russian expansion in the Northeast. Verkhneudinsk occupied a roughly similar position in Transbaikalia. The penetration of the Amur Basin converged from both strongpoints.

Provisions as much as pelts sparked early Russian interest in the Amur. Food shortages posed a serious threat to Eastern Siberia, where a lack of fresh fruits and vegetables gave rise to scurvy, pellagra, and beriberi, and periodic shortfalls of grain forced people to eat grass, roots, and in extreme cases each other.[3] Hunger created a ready audience for stories circulating in Yakutsk about "Dauria," a land south of the mountains, where corn and grain grew in fertile valleys. To investigate these reports, Golovin dispatched a party in 1643 under Vasily Poyarkov, a serving man who had established his credentials the previous year pacifying Yakuts. From the Lena Poyarkov ascended the Aldan, crossed the Stanovoi Range, and descended the Zeya to the Amur. After following the great river to its estuary, Poyarkov returned to Yakutsk overland from the Okhotsk seaboard. His three-year, 3,000-mile trek claimed 130 of the expedition's 150 men.[4] Those who did not die from disease, cold, or malnutrition succumbed to flogging.[5] Poyarkov dealt summarily with native resistance along the Amur. When a Diucher settlement refused to yield yasak, he dispatched scores of inhabitants, including the chief and his entire family.[6] Back in Yakutsk, Poyarkov reported that although local tribes were paying yasak to a southern "khan" (the Manchu emperor), Dauria could be conquered with 300 men.[7]

Poyarkov was followed by Erofei Khabarov, a peasant turned promyshlennik, who with a mandate from the Yakutsk voevoda led twenty-one serving men and 107 promyshlenniki via the Olyokhma and Stanovoi watershed into Dauria in 1649. Khabarov spent three years collecting yasak with methods pioneered by Poyarkov, killing 661 Daurians in one episode alone.[8] In 1925 a Soviet historian denounced Khabarov's "uncontrolled barbarity," but by 1969 he was said to have committed only "isolated excesses."[9] Since then, those excesses have been recast as a disposable footnote to his achievement of "uniting" the Amur region with Russia.*

*The phrase "isolated excesses" (*otdel'nye ekstsessy*), which V. A. Aleksandrov used in *Rossiia na dal'nevostochnykh rubezhakh* (1969), was dropped in the 1984 revision of his book. As Khabarov's depredations have been minimized, his services to the Russian state have been magnified. From no mention of territorial annexations in prerevolutionary and early Soviet accounts,

In the wake of Poyarkov and Khabarov, Cossacks, peasants, traders, hunters, deserters, fugitives, and vagabonds flocked to the Amur in search of land, freedom, and fortune. Cossacks ensconced themselves at Albazin (1651; 1665 in some accounts) and built several small forts downstream. Nerchinsk ostrog (est. 1654), superseding Yakutsk in 1658 as the administrative center handling Daurian yasak, served as Russia's principal gateway to the Amur for the next thirty years.

The Manchu Response, 1650–87

Manchu officials on the Amur, without interfering with Poyarkov and Khabarov, reported to Beijing that "man-devouring demons" had infested the Northeast. Beijing's reaction to these reports was conditioned by a Confucian world view,* by Dauria's proximity to the Manchu homeland, and by an unstable situation in Mongolia, where the Qing dynasty was attempting to subdue recalcitrant tribes, some of whom were in contact with Russians. Moscow for its part was endeavoring to open overland trade with China through Central Asia and Mongolia. The Amur Basin became one of several arenas of encounters between two converging empires and cultures, neither of which fully understood the other's values, objectives, and territorial magnitude.

The Qing first offered Moscow trade as a quid pro quo for withdrawal from the Northeast,[10] a tactic that incorrectly assumed Moscow controlled the behavior of its subjects in Dauria. When linkage failed to produce results, the Manchus resorted to force. From a newly established military governorship at Ninguta, 240 miles south of the Amur, Manchu forces

---

he has progressively been credited with creating "preliminary conditions" for the acquisition of the middle Amur (late 1950s), with annexing the Amur as far downstream as the Zeya junction (1968), and with "assimilating" the entire Amur Basin into Russia (1980s). The last is patently overblown, for Khabarov did not get beyond the junction of the Amur and Zeya rivers and thus never reached the site of the city that today bears his name. Aleksandrov, *Rossiia na dal'nevostochnykh rubezhakh* (1984), p. 25; Russia, *Aziatskaia Rossiia*, 1: 12; Bakhrushin, *Kazaki na Amure*, pp. 97–98; Kabanov, *Amurskii vopros*, p. 12; N. I. Riabov and Shtein, *Ocherki istorii russkogo Dal'nego Vostoka*, p. 32; *Istoriia Sibiri*, 2: 54; Sergeev, *Kazachestvo na russkom Dal'nem Vostoke*, p. 18; Nesterov, *Sviaz' vremen*, p. 88.

*The Qing followed Chinese tradition and dealt with the outside world through the tribute system, a mechanism grounded on the identification of China as the "Middle Kingdom" to which "barbarians" around the periphery submitted tribute in return for legitimation by the Son of Heaven.

attacked ostrogs along the Amur and in 1658 destroyed a band led by Stepanov, killing him and capturing over 200 of his followers.[11] They then withdrew from the Amur, taking along a better part of the Daurian and Diucher population on the assumption that the "demons" would withdraw for lack of sustenance. Again, the Manchus miscalculated. During the next twenty years, over 4,000 peasants, exiles, vagabonds, and rebels made their way to Dauria. Fugitive Cossacks took over Albazin in 1665 and defied Nerchinsk, forwarding yasak proceeds directly to Moscow to secure the tsar's indulgence.[12]

For several years Beijing took no active steps against the "demons," ignoring appeals for help from aborigines as far away as the Okhotsk seaboard.[13] The Manchus at this stage were more concerned about preserving the ethnic purity of their homeland, for which purpose they erected a "willow palisade" across southern Manchuria demarcating the northern limits of Han Chinese settlement. However, when a Mongol tribal chief renounced Qing suzerainty and sought Russian protection in 1667, the Kangxi emperor revived the tactic of using trade as an incentive to enlist Muscovite cooperation on the Amur. Once again Beijing overestimated Moscow's readiness and ability to restrain Russian subjects in Dauria.[14]

While leaving the door open to diplomacy, the Kangxi emperor prepared to take tougher measures in the Northeast. Starting in 1680, forts and roads were built along southern approaches to the Amur. When Moscow dispatched 2,000 serving men to Albazin in 1684, Beijing sent emissaries with a note for the voevoda Tolbuzin ordering the Russians to go back to Yakutsk and not "intrude any more into our lands." When the note failed to elicit the desired response, several thousand Manchu, Chinese, Daurian, and Diucher troops surrounded Albazin in 1685.[15] After a siege of four days, the defenders surrendered and were allowed to retire, without arms, to Nerchinsk.*

When word of Albazin's fall reached Moscow in late 1685, the government decided to abandon the Amur and secure a trade agreement with China. Meanwhile, however, Tolbuzin had slipped back into Albazin and prepared for a siege. Upon learning of this, the Kangxi emperor ordered the fort recaptured. A Qing force of 5,000 men attacked Albazin in the summer of 1686, killed Tolbuzin, and after a thirteen-month siege, retook the fort.

---

*About fifty defenders opted to become Qing subjects and resettled in Beijing to join other Russian prisoners and defectors, collectively known as "Albazinians."

Barely seventy of 900 defenders remained alive, half of whom soon succumbed to disease and starvation. The Kangxi emperor thereupon reverted to diplomacy and signaled Moscow that he was prepared to discuss trade within the context of a Russian withdrawal from the Amur.[16]

Moscow responded by dispatching Count Fyodor Golovin to Nerchinsk with plenipotentiary powers to secure a trade agreement and, if possible, a frontier along the Amur. Failing an Amur frontier, Moscow was prepared to accept the Bureya (leaving China in possession of the lower Amur) or at worst in "the environs of Albazin" (leaving China in control of the middle and lower Amur).[17] Moscow simultaneously vested Golovin with administrative responsibility for southeastern Siberia, thereby establishing a precedent for combining gubernatorial and diplomatic functions in a single person.[18]

The Treaty of Nerchinsk

When the Muscovite and Manchu delegations finally met at Nerchinsk in August of 1689 (Golovin arriving a month and a half late), both claimed lands that neither knew much about. Golovin proposed an Amur River frontier, whereupon the Manchu plenipotentiary, Prince Songota, countered with Lake Baikal. Golovin then suggested the Bureya, and Songota came back with Nerchinsk. Two Jesuits attached to the Manchu delegation then offered what they called a compromise: the Gorbitsa River, which flowed into the Shilka about midway between Nerchinsk and Albazin. Golovin balked at a "compromise" that would exclude Russia from the Amur, but the clank and clamor of 15,000 Manchu troops deployed around Nerchinsk helped him to reconsider.

Russian, Manchu, and Latin texts of the Treaty of Nerchinsk were signed on 6 September 1689. Moscow got its coveted caravan trade and gave up the Amur Valley. The frontier, still undemarcated, was to run along the Argun, Shilka, and Gorbitsa rivers and the crest of the "stone mountains." Areas drained by rivers flowing into the Amur were to belong to the Middle Kingdom, and areas drained by rivers flowing on the other side of the "stone mountains" were to belong to the Russian Empire.

Expulsion from the Amur does not seem to have unduly troubled Moscow, where prospects of lucrative commerce carried more weight than remote real estate.[19] Tsar Peter showed no signs of displeasure other than at the fact that his imperial seal followed rather than preceded that of the Kangxi emperor's, a condition remedied by reversing the sequence in subsequent documents.[20] Golovin's career continued its upward trajectory. Only in the nineteenth century did Russian writers deploring the "loss" of the Amur score Golovin for faintheartedness and Jesuit casuistry.[21] When relations with China deteriorated after 1960, Soviet commentators discovered that the Nerchinsk Treaty had been negotiated under duress and was a product of a "cold war" waged by China to seize the "Siberian Ukraine" and thereby gain "hegemony" over Russia.[22]

Seventeenth-century ambiguities about Northeast Asian geography left ample latitude for divergent interpretations of Nerchinsk's boundary clause. The Chinese asserted that the "stone mountains" and the "ocean" referred to the Yablonovy-Stanovoi ranges and the Sea of Okhotsk.[23] Soviet commentators countered that the "stone mountains" are in fact the Bureya Range and the "ocean" the Amur-Sungari junction.[24] Moreover, they argued that the absence of any mention of Sakhalin and the Primorye in the treaty indicated that these territories did not belong to China.[25]

However one construes the Nerchinsk frontiers, Russia's Amur setback stemmed from priorities, logistics, and economics rather than from "Manchu-Qing aggression."[26] Preoccupied by military commitments in the West and more interested in trade than in territory, Moscow did not place the Amur high on the hierarchy of state objectives for good reasons. Separated by thousands of miles of trackless taiga, the Russian state could match neither Qing power nor Qing munificence in Dauria. Four thousand Russian colonists and a few thousand Cossacks constituted a slender presence in a region the size of France. Beijing enjoyed more prestige among Daurians and Diuchers, for Manchus rewarded tribute with gifts of brocade, titles, and wives, whereas Cossacks, lacking carrots, relied on sticks.

Not long after Nerchinsk, in composing *Robinson Crusoe*, Daniel Defoe had his hero pass through Dauria en route home. Defoe wrote that the Argun [Amur] flowed into a "Chinese Ocean."[27] Small wonder that a Brezhnev-era pedagogue labeled Crusoe "a true bourgeois."[28]

5

« « » »

Pacific Window

Should I go to Okhotsk without provisions, or should the
provisions go to Okhotsk without me?
— Vitus Bering (1737)

Deflected from the Amur, Russian energies were directed for over a century toward the Okhotsk seaboard, Kamchatka, Chukotka, the Kurile Islands, and eventually North America. Although the Russians found more pelts and met less resistance in the "Eastern Ocean" (as they first called the Pacific) than in Dauria, they encountered formidable problems with provisioning North Pacific settlements. Climatic conditions around the Okhotsk seaboard, Kamchatka, Chukotka, and what is today Alaska all but precluded agriculture. Grain imported from Western Siberia not only cost a lot but took nearly a year to deliver. As the quest for sea otters drew Russians into North America after 1740, attempts were made to secure food supplies by resettling peasants from Siberia, by searching for Asia-Pacific trade partners, by establishing agrarian colonies in California and Hawaii, and by relying on the Imperial Navy. None of these expedients proved satisfactory, and some generated diplomatic embarrassment.

Although less than successful in getting wheat and corn, these efforts produced a rich harvest of knowledge. Navigators and scientists made important contributions to cartography, ethnography, and natural history. The first steps were taken by a trio of Cossacks — Semyon Dezhnev and Fedot Alekseyev, who in 1648 made their way along Siberia's arctic coast and around the tip of Chukotka into the "Eastern Ocean," and Ivan Kozyrevsky, who explored the Kurile Islands in 1711–13. Their successors extended the range of discoveries to North America, Japan, and Oceania, bequeathing an array of Russian place-names to Polynesia.

Partly because of the increasing power of the Russian state and partly because enterprise on the Pacific coast required a magnitude of investment beyond the range of merchant capital alone, St. Petersburg (the seat of government from 1703) played a more active role in the east during the eighteenth and early nineteenth centuries than Moscow had during the seventeenth century. Imperial priorities shifted in accordance with (among other things) the idiosyncrasies of Peter I (1689–1725), Catherine II (1762–96), Paul (1796–1801), and Alexander I (1801–25).

Petrine Initiatives, 1711–50

Peter's Westernizing drumbeat for a while echoed faintly and belatedly on the eastern periphery. Although the tsar gave a European form to Siberian administration in 1708, it was not until 1719 that the Yakutsk district came under the jurisdiction of Irkutsk Province.[1] Proposals for expeditions to Kamchatka at first met a tepid response. However, as Peter began to see the Pacific as a source of wealth and power, his interest picked up. Reports by Vladimir Atlasov and Kozyrevsky about Japan evoked bold imperial scenarios of Siberian springboards to China and India. Peter had such considerations in mind in 1711 when he ordered a sea route opened to Kamchatka. Founded in 1647, Okhotsky ostrog was the earliest Russian settlement on the Sea of Okhotsk (or "Big Sea," as it was called at the time), but it turned out to be more of a chink than a window on the Pacific. Connected to Yakutsk by a 500-mile track over the Dzhugdzhur Range, it had no natural harbor and was ice-bound for half the year. When navigation between Okhotsk and Bolsheretsk opened in 1716, travelers to Kamchatka no longer had to make an arctic detour to avoid unfriendly Koryaks along the Okhotsk seaboard.[2]

Although Peter did not live to witness it, he set in motion the First Kamchatka Expedition (1725–30), which sought to clarify the geopolitical configuration of the North Pacific.[3] Led by Captain Vitus Bering, a Dane in Russian service, the expedition was plagued by setbacks and yielded what some contemporaries considered modest dividends. Two Okhotsk-built ships, captained respectively by Bering and Aleksei Chirikov, sailed along the Pacific coast of Kamchatka and Chukotka, passed through the [Bering] strait into the Arctic Ocean, and followed the Siberian shore for about 100 miles, not finding the "Big Land" (Alaska) but confirming that Kamchatka offered the most serviceable site for a Pacific port.

Their Second Kamchatka Expedition (1733–43), more ambitious and multifaceted, explored the Siberian arctic and North Pacific littorals, investigated Northeast Asia's natural and human environment, made a bid to open trade with Japan, and established a Russian foothold along the northwest coast of North America. Although the expedition claimed the life of its leader, it dramatically increased Russia's knowledge of the North Pacific. In addition to clarifying Asia's relationship to America, Bering and Chirikov surveyed the Aleutian Islands and the southern coast of Alaska. Martin Spanberg charted the Kurile Archipelago and made the first Russian landing on Honshu, Japan's main island.[4] Dmitry Laptev explored a section of Russia's arctic coastline.

Scientists and scholars with the expedition made lasting contributions to this fund of knowledge. Georg Wilhelm Steller and Stepan Krasheninnikov wrote classic accounts of the North Pacific and Kamchatka, respectively.[5] Gerhard Friedrich Müller produced the first general history of Siberia.[6] Johann Georg Gmelin pioneered the study of Siberian flora. Such works brought Siberia and the North Pacific into the mainstream of European intellectual discourse. Finally, in 1740 the expedition founded the port of Petropavlovsk, named after Bering's and Chirikov's ships *St. Peter* and *St. Paul*. Located in Avacha Bay on the eastern coast of Kamchatka, Petropavlovsk had two major advantages over Okhotsk: a well-protected anchorage and unobstructed access to the Pacific. The Kamchatka expeditions indirectly promoted the colonization of Northeastern Siberia as agricultural settlements grew up around Okhotsk and Petropavlovsk.[7]

Thanks to Petrine initiatives, Russia gained a half-century head start over England and France in the North Pacific. Spanish galleons had occasionally strayed north of the Manila-Acapulco axis, and Dutch navigators had groped their way around the Kuriles and Sakhalin in 1643, but as Georg Steller wrote in 1745, Russia had a strategic opportunity in the North Pacific to control the southern Kuriles and exert influence over Japan and China.[8] Ironically, by moving into the southern Kuriles later in the century, Russia inspired in the Japanese imagination the durable notion of a "northern threat."

Searching for Direction, 1750–98

During the second half of the eighteenth century, St. Petersburg looked in vain for a satisfactory administrative arrangement for its vast but sparsely settled eastern territories. Irkutsk Province, sprawling over a third of the Russian Empire, underwent a series of reorganizations. In 1732 the Okhotsk Administration (*Okhotskoye upravlenie*) was established at Okhotsk (subsequently moved to Anadyr and then Yakutsk) with elastic boundaries encompassing the Okhotsk seaboard and Kamchatka. A Yakutsk District (oblast) was created in 1775, but unstable boundaries and overlapping jurisdictions continued to plague the Northeast up to and after 1917.[9]

During the mid-eighteenth century Siberian governors attempted to revive Petrine momentum by supporting peasant resettlement, cartographical surveys, schools for navigation, and agricultural experiments in the Northeast. These efforts aroused scant interest in St. Petersburg but dovetailed with private initiatives being launched toward North America and Japan in search of pelts and trade. Russian merchants carried out eighty-eight voyages to the Aleutians and Alaska between 1743 and 1797.[10] One of the boldest entrepreneurs, Grigory Shelikhov, organized a company in 1775 for the North Pacific fur trade and founded the first Russian settlement in North America, while his partner financed probes along the Kurile Islands in the hope of engaging the Japanese in commerce. But it soon became apparent that Russian enterprise alone could not provision North Pacific settlements, and that private trade missions to northern Japan could not breach the barriers raised by shogunal policies.

By the end of the eighteenth century, Russia no longer had the North Pacific to itself. In 1778 James Cook surveyed the northwest coast of North America and passed through the Bering Strait into the Arctic Ocean. His successor James King called twice at Petropavlovsk in 1779 while reconnoitering the Northeast's littoral. In 1787 Jean François de La Pérouse sailed from the Sea of Japan into the Tatar Strait, passed between Sakhalin and Hokkaido, and looked over some of the Kurile Islands. William Broughton covered a similar route a decade later. In the 1780s New England merchants (collectively dubbed "Bostonians") appeared along the northwest American coast, and the commercial visionary John Ledyard showed up in Irkutsk.[11] From the 1790s "Bostonians" collected furs from the Indians of the northwest coast in exchange for trinkets, cloth, rum, and guns, the last of which they occasionally discharged at Russians. Pelts that might have been bartered at Kiakhta were siphoned off by American interlopers for resale in Canton.

St. Petersburg reacted fitfully and ineffectively to encroachment on its North Pacific empire. Catherine II expelled the inquisitive John Ledyard from Russia and in 1786 proclaimed imperial sovereignty over an arc extending from the Kurile Islands to what is today the southern tip of the Alaskan panhandle. The empress dispatched a naval expedition to the Pacific in 1787 to enforce this decree, but recalled it while it was en route when war broke out with Sweden and Turkey. Local officials had to make do with a consignment of gun emplacements at Petropavlovsk, leaving Russia's North Pacific as vulnerable as ever.

Bold Projects, 1799–1824

Official interest in the North Pacific revived during the brief reign of Catherine's son Paul, who in 1799 issued a charter to the Russian-American Company and established a small naval squadron to service the Pacific coast. The Russian-American Company claimed a monopoly of resources along the North Pacific littoral but relied on foreign merchants and the Russian Navy for supplies.

As in the previous century, science outpaced provisioning. Between 1803 and 1830 a series of Russian naval expeditions in the Pacific clarified the contours of the Okhotsk seaboard, the Kurile Islands, Kamchatka, and Chukotka.* Ivan Kruzenshtern failed to discover a navigable channel between Sakhalin and the mainland, but he refined the earlier surveys of La Pérouse and Broughton. Ferdinand Wrangel and others charted Siberia's arctic littoral. These mariners displayed impressive intellectual curiosity as well as professional competence, imparting prestige to a Pacific service whose veterans formed an elite within the Imperial Navy.[12]

So as not to rely entirely on the navy for provisions, officials in Siberia and Russian America attempted to open trade with Japan, China, the United States, Spanish colonies (the Philippines, California, Peru), and Hawaii. Even India was considered.[13] Such inventiveness created more problems than it solved. An impulsive demarche toward Japan led to a series of misunderstandings that, to paraphrase the poet Mikhail Lermontov, would have been funny if they were not so sad. In 1804 the energetic director of the Russian-American Company, Nikolai Rezanov, sailed to Nagasaki and pressed shogunal officials to sanction commerce. When re-

---

*The principal expeditions were led by Ivan Kruzenshtern (1803–6), Yury Lisiansky (1803–6), Vasily Golovnin (1807–9, 1817–19), Otto Kotsebue (1815–17, 1823–26), Fadei Bellingshausen (1819–21), Mikhail Lazarev (1819–21), Ferdinand Wrangel (1825–27), and Fyodor Litke (1826–29).

fused after having been kept waiting for an answer in Nagasaki harbor for six months, Rezanov allowed vexation to override his better judgment. Before setting out on a fatal attempt to cross Siberia, he issued nebulous instructions to a couple of unsophisticated ensigns (Khvostov and Davydov) to teach the obstreperous Japanese a lesson by torching their settlements on Sakhalin and the southern Kuriles. After some hesitation, these naive instruments of Rezanov's pique carried out raids in the fall of 1806 and spring of 1807, thereby earning Japan's wrath against Russia and a court-martial for themselves. The court of history has yet to pass final judgment on this incident, which is still variously characterized as patriotism, piracy, or opera bouffe.[14]

St. Petersburg's embarrassment at Rezanov's gaucherie did not discourage emulators. In 1812 an American named Peter Dobell showed up at Petropavlovsk with two provision-laden ships from Manila. Impressing officials with a plan for a trade network encompassing Siberia, Alaska, California, Japan, Canton, and the Philippines, Dobell wrangled an appointment as consul-general in Manila but achieved little other than promoting himself to "Russian consul-general to the Pacific Ocean."[15] Efforts by the Russian-American Company to establish bases in California and Hawaii came up with more tangible but still disappointing results. An agricultural colony founded in 1812 north of San Francisco produced some wheat and corn before being sold in 1841. A scheme by an irrepressible Teutonic doctor to bring a Hawaiian island into the Russian Empire in 1815–17 went awry, leaving St. Petersburg to distance itself yet again with disavowals.[16]

For lack of alternatives, the Russian-American Company came to depend on Americans. Once the company started exchanging pelts for supplies with "Bostonians" in 1803, the New Englanders gained a foothold in Russian America that they soon extended to Northeast Asia. By 1820 Yankee traders and whalers were operating along the coasts of Chukotka, purveying rum and trinkets for furs, tusks, and sex.[17] To contain these impudent interlopers, the Russian-American Company forbade aborigines to trade with foreigners, backed by an 1821 ukase issued by Alexander I barring foreign vessels from most of the North Pacific littoral. These proprietary gestures were neutralized when larger imperial calculations led to the Russian-American Convention of 1824 restoring American access to Russia's North Pacific shores.[18]

Siberian Reforms and the Northeast

St. Petersburg's plenipotentiaries compiled a mixed record in Northeast Asia during the first four decades of the nineteenth century. On the one hand Prince Gagarin, the first governor-general of Siberia (1711–17), defrauded the state treasury and wound up on the gallows.[19] Governor-General Ivan Pestel, enjoying the emoluments of office without subjecting himself to the hardships, resided for most of his term (1806–19) in St. Petersburg.[20] On the other hand, during his brief tenure as governor-general (1819–22), Mikhail Speransky introduced rationalist ideas of the Enlightenment into Siberian administration by defining official prerogatives and duties, imposing legal constraints on the treatment of exiles, codifying regulations for salt and alcohol monopolies, and promoting immigration by free peasants.[21] Speransky also set up tribal councils to encourage aboriginal self-rule, laying the basis for native land rights.[22] These fresh breezes reached distant Kamchatka, where more land was brought under cultivation and an agricultural school was opened at Petropavlovsk.[23]

Kamchatka was on Alexander Pushkin's mind in the final days of his life in 1837. The great poet's imagination anticipated utopian visions about Siberia among his radical contemporaries and adumbrated a redirection of Russian energies from America to Asia, from Alaska to the Amur.[24]

6

«« »»

Return to the Amur

Every time Russia finds herself checked in Europe she intensifies her drive in Asia.
— Prince Andrei Lobanov-Rostovsky (1933)

In the mid-nineteenth century, Russia dramatically enlarged its territory in the Far East by acquiring the Priamur and the Primorye. Russia's return to the Amur was marked by infiltration rather than force. Provincial bureaucrats, naval officers, scholars, and diplomats, as well as Cossacks, exiles, and peasants, took part in the advance. Like their seventeenth-century predecessors, Far Eastern activists made use of poor communications and imperial vanities to conceal and then legitimize unauthorized initiatives. Unlike *their* predecessors, Manchu leaders found their efforts to deal with Russian encroachment undercut by internal upheavals.

From Nerchinsk to Nanjing

Between the Treaty of Nerchinsk (1689), which excluded Russia from the Amur Basin, and the Treaty of Nanjing (1842), which inaugurated incremental partition of China, the Priamur and the Primorye remained quiescent. Portrayed by some historians as a symptom of neglect,[1] this quiescence derived from a Qing policy of insulating the Manchu homeland from Han Chinese.

Qing relations with Priamur aborigines continued to be defined after 1689 by the tribute system, with furs being sent to Beijing in return for gifts and legitimation.[2] In the early eighteenth century, Qing authorities introduced the practice of marrying Manchu girls to tribal chiefs on the lower Amur. After 1750 Gilyak chiefs from Sakhalin journeyed to Beijing to be invested with brides, surnames, and ranks.[3]

Meanwhile, following surveys of the Priamur, the Primorye, and Sakhalin in 1709, permanent military strongpoints and seasonal tribute collection posts were established along the Amur. Manchu officials descended the Sungari each summer from Sanxing to collect pelts and confer gifts and titles on Amur natives. In 1809 the Japanese surveyor Mamiya Rinzō visited a Manchu tribute post near what is today Komsomolsk, noting that it was staffed only in summer months.[4]

Notwithstanding restrictions imposed by Beijing and enforced at Manchu checkpoints along the Sungari, Chinese made their way to the Priamur for ginseng in the Sikhote Alin, trepang in Haishenwei ("Trepang Bay"), and fur-bearing animals in the Ussuri taiga, living in seasonal huts and worshiping at makeshift shrines.[5] Chinese peasants migrated from drought-wracked Zhili, Shandong, and Shanxi provinces and formed permanent communities along the Bureya, Zeya, Ussuri, and Suifen rivers (see Map 5). About 6,000 Chinese agriculturalists lived in the Priamur in 1854, raising crops of wheat, corn, millet, barley, cucumbers, cabbages, onions, and garlic.[6]

For several decades after 1689, official Russian policies toward the Priamur were constrained by reluctance to jeopardize the caravan trade through Kiakhta. St. Petersburg did little more than periodically ask Beijing for permission to navigate along the Amur.[7] Privately, bolder initiatives were urged. In 1757 a German in Russian service advised that the Nerchinsk treaty be revised in such a way that the Sino-Russian frontier would run along the Amur.[8] Beijing would have none of it, and St. Petersburg was not inclined to press the issue. When John Cochrane made his way by foot through Siberia to Kamchatka in 1820–22, he was struck by the general indifference to the Amur.[9]

Serious interest in the Amur manifested itself first in Transbaikalia, whose eastern reaches suffered economically from lack of access to the Sea of Okhotsk. Viewed from Nerchinsk, the Amur presented itself as a natural artery along which Transbaikalian grain could be shipped to the Okhotsk seaboard and Kamchatka.[10] Political as well as economic calculations promoted Transbaikalian interest in the Amur. The Chita visionary Dmitry Zavalishin and other exiled Decembrists (military officers who had taken

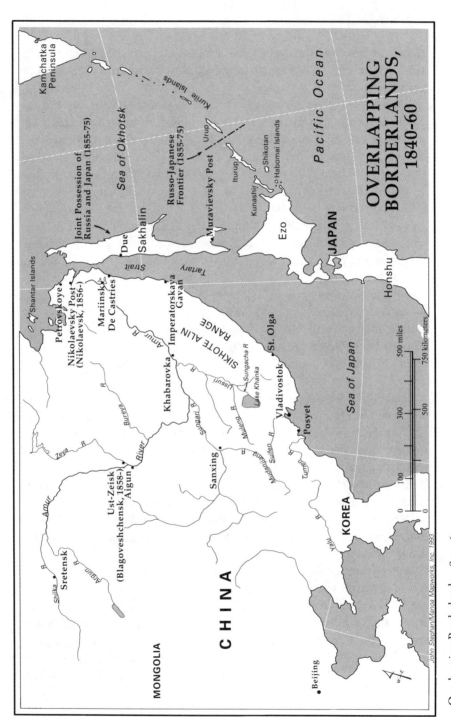

5. Overlapping Borderlands, 1840–60

part in an abortive uprising against Nicholas I in December 1825) in Irkutsk and Transbaikalia nurtured the notion that with an Amur channel to the Pacific, Siberia could become a laboratory for revolution.[11]

The Opium War (1839–42) called St. Petersburg's attention to the Amur by exposing Northeast Asia's vulnerability to British sea power. When the Treaty of Nanjing awarded Great Britain a foothold on the China coast, some Russian officials wondered whether the Amur might not attract predatory designs, a scenario that acquired an uncomfortable plausibility as British, French, and American naval activity mounted in the North Pacific.

Social and economic as well as strategic forces converged to reopen the Amur question in the mid-1840s. Caution reigned in St. Petersburg, but on the periphery officers, merchants, scientists, and political exiles began to coalesce around a governor-general of Eastern Siberia into an unstable partnership of Amur activists who came to be known as *amurtsy*.

Probes, 1843–48

Within a year of the Treaty of Nanjing, a special committee convened in St. Petersburg to reassess Russia's position in the Far East.[12] It was agreed that the undemarcated frontiers needed clarification, although the foreign minister, Count Karl Nesselrode, wanted no territorial aggrandizement at China's expense and insisted that every precaution be taken not to jeopardize relations with Beijing. The most convenient instrument to investigate the Far Eastern frontier zone turned out to be Professor Alexander von Middendorf, then in Yakutsk studying permafrost under the auspices of the Russian Academy of Sciences. Instructed to survey the Okhotsk seacoast in the region of the Shantar Islands, von Middendorf on his own initiative sent a reconnaissance party over the Stanovoi Range to the Amur, establishing a behavioral pattern that became emblematic of the amurtsy.[13]

Von Middendorf's boldness unsettled Nesselrode but piqued the navy's curiosity for finding a navigable channel from the Amur to the Sea of Okhotsk and the Sea of Japan.* Accordingly, Lieutenant Aleksandr Gavrilov was dispatched to the Amur from Ayan (which in 1845 had replaced Okhotsk as a naval base) on a Russian-American Company ship. To avoid

---

*When Mamiya Rinzō surveyed the lower Amur in 1809, he confirmed Sakhalin's insularity and prepared a chart of the estuary. The shogunate tried to keep Mamiya's discovery secret, but a map incorporating his chart was smuggled out of Japan by Philipp Franz von Siebold in 1829 and shown to the Russian navigator Ivan Kruzenshtern in 1834.

arousing Chinese suspicions, crewmen were supplied with Virginia tobacco and told to pass themselves off as Americans should they be questioned. Such precautions proved to be as superfluous as the voyage itself. Finding the estuary to all appearances blocked by sand bars, Gavrilov concluded that the Amur was inaccessible to ocean-going vessels. Gavrilov's "discovery" undercut the strategic rationale for further reconnaissance, prompting Nicholas I to declare the matter closed, much to Nesselrode's relief.[14]

Russian momentum toward the Amur revived under the impetus of a thirty-eight-year-old officer named Nikolai Muraviev, who, having distinguished himself in combat in the Caucasus and having attracted the favorable attention of Nicholas I while serving as governor of Tula, won appointment in 1847 as governor-general of Eastern Siberia. Muraviev was a convinced expansionist, yet his imperial convictions were leavened by a progressive credo that included liberation and land for serfs, a public judiciary and jury system, and freedom of the press. Autocratic by nature, he recognized and rewarded talent without regard to antecedents. Among officers and exiles with whom he mingled in Irkutsk, the governor-general evoked contradictory reactions. The exiled anarchists Mikhail Bakunin (a distant relative) and Peter Kropotkin praised Muraviev for his humane and respectful treatment of Decembrists and Poles, some of whom he appointed to his staff. Dmitry Zavalishin and others, however, were less charitable in their assessments.[15]

Muraviev regarded the Amur as a vehicle to project Russian power and prestige into the Pacific, a vision that drew sustenance from a sense of personal destiny (his great-grandfather had served under Vitus Bering).[16] Hoping to impress on Nicholas the river's geopolitical significance, Muraviev wrote him that "whoever shall control the mouth of the Amur will control Siberia."[17] The tsar was not persuaded. Rather than belabor the point, the governor-general acted on it.

The Amur Estuary and Sakhalin, 1849–53

Muraviev's ally in reopening the Amur question turned out to be a young naval officer, Gennady Nevelskoi, who doubted Gavrilov's conclusions and in the summer of 1849, with the governor-general's backing, sailed into the Tatar Strait, confirmed Sakhalin's insularity, and charted a navigable channel into the Amur.[18] Nevelskoi's actions evoked mixed feelings in St. Petersburg. The navy welcomed a strategically useful discovery, but Nesselrode and the finance minister opposed further moves toward the

Amur as diplomatically risky, fiscally extravagant, and politically imprudent. Nesselrode argued that Siberia should remain a "deep net" into which troublemakers could be securely consigned. Acquiring the Amur, he warned, would untie the net and allow dangerous people out and subversive ideas in. The governor-general of Western Siberia agreed, urging that "it is important above all to keep the inhabitants of Siberia away from immediate contact with foreigners, contact which could easily turn into fatal propaganda."[19]

Undeterred by such qualms, Nevelskoi returned to the Amur during the summer of 1850 and founded two outposts near the estuary: Petrovskoye and Nikolaevsky Post. For good measure he informed the local aborigines that all territory "to the Korean frontier" belonged to Russia.[20] This unauthorized appropriation of a thousand miles of Chinese coast by the young officer and his patron ruffled bureaucratic vanities, but the absence of Manchu forces and of any protest from Beijing (which remained blissfully unaware of what was happening) somewhat assuaged ministerial misgivings, particularly after the tsar ruled out retreat from his namesake Nikolaevsky Post, declaring that wherever the Russian flag had been raised it must not be taken down.

Acting quickly lest St. Petersburg relent or Beijing awake, Muraviev had Nevelskoi organize surveys of the Amgun, the lower Amur, the Tatar Strait, and Sakhalin. These were carried out during 1851–53 by Nikolai Boshnyak, Pyotr Kazakevich, Voin Rimsky-Korsakov (older brother of the composer), and Nikolai Busse, talented officers all save the last. Independently of Muraviev, Rear Admiral Efimy Putiatin opened frontier negotiations with Japan in 1853.[21] Russian outposts sprang up along the lower Amur (Mariinsk, Sofiisk), the Primorye coast (De Castries, Imperatorskaya Gavan), and on Sakhalin (Due, Muravievsky Post). Japanese, Chinese, and Koreans in these areas learned that they were on Russian territory, and the aborigines found themselves subjects of the tsar.[22] Imperial rhetoric belied the fragility of these footholds. Plagued by shortages of food in general and fresh vegetables in particular, one isolated Russian garrison succumbed to scurvy during the winter of 1853–54.

The Amur Expeditions, 1854–57

International developments helped Muraviev gain St. Petersburg's approval to act more boldly in the Priamur. The Taiping Rebellion that erupted in China in 1850 distracted Qing authorities who might otherwise have detected an intrusion in the Northeast. Meanwhile, the mounting presence of foreign warships in the North Pacific enabled Muraviev to cite Siberian security as justification for his own encroachment.

Deftly maneuvering between St. Petersburg's caution and Beijing's caducity, Muraviev correlated defense with expansion, strengthening Russia's periphery while preparing to breach China's. In 1851 he moved Kamchatka's military governor, Vasily Zavoiko, from Ayan out to Petropavlovsk and set up a regional administration in Transbaikalia. Because St. Petersburg would not provide levies, Muraviev raised his own Amur "shock troops" by organizing a Transbaikal *kazachestvo* (territorially based Cossack unit) from descendants of Don and Zaporozhe Cossacks supplemented by peasant recruits and convicts.[23]

With his forces in place, Muraviev asked St. Petersburg for permission to send an expedition down the Amur on the grounds that the international situation warranted reinforcing the empire's exposed Pacific outposts. St. Petersburg acceded, conditionally. In January 1854 Muraviev was given a mandate to descend the Amur, but he was forbidden to resort to force should the Manchus block his passage. Nicholas wanted "no smell of gunpowder."[24] The smell of gunpowder, however, filled the air after England and France declared war on Russia in March. As Anglo-French naval squadrons converged on Kamchatka and Sakhalin, Muraviev used wartime exigencies as a pretext to encroach on Chinese territory in the name of Sino-Russian security.

The first Amur expedition embarked from Sretensk in June 1854 in fifty barges and rafts. Provisioned with supplies requisitioned from Irkutsk merchants and escorted by 800 Cossacks and troops, the governor-general, his cousin the governor of Transbaikalia Mikhail Korsakov, and the flotilla commander Pyotr Kazakevich drifted down the Amur without incident as far as Aigun, where a Manchu garrison commander asked what they were doing. Muraviev explained that he was en route to the Pacific to defend Russian settlements from Anglo-French marauders, adding that it would be in China's interests if he were allowed to pass. He was, reluctantly.

Disembarking at Nikolaevsky Post, Muraviev sent most of the men on to Petropavlovsk, where they arrived in time to help Zavoiko repulse Anglo-French assaults on 31 August and 4 September.[25] Victory at Petropavlovsk, doubly welcome in St. Petersburg amid setbacks in the Crimea, renewed Muraviev's imperial mandate and opened the way for a second Amur expedition in the summer of 1855. This time the governor-general brought along 500 peasant settlers and the Imperial Russian Geographical Society's Richard Maak, whose surveys yielded data that proved useful during subsequent negotiations with Qing authorities.

Events outside of the region during 1855–56 proved decisive for the success of Muraviev's plans. Rear Admiral Putiatin concluded a frontier treaty with Japan,* enabling Muraviev to focus on China. Death claimed Nicholas I and Nesselrode, whose successors, Alexander II and Aleksandr Gorchakov, favored a more active policy in Asia to compensate for disappointments in the Balkans. Beijing had become cognizant of a problem in the Northeast but failed to act, thereby losing any chance to break Russia's grip on the Amur without external help.[26]

British naval surveys between Korea and Sakhalin in 1855–56 prompted Muraviev to move without delay into the Primorye after first coming up with an administrative contrivance to provide a veneer of legitimacy.† In November 1856 the governor-general established a new territorial unit, the Maritime District (Primorskaya oblast) based at Nikolaevsky Post (upgraded for the occasion to "Nikolaevsk") and governed by the Siberian flotilla commander Kazakevich. Embracing Chinese as well as Russian territory, the Maritime District served as an elastic fig leaf for encroachment.[27]

While preparing to advance into the Primorye, Muraviev established an outpost at Ust-Zeisk, strategically located at the confluence of the Amur and Zeya upstream from the Manchu fort at Aigun. Taking advantage of Beijing's war with England and France, the governor-general carried out a third Amur expedition in the spring of 1857, setting the stage for annexation.

Annexation, 1858–60

Russia absorbed the Priamur and the Primorye by a combination of encroachment, diplomacy, and luck. Empowered by St. Petersburg to negotiate a frontier agreement, Muraviev notified Manchu officials in Aigun

---

*The Treaty of Shimoda (7 Feb. 1855), which designated Sakhalin as a joint possession and defined the Russo-Japanese frontier in the Kurile Archipelago running between Iturup (Etorofu) and Urup.

†The surveys left a trail of English place-names along the Primorye coast: Barracouta Harbor (later Imperatorskaya Gavan), Port Seymour (later St. Olga), Port May (later Zolotoi Rog, the main harbor of Vladivostok), Victoria Bay (later Peter the Great Bay), Prince Albert Peninsula (later Muraviev-Amursky Peninsula). For an account by a member of the expedition, see Tronson, *Personal Narrative*.

in early 1858 that he intended to visit them and discuss border questions. The governor-general could hardly have picked a more propitious moment to press his case. War with England and France (October 1856–June 1858) distracted Beijing and promoted appeasement in the Northeast. Arriving by barge at Ust-Zeisk with a well-armed escort, the governor-general crossed the river to Aigun and met with Prince I-Shan who endured a week of blustery bonhomie before affixing his seal on 28 May to a document known as the Treaty of Aigun.

The 1858 treaty awarded the left bank of the Amur to Russia and the right bank as far as the Ussuri to China. Below the Ussuri, the Amur's right bank was defined as jointly held, subject to demarcation following the treaty's ratification. Navigation on the Amur, Sungari, and Ussuri was restricted to subjects of the two signatories. Manchus and Chinese living in some sixty-four settlements north of the Amur (i.e., on Russian territory) were allowed to retain their residence and citizenship.[28] Pleased with the treaty, Muraviev renamed Ust-Zeisk Blagoveshchensk ("Good Tidings").[29] Not letting euphoria slow his momentum, Muraviev ordered a military post established downstream at the Amur-Ussuri junction. This was promptly done at the site of a Manchu-Tungus hamlet called Boli, renamed Khabarovka in honor of a seventeenth-century promyshlennik whose exploits belied his namesake's cozily diminutive appellation.

Provisions for demarcating Sino-Russian frontiers were incorporated into the Treaty of Tianjin concluded by Putiatin a month after Aigun. Inattention to textual nuance and an underestimation of Muraviev's élan let Beijing in for some unpleasant surprises. Whereas the Manchu text stated that undemarcated lands lay close to the frontier, which Manchu officials took to mean between the Tatar Strait and the Amur-Ussuri junction, the Russian text could be construed as defining undemarcated territory between the *entire course* of the Ussuri and the Sea of Japan. Not content with this generous helping, Muraviev had his sights on a common frontier with Korea, thereby cutting off China from the Sea of Japan.[30] The governor-general lost no time in taking advantage of the ambiguity: he quickly dispatched Cossacks, troops, and naval officers to the Primorye, equipped with geographical data previously gathered by Maak and Venyukov.[31]

To press his advantage in the Primorye, Muraviev staked out 250 miles of coastline aboard the New York–built corvette *Amerika* during the summer of 1859, replacing British names that had barely been in place two years. Victoria Bay became Peter the Great Bay, and Prince Albert Peninsula became Muraviev Peninsula. Perhaps in consolation for Russia's elusive quest for Constantinople, Muraviev rechristened the inlet etched at the tip of the peninsula, long called Haishenwei by the Chinese and dubbed Port May by the British, the Golden Horn (Zolotoi Rog) and the straits to the south, Eastern Bosphorus. An officer accompanying Muraviev named the Golden Horn anchorage Port Vladivostok, but it was not until the summer of 1860 that the Russian imperial standard was raised over a cluster of huts, marking the official birth of Vladivostok.[32]

Muraviev's infiltration of the Primorye took place without Beijing's knowledge. When informed, Qing authorities were appalled to learn that the "jointly held territory" they had agreed to extended as far south as Korea.[33] Eastern Manchuria might have been salvaged had Beijing refused to ratify the 1858 treaties, but perils at home all but precluded this option and afforded St. Petersburg a providential opportunity to legitimize Russian encroachment under the guise of aid. When British and French forces occupied Beijing in October 1860, the twenty-eight-year-old Russian envoy, Nikolai Ignatiev, offered his country's good offices in mediating an Anglo-French withdrawal in exchange for a territorial adjustment in the Northeast, an offer that, under the circumstances, Manchu leaders found inexpedient to refuse.

By the Treaty of Beijing (14 November 1860), the Qing emperor ratified what had been signed at Aigun and Tianjin, thereby surrendering the Primorye and access to the Sea of Japan.[34] The river and land boundaries were to be demarcated the following year. When the Manchu surveyors failed to show up in 1861, Governor Kazakevich had his men place border markers on the Chinese banks of the Amur and Ussuri as if the rivers themselves belonged to Russia. Kazakevich was less successful in repeating this coup on the stretch between Lake Khanka and the Tumen River, which he hoped to push inland to the Muleng River, thus giving Russia a convenient water route from eastern Manchuria to the Ussuri. This time Qing authorities, painfully aware of the consequences of inaction, fielded surveyors who managed to contain the "Muleng bulge."[35]

Postmortem

When terms of the Aigun treaty became known in Europe, Friedrich Engels sardonically complimented Russia for "despoiling China of a country as large as France and Germany put together" without spilling a drop of blood.[36] Marx commented in a similar vein. Citing these passages, Soviet writers of the 1920s condemned the annexation of the Priamur and the Primorye and denounced Muraviev as an agent of tsarist imperialism, only to discover with the help of Stalin in the 1930s that Marx and Engels had in fact stressed the "progressive" role of Russia in the Far East.[37] Well before these historiographical somersaults, Muraviev's reputation had undergone several vicissitudes. Honored, reviled, and ignored while alive, he was accorded a measure of posthumous glory in 1891, when the future tsar Nicholas II unveiled his statue at Khabarovka.* After the establishment of Soviet rule, the statue was removed and destroyed, but in 1992, following the dissolution of the USSR, a replacement was cast from the original molds and erected on the same pedestal, which in the interim had supported among other objects an elfish plaster Lenin.

*The statue was the work of Aleksandr Opekushin (1838–1923), creator of the Pushkin monument in Moscow. Destined for Blagoveshchensk, the statue was diverted at the last moment to Khabarovka.

1. Tortoise and stelae in front of Khabarovsk Museum, ca. 1918, described by Vladimir Arseniev as the "tomb of a Chinese nobleman."

2. Tortoise with stelae removed after the Sino-Soviet split. Photographed by the author in 1972.

3. Gennady Nevelskoi

4. Nikolai Muraviev-Amursky

5. Monument to Muraviev-Amursky, Khabarovsk, ca. 1910

6. Lenin on Muraviev's pedestal, Khabarovsk. Photographed by the author in 1972.

Ороченъ Тонга (крещеный) За зиму 1909/1910. убилъ 3 тигра, 5 собачей, 20 козуль, 3 оленя, 35 кабановъ, 150 бълокъ, 28 изюбрей, кабъ = 7 изюбрей. 1910.

7. Orochen youth with Ussuri tiger trophies

8. Chinese temple, Vladivostok

9. Chinese ginseng gatherers in Ussuri taiga

10. Chinese couple with children

11. Chinese man, Russian woman in Amur goldfields

12. *Novosely* ("new settlers")

13. Representatives of ethnic groups in the Priamur, ca. 1910

14. Molokan women, Amur District

15. Japanese stores on Muravievo-Amursky Prospekt, Khabarovsk, 1903

16. Rural branch of Kunst & Albers

17. Advertisement for Enoch Emery's Amur Steam & Navigation Company

18. Oriental Institute, Vladivostok

19. United States Consulate-General, Vladivostok

20. Stepan Makarov

21. Nikolai Baikov, ca. 1935

22. Vladimir Arseniev, ca. 1927

23. Aleksandr Krasnoshchekov and children, ca. 1918

24. Allied Troop parade along the Svetlanskaya, Vladivostok, 1918

25. American doughboys showing the flag, Vladivostok, 1918

26. General Oi Shigemoto and Colonel Henry Styer and staff, Khabarovsk, 1918. Colonel Charles Morrow is seated on the extreme left.

27. Japanese parade, Khabarovsk, 1919

28. A doughboy and Chinese troops, Primorye, 1919

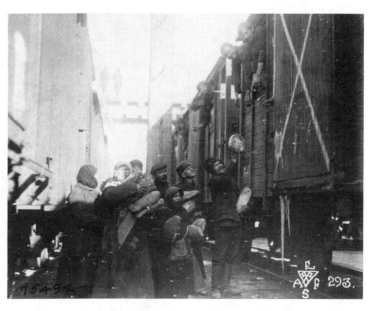

29. Peasants giving bread to "Bolshevik" prisoners, Nikolsk-Ussuriisk, 1919

30. Women and children waiting for slops outside American kitchen, Vladivostok, 1919

31. Washing clothes in the street, Khabarovsk, 1919

PART II

The Russian Far East

7

« « » »

Toward a Far Eastern Viceroyalty

The wings of the Russian eagle are spread too far over Asia
to leave the slightest doubt as to their presence. Our
organic connection with all these countries is the warrant
of our future, when the term "Asiatic Russia" will signify
the whole of Asia. — Prince E. E. Ukhtomsky (1900)

Once the exhilaration of festivities, honors, and promotions had worn
off, amurtsy experienced the inevitable letdown. Personal differences hardened into estrangement. Muraviev's prestige eroded under a stream of criticism by radical intellectuals, some of it justified, some inspired by envy. The
Utopian Socialist Mikhail Petrashevsky denounced the governor-general as
a "tyrant" in a London émigré newspaper.[1] From his perch in Chita, the
Decembrist Dmitry Zavalishin accused Muraviev of appropriating his
(Zavalishin's) "Amur idea."[2] From Irkutsk exile the historian Afanasy
Shchapov wrote Alexander II that Muraviev fancied himself a "Siberian
tsar."[3] Embittered, Muraviev resigned and moved to Paris, where he died of
gangrene in 1881. While Kazakevich and Venyukov went on to distinguished careers in administration and science, respectively, other amurtsy
fared poorly. Nikolai Busse, governor of the Amur District, died of syphilis
in 1866. Muraviev's cousin Korsakov passed away in 1871 after compiling
an indifferent record as governor-general of Eastern Siberia. Nevelskoi lost
money in investments and succumbed to a heart attack in 1876.[4] Putiatin
scalded himself to death in a Paris hotel bath.[5] Boshnyak suffered a nervous
breakdown and spent the last twenty-eight years of his life in an Italian
insane asylum.[6]

Search for a Regional Leadership

During the 1860s and 1870s, imperial priorities drifted away from Pacific Asia. Alaska was sold to the United States in 1867. The central and northern Kuriles were handed over to Japan in exchange for outright possession of Sakhalin in 1875. As Russian armies advanced into Bukhara and Samarkand, Central Asia usurped the Amur's erstwhile topicality in chancelleries and salons.

Against this background the Far East stagnated as a neglected ward of the governor-generalship of Eastern Siberia. Irkutsk-based governor-generals between 1861 and 1879 took no major initiatives in the area. A veteran of Putiatin's Japan Expedition (1853–55), Konstantin Posyet, made a bid to promote Far Eastern development on the eve of his appointment as communications minister. On his return from Vladivostok in 1874, Posyet proposed the construction of a railway from the Volga to the Amur, the abolition of the exile system, and the establishment of economic relations with Korea to develop a food base for the Primorye.[7] Requiring major budgetary outlays not to mention an overhaul of the penal system, Posyet's proposals went against bureaucratic instincts and failed to win support from a reform-jaded Alexander II. The tsar and his ministers approved the railway idea in principle but took no measures affecting the Far East. Appointed governor-general of Eastern Siberia in 1880, Dmitry Anuchin favored colonization, but unlike Muraviev, he would not take a bold initiative without the Center's approval. Writing in 1881, one observer characterized the Far East in bleak terms: Nikolaevsk was completely rundown; communications around the Okhotsk seaboard were haphazard; foreigners dominated commerce everywhere; and bandits from Manchuria raided at will.[8]

At this juncture a combination of external and internal developments forced St. Petersburg to upgrade the Far East in imperial priorities. An escalating Anglo-Russian rivalry in the Balkans, the Middle East, and Central Asia spilled over into Northeast Asia. Seeking dynastic revitalization through "self-strengthening," Beijing loosened its restrictions on Han Chinese immigration to Manchuria in 1878 and having checked Russian encroachment in the Ili district of Chinese Turkestan in 1881, flexed its muscles in the Northeast. Following the overthrow of the Tokugawa shogunate in 1868, Japan's oligarchs fashioned a centralized bureaucratic state and embarked on a purposeful program of economic modernization coupled with cautious self-assertion as a regional power. Both Beijing and Tokyo had their eyes on Korea, whose faction-ridden monarchy and aristocrats could not cope with the erosion of a Confucian East Asian order. In St. Petersburg the accession of Tsar Alexander III in 1881 and the appointment of Asiatic Department chief Nikolai Giers as foreign minister the following year ushered Northeast Asia into the calculus of Russian *Weltpolitik*.[9]

When St. Petersburg recognized that territory from the Korean frontier to the Bering Strait had a new geostrategic significance, it detached the Transbaikal, Amur, Maritime, and Sakhalin districts from the Eastern Siberian governor-generalship and placed them in a newly created Priamur governor-generalship in 1884 (see Map 6). The Priamur governor-generalship gave the Far East its first separate, unified administration and provided an institutional framework for a regional identity distinct from that of Siberia. Personally selected by and accountable only to the tsar, Priamur governor-generals wielded extraordinary powers. They commanded police and military forces (including the Amur and Ussuri *kazachestvos*), administered justice, collected taxes, oversaw economic development, and conducted diplomacy with neighboring countries.[10] In the Far East as in the Caucasus, "governor-general" carried strong military overtones. Of eight governor-generals, seven were army officers. The military monopoly over the highest reaches of the regional administration endured until 1910 when the first civilians were appointed to both this post and the governorship of the Maritime District (see Appendix C).

Military considerations underlay the choice of Khabarovka (1884 pop. 5,000) as headquarters of the Priamur governor-generalship. Strategically situated on the Amur-Ussuri junction, it was neither vulnerable to naval attack like Vladivostok nor exposed to Manchuria like Blagoveshchensk. Khabarovka took shape along three parallel ridges meeting the Amur at perpendicular angles and overlooking low-lying land to the west and southwest. Along the ravines between the ridges flowed two streams, the Plyusninka and the Chardymovka, named after local merchants. Along the top of the central ridge ran a broad, unpaved street named after Muraviev-Amursky.[11] Khabarovka was semantically upgraded to Khabarovsk in 1893 and gradually showed signs of deserving an urban nomenclature. An influx of troops, officials, and Chinese merchants and laborers pushed the population up to 15,000 in 1897. By 1900 Khabarovsk had a Russian Orthodox cathedral, a Roman Catholic church, a synagogue, a woman's academy, and several church schools. Education and cultural life took sustenance from

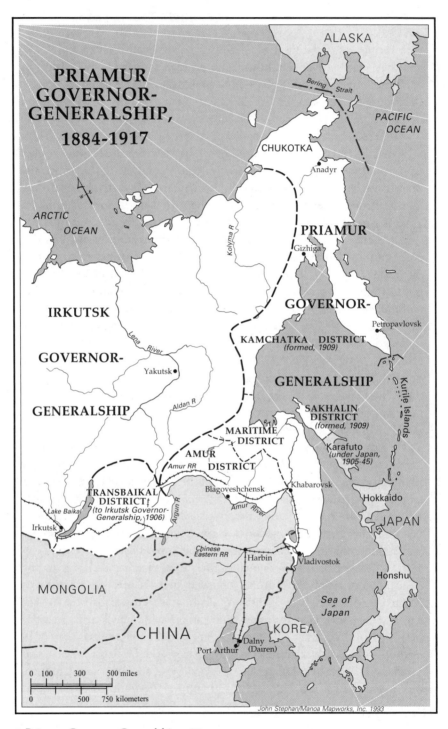

6. Priamur Governor-Generalship, 1884–1917

local philanthropists. Three prominent merchants, Andrei Plyusnin, Mikhail Chardymov, and Illiodor Rafailov, founded and funded schools. Rafailov opened to the public his botanical garden of exotic plants from around the world.[12]

The first Priamur governor-general, Baron A. N. Korf, actively involved himself in economic and cultural matters. He brought together community leaders at conferences in 1885, 1886, and 1893 to discuss ways of promoting regional development. He encouraged colonization and commerce consistent with the maintenance of public order and protection of marine life. He donated 100,000 rubles and an ethnographical collection to what became the Grodekov Museum (today the Khabarovsk Museum of Regional Studies). Korf's successors, Sergei Dukhovskoi and Nikolai Grodekov, allowed the conferences and gala balls to lapse but continued to subsidize education and patronize the arts.

Unlike the explorer Nikolai Przhevalsky, who in 1886 wrote Alexander III, "Give me a company of soldiers and I'll conquer China,"* Korf, a professional cavalry officer fully aware of the costs involved, had little enthusiasm for military adventures. In 1887, skeptical of annexationist designs on Chinese territory south of the Amur, the governor-general presciently warned against getting involved in Korea. He differed with Communications Minister Posyet and later Finance Minister Sergei Witte about the functions of railroads. Arguing that they should serve regional development rather than project imperial power into non-Russian Asia, he favored linking Vladivostok to Khabarovsk and the upper Amur before constructing a line across Siberia.[13]

Korf's caution derived from a knowledge of the Priamur's vulnerability. In 1885 only 15,000 troops were deployed east of Lake Baikal, and the closest Russian railhead was 3,000 miles from Khabarovka. The Pacific Squadron depended on imported coal and winter anchorages in Nagasaki. The British Navy had occupied three Korean islands in readiness for operations against Vladivostok. Beijing had asked St. Petersburg to give back the Posyet district so as to restore China's outlet to the Sea of Japan. Korf's low estimation of the Priamur's defenses was shared by a Chinese spy, who reported to the military governor of Jilin in 1885 that Boli (Khabarovka) could be seized with little difficulty.[14]

Obzor russkoi periodicheskoi pechati, 4: 43. Such bluster was more likely an expression of exuberant gamesmanship than of arrogant disdain for China. According to Khisamutdinov, *Terra incognita*, pp. 145–46, Przhevalsky funded an opulent edition of his Primorye travel diary with money won from card games and wagers in Nikolaevsk during the winter of 1868–69.

Vulnerability was far from people's minds in May and June of 1891 when the tsarevich Nicholas Alexandrovich passed through the Priamur on his way back to St. Petersburg from a tour of Siam, China, and Japan.[15] The crown prince was accompanied by Prince Esper Ukhtomsky, whose rhetoric about Russia's historic mission in Asia left an imprint on the twenty-three-year-old future autocrat no less telling than the head wound inflicted by a sword-wielding Japanese policeman two weeks before he arrived in Vladivostok. The visit bristled with imperial symbolism. On 31 May the tsarevich, who within a year would become chairman of the Committee for the Trans-Siberian Railroad, officially inaugurated the construction of the Ussuri Line by shoveling dirt into a wheelbarrow and hauling it to a nearby embankment. As Nicholas moved through the Priamur, authorities held military reviews and banquets while adoring crowds greeted him with bread, salt, and icons. Triumphal arches were erected in his honor at Vladivostok, Khabarovka, and Blagoveshchensk. This rapturous reception probably nourished the young man's illusions about Russia's capabilities in Northeast Asia, but Korf did not live to see how these illusions led St. Petersburg to gamble Russia's resources and prestige in Manchuria at the expense of the Priamur. In 1893 the sixty-seven-year-old baron collapsed during a gala ball in Khabarovsk and expired on the spot.[16]

Manchurian Magnet, 1894–1904

Starting around 1894, with Nicholas's ascension to the throne, the Priamur became a staging ground for Russian penetration into Manchuria. In contrast to the 1840s and 1850s, when amurtsy could present St. Petersburg with a fait accompli, St. Petersburg now took initiatives and thrust them on the periphery. Korf's successors carried little weight at the Center. Dukhovskoi was not even consulted when St. Petersburg joined with France and Germany in the Triple Intervention of 1895 forcing Japan to relinquish the Liaodong Peninsula, trophy of a recently concluded war with China. Nor did he have much of a say about railroads. When Witte devised the strategy of building a line from Transbaikalia across Manchuria to Vladivostok,* Dukhovskoi tried to argue that the Priamur was too weak to support

---

*Earlier, in 1892, Witte had envisioned a railroad entirely on Russian territory along the Amur to link up with the Ussuri Line, but he changed his mind in 1893 when surveys revealed the engineering problems posed by some 200 rivers and marshy stretches between Sretensk and Khabarovsk. Romanov, *Rossiia v Man'chzhurii*, pp. 82–83; Valliant, pp. 96–98.

expansion into northeastern China and would suffer from a trans-Manchurian line. As an alternative, Dukhovskoi proposed a route from Sretensk to Blagoveshchensk via Hailar, arguing that it would promote Russian settlement of the Amur District and strengthen defenses against Japan.[17] Nicholas rejected Dukhovskoi's proposal in favor of Witte's. Accordingly, work on the Chinese Eastern Railroad (CER) started in 1896, after Witte engineered a Russo-Chinese alliance and set up a Russo-Chinese Bank directed by Prince Ukhtomsky.[18]

Witte's triumphs of 1895–96 drew Russia into Korea and southern Manchuria. The finance minister preferred to reach a modus vivendi with Japan over Korea, but bureaucratic rivals derailed his plans by going after a warm water port in southern Manchuria, extracting from Beijing in 1897 a twenty-five-year lease of the Guandong Territory (1,300 square miles at the tip of the Liaodong Peninsula, including a naval base at Port Arthur [Lüshun] and a commercial port at Dalny [Dalian, during 1905–45 Dairen]) and a CER spur from Harbin to Port Arthur. Russia thereupon took de facto possession of 2,000 square miles of northeastern China, including territory that St. Petersburg had forced Japan to return to China in 1895. Defense of the CER zone north of Mukden fell to the Priamur governor-general,* while Witte himself assumed command of the CER zone border guards, whom some wit dubbed "Matilda's Guards" after the minister's spouse. The Guandong Leasehold came under a separate military administration in Port Arthur.

The appearance of a Russian military presence in Northeast Asia independent of the Priamur disturbed Nikolai Grodekov, who succeeded Dukhovskoi as governor-general in 1898. An infantry general who had spent a decade campaigning around Russian Turkestan and Afghanistan, Grodekov was a man of action. The governor-general also had an acute sense of his own niche in history, and while posted to Khabarovsk as Dukhovskoi's executive assistant (1893–98) steeped himself in the amurtsy tradition. The hour of opportunity seemed to have come in the summer of 1900, when reacting against the latest round of China's dismemberment, antiforeign violence in the form of the Boxer Rebellion threatened Russian lives and property in Manchuria. Amid rumors of imminent Boxer attacks on Blagoveshchensk and Vladivostok, Grodekov ordered the military governors of

---

*Mukden is now called Shenyang. Strictly speaking, the CER extended to about 40 miles north of Mukden.

the Amur and Maritime districts to be ready for any contingency. The former overreacted and after precipitating a noyade of Blagoveshchensk's Chinese,* occupied and proclaimed Russian sovereignty over adjacent parts of Manchuria. Perhaps thinking that he could carry off a Muravievian fait accompli, Grodekov cabled War Minister Aleksei Kuropatkin comparing his subordinate with Nevelskoi.[19]

Grodekov's bout with latter-day Amur activism was symptomatic of Russia's East Asian policy as it fell hostage to jurisdictional and factional disputes.[20] Witte urged reliance on trade and investment to project Russian influence into Manchuria so as not to provoke Chinese resistance or international complications. Kuropatkin favored annexing northern Manchuria so as to straighten out the frontier between Transbaikalia and Vladivostok. Court adventurers hatched schemes for Korea. Nearly everyone, except Witte if we are to believe his memoirs, dismissed the risk of provoking Japan.[21]

Factions in St. Petersburg had their counterparts in the Far East, where administrative jurisdictions overlapped between Khabarovsk and Port Arthur. Successive Priamur governor-generals and Guandong Leasehold commanders haggled over who took precedence in matters of taxation and justice along the CER strip. The balance of forces gradually tilted in favor of Port Arthur. By 1902 there were more Russian troops in Manchuria (100,000) than in the Priamur (80,000), and by 1903 the Priamur had been pushed into the background.[22] Russian colonists and French capital poured into Manchuria rather than into the Priamur. Rail traffic on the CER flowed through Dalny rather than Vladivostok, and important consultations were held in Port Arthur rather than Khabarovsk. Harbin surpassed both Khabarovsk and Vladivostok as a transport hub and commercial center. Although Far Eastern commitments claimed a third of the state budget in 1903,[23] very little of that went into the Priamur.

The primacy of Manchuria received institutional expression in August 1903, when Nicholas II created the Viceroyalty (*Namestnichestvo*) of the Far East, uniting the Priamur governor-generalship, the CER zone, and the Guandong Leasehold into a single administrative unit based at Port Arthur.

---

*When Blagoveshchensk came under sporadic bombardment from Sagalian across the Amur in July 1900, Governor K. N. Gribsky ordered all local Chinese deported to Manchuria. Cossacks rounded up 3,500 men, women, and children and drove them into the river, shooting and hacking laggards. Approximately 100 reached the Manchurian bank alive. An additional 7,000 were killed in villages around Blagoveshchensk.

The Priamur governor-general thereupon became a subordinate of the Far Eastern viceroy (*namestnik*), Admiral Evgeny Ivanovich Alekseyev, sixty-year-old uncle of Nicholas II.* Alekseyev was also entrusted with responsibility for diplomatic relations with neighboring countries, further complicating the tangle of ministerial jurisdictions.[24] Generously endowed with arrogance and incompetence, Alekseyev managed to alienate a large number of senior officers in his sprawling bailiwick. More seriously, by confirming Tokyo's worst suspicions, the Viceroyalty hastened the onslaught of a war for which Russia was woefully unprepared. Within a year of his appointment, Alekseyev had taken refuge in Harbin as Japanese armies converged on the Liaodong Peninsula. After the fall of Port Arthur in January 1905, the viceroyalty lost its raison d'être. Its abolition on 1 July passed unnoticed and unlamented.[25]

Defeat begot new illusions. An army general-staff report compared withdrawal from southern Manchuria in 1905 with withdrawal from the Amur in 1689, implying that it was a case of *reculer pour mieux sauter*.[26] Some Priamur bureaucrats expected Khabarovsk to regain its administrative preeminence, while some Primorye businessmen imagined that Vladivostok would recapture commerce from Dairen, as Dalny was renamed by the Japanese. Some radicals thought that Russia's humiliation at the hands of Japan sounded the death knell of autocracy. Prince Ukhtomsky had fallen silent, but scaled-back visions of a Russian cultural ecumene in Northeast Asia animated the imaginations of latter-day amurtsy. At least one academic publicly predicted that Russia's presence in the Asia-Pacific region would revitalize the Empire.[27] All of the above scenarios materialized, but not at the time or in the way that their authors imagined.

---

*Notwithstanding the patronymic, Alekseyev was the illegitimate son of Alexander II.

« « » »

Patterns of Settlement

The last exile on the Amur breathes more easily than the
first general in Russia.   — Anton Chekhov (1890)

B etween 1859 and 1917 over half a
million people moved to what some
called a "New America."* Though the Far East did not match Western Sibe-
ria in volume, it held its own in diversity, accommodating besides Russians,
Ukrainians, Belorussians, Cossacks, Finns, Estonians, Latvians, Germans,
Jews, Chinese, Japanese, Koreans, and Americans, not to mention the stray
Swiss and Scot. Immigration transformed the region's demographic profile.
In the Priamur and the Primorye, aborigines declined precipitously in relative terms, numbering merely 45,000, or 5 percent of the inhabitants in 1911.
Only in the Northeast and Transbaikalia did indigenous peoples constitute a
significant proportion of the population, and only in Yakutia did they retain
their numerical preponderance. Immigrants boosted the Slavic portion of
the population from 66 percent in 1897 to 80 percent in 1917.[1]

Cossacks

The Amur and Ussuri kazachestvos, established respectively in 1859 and
1860, formed a distinct socioeconomic stratum, with generous land allotments, tax exemptions, and a separate military administration. Leavened
with convicts and penal battalion incorrigibles, they offered unpromising

*This phrase, quoted in a major 1909 study of the Far East, was attributed to Niels E. Hansen,
a University of South Dakota professor who conducted first-hand observations of Siberian
settlement in 1894, 1897, 1905, and 1906 for the U.S. Department of Agriculture. *Priamur'e*,
p. 848.

material for any colonizing venture. Muraviev's hopes that they would build healthy agrarian communities proved illusory, although Cossack villages near Blagoveshchensk appeared orderly and clean to one observer in 1866.[2] Amur and Ussuri Cossacks cultivated less than 1 percent of their holdings, and some abandoned the land altogether in favor of part-time labor or brigandage.[3] It was not unheard of for men to sell the favors of their wives and daughters for provisions and drink.[4]

Free, self-governing, and self-sustaining Cossack communities did not develop in the Far East as they had along the Don. Inexperienced as agriculturists and overextended by military, constabulary, and postal duties, most Cossack households just managed to subsist.[5] Governor-Generals Dukhovskoi and Grodekov tried to reinvigorate Cossack communities by resettling families from the Don, Orenburg, Kuban, and Urals along the Ussuri and around Lake Khanka, but these efforts did not stem the decline of Cossacks as a percentage of the Far East's population: from 85 percent (1859) to 18 percent (1897) in the Amur District; from 43 percent (1869) to 6 percent (1897) in the Maritime District.[6]

Land became a source of tension between Cossacks and peasants. Because most of the former were unable or unwilling to cultivate all of their allotments, some settlers started to move in and clear homesteads for themselves around the edges. The Cossacks regarded this as encroachment, but their appeals to higher officials to exclude peasants from frontier areas fell on deaf ears because the Priamur governor-generals were more interested in promoting Slavic colonization and expanding the regional food base than in preserving the integrity of underutilized parcels. Dukhovskoi and Grodekov offered peasants land near the frontier on condition that they share certain duties with Cossacks. The last governor-general, Nikolai Gondatti (1911–17), went further and distributed frontier plots to peasants without attaching service obligations.[7]

Meanwhile, the Amur and Ussuri Cossack communities themselves underwent structural changes. What started out as a motley aggregation in 1860 differentiated into atamans (officers drawn from regular army units), cavalrymen, policemen, and agriculturists. Successful Cossack farmers hired substitutes to discharge their military service obligations, thereby freeing themselves to consolidate their advantages as cultivators. Some Ussuri Cossacks hired Koreans and Chinese to till their fields. Economic stratification gave rise to envy and resentment, but whether this merited the name "class struggle" is a matter of debate.[8]

Peasants

Peasant migration to the Far East fell into three phrases: (1) 1859–82, (2) 1882–1907, and (3) 1908–17. Each phase was characterized by distinctive government policies, modes of transport, and types of immigrants.

Although St. Petersburg removed some statutory obstacles to peasant migration in 1859, colonization got off to a slow start. Only 250 families came to the Far East in the years 1859–61.[9] Eastward movement picked up in conjunction with Alexander II's Great Reforms in general and the emancipation of serfs in particular. In 1862 an imperial edict granted settlers to the Far East 100 *desyatins* (one desyatin = 2.7 acres) of land per household, exemption from conscription for ten years, and exemption from taxation for twenty years.[10] During the next decade about 5,000 "hundred desyatiners" moved to the Priamur from Western Siberia, Transbaikalia, the Volga, and the Urals, forming the nucleus of the region's prosperous peasantry.[11] Although an overwhelming majority of these newcomers were Russians, Finnish and Estonian colonies cropped up along the shores of Peter the Great Bay starting in 1869.[12] Settlers fared variously depending on the location of allotments. In the middle Amur, peasants found their grain and vegetables in demand in Blagoveshchensk and the Zeya goldfields. Conditions were less favorable along the lower Amur, where enterprising immigrants gave up their original allotments in favor of the warmer climes, richer soils, and ready markets of the southern Primorye.[13]

Among the 14,000 peasants who migrated to the Far East between 1859 and 1882, the Khudyakov family showed what could be achieved by ingenuity, energy, and good fortune. Forty-one-year-old Leonty arrived in the Primorye from Tomsk in 1877 with his wife and five sons ranging in age from three to eleven. Draining his parcel of land near Razdolnoye, he planted and harvested crops of grain and vegetables, assisted by his growing children. Eventually the boys married and had sons of their own until three generations worked together on adjacent farms. Seeing a commercial opportunity, the Khudyakovs cultivated ginseng with the help of a Chinese whom they had saved from Manchurian bandits called *hong huzi*.* Father and sons built a five-ton schooner and descended the Suifen River to fish in Amur Bay. Venturing farther afield each year, by 1910 the sons were bring-

---

*The term *hong huzi* (literally "red beards") may have been coined by Manchus and Chinese in reference to "red-bearded" Russians who preyed on Amur natives during the 17th century. Harvey J. Howard, *Ten Weeks with Chinese Bandits* (New York: Dodd, Mead, 1926), pp. 2–3.

ing back sealskins and walrus tusks from the Sea of Okhotsk. To cope with the ubiquitous *hong huzi*, the Khudyakovs erected watchtowers, dug underground bunkers, and kept their powder dry, enabling them to repulse periodic assaults. Less provident homesteaders took fatal risks. One day in 1879 a Finnish sea captain, Fridolf Heeck, returned to his home at Sidemi on an Amur Bay peninsula opposite Vladivostok to find the house in ruins, his common-law wife and manservant slaughtered, and his seven-year-old son abducted.[14] What befell the Khudyakov and Heeck families threatened isolated southern Primorye settlements well into the twentieth century.

The second phase of peasant migration (1882–1907) was shaped by the advent of maritime transport to the Far East. Almost all arrivals before 1882 had come across Siberia and down the Amur, an undertaking so time-consuming and arduous that one St. Petersburg bureaucrat preferred to travel to and from his Maritime District post via New York and San Francisco.[15] Until the railroads reached Transbaikalia and Manchuria in the 1890s, emigrants from Central Russia and the Ukraine favored the Volunteer Fleet, an offspring of the Anglo-Russian war scare of 1877. Looking for vessels to use as raiders against British commerce, St. Petersburg ordered several 5,000-ton steamers from German shipyards. When the war scare subsided in 1878, the steamers were purchased with funds raised by public subscription in the name of the Volunteer Fleet Company, with offices in Odessa and Vladivostok. The first group to capitalize on the new service arrived in 1882 when the *Rossiya* steamed into the Golden Horn after a record-setting forty-six-day journey from Odessa via the Dardanelles, Suez, the Indian Ocean, the East China Sea, and the Sea of Japan.[16]

Meanwhile, on taking office as the governor-general of Eastern Siberia, Dmitry Anuchin had been trying to persuade St. Petersburg of the benefits of resettling peasants from overpopulated southwestern provinces of the Empire to the strategically sensitive southern Primorye.[17] Anuchin's efforts were rewarded in 1882 by the South Ussuri Resettlement Law, providing land allotments (fifteen desyatins per person, with a maximum of 100 per family), five years of tax exemption, food supplies for eighteen months, and free tools, construction materials, agricultural implements, and transportation from Odessa to Vladivostok. To administer the program, a South Ussuri Resettlement Office opened in Vladivostok, headed from 1883 by a member of the Primorye governor's staff, Fyodor Busse.

From 1882 through 1907 about 243,000 peasants arrived in the Far East from the Ukraine (64%), Siberia (17%), and central Russia (11%), with small contingents from Belorussia, the lower Volga, and the Urals.[18] Whereas the Amur region absorbed most immigrants before 1882, about 75 percent in this second phase made their homes in the Primorye, thanks to the Volunteer Fleet and, from 1901, the Chinese Eastern Railroad.[19] The preponderance of Ukrainians made itself felt in village names like Poltavka, Kievka, Chernigovka, and Chuguyevka, giving birth to the expression "Ukrainian Far East."[20] The Ukrainian connection acquired political significance after the establishment of Soviet rule.

Most settlers arriving before 1900 came from the middle strata of the rural population. The government discouraged poor peasants from using the Volunteer Fleet by requiring each family to make a 600-ruble deposit in Odessa, an obstacle that some families circumvented by pooling their resources to pay the deposit and traveling as a putative "family," then dividing up the refund and the land allotted to them by the Resettlement Office in Vladivostok.[21] In 1901, in conjunction with the penetration of Manchuria, St. Petersburg broke with precedent and resettled poor peasants from European Russia and the Ukraine in the Sikhote Alin and along the Primorye coast.[22]

During the third stage (1908–17) some 300,000 settlers moved to the Far East, more than during the previous half-century. Reflecting Prime Minister P. A. Stolypin's attempt to create a class of peasant proprietors throughout Russia, immigration at this time is referred to as the "Stolypin wave." Many emigrants of this period came by train in "Stolypin cars" divided into equal sections for humans and livestock.[23] They were largely Russian and Ukrainian poor peasants and agricultural laborers who were less technologically literate and less entrepreneurial than their predecessors.[24] *Novosely* ("new settlers") who received good land in the Bureya and Zeya valleys helped double grain production in the Amur District between 1906 and 1913.[25] On the less hospitable lower Amur, about 15 percent of the newcomers abandoned their allotments.[26]

In the southern Primorye the "Stolypin wave" collided with commercialization. *Starozhily* ("old settlers") and Cossacks were renting out part of their allotments to Chinese and Korean tenants, and the state was selling land to merchants, shipowners, retired military officers, officials, and naturalized foreigners. Novosely had three choices: to cultivate parcels in marginal areas, become tenants, or hire themselves out as seasonal laborers on commercial farms.[27] Feelings between starozhily and novosely varied among districts and individual households, but here too some historians have perceived symptoms of "class struggle."[28]

Social differentiation should not obscure the fact that the Priamur was one of the most economically dynamic provinces of Imperial Russia during the last decade of tsarist rule. Land under cultivation increased 42 percent between 1911 and 1917, a rate outstripping the United States, Canada, and Australia.[29] The Far East had the second highest birthrate in Russia (after Siberia) and a lower death rate than France.[30] Village organizations were stronger than in European Russia.[31] Peasant cooperatives allowed cultivators to pool their resources when selling crops and buying provisions, to operate their own dairies and machinery repair shops, to run their own schools, and to negotiate their own contracts with American, German, Japanese, and British firms.[32]

Sectarians

Religious sectarians occupied a special position among peasant migrants to the Far East. Following the Great Schism within the Russian Orthodox Church in 1658, many of those unreconciled to new liturgical forms, referred to variously as "Old Believers" or "sectarians," crossed the Urals to continue their practices undisturbed. During the eighteenth century *Skoptsy* (from the word "eunuch," a sect stressing sexual abstinence) and *Dukhobors* (lit. "soul strugglers," who emphasized the supreme authority of inner experience and believed that the Spirit was embodied in their leaders) founded communities that acknowledged the authority of neither the Russian Orthodox Church nor the Russian state.[33]

Sectarians migrated to the Far East in increasing numbers during the 1860s, attracted by the opening of 470,000 desyatins of imperial domains along the middle Amur. Dukhobors and Molokans (a Dukhobor offshoot, whose dietary laws permitted the drinking of milk during Lent) gravitated to the environs of Blagoveshchensk. German Mennonites and Baptists settled along the Zeya and Bureya. By 1880 Old Believers accounted for half the population of the Amur district, which had more religious sectarians than any province in Russia.[34] Smaller communities clustered in the Sikhote Alin and on the Khanka Plain.[35]

Shunning alcohol and tobacco and stressing hard work, sobriety, and self-reliance, sectarians built strong and stable communities. Their abundant harvests and sturdy homes with "German corners" (*nemetskie ugli* was a Priamur idiom for solid construction) contrasted with the unworked fields and rundown structures characteristic of Cossack lands.[36] Molokans were quick to take advantage of new technology, and by the 1890s their imported harvesters and reapers gave the Amur district more agricultural machinery per capita than any province in the Russian Empire. Credited by Prime Minister Stolypin with making the Amur District a model of modern agriculture, Molokan farmers were enlisted to grow crops on Kamchatka.[37] Molokans also showed themselves to be good businessmen, operating their own Amur steamship lines and Blagoveshchensk flour mills. Success bred envy, and stereotypes of tight-fisted, money-loving Molokans outlived the communities themselves.[38]

Convicts and Exiles

The living conditions of the three million people forcibly sent to Siberia between 1584 and 1917 varied by place and time. Officials who had fallen from favor or wound up on the losing side of a factional struggle might be given administrative exile beyond the Urals, a harder blow to amour propre than to well-being. At the other end of the spectrum, a person condemned to convict labor (*katorga*) stood a fair chance of losing his health if not his life. Political exiles, about 10 percent of the total, experienced anything from arctic bleakness to Altai bucolics, from physical drudgery to literary soirées.

About a fifth of those sent beyond the Urals wound up east of Lake Baikal, a region that gained special notoriety, thanks to books by Anton Chekhov and Vlas Doroshevich about Sakhalin and by George Kennan about Transbaikalia.* At the time they wrote, political exiles as a rule fared better than common criminals, for many of the exiles were allowed to live independently. One revolutionary recalled that he took along his books, enjoyed freedom of movement within several thousand square miles, and was supplied at government expense with writing paper, weather-recording instruments, and a Winchester rifle, pistol, and shotgun.[39] When socialist exiles in Yakutsk rose up to protest travel restrictions in 1904, they wielded Browning automatic pistols and hunting guns previously issued to them by the local police.[40]

Escape was common and usually successful, at least in the short run. In 1861 Mikhail Bakunin rode a barge down the Amur and boarded an American schooner at De Castries Bay for San Francisco. During the next half-

---

*Tsarist authorities, who had given Kennan access to Siberian penal facilities in 1885–86 under the impression that the American was a "friend of St. Petersburg," proscribed *Siberia and the Exile System* when it appeared in 1891 but lifted the ban in 1905.

century, a number of revolutionaries followed his example, including the prominent Menshevik Lev Deich, who left Blagoveshchensk by river steamer. In 1901 Leib Bronshtein secured a blank passport in Irkutsk, inscribed "Leon Trotsky" as the name of his Odessa jailer, and embarked for London. Thousands of convicts took off into the taiga and became vagabonds, or in local vernacular, "joined General Cuckoo's Army." "Cuckoo's troops" usually turned up in the spring thaw as "snowdrops," a floral euphemism for corpses. To survive, one had to have "the cleverness of a Chinaman, the nose of a dog, the eyes of a falcon, the ears of a rabbit, and the dexterity of a tiger."[41] The Sikhote Alin, rarely visited by officials, offered vagabonds ample scope for malfeasance. While surveying the range in 1906, Vladimir Arseniev encountered a self-styled "promyshlennik," who confided that he "hunted grouse and swans" (shot Chinese and Koreans).[42]

Employment offered an alternative to escape. A fair number of political exiles sublimated revolutionary impulses into science, education, and business in the Priamur and the Primorye. People's Will exiles arriving in Vladivostok from Sakhalin during 1896–1903 added yeast to local intellectual life. Lyudmila Volkenshtein devoted herself to education and social work. Gilyary Gostkevich promoted a trade union movement while working in the Ussuri Railroad administration. Boris Orzhikh dabbled in journalism before emigrating to Japan where he established a populist Russian-language newspaper.[43] Mikhail Yankovsky, sentenced to hard labor for involvement in the 1863 Polish uprising, enlivened the southern Primorye from 1879 until 1910, when at the age of sixty-nine he eloped with a young woman to Sochi. During these three decades, Yankovsky raised a family, bred horses and reindeer, and cultivated ginseng at a picturesque farm at Sidemi on a peninsula across Amur Bay from Vladivostok. An elaborately unpretentious retreat for upwardly mobile families and their friends, Sidemi resembled a Russian Hyannis Port. The guest roster featured the ethnographer Vladimir Arseniev, the poet Konstantin Balmont, the governor of the Ussuri District Aleksandr Sukhanov, and the Swiss entrepreneur Yulius Bryner, who married Yankovsky's cousin. Yulius's grandson is said to have romped barefoot around Sidemi as he would on the stage decades later in *The King and I* under the name Yul Brynner.[44]

Far Eastern exile had a way of channelling outrage into creativity. Nikolai Chernyshevsky and Vladimir Korolenko found literary inspiration in Yakutia. An earnest would-be regicide, Konstantin Kurteyev, reinvented himself as a monarchist newspaper editor in Khabarovsk. The Polish nationalists Alexander Czekanowski and Iwan Czerski embarked on geological expeditions in Yakutia, and no one objected when Benedykt Dybowski went off to study the zoology of Transbaikalia. Waclaw Sieroszewski spent part of his exile touring the Priamur under the auspices of the Imperial Russian Geographical Society. Vladimir Yokhelson, Vladimir Bogoraz, Lev Shternberg, and Bronislaw Pilsudski (older brother of Poland's future president) built international reputations on the basis of ethnographic research conducted while exiled to Yakutia and Sakhalin. In 1894–96, Bogoraz participated in an expedition financed by the merchant Innokenty Sibiryakov, and in 1900 he and his friend Yokhelson joined a North Pacific expedition sponsored by the merchant and banker Morris Ketchum Jesup on behalf of the American Museum of Natural History in New York. All eventually left the Far East, but not before most had availed themselves of Yankovsky's hospitality at Sidemi.[45]

« « » »

East Asian Communities

I prefer a Russian desert to a Korean-made paradise.
— Governor-General P. F. Unterberger (early 1900s)

On the eve of the First World War, thousands of Chinese, Koreans, and Japanese resided or sojourned within the Priamur governor-generalship. Unnerved by defeat at the hands of Japan in 1905, and susceptible to "Yellow Peril" cassandras, authorities came to regard these minorities with suspicion. Yet dependence on Asian labor and enterprise precluded an administrative solution. Meanwhile, East Asians shaped regional development and added a cosmopolitan hue to Russian provincial life.

Chinese

Chinese continued to trickle into the Priamur and the Primorye after their annexation by the Russian Empire in 1858–60. The trickle swelled into a torrent after Beijing loosened restrictions on access to Manchuria in 1878. During the next thirty years, an estimated 200,000 entered the Russian Far East.[1] Because of their high mobility, census-takers could only estimate their numbers in Vladivostok (27,000 in 1912), Nikolsk (4,000), and Khabarovsk (3,700), and did not even try to count them in the Sikhote Alin. Chinese moved freely across the Manchurian frontier and commuted to Japan and Korea without bothering to inform Russian authorities.[2]

Although Chinese settlements in the Priamur and the Primorye legally remained under Qing jurisdiction after 1860, they were in practice self-governing. Guilds (*hui fang*) led by elders regulated affairs in each community and acted as a link with Beijing. *Hui fang* in the Sikhote Alin dispensed justice and organized local defense forces. As well as governing themselves, Chinese exercised power over aborigines, many of whom depended on them for provisions and employment.[3]

Furs, ginseng, and antlers had drawn Chinese to the Sikhote Alin for centuries. Deer antlers, obtained from natives in exchange for provisions, alcohol, and opium, were ground into powder and sold as tonics and aphrodisiacs. The ginseng root, prized for its medicinal qualities south of the Great Wall, was both collected in the wild and cultivated in jealously guarded taiga oases. In 1907 a forester stumbled across an enormous natural root cluster forty miles southeast of Khabarovsk, precipitating a "ginseng rush" from hundreds of miles around.[4]

When Russian settlers moved into the Priamur and the Primorye regions in the 1860s, they found Chinese agricultural settlements along the Zeya and Suifen river valleys and on the Khanka Plain.[5] It was not long before Chinese farmers were supplying grain, fruits, and vegetables to Blagoveshchensk, Khabarovka, and Vladivostok.[6] Foreigners traveling on steamers along the Amur noted how the rich crops of corn and wheat around Chinese settlements contrasted with the unkempt fields of Cossacks.[7] Few visitors realized that in less-frequented corners of the Primorye Chinese farmers produced opium for export to their homeland. Thanks to constabulary indulgence, poppies bloomed in full view of at least one district police station.[8]

Chinese merchants took advantage of the free trade zone on both sides of the border and did a thriving business in Blagoveshchensk, Khabarovsk, Nikolsk, and Vladivostok.* Vladivostok attracted merchants, tradesmen, and peddlers from Shanghai and Canton as well as seasonal labor from Shandong and Shanxi.[9] Shops and bazaars sold ginseng, kelp, trepang and crab, dry goods, groceries, and "Chinese vodka."[10] Chinatown ran along the shores of Amur Bay in a district called Millyonka, where huts and tile-roofed brick buildings housed artels, prefectural societies, public houses, gambling parlors, opium dens, and a Buddhist temple. Chinese merchants adhered to their own organizations with the notable exception of the influential trader and naturalized Russian subject Ji Fengtai, known among fellow guild members as Tifontai.[11] The Chinese community in Khabarovka constituted about a third of the town's population until 1900. Most lived in the Kitaiskaya sloboda ("Chinese village") along the Amur or in the

*The Far Eastern free trade zone, created in 1862 by supplementary articles to the Treaty of Beijing, endured until 1900, was revived in 1906, and then was incrementally reduced in 1909 and 1913.

smaller Kitaiskaya slobodka behind the railroad station. Chinese built and managed the river piers and most of the stores. Their kilns produced bricks and tiles emblematic of local buildings.[12]

Starting around 1890, coolies recruited in Shandong by Chinese contractors were leased to Russian enterprises and worked under the supervision of Chinese foremen.[13] The proportion of coolie labor in the Amur goldfields rose from 15 percent in 1900 to 76 percent in 1915.[14] By 1900 nine of ten workers in the Vladivostok shipyards were Chinese — as were almost all the unskilled laborers on the Ussuri Line, the Chinese Eastern Railroad, and the Amur Line.[15]

Chinese entrepreneurship found an outlet in smuggling, which flourished along Far Eastern frontiers with little interference from authorities. Neither border guards, deployed only in ports and towns, nor the understaffed Amur Flotilla presented much of an obstacle.[16] Instead of guarding the frontiers against smugglers, Cossacks relied on them and contrived to import contraband spirits from Manchuria.* Gold smuggled out of the Far East by the Chinese has been estimated as 20 percent to 60 percent of annual production between 1890 and 1916.[17] Coolies sold their diggings on the sly or contrived ways to take them home. An embalmed cadaver en route to its ancestral land might have a skull sprinkled with gold dust blown up the nostrils, or a baby in the arms of a young mother might be a nugget-stuffed corpse.

Although *hong huzi* dabbled in contraband, they preferred to enrich themselves by more direct means. From bases in sparsely inhabited border areas, these Sino-Manchurian bandits preyed on frontier settlements. From time to time they moved inland and attacked homesteads on the Khanka Plain and along Peter the Great Bay. During the "Manza War" (1868) over Askold Island gold deposits, *hong huzi* destroyed several villages around Vladivostok.†

Russian attitudes toward the Chinese varied from person to person. On the one hand, the birth of Russo-Chinese pidgin reflected a considerable interaction in the mundane matters of daily life. On the other, prejudice infected all reaches of society, from peasants to governors. Although the

*When Molokans celebrated Epiphany and brought holy water from Sagalian across the Amur to Blagoveshchensk, Cossacks were wont to join the procession, lustily chanting and carrying buckets of alcoholic "holy water" past unsuspecting customs officials.

†Chikhachev, "Kaliforniia i Ussuriiskii krai," p. 559; Malozemoff, *Russian Far Eastern Policy*, pp. 5, 19; Solov'ev, *Kitaiskoe otkhodnichestvo*, pp. 86–90. *Manza*, local Russian slang for a Chinese, probably derived from a colloquial appellation for Manchu.

regional press expressed remorse over the massacre of Chinese in and around Blagoveshchensk in 1900, Chinese continued to suffer casual indignities. In Vladivostok Chinese were mimicked, muddied, and mulcted. Such hooliganism was publicly deplored but officially winked at.* In 1900 the newspaper *Vladivostok* sardonically editorialized that "beating the *manza* has become a custom with us. Only the lazy don't indulge in it."[18] Such treatment may explain why Chinese generally sympathized with Japan during the war of 1904–5. Out of sight of Russians, many Chinese did not conceal their satisfaction at each Japanese victory. Some eagerly awaited an invasion of the Primorye, assuming that the Mikado would restore lands stripped from the Celestial Empire in 1858–60.[19]

Russians and Chinese nonetheless lived together for the most part peacefully. Russians bought food and household goods in Chinese stores or from Chinese hawkers at local bazaars. Russians and Chinese worked side by side on railroads, on the docks, and in search of gold. In 1883 some 12,000 Russian and Chinese prospectors went so far as to set up a short-lived "Zheltuga Republic" in northern Manchuria.[20] Chinese tenant farmers on Russian and Ukrainian allotments sold vegetables to their landlords, some of whom provided their tenants with imported agricultural machinery.[21]

Although Chinese immigrants did not readily assimilate, members of the second generation adopted Russian or Ukrainian dress and acquired at least a rudimentary knowledge of Russian. One affluent Chinese family in Vladivostok hired a live-in Russian tutor for the children.[22] There are no statistics for intermarriages, but a British visitor noted on the eve of the First World War: "the Russian woman does not object to the Chinese as a husband, and the Russian takes a Chinese wife."[23]

Koreans

Long before Russians arrived, Koreans had raised crops of millet and beans in the Posyet region and harvested kelp along the Primorye coast.[24]

---

*According to an Englishman visiting Vladivostok in 1903 (Gerrare, pp. 214–15), local Chinese were required to purchase a miniature portrait of the chief of police to insert in their passports. Chinese were not the only victims of thuggery and squeeze in a port teeming with vagrants and demobilized as well as active-duty military personnel. The shortage of women created an atmosphere redolent of a Rocky Mountain mining camp. Couples imprudent enough to venture into the sailors' quarter (Matrosskaya slobodka) were greeted with catcalls and lascivious gestures. There were cases of wives being pulled out of carriages in front of their husbands.

Their numbers increased after 1860 as several thousand refugees from famine-stricken Hamgyondo Province crossed the Tumen River settled around Posyet Bay. Russian authorities welcomed these migrants and made land available to them along the Suifen, Suchan, and Ussuri rivers. In 1871 the governor-general of Eastern Siberia distributed hundred-desyatin parcels to Korean families along the middle Amur.[25] Immigration swelled after the Japanese annexation of Korea in 1910. According to official statistics, Koreans in the Primorye increased from 24,000 in 1900 to over 64,000 in 1914, not including thousands who did not register.[26]

Koreans had no legal status in the Russian Far East until 1884, when St. Petersburg and Seoul concluded a trade treaty. Thereafter, pre-1884 immigrants were given the right to acquire Russian citizenship and a fifteen-desyatin (forty-acre) parcel of land. Those arriving after 1884 were allowed to become Russian citizens provided that they had lived in the region for at least five years, enjoyed good health, and pursued a useful occupation. Those who came for temporary employment were required to apply for residence permits annually. Between 1898 and 1917 roughly one-quarter of Koreans in the Priamur governor-generalship had Russian citizenship.[27]

Regardless of citizenship, Koreans demonstrated energy, enterprise, and adaptability. Like the Chinese, they kept Vladivostok and Khabarovsk supplied with fresh vegetables. In addition to farming their own parcels, they cultivated the lands of their Cossack, Russian, and Ukrainian landlords, leading an official to remark in 1906 that "Koreans work hard and always get better harvests than Russians."[28] Koreans assimilated more quickly than the Chinese. Most came as settlers rather than sojourners, studied Russian, and embraced the Orthodox faith. Parents sent their children to Russian schools or to Korean schools with a Russian curriculum.[29] From the second-generation emerged traders, shopkeepers, telegraph office employees, postmen, veterinarians, and schoolteachers, forming the nucleus of a Russian Korean bourgeoisie. All the same, national identity and ties with the ancestral land remained strong. In Vladivostok the Korean community had its own administration, which collected taxes, distributed charity, ran an employment bureau, and organized festivals. Immigrants sent money to relatives in Korea and revisited their old villages.[30] Efforts by the government to russify Koreans reinforced their attachment to the ancestral language and culture.[31]

Koreans got along reasonably well with the Slavic majority. Russian laborers generally felt more at ease with them than with Chinese, who tended to socialize only with members of their own work gangs.[32] Yet their diligence and growing prosperity exposed Koreans to epithets such as "yellow yids" (*zhyoltye zhidy*).[33] Even the "progressive" writer N. G. Garin-Mikhailovsky indulged in caricatures when he skirted Korean settlements in the southern Primorye in 1898.[34]

As Tokyo tightened its grip on the peninsula after 1905, Korean exiles in the southern Primorye stepped up their political agitation, trained military units, roughed up local Japanese, and in 1908 carried out an armed foray across the Tumen River. When a Vladivostok Korean assassinated the elder statesman Itō Hirobumi in Harbin in 1909, Tokyo put pressure on St. Petersburg to crack down on Korean expatriates. Authorities responded by prohibiting military training and removing a few activists to Irkutsk, but Korean nationalists were neither extradited nor prevented from publishing vernacular newspapers.[35]

Japanese

Japanese links with the Priamur are of comparatively recent origin despite imaginative claims that an imperial commander (Abe Hirafu) and a Buddhist priest (Nichijin) pacified the Amur in the seventh and thirteenth centuries, respectively.[36] Japanese may have set foot on Sakhalin and the Kuriles in the seventeenth century, but their earliest documented debut on the Amur came in 1809, when the surveyor Mamiya Rinzō visited a Manchu post about forty miles downstream from what is today Komsomolsk.

The Japanese presence in the Priamur grew slowly during the last four decades of the nineteenth century, starting in Nikolaevsk, where a Hakodate merchant named Takeda showed up in 1861 with a boatload of provisions.[37] Japanese took up residence in several towns during the next two decades, but their total number did not exceed 4,000 before 1900.[38] For all its proximity, the Russian Far East could not compete with Hawaii and California. Moreover, the prefectures along the Sea of Japan facing the Primorye were thinly populated. About 70 percent of Japanese in the Russian Far East came from Nagasaki, whose entrepreneurs opened dry goods stores and offered their services as contractors in Vladivostok during the 1870s. Nagasaki for its part accommodated a Russian community of naval personnel (the Pacific Squadron wintered there from 1878 until 1894) and summer sojourners from Vladivostok.[39]

What Japanese in the Far East lacked in numbers (5,000 in 1901, 3,000 of whom were in Vladivostok), they made up for in organization. The Vladivostok Resident Society, established in 1876, maintained branches in Razdolnoye, Nikolsk, Iman, Khabarovsk, Blagoveshchensk, Nikolaevsk, Aleksandrovsk (Sakhalin), Zeya, Nerchinsk, Sretensk, Chita, and Irkutsk. The Society looked after local Japanese community affairs and acted as an intermediary between Japanese citizens and Russian authorities. All residents were obliged to register and pay dues. Because St. Petersburg refused to permit the establishment of a consulate in Vladivostok until 1907, Tokyo relied on "commercial agents" such as Sewaki Hitosa and Kawakami Toshihiko.*

Japanese immigrants shunned agriculture in favor of trade and service. By 1900 no town east of Lake Baikal and south of the Stanovoi Range was without a Japanese barber, carpenter, joiner, launderer, coal merchant, domestic servant, bathhouse attendant, watch repairman, draper, and photographer. Russians loved to have their pictures taken and regarded Japanese as destined for that calling. Few visitors to Khabarovsk failed to pose for a Japanese photographer at the base of Muraviev's statue. Shortly before the turn of the century, Japanese hotels made their appearance in Khabarovsk and Vladivostok, and Japan Mail Lines inaugurated service between Vladivostok and Otaru, Hakodate, Niigata, Tsuruga, Nagasaki, and Shanghai. Firms such as Mitsui, Mitsubishi, and Kuhara opened branch offices in Vladivostok. Priamur governor-generals permitted the Japanese to operate a school in Vladivostok but, in contrast with their indulgence of Korean journalistic enterprise, not to publish a vernacular newspaper.[40]

In sharp contrast to Chinese and Koreans, most Japanese sojourners in the Far East were women. These "forerunners of Japanese economic expansion,"[41] daughters of impoverished fishermen and peasants, had been sold to contractors and indentured as domestic servants or prostitutes. Girls as young as thirteen worked as maids in Russian families, some following their employers from Vladivostok to Harbin. Nagasaki entrepreneurs, noticing that Russian sailors treated the licensed quarter as a "second homeland," saw a commercial opportunity across the Sea of Japan. A decade after these entrepreneurs opened their first brothel in Vladivostok, in 1883, prostitutes constituted the largest category of Japanese residents.[42] By 1901 "rice ladies" could be found in every Priamur town and CER construction site. Their access to areas (especially in Manchuria) off-limits to Japanese mer-

* See Appendix D for biographical information.

chants and their popularity among Russian officers inevitably attracted the attention of Japanese Army Intelligence.[43]

The Priamur offered Tokyo an easy target for penetration. Open frontiers afforded unhindered access, and official complacency anesthetized vigilance. The Japanese Army staff began sending agents to Vladivostok in 1882. Young Ōba Kakō lived there for three years perfecting language skills that qualified him as interpreter for the Army staff during the Russo-Japanese War. In 1892–93, Captain Fukushima Yasumasa completed an unescorted equestrian reconnaissance mission across European Russia, Siberia, Mongolia, Manchuria, and the Primorye. Nationalist organizations such as the Genyōsha (Black Ocean Society) and the Kokuryūkai (Amur River Society) provided additional eyes and ears, fielding Chinese- and Korean-speaking agents posing as commercial photographers, barbers, tailors, launderers, martial arts instructors, and Buddhist priests. In 1896, Kokuryūkai co-founder Uchida Ryōhei set up a judo school in Vladivostok while Imperial Army Intelligence set up field headquarters at the local Nishi Honganji Temple, whose Abbot Ōta Kakumin demurely blended philanthropy and espionage. Japanese brothels scattered throughout the Priamur governor-generalship provided both data and shelter, earning their employees the collective sobriquet "Amazon army" (*jōshigun*) in Kokuryūkai literature.[44]

Japanese fished along the entire Far Eastern littoral. Liberally interpreting the right to operate "off the coasts of Sakhalin" conferred in the Treaty of St. Petersburg (1875), they entered the Amur estuary and set up warehouses and processing facilities at Nikolaevsk. The Treaty of Portsmouth (1905) and the Fisheries Convention (1907) not only guaranteed the Japanese access to Far Eastern waterways but allowed them to employ their own labor on Russian soil, a privilege that entrepreneurs exploited with particular vigor on Kamchatka.[45]

The growing international prestige of the Rising Sun found its reflection in the Priamur Japanese, who set themselves apart from the Chinese and Koreans. A Russian recalled that "their cultural standards, neatness, dexterity, and taste put them in the same category as Europeans."[46] Japanese women married into prominent foreign families in Vladivostok, such as the Bryners, Coopers, and Denbighs. Yet social equality among the elite did not translate into amity among the masses. As one observer noted in 1901, "tolerant as the Russians are of other races, their hatred of the Japanese is pronounced and apparently instinctive."[47] Around this time one Russian family in Vladivostok, convinced that Japan would take over the Primorye, emigrated to California.[48] Admiral Tōgō Heihachirō's surprise attack on Port Arthur in February 1904 gave birth to the stereotype of Japanese duplicity among Russians much as Pearl Harbor did among Americans thirty-seven years later. Few residents of Vladivostok forgot that on the night of the attack Tokyo's official representative was the guest of honor at a gala dinner hosted by municipal leaders.[49] St. Petersburg's rapprochement with Tokyo after 1906 elicited official manifestations of cordiality but did not dissipate popular distrust, activated whenever local Japanese exhibited the least tendency toward proprietary behavior.[50]

Dealing with the "Yellow Peril"

Confronted by Chinese and Korean numbers and by Japanese power, successive governor-generals looked for ways to reverse the "Asianization" of the Priamur. In 1886 Baron Korf ordered the expulsion of all Chinese living more than thirty-four miles from the frontier. Over the next two decades, thousands of Chinese were flushed out of the Sikhote Alin and Zeya Valley. Dukhovskoi and Grodekov continued Korf's offensive by disbanding some Chinese organizations in Khabarovsk and Vladivostok, by attempting to russify Korean youth, and by relocating Koreans from the strategically sensitive Posyet region to lands along Ussuri tributaries in the Sikhote Alin.[51]

The "Yellow Peril" notion, cropping up in Russian discourse in the 1890s, grew teeth in the Far East during the Russo-Japanese War when it became known that Japan was recruiting Chinese and Koreans as agents. In St. Petersburg the "Yellow Peril" took the form of a Sino-Japanese alliance against Russia, but in the Far East it assumed a demographic and commercial guise.[52] In the words of Governor-General P. F. Unterberger, "we didn't occupy this region so that it could be colonized by yellows."[53] Unterberger targeted Koreans, ignoring the fact that they were victims rather than accomplices of Japanese imperial expansion. Koreans, he asserted, were more dangerous than Chinese, who only sojourned whereas the Koreans stayed. He accused the Koreans of creating "a state within a state" and warned that they provided "convenient soil for our foreign enemies to organize wide-ranging espionage."[54] Reversing Grodekov's russification policies, Unterberger looked for ways to squeeze Koreans out of the Primorye.

Unterberger's diagnosis and prescriptions did not go unchallenged within the bureaucracy. Nikolai Gondatti, governor of Tomsk, who had worked for a decade in the Priamur governor-generalship after traveling in China and Japan, came up with different conclusions while leading the Amur Expedition (1909–10). While noting that some Koreans evaded taxes and conscription, Gondatti asserted that the community as a whole was loyal, productive, and assimilable.[55] Prime Minister Stolypin was sufficiently impressed with his protégé to recommend to Nicholas II in 1910 that Gondatti be appointed to succeed Unterberger.

But once in office, Gondatti started expressing views on Asians uncannily similar to those of his predecessor. "My task is to make sure that there are lots of Russians and very few yellows here," he declared in 1911.[56] This was easier said than done. Efforts to introduce a passport system for Chinese coolies precipitated a mass exodus into the taiga.[57] Looking around for other expedients, Gondatti asked the American consul-general at Vladivostok how the United States had managed to exclude Orientals.[58] The first civilian governor-general considered welding identification bracelets on "legal" Chinese and deporting all the rest.[59] Gondatti met strong opposition in the State Duma, where Bolshevik delegates joined representatives of the gold industry to oppose any restriction of Chinese immigration. Ultimately, the laws of supply and demand prevailed. When war broke out in 1914, Gondatti was forced to sanction the recruitment of Chinese laborers in Harbin in order to alleviate manpower shortages. With the gates open, some 50,000 Chinese entered the Priamur in 1916 alone.[60] It took another generation and harsher ideology to achieve Gondatti's goal of a Far East with "many Russians and very few yellows."

10

《《 》》

International Emporium

The Far East acts like an independent country in its trade
with foreigners.   — Kliment Olan'on (1902)

From the 1850s until the First World War, foreign involvement in the Far East developed in the context of mounting international economic activity in Northeast Asia. British commerce, while concentrated in Hong Kong and the Yangzi River basin, moved northward as the Anglo-Japanese Alliance (1902) and Anglo-Russian Convention (1907) sorted out imperial rivalries. German enterprise converged on the Priamur from European Russia and North China. American trade in Northeast Asia grew in conjunction with the completion of transcontinental railroads and the acquisition of Pacific territories (California in 1848; Alaska in 1867; Hawaii, Guam, and the Philippines in 1898). Japan harnessed overseas trade to imperial expansion in the Ryukyu Islands (1879), Taiwan (1895), southern Manchuria and southern Sakhalin (1905), and Korea (1910). To stave off Japanese and Russian encroachment, Beijing removed barriers to Han Chinese immigration and foreign investment in Manchuria. The Manchurian magnet both energized and short-circuited the Priamur economy.

An International Artery

The Crimean War prepared the groundwork for international enterprise on the Amur. Californians running the British blockade to supply Russian settlements around the Okhotsk seaboard came to see the river's commercial potential as an artery between China and the Pacific. At the same time, St. Petersburg's search for a counterweight to Britain in the Pacific created a more receptive atmosphere to American initiatives. Shortly after the war ended in 1856, a San Francisco merchant named Bernard Peyton traveled to Irkutsk to ask Governor-General Muraviev for an American monopoly of commerce on the Amur.[1] Peyton was accompanied by another Californian, Perry McDonough Collins. This self-styled "Commercial Agent of the United States for the Amoor River" tried to persuade Muraviev to let Americans manage Russo-Chinese trade, handle Russia's Pacific shipping, construct a railroad from Lake Baikal to the Amur, and colonize the Amur valley. Muraviev was at first receptive to some of these ideas. He admired Yankee enterprise and was not unmindful of sympathy among his staff officers for the young republic. At a practical level he calculated that American commerce could be used to promote Russian settlement of the Pacific perimeter.

Although St. Petersburg balked at the idea of a Siberian-Pacific railroad, it saw no immediate reason to deny American merchants access to the Amur.[2] Bostonians and Californians soon made themselves at home in Nikolaevsk, opening an American club and marketing Havana cigars, French pâté, and Jamaican rum. Townsmen were divided about the Yankees. Some welcomed the competition to price-gouging Siberian merchants, but others considered the Amur a Russian river whose commerce should be in Russian hands.[3] Muraviev gradually came to share the latter view for pecuniary as well as patriotic reasons. Co-founding the Amur Company in 1858, he restricted foreign commerce on all but the lower courses of the river.[4]

Muraviev's successors concluded that free trade was a more efficient way to develop the eastern periphery and restored a degree of access. A year after the free trade zone was established along the Sino-Russian frontier (1861), Russian Far Eastern coastal towns were designated open ports. Far Eastern imports destined for the interior underwent customs inspection at Irkutsk.

For approximately a decade Nikolaevsk reaped the benefits of free trade. Bostonians and Californians were joined by merchants from Hamburg, Bremen, and Honolulu, the last doubling as a consular representative of the Hawaiian Kingdom.[5] In 1867 Ivan Yakovlevich Churin established a trading firm, I. Ya. Churin & Co., that in time became a household word throughout the Priamur and, after a Harbin branch opened in 1898, throughout Manchuria. But Nikolaevsk suffered drawbacks that enterprise and ingenuity could not overcome. The Amur estuary froze over for half the year, and for the other half was inaccessible to deep-draft vessels. By the time that the Priamur governor-generalship had been created in 1884, the navy had abandoned Nikolaevsk in favor of Vladivostok; the Maritime District administration had been transferred to Khabarovka (as Khabarovsk was then called); and Churin & Co. had moved its head office to Blagoveshchensk.[6]

Located at the confluence of the Amur and Zeya across from the Manchu-Chinese town of Sagalian, Blagoveshchensk was well situated to take advantage of domestic and international commerce, thriving as an entrepôt for Zeya gold, Manchurian and Amur grain, and Transbaikalian and Mongolian livestock. Blagoveshchensk prided itself on its broad, straight streets, handsome homes, big stores, and telephones (the first in the Far East). By 1900 the town's population (50,000) exceeded that of Vladivostok and Khabarovsk combined. When U. S. Senator Albert Beveridge visited Blagoveshchensk in 1901, he noted that the living conditions of local mill workers matched those of their American counterparts.[7]

Blagoveshchensk's main rival on the Amur was Khabarovsk. Although primarily an administrative center, Khabarovsk hosted local branches of Churin & Co., Kunst & Albers, the Yaroslavl & Kostroma Land Bank, and the Russo-Chinese Bank (renamed the Russo-Asiatic Bank in 1905). Chinese and Japanese enterprises abounded. The largest local firm, Plyusnin & Company, operated lumber and flour mills, vineyards, and retail businesses, and had branches in the Primorye and Manchuria. The Plyusnin family was also active in philanthropy, and one member served in the municipal duma from the time of its creation in 1894.[8]

Operating out of Nikolaevsk, Blagoveshchensk, and Khabarovsk, foreigners dominated freight and passenger transport along the Amur. Massachusetts-born Enoch Emery, who arrived in Nikolaevsk as a cabin boy around 1860, spent over forty years in the Far East marketing and operating American paddle-wheelers. In 1895 Emery founded the Amur Navigation Company, which until completion of the Amur Railroad in 1916 provided passenger and freight service between Sretensk (terminus of the Transbaikal Line) and Nikolaevsk.[9] Among a hundred American, British, German, Belgian, French, Swedish, and Japanese vessels on the Amur in 1914, the English-owned *John Cockerill* was the most sumptuously appointed, offering first-class passengers a mahogany-paneled lounge, a well-stocked library, and a table d'hôte in which sturgeon caviar was served "like marmalade on a British breakfast table."[10]

Vladivostok

Perched at the tip of a twenty-mile peninsula and connected to the interior by a cow path, Vladivostok in the 1860s and 1870s endeared itself neither to the Imperial Navy nor to merchants. Although a telegraph line to Khabarovsk was completed in 1866 and an undersea cable laid to Nagasaki and Shanghai by a Danish firm in 1871, there was a sense of isolation not attributable solely to the circumstance that the Golden Horn from December to April was covered by ice thick enough to discourage sailing vessels and small steamers. The navy on more than one occasion considered moving the fleet to Posyet or St. Olga, but the former had no wood and the latter was even more isolated from the interior.[11]

Vladivostok belied its grandiloquent name. A few wooden piers, an Orthodox church, a Chinese temple, and huts clung to scrubby slopes rising from a dirt track originally called Amerikanskaya and renamed Svetlanskaya in 1873 in honor of the frigate *Svetlanka* that brought Grand Duke Aleksei Aleksandrovich into the Golden Horn. Until the 1880s Amerikanskaya-Svetlanskaya was the only recognizable street. Rains turned pathways and gullies into sewers. Refuse polluted wells and eventually all the nearby streams, obliging residents to import drinking water from Japan, Korea, and Shanghai.[12] Cultural amenities were scarcer than potable water, and boredom easily gave way to restlessness. Amateur theatrical productions often ended in brawls. Young officers diverted themselves by taking turns shouting "Tiger!" in a darkened room filled with companions who discharged their pistols in the direction of the noise.[13] Its very dullness may have spared Vladivostok during the war scare of 1877, when the British War Office considered seizing Russky Island and turning it into a "northern Gibraltar" but then decided that St. Petersburg should continue to bear the consequences of its "costly mistake" of having occupied the Primorye.[14]

Russian laws prohibiting foreign investment and landownership were easily circumvented. When an agent of the military governor of Jilin predicted in 1885 that Haishenwei (Vladivostok) would someday be another Shanghai, he had the numerical and commercial preeminence of local compatriots in mind.[15] In 1877 four of every five civilians in Vladivostok was Chinese or Korean, a proportion that did not dramatically change for the rest of the century. Chinese and Koreans supplied most of the unskilled labor, owned the bulk of small stores, and controlled local supplies of fresh water, firewood, and animal feed. Western merchants circumvented restrictions by equipping themselves with Russian citizenship, Russian business partners, and Russian wives. A Swede, Otto Lindholm, built and operated the district's biggest grain mills. A Scot, George Denbigh, teamed up with the local "seaweed king" Yakov Semyonov and organized Vladivostok's largest food wholesaler, Semyonov & Denbigh Co. A French flag flew over the De Louvre Hotel. Scandinavians, Germans, and Japanese had the lion's share of cabotage as well as international shipping. The Pacific Squadron was able to avoid complete dependence on Vladivostok's foreign merchants only by buying its ordnance in San Francisco and undergoing repairs in Nagasaki.[16]

Vladivostok's flagship firm was founded in 1864 by two Hamburg merchants, Gustav Kunst and Gustav Albers, whose partnership accommodated a naturalized Russian from Thuringia named Adolf Dattan in 1886. By 1914 Kunst & Albers had thirty branches in the Priamur and offices in St. Petersburg, Moscow, Odessa, Riga, Warsaw, Kobe, and Nagasaki. From selling provisions, the firm diversified into agricultural machinery, shipping, and insurance. Combining baroque opulence with modern technology, Kunst & Albers department stores in Khabarovsk, Vladivostok, and Blagoveshchensk featured marble interiors and electric lights (the Vladivostok store set the pace in 1893 by installing its own steam-driven generator). Waited upon by multilingual clerks, favored patrons inspected Swiss timepieces, sampled French clarets, and kept up with the latest fashions from Paris and Savile Row. The firm's 800 German employees sustained a brewery in Blagoveshchensk.* After the death of the original partners, Albers' son Alfred and Dattan carried on the business until 1914, when wartime conditions obliged them to deposit the firm's liquid assets in the Harbin branch of the Russo-Asiatic Bank and to place immovable properties in the custody of Churin & Co., whose local manager Karl Richter, a former Kunst & Albers clerk, looked after them until the Armistice.[17]

Bryner & Co. avoided some but not all of the vicissitudes experienced by Kunst & Albers thanks to the nationality and foresight of its Swiss founder, Yulius Bryner. Bryner showed up in Vladivostok in 1880 and wasted little time turning a series of picaresque encounters into the filaments of a busi-

---

*In 1909 the Schlitz Beer Company of Milwaukee, Wisconsin, protested through the Department of State about the Schlitz label on lager bottled in Blagoveshchensk. U.S. Consul Lester Maynard, Vladivostok, to Sec. State, 22 Oct. 1909. U.S. State Dept. Archives, M862, roll 1131, item 22363.

ness network: Chinese associates in Hong Kong, a British partner and a mistress in Japan, and influential friends in Korea. Starting as a trading concern, Bryner & Co. diversified into Amur timber, Sakhalin coal, and Tetyukhe lead. Cultivating his contacts in Seoul, Bryner in 1898 secured a 1,800-square-mile timber concession from the king of Korea along the Yalu and Tumen rivers, a coup that might have yielded handsome dividends had it not fallen victim to international rivalries.[18]

The completion of the CER spur from Harbin to Port Arthur in 1901 challenged Vladivostok's regional preeminence. Russian and foreign firms alike opened branches in Manchuria and diverted shipments to Dalny, a port that skeptics dubbed Lishny ("superfluous").* Russia's loss of the Guandong Leasehold to Japan in 1905 raised hopes that Vladivostok could regain its role as the center for exports of Manchurian soybeans, wheat, oats, and hops. Thanks to favorable CER freight rates, bean and beancake shipments through Vladivostok rose after 1906 until they constituted 80 percent of the port's exports by 1913.[19] Dairen (as Dalny was called after 1905) nonetheless lengthened its lead over Vladivostok by providing better storage facilities and more reliable service. Transcontinental travelers generally opted for Dairen or Pusan over Vladivostok to limit their exposure to Russian "squeeze."

In cosmopolitanism if not commerce, Vladivostok held its own with Dairen. China, Japan, Great Britain, France, the Ottoman Empire, Greece, the Netherlands, Denmark, Norway, Italy, and the United States maintained consulates along the embankment and hills overlooking the Golden Horn. A dozen languages echoed in local stores, banks, hotel lobbies, and brothels. Only Harbin matched Vladivostok in celebrating the New Year four times in accordance with the Julian, Gregorian, Chinese, and Japanese calendars.[20]

Americans

The origins of American enterprise in the Russian Far East can be traced to New England whalers looking for fresh water, wood, and shelter on Chukotka in 1819. Finding what they needed at Avacha Bay, Americans began to winter in Petropavlovsk rather than Honolulu. Their numbers sharply increased when the Russian-American Convention of 1824 granted

---

*Tifontai, a prominent Chinese merchant in Vladivostok, invested heavily in Port Arthur and Mukden but apparently not in Dalny.

them access to the Northeast. As crews came into contact with Chukchi, Koryaks, Evenki, and Eskimos, they exchanged ironware, utensils, crockery, trinkets, and rum for fish, furs, whale oil, tusks, and sex. As noted earlier, Americans reinforced their position during the Crimean War, when they ran the British blockade to supply Russian settlements from Ayan to Sitka.[21]

North Pacific whaling declined after the 1850s, leaving the way open for traders and poachers colloquially called "Americans." In fact ship captains were mostly Englishmen, Finns, Swedes, and Norwegians, and their crews were made up in the main of Russians, Chinese, Japanese, Hawaiians, and Portuguese from Macao. The Hudson's Bay Company, the largest trading firm operating in Chukotka, was Canadian. Alcohol and disease also boasted a cosmopolitan pedigree. "Americans" who purveyed rum for furs, walrus tusks, and reindeer antlers followed a precedent pioneered by Cossacks, who with spirits distilled from local parsnips and bog whortleberries had encouraged aborigines to part with pelts in the seventeenth century. Siberian merchants bought Chukchi girls for less than the cost of a reindeer and resold them in mining-camp brothels.* Russian-carried smallpox and syphilis decimated the Chukchi, Koryaks, and Yukagirs.[22]

American tinned fruit, dried milk, textiles, hardware, and toys circulated around the Northeast from the middle of the nineteenth century. Virginia chewing tobacco was prized by the Chukchi and occasionally used to pacify infants.[23] While surveying Kamchatka and Chukotka in 1865–67 for Western Union's planned telegraph route under the Bering Strait, George Kennan came across American cooking utensils, linen, magazines, lithographs, and music.[24] A visitor to Petropavlovsk in 1866 noticed that houses had ceilings of California redwood.[25] Thirty years later another traveler recorded that the most prestigious possession of an Okhotsk seaboard housewife was a Singer sewing machine.[26] A visitor from St. Petersburg on the eve of the First World War complained that the only signs of civilization on Kamchatka were American gramophones and records.[27]

Language followed commerce. A visitor to Anadyr in 1866 reported that local officials used English to communicate with Koryaks and Chukchi.[28] Though St. Petersburg regarded Chukotka as an overseas colony, bureaucrats looked askance at English becoming a lingua franca among people who used the word "Russian" to mean "criminal."[29]

---

*According to Evgeny Rozhkov in *Russian Far East* (Dec. 1992–Jan. 1993), p. 22, affluent Chukchi herd owners bought Russian girls.

Tsarist policies toward Americans oscillated between equally unsuccessful attempts at exclusion and regulation. St. Petersburg routinely vetoed attempts to organize joint whaling operations in the North Pacific, yet in 1871 gave an American firm, Hutchinson, Kohl & Company, a twenty-year license to hunt seals in the Commander Islands and on Tyuleny Island off the eastern coast of Sakhalin.[30] St. Petersburg tried to curtail the American presence in 1877 by prohibiting natives from bartering furs for food, only to relent within a year as famine gripped Chukotka.[31] By 1879 the prominent jurist Konstantin Pobedonostsev was warning the future Tsar Alexander III that unless warships were dispatched to the Northeast, local natives "will altogether forget that they belong to Russia."[32]

After the establishment of the Priamur governor-generalship in 1884, Baron Korf and his staff concluded that foreign interlopers could be contained by taxation, regulation, and competition. To implement these policies, as well as to give the government visibility on Chukotka, the Anadyr District was created in 1889. Its first governor succumbed to depression, but his young and energetic successor, Nikolai Gondatti, relished the assignment, studying the Chukchi language, surveying Chukotka, encouraging Russian enterprise, and stocking provisions in government warehouses that natives could buy at subsidized prices.[33] The fruits of Gondatti's exertions did not long survive his departure in 1897. The gold rush fever that swept the Yukon Territory in 1898 brought prospectors and adventurers across the Bering Strait in search of a Chukotka Klondike. Among them was Washington B. Vanderlip, a flamboyant Californian promoter calling himself the "Siberian representative" of the "Russian-American Trading Company of New York and Gizhiga."[34] Vanderlip's Russian analogue, a mercurial cavalry officer named Vladimir Vonliariarsky, used court connections to set up in 1902 a short-lived "Northeast Siberia Company" in partnership with a Seattle promoter, John Rosene.[35] Vanderlip and Vonliariarsky did little for Chukotka, but their rhetoric set the tone for later promoters on both sides of the Bering Strait.

Government authority in the Northeast revived in 1909, when Kamchatka was detached from the Maritime District and given its own administration. Governor Vasily Perfiliev, like his rival Gondatti an able and energetic administrator, weeded abuses out of local trade, boosted Siberian Flotilla patrols against poachers, oversaw the construction of a telegraph line from Petropavlovsk to Nikolaevsk, and persuaded the Volunteer Fleet to offer regular service from Vladivostok to Chukotka.[36]

When Henry Adams wrote in 1891 that the americanizing of Siberia was the only worthwhile challenge the Pacific region offered to the United States,[37] American interest in the Priamur was at a low ebb. Enoch Emery lamented in 1897 that American shipping in Vladivostok had "practically stood still" since 1860 while that of Europe and Japan had undergone an "enormous expansion."[38] American business discovered the Primorye in 1898, when St. Petersburg lifted import duties on agricultural machinery and President William McKinley appointed a prominent black jurist, Richard T. Greener, as the first U.S. consul in Vladivostok. During the next decade peasant migration and railroad construction created an insatiable demand for American rails and rolling stock, foodstuffs, bicycles, tools, pianos, stoves, elevators, streetcars, harbor dredgers, and wood-processing and mining machinery. Corrugated steel roofs were hot items in the Amur District, where every izba seemed to have one.[39] As the advertisements of the McCormick and Deere companies appeared in the remotest settlements, American reapers, harvesters, sowers, binders, and gins found a ready market in the Priamur, where iron ploughs were called *amerikanki*. So robust was demand, noted Consul Greener in 1903, "that private firms cannot fill orders."[40]

The Far East, however, was no "new California" for American capital. Hopes raised by rich mineral deposits, geographic propinquity, and promotional rhetoric were monotonously disappointed by political and economic realities. Western Union's project to build a telegraph line from Seattle to Europe via Alaska, Chukotka, Kamchatka, and Yakutia was made redundant by the Atlantic cable in 1869. The vision of direct rail service from Chicago to Paris via the Bering Strait generated little more than bombast. Geopolitical calculations and national sensitivities in Russia and Japan cooled receptivity to American investment in Northeast Asia. American bids to develop Sakhalin cropped up periodically but got nowhere in St. Petersburg, although during the Russo-Japanese War there was talk in court circles of selling the island to the United States to keep it out of Japanese hands. In October 1905, when the railroad magnate E. H. Harriman came up with a plan to create a globe-girdling transportation network by linking the Union Pacific and Pacific Mail Steamship Company with the South Manchurian, Chinese Eastern and Trans-Siberian lines, Tokyo turned it down. Nor did anything come of discussions during 1905–6 between the Russian finance ministry and potential American investors in the Ussuri Line.

Debates over Accessibility

International accessibility to the Far Eastern market came under attack during the last decade of tsarist rule. There was metropolitan resistance against Russian Jews who, to circumvent restrictions imposed by the tsarist regime, emigrated to the United States, became naturalized citizens, and then appeared in the Priamur to engage in commerce under the protection of the American flag. While the re-émigré issue troubled relations between St. Petersburg and Washington, an internal public debate revolved around whether the Far East should maintain the free trade zones established in the early 1860s along the Chinese frontier and in ports along the Pacific littoral. As early as 1883, Military Governor of Vladivostok Aleksandr Feldhausen urged that Vladivostok's free trade status be abolished so as to curtail imports, spur domestic enterprise, and increase state revenues.[41] The issue divided Far Easterners, and no consensus emerged on which products should be subject to duties. Amur wheat farmers wanted to limit imports of Manchurian grain (millions of peasant settlers from North China were turning the Sungari Plain into the richest granary in Asia). Blagoveshchensk and Nikolsk mill owners welcomed cheap Manchurian grain but not Manchurian flour. After much wrangling St. Petersburg abolished the free port status of Vladivostok and Nikolaevsk in 1900, squeezing out American but not Manchurian agricultural imports.[42] The duty-free status of both ports was restored in 1904 as an incentive for neutrals to run the wartime Japanese blockade. Many did, including President Roosevelt's daughter Alice, who took time off from an East Asian tour with War Secretary William Howard Taft to slip into the Golden Horn during the summer of 1905.[43]

Debates over free trade resumed in 1907, dividing Far Eastern merchants, editors, and delegates to the Imperial Duma.[44] A compromise was reached in 1909, whereby ports south of the Amur lost their free trade status while those to the north retained it. In 1913 the free trade zone along the Sino-Russian frontier was abolished, but a year later war forced St. Petersburg to relent. With the Central Powers blockading both the Baltic and the Black Sea, Vladivostok became the only major port through which Russia could obtain supplies. As the Pacific gate swung open and the Priamur slipped into the magnetic field of Japanese-American rivalry, words written in 1906 acquired fresh relevance: "Our weakness dooms the region [Far East] to be seized. We are left only with a choice. Should it be taken by Japanese or Americans?"[45]

11

《 《　》 》

Stirrings of a Regional Consciousness

Far Easterners would rather give up St. Petersburg than
lose Vladivostok.　　　　　　　 — Cao Tingjie (1885)

A Moscow editor warned in 1909 that if St. Petersburg imposed tariffs on Far Eastern ports, it would reap the same consequences that overtook the British Empire when London levied tariffs on its North American colonies.[1] In dramatizing a provincial grievance, the remark advertised a metropolitan conceit and revealed a metropolitan fear. Within the Center's conception of the eastern periphery as a colony lurked the specter of a vast, untamed, and unpredictable frontier. In the seventeenth century Moscow put up with jurisdictional confusion east of the Urals rather than run the risk of concentrating power in the hands of an ambitious Siberian viceroy.[2] St. Petersburg rejected an American's proposal for a Baikal-Amur railroad in 1857 out of an awareness of such a project's centrifugal potential.[3] Insinuations that Governor-General Muraviev was grooming himself as a "Siberian tsar" or that Finance Minister Witte was organizing a separate Manchurian state were calculated to invoke the same bogey.[4]

Siberian regional consciousness grew from both reformist and revolutionary impulses, but its predominant thrust was toward autonomy rather than outright independence. When Governor-General Mikhail Speransky pointed out in 1820 that Siberian needs were being neglected by metropolitan authorities, he adumbrated its central rationale.[5] Siberian aspirations were most fully articulated between the 1860s and the 1890s by Grigory Potanin and Nikolai Yadrintsev under the rubric of *oblastnichestvo* ("regionalism"). Potanin and Yadrintsev were arrested and imprisoned in 1865 for allegedly plotting to detach Siberia from Russia and form an

American-style republic. In fact they sought to transform Siberia from a dumping ground for undesirables into a region empowered to pursue its own social and economic development. In concrete terms this meant abolishing the exile system, establishing a Siberian university, and installing officials who had Siberian interests uppermost in mind.[6]

By 1914, oblastnichestvo had outgrown the original circle of Tomsk and Omsk intellectuals to embrace merchants, teachers, journalists, physicians, and prosperous peasants between the Urals and the Pacific. As Siberians discovered their own needs, they became aware of where their priorities diverged with those of European Russia and grew bolder in expressing dissatisfaction with metropolitan conceits and central policies. The consciousness of being Siberians as well as Russians was compared to the sentiments of English settlers in Canada.[7] Siberian self-assertiveness worried Prime Minister Stolypin, who in 1910 warned that something must be done lest "a rough democratic society" grow up east of the Urals and "crush European Russia."[8]

The Far East had an ambiguous relationship with Siberia after 1884 (when the Priamur governor-generalship was established), as it did with Manchuria after 1896. In some contexts it was subsumed in both. In others it stood apart. Oblastnichestvo in Vladivostok grew distinct from oblastnichestvo in Tomsk, especially when the negative repercussions of Russian penetration into Manchuria forced Far Easterners to take cognizance of their own interests.[9]

Birth of a Far Eastern Intelligentsia

During the 1880s and 1890s, an embryonic regional intelligentsia took shape in Blagoveshchensk, Khabarovsk, and Vladivostok. At first glance redolent of counterparts in Omsk, Tomsk, and Irkutsk, it stood apart in both composition and agenda. The presence of naval officers and sea captains gave it a maritime coloration. East Asia and the Pacific loomed prominently in its concerns and discourse.

Distance from metropolitan cultural life bred a sense of isolation behind which lurked boredom, belligerence, dissipation, and depression. Far Eastern intellectuals found inventive ways to ward off these afflictions, throwing themselves into journalism, ethnographic research, local history, and myth-making. Some called themselves amurtsy and celebrated their spiritual kinship to the Muravievian pleiad in after-dinner speeches.[10] Distance from the Center had its compensations, among them the relative scarcity of bureaucrats and the relative accessibility of visiting luminaries such as Anton Chekhov, the noted explorer Fridtjof Nansen, and the indefatigable world traveler Isabella Bird Bishop.[11]

Far Eastern intellectual life revolved around two organizations promoting the study of regional geography, history, and ethnography. One was the Society for the Study of the Amur Region (henceforth Amur Society),* founded in Vladivostok in 1884 by the head of the Resettlement Office Fyodor Busse (not to be confused with his cousin Nikolai Busse, who served under Muraviev). The other was the Priamur Branch of the Imperial Russian Geographical Society (henceforth Priamur Branch), founded in Khabarovsk in 1894. Both organizations maintained museums and libraries. The Amur Society Museum was started in 1890; Anton Chekhov attended the stone-laying ceremony. The Priamur Branch opened the Nikolaevsk Library and Grodekov Museum in 1896. The former was launched with a gift of 500 volumes from Nicholas II; the latter was endowed by Governor-General Grodekov, fluent in several Central Asian languages, author of an 1879 study of Afghanistan, and patron of the Nikolaevsk Library to which he donated his personal book collection.[12]

The Amur Society supported itself by members' dues and built up a library through donations of books from, among others, Przhevalsky, Venyukov, Bronislaw Pilsudski, Dybowski, Shternberg, Yokhelson, Chekhov, and Nansen. In a move symptomatic of rivalry between Vladivostok and Khabarovsk, the Far East's "St. Petersburg" and "Moscow,"† Governor-General Dukhovskoi tried to absorb the Amur Society into the Priamur Branch in 1894, but Busse frustrated the maneuver by appealing to powerful officials in St. Petersburg. The incident proved to be the first of several attempts by bureaucrats to take over the Amur Society.[13]

Both the Amur Society and the Priamur Branch won international respect for promoting knowledge about Northeast Asia. Scholars in Berlin, Paris, and Vienna cited their publications. Foreign visitors marveled at the Grodekov Museum, although one Englishman uncharitably quipped that

*As used here and in other nineteenth-century lexical contexts, "Amur Region" embraced the Priamur and the Primorye.

†Graduates of St. Petersburg University figured prominently among Vladivostok elites. They very likely transposed, or abetted the transposition of, Pushkin's metaphor of an imperial capital on the Gulf of Finland ("a window on Europe") to a port on the Sea of Japan ("a window on the Pacific").

the best pieces had been looted from Manchuria and Beijing.[14] Through publications, exhibits, and lectures, the Amur Society and Priamur Branch called attention to the fragility of the Far East's natural environment. Amur Society member Bronislaw Pilsudski struck a note of environmental activism in 1907 when he called for popular opposition to an Anglo-German-Russian syndicate proposing to drill for oil in northern Sakhalin.[15]

Leading editors took an active part in both organizations, testifying to the centrality of journalism in regional intellectual life. The labels "conservative" and "liberal" are of limited utility in explaining the editorial slants in the debates over free ports and East Asian immigration. The most influential editors themselves defied categorization. The onetime revolutionary Konstantin Kurteyev sang the praises of Governor-General Gondatti in Khabarovsk, while in Vladivostok the monarchist Viktor Panov called Russia's imperial advance into southern Manchuria "a major historical mistake."[16] Private feuds often underlay public polemics.

Educational institutions also set the tone for Priamur cultural life. Traditionally a domain of the Church, regional education grew more secular in the twilight of tsarist rule. There were over 400 elementary schools in the Priamur in 1914.[17] Virtually every village had a school and teacher.[18] In Khabarovsk and Vladivostok, gymnasia prepared boys for matriculation in the universities at Tomsk, Moscow, and St. Petersburg while academies offered women instruction in literature, accounting, and foreign languages preparatory to employment as clerks or cashiers in such firms as Denbigh & Semyonov, the Russo-Asiatic Bank, Churin & Co., and Kunst & Albers. Technical curricula were offered by a navigation school in Blagoveshchensk, a railroad institute in Khabarovsk, and a commercial school in Vladivostok. Cadets at the Muraviev Academy in Khabarovsk, all on state scholarships, could study Japanese as well as French, German, and English. The Nikolaevsk (Khabarovsk) and Gogol (Vladivostok) libraries and the Grodekov and Amur Society museums were open to the public. The privately financed Philanthropical Society (Khabarovsk) and People's House (Vladivostok) offered free adult education.[19]

Oriental and Marine Studies

Proximity to Japan, China, and Korea made Vladivostok a natural site for "oriental studies" (*vostokovedeniye*), which in this context meant the study of Northeast Asia, an area assuming strategic and economic significance as Russian railroads, settlers, and troops moved into Manchuria. Following three years of discussions, Governor-General Grodekov approved the creation in Vladivostok of an Oriental institute. The Vostochny Institut opened on 2 November 1899, with sixteen professors and lecturers, sixty students, and a library of 16,000 volumes.[20]

The Oriental Institute recruited its teaching staff primarily from graduates of St. Petersburg University, bright young men drawn to the Priamur by the prospect of scholarly and professional opportunity. China, Korea, Japan, and Mongolia were next door, tantalizingly accessible. Promotion in rank came with the job. Lecturers from St. Petersburg woke up as professors in Vladivostok. Most took their responsibilities seriously, judging from the volume and quality of scholarship published in the institute's journals. Within a decade the faculty roster read like a Who's Who of East Asian studies in Russia: sinologists Peter Schmidt, Apollinary Rudakov, Pavel Shkurkin, Nikolai Kyuner, and Aleksandr Grebenshchikov; Japan scholars Dmitry Pozdneyev and Evgeny Spalvin; Aleksei Pozdneyev and Gonbozhab Tsybikov, specialists in Mongolia and Tibet respectively; and the founder of Korean studies in Russia, Grigory Podstavin.[21]

Practical language instruction formed the core of the Oriental Institute's curriculum. Students were expected to acquire proficiency in English, Chinese, and an additional eastern language in a three-year program at the institute followed by a year of residence in an Asian country. In language instruction the institute pioneered what is now called "total immersion." Native speakers on the faculty taught in the vernacular, as did guest lecturers from Japan and China. For their second Asian language, most students chose Manchu, considered easier than Chinese to read.[22] Foreign residency enabled students to acquire skills, even if not always those intended by the program's architects.[23]

Students came from diverse backgrounds. Sons of peasants accounted for the largest number, making up over half the student body, followed by offspring of officials, aristocrats, shopkeepers, clergy, merchants, and Cossacks. Those in need of financial assistance were looked after by a scholarship committee chaired by Yulius Bryner. Military officers, composing about 20 to 30 percent of each class, received stipends from the Priamur governor-general.[24]

Though spared disturbances afflicting metropolitan universities, the Oriental Institute had its share of excitement. In 1903 students petitioned the rector, Aleksei Pozdneyev, to improve living conditions. When Pozdneyev expelled the signatories, the aggrieved young men appealed to Priamur Governor-General N. V. Linevich and then to War Minister Kuropatkin, who ordered an investigation. Pozdneyev thereupon resigned and was succeeded by his younger brother Dmitry. Dmitry departed three years later under similar circumstances. Apollinary Rudakov assumed the rectorship in 1906 and retained it until 1917, by which time 300 graduates were working as interpreters, diplomats, teachers, academics, journalists, and military intelligence officers throughout Northeast Asia. Some found employment in the CER administration, the Russo-Asiatic Bank, and Russian Orthodox missions in Beijing, Seoul, and Tokyo.[25]

Vladivostok also served as a forward base for marine sciences. Between 1886 and 1901 Stepan Makarov, Amur Society member and Russia's most illustrious naval officer, conducted hydrographic expeditions in the Pacific and Arctic oceans. Makarov's reports attracted international attention and sparked a debate with the chemist Dmitry Mendeleyev about whether the proposed Northern Sea Route should pass along the Siberian coast or across the North Pole. Among the junior officers who won Makarov's esteem was Ensign Aleksandr Kolchak, who came to Vladivostok in 1895 and served in the Pacific Squadron for four years. Kolchak traveled to Norway in 1899 to study under Nansen and a year later joined an arctic expedition led by Baron Eduard Toll. Fate dealt harshly with Kolchak's patrons as it would with him a generation later. Toll perished on an ice floe in 1902, and Makarov went down with his flagship in 1904.[26]

Parallel Lives

The navy had no monopoly of scholarly officers in the Far East. From Caucasian and Polish cantonments emerged two army lieutenants whose intellectual curiosity matched that of Stepan Makarov and whose literary gifts put them in a class by themselves. Assisted by a letter of introduction from Mendeleyev, Nikolai Baikov joined "Matilda's Guards" along the CER in 1901 and immersed himself in the Manchurian taiga. Transferred at his own request to Vladivostok in 1900, Vladimir Arseniev parlayed hunting skills into assignments in the south Ussuri taiga. Baikov and Arseniev came to an understanding about a division of labor between eastern Manchuria and the Primorye. Over the course of the next thirty years, both won international distinction as intrepid explorers and sensitive interpreters of Northeast Asian life.[27]

Arseniev's career advanced more quickly than that of Baikov thanks in part to connections with important regional figures. Through a former secretary of the Amur Society, he was introduced to Pavel Unterberger whose formidable knowledge of the Far East rested on more than a decade of research and administrative experience. Favorably impressed by the young officer's intelligence and capacity for hard work, the governor-general sent Arseniev on three expeditions into the Sikhote Alin during the years 1906–9, arranging their sponsorship by the Russian Geographical Society, a circumstance that attached to them a prestige absent from Baikov's contemporaneous treks about eastern Manchuria. Arseniev carried out the assignments to the satisfaction of Unterberger, who in 1910 appointed his protégé director of the Grodekov Museum. Lev Shternberg, now a free man and respected ethnographer, met Arseniev that year and became his mentor. By then a Khabarovsk newspaper editor had recognized Arseniev's literary talent and was publishing his field notes to a growing readership.[28]

The expeditions of 1906–9 engaged Arseniev in three ways. As an officer, he surveyed uncharted territory for possible Japanese invasion routes. As an ethnographer, he observed aborigines, ginseng-collectors, hunters, *brodyagi* ("vagabonds"), and *hong huzi*. As an artist, he was captivated by the Ussuri taiga, which came to symbolize for him primordial Nature: mysterious, ineffably beautiful, elusive, threatening, and threatened. The expeditions awakened in Arseniev a poetic sensibility that later drew on his encounters with a Nanai named Dersu Uzala. Arseniev met Dersu in August 1906 and saw him intermittently over a period of nineteen months, until Dersu was murdered by robbers. A decade later Arseniev used his field notes to create a mythic Dersu, a composite of taiga denizens, including his principal guide, who happened to be Chinese.[29]

Arseniev's growing stature exposed him to unpleasant realities that darkened the last quarter of his life. In St. Petersburg to address the Imperial Russian Geographical Society in 1910, he was shocked by the vanity and petty vindictiveness of the metropolitan intelligentsia. He yearned to get back to the Far East and resume his ethnographic studies undisturbed, but politics and personalities again intervened. Late in 1910 Arseniev's patron Unterberger was replaced by Nikolai Gondatti, who, possibly out of jealousy (Gondatti's work on Chukotka had won him recognition as an ethnographer), showed less readiness than his predecessor to let a gifted subordinate indulge in scholarship.[30]

Fragile Ecumene

Between 1896 and 1914 amurtsy evolved into *zaamurtsy* ("trans-Amurians"), a word connoting Manchuria, as well as the Priamur. Army officers (Baikov, Arseniev), orientalists (Rudakov, Grebenshchikov, Spalvin, the Pozdneyev brothers), editors (Panov, Matveyev, Orzhik), and Amur Society officials (including Nikolai Solovyov), together with entrepreneurs such as Yankovsky, inhabited a Northeast Asian Russian ecumene. Moving between the Priamur and China, Korea, and Japan, zaamurtsy wove a web of Northeast Asian trajectories. Nikolai Matveyev commuted to Japan, his "second homeland."* Dmitry Pozdneyev and Boris Orzhik found it politically and economically expedient to publish in Yokohama. Mikhail Yankovsky joined a young botanist named Vladimir Komarov to pursue his ornithological hobby in Korea. Rudakov, Grebenshchikov, and Spalvin took their students on field trips to Manchuria, co-founded the Society of Russian Orientalists in Harbin (1907), and two years later inaugurated a journal featuring the work of Russians living in China, Japan, and the Priamur.[31] Occasionally summering in Nagasaki, as did other members of the Vladivostok bourgeoisie, zaamurtsy renewed their friendships (and rivalries) with former exiles from Transbaikalia, Yakutia, and Sakhalin living in Japan.

The ecumene embraced foreigners residing or sojourning in the Far East. While conducting research on the lower Amur, Sakhalin, and China between 1898 and 1910, the young German-American ethnographer and orientalist Bernard Laufer worked with Grebenshchikov and Rudakov. Business took Albers to Harbin, Shanghai, Kobe, and Hakodate, and Nagasaki (Kunst was more partial to Hawaii, where he built himself a winter home on Honolulu's Waikiki Beach). Bryner, Kunst, Albers, Dattan, and Denbigh took Russian citizenship to circumvent laws barring aliens from owning real estate, but they became deeply attached to their adopted land. Bryner married a Russian-Mongol woman, and Maeda Kiyotsugu, a language instructor at the Oriental Institute, married a Russian librarian. When war broke out in 1904, Maeda declined repatriation, an act that incensed some of his compatriots and led to his assassination three years later on a Tokyo street.[32] The unassuming cosmopolitanism of zaamurtsy might have become the hallmark of Far Eastern identity had it been able to withstand the visceral pull of class and country and the corrosive acid of envy.

---

*According to A. Khisamutdinov in *Zotik Nikolaevich Matveev*, p. 33, Matveyev was the first Russian born in Japan.

« « » »

Rumblings

Nowhere in Russia were there so many armed revolutionaries. Nowhere were local tsarist officials so helpless.
— A History of the 1905 Revolution
in the Far East (1956)

U ntil the Russo-Japanese War, the
Far East offered unpromising soil
for revolution. Less than 20 percent of the peasants were poor. Proletarians
were scarce and scattered in small-scale family enterprises, railroad shops,
and docks. Military personnel were ubiquitous, disciplined, and loyal. The
soil was enriched after 1900 by an influx of poor peasants, who gravitated
into cities and towns, to give the Far East the highest proportion of urban
inhabitants of any Russian province.[1] Workers concentrated in the Zeya-
Bureya goldfields and at Chita, Nikolsk-Ussuriisk, Khabarovsk, and Blagoveshchensk. Vladivostok harbored a volatile combination of port and railroad workers, former exiles, ex-convicts, active duty and demobilized
troops, and sailors. Symptoms of unrest appeared during the 1890s, when
Amur boatmen staged slowdowns and miners periodically struck at the
Zeya-Bureya goldfields.[2] Arising from economic grievances, these disputes
acquired political overtones as two parties attempted to channel discontent
into class consciousness and revolutionary action.

Socialist Revolutionaries (SRs) gained adherents among teachers, veterinarians, engineers, physicians, and clerks in the years preceding the
Russo-Japanese War. Though not at first receptive to the idea of regional
autonomy, SRs professed respect for political freedoms and improved living conditions for peasants and workers. Committed to agrarian socialism,
SR activists operated out of Khabarovsk, Blagoveshchensk, and Vladivos-

tok.[3] The Russian Social Democratic Workers' Party (RSDRP) made its debut in the Far East in 1901, when its pamphlets started circulating among Nikolsk-Ussuriisk railroad workers and Vladivostok stevedores. In the same year, the son of a Blagoveshchensk physician, Vladimir Shimanovsky, formed the RSDRP Siberian Union at Tomsk University. A year later in Chita, a local activist named Emelyan Yaroslavsky organized a RSDRP cell whose members intermittently recognized the authority of the Siberian Union.[4]

An unpopular war with Japan created favorable conditions for political agitation. Being close to the war zone, the Maritime District was put under martial law in 1904, subjecting residents to annoying constraints. Martial law was extended to the Amur District in 1905 in response to a strike by railroad workers protesting Bloody Sunday.* Conscription placed a special burden on peasants and Cossacks. Inflation and shortages hurt all but the most affluent. Morale sagged with each reverse: the brazen bombardment of the Golden Horn by a Japanese squadron, the death of popular Admiral Makarov and 700 officers and men of the *Petropavlovsk*, the fall of Port Arthur, the retreat from Mukden, the destruction of the Baltic Squadron, and the Japanese occupation of Sakhalin and the lower Amur. Frustrations building up during the war erupted after the conclusion of peace at Portsmouth on 5 September 1905.

Reservists posed the most serious threat to public order. Less disciplined than army regulars, they were susceptible to aspirations that if unfulfilled transmogrified into grievances. Reservists expected to receive priority in demobilization and repatriation to European Russia, but logistical obstacles precluded this from happening. It would normally have required months to transport some 900,000 troops from the Far East to metropolitan Russia over 5,000 miles of single track. Normal conditions did not obtain in late 1905, because the war had taken a toll on both equipment and personnel. Even assuming official cooperation, the railroad was not up to the task. RSDRP activists wanted to exploit the situation to provoke a rebellion, but they lacked the wherewithal to carry out such an ambitious program. There were fewer than 400 Social Democrats in the Priamur and Harbin combined and not a single RSDRP cell in the Manchurian Army, the Vladivostok garrison, or the Pacific Squadron.[5]

Before either the Social Democrats or the SRs could organize, disorder

---

*On 22 Jan. 1905 Cossacks fired on a procession of workers demanding bread outside the Winter Palace in St. Petersburg, killing 70 and wounding 240.

spread spontaneously through the Priamur and Transbaikalia in the three months following proclamation of the October Manifesto.* Reservists commandeered westward bound trains and rampaged around stations as railroad workers stood aside. Officers who tried to intervene were beaten up and in some cases shot.[6] Postal and telegraph workers struck in Blagoveshchensk, Khabarovsk, and Vladivostok. Miners proclaimed a short-lived "Zeya Republic" in the Amur goldfields. A Harbin strike committee briefly took over the CER. Communications between the Far East and metropolitan Russia were severed for several weeks.[7] Each town experienced an insurrectionary spasm. Disaffected military and railway personnel temporarily seized power in Vladivostok and Chita. Arsenal workers and stevedores went on strike in Khabarovsk and Blagoveshchensk. Rural areas for the most part remained outwardly calm during the critical months of November 1905 to January 1906.[8]

Insurgency at Vladivostok

Wartime Vladivostok contained ample ingredients for unrest. The port teemed with disgruntled and politically active sailors, for commanders of other fleets had availed themselves of the chance to rid themselves of troublemakers when sending reinforcements to the Pacific. Shortages exacerbated relations between officers and the ranks. The former enjoyed access to prized commodities at a time when subordinates suffered from a lack of fruit and fresh vegetables. Sailors resented having to labor on local fortifications and were humiliated by municipal ordinances prohibiting them from riding in carriages or walking near flower beds along the Svetlanskaya.[9] Peace eroded what was left of wartime discipline by raising expectations for demobilization and flooding the city with 90,000 restless soldiers and sailors, including politicized Russian prisoners of war repatriated from Japan. As waiting for homeward-bound trains stretched into the third month Vladivostok erupted.

Mob violence of uncertain origin engulfed the city on 12 November as over 10,000 reservists, garrison troops, sailors, and stevedores, joined by inmates freed from municipal prisons, burned the navy court, private shops, and a library. Several officers were killed in what was described by

*Issued by Nicholas II on the advice of Sergei Witte (who composed it) after a general strike had paralyzed the government, the manifesto granted a constitution, invested a representative assembly (duma) with legislative powers, and extended the franchise and civil liberties.

Vladivostok Military Governor Nikolai Greve as "complete anarchy." The following day a crowd of 1,000 gathered outside a cathedral on the Svetlan-skaya and demanded public readings of the October Manifesto, the immediate discharge of all reservists, freedom to attend political meetings, and civil behavior by officers. Vladivostok's garrison commander, General G. N. Kazbek, responded with a combination of diplomacy and force. He left the crowds alone, persuaded garrison troops to return to their barracks, and then called in detachments of Ussuri Cossacks who managed to restore order on 15 November. All together thirty-eight people (24 insurgents and 14 loyalists) lost their lives.[10]

Signs of unrest reappeared in early December when postal, telegraph, and railroad workers went on strike, cutting communications with Khabarovsk. With the Transbaikal section of the Trans-Siberian already paralyzed by disorders, Vladivostok became isolated from both the imperial and the Priamur capital. Meanwhile, General Kazbek had been replaced by Andrei Selivanov, who had instructions to take any measures necessary to maintain order.*

When news of the arrest of members of the St. Petersburg Soviet reached Vladivostok on 17 December, local garrison troops joined by Kadets, SRs, and Social Democrats formed an organization called the Executive Committee of Lower Ranks of the Vladivostok Garrison (henceforth Executive Committee).[†] Leadership of the Executive Committee was entrusted to one SR and two Kadets.[11] The committee found itself caught between pressures for action and official intransigence. When Moscow workers rose against the regime on 22 December, some Vladivostok garrison troops and the more militant SRs and Social Democrats prepared for action. General Selivanov thereupon prohibited political meetings and ordered the Executive Committee to disband.

Matters came to a head on the first anniversary of Bloody Sunday.[12] On 23 January 1906 several thousand armed sailors, garrison and railroad troops, railroad and port workers, women, children, and assorted spectators gathered in Railroad Station Square. After a few speeches, voices called

---

*Nicholas II and Governor-General Unterberger had expressed displeasure at the lack of firmness of local authorities dealing with the disorders in Vladivostok. Unterberger, *Priamurskii krai*, p. 401. Nesterov, p. 180. *Istoriia Sibiri*, 3: 287. Ascher, p. 270.

†The St. Petersburg soviet was a council of workers' deputies. "Kadets" was the familiar name for members of the Constitutional Democratic Party formed in 1905 and led by Pavel Milyukov. The Kadets advocated a constitutional monarchy and political and economic freedoms, views popular within Russia's fledgling middle class and among the bourgeoisie of Blagoveshchensk, Khabarovsk, and Vladivostok.

for a march on General Selivanov's headquarters to demand the immediate release of all political prisoners. The crowd roared approval and formed into a procession. Armed men took their place behind women, children, and a band. In the front ranks strode the publicist Lyudmila Volkenshtein, whose revolutionary fervor had not been dampened by fifteen years of imprisonment and Sakhalin hard labor. Reinforced by contingents of East Siberian Sharpshooters and Transbaikalian Cossacks, General Selivanov blocked their path. As the procession approached a central intersection, sharpshooters and Cossacks opened fire with machine guns. The marchers scattered, leaving behind thirty dead, including Volkenshtein and a local gymnasium student.

Once the demonstrators had recovered from the shock, they reacted explosively. Brushing aside the Executive Committee's appeals for restraint, garrison troops and sailors stormed the fortress and shot General Selivanov and a number of other officers. The sharpshooters and Cossacks withdrew to Pervaya Rechka, about a mile north of the Golden Horn, leaving Vladivostok in insurgent hands. On 25 January a crowd of 20,000 attended a funeral for the fallen demonstrators as rebel-held batteries fired salutes. Neither the Executive Committee nor the insurgents had any idea what to do next.

While the insurgents hesitated, the tsar appointed a veteran cavalry officer then commanding a Cossack division in Manchuria, General Pavel Mishchenko, "Special Governor-General of the Vladivostok Fortified Zone" and ordered him to use every means at his disposal to restore order. Mishchenko handled the assignment deftly, opening negotiations with the Executive Committee and rebel units as a way of ascertaining whom to neutralize. Using promises and threats, Mishchenko managed to lure rebel troops piecemeal from Vladivostok and to enter the city without incident on 27 January. He then dissolved the Executive Committee and arrested 1,967 troops and sailors as mutineers and put them on trial at Spassk. Of these, 1,550 were released, 332 received prison terms, and eighty-five were sentenced to death. In the end, fifty-four of the death sentences were carried out, the others were commuted to hard labor.[13]

The "Chita Republic"

Whereas Kadets and SRs loomed prominently in Vladivostok, Social Democrats played a leading role in Chita (1907 pop. 39,000), administrative center of Transbaikalia. Chita lay just west of Karymskaya, junction of the Sretensk spur (until the completion of the Amur Line in 1916, travelers used river steamers from Sretensk to reach Blagoveshchensk, Khabarovsk, and Nikolaevsk) and the trunk line leading to Manchuria. Mindful of Chita's strategic location astride lines of communication from Manchuria and the Priamur, RSDRP activists focused their propaganda on local Cossacks, garrison troops, railroad workers, ex-convicts, and exiles.

During the last three months of 1905, the Chita cell (now grown to committee size) supported RSDRP propaganda efforts in Transbaikalia and Manchuria by printing leaflets and publishing a newspaper.[14] The leadership of the committee had passed from its organizer Emelyan Yaroslavsky, to three Social Democrats fresh from Yakutian exile: Ivan Babushkin, Anton Kostyushko-Volyuzhanich, and Viktor Kurnatovsky. The trio appealed to a variegated constituency by addressing each group's grievances (an eight-hour workday for railroad workers, rights for rank and file troops, elimination of ataman privileges for poor Cossacks) and identified the fulfillment of everyone's aspirations with the struggle against tsarist autocracy. Troops passing through Chita from Manchuria proved less receptive to RSDRP propaganda, but the freight cars yielded ordnance to equip units of armed workers.

Events in Chita moved quickly from late November, when railwaymen went on strike, blocking east-west movement. A strike committee under Babushkin, Kostyushko-Volyuzhanich, and Kurnatovsky induced the local garrison and postal and telegraph employees to join the walkout, and on 5 December a "Soviet of Soldiers' and Cossacks' Deputies" chaired by Kostyushko-Volyuzhanich proclaimed the formation of a "Chita Republic." Armed workers released prisoners from the local jail and placed Transbaikalia Governor Ivan Kholshchevnikov, brother-in-law of War Minister Aleksandr Rediger, under house arrest.[15]

Only after putting down an uprising in Moscow did the government turn to deal with Siberia. On 7 January 1906 the Trans-Siberian Line was put under martial law, and armored trains departed Moscow and Harbin commanded respectively by Aleksandr Meller-Zakomelsky and Pavel Rennenkampf. As they converged on Chita, the generals "reestablished order," Rennenkampf displaying more restraint than Meller-Zakomelsky, who confused military efficiency with summary execution. The armored trains pulled into Chita from east and west on 6 February, extinguishing the short-lived republic. Some 400 railway workers and soldiers went on trial, of whom 147 were found guilty. Of these, nine were shot and seven hanged.[16]

Babushkin and Kostyushko-Volyuzhanich were not among them, having been captured and executed outside of Chita. Kurnatovsky was more fortunate. Rennenkampf commuted his death sentence to hard labor. Before he could begin a new life as a convict, Kurnatovsky escaped from a Verkhneudinsk hospital and made his way to Australia where he settled down as a dishwasher until summoned by Lenin to Paris in 1910 to give a first-hand account of the Chita Republic. Governor Kholshchevnikov emerged from house arrest physically unscathed and was promptly court-martialed and imprisoned for dereliction of duty, thereby earning the unenviable distinction of having been incarcerated by revolutionary and tsarist authorities in that order.[17]

Repercussions

The upheavals of 1905–6 profoundly shook two groups within the region's small middle class: adults who regarded themselves as "progressive" and impressionable youngsters who conceived a hatred for autocracy. The former flirted with reform but remained politically passive. The latter embraced the illusion of revolutionary short-cuts to economic well-being and social justice.

The suppression of what came to be called the Revolution of 1905 triggered gestures of protest within the Vladivostok bourgeoisie. In January 1907 Amur Society members voted to confer a gold medal on their former secretary, Ferdinand Ossendowski, then sojourning in a Harbin prison for having chaired a CER strike committee. Liberal newspaper editor Nikolai Matveyev published a poem in memory of Lyudmila Volkenshtein.* Such displays of defiance lacked a political agenda. On the whole, the members of the Amur Society, including Matveyev, rejected revolution, although some later showed themselves capable of adapting to it.

The shooting of demonstrators on 23 January 1906 profoundly affected two Vladivostok youngsters born into privilege: Zotik Matveyev, seventeen-year-old son of Nikolai, and Kostya Sukhanov, the twelve-year-old son of South Ussuri District Governor Aleksandr Sukhanov. Both boys knew

---

*It is conventionally maintained that Matveyev spent eighteen months in prison for publishing this poem. According to Amir Khisamutdinov, the term was six months; moreover, this was not for the poem but for being the addressee of seditious literature that Nicholas Sudzilovsky-Russel, a political exile in Japan, had entrusted to Ōba Kakō, a Japanese journalist who had recently served on the Imperial Army staff as a Russian interpreter. Khisamutdinov, *Russian Far East*, p. 47.

the fatally wounded gymnasium student and were stunned to learn that he had been gunned down by men wearing the uniform of the Imperial Russian Army. For Kostya, shock gave way to an anger that led him to the RSDRP underground. For the gentler and more reflective Zotik, the incident catalyzed a devotion to the ideals of Lev Tolstoy.[18] Both reactions were emblematic in a generation that came to maturity in the following decade of war and revolution.

In the aftermath of Vladivostok and Chita, Far Eastern SRs and Social Democrats tried to regroup amid factionalism within their respective parties. As one faction of the Socialist Revolutionary Party engaged in terrorism in the Center, Far Eastern "Maximalists" planned direct action against the regime on the periphery. Meanwhile, Far Eastern Social Democrats shrugged off Bolshevik-Menshevik polemics and went about the practical task of putting together a regional network. A tiny RSDRP organization materialized in Vladivostok in 1906, consisting largely of fugitives from Chita. In 1907 the Vladivostok RSDRP Committee, styling itself a Far Eastern "center," convened a conference at Nikolsk-Ussuriisk; it was attended by sixteen delegates representing 300 comrades, a third of whom were in Harbin.[19] The Vladivostok Social Democrats concentrated on building their constituency, conducting "open" educational programs at People's House and propagandizing sailors and garrison troops, local trade union workers, and students at the Oriental Institute.[20] To avoid tsarist censorship, they bought shares in a local newspaper founded by S. A. Garfield, nephew of the American president.[21] Maximalists looked for a time and place to ignite a revolutionary explosion.

Vladivostok in 1907 had some characteristics of a tinderbox. The port overflowed with politically conscious workers from Moscow, St. Petersburg, and Odessa, unwittingly recruited by Governor-General Unterberger in his effort to offset reliance on Chinese labor. Discontent over harsh discipline and poor food simmered in the Pacific Squadron, whose torpedo-boat crews were exercised over the incarceration of some shipmates. The Maximalists exhorted the sailors to act, hoping to foment a general mutiny in the Pacific Squadron. On 30 October three torpedo-boat crews obliged and raised red flags over their vessels. Two of the crews had an immediate change of heart and pulled them down again. The third ran their ship aground trying to steam out of the Golden Horn. As the sailors were marched off to jail, the Maximalist instigators applauded from the sidelines, then hastily departed for Nagasaki to exchange recriminations.[22]

The state's secret police allowed Far Eastern Social Democrats little time to savor the Maximalist fiasco. Agents of the Okhranka infiltrated and shattered RSDRP organizations in Khabarovsk (1908), Vladivostok (1909), and Harbin (1910). Members were either jailed, coopted, or induced to emigrate. At the outbreak of the First World War, the Social Democrats had no base in the Far East.[23] They fared better in Yakutsk, owing to the organizational talents of the Chita veteran Emelyan Yaroslavsky following the 1912 Lena goldfields massacre.*

In the long run, tsarist authorities unwittingly prepared the Far East for revolution. State-subsidized resettlement after 1907 brought in thousands of poor peasants and laborers with little stake in the existing order. After war broke out in 1914, military and labor conscription depleted the region of over 500,000 residents, nearly half the farming population.[24] Meanwhile, the influx of several hundred thousand refugees from the Ukraine and the Baltic provinces, together with thousands of Austro-Hungarian and German prisoners of war, further weakened the social foundations of political stability.[25]

Sensing opportunity in these developments, the Petrograd RSDRP Committee decided in 1916 to conduct antiwar propaganda among Vladivostok port workers in order to interdict the flow of supplies reaching the Russian Army from the Pacific. Chosen for the task was the gymnasium student of ten years earlier, Kostya Sukhanov, now a Party organizer at the University of St. Petersburg. Equipped with a medical exemption from military service, Kostya returned to Vladivostok that summer, almost married the youngest daughter of Yulius Bryner, made a few speeches, and landed in jail. Kostya's father, Ussuri District Governor Aleksandr Sukhanov, got around to bailing out his wayward son on 27 February 1917, just nine days before his own career collapsed together with the Romanov dynasty.[26]

False Dawn

The twilight of Imperial Russia masqueraded as dawn in the Far East under the artificial radiance of technology and construction. Telephones and electric lights appeared in urban centers, as did horseless carriages from the Baltic Machine Works. In 1913 Belgian trams started clattering along

*On 17 April 1912 troops at Bodaibo on the Vitim River fired on 3,000 workers demanding the release of arrested members of a strike committee, killing 270 and wounding 250.

Vladivostok's Svetlanskaya amid a forest of new structures: Kunst & Albers and Churin department stores, Bryner & Company's offices, a Japanese consulate, Lutheran and Catholic churches, a cinema called "Illusion," and a monument to the hero of Petropavlovsk, Admiral Zavoiko. That summer, in celebration of the Romanov tricentennial, Governor-General Gondatti opened an agricultural exhibition at Khabarovsk. As a military band struck up the "Preobrazhensky March" and a French Blériot monoplane circled above, crowds flocked toward flag-festooned pavilions and open-air restaurants.[27] The Norwegian explorer Fridtjof Nansen, stopping in Khabarovsk after a Siberian tour, forecast a bright future for civilization in general and the Priamur in particular.[28]

Few Far Easterners paid much attention to the Balkans during the summer of 1914. Local, not European, temperatures were on their minds, propelling them to beaches rather than kiosks. Shrugging off Sarajevo, Arseniev took a group of students on an excursion into the Khektsir Hills south of Khabarovsk. When St. Petersburg announced all-out mobilization on 31 July, some assumed it was against Japan. From Vladivostok, Berlin looked less threatening than Tokyo. True, there were those who complained that Governor-General Unterberger had favored Balts in his staff appointments, those who bridled at the Teutonic pedantry of Kunst & Albers clerks, and those who eventually abetted or succumbed to spy hysteria.* Yet in July 1914 few Far Easterners wanted or expected to fight the Kaiser. Local distractions kept the illusion of normalcy alive after war engulfed Europe. Tannenberg was far away, and the fifteen-year-old violin prodigy Jashcha Heifetz was playing to full houses in Khabarovsk, where the only "Lenin" anyone knew was a local impresario. As summer gave way to autumn, reality intruded in the form of conscription, casualty lists, and an anti-alcohol campaign. Yet curiosity and hospitality never flagged. Rumors of an imminent visit by Maksim Gorky circulated around the Far East during the spring of 1916. When instead of a lionized proletarian writer, a faintly passé symbolist poet turned up at the Golden Horn, the welcome was no less

---

*In Oct. 1914 zaamurets Ferdinand Ossendowski wrote a series of articles under the pseudonym "Mzura" in the Petrograd newspaper *Vechernee vremia*, calling Kunst & Albers director Adolf Dattan a German agent. Dattan was arrested and released but forced to move from Vladivostok to Narym (Tomsk District). The Vladivostok editor Viktor Panov publicly defended Dattan and accused Ossendowski of slander. Dattan was officially cleared of all charges by the Provisional Government in 1917. It is interesting to note in this context that Vladivostok-born Alfred Gustafovich Albers joined the Imperial Russian Army and served at the front. Panov, *Amerikanskie podlozhnie dokumenty*, pp. 7, 14.

effusive. Local audiences devoured Konstantin Balmont's declamations on love and death, prompting the normally melancholy poet to remark in an uncharacteristically upbeat letter home that Vladivostok's reception was the warmest of any town in Siberia.[29]

War brought the hitherto more or less parallel lives of the officer-ethnographers Arseniev and Baikov to a crossroads. Lieutenant-Colonel Baikov left Manchuria for the European front. Lieutenant-Colonel Arseniev sequestered himself in a Ussuri village and composed a fictional memoir about Dersu Uzala. Gondatti found it increasingly difficult to tolerate Arseniev's scholarly indulgences and in 1916 reprimanded his subordinate for neglecting his duties in the Resettlement Office. When not long thereafter Arseniev went off to Harbin to read a paper for the Society of Russian Orientalists, Gondatti fired him.[30]

Eight days later, on 18 October 1916, Gondatti presided over a ceremony celebrating the completion of a mile-long railroad bridge across the Amur at Khabarovsk. Trains from metropolitan Russia could at last reach Vladivostok without passing through Manchuria, fulfilling Baron Korf's vision of a rail line from Transbaikalia to the Primorye entirely on Russian soil. Ironically, the fulfillment of Korf's dream set the stage for Gondatti's nightmare, for the ribbon of steel linking the Far East to the Center served as a lightning rod for revolution.

13

《 《 》 》

Revolution

Life in the Far East began in earnest only after the Great
October Revolution.   — Vladimir Klipel (1976)

Reactions to the February Revolution
(8–12 March 1917) varied among
the 1,700,000 inhabitants of the Priamur governor-generalship. For senior
officials, military officers, policemen, cadets, and priests,* the abrupt ab-
dication of the tsar and unceremonious end of the imperial Russian state
came as a painful shock. "Revolution" meant little to aborigines who still
had to deal with Russians.[1] Most peasants, Cossacks, merchants, teachers,
workers, exiles, soldiers, and sailors welcomed the end of Romanov rule. As
the Provisional Government proclaimed civil liberties and social equality,
each Far Eastern constituency thought it saw the imminent fulfillment of its
own aspirations. Prosperous peasants saw the February Revolution as an
opportunity to gain more control over their own lives through the institutions of self-government called *zemstvos*. Opposed by Unterberger, these
organs of local self-government did not exist in the Far East until 1916,
when Gondatti convened a congress of zemstvo councils in Khabarovsk.[2]
Following the February Revolution, newly established zemstvos assumed
jurisdiction over police activities as well as education, health, and public
works. The urban middle classes cautiously approved of the Provisional
Government but saw their immediate interests represented in municipal
dumas. Amur and Ussuri Cossacks regarded the February Revolution as an
opportunity to achieve greater autonomy, but among Cossacks returning
from service at the front, some interpreted the collapse of the old regime as
a signal to challenge their own atamans. The Far Eastern proletariat, about

---

*In 1915 the Russian Orthodox Church was represented in the Priamur governor-generalship
by 785 churches, ten monasteries, and 1,615 ecclesiastics. Kandidov, pp. 14–15.

97,000 railwaymen, miners, stevedores, ship repairmen, metalworkers, millers, tanners, and fish-processing workers, viewed the Provisional Government with skeptical detachment. Among 190,000 Koreans, those with Russian citizenship (about 20 percent) tended to support the Provisional Government, while the recently arrived and generally poorer compatriots gravitated toward the Socialist Revolutionary Party.[3]

SR-Menshevik Dominance, March–July

Several political parties jockeyed for position in the Far East during 1917, an uncoordinated scramble in a fluid domestic and international environment. Notwithstanding their coolness to regional autonomy, Kadets attracted a following within the middle class.[4] SRs dominated peasant cooperatives and zemstvo organs.[5] Despite signals from Petrograd to adhere to Bolshevik or Menshevik factions, the local Social Democrats worked together into the summer of 1917. Although some Far Eastern Bolsheviks attuned their rhetoric so as not to ruffle the sensibilities of regionalists and independent peasants, the Mensheviks had a stronger Far Eastern base and dominated trade unions in Vladivostok and Nikolsk-Ussuriisk while maintaining networks in Khabarovsk, Blagoveshchensk, and Chita.[6] Yet within nine months of the February Revolution, Bolsheviks were in power in Vladivostok and Khabarovsk, an achievement that would not have been possible without painstaking organizational efforts and a quickness to exploit shifting popular moods.

During the spring of 1917, ad hoc organs of local administration called committees of public safety sprang up in all Far Eastern towns. Individual committees varied in political complexion, but Kadets, SRs, and Mensheviks were consistently well represented in municipal dumas, zemstvo councils, and peasant cooperatives.

The February Revolution removed only the apex of the Priamur governor-general's administration. Atamans, army officers, and civil servants remained at their posts. Many a bureaucrat adapted to the new circumstances by adopting the title "commissar."[7] Changes in the countryside were also cosmetic. Zemstvo leaders assumed the prerogatives of rural administrators, and district elders rechristened themselves district commissars.[8] Governor-General Gondatti was in Vladivostok when the tsar abdicated on 15 March. The local committee of public safety treated him civilly and raised no objections when he embarked for Khabarovsk to rejoin his family.

A different atmosphere greeted him in Khabarovsk where the committee of public safety was under the sway of the Social Democrat Aleksandr Malyshev and Left SR allies. Malyshev had Gondatti arrested, most likely to give credibility to his own claim to jurisdiction over the entire Far East.[9] The maneuver backfired, for Gondatti still enjoyed respect, especially in rural areas where he had distributed Cossack lands to peasants and empowered zemstvo councils. The Khabarovsk soviet, chaired by a Menshevik (Nikolai Vakulin), distanced itself from Malyshev, while a former schoolteacher and Right SR named Aleksandr Rusanov challenged Bolshevik–Left SR influence in the Khabarovsk committee.[*] As the Provisional Government's new Commissar for the Far East, Rusanov in April transferred Gondatti to Petrograd (where he was released following an investigation) and in May engineered Malyshev's resignation from the committee of public safety.[10]

Mensheviks dominated the political scene in Vladivostok, sharing power with SRs and Kadets on the committee of public safety, presiding over the municipal duma, chairing the Intersocialist Bureau and its offspring, the Vladivostok soviet (formed on 17 March), and occupying visible posts in the local RSDRP organization. Kostya Sukhanov did not advertise his Bolshevik affiliations, because Lenin's "April Theses"[†] had little appeal in the Far East where local soviets were not inclined to challenge the Provisional Government, where support for the war remained strong, and where most peasants owned their own fields. When the First Congress of Far Eastern Soviets convened in May 1917, it repudiated Lenin by endorsing a Menshevik program and electing a Menshevik-SR team led by Luka Gerasimov to the soon-to-be-formed People's Commissariat of Far Eastern Soviets (Dalsovnarkom).[11]

The failure of a Bolshevik uprising in Petrograd in mid-July marked a high point for Far Eastern Mensheviks and their allies.[‡] The Vladivostok, Khabarovsk, and Blagoveshchensk soviets all supported Menshevik motions denouncing the insurrection for "betraying the revolution."[12] As local RSDRP

---

[*]*Dal'istpart*, 3: 10. The spectacle of an organ of the Provisional Government behaving in a more "Bolshevik" manner than an organ of soviet power was an anomaly not confined to the Far East.

[†]On 17 April (the day after his return from exile in Geneva) Lenin called for the transfer of power from the "bourgeois" Provisional Government to the soviets, for ending Russia's participation in the war, for the expropriation and distribution of the land to peasants, and for the establishment of "worker control" over industry.

[‡]The Petrograd Bolsheviks had broken with the Mensheviks in April and, unwilling to give up their party name, styled it the RSDRP(b), "b" denoting *bolshevikov*.

committees declared their support for the Provisional Government and Mensheviks consolidated their position in Dalsovnarkom, Vakulin replaced the increasingly left-leaning Gerasimov as chairman in August (Gerasimov openly affiliated himself with the Bolsheviks the next month).[13]

Bolshevik Ascent, August–November

The Bolsheviks enlarged their political base in the Primorye during the summer and fall of 1917 by pragmatically adapting to local conditions rather than blindly following directives from Petrograd. Their efforts were assisted by six Russian-born émigrés from Chicago: Arnold Neibut, Vladimir ("Bill") Shatov, Grigory Rayev, Andrei Chumak, Moisei Delvig, and Aleksandr Krasnoshchekov.[14] In Vladivostok the Bolsheviks concentrated on organizing port and railway workers, sailors, garrison troops, and miners, outwardly maintaining an alliance with Menshevik "internationalists." Rayev was elected chairman of the municipal trade union bureau, while Neibut took over the RSDRP daily, *Krasnoye znamya*. Bolsheviks gained influence in the soviet's military commission and coached stevedores on how to set up "workers' control" committees in local enterprises.[15] Outside of Vladivostok the Party's gains were less impressive. Delvig did his best to organize coal miners in Suchan. Krasnoshchekov chaired the Nikolsk-Ussuriisk soviet, but Menshevik "defensists" dominated the Blagoveshchensk soviet, and a Menshevik-SR alliance held sway in Khabarovsk.[16]

Mensheviks rather than Bolsheviks took the initiative in establishing soviet rule in Vladivostok. When news of General Lavr Kornilov's attempted coup against the Kerensky government reached the Far East on 10 September, another Chicago émigré, A. F. Agarev, chairman of the Vladivostok soviet, proposed that the soviet assume power to defend the Provisional Government. Taken by surprise, Bolshevik delegates had little choice but to support the motion.[17] Agarev's initiative convinced Neibut and Sukhanov that the time had come to break with the Mensheviks. At the Second Far Eastern Conference of the RSDRP in September, Neibut denounced Agarev, whereupon seven Menshevik delegates walked out, leaving seven Bolsheviks to open the First Far Eastern Conference of the RSDRP(b). Other Far Eastern Social Democrats did not rush to follow Vladivostok's example, and Neibut got a frosty reception when he visited Khabarovsk in October.[18]

Undaunted, Vladivostok Bolsheviks set out to build a regional organization, but they soon found themselves contending with both local mavericks and the Irkutsk-based Central Executive Committee of Siberian Soviets (Tsentrosibir), Lenin's instrument to gain control of Far Eastern soviets and Party committees. Three emissaries, Meier Trilisser, Pavel Postyshev, and Boris Shumyatsky, arrived in Blagoveshchensk, Khabarovsk, and Vladivostok, respectively, attempting with mixed results to coordinate local tactics with a central agenda.

The October Revolution

Ten days that shook the world only ruffled the Far East. In Khabarovsk neither the committee of public safety nor the soviet recognized the regime created by the 7 November coup in Petrograd. Zemstvo councils and rural soviets continued to function under the same leaders, as did organs of the Provisional Government. News of the "October Revolution" did not reach remote areas for weeks. Arseniev only learned about it on 5 February 1918, on returning to Khabarovsk from the taiga. Most inhabitants of the Commander Islands remained in ignorance for months because those who had access to the only wireless decided not to tell them.[19]

During November and December the Bolsheviks tried to take power in several Far Eastern cities. They succeeded in Vladivostok on 18 November, but an attempt to seize control in Harbin wilted under the barrels of Chinese guns.[20] In Khabarovsk Luka Gerasimov and Aleksandra Kim, recent recruits to the Bolshevik faction, organized arsenal workers, Amur Flotilla sailors, garrison troops, Koreans, and "internationalists" (German and Austro-Hungarian POWs) into Red Guard units that marched around the city demanding immediate submission to the "Soviet" regime in Petrograd. Provisional Government Commissar Rusanov, backed by the municipal duma, soviet, and zemstvo councils, refused to endorse any transfer of power until after the upcoming elections for the Constituent Assembly. A telegram from Lenin did not shake his resolve. When elections were held on 16 December, Bolsheviks received only 15 percent of the Khabarovsk vote.* Frustrated at the polls, local Bolsheviks and their allies on 24 December

---

*They received 49% of the vote in Vladivostok, 46% in Harbin, 40% in Nikolsk-Ussuriisk, and 19% in Blagoveshchensk and Nikolaevsk. Their share of the Far Eastern total was about 25% (54,660 of 212,000 votes). In Siberia, they garnered only 10%, a fact that Lenin ascribed to the "satiety" (*sytost*) of Siberian peasants. Nikiforov, p. 26. *V. I. Lenin: Polnoe sobranie sochinenii*, 5th ed., vol. 40 (Moscow: Inst. Marksizma-Leninizma, 1963): 16.

arrested Rusanov and occupied police headquarters, post and telegraph offices, banks, the railroad station, and newspaper offices.[21] The next day, they convened a Third Congress of Far Eastern Soviets that declared the entire Far East under Soviet rule and installed Krasnoshchekov as chairman of Dalsovnarkom.* For the time being, these proclamations carried little weight outside of Vladivostok, Khabarovsk, and Suchan.[22]

Far Eastern Bolsheviks did not flinch from resorting to force against real and potential opponents. Military-revolutionary committees in Vladivostok and Khabarovsk arrested bank directors, customs officials, labor exchange officers, heads of the post and telegraph offices, and conservative newspaper editors such as Panov. Former Imperial Army officers were rounded up, accused of plotting with Japan, and tried amid demands by Aleksandra Kim that they be shot.[23] As each side resorted to harsher methods during the first three months of 1918, the political struggle escalated into civil war.

Yakutia and the Northeast

Geography and ethnicity conditioned Yakutia's responses to 1917, setting it apart from those of the Priamur. Neither railroads nor roads cut through the taiga between the Lena Basin and the Bering Strait. Hunters, reindeer herders, and traders formed the bulk of the population. Yakut elites took advantage of the February Revolution to press demands for self-determination, representation in the Constituent Assembly, and native control over former imperial lands. SRs had a larger political constituency than Social Democrats. Although two Social Democrats, Emelyan Yaroslavsky and Vladimir Vilensky, briefly chaired the Yakutsk soviet, both soon left for the Center. After the Bolshevik coup in Petrograd, the SR-dominated Yakutsk soviet refused to recognize the new regime. Armed with a mandate by elections for the Constituent Assembly, Right SRs in alliance with zemstvo officers formed their own organ of government, the Yakutsk Regional Soviet, and ignored telegrams from Petrograd and Irkutsk ordering it to dissolve. Unable to move against them in winter, Tsentrosibir bided its time until weather conditions permitted the dispatch of Red Guards in the spring of 1918. A seesaw struggle for Yakutia ensued. Barely had Red Guards from

*The acronym remained unchanged but henceforth stood for Far Eastern Regional Committee of Soviets of Workers', Soldiers', and Peasants' Deputies and Self-Administrations (*samoupravleniia*), the last being appended to win over zemstvo councils and municipal dumas.

Irkutsk disbanded the Yakutsk Regional Soviet in June 1918 when White forces arrived and drove them out of town. For the next two years, Yakutia was governed by a coalition of zemstvo officials, local merchants, Yakut chiefs, and former tsarist officers.[24]

Neither the February nor the October Revolution made much of a stir in the Northeast. At Petropavlovsk and Anadyr chancelleries went through the motions of governance as bureaucrats came to understandings with local merchants, doctors, and lawyers. Local leaders adapted titles and rhetoric to each vicissitude on the "mainland." Whether local organs of government were called committees of public safety or soviets, power stayed within the circle of family, friends, and business associates.[25]

When "mainland" authorities got around to checking out the Northeast, the locals showed that they could accommodate to every shift in the political winds. In September 1917 the Vladivostok soviet sent a Left SR, Ivan Larin, to Kamchatka to ascertain what was happening there. Galvanized by the Petrograd coup, Larin set up a Petropavlovsk soviet, whereupon the local elites proposed to work out mutually agreeable modus vivendi. Larin refused and on 28 February 1918 proclaimed Kamchatka under Soviet rule, whereupon local worthies dissolved the soviet, placed Larin in custody (the local constabulary was on their payroll), and resumed their usual routines until the arrival of some White officers in early 1919 occasioned a show of reactionary solidarity.[26] On Chukotka officials appointed by the Provisional Government in 1917 stayed in office until the end of 1919, adding or dropping the word "soviet" from their nomenclature as circumstances required.[27]

14

« « » »

Civil War

Cut all Bolshevik throats or they'll cut yours.
— Ivan Kalmykov (1918)

Although Far Eastern Bolsheviks succeeded in outmaneuvering their rivals during 1917, they remained in a precarious position during the first half of 1918. The regional Party organization was small, disorganized, and divided. Dalsovnarkom in Khabarovsk competed with Tsentrosibir in Irkutsk. Neither worked well with headstrong comrades in Vladivostok. These weaknesses forced the Bolsheviks to rely on ungovernable allies such as Left SRs, whose unpredictable impulses could be a liability.[1]

During the first three months of 1918, the Bolsheviks made few friends. Their dissolution of municipal dumas antagonized not only Mensheviks and Right SRs but also white-collar workers.[2] Their attempt to dissolve zemstvo councils upset a rural constituency without achieving its purpose, for the councils were quietly reorganized as county soviets. Their land redistribution programs got a cold reception from Cossacks, *starozhily* ("old settlers"), and religious sectarians. Ominously, they encountered hostility when they tried to requisition grain from peasants unaccustomed to confiscatory methods (before 1917 taxes were low and in some cases nonexistent; peasants often sold their produce to the Imperial Army).[3]

Fortunately for the Bolsheviks, their opponents were disorganized. Cossacks, prosperous farmers, priests, officers, merchants, shopkeepers, civil servants, lawyers, and journalists had little enthusiasm for "Soviet" rule, but narrow self-interest and mutual suspicions prevented these disparate groups from finding a common language beyond exhortations to restore the Constituent Assembly (which the Bolsheviks had forcibly disbanded some two months after seizing power).[4]

The Socialist Revolutionary Party enjoyed more support in rural areas than any group in the Far East during 1917 and 1918. Left SRs allied with the Bolsheviks in late 1917, but others looked askance at a regime that had dispersed the Constituent Assembly with bayonets in January 1918. SRs dominated both the Peasant-Cossack Congress and the Second Congress of All-Russian Korean National Organizations, held at Nikolsk-Ussuriisk in April and May 1918, respectively. Yet they shrank from a direct confrontation with the Bolsheviks, neither organizing resistance to grain requisitions nor supporting a strike of dissident white collar workers in Khabarovsk.[5]

The first counterattacks against the Bolsheviks and their allies came not from SRs but from Cossacks and tsarist army officers in Transbaikalia, Blagoveshchensk, and Grodekovo. These separate offensives coincided with the birth of several White armies in European Russia and the Ukraine. Lacking coordination and supplies, the Far Eastern Whites had little chance of success without major support from abroad.

Revolt in Transbaikalia

Transbaikalia occupied an axial position between Siberia, the Priamur, Mongolia, and Manchuria, lying astride routes between the eastern periphery and the Center. In 1917 its 825,000 inhabitants included 300,000 Russians, 264,000 Cossacks, and 210,000 Buryat Mongols.

The October Revolution left Transbaikalia deeply divided, ruled from Chita by a fragile coalition of Bolsheviks, Mensheviks, and SRs who formed a People's Soviet. Poor peasants and Cossacks, railroad workers, and demobilized troops supported the People's Soviet. Former tsarist officers together with more affluent Cossacks and peasants distrusted it. Grigory Semyonov undertook to destroy it.

Son of a Transbaikal Cossack and a Buryat mother, Semyonov served in the First World War as a Cossack captain and in June 1917 was appointed military commissar of Transbaikalia, with orders to raise a detachment of Cossacks and Buryats for service on the Western front. The October Revolution left this detachment the strongest anti-Bolshevik force east of Lake Baikal. In December Semyonov tried and failed to overthrow the People's Soviet. Retreating into Manchuria, he was granted asylum by the CER's director, General Horvath, and local Chinese authorities. With subsidies from the Japanese Army, Semyonov promptly recruited Buryat Mongols, tsarist officers, and Khabarovsk cadets into a fighting force called the Special Manchurian Detachment, and in January 1918 he reentered Trans-baikalia, declaring himself a champion of an autonomous Buryat Mongolia. As the Special Manchurian Detachment advanced toward Chita, local SRs, Mensheviks, peasants, and Cossacks prematurely declared their support for their would-be liberator, only to be crushed by Red Guards and "internationalists" under Sergei Lazo. A skilled tactician as well as a ruthless enforcer, Lazo then turned on Semyonov and chased the Special Manchurian Detachment back to its namesake. Launching a second assault on Transbaikalia in April, Semyonov managed for a while to preside over a "Provisional Transbaikalian Government" in a town southeast of Chita, but the self-styled ataman soon found himself again headed for Manchuria with Lazo at his heels.[6]

Counterrevolution in Blagoveshchensk

Blagoveshchensk (pop. 70,000) was the most stable city in the Far East in 1917. Its middle class was comparatively large and affluent. Its workers were economically better off and politically less radical than those of Vladivostok. Bolsheviks were few and uninfluential. The local soviet, dominated by Right SRs and Mensheviks, cooperated with the town duma and the Amur District commissar of the Provisional Government. These groups opposed Bolshevik–Left SR efforts to take power after the October Revolution, refusing to recognize any regime until after the elections for the Constituent Assembly. When the Bolsheviks received only 19 percent of the vote in those elections, they organized Amur Flotilla sailors and metalworkers while demanding new elections to the local soviet. Claiming victory in contested elections to the local soviet held on 18 January, the Bolshevik–Left SR coalition proclaimed Soviet rule on 1 February. A congress of peasants recognized the local soviet on 25 February, setting the stage for Krasnoshchekov's arrival from Khabarovsk with a squad of Red Guards to consolidate the authority of Dalsovnarkom.[7]

Meanwhile, counterrevolution brewed across the Amur at Sagalian, swollen by anti-Bolshevik refugees from Khabarovsk.[8] Zemstvo officials, town duma members, former tsarist army officers, former Provisional Government commissar of the Amur District Nikolai Kozhevnikov (a Right SR), and Amur Cossack ataman Vasily Gamov planned an assault from Sagalian in conjunction with assistance from Chinese and Japanese militia in Blagoveshchensk, hoping to ignite an uprising of peasants and Cossacks around the town. On the night of 6–7 March the insurgents seized Blago-veshchensk, drove out the Red Guards, and captured Krasnoshchekov. Ominously, few Cossacks heeded Ataman Gamov's appeal. Within Blago-veshchensk, only a handful of Chinese and Japanese residents took up arms. The town bourgeoisie watched from the sidelines, hoping for a White victory but unwilling to risk anything by getting involved.[9]

While Gamov looked in vain for help, trainloads of Red Guards, Austro-Hungarian and German "internationalists," and Amur Flotilla sailors ap-proached from Khabarovsk, joined en route by Ukrainian *novosely* ("new settlers"), who swelled the attacking force to 12,000. Inside Blagovesh-chensk, about 800 officers, 700 Cossacks, and 30 Japanese militiamen pre-pared makeshift defenses. The Red assault started on 9 March and lasted three days. As the attackers closed in, 10,000 fled across the frozen Amur to Sagalian, Gamov and Kozhevnikov among them.[10]

The victors plundered homes and stores and shot captured officers and Japanese militiamen. Informants surfaced to denounce "collaborators," who were summarily executed. According to one eyewitness, women orga-nized lynchings. A poet committed suicide. Krasnoshchekov emerged from captivity unscathed.[11] Amid the butchery, an anti-Bolshevik underground took shape, preparing its own lists of collaborators. Blagoveshchensk be-came a harbinger of retributive fury.

The Grodekovo Front

Ussuri Cossacks, numbering about 44,000 at the beginning of 1918, fell into three categories. The more affluent accepted the Provisional Govern-ment, rejected the October Revolution, and looked askance at local soviets. Poor Cossacks and many of the 3,000 returned frontline troops supported local soviets and welcomed Dalsovnarkom's land redistribution program. Middle-level Cossacks, the bulk of the community, wavered. During the spring and summer of 1918, part of the first and third categories followed a 27-year-old veteran from the Western front, Ivan Kalmykov.

Son of a Ussuri Cossack officer, Kalmykov was born and raised in Gro-dekovo, a town on the CER line 90 miles north of Vladivostok and seven miles east of the Chinese frontier. During the First World War, he served at the front, was wounded and decorated, and attained the rank of captain. Returning to Grodekovo in the summer of 1917, he threw himself into politics and was elected to a minor office. Four months later, in a contested election, he took the title of ataman. Kalmykov's emergence split the community. A minority followed him. Another minority coalesced around another Grodekovo veteran from the front, Grigory Shevchenko, who raised a Cossack detachment to defend Soviet rule in Vladivostok.

Disliked by CER director Dmitry Horvath, tolerated by the Manchurian warlord Zhang Zuolin, and subsidized by the Japanese Army, Kalmykov prepared a base of operations at the CER station of Pogranichnaya, just inside Manchuria, in February 1918. In March he crossed the frontier with about 100 men and advanced on Grodekovo. The Vladivostok soviet rushed Red Guards and a battalion of "internationalists" to the "Grodekovo front," where fighting continued inconclusively for the next three months.

By themselves, Semyonov, Gamov, and Kalmykov stood no chance of overthrowing Soviet rule in Transbaikalia, the Amur District, and the Primorye, for the peasantry and bourgeoisie stayed on the sidelines. Foreign involvement on behalf of both Reds and Whites redefined this correlation of forces.

Internationalists and Interventionists

In March 1917 there were over five million foreigners in Russia: 2.8 million refugees (Poles, Balts, Rumanians, Persians, Chinese, Koreans) and 2.3 million prisoners of war (Austrians, Hungarians, Germans, Czechs, Poles, Serbs, Bulgarians, Turks). Some POWs, the "bacilli of Bolshevism" as Lenin called them,[12] threw themselves into the struggle for world revolution, but most just tried to fill their stomachs and stay alive. Half got home; the rest succumbed or sojourned. In the Soviet political lexicon, POWs who fought for the Reds were "internationalists" and POWs who fought for the Whites were "interventionists." This semantic distinction may have forensic utility, but it throws little light on why individuals wound up in one category or another.

Take, for example, the case of Béla Kun, a Hungarian socialist who had been conscripted into the Austro-Hungarian Army. Corporal Kun formed Marxist discussion circles among his fellow prisoners and after November 1917 offered his services as a POW recruiter for the Soviet regime. With Lenin's approval, he was made chairman of the All-Russian Prisoner-of-War Committee and secretary of the Hungarian Section of RSDRP(b). Thanks in part to Kun's organizational talents, 85,000 of the 500,000-odd Hungarian POWs had joined Red military units by May 1918.[13]

Although German and Austro-Hungarian internationalists had helped the Bolsheviks seize power in Khabarovsk in December 1917, their full potential as a military force was not reached until 1918, when party activists systematically recruited at camps in Chita, Blagoveshchensk, Khabarovsk, and Nikolsk-Ussuriisk.[14] If proletarian internationalism prompted some POWs to take up arms for the October Revolution, so did hunger, homesickness, and political opportunism.[*] Armed POWs performed useful services for Dalsovnarkom during the first half of 1918, helping to drive Semyonov out of Transbaikalia, to crush counterrevolution in Blagoveshchensk, and to block Kalmykov at Grodekovo. With the advent of warm weather, however, some internationalists joined "General Cuckoo's Army" and slipped into Manchuria.[15]

Whereas Hungarian, Austrian, and German POWs tended to side with the Reds, most Czechs and Slovaks were staunch "interventionists." As disenfranchised Slavic minorities within the Austro-Hungarian Empire, Czechs and Slovaks had little enthusiasm for the Central Powers during the First World War. Of 100,000 drafted into the Austro-Hungarian Army, 60,000 surrendered to the Russians during 1914–16. Emancipated from POW status by the February Revolution, stirred by Wilsonian rhetoric about national self-determination, and encouraged by the Czech National Council in Paris, thousands of Czechs and Slovaks joined a special military unit to fight alongside the Russian Army against the Austrians and Hungarians on the southwestern front. This so-called Czech Legion consisted of two divisions totaling 30,000 men when the Bolsheviks seized power in November.

The disintegration of the Russian Army and the outbreak of civil war subjected the legion to conflicting pressures. The Czech National Council declared a policy of noninvolvement in the civil war, but this neutrality was eroded by the Bolsheviks' recruitment of Czech internationalists,[†] by the anti-Bolshevik sentiments of the legion's officers, by Anglo-French diplomatic maneuvers, and by Lenin's conclusion of a separate peace with Ger-

---

[*]All of these considerations may have motivated the German POW Roland Freisler to declare himself an internationalist. After two years as a self-professed Communist, Freisler escaped from Siberia and returned to Germany, where he joined the Nazis and found employment in the Prussian Ministry of Justice as an anti-subversion expert. Hitler was at first skeptical about the Siberian veteran and disdainfully referred to him as a "Bolshevik," but in 1942 Freisler's fanatic loyalty and prosecutorial zeal were rewarded by an appointment to the post of chief justice of the Volksgericht ("People's Court"), the most feared tribunal in the Third Reich. Freisler's savage treatment of members of the German resistance on trial for treason in 1944–45 prompted Hitler to call him "our Vishinsky." *Hitler's Table Talk, 1941–1944* (London: Weidenfeld and Nicolson, 1953), p. 376; William L. Shirer, *Rise and Fall of the Third Reich* (New York: Simon and Schuster, 1960), p. 1070.

[†]The Reds anticipated the White use of Czechs in the civil war by recruiting them into the Vladivostok International Battalion on the Grodekovo front in April 1918.

many at Brest-Litovsk on 3 March 1918. Informed of Brest-Litovsk, the legion's chief-of-staff, General Mikhail Dieterichs, ordered an evacuation of Czech troops from the Ukraine toward Vladivostok, where Allied ships were to transport them to Europe for redeployment on the Western front. Dieterichs and the first contingent of legionnaires reached Vladivostok on 4 April, and by early May a further 12,000 had arrived. Contrary to rumor, Good Soldier Schweik was not among them.*

During March and April Soviet leaders pondered what to do about the Czechs, whose presence in Russia threatened to complicate relations with both Berlin and the Allies. At first Moscow declared its readiness to expedite the legion's movement toward Vladivostok if the Czechs would surrender their arms en route, a condition designed to reassure the Siberian soviets, which felt anxious about the passage of foreign soldiers under anti-Bolshevik officers. However, when Berlin demanded that the Czechs be sent out of Russia via Arkhangelsk rather than Vladivostok, Moscow reversed itself and on 21 April 1918 instructed the Siberian soviets to halt the eastbound trains.

This order caught 45,000 armed Czechs along the rail lines between the Volga and Vladivostok. Suspecting the worst and encouraged by the Czech National Committee and the Allies, Czech and Russian officers decided to proceed to Vladivostok despite the risk of collisions with local soviets. When, on 14 May Czechs and Hungarians opened fire on each other at Chelyabinsk, the legion's senior officers met and resolved to push toward Vladivostok by force. War Commissar Leon Trotsky thereupon ordered local soviets to disarm all Czechs and shoot anyone who resisted. When the local soviets tried to comply, legionnaires seized a dozen stations between Samara and Irkutsk, transforming the political geography of Siberia by overthrowing Soviet rule and allowing zemstvo organs, peasant coopera- tives, and town dumas to re-establish themselves. Although these boulever- sements did not immediately affect areas east of Lake Baikal, they por- tended trouble for Dalsovnarkom.

Czech Coup in Vladivostok

As the gateway for matériel bound for European Russia from Japan and the United States, Vladivostok teemed with foreigners in late June 1918:

---

* In 1959 a Vladivostok newspaper announced with tongue in cheek that Good Soldier Schweik had passed through in 1918, but Schweik's creator, the Czech novelist and short-story writer Jaroslav Hašek (1883–1923), got no further east than Irkutsk. Lerman, *Po serdtsu blizkie druz'ia*, pp. 33–34.

some 15,000 Czech legionnaires, 10,000 Japanese civilians, 30,000 Chinese and Koreans, and 1,000 Europeans and North Americans. Prominent among the last group was a former Congregationalist minister, Albert Rhys Williams, bearing a letter from Lenin to American "socialists-internationalists." Ohio-born Williams had impeccable internationalist credentials, having enlisted in the Red Army the previous February.[16] Waiting through the month of June for passage home from the Golden Horn, the former Congregationalist minister delivered a fulsome oration to the Vladivostok soviet, eliciting what could be interpreted as a compliment from its secretary Vsevolod Sibirtsev.* Whatever they thought of the voluble American, Sibirtsev and Kostya Sukhanov (chairman of the soviet) instinctively distrusted the presence of growing numbers of armed Czechs and Japanese in their midst. Yet they restrained comrades from taking precipitate action, not just because Lenin had warned against giving Tokyo a pretext to intervene, but because sympathetic port workers were provisioning the soviet with Allied foodstuffs, clothing, automobiles, and ordnance pilfered from local warehouses. General Dieterichs and the legion's officers were less patient. On 29 June, prompted by reports of Austro-Hungarian POWs being armed at Nikolsk-Ussuriisk or using such reports as a pretext to follow a script written in Paris or London, Czech officers handed an ultimatum to the Vladivostok soviet, demanding the immediate disarmament of Red Guards and Austro-Hungarians. When no reply was forthcoming, some 6,000 Czechs and a few hundred Russians wearing the green and white colors of Siberian autonomists assaulted municipal facilities, while several dozen Japanese marines seized the arsenal and a British contingent occupied the railroad station. By evening Soviet rule in Vladivostok had expired, as had four Czechs, eleven Hungarians, and forty-nine Red Guards.[17] The city divided into quiet celebrants and loud mourners, some citizens welcoming the end of arbitrary arrests and requisitions, others venting their anger and grief in a mass funeral.

The Czech sorties of May-June 1918 galvanized anti-Bolsheviks throughout Siberia, the Far East, and Manchuria. SRs, Mensheviks, monarchists, and atamans lost no time staking out their political turf. Pyotr Derber, who had taken refuge in Harbin after the Bolsheviks had dissolved a Siberian Regional Duma at Tomsk on 6 February,[18] presciently moved his headquar-

---

*Sibirtsev allowed that Williams was "not a bad propagandist of Soviet rule." Quoted in Lerman, *Po serdtsu blizkie druz'ia*, p. 26.

ters to Vladivostok in April and, following the Czech coup, proclaimed himself head of a Provisional Government of Autonomous Siberia. Meanwhile, Semyonov embarked on another foray into Transbaikalia, and Kalmykov advanced from Grodekovo onto the Khanka Plain.

The Primorye Bolsheviks had been dealt a serious but by no means fatal blow. Sukhanov fell,* but Sibirtsev and others escaped and went underground. Albert Rhys Williams was allowed to embark for Shanghai, from where he returned to New York and lived up to Sibirtsev's appraisal of him. Although few realized it at the time, the Czech coup set the stage for a Red victory by staining the White cause with Russian blood drawn by foreign bayonets.

---

*Captured on 29 June, Sukhanov was shot on 17 Nov. while in transit to another prison, thereby becoming the Far East's first serviceable revolutionary martyr and namesake of Sukhanov Street in Vladivostok.

15

« « » »

Intervention

Morphine, cocaine, prostitution, blackmail, sudden riches and ruin, dashing autos, a cinematic flow of faces, literary cabals, bohemian lifestyles, coups and countercoups, Mexican political morals, parliaments, dictators, speeches from balconies, newspapers from Shanghai and San Francisco, "Intervention girls," uniforms from every kingdom, empire, republic, monarchist clubs, leftist rallies, complete isolation from Moscow.

— Konstantin Kharnsky describing
Vladivostok in 1919

On 4 July 1918, some 6,000 demonstrators carrying red banners gathered in front of the American consulate-general in Vladivostok and cheered. Having spotted what looked like a black flag fluttering over the cruiser *Brooklyn* anchored in the Golden Horn, someone spread the word that the United States was showing its solidarity with workers mourning the Red Guards killed in the Czech coup several days earlier. The "black flag" was in fact Admiral Austin Knight's blue ensign, hoisted to celebrate the Fourth of July.[1] Inconsequential in itself, the incident captured an essential quality of a chapter in Far Eastern history rich in self-delusion and misdirected emotion.

The Demonology

Much has been written about why the Entente Powers sent troops to Siberia during the final months of the First World War. British, American,

Japanese, Chinese, and Canadian decision-making has been meticulously scrutinized. Each government justified its actions by citing a German threat and the Czech plight. Some historians, justifiably doubtful of official palaver, have gone to the opposite extreme and suggested that Germany and the Czechs served merely as a camouflage for anti-Soviet and annexationist agendas. Indeed, some Japanese had sought unobstructed access to the Amur-Sungari water route for Manchurian exports, and others hankered after North Sakhalin or Kamchatka, but it requires a considerable effort of the imagination to believe that Woodrow Wilson plotted to make the Russian Far East an American colony by creating a "Russian United States," complete with Jeffersonian constitution.[2] American and Japanese interests in the Far East did bear on the region's painful trials during 1918–22, for the shadow of Japanese-American rivalry hung over deliberations about Russia in Washington and Tokyo.

Japan steadily expanded its footholds in the Far East under the rubric of collaboration. A military alliance concluded in 1916 awarded Tokyo extensive economic privileges that carried proprietary overtones, such as freedom of navigation on the Sungari and lower Amur. Diplomatic pressure for further concessions gave rise to speculation in the Japanese press about the cession of northern Sakhalin and dismantling of Vladivostok fortifications. When the Provisional Government lifted restrictions on foreign economic activity in the spring of 1917, Japanese enterprise went into high gear. Banks and trading firms bought up stores, buildings, utility companies, and newspapers throughout the Priamur and the Primorye.[3]

The establishment of Soviet rule in Vladivostok prompted Tokyo to take a precautionary measure to protect Japanese investments and residents; the cruiser *Iwami* was dispatched to the Golden Horn in January 1918 in a demonstration of strength. Japanese community spokesmen in the Priamur and Manchuria voiced demands for more substantive forces following the execution of Japanese militiamen at Blagoveshchensk in March and an assault on two Japanese in Vladivostok in April. But though some army officers seem to have favored active intervention, senior politicians in Tokyo would not send an expeditionary force to Russia without American participation.[4]

Washington's declaration of war on Germany in April 1917 created dilemmas for American Far Eastern policy. The United States became an ally of both Russia and Japan, but there was concern in some circles that Japan would take advantage of Russian weakness in Northeast Asia. Consequently, American aid to the Provisional Government during 1917 sent signals to Tokyo as well as to Petrograd. These currents swirled around Vladivostok, the main port of entry for American and Japanese assistance to Russia. Closely observed by Tokyo, two American missions invited by the Provisional Government passed through the Golden Horn in the spring of 1917. The Stevens Commission headed by an engineer, John Stevens, was empowered by Petrograd to keep the Trans-Siberian Railroad running. The Root Mission, led by former secretary of state Elihu Root, took stock of Russia's material needs.

Following the October coup, American policy toward Russia was in some ways hostage to Washington's preoccupation with the struggle against Germany. Though hostile to Bolshevism, especially after Lenin had concluded a separate peace with Germany, President Woodrow Wilson had no desire to involve the United States in the Russian civil war and, during the first half of 1918, resisted Anglo-French pressures for a Japanese-American expedition to Siberia. His dispatch of Admiral Knight on the cruiser *Brooklyn* to Vladivostok in January 1918 reflected a willingness to join Britain, France, Japan, and China in demonstrating concern for the safety of their nationals in the city. Whatever misconceptions Wilson may have had about the Soviet regime and its enemies, there is no evidence to support allegations that he plotted with either Communist "renegades" (Leon Trotsky, Nikolai Bukharin) or Right SRs to take over Siberia.[5]

Events in Europe and Asia during the spring of 1918 eroded Wilson's noninterventionist resolve. On 21 March, less than three weeks after Soviet Russia and Imperial Germany concluded the Treaty of Brest-Litovsk taking the former signatory out of the war and enabling the latter to transfer forces to the West, General Erich Ludendorff opened a general offensive in France. The Germans broke through Allied lines during April and May, reaching the Marne on 6 June. German successes in France gave an ominous coloration to the outbreak of fighting between Czech legionnaires and Hungarian internationalists at Chelyabinsk in the eastern foothills of the Urals. Meanwhile, as if to confirm a worst-case scenario, American consuls in Irkutsk and Harbin reported that thousands of armed German and Austro-Hungarian POWs were operating across Siberia to the borders of Manchuria, presumably preparing bases for Teutonic power on the Pacific.

The confluence of real German victories in the West and spectral German maneuvers in the East brought Wilson under pressure from European allies. Presidential action also seems to have been prompted by images, purveyed by journalists as well as diplomats, of beleaguered Czechs valiantly striving to free themselves from the coils of Kaiser-Bolshevik collusion in the depths of Siberia. Ironically, legionnaires had already seized the railroad between the Volga and Lake Baikal and taken control of Vladivostok when, on 5 July, Wilson announced American participation in an Allied expedition to help the Czechs leave Russia and to keep Allied military stores in Vladivostok from falling into German hands. Wilson's decision enabled Japan, unwilling to move unilaterally, to proceed with its own agenda.

The Collapse of Soviet Rule

During July and the first half of August 1918, Vladivostok filled up with a kaleidoscopic array of military forces: Czech legionnaires, Siberian autonomist "Greens," Kalmykovian Cossacks, Chinese Eastern Railroad guards, 14,000 men of the Japanese 3rd and 12th divisions, 800 men of His Majesty's Middlesex Regiment in Hong Kong, 9,000 doughboys of the American Expeditionary Force (AEF) put together from units in the Philippines and Hawaii, 500 *poilus* from the French garrison in Beijing, Italians, Canadians, Chinese levies of the Manchurian warlord Zhang Zuolin, sailors from a half-dozen navies, and stray tsarist officers. On 19 August, as a Japanese military band repeatedly played Sousa's "Washington Post March," all of the above, joined by ad hoc formations of Rumanians, Serbs, and Poles in British uniforms, marched along the Svetlanskaya past a reviewing stand bristling with foreign and local dignitaries. Non-Bolshevik socialists joined with the local bourgeoisie in applauding the arrival of foreign troops.[6]

As the senior officer present, Lieutenant-General Ōtani Kikuzō appointed himself commander of the Allied expeditionary forces. The AEF commander, Major-General William S. Graves, was still en route from Kansas City, where he had received instructions on 4 August. In his absence, the acting commander, Colonel Henry Styer, outranked and politically out of his depth, acquiesced to General Ōtani's unilateral dispositions, thereby placing American troops under Japanese control for two eventful weeks.[7] The Japanese had a clear plan of action: drive north along the Ussuri Line, capture Khabarovsk, clear Reds from the Amur Line, and link up with Ataman Semyonov in Transbaikalia.[8] Japanese and Czechs lost no time occupying Nikolsk-Ussuriisk, moving against Dalsovnarkom's motley forces on what was now called the "Ussuri front." Directed by General

Ōtani to bring up the rear of the Czech-Japanese advance, Colonel Styer ordered Lieutenant-Colonel Charles Morrow to proceed with units from the 27th Infantry Battalion ("Wolfhounds") to the Ussuri front. Left to fend for themselves without transport, Morrow's Wolfhounds could not keep up with the Czech-Japanese advance and covered much of the 480 miles to Khabarovsk on foot. Doughboys took no part in combat (the identity of the enemy remained unclear) but took casualties from heat, dysentery, and *hong huzi* bullets. As soon as General Graves arrived in Vladivostok on 2 September, he removed the AEF from General Ōtani's authority and ordered Colonel Styer and other subordinates to stay out of Russia's internal affairs.[9]

Faced with a serious challenge in the Primorye, Dalsovnarkom had neither the time nor the resources to prepare for the Allied advance on Khabarovsk. Krasnoshchekov, after obtaining American passports for his wife and two daughters, turned to the unpromising task of shoring up a crumbling edifice.[10] Declaring a state of emergency, he tried to mobilize all able-bodied adult males, but peasants who had tasted Soviet rule showed little enthusiasm to die for it. The only reliable forces at Krasnoshchekov's disposal were several thousand Red Guards and about 10,000 internationalists in Avgust Goldfinger's Hungarian Cavalry, Béla Frankl's Revolutionary Regiment, and the Erno Svetets Brigade. These units had acquitted themselves well against small forces fielded by Semyonov, Gamov, and Kalmykov, but they proved to be no match for disciplined and well-armed troops.[11]

The Ussuri front collapsed on 24 August, when Czechs and Japanese drove northward from Spassk with Kalmykov's cavalry on the right (eastern) flank. Panic gripped the Red Guards at the sight of Japanese troops. Commissars tried in vain to restore morale by telling the men that they were facing Chinese in Japanese uniforms. The Allies reached Iman on 29 August, triggering anti-Bolshevik uprisings of peasants and Cossacks in Vyazemsky and Bikin as well as a mutiny in the Amur Flotilla, exposing river approaches to Khabarovsk.[12] At this, Krasnoshchekov and the Tsentrosibir emissary, Postyshev, decided to abandon Khabarovsk and relocate Dalsovnarkom to Alekseyevsk 400 miles to the northwest, where the Amur Line crosses the Zeya River. Moving out on requisitioned trains and steamers, the pillars of Soviet rule — Party activists, Dalsovnarkom staff, Red Guards, internationalists, and their dependents — evacuated the city between 30 August and 3 September.[13]

White rule came to Khabarovsk on 5 September, when Czech, Japanese, and Kalmykov cavalry entered the town to the peal of church bells. After a company of footsore Wolfhounds showed up two days later, the Stars and Stripes was run up alongside the Rising Sun flag atop the railroad station, belying imbalances and tensions between the two expeditionary forces. Kalmykov lost no time rounding up and dispatching "Bolsheviks." Most of the genuine Bolsheviks escaped except for Aleksandra Kim, who after fleeing Khabarovsk on the *Baron Korf* was intercepted upstream by Cossacks and handed over to Kalmykov.[14]

During the remainder of September, a Czech-Japanese-Cossack offensive swept away Soviet rule along the Amur and Transbaikal lines. Semyonov's Special Manchurian Detachment entered Chita, and Right SRs led by Aleksandr Alekseyevsky took over Blagoveshchensk. When it became apparent to Dalsovnarkom leaders that they could not expect to hold out in Alekseyevsk, they resolved to go underground. Krasnoshchekov fled up the Zeya River and on 17 September formally dissolved Dalsovnarkom, which for all practical purposes had ceased to exist.[15] As the Bolshevik leaders scattered,* Red Guards and internationalists melted away. Whole units went over to Semyonov and Kalmykov. Peasant conscripts headed back to their villages. Internationalists who took to the taiga were with few exceptions hunted down. A fortunate few surrendered to SR authorities in Blagoveshchensk and, thanks to the intercession of the International Red Cross, were released and repatriated.[16]

A Bazaar of Nations and Illusions

The collapse of Soviet rule left several governments claiming overlapping jurisdictions east of Lake Baikal: Semyonov's Buryat Mongol Republic at Chita, Alekseyevsky's SR regime at Blagoveshchensk, Kalmykov's regime at Khabarovsk, and Horvath's CER administration at Harbin. "Rulers" came and went in Vladivostok: members of Derber's Provisional Government of Autonomous Siberia (July–September 1918), representa-

---

*Krasnoshchekov wandered around Siberia and the Volga region under an assumed name. Picked up as a vagrant in the summer of 1919, he languished in an Irkutsk prison until he was released in December. Meanwhile, his wife Gertrude Tobinson and their two daughters, having boarded a steamer in Vladivostok for San Francisco, settled in New York. For details see Krasnoshchekova, "Iz vospominaniia," pp. 139–43; Canfield F. Smith in *Modern Encyclopedia of Russian and Soviet History*, 18 (1980): 42–46.

tives of a coalition government in Omsk (July–November 1918), and two plenipotentiaries of the coalition's successor Kolchak government, Pavel Ivanov-Rinov (November 1918–September 1919) and Sergei Rozanov (September 1919–January 1920).*

Superimposed upon these "governments" were eleven foreign expeditionary forces of varying sizes, sympathies, and agendas. Leading the list were 73,000 Japanese, followed by 55,000 Czechs, 12,000 Poles, 9,000 Americans, 5,000 Chinese, 4,000 Serbs, 4,000 Rumanians, 4,000 Canadians, 2,000 Italians, 1,600 British, and 700 French. These expeditions were deployed in less than 5 percent of the Russian Far East; most clustered around Vladivostok. Japanese garrisons were stationed in Chita, Khabarovsk, Nikolaevsk, Suchan, and Olga. The Americans were concentrated at Vladivostok, but maintained a presence along the Transbaikal, Amur, Ussuri, and Suchan lines.

Vladivostok was a world unto itself, a unique blend of provincial Russia, treaty-port Shanghai, and the American Wild West. A dozen languages reverberated in the lobby of the Versailles Hotel, and more than a dozen currencies circulated. In addition to U.S. dollars, Chinese yuan, and Japanese yen, people used Japanese military script, Japanese company script (one merchant printed money bearing his own portrait), Kunst & Albers vouchers, and seven types of rubles (tsarist, "Kerensky," Soviet, "Horvath," "Kolchak," "Zemstvo," "Semyonov," and "SR"). Kiosks sold New York, Tokyo, and London newspapers together with Vladivostok's own Japanese, American, monarchist, SR, Menshevik, and Communist papers, including Russian, English, Japanese, and Chinese editions of *Business Siberia*.[17] Chinese guilds and Japanese trading houses rubbed shoulders with the National City Bank, International Harvester, the YMCA, the Knights of Columbus, the American Red Cross, and the Chicago Cafe.[18]

War, revolution, and intervention filled Vladivostok with transients, among whom from time to time surfaced a metropolitan cultural celebrity such as the Symbolist poet Konstantin Balmont. Somerset Maugham, traveling under the name Somerville as he made his way to Petrograd on behalf of the British Foreign Office in August 1917, paused long enough to sip cabbage soup and down a shot of vodka at the station cafe. In 1918 the late tsarina Aleksandra Fyodorovna's French poodle "Joy" passed through town

---

*After a rightist coup toppled the coalition government in Omsk on 18 Nov. 1918, its war minister, Admiral Aleksandr Kolchak, declared himself the "Supreme Ruler of Russia."

to share exile with its new owner in China. William Gerhardie turned up with the British Military Mission and gathered material for a novel (*Futility*) that earned him the sobriquet "English Chekhov." The poets Arseny Nesmelov, Nikolai Aseyev, and Sergei Tretyakov, and the cubist painter David Burliuk arrived from Moscow and, at the initiative of a local newspaper editor, Nikolai Chuzhak, founded a futurist group called *Tvorchestvo* ("Creativity").[19] From Khabarovsk seeking refuge from Whites and Reds alike came the conservative newspaper editor Konstantin Kurteyev and the ethnographers Vladimir Arseniev and Ivan Lopatin. This concentration of talent assumed an institutional expression on 1 April 1920, when a committee of civic leaders established the Far Eastern State University (DVGU) on the basis of the Oriental Institute and selected the Korea specialist Grigory Podstavin as rector.[20]

Vladivostok's social life acquired a Danubian exuberance, thanks in part to the Japanese and American Red Cross teams who fed thousands of Germans, Austrians, and Hungarians in nearby camps. After the Armistice former POWs were free to leave, but few did because they were better fed and cared for "in custody." As news of the good life spread, Russians began surrendering as "escaped prisoners," prompting one warden to issue passes to "genuine prisoners" entitling them to readmission after weekend leaves.[21]

Fraternization and Friction

Although Americans enjoyed a degree of immunity from popular hostility,* their affluence aroused envy and resentment. Doughboys ate incomparably better than did all but the most privileged Russians, and the insouciant profligacy with which they wasted food attracted hangers-on but also offended proud sensibilities.[22] Child scavengers formed the AEF's retinue, posting themselves outside mess halls to rummage through freshly filled slop-pails. Bedraggled Russian children hovered around picnics to stare at white bread, sausages, cheese, fruit compotes, and chocolate.[23] Doughboys adopted waifs as mascots, outfitting them with campaign hats and khaki

---

*One partisan confided to the journalist Marguerite Harrison that "we never fought with our hearts in it when we were against the Americans." When a doughboy asked a Spassk sawmill worker the meaning of Bolshevism, the man answered: "It means we want to be the same as you Americans." A Ussuri District village reportedly sent a petition to President Wilson requesting annexation. Harrison, *Red Bear*, p. 108; Kindall, *American Soldiers in Siberia*, pp. 69, 248.

tunics, but they were not in a position to emulate the American Red Cross, which collected 780 waifs in the Urals and transported them from Vladivostok via San Francisco to the Karelian frontier, from where most eventually rejoined their parents.[24]

Intimate relationships inevitably developed between foreigners and locals, and since the foreigners were almost always men, the locals tended to be women. To control venereal disease, the Japanese Army issued its own marketable ration cards valid for "comfort visits" to compatriot-run brothels.[25] Russian-speaking Japanese officers socialized with Russian and Cossack women.[26] Oblivious to the language barrier, Americans surrendered themselves to the all-embracing hospitality of Russian families, attending Orthodox Church services and avidly adopting the custom of hugging and kissing at Easter.[27] Many were struck by the inner strength of Russian women. Recalled one doughboy: "Their independence and courage were the most astonishing facts we met with in Siberia."[28] Russian women for their part discovered something not entirely unpleasant in the American male. His boyish innocence, unfeigned enthusiasm, and awkward gallantry flattered feminine self-esteem, promised access to provisions, and held out the shimmering prospect of going abroad. Self-deception blurred motives on both sides of the cultural and sexual divide, but manifestations of love at first sight or foresight were clear for all to see. Some AEF officers fell heir to the venerable practice among metropolitan officials on Siberian assignments of temporarily taking a local "wife."[29] Charles Morrow, now a full colonel as Henry Styer's successor to the command of the 27th Infantry, kept a "duchess" at his Khabarovsk headquarters, an example not lost upon subordinates.[30] Nearly 6 percent of all AEF personnel took matrimonial vows, prompting Congresswoman Jeanette Rankin to propose that Washington purchase a tract of land in Siberia where the couples might settle.[31]

Little love was lost between the AEF and Semyonov and Kalmykov. Graves called the two atamans the most contemptible scoundrels he had ever met.[32] Mutual disdain and sexual jealousy at times erupted into violence. Kalmykov forbade Russian girls to marry Americans. After incidents where doughboys were whipped, Colonel Morrow notified his men that "any son of a bitch who gets hit with the whip of a Cossack and doesn't shoot him will get six months."[33] Such was Morrow's antipathy to Kalmykov that in 1919 he forcefully intervened to prevent the ataman from carrying out the arrest of bona fide Bolsheviks.[34]

"Bolsheviks" (by which Americans generally meant anyone fighting the

Whites) benefited in other ways from anti-Kalmykov and anti-Semyonov sentiment within the AEF. Influenced by émigré-interpreters in the AEF and prompted by the appeals of their Russian girlfriends, doughboys supplied any number of "Bolshevik" bands with food, waterproof tents, machine guns, Colt revolvers, and ammunition.[35] One Russian-born Pennsylvania lad went AWOL, formed his own unit of irregulars, and killed a U.S. sentinel guarding an ammunition depot. Recognized on a Vladivostok street, the deserter was arrested, court-martialed, and condemned to death by a military tribunal in Manila. President Warren Harding commuted the sentence to twenty years following an appeal by a group in New York. Paroled, the miscreant eventually moved back to Vladivostok and joined the Party.[36]

In contrast to the Americans, Japanese troops remained largely inaccessible to Bolshevik propaganda. Literature in the vernacular was not distributed among members of the expeditionary force until 1922. A trading company employee named Satō Michio joined the Party under the alias Sato Asada, but not a single Japanese officer or enlisted man followed his example.[37]

The Partisan Movement

Although eventually subjected to a degree of Bolshevik control, the anti-White movement that developed following the collapse of Soviet rule in the summer of 1918 started out as largely a spontaneous affair. What began as a few hundred poorly trained men and boys grew during the next four years into an army of partisans. But peasant support for the partisans materialized gradually, unevenly, and at times grudgingly. Conscription and grain requisition by Kolchak agents together with "pacification" campaigns by Kalmykov and his Japanese patrons motivated some peasants to join the partisans, though rural youth had the distressing habit of dropping everything and setting off for their villages at harvest time.[38]

Grass-roots attitudes toward partisans were shaped both by predictable socioeconomic factors and by the unpredictable chemistry of encounters among individuals and different bands. The mines at Suchan and Tetyukhe yielded a steady stream of recruits, as did novosely hamlets around Olga and Iman. Starozhily, sectarian, and Cossack settlements around Nikolsk-Ussuriisk and Blagoveshchensk were more aloof. Yet not all prosperous peasants shunned the partisans, nor did all poor peasants welcome them.[39]

By the end of 1919, about 50,000 partisans divided into 200 groups operated in the Far East. Several thousand Chinese and Koreans joined Russian bands or formed their own detachments. Recent immigrants from Korea produced volunteers, and those who spoke Japanese offered their services as agents to both sides, as did Nanai, Ulchi, Evenki, Nivkhi, Koryaki, and Chukchi scouts and guides.[40]

The word "partisan" embraced a heterogeneous and changeable constituency. Criminals called themselves partisans whenever they wanted to confer a patina of legitimacy on plunder. Korean partisans split into pro-Bolshevik and pro-SR factions, the former being ready to fight the Japanese protégés Semyonov and Kalmykov but not Kolchak.[41] Some partisans professed to believe in "freedom" or "democracy" and regarded Bolsheviks as meddlesome outsiders. Bolsheviks looked askance at any independent partisan leader, particularly one as popular as Gavrila (in some sources Ivan) Shevchenko* of the Suchan Valley northeast of Vladivostok.[42] When, in the spring of 1919, the Siberian Party Committee created a "military-revolutionary staff" under Sergei Lazo to bring partisan bands under central control, Lazo proceeded to make plans for a major operation in the Suchan Valley. Nominally designed to immobilize the mines supplying coal for trains carrying supplies to Kolchak, the Suchan operation in fact had a political purpose: to undermine Shevchenko's authority.[43]

A company of Americans was quartered at the village of Romanovka on the Vladivostok-Suchan railroad. The local American commander had come to an understanding with Shevchenko to observe a two-mile-wide neutrality zone on each side of the tracks. As long as partisans refrained from launching attacks within the zone, they could enter it without interference, get provisions, and propagandize Suchan miners.[44] Arriving at the village of Kazanka six miles north of Suchan with a detachment of partisans from Olga, Lazo denounced the agreement as a "trick" and sketched out a plan for a surprise attack on the American cantonment at Romanovka. Shevchenko refused to take part, denouncing the proposal as an unnecessary provocation that would incur retaliation rather than achieving any practical objective. Lazo went ahead with the Olga partisans and some of Shevchenko's men, and personally led a three-hour assault beginning before dawn on 22 June. Six hundred partisans surrounded the tents of the

---

*Not to be confused with Grigory Shevchenko, a Ussuri Cossack active on the Grodekovo front against Ataman Kalmykov during the first eight months of 1918.

200 sleeping men of Company A, 31st Infantry Battalion. After garotting the sentinels, the partisans opened fire, killing or wounding most of the doughboys in their tents.[45]

As Shevchenko had predicted, retribution came with a vengeance. During the next two weeks, American units from Vladivostok drove the partisans from the Suchan Valley. Shevchenko blamed Lazo for this turn of events and declared that he would henceforth under no circumstances cooperate with the "military revolutionary staff."[46] Lazo's Suchan operation embittered the local population against partisans and Americans alike, split the partisan movement in the Primorye, and precipitated a Party vendetta against Shevchenko that defamed and eventually destroyed him.

Atrocities

Both Whites and Reds resorted to terror, but White terror got more publicity, partly because it was visible to Americans (who discounted Japanese testimony about Red terror) and partly because the victors wrote more history books. Unlike the Reds, who killed methodically in the name of a higher principle (class struggle, revolution, human progress), Whites murdered in a wild fury at everything and everyone whom they thought had destroyed their prerevolutionary world. General Graves remarked that the difference between Semyonov and Kalmykov was that the former ordered others to kill and the latter murdered with his own hands.[47] Indeed, Kalmykov seems to have shot almost anyone who aroused his capricious wrath, including two Khabarovsk Cadet Corps instructors for reasons that can only be surmised (because they failed to show sufficient enthusiasm for renaming their school after him?), two Swedish Red Cross representatives for smuggling "Bolsheviks," and an entire musical ensemble for playing the "Internationale" instead of "God Save the Tsar" in a Khabarovsk cafe.*

American atrocities figure prominently in Soviet works published after 1945. AEF "punitive expeditions" destroyed a half-dozen villages. In one episode doughboys cut up a pregnant woman, turned her breasts inside out, and pulled her pigtail into her mouth and out again through a slit throat. In another, they buried peasants alive. At Kazanka they killed over 100, including a pregnant girl who gave birth to a stillborn child in a pool

---

*Noting that the musicians were Hungarians, Kalmykov included at least one Czech in the firing squad.

of her own blood. In Vladivostok they beat the editor of a local newspaper to death and built a latrine over the graves of revolutionary martyrs.[48] These allegations have yet to be verified, but it is unlikely that all are baseless. There is evidence that American troops did commit violence against non-combatants at Kazanka in revenge for Lazo's attack on Romanovka.[49]

Because Japanese units accompanied Semyonov and Kalmykov units on "pacification" campaigns, partisans considered them fair game for ambushes. Neither side took prisoners, but the partisan practice of donning Imperial Army uniforms stripped from corpses was an unforgivable sacrilege in the eyes of officers steeped in Bushido. Frustrated by the enemy's elusiveness and lacking reliable intelligence, Japanese forces were wont to strike indiscriminately at suspected sympathizers, in one case using artillery to level an undefended Amur village.[50]

Partial Exits

The Kolchak regime failed to mobilize grass-roots support in the Far East during its one-year existence. Prosperous peasants and the middle classes were alienated by the Omsk government's arbitrary and brutal methods of conscription and tax collection. To avoid serving in Kolchak's army, some rural youths got medical exemptions by shooting their extremities through a loaf of bread, leaving no telltale powder burns.[51]

When the Red Army broke through the Ural front in September 1919, the Czechs started appropriating eastbound trains. Abandoning Omsk on 14 November, Kolchak withdrew with what was left of his forces. By December the White retreat had turned into a rout. Out of an army that once numbered 800,000, only 20,000 reached Irkutsk with their units intact. In exchange for freedom of passage for Czech legionnaires and French military advisers, Admiral Kolchak was handed over at Irkutsk to a Menshevik-SR coalition called the Political Center. On 21 January 1920 the Soviet Military Revolutionary Committee took over power in Irkutsk and put Kolchak on trial with his prime minister, Viktor Pepeliaev. Both men were shot seventeen days later.

To avoid provoking Japan, Moscow postponed an open bid for power in the Far East and ordered local Bolsheviks to form a tactical coalition with local SRs. This unnatural relationship had already been tried and found wanting in the failed attempt of Vladivostok SRs and an ambitious Czech officer named Rudolf Gaida to overthrow Kolchak's local representative,

General Sergei Rozanov, on 17–18 November 1919. Tactical cooperation with SRs survived the debacle and revived during 25–30 January 1920, when garrison troops, trade unionists, and partisans seized Vladivostok, Nikolsk-Ussuriisk, Spassk, and Grodekovo.[52] The Provisional Zemstvo Government of the Maritime Province that was established on 31 January was under the nominal leadership of the SR chairman of the Vladivostok Zemstvo Board, A. S. Medvedev, but under de facto Bolshevik control. After partisans took over Iman (1 February), Blagoveshchensk (5 February), Vyazemsky (12 February), and Khabarovsk (14–16 February), zemstvo officials adorned visible posts while Bolsheviks ruled from behind the scenes, ushering in an interlude of "pink communism."[53]

Not waiting for partisans to enter Khabarovsk, Kalmykov crossed the frozen Amur to China with a dozen Cossacks, eighty "Kalmykov Corps" cadets, and a personal hoard of gold.[54] Ready to settle scores and not averse to inheriting the gold, the Chinese disarmed and in due course shot the ataman.* Partisans and commissars entered Khabarovsk bearing lists of counterrevolutionaries, soon supplemented with names supplied by zealous informants. Shunning Kalmykovian theatrics, the instruments of revolutionary justice removed the accused to Khor, thirty miles south of Khabarovsk, where they could be inconspicuously dispatched.[55]

Evacuated by the Japanese on 23 February, Blagoveshchensk leapt directly from White to Soviet rule under Meier Trilisser, who after the demise of Tsentrosibir had set himself up as an underground Party organizer in the Amur District. Moscow publicly recognized the Primorye Zemstvo Government but quietly transferred 72,000,000 rubles of gold, platinum, and foreign currency from Vladivostok banks to Blagoveshchensk.[56]

Allied expeditionary forces withdrew according to individual timetables. The Canadians, French, Italians, British, and Chinese departed during 1919. The Czechs left during the first nine months of 1920. American units evacuated Transbaikalia and Khabarovsk at the end of 1919, and on 12 January 1920, President Wilson announced that the AEF was coming home. To the bewilderment of some doughboys, local attitudes warmed perceptibly.[57] The prospect of separation galvanized love and self-interest into precipitous action. Orthodox priests coped with the matrimonial rush

---

*Kalmykov had intermittently fired on Chinese gunboats navigating past Khabarovsk. After his arrest on 8 Mar., the ataman escaped and for a while hid on the grounds of the old imperial Russian consulate in Jilin. Recaptured, he was shot in July while being transferred to Beijing.

by performing ceremonies for up to thirty Russian-American couples at a time.[58]

As the last U.S. transport steamed out of the Golden Horn on April Fool's Day, a Japanese military band, departing from its old standby "Washington Post March," struck up "Hard Times Come Again No More." A dozen moonstruck doughboys stayed behind to look for happiness with Russian paramours. Most found death.

« « » »

The Far Eastern Republic

The people of the Russian Far East were fortunate enough
in that their mother country did not deny them the right
of an independent existence.

— Boris E. Skvirsky (1922)

The fall of Kolchak heralded a new
phase of the civil war and foreign
intervention in the Far East. Soviet rule moved from the Urals to Lake
Baikal. But more than two years elapsed before it reached the Pacific. In the
interim various would-be local governments competed for preeminence
amid maneuvering by Moscow and Tokyo.

Buffer Strategy

A combination of circumstances left Soviet Russia vulnerable in Northeast Asia in the spring of 1920. Offensives by Poland in the Ukraine and by
Baron Pyotr Nikolaevich Wrangel in the Crimea forced the Red Army to
redeploy units from Siberia. Japanese forces remained in the Priamur, the
Primorye, and Transbaikalia, propping up Ataman Semyonov's Buryat
Mongol Republic and covering the anabasis of Kolchak army remnants. SRs
did not give up hope for an autonomous non-Bolshevik polity on the Pacific.

This correlation of forces convinced Lenin that the sovietization of the
Far East would have to be postponed to avoid giving Japan a pretext to
entrench itself in Transbaikalia and the Primorye. Lenin and Trotsky appro-
priated the SR idea of a buffer state and used it to limit Moscow's liabilities
and curb the political impulses of Far Eastern Bolsheviks.[1] Independent and
democratic in appearance, the buffer was also designed to generate domestic and American pressure on Tokyo. Moscow would control the buffer

from behind the scenes through Far Eastern Bolsheviks, the bureau of the Siberian Party Committee (Sibbiuro), and emissaries from the Center. This artful scenario soon fell prey to unpredictable and uncontrollable forces. SRs and Tokyo played their own buffer games. Far Eastern Bolsheviks squabbled with Siberian comrades and among themselves, and Moscow's emissaries had their own preferences and priorities.

Buffer strategy made a debut on 7 March 1920, when on Moscow's instructions ex-Dalsovnarkom Chairman Krasnoshchekov organized a "Provisional Government of Pribaikalia" at Verkhneudinsk in Transbaikalia. Krasnoshchekov was not an ideal instrument to implement a finely nuanced strategy, for he displayed a susceptibility to the notion of a genuinely independent, democratic, and permanent state on the Pacific.[2] Nor was Vladimir Vilensky an ideal central emissary to the Far East, at least to the extent of disagreeing on the Verkhneudinsk site. The former chairman of the Yakutsk soviet backed those Primorye Bolsheviks who felt that the buffer state capital should be located in Vladivostok, a position favored by the SRs, who were counting on diplomatic and economic support from the United States. Moscow strongly opposed Vladivostok as a capital, among other reasons because Lenin intended to use the local Zemstvo Government to distract the Japanese while consolidating Bolshevik control over Transbaikalia.[3] Accordingly, Verkhneudinsk became the seat of a Far Eastern Republic (FER) when it superseded the Provisional Government of Pribaikalia on 6 April 1920 (see Map 7). Krasnoshchekov assumed the FER presidency, drafting a declaration of independence in English, while fellow Chicagoan "Bill" Shatov became minister of war.[4]

Lenin's buffer strategy sorely disappointed those Far Eastern comrades who had no taste for political charades and who saw no need to put off establishing Soviet rule. They were irked at being told to fly a green flag with a plow and anchor (instead of a red flag with a hammer and sickle) and to replace the red star with a green rhombus on their caps.[5] One partisan leader would have none of this and, styling himself a "Red Army commander," upset Moscow's game plan by establishing his own version of Soviet rule at Nikolaevsk.

The Nikolaevsk Incident

Tensions between the Japanese expeditionary force and the partisans escalated during the first four months of 1920 as both sides tried to fill the

7. The Far Eastern Republic, 1920–22

vacuum left by Kolchak's collapse. As victory-flushed partisan bands mopped up isolated White garrisons, Tokyo increased its expeditionary force from 73,000 to 100,000.[6] The first major collision occurred on the lower Amur at Nikolaevsk, a town populated by some 8,800 Russians, 1,400 Chinese, 900 Koreans, and 730 Japanese. The Japanese contingent consisted of a civilian population of 380, including 184 women and children, and the 350 military men stationed in the local garrison and naval communications unit. Consul Ishida Toramatsu had arrived with his wife and children in 1917, and Major Ishikawa Masanori had assumed command of the garrison in 1919.[7]

Compared with Blagoveshchensk and Khabarovsk, Nikolaevsk had been an oasis of calm until January 1920 when a large partisan force under Yakov Triapitsyn approached along the Amur "liberating" one upstream village after another.* Consul Ishida telegraphed his concern to Tokyo, but ice clogging the Amur and the Tatar Strait precluded either withdrawal or reinforcement. Snowballing to 4,000 armed men as it advanced, Triapitsyn's band annihilated small Russian and Japanese detachments sent out to stop it. It reached the outskirts of Nikolaevsk in late January, cut the telegraph line to Khabarovsk, and put the town under siege. Capturing nearby Fort Chnyrrakh, the partisans bombarded Nikolaevsk with field artillery. Against the advice of the Russian garrison commander, Ishikawa negotiated with Triapitsyn. The upshot was an agreement concluded on 28 February that opened the town to the partisans while allowing the Japanese to keep their arms. The next day Triapitsyn triumphantly entered Nikolaevsk, proclaimed Soviet rule, and arrested about 100 Russian officers (the garrison commander committed suicide).

Amid boisterous festivities Triapitsyn requisitioned homes, arrested community leaders, and executed the officers already in custody. On 10 March the partisan chief told the Japanese that they too must surrender their arms. With no way to communicate with the outside world (Triapitsyn controlled the telegraph), Major Ishikawa and Consul Ishida decided to launch a surprise attack on Triapitsyn's headquarters with all available Japanese military personnel and armed civilians. They struck early in the

---

*Triapitsyn appears to have been employed in a Petrograd metal works and to have served as a noncommissioned officer in the Imperial Army before coming to the Far East in 1918. By Nov. 1919 he was leading a band of 1,500 Russians, 300 Chinese, 200 Koreans, some Hungarian internationalists, and local aborigines. Nina Lebedeva, sent by the Red Army Military Revolutionary Staff to keep an eye on him, became his chief of staff and lover.

morning of 12 March, but Triapitsyn survived and counterattacked, killing most of the Japanese population, including Major Ishikawa. Consul Ishida committed suicide with his family. The 136 Japanese survivors, mostly women, children, and wounded, were imprisoned.

When Tokyo learned of the fate of its Nikolaevsk garrison, the Japanese commanders in Khabarovsk and Vladivostok were ordered to render the Bolsheviks "incapable" of injuring Japanese lives and interests, a bureaucratic euphemism for taking revenge.[8] On the night of 4–5 April, three days after the last American troop transport had steamed out of the Golden Horn, Japanese units assaulted known and suspected Red organizations in Vladivostok, Nikolsk-Ussuriisk, Spassk, Posyet, and Khabarovsk. Both sides took heavy casualties: 1,000 Japanese and 3,000 "Bolsheviks," among them Sergei Lazo.[9]

Although officially chairman of the Vladivostok Zemstvo Government's Military Council, Lazo was known to be the top Red partisan commander in the Far East and as such ranked high on the Japanese hit list. Lazo gave a false name when picked up on the night of 4–5 April, but his captors knew better and after several days of questioning transported him and two others (one being former secretary of the Vladivostok soviet Vsevolod Sibirtsev) in mail bags to an Ussuri Line station called Muraviev-Amursky, where the three were handed over to a Don Cossack named Bochkarev. When Lazo struggled as he was being taken out of the bag, Bochkarev's men knocked him unconscious and threw him into a locomotive furnace. His two companions followed, having been first shot inside their bags.*

After the Imperial Army had extracted a measure of revenge, a Foreign Ministry representative apologized for "unauthorized actions" and set up a joint "Russo-Japanese conciliation commission" in Vladivostok. Meanwhile, under Japanese tutelage, a new zemstvo government was installed, presided over by a Menshevik. The Japanese found a cooperative figure in Vasily Boldyrev, a former tsarist officer who had represented the Omsk government in Tokyo, to succeed Lazo as chairman of the military council. On 29 April the new government and Tokyo concluded an agreement

---

*The Bolsheviks lost an energetic commander but gained a revolutionary martyr. In a 1924 poem, "Vladimir Ilych Lenin," Vladimir Mayakovsky depicted Lazo being held by Japanese soldiers, one of whom pours molten lead down his throat as another shouts, "Recant!" Lazo gurgles: "Long live communism!" Lazo's murderers were hardly original. Approximately two years earlier, on 13 June 1918, instruments of revolutionary justice in Perm threw Grand Duke Mikhail Aleksandrovich, his English secretary, and his chauffeur alive into a factory furnace.

dubbed by critics a "Far Eastern Brest-Litovsk," providing for a twenty-mile zone around southern Primorye towns, rail lines, and roads within which only Japanese and Japanese-approved Russian police were permitted to bear arms.[10]

The Japanese sortie of 4–5 April, followed by relief expeditions from Khabarovsk and Otaru (Hokkaido), had fateful results for thousands of hostages in Nikolaevsk. As the relief forces drew near in the last days of May, the partisans put to death their 136 Japanese prisoners, slaughtered approximately 4,000 Russian men, women, and children, and after torching the town, herded a couple of thousand dazed survivors up the Amgun River to Kerbi.[11] When Japanese forces entered Nikolaevsk on 3 June, they found the town in ashes and the river clogged with bloated corpses. Amid journalistically fanned public outrage, Tokyo charged Moscow with responsibility and on 3 July announced that the Imperial Army was occupying northern Sakhalin until the "incident" was resolved.[12]

Triapitsyn's homicidal proclivities concerned Moscow only because their visibility jeopardized the success of its buffer strategy. By arousing a powerful neighbor that Lenin and Trotsky wanted to neutralize, Triapitsyn had made himself an unwanted witness whose testimony could prove embarrassing. Accordingly, Triapitsyn, his mistress Nina Lebedeva, and twenty-three followers were quickly executed at Kerbi on 11 July after having been found guilty of murdering four Communists. The fate of over 4,000 Nikolaevsk residents was not mentioned in the proceedings. Judicial choreography did not deter Tokyo from raising the ante for withdrawing its forces from Russian territory.

The Far Eastern Republic Comes of Age

At various times between 1920 and 1922, five self-styled "governments" claimed jurisdiction over all or part of the Far East. Each had its own political complexion. Each to various degrees was beholden to Moscow or Tokyo. At Vladivostok the Zemstvo Government claimed jurisdiction over the Primorye, northern Sakhalin, and Kamchatka, but its authority was in fact restricted to a 200-mile radius. Operating under Japanese sufferance, it had the trappings of a bourgeois-moderate socialist coalition of SRs, Mensheviks, and independents, but Bolsheviks wielded influence behind the scenes.[13] At Khabarovsk a White regime headed by former municipal duma presidents Konstantin Likhoidov and Aleksandr Plyusnin was supported by vestigial property owners, defended by Japanese bayonets, and policed by Cossacks under the command of Lazo's nemesis Bochkarev.[14] At Blagoveshchensk, Meier Trilisser created a "red island" and flaunted his disdain for Lenin's buffer strategy by refusing to recognize the FER and calling for the immediate sovietization of the Far East. In eastern Transbaikalia the Japanese Army shored up Semyonov's Buryat Mongol Republic and allowed its protégé to obstruct metropolitan communications with the Far Eastern periphery, obliging Moscow emissaries to detour around the "Chita stopper" through Mongolia and Manchuria to reach Vladivostok.

Precarious communications also forced Moscow to rely temporarily on Sibbiuro to bring Far Eastern comrades into line. Sibbiuro in turn created a branch called the Far Eastern Bureau (Dalbiuro), but when this failed to produce any noticeable change in the level of squabbling, Moscow removed Dalbiuro from Sibbiuro's jurisdiction and put it under the Central Committee.[15]

Publicly "recognized" by Moscow as an independent state on 14 May 1920, the Far Eastern Republic gradually acquired a veneer of authority. Trilisser relented and agreed to become the FER plenipotentiary in Blagoveshchensk. Postyshev manfully tried to fit unruly partisans into the People's Revolutionary Army (NRA), the FER equivalent of the Red Army.[16] Wishful thinking helped the FER gain credibility among Whites naive enough to grasp at the mirage of a non-Bolshevik corner of Russian soil. Party operatives did their best to exploit this psychological vulnerability. Pyotr Parfyonov, for one, set his hook for Semyonov in a series of "fishing expeditions" during the spring of 1920. Nibbling at the bait, the ataman intimated that he might be willing to serve as NRA commander-in-chief.[17]

While Parfyonov played on White vanities, FER War Minister Shatov probed Japanese political vulnerabilities, suggesting to the commander of the expeditionary force, General Ōi Shigemoto, that if the Imperial Army evacuated Transbaikalia, the FER would turn the region into a neutral zone closed to the Red Army. After two months of negotiations, Tokyo approved, and in an agreement signed on 15 July 1920 at Gongota, seventy miles southwest of Chita, the FER undertook to contain Bolshevism, and Japan promised to withdraw from Transbaikalia.[18]

The Gongota agreement undercut Japan's protégés in Transbaikalia and the Priamur. When the Imperial Army evacuated Chita in late July, Ataman Semyonov soon followed, transferring the Buryat Mongol Republic to Dauria, ten miles from the Manchurian frontier. When two months later

Japan signaled its intention to withdraw from Khabarovsk, the Likhoidov-Plyusnin regime tottered. No sooner had the last Imperial Army troops left Transbaikalia and Khabarovsk in October than the FER capital moved eastward from Verkhneudinsk to Chita.[19] In November the NRA drove out the last Semyonovite and Kappelite troops from Dauria into Manchuria, completing the occupation of Transbaikalia.[*]

Despite its gains between April and November 1920, the FER did not move immediately to bring the Zemstvo Government under its jurisdiction. Though local Bolsheviks hankered to sovietize Vladivostok, they were warned by Moscow not to rock the boat while Japanese troops were still in the Primorye. Moscow's restraint paid off on 11 December when Vladivostok's Bolshevik-dominated popular assembly recognized the FER, and a Communist newspaper editor, Vasily Antonov, was installed as the head of a scaled-back administration (dubbed "a buffer within a buffer") to deal with Japanese authorities.[20] To lend credence to the image of FER independence, Moscow concluded a boundary treaty with Chita in the last days of 1920.[21]

The first half of 1921 brought new problems for Moscow on the eastern periphery. "Pink communism" did not fool (among others) Right SRs, who remained a political force in Khabarovsk. Far Eastern Bolsheviks, discovering that it was easier to make promises as revolutionaries than to run coalition governments from behind the scenes, expended a good deal of time and energy bickering among themselves. Lenin's repeated calls for discipline elicited the usual gestures of compliance but little else. Central Party leaders grew especially impatient with sovietization hotheads and Krasnoshchekov. The former jeopardized "buffer strategy" by their impetuosity. The latter took "buffer strategy" too seriously. When Krasnoshchekov showed himself to be unmanageable and clashed with Lenin's envoy, Boris Shumyatsky, the ex-FER president was summoned to Moscow and never set foot in the Far East again.[†]

---

[*]The Kappelites were followers of Vladimir Kappel, a General Staff Academy graduate and much-decorated World War veteran who served under Kolchak on the Volga and Ural fronts in 1918 and 1919. Their leader was no longer alive by then, having died of frostbite on 25 Jan. 1920, in the White retreat across Siberia.

[†]Nikiforov, *Zapiski prem'era DVR*, pp. 157, 159; Mukhachev, "Prezident respubliki," p. 137. Krasnoshchekov served briefly as deputy commissar of finance and in 1922 was appointed chairman of Industrial Bank until, accused of mismanagement, he went on trial in 1924 and disappeared from public view for a decade.

White Resurgence

The loss of Transbaikalia and the Priamur did not extinguish the White dream. Several thousand Semyonovites and about 35,000 Kappelites and their families moved into the Primorye via Manchuria in November 1920. The Semyonovites, preferring to be near the Manchurian frontier, clustered at Grodekovo; the Kappelites settled down around Rasdolnoye and Nikolsk-Ussuriisk, reinforcing the anti-Bolshevik demographics of the Khanka Plain.[22]

The influx of battle-tested anti-Bolsheviks buttressed the efforts of Nikolai Merkulov and his brother Spiridon to whiten Vladivostok's increasingly "pink" coloration. Prominent in local commerce and politics well before 1917, the Merkulov brothers began forging a conservative opposition the instant Antonov became head of the scaled-down Zemstvo Government in December 1920. Early in 1921 they founded the Committee for the Salvation of the Fatherland and recruited members from local professional classes, businessmen, civil servants, and former tsarist officers. Unable to reconcile Kappelites and Semyonovites, the Merkulovs used both to seize power. On 21 May, as Japanese forces held off the NRA and partisans, Kappelite troops dissolved the Antonov-led Zemstvo Government, and the Merkulovs proclaimed an anti-Bolshevik "Provisional Priamur Government." Having secured Semyonov's benevolence by promising him the post of commander-in-chief in the new regime, the brothers reneged on the deal and bribed the ataman to entrain for Harbin.[23]

The birth of a "black" buffer in Vladivostok opened an opportunity for Tokyo to apply pressure on the "pink" buffer at Chita. In September 1921 the Foreign Ministry requested that the FER recognize Vladivostok as an international port, grant Japan unrestricted access to Far Eastern natural resources, and accept an indefinite occupation of the Primorye and northern Sakhalin.[24] The FER had less trouble deflecting Japanese importunities than it did dealing with quixotic crusaders calling themselves *belopovstantsy* ("White insurgents"): about 17,000 diehard Kappelites, Semyonovites, Ungernites, and Wrangelites who began converging on Vladivostok from every part of Russia.* These "last of the White Mohicans" fervently believed

---

*The Ungernites were followers of Baron Ungern-Sternberg, commander of the Asiatic Cavalry Corps in Transbaikalia and Mongolia. Wrangelites were remnants of Baron Wrangel's

that Russia could still be saved from Bolshevism. They lived under the illusion, reinforced by uprisings of Baltic Fleet sailors at Kronstadt and peasants in Tambov Province, that Soviet rule hung by a thread and that one or two military victories on the eastern periphery would ignite a chain reaction of anti-Bolshevik explosions across Siberia, opening the way for a "march on Moscow."

These belopovstantsy were led by Viktorin Molchanov, one of the most able White commanders of the civil war. Returning to his native Yelabuga district in the summer of 1918 after four years of frontline duty during which he escaped from German captivity, Molchanov organized local peasants into self-defense units against Bolshevik grain collectors along the Kama River, a tributary of the Volga. In September the Yelabugans were incorporated into Kolchak's army. Although he showed symptoms of neurasthenia, Molchanov was brave, unaffected, and solicitous about the welfare of his subordinates. His combat record and rank-and-file popularity earned him the appointment to lead the Izhevsk Workers' Brigade,* which together with the Yelabugans fought the Red Army between the Volga and Urals until June 1919. After the collapse of the Ural front in the summer of 1919, Molchanov shepherded some 4,000 Yelabuga-Izhevsk survivors and their families across Siberia and Manchuria to the Primorye.[25]

Molchanov's march on Moscow began on 1 November 1921 as Yelabugans moved northward from Spassk while Kappelites cleared partisans out of Suchan and Admiral Yury Stark's Siberian Flotilla secured a beachhead at Olga. As Molchanov approached Khabarovsk, the regional Party organization mobilized young Communists to form a defense line south of the city. Molchanov outflanked the *komsomoltsy* by sending cavalry across the frozen Ussuri to the Chinese shore. This maneuver so shook local FER authorities that they abandoned Khabarovsk on 21 December, after setting fire to military stores, blowing up ice-bound ships, and burning three grounded airplanes.[26]

Disappointment soon dampened whatever exhilaration the belopovstantsy might have felt after having fought their way to Khabarovsk in mid-

Volunteer Army in South Russia, 400 of whom reached Vladivostok from Mesopotamia on the steamer *Ferdinand* in Oct. 1921.
*Peasant and worker volunteers from districts around Izhevsk (Izhevsky Zavod until 1917), a city located eighty miles northeast of Yelabuga. Izhevsky Zavod enjoyed fame during the 19th century for producing shotguns.

winter across 400 miles of taiga. The hoped-for uprisings in Siberia failed to materialize, and peasants along the Ussuri showed no inclination to join in the march on Khabarovsk, let alone Moscow. Having outrun their supplies, the exhausted victors had little choice but to steel themselves for a counterblow.

Birth of a Cohort, Death of a Dream

In the spring of 1921, the NRA was more of a mob than a fighting force. Internationalists, partisans, and re-outfitted Red Army men rubbed shoulders with former followers of Kolchak and Semyonov. Over a third of the officers had served in White armies. SRs and Mensheviks abounded. Indiscipline, thefts, and acrimony flourished. To put things in order, the Politburo appointed Vasily Blücher NRA commander and FER war minister. Born into a family of poor peasants, Blücher had supported himself in St. Petersburg as a metalworker from the age of fourteen and served in the Imperial Army on the front as a conscript and then a noncommissioned officer. Committing to the Bolshevik regime in November 1917, he had compiled an impressive combat record during the next three years as a Red Guard leader along the Volga, a sharpshooter division commander in the Urals, and a co-architect of a successful offensive into the Crimea.[27]

On his arrival in Chita in late June 1921, Blücher found the NRA undisciplined and demoralized. He dismissed hundreds of officers and abolished restive units, cutting the NRA from 90,000 to 79,650 in three months.[28] In building a fighting force, Blücher relied on a small team of military men and civilians: his deputy NRA commander Albert Lapin, and chief of staff Yakov Pokus; the political commissar Postyshev; and four partisan liaison agents, Konstantin Pshenitsyn, Rafail Shishlyannikov, Mikhail Volsky, and Boris Melnikov. With the exception of Postyshev, who was transferred to Moscow in 1924, these men formed the nucleus of the cohort of civil war and FER veterans that were to hold key political and military positions in the Far East after the establishment of Soviet rule.

Although a shrewd judge of human character, Blücher underestimated his adversary, Molchanov. Only on 17 December 1921 did the NRA commander return from a conference with Japanese diplomats in Dairen and assume direct command of a crumbling Amur front. By then it was too late to prevent the belopovstantsy from taking Khabarovsk.

After occupying Khabarovsk, Molchanov sent a cavalry detachment across the Amur to establish contact with the enemy. The detachment followed the Amur Line tracks westward for about fifty miles to a station called In, where it encountered strong NRA units, backed up by an armored train and artillery. Lacking the strength to press on, Molchanov's detachment dug in about halfway between In and Khabarovsk, around a village called Volochayevka.

After peaking around Christmas, the White tide ebbed as the fateful year of 1922 began. Blücher, Pokus, and the local NRA commander Stepan Seryshev brought in reinforcements from Chita until by the end of January the Reds enjoyed a preponderance of troops (15,000–20,000 against 6,000 belopovstantsy) and firepower.[29] In contrast, the Japanese detained trains supplying Molchanov at Spassk, the northern perimeter of the "neutral zone."[30] On 5 February Blücher launched a general assault against Volochayevka. After an artillery bombardment, NRA troops stormed the White trenches. The defenders hung on desperately amid hand-to-hand combat, but the NRA broke through. Blücher wanted to trap the Whites in Khabarovsk, but Molchanov guessed his intentions and skirted the town, taking his men, horses, and supplies across the frozen Amur and Ussuri to safety. Blücher thereupon sent his adversary a letter urging him to switch sides.[31] Molchanov did not reply.

The Battle of Volochayevka destroyed the last hope for an anti-Communist buffer state in the Primorye. Molchanov retreated to Spassk, where on 6 April the NRA momentarily cut off its pursuit when it became clear that the Japanese would not allow hostilities in the "neutral zone." Undeterred, Blücher unleashed partisans, who proceeded to wipe out small White garrisons in villages around Vladivostok and temporarily paralyze the CER and Ussuri lines. Meanwhile, the NRA massed north of Spassk for a final assault into the southern Primorye.

While Blücher engaged external enemies, less visible operators dealt with internal disaffection. In July 1922, Chita criminalized "slander" against FER leaders, thereby preparing the judicial rationale for measures by the FER State Political Security (GPO), a branch of the GPU. In August Dalbiuro created a FER "central troika" empowered to dispense death sentences in political cases. Assisted by civilians organized into "special purpose units" (*chasti osobovo naznacheniya* or CHON), the GPO rounded up Mensheviks and SRs for summary disposal following trial by troika. By criminalizing political opposition, streamlining judicial and punitive procedures, and mobilizing the masses as accomplices, the GPO-CHON-troika partnership formed a prototype engine that would run at full throttle during the next decade.[32]

Meanwhile, the White position in Vladivostok deteriorated precipitously during the summer of 1922. Under diplomatic prodding from Washington, Tokyo announced on 24 June that Imperial Army troops would be withdrawn from the Primorye by the end of October.[33] Instead of closing ranks, Semyonovites, Kappelites, Siberia Flotilla officers, Merkulovites, and members of the Vladivostok duma, popular assembly, and chamber of commerce bickered. Appointing himself voevoda, the former commander of the Czech Legion, Mikhail Dieterichs, resurrected a medieval Russian "estates general," while monarchists sent a missive to Denmark offering Vladivostok to Maria Fyodorovna, mother of Nicholas II.[34] As Whites fantasized, the "neutral zone" contracted. Japanese units started leaving in August and by October were deployed only in Vladivostok, ignoring Dieterichs' pleas for arms and ammunition.[35]

Although their situation had become hopeless, some Whites were not about to give up the last corner of their homeland without a final gesture of defiance. Molchanov and a few hundred troops advanced forty miles northward from Spassk in September, only to receive the full brunt of Operation Primorye, launched early in October by newly appointed war minister and NRA commander Ieronym Uborevich. Spearheaded by 8,000 "shock troops" under Stepan Vostretsov and 5,000 partisans under Volsky, the attackers annihilated 1,600 White defenders at Spassk, opening the gates to the Khanka Plain.[36] As Molchanov fell back along the Ussuri Line and Semyonovites withdrew into Manchuria, Reds swept through Nikolsk-Ussuriisk toward Vladivostok. Vladivostok won a brief reprieve on 19 October, when Uborevich ordered Vostretsov and Volsky to suspend operations until the Japanese had completed their withdrawal. Four days later Uborevich met with the U.S. consul and agreed that order would be preserved as Whites left and FER forces entered the city.[37]

There was little order to preserve during the last days of White rule. Dieterichs departed for Japan, and Admiral Stark brought the Siberian Flotilla into the Golden Horn to evacuate thousands of refugees. Bolshevik activists organized a general strike, and Siberian autonomists founded yet another government amid rumors that Tokyo would finance a White redoubt on Kamchatka.[38]

Four hours after the last Japanese transport cleared Cape Egersheld at midday on 25 October, the NRA and partisans swept into Vladivostok, marching down the Svetlanskaya along which Allied formations had paraded four years earlier. The GPO lost no time arresting two senior figures in the former Zemstvo Government: President Medvedev and Military Council Chairman Boldyrev.* Hundreds of less prominent people were rounded up, interrogated, and sentenced by troikas. Some were shot, but most went into holding camps outside Vladivostok and Khabarovsk until they could be put to work.[39]

While Vladivostok celebrated, 25,000 men, women, and children made their way abroad. One group around Grodekovo moved along the CER tracks to the Manchurian border. Some 9,000 refugees who had gathered around Posyet reached Manchuria by walking along a rain-soaked track to Hunchun. After confiscating arms and valuables, Chinese authorities distributed food and provided temporary shelter. A third group of 5,000 refugees crossed the Tumen into Korea where Japanese officials and Red Cross workers accommodated them in Genzan. A fourth group of 8,000 boarded Admiral Stark's motley flotilla in the Golden Horn and sailed to Shanghai. Uborevich forbade any interference in the White exodus, declaring that defeated adversaries should be allowed to leave in peace. A few did so in style. A company of Cossacks, finding themselves stranded by the Red tide, altered their uniforms and fell in with a column of NRA troops marching toward the Chinese frontier. They not only arrived undetected but lived off NRA rations en route.[40]

Although most refugees from the Primorye resettled in Manchuria, Shanghai, Hong Kong, Korea, or Australia, some made the odyssey from Golden Horn to Golden Gate. Leaving all but 900 passengers in Shanghai, Admiral Stark sailed via Taiwan to the Philippines, from where most continued on to San Francisco with the help of the U.S. Navy. Among those reaching California were Yelabugans who had fought their way under Viktorin Molchanov from the Volga to the Pacific. Joining the Russian community in the Bay Area, they cherished proud memories and kept in touch. "General" Molchanov wound up in Petaluma as a chicken farmer and passed away in 1974 at the age of eighty-eight.[41]

---

*Medvedev was sent to a Solovetsky Islands camp where he soon perished. Sent to Petrograd for interrogation, Boldyrev was incarcerated in Novonikolaevsk (Novosibirsk), amnestied following his 1923 appeal to the Central Committee, and shot in 1933 on charges of being a member of a "terrorist organization" that OGPU scenarists labeled the "West Siberian Counterrevolutionary Center."

Having served its purpose, the Far Eastern Republic was absorbed into Soviet Russia on 15 November 1922. NRA personnel exchanged green rhombi for red stars on their caps. FER officials transferred to the Soviet state apparatus. Members of the GPO switched one letter to become part of the GPU. Successful in expediting a Japanese withdrawal, Lenin's buffer strategy returned to haunt Moscow, for the independence charade had infected some players with a regionalist virus.

32. General William S. Graves, Ataman Grigory Semyonov, and their staffs in
Vladivostok, 1918

33. Ataman Grigory Semyonov

34. Ataman Ivan Kalmykov

35. Ataman Kalmykov and entourage

36. "White Argonaut" of Yakutia, Anatoly Pepeliaev

37. Leader of the "March on Moscow," Viktorin Molchanov

38. Special Far Eastern Army skiers about to set off for Moscow to celebrate the successful campaign in Manchuria, Khabarovsk, 1929

39. OKDVA Commander Vasily Blücher (left) with NKVD Commissars Semyon Zapadny and Terenty Deribas

40. Yan Gamarnik, Vasily Blücher, and Ivan Fedko at OKDVA review in Voroshilov (Ussuriisk), September 1936

Left: 41. Writer, orientalist, and intelligence officer Oskar Tarkhanov
Right: 42. Doomed foursome: Lavrentiev, Krutov, Deribas, Berzin in Magadan, August 1936

43. Valentina Khetagurova with Stalin and Voroshilov at the All-Union Conference of Wives of Army Commanders in Moscow, December 1936

44. Ex-NKVD Commissar Genrikh Lyushkov at Sanno Hotel, Tokyo, July 1938

45. Blücher's successor: Grigory Shtern, 1939

46. Pacific Fleet sailors during a lighter moment, 1939

47. Vice-President Henry Wallace and NKVD Commissar Sergei Goglidze in Kolyma, 1944

48. Monument to victims of American "air pirates,"
Vladivostok, 1980

49. Border guards patrolling the KSP ("control tracking strip"), ca. 1982

50. Nikita Karatsupa surrounded by chekist admirers, ca. 1982

51. Young Friends of Border Guards on patrol, ca. 1985

52. Alaska Governor Steve Cowper and KGB escort, Big Diomede Island, Bering Strait, 1988

«« PART III »»

The Soviet Far East

<< << >> >>

Anomalous Enclave

Though Vladivostok is a long way off, it is after all one of our own towns.   — V. I. Lenin (1922)

When Lenin called Vladivostok "our own," the Far East was still largely outside Moscow's control. Japanese forces occupied northern Sakhalin. White bands infested the Northeast and infiltrated the Priamur and the Primorye from Manchuria. Independent-minded peasants and Cossacks clung to their lands. Soviet rule so little touched the Northeast that some Chukchi assumed Chukotka had been sold to the United States.[1] When a Soviet gunboat steamed into Provideniya Bay in 1924, a local constable came aboard and declared the captain and crew under arrest for flying a red flag.[2]

Moscow could spare neither capital nor personnel for its most distant province, so the task of liquidating Whites, patrolling frontiers, and rebuilding the economy fell to local Party and soviet organs. Regional authorities had no practical alternative but to rely on foreign capital, to tolerate private enterprise, and to employ "bourgeois experts." Expedience acquired a momentum of its own, and the New Economic Policy (NEP) persisted on the Pacific for two years after 1928 when it was discarded in metropolitan Russia.

Initially, the whole of the Far East was administered by district revolutionary committees (*revkomy*) accountable to the Far Eastern Revolutionary Committee (Dalrevkom) in Khabarovsk. By 1926, soviets had superseded revkomy in the Priamur and the Primorye, but the latter continued to rule parts of the Northeast until 1931.[3] Former Far Eastern Republic officials occupied key positions. Pyotr Kobozev, chairman of the FER Council of Ministers, headed Dalrevkom. Postyshev chaired the Pribaikal revkom. Uborevich coordinated Dalrevkom military operations. Volsky headed the regional GPU. Pshenitsyn became deputy chairman of the Primorye revkom. Shishlyannikov chaired the Sakhalin revkom. To head the Far Eastern Party organization (Dalbiuro), Moscow sent Nikolai Kubiak, a stalwart of the anti-bureaucratic "workers' opposition" within the Party.[4]

White Afterglow

Waves generated by the fall of Kolchak reached the Northeast as ripples. As was their habit, local authorities trimmed their sails to prevailing political winds. At Petropavlovsk the Left SR Ivan Larin and his followers shot a few officers of the local garrison on 9 January 1920 and created a "Kamchatka Revolutionary Committee" that genuflected alternately to Vladivostok, Chita, and Moscow while its members set their families up in comfortable circumstances. At Anadyr two Vladivostok Bolsheviks and a wayward American sailor shot a few officials in December 1919 without changing much or saving themselves from retribution. To keep in step with political nomenclature on the "mainland," Anadyr's local elites formed their own "Soviet of Chukotka Deputies."[5]

Semantic complaisance did not fool Bochkarev, the Cossack enforcer whose henchmen had stuffed Lazo into an engine furnace. Intent on turning the Northeast into a White redoubt, Bochkarev landed on Kamchatka at the head of a 200-man "death battalion" and marched into Petropavlovsk on 28 October 1921, to the ostensible delight of local inhabitants. To almost everyone's relief, he set out the following July to conquer Chukotka. Members of the erstwhile Chukotka soviet greeted him in Anadyr with protestations of loyalty as two bona fide Communists fled to Alaska.* Bochkarev's luck ran out after Volsky showed up in Petropavlovsk in December with a well-armed GPU pacification squad. The chekists pursued, cornered, and on 13 April 1923 executed Bochkarev fifty miles outside of Gizhiga, where he had taken refuge with his wife and a handful of followers.[6]

As the GPU completed its "cleansing" of Kamchatka, counterrevolution

---

*A. M. Bychkov and G. G. Rudykh could well have been — until 1991 — the only Communists who sought asylum in the United States from anti-Communists in Soviet Russia. Bychkov and Rudykh made their way back to Moscow via New York, but it is not clear whether they ever returned to the Far East, let alone Chukotka.

flared up in Yakutia, where a group of Yakut intellectuals and Siberian autonomists captured Yakutsk, proclaimed a "Provisional Yakut People's Government," and annihilated a Red Army column advancing from Irkutsk.[7] Yakutsk was recaptured in late 1922, but Yakut nationalists and their Russian allies held out in Verkhoyansk and Aldan. Stirred by their tenacity and moved by their appeal for assistance, a force of 700 volunteers mustered in Harbin and Vladivostok by Anatoly Pepeliaev (a brother of Kolchak's last prime minister) sailed from the Golden Horn in September 1922 under the green-and-white banner of Siberian autonomy.[8] From Ayan the "argonauts of the White dream" marched in midwinter across the Dzhugdzhur Mountains toward Yakutsk, coming to within 100 miles of their goal before being attacked by a Red force led by Ivan Strod. In the meantime a Red Army infantry regiment and artillery battalion commanded by Stepan Vostretsov landed at Ayan, cutting off Pepeliaev's retreat. A handful of "argonauts" escaped to Hokkaido, but most perished at the hands of chekist mop-up squads guided by an ethnographer named Albert Lipsky. Twenty-seven officers, including Pepeliaev, were brought before a revolutionary tribunal in Yakutsk. All were condemned to death and shot except for Pepeliaev, whose sentence was commuted to ten years' imprisonment after he had publicly recanted. Apostasy spared the White argonaut until 1938, when he and his Red antagonist Strod were both shot as "enemies of the people."[9]

Pepeliaev's defeat did not extinguish the flame of White resistance in Yakutia and the Northeast. As late as 1925, anti-Communists periodically rose up around the Okhotsk seaboard, ambushing Red Army and GPU (OGPU after 2 November 1923) detachments sent out to destroy them.[10] In 1926 Yakut nationalists formed an underground anti-Communist organization. The OGPU neutralized it the next year by announcing a general amnesty and liquidating those who came out of hiding.[11]

Unlike Yakutia, Wrangel Island accepted Soviet rule without complaint. Eighty-five miles off the Siberian coast, Wrangel (half again as large as Rhode Island) had at various times been claimed by Americans, Canadians, and Russians before catching the attention of the arctic explorer Vilhjalmur Stefansson as a potential refueling stop for transpolar flights. With the approval of Canadian Prime Minister Arthur Meighen, Stepansson deposited five Canadians and an Eskimo woman on Wrangel in the fall of 1921, but only the woman remained alive when he returned two years later. Ottawa thereupon dropped its claim, and Stefansson "sold" Wrangel to a

Nome, Alaska, merchant, who planned to turn it into a reindeer farm. In the meantime Dalrevkom, alerted to capitalist encroachment, dispatched a gunboat. On 19 August 1924 Red Army troops stormed ashore, seized four bewildered Eskimos, and raised the hammer-and-sickle. The feat was commemorated by bronze medals cast with the inscription "For the Liberation of Wrangel Island."[12]

Porous Frontiers

During most of the 1920s, Far Eastern state frontiers existed mostly on paper. Aborigines and traders moved freely back and forth across the Bering Strait, while the U.S. Geodetic Expedition surveyed Chukotka, leaving behind bronze markers warning "$250 fine for removal."[13] Protected by the Imperial Navy, Japanese fished and landed at will along the coast from the Primorye to Kamchatka. Koreans commuted across the Tumen. *Hong huzi* and White partisans from Manchuria made a nuisance of themselves along the Amur and Ussuri. Two-thirds of Amur gold found its way to China.[14] Smugglers supplied Priamur and Primorye settlements with vodka, hunting guns, clothing, kitchenware, and farm implements, outwitting border guards by employing decoys and other tricks, like substituting alcohol for water in engine boilers.[15]

All of this was despite the authorities' best efforts, for borders in fact ranked high in Dalrevkom priorities. In September 1923 the GPU assumed direct control of a fourteen-mile-wide strip along the entire Far Eastern periphery. No Soviet citizen was allowed to approach within ten miles of a state boundary without a special pass. Within a five-mile zone, border guards (*pogranichniki*) could open fire on anyone not responding to two challenges. Nonetheless, trespassers and fugitives had little trouble crossing the frontier, for there was but one pogranichnik for every three miles of land border and one for every sixty miles of Pacific coastline.[16]

The man who bore the brunt of this responsibility, Aleksei Flegontov, commander of Far Eastern frontier forces, knew that smuggling thrived because peasants had little choice but to sell produce and buy provisions illegally.[17] Setting out to build a symbiotic relationship between border guards and frontier zone inhabitants, he set up trading enterprises operated by state security organs, empowered local residents to detain suspicious strangers, and encouraged each village to adopt a pogranichnik. Thanks to Flegontov's exertions, a border guard assumed something of the role of a village priest in a frontier settlement: "no festivities, even intimate family affairs, took place without him."[18]

Although the OGPU recruited Chukchi and Eskimos to hunt fugitives attempting to reach Alaska,[19] people and goods continued to move illegally across the Bering Strait because everyone wanted American canned milk and fruit, crockery, linoleum tiles, kerosene lamps, aluminum pots, and whiskey (spirits were smuggled in ship boilers). When the Rockefeller family yacht *Mary Ann* called unannounced at Uelen in 1928, constabulary vigilance dissolved at the sight of fresh oranges.[20]

Reconstruction

Four years of civil war and foreign intervention left the Priamur and the Primorye in shambles. Nearly half the land under cultivation was abandoned and more than half the livestock slaughtered. Gold production plummeted to a tenth of prewar levels. Amur and Ussuri rail lines were left inoperable, and what was left of the Volunteer Fleet and Siberian Flotilla, scattered in ports around the world, defied repossession.[21] The Far East's population fell by 200,000 between 1913 and 1926.[22] Estimates of the victims of White Terror range from 44,000 to 50,000.[23] The Red Terror claimed no less, if we recall that Nikolaevsk in 1926 had just over half of its 1913 population.[24]

Foreign enterprise survived the establishment of Soviet rule. Kunst & Albers, Semyonov & Denbigh, and Bryner & Co. continued to do business, albeit on a smaller scale and under OGPU supervision. Chinese merchants retained their hold over the retail trade, particularly in the Primorye. In May 1923, a few days after Charles Stephan closed the U.S. consulate-general in Vladivostok, Wilhelm Wagner and his assistant Georg Kühlborn opened the consulate-general of the Weimar Republic. While maintaining a representative in Vladivostok under a veteran Russian specialist, Watanabe Riye, Tokyo upon normalizing relations with Moscow in 1925 opened consulates in Khabarovsk, Blagoveshchensk, Petropavlovsk, and Aleksandrovsk (northern Sakhalin). Japanese consortia operated lumber, ore, and fur concessions; dominated banking and shipping; and controlled 90 percent of Far Eastern fisheries (employing 22,600 Japanese in 1925 and 38,600 in 1930). On Kamchatka, seasonal Japanese workers outnumbered the local population. Yen circulated throughout the Far East legally until 1924 and illegally thereafter.[25]

Statistics testify to the survival of capitalism in the Far East during the early years of Soviet rule. Private firms handled 88 percent of the Far East's internal commerce (60 percent of the turnover value) in 1924. Of 2,814 trading concerns registered as of 1 April 1925, 96 percent were private, 3 percent were cooperatives, and 1 percent were state-owned.[26] Notwithstanding the proliferation of state agencies (Dalbank, Dalplan, Dalprombiuro, etc.), authorities depended on private enterprise and recruited scores of "bourgeois experts," including the former head of the short-lived Provisional Siberian Autonomous Government, Pyotr Derber.[27]

Derber and his assistants came up with a strategy for Far Eastern economic development that stressed forging links with Pacific neighbors. To improve communications and transport, they recommended constructing new railroad lines, establishing a merchant marine, and relocating Russia's Pacific gateway from Vladivostok to Posyet, whose location promised better access to Manchuria. Exports of natural resources developed by foreign concessionaires would pay for imports of technology and equipment. Derber urged that Far Eastern authorities take advantage of the U.S. Exclusion Act (1924) and encourage East Asian immigration to the Primorye.[28] Chinese, Japanese, and Koreans could cultivate rice on the Khanka Plain for export to Japan. Derber's basic idea was echoed by the economist Nikolai Arkhipov, who wrote in 1926 that "the pull toward Pacific markets is the main economic force of the Far Eastern region."[29] Successive Dalrevkom chairmen also expressed support for regional engagement with Asia-Pacific economies and revived the vision of Vladivostok competing with Dairen as an international port.[30]

Foreign Concessions

Foreign concessions loomed more prominently in the Far East than in any other part of Soviet Russia,[31] for they fulfilled a political as well as economic purpose. Lenin regarded Far Eastern concessions as a means of gaining diplomatic recognition and a way to prevent Japan and the United States from forming a common front against the Soviet regime.[32] The origins of Lenin's "concession strategy" can be traced to May 1918, when he unveiled a "preliminary plan" for awarding the United States a timber concession in Kamchatka and the right to build a railroad from Lake Baikal to Nikolaevsk.[33] "Concession strategy" was the handmaiden of Lenin's "buffer strategy" during 1920–22, when delegations from the Far Eastern

Republic visited the United States to assure business and government leaders that American capital would find a warm welcome in the FER.[34]

"Concession strategy" went awry in 1920, when Washington B. Vanderlip, who twenty years earlier had brokered evanescent joint ventures in Chukotka, parlayed a surname (shared with a prominent banker)* into a brief fling on the stage of international politics. Persuading FER officials visiting California that he represented a financial consortium and enjoyed the personal confidence of Republican presidential hopeful Warren G. Harding, Vanderlip intimated that if Moscow would rent him the Northeast, he would see to it that the Harding administration extended diplomatic recognition to the Soviet regime.[35] Moscow took the bait, and Vanderlip gained a private audience with Lenin who provisionally endorsed giving the Hollywood impresario a sixty-year concession to develop coal, oil, and fish resources in Kolyma, Kamchatka, and Chukotka. When the Western press revealed that Vanderlip had been talking through his hat, Lenin took the sting in stride and with sardonic humor told an assemblage of party secretaries that the Cheka, having not yet seized the "Northern States of America," could not keep all the Vanderlips straight.[36]

The Vanderlip flap notwithstanding, foreign concessionaires proliferated under the supervision of the Cheka and its chief, Feliks Dzerzhinsky. In the Far East they included familiar names such as Bryner & Company (presciently incorporated in Hong Kong) as well as new British, American, German, Norwegian, and Finnish firms. In 1925 London consortia signed thirty-six-year contracts to develop the Tetyukhe lead mines and Lena goldfields. The Japanese, the only concessionaires allowed to employ their own laborers, overshadowed all others on northern Sakhalin, the Primorye, the lower Amur, and Kamchatka.[37]

Lenin used concessions in areas under real (northern Sakhalin) or potential (Kamchatka) Japanese occupation as instruments to exacerbate relations between Tokyo and Washington. This strategy led the FER, acting as a cat's-paw for Moscow, to grant the Sinclair Oil Company in 1922 a thirty-six-year lease of North Sakhalin oil fields. When Sinclair geologists tried to land at Aleksandrovsk in February 1924, they were met by Japanese troops who escorted them off the island. Sinclair duly complained to Washington, but the State Department declined to get involved. Sinclair's utility to Moscow came to an end in 1925 when Japan and the Soviet Union, nor-

*Frank Arthur Vanderlip (1864–1937), president of the National City Bank, New York.

malizing relations, struck a deal over North Sakhalin: in exchange for withdrawing their troops, the Japanese were awarded oil and coal concessions.
Sinclair protested, but to no avail, for the Soviet Supreme Court nullified
the contract on the grounds that the American company had failed to fulfill
it.[38]

American entrepreneurs fared better in the Northeast, where locals depended on foreign supplies. Unable to provision Kamchatka and Chukotka, Dalrevkom chartered the Kamchatka Company (AKO) in 1924 to assume responsibility for (among other things) foreign commerce. Enjoying
more autonomy than any comparable Soviet government agency, AKO
turned to Olaf Swenson for provisions despite the fact that the veteran
Norwegian-American trader had done business with the likes of Pepeliaev
and Bochkarev. To atone for affiliations with reactionaries, Swenson indulged in largesse toward the instruments of progress. His sympathetic
understanding of the venerable custom of "feeding" (*kormlenie*) allowed
many a Soviet guardian of native welfare to outfit himself with American
corduroy breeches, leather boots, and mackinaw.[39]

While they lasted, foreign concessions had a generally positive impact on
the Far East. They helped people feed and clothe themselves at a time when
Moscow could provide neither goods nor subsidies. They jump-started
economic recovery by investing capital, by modernizing the mining and
fisheries industries, and by offering overseas markets for regional exports.
Seen from Moscow, however, foreign concessions carried ambivalent overtones. Although they brought millions of rubles to the state treasury, they
also reinforced cosmopolitan habits and animated local aspirations that
proved troublesome as the central bureaucracy tried to impose control over
a distant periphery.[40]

Rural Intractability

According to an Amur folktale, a high official once stumbled upon a
prosperous village deep in the taiga. When asked the reason for such well-
being, the village headman prostrated himself and replied, "Your Excel-
lency, because we're far from the authorities!"[41] Indeed, most Far Eastern
peasants wanted nothing more than to be left alone and regarded all authorities, whether tsarist, White, or Red, as afflictions to be endured and —
when circumstances allowed — hoodwinked.

In 1917 Far Eastern peasants were for the most part politically uncommitted. Anti-Bolshevik sentiment grew in the first half of 1918 as Dalsovnarkom broke up zemstvo councils and requisitioned grain. Accustomed to being paid for their grain before 1917, peasants balked at unremunerated levies. In the southern Primorye the Khudyakov brothers prepared to abandon their family farm on the Khanka Plain and emigrate to New Zealand, but they decided to stay after the overthrow of Soviet rule in August 1918. Four years later they and other peasant families found themselves the objects of confiscatory forays by strangers acting in the name of Dalrevkom. Ominously, chekists appeared on the farm and arrested one of the brothers for possessing a rifle, labeling him a "bandit."[42]

Mounting grain requisitions in 1923 antagonized middle as well as prosperous peasants who responded by underreporting harvests and planting crops of sunflower, flax, and hemp instead of grain.[43] Chinese and Korean truck farmers around Vladivostok let their vegetable plots lie fallow. Resistance assumed serious political overtones in January 1924 when Communist officials were expelled from Russian, Ukrainian, and Molokan villages around Blagoveshchensk. Resorting to guile, Dalrevkom proclaimed an amnesty for all but the leaders. Rounding up the credulous, the OGPU proceeded to shoot several hundred "kulak insurgents" and to exile several thousand survivors, precipitating an exodus to Manchuria and halving the population of a dozen Amur villages.[44] Sensing danger, Yury Yankovsky and his family abandoned Sidemi and made their way along the coast to Korea. As the region's most productive cultivators resisted or fled, grain output plummeted, and the Far East lost once and for all the ability to feed itself.[45]

Rural resistance also expressed itself in the vitality of religious faith. Although Dalrevkom confiscated icons, demolished churches, and disseminated atheist literature, the anti-religion campaign made little headway outside the cities. Terror against ecclesiastics provoked popular anger. Peasants infuriated by the execution of a local priest disrupted a speech by USSR President Mikhail Kalinin at Skorovodino (Amur District) in 1923.[46] Resourceful clerics deftly refashioned atheist propaganda to serve religious ends. Baptists inserted biblical lyrics into the "Internationale" and turned "Lenin corners" (areas in factories, offices, barracks set aside for reading selected works of Marx, Engels, Lenin, and Stalin) into "Christ corners." At a regional Party conference in 1929, one delegate complained that Baptists were doing more than the Komsomol to motivate youth.[47]

Cosmopolitan Twilight

The advent of Soviet rule delivered a heavy blow to the fragile Russian ecumene that had grown up in Northeast Asia since the 1890s. As they consolidated their power after 1922, Party and state organs took measures to control the movement of people and information. Dalrevkom restricted foreign travel, introduced postal censorship, and set up check points around Vladivostok, Khabarovsk, and Blagoveshchensk. Unauthorized fraternization with foreigners, tolerated for the time being, was discouraged in the school curricula and media, by Party discipline, and by peer pressure.

Far Eastern intellectuals reacted variously to Soviet rule. The Japanologist Konstantin Kharnsky demonstratively welcomed it, although he had cavorted with Whites in their heyday. Zotik Matveyev placed his youthful hopes for social and economic justice on the new regime and served it faithfully as head librarian of the Far Eastern State University (DVGU). Zotik's teacher Evgeny Spalvin to all appearances embraced Marxism and was appointed acting DVGU rector when Grigory Podstavin embarked for Harbin in 1923. Aleksandr Grebenshchikov sounded out his friend and fellow orientalist Berthold Laufer (curator of the Chicago Field Museum since 1915, visiting China and Japan in 1923) about an academic post in the United States but for reasons that are not clear stayed in Vladivostok. The ethnographers Vladimir Yokhelson and Ivan Lopatin emigrated and wound up at the American Museum of Natural History and the University of Southern California, respectively.[48] Among prominent prerevolutionary newspaper editors, the liberal Nikolai Matveyev (Zotik's father) settled in Japan while the conservative Konstantin Kurteyev mastered a new political script in Vladivostok. Arseny Nesmelov dithered for over a year while friends warned him against remaining in Vladivostok as a known former White officer who had published in a White literary journal in Vladivostok six weeks before the Reds took over the city.[49] Then, after secretly consulting with Arseniev about unguarded trails, the poet slipped across the frontier into Manchuria.[50]

The prospect of abandoning familiar surroundings for an uncertain life in exile deterred some would-be émigrés, as did wishful thinking. Those with a higher education tried to get along with the new regime in the hope that life would return to "normal." Technical skills qualified some of them for employment by state agencies as "bourgeois specialists" until replacements of working-class background could be trained. There are no statistics on how many people broke under the strain of serving a regime that labeled them "class enemies." A senior physician at a Vladivostok hospital committed suicide in 1924 after being rebuked at a union meeting for his "unsocial attitude."[51]

The Sovietization of DVGU did not proceed smoothly notwithstanding the earnest efforts of Party watchdog Konstantin Kharnsky. Even the installation of a Communist rector, Vladimir Ogorodnikov, along with the removal of "anti-Soviet" elements on the faculty, the expulsion of 500 out of 600 students, and the recruitment of "working-class" replacements, failed to make the university manageable. A lack of enthusiasm for Marxism-Leninism among professors could be explained by the faculty's bourgeois character. But it came as a shock when class affiliation proved unreliable as a guide for the behavior of Soviet youth. In 1926 students with impeccably proletarian and peasant pedigrees issued a statement calling for the defense of academic freedom. Catching a whiff of subversion, Party organs turned the matter over to the OGPU, which with professional foresight had prepared a facility six miles north of the campus.[52]

Between 1924 and 1927 Party organs tightened their hold over Far Eastern education and research. FER Nationalities Minister Karl Luks succeeded Arseniev as director of the Khabarovsk Museum. At DVGU, Kharnsky groomed NRA veterans and ex-partisans such as Vasily Voiloshnikov to replace "bourgeois" orientalists. The Amur Society avoided a takeover bid by DVGU Rector Ogorodnikov in 1923, but the following year was nationalized and absorbed into the Russian Geographical Society (USSR Geographical Society from 1938). By 1927, the year that the DVGU Oriental Faculty graduated its first student (N. V. Pak), all Far Eastern scholarly and cultural organizations were accountable to the Agitprop Section of Dalkraikom.[53]

Defying obstacles and hazards, intellectuals contrived to maintain ties with émigré colleagues. A Siberian literary journal published verse sent from Harbin by Arseny Nesmelov. Vladimir Arseniev kept in touch with Nikolai Baikov, a resident of Harbin from 1922, whose research on the Manchurian taiga had for two decades paralleled Arseniev's on the Sikhote Alin. Arseniev let neither antecedents (both men had been tsarist officers) nor politics (Baikov had little sympathy for the Soviet regime) interrupt scholarly discourse. At an institutional level, the Amur Society exchanged publications and letters with émigré counterparts in Harbin, Prague, and Riga. Editors of a projected encyclopedia of the Soviet Far East invited Vladimir Yokhelson to contribute articles on ethnographic topics despite the fact that the former Siberian exile had become a naturalized American citizen and lived in Washington, D.C. Zotik Matveyev corresponded with his father Nikolai until 1927 when an intuitive sense of impending danger prompted him to send no more letters to Japan.[54]

Vladimir Arseniev came through revolution and civil war unscathed, quite an achievement for an Imperial Army officer with principles and a conscience. He welcomed the February Revolution and was appointed Far Eastern nationalities commissar by the Provisional Government. The October Revolution repelled him, but he stayed out of trouble by keeping a low profile working in a fisheries trust. In his spare time, Arseniev continued his research and writing, helped by the secretary of the Amur Society, Nikolai Solovyov, and his daughter Margarita Nikolaevna, whom he married in 1918 after divorcing his first wife. In 1921, with a subsidy from his father-in-law, Arseniev's *Dersu Uzala* came out in Vladivostok. Its author was with difficulty dissuaded from dedicating the book to his late patron, former Governor-General Unterberger. The following year, on an expedition along the Okhotsk seaboard, Arseniev narrowly avoided falling into the hands of the Cossack Bochkarev.[55]

Arseniev's good fortune did not abandon him after the establishment of Soviet rule in 1923. As a former tsarist officer and Provisional Government official he had to show his face every two weeks at Vladivostok OGPU headquarters but was not otherwise persecuted. He was allowed to continue his research, to lead expeditions into the taiga, and even to visit Japan. He retained his lectureship at DVGU while holding honorary membership in the Society of Russian Orientalists in Harbin. No one interfered when he socialized with Consul-General Watanabe Riye. No one objected when, in 1924, a Berlin publisher brought out *Dersu Uzala* with a preface by the 1922 Nobel Peace Prize laureate, Fridtjof Nansen, and encomiums by the illustrious explorers Sven Hedin and Georg Schweinfurth. Arseniev continued to enjoy the support of his old teacher Lev Shternberg, who had become an acknowledged leader of Soviet ethnography.[56] In what must have looked like an unimpeachable endorsement, the Vladivostok Party paper in 1928 published Maxim Gorky's letter comparing the author of *Dersu Uzala* to James Fenimore Cooper.[*]

The threads of Arseniev's public triumphs were caught up in an invisible

---

[*]*Krasnoe znamia*, 25 Feb. 1928, cited in Tarasova, *Vladimir Klavdievich Arsen'ev*, pp. 41, 50–51. Gorky stayed abroad for much of the 1920s, but he enjoyed the status of literary elder statesman in Soviet Russia. While Lenin lived, Gorky interceded successfully on behalf of intellectuals who had fallen into the maws of the security organs, including Lev Shternberg and Vladimir Yokhelson.

tangle of personal envy and bureaucratic politics. Although the public campaign against Arseniev as a "Great Russian chauvinist" began only after his death, the groundwork was prepared much earlier by ambitious youngsters who abused his trust for the sake of their own careers. One was a certain Petrovsky, who on the basis of campfire conversations during an expedition in 1926 denounced him to the OGPU for spreading "anti-Soviet propaganda."[57] Another was Elpidifor Titov, who accompanied Arseniev on an expedition into the Sikhote Alin in 1925, moved to Harbin in 1927, and upon returning to the Soviet Union in 1932, criticized his former teacher in order to establish his own political reliability.[58] Neither Petrovsky nor Titov could match Albert Lipsky, whom Arseniev accepted as a student in 1917 and nominated to the Priamur Branch of the Russian Geographical Society in 1918.[59] Envy drove Lipsky to denigrate Arseniev within a year. Taking advantage of his teacher's absence from Khabarovsk in 1919, Lipsky confided to the visiting University of Tokyo ethnographer Torii Ryūzō that Arseniev "doesn't understand anything."[60] After offering his services to the GPO as an informant in 1920, Lipsky secured for himself a double appointment as director of the Khabarovsk Museum and FER minister of nationalities, placing him in a position after the establishment of Soviet rule in the Primorye to accuse Arseniev of selling artifacts to American "interventionists."[61] Lipsky's career continued to blossom under chekist patronage. He was made plenipotentiary for aboriginal affairs on the lower Amur in 1924 and was appointed secretary of the premier Soviet ethnographic journal in 1926. Perhaps intimidated by Lipsky's scathing denunciation of Ivan Lopatin's work in 1925,[62] Arseniev withdrew into research and showed his manuscripts only to trusted friends like Lev Shternberg. Shternberg wrote Arseniev in May 1926 advising him not to fear Lipsky,[63] but by then the bureaucratic gears had already begun to grind. On 26 October 1926 Arseniev was summoned by the Vladivostok OGPU for questioning about Petrovsky's denunciation. As if on cue, his friend Vladimir Komarov, now a politically perspicacious academician, stopped corresponding with him. A photograph of Arseniev seeing off Watanabe Riye as the consul-general embarked for home in 1929 served as the basis for an espionage "case" against Arseniev by the OGPU. An order for Arseniev's arrest was drawn up but his heart gave out on 4 September 1930 before it could be delivered.[64]

As Arseniev's experiences suggest, zaamurtsy were in general better prepared than the next generation to foresee the toll that the new age would extract on intellectual honesty and personal integrity. For true believers like

Zotik Matveyev, pricks of conscience may have punctured some illusions, but doubt remained hostage to fear. For careerists like Elpidifor Titov and Albert Lipsky, the system's mounting appetite for scapegoats offered opportunities for self-advancement. Ironically, in burying religion and traditional morality, idealists and cynics alike dug — among others — their own graves.

As surviving zaamurtsy emigrated, adapted, or fell silent, Northeast Asian cosmopolitanism migrated to Harbin, Shanghai, and Kobe, leaving the Priamur and the Primorye under the banner of proletarian internationalism. Russian and Soviet cultures nurtured their own myths and illusions in proximity to each other, insulated by mutual suspicion, traumatized in different ways by Japanese continental expansion. While Yury Yankovsky hosted émigré artists and writers at his hunting lodge in the mountains of northeastern Korea, two hundred miles away at Vladivostok, Comintern and Profintern (Red International of Labor Unions) bureaucrats shuffled earnest comrades to and from anti-colonial struggles in China and Imperial Japan (including Korea).[65] While émigrés encountered East Asian cultures in Harbin, Dairen, and Kobe, East Asians studied Marxism-Leninism at DVGU. While White Russian children were taught to shout "Dai Nippon banzai!", foreign Friends of the Soviet Union in Vladivostok learned to bleat the praises of Lenin and Stalin.[66]

Illusions of Japan-assisted counterrevolution rampant in the Russian diaspora had their counterpart in illusions of proletarian internationalism in the Far East. In 1924 Dalrevkom officials welcomed Chiang Kai-shek at Vladivostok, calling him a leader of China's anti-imperialist struggle. Three years later, a Posyet District Party secretary named Afanasy Kim petitioned Moscow to create a "Korean people's republic" in the southern Primorye.[67] Who could foresee that such behavior would someday serve as prima facie evidence of treason?

18

« « » »

The Far Eastern Cohort

The slightest insincerity in our movement is like a drop of
tar in a barrel of honey.   — Yan Gamarnik (ca. 1931)

From 1926 to 1938 the Far East
formed a province officially called
Dalnevostochny krai ("Far Eastern region") and colloquially called DVK
or Dalkrai. At no time after that were Party, state, army, and security organs
all organized around the same territorial unit. At no time did regional
leaders exert such a profound influence over the Far East's economy and
political culture.

Leadership in the Far East devolved on men with shared experiences and
to some extent common outlooks. Most had been born between 1890 and
1900, had fought in the civil war, had lived longer than anyone under White
rule, had temporized with interventionists, and had grown accustomed to
unsupervised contacts with Asia-Pacific neighbors. Necessity had made
them self-reliant, for Lenin's "buffer strategy" had taught them that Moscow was prepared to sacrifice regional interests on the altar of central strategies.

Center-periphery tensions were not peculiar to the Far East. Forced
during the civil war to tolerate various degrees of autonomy by regional
secretaries, the Central Committee secretariat attempted to impose control
over provincial Party organizations during the 1920s. But as a rule, central
control decreased with distance from urban centers in general and from
Moscow in particular.[1] Dalkrai was farthest of all from Moscow and closest
to Japan, China, and the United States, a circumstance bound to raise
eyebrows at the Center.

A Haven for Mavericks

The Far East was traditionally a haven as well as a receptacle for mavericks: convicts and exiles, escaped serfs, hunters and trappers, and gold prospectors. Cossacks and sectarians made up fiercely independent communities. Priamur and Primorye lands attracted the more restless elements of the Ukrainian and Russian peasantry. Whatever their background, Far Easterners did not readily take to regimentation, and most of them had a low tolerance for bureaucrats.

Political dissidents and misfits continued to flow into the Far East after the establishment of Soviet rule. Mensheviks and SRs found a temporary refuge in Vladivostok.[2] Trotskyists were well represented in the Far Eastern Party organization and CER administration,[3] as were sympathizers of Evgeny Preobrazhensky, a former Chita activist and erstwhile Central Committee member who openly questioned Stalin's qualifications and in 1923 called for a restoration of democracy within the Party. Reinforcing the centrifugal dynamic, Stalin's Central Committee secretariat moved opponents from metropolitan to provincial posts. Two members of the Zinoviev faction who were expelled from the Party at the Fifteenth Congress in 1927, Deputy Gosplan Chairman Ivar Smilga and Komsomol Secretary Oskar Tarkhanov, found themselves assigned to new duties in the Far East. Smilga was named director of the Far Eastern Bank (Dalbank), and Tarkhanov was seconded to the Special Far Eastern Army.[4] Several thousand demonstrators, including Trotsky and Zinoviev, showed up at Moscow's Yaroslavl Station when Smilga embarked for Khabarovsk. There were analogous displays of sympathy in the Primorye.[5]

As oppositionists found niches in Far Eastern Party and state organs, particularly in those dealing with trade and finance, they came into contact with an impressionable rank and file, almost half of whom were illiterate.[6] Few Far Eastern Communists had even glanced at the works of Marx or Lenin, but Trotsky's "Lessons of October" circulated widely, and oppositionist appeals for intra-Party democracy struck a chord among younger comrades.[7]

Stalin and his entourage had no intention of letting oppositionists entrench themselves in the Far East, but for most of the 1920s Moscow was not always able to assert its will on the periphery. Although never openly opposed, Central Committee decrees that impinged upon the interests of provincial cliques were imaginatively emasculated amid gestures of sedulous compliance. For example, in 1924 the Central Committee instructed Dalbiuro to root out Trotskyism among young Communists throughout the Far East. Dalbiuro duly denounced "Lessons of October" and removed expendable Trotskyists from the regional Komsomol organization. When a Central Committee apparatchik, Andrei Andreyev, arrived in Khabarovsk to verify that Moscow's instructions were being carried out, Dalbiuro in a show of zeal launched a noisy campaign to "liquidate political illiteracy." "Political literacy schools" sprouted in Vladivostok and Khabarovsk while peripatetic "illiteracy liquidators" scoured the countryside for signs of the Trotskyist heresy. Privately, however, Dalbiuro Secretary Kubiak dismissed the whole campaign as empty phrase-mongering.[8]

Oppositionists posed less of a challenge to Stalin in the Far East than did emerging regional networks whose members paid lip service to Moscow while consolidating their local power. Far Eastern delegations to Party congresses in Moscow between 1919 and 1921 were made up of roughhewn men of action — partisans and underground operatives — rather than bureaucrats. After 1921 many of these delegates assumed administrative positions, to which they brought a dislike of paperwork, an impatience with procedural formalities, and a distrust of rhetoric.[9]

Vasily Blücher, former FER war minister and NRA commander, possessed qualities that appealed to such men. His directness and fairness had won him the dedication of his teamworkers in 1921–22: Albert Lapin, Yakov Pokus, Konstantin Pshenitsyn, Rafail Shishlyannikov, Mikhail Volsky, and Boris Melnikov. His absence from the Far East between 1922 and 1929 did not break up this team. Lapin accompanied Blücher to China. Melnikov went into the diplomatic service but kept in touch with Blücher as consul-general in Harbin. Pokus, Pshenitsyn, Shishlyannikov, and Volsky took up posts in Dalrevkom, while retaining their positions in Dalbiuro. Pokus commanded army units in the Priamur. Pshenitsyn became deputy chairman of the Primorye revkom. Shishlyannikov chaired the Sakhalin revkom. Volsky headed the Kamchatka and then the Priamur OGPU.[10]

Less than a year elapsed between the departure of Blücher in 1922 and the arrival of Yan Gamarnik from the Ukraine in 1923. As Gamarnik succeeded Kobozev as chairman of Dalrevkom in 1924 and then Kubiak as secretary of Dalkraikom in 1927, he built up a personal network and in the process "inherited" local members of Blücher's team.

Gamarnik: Network and Projects

One of Stalin's luckier cronies, Anastas Mikoyan, remarked in 1967 that Gamarnik had used the Far East as a base for a political career.[11] No novice in the art of political survival, Mikoyan neglected to mention that Gamarnik's career strategy made no provision for pretence, sycophancy, or chumminess. Even with colleagues he maintained a certain distance, addressing all but a handful with the formal "you." Yet he inspired trust and loyalty by making himself accessible, knowing how to listen, and treating subordinates as individuals.[12]

When Gamarnik arrived in the Far East in 1923, Party-soviet and Center-periphery relationships were in transition. The Far Eastern Party organ Dalbiuro, renamed Dalkraikom on 16 November 1925, was assuming powers hitherto wielded by Dalrevkom, reconstituted as the Far Eastern Executive Committee, or Dalkraiispolkom, on 4 January 1926. At the same time Moscow was seeking to extend its control over the Far Eastern periphery by displacing provincial cliques. While allowing regional Party conferences to elect their own committees, Moscow started appointing and dismissing regional secretaries and using the Party Control Commission to scrutinize the activities of provincial comrades.[13] Gamarnik was the major beneficiary of these dynamics. As chairman of Dalrevkom and first secretary of Dalkraikom, he held the reins of regional networks. As a full member of the Central Committee, he had direct access to Stalin.[14]

Gamarnik's position at the top of both Party and state hierarchies facilitated his consolidation of a regional power base. The offices of Dalkraikom and Dalkraiispolkom were accommodated in the same Khabarovsk building, a spatial arrangement reflecting their overlapping membership. Since the full Party and executive committees convened only two or three times annually, day-to-day business was handled by Gamarnik, assisted by members of Blücher's old team and a newcomer, Georgy Krutov. Though in time Gamarnik brought his own team from the Ukraine, on a personal basis he was closest to Pshenitsyn, reserving for him alone the familiar "thee."[15]

Gamarnik's regional network embraced not only Party activists and administrators but also teachers, agronomists, engineers, journalists, scholars, and members of national minorities with whom he came in contact in villages, factories, mines, schools, and garrisons from Transbaikalia to Kamchatka. Endowed with a rare ability to spot talent, he personally recruited hundreds of people for a Far Eastern encyclopedia and a Far Eastern Olympiad.[16]

Scarcely any major economic, social, scientific, or cultural initiative was undertaken in the Far East between 1923 and 1928 without Yan Gamarnik's direct participation. Constantly on the move, he studied local conditions in order to make the Far East secure and self-supporting. He felt that through foreign investment and international trade the Far East could develop without help from or control by the Center. Arguing that regional development was a regional responsibility, Gamarnik criticized Moscow bureaucrats for their ignorance of Far Eastern conditions and took steps to enlist Japanese and Chinese expertise to promote regional development. In 1926 he invited economists from Beijing and Tokyo to Khabarovsk for a conference on how best to realize the Far East's economic potential. Convinced that exports of timber, fish, and rice could finance imports of ships, agricultural machinery, and canning equipment, Gamarnik channeled investment into forestry and fisheries industries and expanded rice cultivation around Lake Khanka with the Japanese market in mind.[17]

For Gamarnik, economic engagement with the Pacific was inseparable from colonization and improved transport. In 1925 he had Dalrevkom prepare a Far Eastern ten-year plan that envisioned the resettlement of 400,000 peasants from his native Ukraine, the upgrading of the Amur and Ussuri rail lines, the construction of a railroad from Khabarovsk to Sovetskaya Gavan, the expansion of port facilities at Vladivostok, and the establishment of a Far Eastern merchant marine.[18] This program got under way in 1926. About 30,000 settlers arrived during the first year. The Khabarovsk-Sovetskaya Gavan railroad route was surveyed, and a small merchant marine created. Trade with China and Japan reached levels in 1928 that would not be seen again until after the Second World War.[19]

Although he applauded the installation of American equipment in Vladivostok's radio station in 1925, Gamarnik was no cosmopolitan. He stripped the Amur Society of its vestigial independence, subordinated all cultural organizations to Dalrevkom, and dissolved the non-Communist press. Presiding over a Khabarovsk conference of journalists in 1925 with the Central Committee's press chief, Yosif Vareikis, Gamarnik stressed the strategic importance of Party guidance on a sensitive borderland.

Tenuous control of rural areas convinced Gamarnik of the urgency of achieving universal literacy, a formidable task in a region where only 37 percent of adults could read in 1923. Undeterred, Gamarnik launched teacher-training programs in Khabarovsk, Vladivostok, and Blagoveshchensk. It was not long before cultural shock troops began fanning out to remote hamlets, armed largely with enthusiasm, to establish "illiteracy liquidation bases" (*likbazy*).[20] Special efforts were directed toward the "little peoples of the North," for according to Education Commissar Lunacharsky not a single Orok, Nivkh, Nanai, Chukcha, Koryak, Kamchadal, Evenk, Eskimo, Aleut, Yukagir, or Negidal was capable of reading or speaking Russian properly.[21] To catapult the "little peoples" from "feudalism" to "socialism," Gamarnik in 1924 created within Dalrevkom the Committee for Assistance to Peoples of Northern Borderlands under the chairmanship of his friend Karl Luks, a Latvian and former partisan and NRA commander in Transbaikalia.[22] In 1925 Luks and Gamarnik set up a Pedagogical Institute for Peoples of the North in Khabarovsk.* That year they convened the First Congress of Far Eastern Aborigines.[23] Gamarnik stressed the importance of recruiting "little peoples" into the Party, asserting that in the event of war they would be the Red Army's best sharpshooters.[24]

The most visible fruits of the Luks-Gamarnik effort were effusive expressions of gratitude from showcase aborigines like Tevlyanto, Chukcha delegate to the Supreme Soviet. Judging from the earnest palaver about "nomadic soviets," in which Party pedagogues recited Marxist-Leninist catechisms while tagging along with reindeer herds, the campaign for universal literacy produced intellectual semi-literacy without doing much to eliminate venereal disease, tuberculosis, or trachoma.[25] Real conditions in aboriginal communities belied official rhetoric, because social and cultural realities did not fit Marxist categories.[26] Human nature as usual proved resistant to social engineering. Natives were more interested in provisions than in pamphlets, and many were prone to see modern technology through their own cultural prism. When a radio station at Uelen stood unused because no one could operate the equipment, local Chukchi concluded that the antenna was a Soviet totem pole.[27]

Departure Without Discontinuity

After five years and five months in the Far East, Gamarnik left in November 1928 for Minsk to become first secretary of the Belorussian Party Com-

---

*Affiliated with the Leningrad Institute of Peoples of the North, then directed by Pyotr Smidovich. The institute opened in 1927 with forty-three students (twelve Kamchadals, twelve Yakuts, eleven Tungus, four Nivkhi, one Yukagir, one Nanai, one Aleut, and one Eskimo). It moved to Nikolaevsk in 1932 and was taken over by the Northern Sea Route Administration in 1935.

mittee. He was appointed Army Political Administration head (October 1929) and Deputy Defense Commissar (June 1930), overseeing the delicate assignment of maintaining army discipline during forced collectivization. These rapid promotions suggest that Gamarnik had earned the trust of the Politburo (dominated but not yet controlled by Stalin) for engineering Dalkrai's economic recovery, eradicating White remnants, and denouncing oppositionists at the Fifteenth Party Congress (1927).[28]

Gamarnik retained personal links with the Far East after leaving the region. His successor as Dalkraikom secretary turned out to be a personal friend and fellow veteran of the Odessa underground, Ivan Perepechko. More important, appointed chairman of the Special Commission for Far Eastern Development and Defense in 1931, Gamarnik traveled frequently to Dalkrai as a plenipotentiary of the Politburo. Between 1931 and 1936 he spent four to six months annually in a specially equipped rail car keeping in touch with a dispersed Far Eastern constituency.[29]

The team that Gamarnik had led during 1923–28 was "reinherited" by Blücher, who returned to the Far East in 1929. By fostering a cohort held together by common civil war experiences, personal friendships, and shared views on regional development, Gamarnik and Blücher prepared the foundations for an autonomous power base on the Pacific.

19

« « » »

Red-Bannered Satraps

[Blücher] had none of the traits associated with
Bolsheviks.   — Chiang Kai-shek (1957)

As guardians of an imperial outpost on the Pacific, the military had special stature in the Russian Far East. The Priamur governor-generals, army officers all save one, behaved like satraps.[1] Soviet leaders built on this tradition by creating in 1929 the Special Far Eastern Army (OKDVA), which bestrode a quarter of the USSR, attracted a formidable concentration of talent, and shaped the region's economy, society, and culture.*

Led by Vasily Blücher, the OKDVA exuded an esprit not unlike that of the British Indian Army or the Kwantung Army that controlled Manchuria (1932–45).[2] First-hand contact with Far Eastern conditions bred an awareness of regional needs and in some cases a readiness to champion policies at variance with those of the Center. A committed Communist, Blücher nonetheless felt the undertow of regional attachments. According to his Khabarovsk-born second wife, he "passionately loved the Far East" and "never sought work in the central part of the country."[3]

Birth of the Special Far Eastern Army

Military units east of Lake Baikal underwent periodic reorganizations during the early 1920s, reflecting the dissolution of the FER, demobiliza-

---

*It was called Osobaya Dalnevostochnaya Armiya (ODVA) until "Red-bannered" (krasnoznamennaya) was added on 1 Jan. 1930. According to GVVI (1987), p. 69, the "O" of OKDVA stood not for Osobaya ("special") but for Otdelnaya ("separate"). Eight OKDVA "alumni" achieved the rank of Marshal of the Soviet Union: Leonid Brezhnev, Vasily Chuikov, Ivan

tion, and the struggle between Trotsky and Stalin. As international tensions in Northeast Asia relaxed after 1923, the Far East became something of a military backwater. The number of troops fell from 80,000 in 1922 to fewer than 20,000 in 1925, as Khabarovsk slipped from military stronghold to a secondary garrison town within the Siberian Military District.[4]

Friction with a Manchurian warlord over the CER paved the way for regional rearmament. Although Stalin was once credited with creation of the Special Far Eastern Army,[5] the idea originated with the Red Army's chief of operations, Mikhail Tukhachevsky, who in July 1929 ordered a survey of Far Eastern frontiers and presented the results to the Revolutionary Military Council. A month later, the council announced the formation of the Special Far Eastern Army under Blücher.[6]

No senior officer possessed Blücher's experience in Northeast Asia. In 1921–22, he had turned the NRA into a credible force, which proved itself against Molchanov at Volochayevka. As head of the Soviet military mission to China during 1924–27, Blücher became something of a legend under the alias "Galen"[*] and retained Chiang Kai-shek's high regard after the Soviet-trained leader of the Guomindang (Nationalist Party) broke with Moscow in 1927. Blücher brought to the Far East a team that had worked with him at various times in the Urals and Transbaikalia during 1918–22. Mikhail Kalmykov and Grigory Khakhanian became OKDVA corps commanders. Lazar Aronshtam was appointed OKDVA political commissar. Vitovt Putna, after a stint as military attaché in Tokyo, assumed command of OKDVA forces in the Primorye. Mikhail Sangursky acted as OKDVA liaison officer with Dalkraikom. Albert Lapin became OKDVA chief of staff. Putna, Sangursky, and Lapin had accompanied Blücher to China and were known as "Blücher's pupils."[7] The OKDVA commander inspired loyalty beyond his immediate circle by an unfeigned concern for the welfare of subordinates. Distance from Moscow's hot-house atmosphere and proximity to potential war zones gave Blücher breathing space to test new ideas about strategy and to concentrate on combat rather than politics.[8]

Konev, Nikolai Krylov, Rodion Malinovsky, Konstantin Rokossovsky, Aleksandr Vasilevsky, and Georgy Zhukov. An OKDVA tank school political commissar in 1935, Brezhnev acquired his marshalship in 1976, according to wits, "for taking the Kremlin."

[*]"Galen" derived from the given name of Blücher's first wife, Galina Pavlovna Pokrovskaya (also known as Galina Aleksandrovna Kolchugina), whom he divorced while in China. The orthography followed that of a French journalist.

The CER Campaign, 1929

Russian prerogatives on the Chinese Eastern Railroad dated from 1896, when Beijing and St. Petersburg signed an agreement to build and operate a line across Manchuria. The October Revolution did not dislodge the Harbin-based CER administration, whose political complexion remained distinctly White. Although Moscow renounced tsarist concessions in China in 1919, it soon asserted proprietary claims to the CER and in 1924 concluded an agreement with the Beijing government (one of two governments in China at the time) putting the CER under joint Sino-Soviet management. Playing off Beijing, Moscow, and Tokyo, Manchuria's warlord Zhang Zuolin turned a blind eye to White Russian harassment of Soviet CER employees. As nationalism swept across China in 1928 in the wake of Chiang Kai-shek's Northern Expedition against refractory warlords and erstwhile Communist allies, Zhang's son and successor, Zhang Xueliang, tried to squeeze Soviets out of the CER administration. Defense Commissar Kliment Voroshilov had wanted to march into northern Manchuria as early as 1926, but Stalin would not risk provoking Japan, whose restive Kwantung Army guarded the Kwantung Territory and the South Manchurian Railroad strip from Port Arthur to a small station about 125 miles south of Harbin. Only when Tokyo signaled that it would not object to a Soviet thrust into northern Manchuria did Stalin give Blücher the green light.

Commanding fewer than 30,000 troops and confronted with local peasant resistance to conscription, Blücher was obliged to import and improvise. Moscow sent him some "territorials" from Perm, Barnaul, Novosibirsk, and Tomsk, and five companies of Volga Germans.* To supplement these he raised a Buryat Mongol regiment and a battalion of Koreans.[9] Chinese-speaking DVGU alumni such as Vasily Voiloshnikov were mobilized as interpreters. With these heterogeneous forces, Blücher launched a series of strikes into Manchuria during October and November. Lapin took gunboats up the Sungari and Muleng rivers, while Vostretsov opened an air and ground offensive against Manchouli and Hailar. Zhang understood the language of force, and on 22 December his representatives signed a protocol at Khabarovsk reaffirming Soviet rights to the CER.[10]

The CER campaign attracted world attention and won Blücher plaudits

*"Territorials" were units of workers and peasants who spent part of each year in military service.

in the Soviet press, which reported that Chinese POWs boasted at having been captured by "General Galen."[11] When Blücher addressed the Sixteenth Party Congress at the Bolshoi Theater on 26 June 1930, he got a standing ovation.[12] Voroshilov pinned the Order of the Red Star on Blücher's tunic. Stalin sent him a Buick sedan and assigned the former Chinese consulate in Khabarovsk for his personal use.[13] But gratifying as the CER campaign was for Blücher, it had unsettling consequences. It stirred up popular feelings against local Chinese and precipitated some ugly incidents.[14] More important, by exposing Zhang's military weakness and international passivity in the face of aggression, it gave ideas to Kwantung Army activists.

The Manchurian Incident and Its Repercussions

Barely two years after Blücher had reasserted Soviet rights on the CER, the Kwantung Army turned Manchuria into a Japanese protectorate. Following a staged "incident" at Mukden on 18 September 1931, Japanese troops fanned out across Manchuria and in February 1932 entered Harbin, greeted by jubilant crowds of Russian émigrés. To cover the fruits of aggression with a fig leaf of legitimacy, the Kwantung Army created the puppet state of Manchukuo (see Map 8) and installed as its sovereign the last Manchu emperor.

Cautioned by Moscow not to intervene, Blücher and his staff watched Japan enlarge its continental base and confront Dalkrai with a strategic threat more serious than the ones that hung over the Russian Far East in 1904–5 and 1918–22. The Kwantung Army had advanced to the Amur and Ussuri rivers, leaving the Primorye dangerously exposed. Occupying Inner Mongolia in 1933–35, the Japanese positioned themselves to strike Transbaikalia and isolate Dalkrai. In mid-1932 the Kwantung Army fielded 130,000 troops bolstered by 127,000 "Manchukuoan" levies, vastly outnumbering the forces at Blücher's disposal, 90,000 OKDVA troops plus 20,000 border guards.[15] Manchukuo's population (30,000,000) dwarfed that of Dalkrai (800,000, including some 200,000 Koreans and Chinese).

Citing the Japanese threat, Blücher demanded massive reinforcements and discretionary powers. He got both. Between 1932 and 1936 the OKDVA grew from six to fourteen divisions.[16] Transbaikalia was detached to form a separate military district in 1935, but Blücher still commanded 300,000 men or 15 percent of the Red Army.[17] Blücher was also given broad powers to engineer economic and social development. He took full advan-

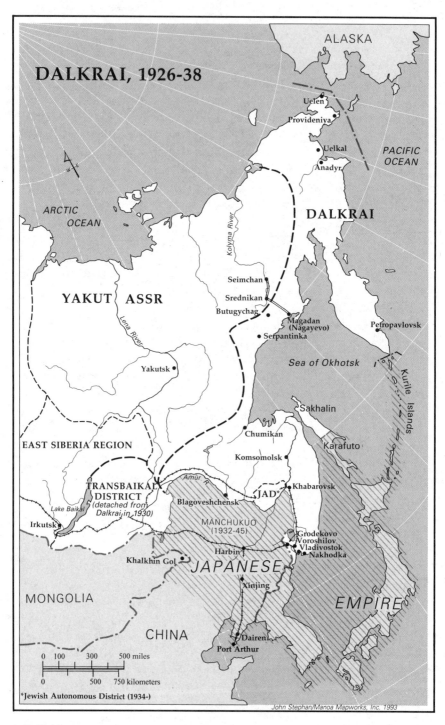

DALKRAI, 1926-38

ALASKA

Uelen

Provideniya

Uelkal

Anadyr.

PACIFIC
OCEAN

ARCTIC
OCEAN

DALKRAI

Kolyma River

Seimchan

Srednikan

Butugychag

Magadan
(Nagayevo)

Petropavlovsk

YAKUT ASSR

Serpantinka

Lena River

Yakutsk

Sea of Okhotsk

Kurile Islands

Sakhalin

Chumikan

EAST SIBERIA REGION

Komsomolsk

Karafuto

TRANSBAIKAL
DISTRICT
(detached from
Dalkrai in 1930)

Amur R.

JAD*

Khabarovsk

Blagoveshchensk

MANCHUKUO
(1932-45)

Lake Baikal

Irkutsk

Grodekovo
Voroshilov
Vladivostok
Nakhodka

Khalkhin Gol

Harbin

JAPANESE

MONGOLIA

Xinjing

EMPIRE

CHINA

Dairen

Port Arthur

0   100   300   500 miles

0   500   750 kilometers

*Jewish Autonomous District (1934-)

John Stephan/Manoa Mapworks, Inc. 1993

8. Dalkrai, 1926–38

tage of this mandate in partnership with Yan Gamarnik to overcome Dalkrai's demographic deficit. Far Eastern resettlement was disrupted during 1929 and 1930 by collectivization, but the pace picked up late in 1931. After 1933 entire collective farms were transferred from the central provinces. A million people (not including forced laborers) came to the Far East during 1931–39, one out of every three who crossed the Urals. This influx, together with a high fertility rate, made Dalkrai the fastest growing province in the Russian Republic, with a 1939 population (2,562,000, not including labor camp inmates) double that of 1926.[18]

Together with migration from rural areas to towns within the Priamur and the Primorye, immigration gave the Far East an urban and industrial character. Factory workers increased their share of the population from 2 percent in 1926 to 30 percent in 1940. Between 1926 and 1938 the population of Vladivostok nearly doubled (from 108,129 to 206,432), while that of Khabarovsk almost quadrupled (52,045 to 199,364). Komsomolsk, founded in 1932, had 71,000 inhabitants by 1939.[19]

Following the tsarist precedent of offering land and subsidies to keep military personnel in the Far East, Gamarnik set up an agency to settle demobilized troops and established army communes around Lake Khanka, providing them with livestock, timber rights, and exemption from taxes.[20] Blücher worked closely with Gamarnik to put soldiers on the land, setting aside choice acreage for OKDVA collective farms and making sure that they got the best equipment. He shared Gamarnik's view that the Far East should develop an independent economic base and that farmer-soldiers could help Dalkrai achieve self-sufficiency in foodstuffs.[21] To institutionalize an OKDVA link with the land, he proposed to the Politburo a plan to create a special collective farm corps, offering soldiers a chance to bring their families to the Far East. The Politburo approved the proposal on 17 March 1932, giving birth to a special OKDVA unit, the Kolkhoz Corps, under the command of Mikhail Kalmykov, a member of Blücher's inner circle. In addition to "rooting" the OKDVA in the Far East, the Kolkhoz Corps served as a vehicle to train political commissars for regular OKDVA units.[22]

Birth of the Pacific Fleet

Early Soviet attempts to establish a naval presence in the Pacific fell victim to a gap between conception and achievement. As NRA troops approached Vladivostok in 1922, the Central Committee apparat worked out a plan to assemble a Pacific squadron by repairing available vessels, but when welders and fitters reached the Golden Horn, they found no ships to repair. Undiscouraged, they cabled Moscow: "People's Revolutionary Fleet will direct its efforts to laying the basis of naval power in the Pacific."[23] "Laying the basis" took over a decade. Only in 1924 did the "fleet" acquire its first vessel, the fugitive yacht *Admiral Zavoiko*, in Shanghai. When Japan seized Mukden seven years later, Dalkrai naval forces consisted of four gunboats, one salvaged minelayer, and two refurbished river steamers, a state of affairs that ensured Moscow's inactivity during the Manchurian crisis.[24] The establishment of the Pacific Fleet is commonly dated to 21 April 1932, when the "Commander of Maritime Forces in the Far East," Mikhail Viktorov, issued an order reorganizing the meager units in his bailiwick.[25] Later, Viktorov sardonically recorded his impressions of these forces upon arriving in Vladivostok: "There was a commander, there was also a Pacific, but no Pacific Fleet."[26]

What there was of the Pacific Fleet owed much to Weimar Germany and Fascist Italy. From 1926 to 1933 German military engineers upgraded naval installations at Vladivostok and taught Soviet apprentices how to operate German submarines shipped across Siberia on flatcars.[27] When the Germans left after the advent of Hitler in 1933, Moscow placed an order for submarines with an Italian firm and sent Vladimir Kukel (head of the OGPU maritime border guards and grandson of the Amur navigator Nevelskoi) to Genoa to negotiate the sale. Mussolini approved the deal, and "Lenin-class" Italian submarines reached Vladivostok in 1934. When Stalin noted at the Seventeenth Party Congress that relations with Rome "have indisputably become satisfactory," he probably had naval cooperation in mind.[28]

The Italian connection did not survive the Abyssinian War (1935–36), leaving the Pacific Fleet a weak instrument in Stalin's quadrille with China, Japan, and the United States during the remainder of the decade. By itself, the Fleet did not pose a credible deterrent against Japanese expansion in China, but Moscow seems to have calculated that a gesture of association with the U.S. Navy might give Tokyo pause. Accordingly, within three weeks of the outbreak of Sino-Japanese hostilities at Marco Polo Bridge on 7 July 1937, the U.S. Asiatic Fleet paid a courtesy call at Vladivostok. As the five-vessel American squadron led by the cruiser *Augusta* traversed Peter the Great Bay on 28 July, it was escorted by the destroyer *Stalin* to the Golden Horn. Asiatic Fleet Commander Admiral Harry Ervin Yarnell was greeted by Pacific Fleet Commander Grigory Kireyev (Viktorov had been appointed Navy Commissar a month previously), Fleet Political Commissar Georgy Okunev, chairman of the Vladivostok executive committee, a representative of the Commissariat of Foreign Affairs, and the American military attaché Colonel Philip R. Faymonville. For five days (28 July–1 August), the Russians and Americans entertained each other with banquets, music, and sports (soccer and softball). Yarnell and Kireyev did not, however, engage in substantive talks about an object of mutual concern — Japan.* Soviet-American fraternization at Vladivostok caught Tokyo's eye but did not slow the Imperial Army's advance into China.[29]

Overlapping Networks

Shielded by distance from Moscow, commanding a special army, glorified by settlements and collective farms that bore his name, Blücher struck some observers as a regional dictator.[30] Appearances notwithstanding, Dalkrai was controlled by overlapping local networks loyal to Gamarnik as well as to Blücher. Gamarnik wielded power in the Far East through the army political commissariat and regional Party and state organs. His network was reinforced by the arrival of new appointees from the Ukraine. Dalkraikom First Secretaries Perepechko and Lavrenty Lavrentiev had both worked with Gamarnik in Kiev and Odessa in the revolutionary underground and fought together in the civil war. Lavrentiev had shared a prison cell with Gamarnik and maintained close ties thereafter.[31]

Although it is not clear when Gamarnik first met Blücher, they developed a mutual respect and perhaps affection.[32] Their acquaintance could have dated from the first half of 1921, when Blücher commanded the Odessa garrison. They may have been introduced by Ivan Fedko, who befriended both men, having commanded a division in which Gamarnik was political commissar in 1919 and worked under Blücher in the NRA in 1921. Blücher and Gamarnik were also linked by men who worked at various times with them between 1918 and 1937 in the Ukraine, the Urals, the Far East, and China.[33]

---

*As a member of the Navy Planning Committee in 1918, Harry Yarnell sent to the Chief of Naval Operations a memo opining that: "A possible solution [to Japanese-American rivalry over Pacific islands] might be to give Japan a free hand in Eastern Siberia. This is a territory very sparsely settled by Russians, and was acquired by Russia under the old methods of exploration and announcement of ownership. . . . It must be born in mind that it is of vital interest to the United States to turn Japan toward the continent of Asia." David Hunter Miller, *My Diary at the Conference of Paris* (New York: Appeal, 1924), 2:101–7. I am grateful to John Charles Schencking for calling this memo to my attention.

From 1929 until 1937, Far Eastern security organs were headed by Terenty Deribas who, like Gamarnik, was Jewish and from Odessa. Deribas cooperated with Blücher and Gamarnik on questions of internal security and foreign intelligence. For helping Deribas to intercept Japanese agents infiltrating Dalkrai from Manchukuo, Blücher was awarded the title "honorary chekist" (*pochyotny chekist*).* Tapping the reservoir of prisoners under his jurisdiction, Deribas supplied Blücher and Gamarnik with labor for construction projects. At a lower level OGPU border guards lived in OKDVA communes, while Komsomol and Party cells in OGPU units came under the jurisdiction of Dalkraikom.[34] Starting in 1932, Gamarnik, Blücher, and Deribas collaborated in building an industrial base on the Amur christened "Komsomolsk" in honor of *komsomoltsy* who came to the Far East from throughout the Soviet Union looking for a radiant future. By a happy coincidence, Deribas's son Andrei happened to be a Komsomol secretary. This father-son team set the tone for a selectively publicized saga. While Andrei posed with earnest young Communist shock brigaders for the edification of domestic and international audiences, Terenty unobtrusively saw to it that tens of thousands of expendable Cossacks, religious sectarians, "kulaks," Mensheviks, SRs, ex-Communists (political etiquette required that expulsion from the Party precede arrest), and common criminals fulfilled their work norms.[35]

Relations between the OGPU and the OKDVA were complicated by the fact that the former bore responsibility for monitoring the loyalty of the latter. Tensions that might have arisen from this circumstance seem to have been kept in check by Deribas's acquiescence to Blücher's authority. The chekist-army relationship came under strain after 1934 under the influence of an escalating vigilance campaign to unmask internal enemies. Ironically, the media exerted itself to cultivate an image of interservice fraternity. In May 1937, as the security organs prepared to liquidate "traitors" among OKDVA officers, *Pravda* hailed chekist wives for liquidating illiteracy among OKDVA conscripts.[36]

Pogranichnik, 10 (1976): 87, cited in Ianguzov, *Zabven'ia net*, p. 284. From circumstantial evidence, the award was conferred in 1935 or 1936. Blücher does not appear to have taken part in Deribas's major intelligence coup: the recruitment in 1930 of Izumi Kōzō (1890–1956), a Russian specialist at the Japanese consulate in Blagoveshchensk, who served as an informant in Japan and abroad until 1952. Japan, Keishichō, Kōanbu (Police Office, Public Security Division), "Rasutoborofu jiken sōkatsu" (Conspectus of the Rastvorov Incident). Typescript. April 1969, pp. 302–17. Provided courtesy of Hata Ikuhiko.

« « » »

Building Socialism on the Pacific

Forward! To blindingly bright, shimmering summits of a
Communist tomorrow, a cloudless world of human joys.
— Khabarovsk Agitprop refrain (1939)

The Far East occupied a special niche
in the firmament of national myths
during the decade of "socialist construction" (1928–38). In addition to
scaling the heights of collectivization and industrialization, Far Easterners
were cast in heroic roles played out in exotic milieux. Komsomoltsy transformed tiger-infested taiga into a modern city. Pogranichniki defended far-
flung frontiers from Chinese bandits and Japanese "samurai." Geologists
unlocked Nature's secrets in arctic tundra. Dalkrai role models cropped up
regularly in the media: chekists tutoring aborigines, Stakhanovites boiling
whale blubber, and "little peoples" graduates of the "Tent of Miracles"
expressing gratitude to Comrade Stalin for their happy lives.* Behind these
bracing images, Dalkrai offered a study in contrasts between public triumphs and private tragedies, herd morality and solitary courage.

Five-Year Plans and Collectivization

Distance, competing priorities, and a shortage of capital and trained
cadres blunted the impact of the First Five-Year Plan (1928–32) on the Far

---

*"Stakhanovites," a term coined in 1935 in honor of the Donbass coal miner Aleksandr Stakha-
nov (1905–77), was conferred on workers for norm-breaking output. The "Tent of Miracles"
was a name for the Institute of Peoples of the North in Leningrad whose most celebrated role
model at this time was the Chukcha Tevlyanto, Chairman of the Chukotka Executive Committee and delegate to the Supreme Soviet.

East. The plan allocated over a billion rubles (about 5 percent of total capital investment in the USSR) to Dalkrai, an amount supposedly exceeding total investment in the Far East between 1847 and 1917, but less than a third of what was allocated to Western Siberia. Expected to exploit oil, coal, and gold while becoming self-sufficient in foodstuffs, Dalkrai met none of its targets.[1]

Japan's seizure of Manchuria boosted the Far East's priority in the Second Five-Year Plan (1933–37). Moscow allocated over seven billion rubles to Dalkrai, 10 percent of total national investment, for among other things a metallurgical base at Komsomolsk, a Baikal-Amur railroad, and sea and air routes to the Center.[2] Formal responsibility for overseeing the second plan in Dalkrai was invested in Yosif Kosior, Far Eastern plenipotentiary of the Council of People's Commissars, but practical work was handled by Gamarnik, Blücher, Deribas, Dalkraikom Secretary Lavrentiev, Dalkraiispolkom Chairman Krutov, and Krutov's assistant, Elizar Raikhman.

As we have seen, efforts to transform Far Eastern rural society from 1923 to 1927 foundered on resistance to social engineering and weak grass-roots support for land redistribution. Warned by Gamarnik against alienating middle peasants, authorities toned down the anti-kulak offensive in 1925, leaving many villages with their traditional social structures and property ownership virtually intact.[3] This laissez-faire attitude came under assault in early 1928 when Stalin toured Western Siberia and told local leaders to adopt tougher attitudes toward "kulaks," intimating that extraordinary measures should be taken to deal with "sabotage" of grain deliveries.[4] At first Far Eastern officials did nothing, but the consequences of inaction made themselves painfully manifest by the end of the year, when only 15 percent of the region's grain plan had been fulfilled.[5] After Stalin called for the employment of the "Uralo-Siberian method of grain collection" in April 1929, Dalkraiispolkom mobilized trade union and Komsomol activists to expropriate grain and livestock and began forcing peasants into communes. At this time the Khudyakov family farm outside Razdolnoye was turned into a kolkhoz. The Khudyakov brothers did not resist, but others did. Peasants burned grain, destroyed livestock, set up cosmetic communes, or turned rural soviets into anti-Communist forums. Party activists were attacked and in some cases killed.[6]

Retribution was quick and harsh. Liquidating 131 "kulak bands" in 1929 alone, chekists machine-gunned peasants, took hostages, executed suspects, and exiled survivors.[7] Repression moved into high gear in November 1929,

with the Central Committee's order to Dalkraikom to carry out "total collectivization" by 1932. Although Stalin's "Dizzy with Success" speech (2
March 1930) prompted the Central Committee to instruct regional Party
secretaries to rein in overzealous comrades, Deribas went on crushing real
or putative uprisings.[8] On 28 June 1931, seventy-five Amur peasants were
tried by a troika and shot. In 1933 the OGPU uncovered "conspiracies"
among Amur Cossacks and Old Believers and destroyed a "Worker-Peasant
Party." Between 1929 and 1935 the OGPU killed 6,000 peasants and Cossacks and forcibly relocated 30,000 survivors to Yakutia and Kazakhstan.[9]

Rural unrest afforded Arseniev's nemesis Albert Lipsky an opportunity
to upgrade his chekist credentials. As plenipotentiary of aboriginal affairs
along the lower Amur from 1924 to 1938, Lipsky had the authority to
suppress local "uprisings" (a catchword for lack of enthusiasm for collectivization). In April 1931 the "ethnographer with a pistol" (as he was called)
conducted a pacification campaign in the Chumikan district, dispensing
summary justice with a mobile troika and spraying stray indigenes from the
air with a hand-held machine-gun.[10]

The OKDVA took part in these "anti-kulak" operations, putting Gamarnik and Blücher in a delicate position.[11] As chief of the Army Political
Administration Gamarnik bore responsibility for ideological discipline in a
force made up predominantly of peasant conscripts. Although Gamarnik
did not relish using violence against peasants, he appears to have kept his
own counsel. But Blücher spoke out, warning Moscow that unless Far
Eastern peasants were exempted from further levies, he could not be responsible for the security of the Primorye. Whether or not as a result of
Blücher's bluntness, Moscow lowered Dalkrai grain quotas.[12]

Blücher's intervention only marginally attenuated the human suffering
and economic losses wrought by "dekulakization" between 1929 and 1938.
The campaign broke up and expelled the region's most productive peasant
households. Tens of thousands of men, women, and children were torn
from their homes and loaded onto special trains bound for logging camps,
mines, and construction sites. Thousands sought refuge in the taiga. From
10,000 to 50,000 Soviet Koreans migrated to Manchukuo's Jiandao District
north of the Tumen River.[13] Cossacks, religious sectarians, and Buryat
Mongols also found new homes in Manchukuo.[14] Soviet "boat people"
turned up in Hokkaido.[15]

The Khudyakov brothers and their dependents could count themselves
fortunate. Although all of their possessions were confiscated, no one was

shot. Husbands, wives, and children were transported to the upper Zeya River in 1930, where local authorities scattered the family among collective farms. Shortly before his death in 1939, Yustin Khudyakov managed to steal away from the Stalin Kolkhoz long enough to take one last look at the family farm where he had grown up and spent the best years of his life.[16]

A Far Eastern Jewish Homeland

The idea of creating a Jewish homeland in Soviet Russia sprang from practical motives: to find work for unemployed Jews, to counter Zionist proclivities within the Party's Jewish Section, and to extract hard currency from overseas Jews.[17] The Jewish Section preferred Crimea while giving consideration to the Ukraine and Kazakhstan, but the Agriculture and Defense commissariats favored the Far East because of its untenanted acreage and strategic location. At first doubtful, Stalin eventually gave the Far East the nod. Surveys began in 1925, focusing on 13,000 square miles west of Khabarovsk thinly populated by 34,000 people — of whom 70 percent were Russians, 20 percent Ukrainians, and 7 percent Koreans. Adjacent lands along the Amur had been settled in the 1860s by Transbaikal Cossacks, and sixty years later their descendants still tilled the soil. Consequently, Jewish immigrants were concentrated on lands along the Amur Railroad. Internal colonization was administered by the government's Committee for Settling Jewish Workers on the Land, while an ostensibly private organization called the Society for Settling Jewish Workers mobilized foreign financial support and arranged visits by, among others, the president of the University of Utah. The Birobidzhan National District was formally created in 1930, named after the Amur tributaries Bira and Bidzhan. Its capital was Tikhonkaya Stantsiya (renamed Birobidzhan), 100 miles west of Khabarovsk where the Amur Line crosses the Bira River.[18]

Birobidzhan evoked mixed feelings among would-be constituents. Jewish Party officials who had pushed for a Crimean homeland were less than enthusiastic, and Jewish intellectuals deplored Birobidzhan's remote location (the closest Jewish community was in Harbin, 300 miles up the Sungari) and inhospitable climate. Yan Gamarnik refrained from public comment, but Ilya Ehrenburg called Birobidzhan a new ghetto. Fewer than half of the 20,000 arrivals between 1928 and 1933 stayed.[19] During these years Birobidzhan attracted 1,400 Jews from the United States, Lithuania, England, Argentina, and Palestine, many of whom worked on a collective farm called Waldheim. A Los Angeles educator, Charles Kuntz, organized the American Association for Jewish Colonization in the Soviet Union (IKOR) and spent a year in Birobidzhan as chairman of the IKOR kolkhoz.[20]

Moscow tried to revive demographic momentum by upgrading the national district to the Jewish Autonomous District (oblast) in 1934 (see Map 8), and by sending Politburo member Lazar Kaganovich to inspect and act as "guardian" of the region in 1936. The proportion of Jews declined after peaking at 23 percent in 1936, and the Second Five-Year Plan ended in 1937 with 19,000 Jews in Birobidzhan against a projected 150,000.* Of some 20,000 Jewish refugees from Germany and Poland arriving between 1936 and 1941, most went on to Shanghai.[21]

Epics of Transport

Distance posed a perennial obstacle to the development, security, and control of the eastern periphery. In the struggle against space, the tsarist regime had relied on railroads and telegraph while experimenting with arctic navigation. The Soviet regime proclaimed the conquest of distance in a series of transport extravaganzas but by 1941 had made only moderate progress toward overcoming the Far East's isolation from European Russia.

The Northern Sea Route cut the maritime distance from European Russia to the Far East by half. Vladivostok lay 16,800 miles from Kronstadt via Suez but only 8,100 miles from Arkhangelsk via the Bering Strait. Interrupted by revolution and civil war, arctic navigation resumed in the 1920s, when the polar explorer and scientist Otto Schmidt carried machinery on German freighters to Ob and Yenisei river ports and brought back cargoes of Siberian grain. In 1932 Schmidt organized the first single-season run from Arkhangelsk to Vladivostok on the icebreaker *Aleksandr Sibiryakov*.† Later that year he was appointed head of the Northern Sea Route Administration, which assumed responsibility for arctic shipping, Taimyr salt

*From 5,000 Jews (11% of the region's population) in 1931, the figure climbed to 7,500 (15%) in 1934, and 18,000 (23%) in 1936. Their representation fell off significantly in the postwar period: 14,300 (9%) in 1959; 11,500 (7%) in 1970; 10,200 (5%) in 1979; 9,000 (4%) in 1990. Pinkus, *Jews of the Soviet Union*, p. 75; Levin, *Jews in the Soviet Union*, pp. 290, 896.

†Built in 1909, the ship was named after a Siberian merchant who had financed a similar expedition by the Swedish navigator A. E. Nordenskiöld in 1878–79. At the time of the *Aleksandr Sibiryakov*'s historic voyage in 1932, the ship's namesake was an indigent émigré in Nice.

mines, and Kamchatka canneries.[22] The Northern Sea Route captured world attention in February 1934, when the icebreaker *Chelyuskin* was trapped and crushed off Chukotka on its maiden voyage. In a dramatic rescue operation, Soviet pilots located the stricken ship, landed on the ice, and ferried out crew, dogs, and equipment.[23]

Dramatizing Soviet heroism and technology, the *Chelyuskin* rescue triggered a series of high visibility exploits across Far Eastern skies. By 1938 transcontinental and transpolar flights had made the names Levanevsky, Chkalov, and Osipenko household words. By 1939 all three aviators had perished in crashes, testifying obliquely to the chanciness of a form of transportation in which every passenger could feel like a hero. "Regular" flights between Khabarovsk and Moscow, inaugurated in 1934, in principle took three days to complete but in practice featured leisurely, unscheduled stopovers owing to weather conditions, mechanical problems, navigational errors, and red tape. When given a choice, Blücher and Gamarnik traveled by train.

Convinced that railroads were indispensable to Dalkrai's security, Blücher and Gamarnik were stunned to learn in 1932 that Stalin planned to sell the CER in order to remove a source of friction with Japan. For Blücher, giving up the line made the 1929 Manchurian campaign meaningless and deprived the OKDVA of an invaluable base for collecting intelligence about China and Japan. Nonetheless, Moscow sold the line to Manchukuo in 1935 for less than it had cost to build.[24]

At that point, Moscow had already decided to build a railroad of its own north of and parallel to the eastern section of the Trans-Siberian Line under the catchy acronym BAM (Baikal-Amur Mainline). To fill manpower needs, the OGPU prepared a cluster of camps (Bamlag) accommodating thousands of "kulaks," criminals, and Cossacks collectively dubbed *bamovtsy* (then a synonym for "prisoner"). Despite inexhaustible reserves of labor, BAM fell victim to the gap between rhetoric and reality. At the Seventeenth Party Congress (1934), Vyacheslav Molotov announced that BAM would be completed in 1937. By 1937 the route had yet to be surveyed. At the Eighteenth Party Congress (1939), Molotov asserted that BAM would be a reality by 1942. It was, on foreign maps.[25]

Cultural Mobilization

Distance did not shield Dalkrai from the cultural component of the Great Transformation of 1928–32.[26] In the Far East the cultural revolution coincided with militarization, reinforcing regimentation. Appearances notwithstanding, the relationship of public rhetoric and private behavior grew even more tangled, for what played to populist instincts in European Russia plucked pragmatic chords on the periphery, where local elites camouflaged their perquisites while bleating the litany of class struggle. An epidemic of moral compromises marked another milestone in the degradation of regional culture and groomed Far Eastern intellectuals as accomplices, perpetrators, and victims of Stalinist terror.

The cultural revolution first made itself felt in education, where vestiges of academic independence lingered among "bourgeois specialists" in the Oriental Institute, Amur Society, and Priamur Branch. DVGU came under attack from "above" and "below" in 1929 for failing to engage in socialist construction.[27] "Socially alien elements" were trimmed from the faculty and replaced by former partisans, Red Army personnel, and komsomoltsy like Vasily Voiloshnikov, who took over as rector, and Nikolai Ovidiev, who became head of the Japan Department.[*] The word "university" assumed a new meaning in 1930 with the opening of the Far Eastern Communist University in Khabarovsk to train shock troops of collectivization. Dozens of Far Easterners were sent to incubators of "massive cadres of intelligentsia" in Moscow at the Stalin Communist University of Workers of the East and the Stalin Communist Agricultural University.[28] Meanwhile, a crash program to catapult "little peoples" from savagery to socialism by achieving universal primary education by 1933 and universal literacy by 1935 got under way at the Institute of Peoples of the North in Leningrad.[29]

The cultural revolution bureaucratized literature, replacing several fractious groups, including the Russian Association for Proletarian Writers, which gave way in 1932 to a well-oiled machine called the USSR Union of Writers. Responding to cues from the Center, Dalkraikom formed a Far Eastern branch of the union around a core of two *Tikhookeanskaya zvezda* editors, I. Shatsky and I. Shabanov, and an OKDVA officer, Oskar Tarkhanov. The trio lost no time in publishing their own works in a 1933 almanac called *Na rubezhe* ("On the frontier"), edited by Shatsky, Shabanov, ex-oppositionist Tarkhanov (under the alias Oskar Erdberg), Pyotr Kulygin, and Elpidifor Titov. Titov, who, it will be recalled, had returned to Khabarovsk from self-exile in 1932 and denounced his late teacher, Arse-

---

[*]The department's former head, Evgeny Spalvin, avoided much unpleasantness by being attached to the Soviet Embassy in Tokyo from 1925 to 1931 and by being assigned in 1932 to the CER administration in Harbin. He retained the DVGU affiliation in absentia, listed as a subordinate of Ovidiev.

niev, was appointed secretary of *Na rubezhe*. The most famous "Far Eastern" writer, Moscow-based Alexander Fadeyev, criticized the first issue of *Na rubezhe* in *Pravda* on 24 March 1934 for failing to eulogize BAM.[30]

The bureaucratization of literature gathered momentum in 1934 when the Far Eastern Branch of the Writers Union held its first conference at Khabarovsk's Red Army House and elected Shabanov, Tarkhanov-Erdberg, Kulygin, Anatoly Gai, and Vasily Kim to a secretariat and endorsed membership applications from Titov and a young poet named Semyon Bytovoi. Shabanov and Kulygin attended the First Conference of USSR Writers in Moscow in August, joining hundreds of delegates in pledging fealty to the canon of socialist realism. That autumn Fadeyev, Pyotr Pavlenko, and Ruvim Fraerman toured Dalkrai. Pavlenko, approaching the peak of his fame, was collecting material for a novel about chekist vigilance. Fraerman, a former Nikolaevsk partisan, wanted to refresh his memory about the emancipatory impact of the October Revolution on lower Amur aborigines. Before returning to Moscow to resume his ascent toward the secretaryship of the writers' union and membership in Central Committee, Fadeyev reassured local audiences that the Far East was "almost my home."[31]

Aside from silencing survivors of the old intelligentsia and launching some careers, the cultural revolution mobilized youth as purveyors and consumers of utopian kitsch. Its "cultural" heritage turned out to be largely vacuous, for as Nikolai Yadrintsev had pointed out a half-century earlier, "administrative measures create neither life nor culture but only illusions of them."[32]

Birth of a Frontier Cult

Frontier porosity persisted well into the 1930s. Smugglers, Whites (Cossacks, monarchists, fascists), and spies (Japanese, OKDVA, OGPU/NKVD) commuted in and out of Manchukuo. In October 1932 alone, some 20,000 Chinese anti-Japanese fighters in Manchuria sought refuge in Dalkrai. Worried as the authorities were about people illegally entering the USSR, they were equally if not more anxious to keep Soviet citizens from finding their way out or even learning about the outside world. The proximity of traditional Russian communities in Manchuria posed a troublesome problem for guardians of ideological vigilance. Merely two dozen miles — and cultural light-years — separated schools at Pogranichnaya and Grodekovo, consecrated respectively to Nicholas II and Stalin. Considerations of internal control as much as national defense generated a frontier cult epitomized by Blücher's phrase at the Seventeenth Party Congress in 1934: "Frontier under lock and key!"[33] The cult took shape around heroes and rituals designed to glorify chekists and inculcate vigilance. By 1935 the cult had reached a stage where Vladimir Komarov, onetime zaamurets now become president of the USSR Academy of Sciences, could extol the NKVD for "invaluable help to Soviet science."[34]

Stalin used the frontier cult to promote the stature of his crony Defense Commissar Voroshilov as a counterweight to Blücher, who enjoyed more popularity in the Red Army.[35] Alert to signals "from above," Far Eastern pogranichniki petitioned to change the name of Nikolsk-Ussuriisk to Voroshilov, floated "Klim Voroshilov" blimps, and competed among themselves for the title of "Voroshilov marksmen." Voroshilov played his part well, remarking at a Japanese embassy reception in 1936 that it was "only natural" to shoot border violators.[36] An NKVD decree of 17 November 1938 gave his words teeth by turning the entire frontier strip into a free-fire zone.

Quick to exploit the topicality of Bolshevik vigilance and Japanese aggression, writers outdid themselves to apotheosize Far Eastern border guards in 1937–38. Pavlenko called attention to their life-affirming humanism. Ruvim Fraerman taught juvenile readers how they tracked fugitives. Semyon Bytovoi and others evoked their bucolic lifestyles. The composer of "Katyusha," Matvei Blanter, orchestrated their soft footfalls in an operetta that garnered a Stalin Prize.[37]

The frontier cult served Blücher's and Gamarnik's immediate need to strengthen Dalkrai, yet neither man could ignore its lethal potential. By turning chekists into role models and by promoting vigilance as a civic virtue, it laid the moral basis for complicity in repression.

"Girls, Come East!"

The Far East suffered from a perennial shortage of women. In 1923, at a time when there were 119 women for every 100 men in European Russia, the ratio was ninety-three to 100 in the Far East.[38] The imbalance worsened during the next decade, as troops, construction workers, and komsomoltsy poured into Dalkrai. By January 1937 only seventy-three women could be found for every 100 men.[39] The gap hurt morale and, more important, boosted worker turnover rates.

Into this breach stepped Valentina Khetagurova, a photogenic young woman well endowed with energy and contacts. In 1932 the eighteen-year-old Valentina set off from Leningrad for Dalkrai, where she met and married an upwardly mobile OKDVA captain. Throwing herself into cultural work, she set up "Stalin corners" in barracks, a demonstration of political literacy that caught the attention of higher authorities. When the All-Union Conference of Wives of Red Army Commanders convened in Moscow in December 1936, Valentina proudly shared the podium with Stalin and Voroshilov. From there it was but one step to national celebrity, which materialized on 5 February 1937 when *Komsomolskaya pravda* carried a letter under her signature headlined "Girls! Come to the Far East!"

Khetagurova's clarion call brought 27,000 young women to Dalkrai. About 20 percent of them secured work in the OKDVA, Pacific Fleet, and NKVD. The rest wound up on collective farms and construction sites. Whatever their assignments, Khetagurovites had ample opportunities to meet men. An outdoor dance pavilion was erected for this purpose on the site of Khabarovsk's Uspensky Cathedral. Some found marriage partners and settled down to raise families. Others succumbed to alcohol and pimps. As reports of poor housing, scarce food, and rough treatment filtered back to European Russia, prudent lasses detrained west of Lake Baikal.[40]

Radiant Shadow

The "cult of personality" reached the Far East somewhat belatedly. In the Center its symptoms surfaced in December 1929, on the occasion of Stalin's fiftieth birthday, when Voroshilov hailed him as the architect of victory in the civil war and *Pravda* called him "the most outstanding theoretician of Leninism."[41] Such hyperbole did not immediately resonate in Dalkrai. Several circumstances accounted for the delay. Stalin had few ties with the Far East and never set foot east of Baikal. Among his immediate entourage, Voroshilov and Kaganovich did not visit Dalkrai until 1931 and 1936, respectively. The commander of a Red cavalry army during the civil war, Semyon Budyonny had spent nine years as a sergeant-major at Razdolnoye before 1914 and toured Dalkrai in 1929 six months before the birth of the OKDVA. Lesser henchmen made little headway suborning, let alone dislodging, regional elites during the 1920s.

Delayed symptoms, however, did not mitigate the virulence of the disease. After the Seventeenth Party Congress (1934), sycophantic references to Stalin infested the Far Eastern press. A rash of Stalins, Stalinsks, and

Stalinos broke out among collective farms, settlements, schools, districts, streets, and roads. Wage coefficients became "Stalin privileges," and the intermittently passable road between Khabarovsk and Vladivostok "Stalin Highway."

As the cult intensified in 1936, literary hopefuls joined the chorus. Bytovoi put aside bucolics to compose a dithyramb of ejaculatory "Stalins!"[42] The ambitious young poet Pyotr Komarov called him "our happiness, our pride, our joy, our intelligence."[43] Blending the mundane and the sublime, the aviatrix Polina Osipenko credited her survival of a forced landing in the taiga to thoughts of Comrade Stalin and a chocolate bar.

21

« « » »

Center vs. Periphery

Comrade Stalin does not take his eyes off the Far East.
— *Pravda*, 11 Nov. 1936

As Russia's most distant periphery, the Far East posed special problems for central authorities. Communications, essential to control, foundered on natural and technical obstacles. Frontier porosity permitted unauthorized contacts with Asia-Pacific neighbors. Whether as a haven or a receptacle, the Far East brimmed over with mavericks.

Rather than alleviating Center-periphery strains, the October Revolution exacerbated them. Cut off from Moscow by civil war and intervention, Far Easterners learned to fend for themselves. Lenin unwittingly abetted their self-awareness by postponing Soviet rule in favor of a Far Eastern buffer state. Designed as a temporary camouflage, the Far Eastern Republic outgrew its role and became a focus of regional aspirations. Some Far Easterners took the buffer idea so seriously that the Center felt compelled to intervene. When, in 1921, a FER mission to the United States gained observer status at the Washington Conference on naval and Asia-Pacific issues, Moscow tartly reminded Chita that it had no right to take part in international deliberations.[1]

Moscow may have clipped FER diplomatic wings, but it did not always get what it wanted during the first four years of Soviet rule, when the Far East enjoyed de facto economic autonomy. Far Easterners knew that they had engineered recovery without help from the Center by using bourgeois enterprise and foreign investment. The experience suggested that the region's economic potential lay in an Asia-Pacific arena.

In the late 1920s Stalin moved to impose control over provincial party organizations, inaugurating a new stage of Center-periphery dynamics. Because the former partisans and FER officials who formed the backbone of regional leadership did not impress Stalin and his entourage as reliable instruments, the latter delegated broad discretionary powers to Gamarnik and Blücher, who soon found themselves in an awkward position. Appointed as instruments of the Center, they evolved into champions of the periphery and created what amounted to a Far Eastern government.[2] Their local popularity translated into a regional power base resistant to penetration or manipulation, to the chagrin and misgivings of Moscow.

Administrative Assaults

The central Party machine adopted several mechanisms to tighten control over the Far East and other parts of the USSR. An internal passport system was introduced in 1932 for the urban population. "Political sections" jointly administered by Party and security organ personnel were set up during 1933–34 in collective farms, factories, and military units.[3] The effectiveness of these measures depended on how they were implemented by regional and local officials. Since the central Party apparatus judged regional Party secretaries in terms of manageability as well as efficiency, open gestures of intractability were avoided, except in the case of Blücher, who usually got his way by citing the Japanese threat. Far Eastern elites followed their tsarist predecessors and perfected displays of zeal to camouflage inaction. Modern communications constricted the latitude for sleight of hand formerly enjoyed by voevodas and governor-generals, but it should be recalled that until 1938 Moscow had no telephone link with Dalkrai.

On the surface the campaign against "Rightists" in 1928–30 was a struggle of the Party against opponents of the First Five-Year Plan and collectivization, but in the Far East it acted as a cover for complex maneuvers between central and regional power networks. Slogans and labels concealed as much as they revealed about underlying motives and stakes. For example, when in October 1928 the Central Committee instructed Dalkraikom to rid the Far Eastern Party organization of "Right opportunists," Dalkraikom responded by calling for a struggle against "Right opportunists and Trotskyist remnants."[4] By adding "Trotskyist remnants," regional Party leaders gave themselves a task that could be "fulfilled" without threatening entrenched local networks. Accordingly, two administrative "exiles," Dalbank head Smilga and Dalkraikom Secretary Perepechko, were removed while Trotsky sympathizers within the OKDVA underwent self-criticism.[5]

Dealing with "Right opportunists" posed a more delicate problem, for many network members were candidates for that unwelcome rubric. Doubts about the pace of industrialization and collectivization were widespread in the Far East. Enterprise managers and middle peasants had no wish to surrender the discretionary latitude they had enjoyed under NEP in exchange for scrambling after production targets formulated by central bureaucrats. Local economists preferred a Canadian to a Stalinist model of development.[6] Each of the "Rightists" under fire in Moscow—Mikhail Tomsky, Aleksei Rykov, and Nikolai Bukharin—had a Far Eastern constituency. Tomsky enjoyed respect in local trade unions, whose head, Rafail Izmailov, was also a personal friend of Rykov. Bukharin was admired by intellectuals, komsomoltsy, and cultivators; railroad workers openly demonstrated in his defense at Nikolsk-Ussuriisk in 1928.[7]

After Stalin branded Bukharin, Rykov, and Tomsky "Rightists" in February 1929, Dalkraikom dutifully criticized the threesome, removed Izmailov as the head of regional trade unions, and expelled 3,210 "Rightists" from the Party, less than a tenth of total membership. Not content to let Dalkraikom handle the anti-Rightist campaign, Moscow sent Central Committee apparatchiki to purge the Vladivostok and Chita Party organizations and to investigate cases of indulgence toward "kulaks."[8] But even with this intervention, the anti-Rightist campaign yielded disappointing results. The Khabarovsk, Chita, and Vladivostok Party committees underwent some personnel turnover, but Sakhalin and the Northeast remained largely unaffected. Grumbling about the Five-Year Plan and collectivization could still be heard in county and district committees, and Vladivostok officials continued to tolerate NEP-style enterprises.[9]

The failure of the anti-Rightist campaign prompted a new Moscow tact in 1930–32: expelling "alien elements" from the Far Eastern Party organization. Again, regional officials carried out directives from above with demonstrative zeal and negligible results.[10] In response the Central Committee in 1933 empowered a special control commission consisting of the former Chita activist Emelyan Yaroslavsky, Nikolai Yezhov, Lazar Kaganovich, and Matvei Shkiryatov to conduct a thorough purge of regional Party organizations. Faced with such heavyweights, Dalkraikom expelled nearly a quarter of the Far Eastern Party members and accepted no new ones until 1937.[11] Party rolls contracted by a third, but the Blücher-Gamarnik networks remained in place.

Moscow also sent plenipotentiaries to the Far East to make sure that local officials were correctly implementing central Party directives or to carry out such directives themselves. The most prominent of these plenipotentiaries turned out to be chekists: Eduard Berzin was sent out in 1931 to head a new unit, the Far Eastern Construction Trust (Dalstroi), formed to develop the Kolyma Basin and Okhotsk seaboard. Meir Trilisser was dispatched in 1934 as a special commissioner charged with enforcing discipline among local party secretaries.[12] Intended to serve as instruments of the Center, these plenipotentiaries became part of the problem they were supposed to solve. Berzin set up his own administration in the Northeast and established "horizontal" ties with Dalkrai. Trilisser, a former Amur District Party secretary and FER official, does not appear to have imposed much discipline on his old associates.

Blücher ably deflected all attempts by the Center to dilute his authority. When Moscow ordered a purge of OKDVA Party cadres in 1933, Blücher entrusted the matter to a loyal pupil, OKDVA Political Commissar Aronshtam. When Moscow removed Transbaikalia from OKDVA jurisdiction in 1935, Blücher continued to exercise influence there through the local military commander. When Voroshilov sent the head of Red Army Intelligence, Yan Berzin, to investigate OKDVA intelligence operations in 1935, Berzin and Blücher renewed a personal friendship dating from 1922.[13]

The stability and impenetrability of Far Eastern elites eventually doomed them. Stalin and his entourage came to eliminate the distinction between autonomy and separatism, between self-reliance and treason.

Criminalizing Regionalism

Moscow's inability to unravel Far Eastern networks by administrative means during 1928–35 occurred against a background of mounting domestic and international tension. Trials of Shakty engineers (1928), the "Industrial Party" (1930), and Mensheviks (1931) reconfirmed the axiom of revolutionary justice that criminal charges could be leveled against categories of people as well as individuals. That the Far East was a potential category became apparent as early as 1930 when word spread that oppositionists in the regional Party and state organs were alienating the peasantry and sabotaging collectivization.[14] Once the Kwantung Army set up a puppet state in Manchuria, it became possible in Moscow to suspect that oppositionists might turn Dalkrai into a Trojan horse for a Soviet Manchukuo.

As putative linkages between Japan and oppositionists assumed the character of an incubus at the Center, perspicacious Far Eastern OGPU operatives saw an opportunity to demonstrate their vigilance to Moscow by fabricating and then "neutralizing" plots. Accordingly, on 5 May 1933 chekists arrested the former DVGU rector Vladimir Ogorodnikov and a schoolteacher named Prokopy Novograblenov in Petropavlovsk on charges of plotting Kamchatka's "autonomy." Taken to Khabarovsk for interrogation, the accused were induced to implicate the late Vladimir Arseniev. For cooperating with investigators, Ogorodnikov received a ten-year sentence. Novograblenov was condemned to death and shot on 1 January 1934. Arseniev's widow Margarita Nikolaevna, arrested in Vladivostok on 31 March 1934 and taken to Khabarovsk for interrogation, stoutly denied the accusations against her late husband and refused to sign any confession. She was released after a few months for "lack of evidence."[15]

Probably informed about the Kamchatka conspiracy by OGPU Commissar Yagoda, Stalin vented his suspicions about the Far East at the Seventeenth Party Congress early in 1934. Fulsome speeches by Far Eastern delegates (Afanasy Kim described how Korean children drew doodles of their beloved leader) rang no less false than the abject mea culpas of former oppositionists, because Stalin knew that a number of those flattering orators were planning to replace him as general-secretary with first secretary of the Leningrad Party Committee, Sergei Kirov. When Voroshilov told the congress that Comrade Stalin was constantly watching the Far East, the defense commissar meant Dalkrai, as well as China and Japan. By warning that Japanese militarists had their eyes on the Primorye, Stalin let the Far Eastern delegates know that his eyes were on them.[16]

Kirov's assassination on 1 December 1934 brought immediate pressure on Far Eastern Party and security organs to detect and neutralize internal "enemies." Afanasy Kim's ringing phrases at the Seventeenth Congress did not save him from expulsion from the Party in 1935 for "lack of vigilance." By the time that Commissar of Communications Rykov visited Dalkrai in July 1936, the media-stoked animus against former oppositionists prompted survival-minded officials to avoid him.[17] Popular anger escalated still further after the second Kamenev-Zinoviev trial in August 1936.* Confessions of wrecking, murder, and treason by the accused triggered venomous public outbursts. The press, factory meetings, and mass rallies greeted the execu-

*At the first Moscow trial of prominent Old Bolsheviks (January 1935), Lev Kamenev and Grigory Zinoviev received five- and ten-year sentences, respectively, for political complicity in Kirov's murder. In the second trial, accused of treason and terrorism, they and fourteen others were condemned to death. Their executions were announced twenty-four hours after the trial.

tion of all sixteen defendants with exultation.[18] Appetites grew with feeding. Everywhere voices warned about local "enemies of the people" (so far only minor officials) and exhorted citizens to unmask hidden "wreckers."[19]

With directives from above and denunciations from below, Deribas had his hands full during the autumn of 1936 carrying out mass arrests of ethnic Germans, rounding up hundreds of railroad personnel, and taking into custody 144 former party workers including Afanasy Kim.[20] Yet no amount of constabulary zeal could save Deribas after 25 September when Nikolai Yezhov succeeded Yagoda as People's Commissar for Internal Affairs.

The Fall of Gamarnik

No one knows when Stalin began nurturing suspicions about Gamarnik, but it seems safe to assume that by the second Kamenev-Zinoviev trial, the general-secretary had his sights on Gamarnik's friend Vitovt Putna. Having served in Tokyo as military attaché in 1928 and in Khabarovsk as OKDVA liaison with Dalkraikom from 1931 to 1935, Putna had been in a position to bring together the Japanese and Far Eastern threads of a conspiracy. Putna disappeared in August 1936 and for the next ten months was worked over by NKVD interrogators hunting for names of would-be accomplices. Circumstantial evidence suggests that Gamarnik's network figured prominently in his "confession."[21]

In September 1936, while Putna was being tortured in an NKVD prison, Gamarnik made his last trip to the Far East. Accompanied by Blücher and OKDVA political commissar Aronshtam, he reviewed Transbaikalian units at Chita, met Dalkraikom secretary Lavrentiev at Khabarovsk, attended OKDVA maneuvers at Voroshilov (Ussuriisk), and called upon Pacific Fleet Commander Viktorov at Vladivostok.[22] Gamarnik showed signs of nervous strain and before leaving warned Blücher that his young wife Glafira was an NKVD "plant."[23]

Returning to Moscow in October, Gamarnik found himself engulfed in a rising tide of sycophancy and fear attending the trial and execution of Kemerovo engineers. The media reverberated with Stalinist hyperbole. *Pravda* carried florid panegyrics from, among others, two of the Far Easterners he had just visited, Lavrentiev and Viktorov.[24] Gamarnik made himself dangerously conspicuous by standing up for three Old Bolsheviks marked for destruction. At the autumn Central Committee plenum, he voted against investigating Bukharin and Rykov. As 1936 drew to a close,

Gamarnik interceded with Stalin on behalf of former Deputy Commissar of Heavy Industry Georgy Pyatakov, with whom he had many years before shared a tsarist prison cell.[25]

As 1937 opened, Yezhov with Stalin's knowledge (if not at his instigation) was investigating Gamarnik and picking apart his network.[26] On 15 January Lavrentiev was removed as Dalkraikom secretary and replaced by Yosif Vareikis. As a senior Party functionary in Voronezh and Stalingrad, Vareikis had built his own team, half of whom were allowed to accompany him to Khabarovsk.[27] The implications of Lavrentiev's replacement by Vareikis became clear before the end of January when Karl Radek, on trial with Pyatakov and others, implicated Gamarnik's friend Putna as a Japanese agent. Ominous signs multiplied at the February-March Central Committee plenum, when Stalin said that Pyatakov, on whose behalf Gamarnik had interceded three months earlier, had plotted with Japan to detach the Primorye from the USSR.[28] Immediately after the plenum, Gamarnik's closest OKDVA associates, Aronshtam, Sangursky, and Lapin, were dismissed.[29] Men with whom Gamarnik had worked in Vladivostok and Khabarovsk during the 1920s were arrested.[30] While Yezhov unraveled Gamarnik's Far Eastern networks, the press launched a vilification campaign against the Army Political Administration that Gamarnik headed. By the end of April, *Pravda* was describing the Far East as full of spies and warning soldiers to beware of hidden enemies within the Red Army.[31]

Gamarnik hastened his own end by refusing in late May to sit in judgment of Marshal Tukhachevsky, Commander Uborevich, and five other senior officers accused of conspiring against Stalin.[32] Voroshilov thereupon dismissed Gamarnik as deputy defense commissar, and Yezhov's men arrested Avgust Mezis (former OKDVA political commissar), Aronshtam, Sangursky, Lapin, and Pshenitsyn.[33] On the afternoon of 31 May, Blücher and Lavrentiev visited Gamarnik, then confined to his apartment by his diabetes, and informed him of his dismissal that morning as head of the Army Political Administration. As they left, Blücher noticed NKVD operatives waiting outside.[34] When the chekists moved in, Gamarnik committed suicide or was murdered.[35]

The following day *Pravda*'s back page carried a five-line item sandwiched between notices of a football match and a swimming pool opening: "Former CC VKP(b) member Ya. B. Gamarnik, caught up in ties with anti-Soviet elements and evidently fearing exposure, committed suicide on 31 May." Before the week was out, Gamarnik was being denounced as a Trotskyist, a fascist, and a traitor.[36]

Far Eastern Conspiracy?

During the first week of June 1937, Stalin and Voroshilov told the Supreme Military Soviet that the NKVD had uncovered a massive conspiracy in the Red Army.[37] A special military tribunal, with Blücher among its members, convened *in camera* to pass judgment on Tukhachevsky and six senior Red Army officers accused of treason. On 11 June, all seven received death sentences and were shot forthwith. On 12 June the papers began carrying endorsements of the executions from workers, soldiers, collective farmers, scientists, and writers.

Blücher's state of mind during these events has been the subject of considerable speculation. It has been suggested that the NKVD "revelations" about Gamarnik shocked him, and that he emerged from the tribunal deeply shaken but psychologically unprepared to doubt Stalin.[38] The OKDVA commander may well have wondered why he was not among the accused. Reports about his involvement in an anti-Stalin conspiracy had been rife within and outside the USSR for five years. In 1932 a Harbin military analyst had written that Blücher's independent power base was making Stalin nervous. At about the same time rumors were circulating among foreign communists in Moscow that Blücher was plotting to kill Stalin.[39] When Blücher visited Berlin the next year, reports of anti-Stalin feeling in the OKDVA reached Japanese ears.[40]

In June 1937, Gamarnik posthumously replaced Blücher as the central figure in conspiracy theories.[41] Among these, the most detailed and controversial was that offered in the postwar years by a former OKDVA newspaper editor writing in England under the name of Andrei Svetlanin.[42] According to Svetlanin, Gamarnik and Tukhachevsky began plotting in 1932 to overthrow Stalin. Gamarnik prepared the Far East as a redoubt, using the Japanese bogey to build up the OKDVA and the Kolkhoz Corps. The latter's real function was to bring military dependents to Dalkrai and thus deprive Moscow of potential hostages. The conspirators planned to seize Khabarovsk and declare martial law under a "Far Eastern Committee for the Liberation of the Motherland."[43]

Although a chekist who defected in 1937 hinted at Gamarnik's involvement in an anti-Stalin plot, Khrushchev rejected the whole notion by pronouncing Stalin's Red Army victims "unconditionally loyal to Party and motherland" in his secret speech at the Twentieth Party Congress on 24 February 1956.[44] Conspiracy theories thereafter enjoyed little credibility, leaving Svetlanin's scenario to be dismissed as a concoction of Western or

Soviet intelligence agencies.[45] During the 1980s, however, internal opposition to Stalin regained some of its earlier topicality. One study noted the circumstance that "in the Far East the Red Army had its last chance to oppose Stalin."[46] One British and two American historians went further and gave Svetlanin the benefit of the doubt.[47] The Ukrainian antecedents of Gamarnik's network, when taken in conjunction with Ukrainian settlement of the Primorye and Ukrainian nationalist organizations in Harbin and Shanghai, may have played a role in real or imagined plots.[48]

Though the existence of a Far Eastern conspiracy can be neither proved nor disproved on the basis of available evidence, a case can be made for a Center-periphery struggle culminating in the annihilation of Far Eastern elites by "the main conspirator — Stalin himself."[49]

22

"Cleansing" Dalkrai

I have a bright, buoyant feeling when recalling the summer of 1937 in the Far East.
— Valentina Khetagurova (1987)

"Life in the Far East is joyful!" Dalkraikom secretary Lavrentiev proclaimed in 1936.[1] During the next three years, life in Dalkrai was indeed emblazoned with symbols of joyous renewal. Catchwords such as "perestroika" and "inner Party democracy" greeted eye and ear. Far Easterners hailed the "Stalin Constitution," ogled nubile Khetagurovites, applauded quota-busting Stakhanovites, and swelled with pride at "Stalin falcons" making aviation history. They flocked to vote for the "unbreakable bloc" of candidates for the Supreme Soviet. They thronged to glimpse the surviving half of the comic pair "Ilf and Petrov."* They basked in the homilies of visiting *L'Humanité* editor Paul Vaillant-Couturier and savored the prestige of the U.S. Asiatic Fleet paying a courtesy call at Vladivostok.

But behind the public euphoria lurked a pervasive private terror. Unable to manage Dalkrai and obsessed by the specter of conspiratorial separatism, Stalin and his associates "cleansed" the Far East from above and from below. What started at the Center took on a life of its own on the periphery. Moscow provided quotas; local authorities selected victims, except in cases involving members of the central *nomenklatura*. In a macabre parody of participatory democracy, ordinary people fueled the motors of repression by inundating Party committees, security organs, courts, and military tribunals with signed and anonymous denunciations.

---

*Ilya Ilf died on 13 Apr. 1937, to all appearances from natural causes.

"A State of Semi-War"

When Vareikis set off to take up his post as secretary of the Far Eastern Party organization in January 1937, Stalin warned him that Dalkrai was in a "state of semi-war."[2] Vareikis was allowed to bring only part of his own team, so once in Khabarovsk he set about recruiting the followers of Dalkraiispolkom Chairman Krutov and other vulnerable functionaries. Consolidating his position, Vareikis launched a searing attack on Krutov for "lack of vigilance," accusing him of "tolerating internal enemies" and allowing "Trotskyist-Japanese agents" to sabotage the regional economy.[3] Vareikis did not have the field to himself. Barely two months after his arrival in Khabarovsk, Central Committee Secretary Georgy Malenkov dispatched a mission to investigate why so few enemies had been uncovered in Dalkrai and why there had been no trials of railroad officials arrested during 1936. The question assumed a certain piquancy when the chief of the Far Eastern Railroad, Lev Lemberg, shot himself in his Khabarovsk office on 1 April. Deribas took the hint and opened an investigation of Lemberg's subordinates. Two hundred of them were tried and shot by the end of May, but Deribas had been tainted with "lack of vigilance."[4]

News of Gamarnik's "treason" exploded in the midst of a regional Party conference. Nearly everyone desperately tried to distance themselves from the contagion and pointed at Krutov, who was summarily expelled from the Party.[5] A virulent vigilance campaign welled up "from below," acquiring a momentum of its own and putting local Party and state leaders on the defensive.[6] At meetings and mass rallies, crowds roared their approval of the execution of senior Red Army commanders, reviling them and Gamarnik as "vile jerks" (*gady*).[7]

Meanwhile in Moscow Stalin and Yezhov moved to crush what they called a "Far Eastern parallel Rightist-Trotskyist center" embracing Dalkrai's military, political, economic, and cultural elite.[8] Stalin dispatched an NKVD plenipotentiary, Vsevolod Balitsky, and a Party Central Control Commission enforcer, Matvei Shkiryatov, both of whom arrived in Khabarovsk before the end of June. Balitsky, acting on the direct order of Stalin's henchman Vyacheslav Molotov, arrested Krutov but left Deribas alone.[9] Then, a subordinate detected a "lack of vigilance" on Balitsky's part, and acting on his own, persuaded the imprisoned Krutov to give him a list of thirty "co-conspirators," which was duly sent to Moscow.[10] After barely three weeks in the Far East, Balitsky was recalled, arrested, and shot.[11]

Angel of Death

In July 1937 the Far East presented Yezhov with a spectacle of external and internal threats to state security. On 2 July, five days before the outbreak of a Sino-Japanese undeclared war, Japanese and Manchukuoan units sank an NKVD patrol boat on the Amur.[12] Meanwhile NKVD operatives in Moscow had extracted under torture the names of Gamarnik's "co-conspirators" in the OKDVA from the former commander of the Far Eastern Air Force, Albert Lapin. Armed with this "evidence," Yezhov, with Stalin's approval, went after Deribas and surviving Far Eastern elites using NKVD Commissar Genrikh Lyushkov as his instrument.[13] According to Lyushkov's own testimony, he received instructions directly from Stalin on the eve of departing for Khabarovsk in early July. The general-secretary warned him that Gamarnik's connections in Dalkrai were extensive, embracing the OKDVA, the Party, collective farms, and even the NKVD. Lyushkov should find out to what extent Far Eastern chekists had become involved in Gamarnik's treason. Dalkrai was to be "cleansed" of dangerous elements. Blücher was to be placed under surveillance.[14]

During the late summer and autumn of 1937, Lyushkov cut a broad swath through Dalkrai. Quotas of enemies of the people requiring "neutralization" were drawn up for each district and county.[15] Party and state officials, factory managers, and collective farm chairmen were expected to identify a certain number of enemies within their jurisdictions. The NKVD, saddled with its own quotas (ten to twenty cases per investigator per day in December 1937), extracted confessions by torture. Whether or not the accused signed protocols admitting guilt, their cases were sent to regional representatives of judicial organs (military collegia, civilian tribunals), where troikas handed down decisions after deliberating for as little as ten minutes. Repression worked its way through regional, district, municipal, and county Party committeemen, Komsomol secretaries, collective farm chairmen, agronomists, engineers, teachers, peasants, and Cossacks.[16] Anyone who had lived under White or foreign rule was particularly vulnerable, because that circumstance alone raised the possibility of recruitment as a spy. This included former partisans, who were the first to be rounded up in rural areas.[17] Former CER employees repatriated to the USSR in 1935 also fell into this category.[18] Polish, Finnish, and Estonian communities were thinned out by arrests, executions, and deportations. Entire settlements vanished, and it was rumored that peasant-filled barges were towed from the Amur to the Sea of Okhotsk and sunk.[19] The machinery of repression was gender-blind. Anna Lebedeva, the only woman to storm White positions at Volochayevka in 1922, shared the fate of her husband, a former partisan and Party official. Nor were women employees of the Far Eastern Railroad administration spared.[20]

Vareikis's zeal to uncover enemies did not save him. In September 1937, after less than nine months as Dalkraikom secretary, he was recalled to Moscow, where he was arrested on arrival, accused of involvement in a "Far Eastern Rightist-Trotskyist conspiracy," and shot together with Deribas and Krutov.[21] His fall boded ill for members of his team and others who had rushed to attach themselves to what a few months earlier had looked like a rising star.[22]

Expulsion of East Asians

The intellectual progenitor of the forced relocation of East Asians was the author of *Dersu Uzala*. In 1906 Captain Arseniev reported to Priamur Governor-General Unterberger that Chinese along the Primorye coast, being partial to Japan, should be removed as security risks. Twenty-two years later in 1928, Arseniev sent a secret memorandum to Dalkraikom recommending that Koreans be relocated from the Khasan area near the Tumen River border.[23] The Jekyll of an ethnographer's good intentions transmuted into a Hyde of Stalinist expediency.

Although Dalkrai's 165,168 Koreans (1937 census), many of whom were refugees from Japanese rule, had every reason to be loyal to the Soviet regime and to Comrade Stalin (after whom a Korean Club was named in Vladivostok), their concentration around the Posyet frontier zone had from the 1920s made them suspect as cat's-paws for a Japanese takeover of the Primorye.[24] For this reason, Koreans had been resettled to the interior from the southern Primorye in 1928 and from Vladivostok in 1933.[25] In 1933 Deribas presided over the arrest, trial by troika, and execution of three Soviet Koreans charged with espionage on behalf of Japan.[26] Although these three appear to have been innocent, the Kwantung Army did set up a school in Manchukuo in 1936 to train Koreans for espionage and political agitation in the Primorye.[27]

After receiving instructions from Dalkraikom on 21 August, Lyushkov proceeded to round up Koreans during September and October while the Pacific Fleet went on alert to prevent them from fleeing by sea. Lyushkov gave each Korean community six days to pack all portable property and to choose between resettlement within the USSR and deportation to Manchukuo. The vast majority opted for the former and were put in boxcars bound for Central Asia. By late October, as NKVD squads assisted by civilian auxiliaries (*druzhiny*) were flushing the last holdouts from Vladivostok, 135,343 Koreans had been removed on sixty trains.[28] On 20 December *Pravda* announced that the Central Committee had expressed gratitude to Lyushkov for fulfilling an important assignment "in the field of transport."

Having finished with the Koreans, Lyushkov turned to the Chinese, picking up about 19,000 of Dalkrai's 24,589 (1937 census) inhabitants between December 1937 and May 1938. All Chinese domiciled in Vladivostok and within sixty miles of the Manchukuo frontier were rounded up. An ethnic group associated for over a thousand years with the region, constituting 13 percent of its population in 1911, made up less than 1 percent of its inhabitants by 1939.[29]

Not all Koreans were relocated or deported. Among about 25,000 living outside the border zone, most remained in place. So did Party activists executed as traitors, such as Afanasy Kim, who after having been arrested by Deribas in 1936 was accused of having plotted *with* Deribas to detach the Posyet Region from the USSR.[30] Korean chekists took part in repressing members of their own ethnic group, before succumbing themselves.[31] During 1940 and 1941 Korean partisans driven out of Manchuria by Japanese anti-bandit campaigns were placed in a camp north of Khabarovsk. Among them was Kim Il-sung and his wife, who in 1942 gave birth to Kim Jong-il on Soviet soil.

Destroying Blücher

Blücher continued to enjoy official prestige and genuine popularity well into 1938. In December 1937 he led the Far Eastern delegation to the Supreme Soviet, and a month later, he was elected to the Supreme Soviet presidium.[32] On 23 February (Red Army Day), he was awarded the Order of Lenin.[33] A laudatory article on him by the noted writer Konstantin Paustovsky appeared that month in a leading literary journal.[34] He was nominated as a candidate for the RSFSR Supreme Soviet in May and continued to appear in public in Khabarovsk during June.

But beneath a veneer of public honors, Blücher slid into isolation. From the middle of 1937 until the summer of 1938, 4,000 OKDVA officers and military commissars were arrested, among them his closest associates.[35] The OKDVA itself ceased to exist on 1 July, replaced by the Far Eastern Front. Stalin waited until after the Bukharin-Rykov trial (March 1938) before moving directly against Blücher. In April an assassination attempt on the Navy commissar in Vladivostok gave Stalin grounds to dispatch Lev Mekhlis, head of the Army Political Administration, and Mikhail Frinovsky, chief of the NKVD Border Guard, to the Far East. En route they were joined by Grigory Gorbach, head of the Novosibirsk NKVD. The trio arrived in Khabarovsk in mid-June, each on a special train filled with armed escorts and replacements for targeted cadres. Lyushkov was not at the station to greet them. Sensing that his turn had come, the commander of the NKVD in the Far East had decided to remove himself from harm's way and on the night of 12–13 June walked into Manchukuo. Aside from dooming his immediate subordinates, Lyushkov's defection hastened Blücher's destruction.[36]

Blücher's last month in the Far East (mid-July to mid-August 1938) coincided with a complex interaction of domestic and external forces. As Mekhlis and Frinovsky "cleansed" regional cadres, Soviet and Japanese forces clashed on the Manchukuo-Korea-USSR frontier. If Stalin and Voroshilov had been waiting for a chance to settle accounts with Blücher, they found it in the interstices of bureaucratic and border conflicts. In the second week of July, without consulting Blücher, Frinovsky deployed NKVD troops on a ridge of hills between the Tumen River and Lake Khasan. Alerted to what had happened, Blücher sent his own observers to the area and on 24 July remonstrated with Frinovsky for encroaching on Manchukuo territory.[37]

Frinovsky's initiative did not pass unnoticed by Japanese troops. Although the ridge lay within Manchukuo, Japan's Korea Army bore responsibility for defending this narrow wedge of territory along the left bank of the lower Tumen. After making several protests to leaders of the NKVD troops dug in on the ridge, the local Japanese commander concluded that the intruders would have to be dislodged. Korea Army headquarters in Seoul (then officially called Keijō) and the Army Ministry in Tokyo neither permitted nor prohibited the use of force but ruled out the use of air strikes and artillery. In the early hours of 31 July, three battalions crossed the Tumen River, drove the NKVD forces off the ridge, and dug in. Any counterattack could come only along exposed corridors north and south of Lake Khasan.[38]

Blücher found himself confronted at once with a formidable military problem (how to expel the Japanese) and a dangerous political dilemma (how to deal with Mekhlis and Frinovsky). Recapturing the ridge overlooking Lake Khasan would have to be carried out by army and NKVD troops acting in concert, an unpromising exercise. Frinovsky showed no inclination to put his chekists under Blücher's command. To make matters worse, Stalin and Voroshilov telephoned Blücher on 1 August and ordered him to liquidate without delay enemy positions above Lake Khasan. Ominously, Stalin asked the Far Eastern marshal whether he really wanted to fight the Japanese. Blücher thereupon instructed his new chief of staff Grigory Shtern, recently decorated by Voroshilov, to attack immediately. When Shtern's assault on 2–3 August was repulsed with heavy losses, Blücher joined him at Posyet to launch a massive air and ground assault on 6 August that left both Soviet and Japanese troops clinging to the ridge. On the same day Blücher's portrait and name were absent from a mass rally in Khabarovsk.[39]

Summoned to Moscow by Voroshilov on 16 August to give an account of the Lake Khasan fighting, Blücher appeared before Stalin, Voroshilov, Molotov, and Frinovsky on 31 August.[40] Voroshilov and Frinovsky charged him with gross incompetence "bordering on conscious defeatism."[41] Someone said that "enemies of the people" had hidden behind him while subverting the Far Eastern armed forces. Stalin remained silent. Ordered by Voroshilov to Sochi to await "work fit for a marshal," Blücher cabled his wife and younger brother Pavel (a captain in the Far East air force) to join him on the Black Sea. "Work fit for a marshal" turned up on 22 October when NKVD operatives arrested Blücher and his wife at Sochi and took them to Moscow. At Lefortovo Prison, in an interrogation personally supervised by Lavrenty Beria, Blücher was accused of being a Japanese agent since 1921. There are several versions of his death, but the evidence suggests that he was tortured.[42] He expired on 9 November.*

Blücher became a non-person rather than an object of public vilification. Young weathercock Yury Zhukov, who would build a career on Far Eastern themes, praised Blücher in a book printed on 15 July 1938, then removed all references to him in a revised edition appearing in October.[43] Following Blücher's disappearance, rumors circulated that he had been sent back to China to help Chiang Kai-shek fight Japan. Chiang inquired about his former military advisor and was informed by Stalin that he had been executed "for succumbing to the charms of a Japanese woman spy."[44]

---

*Blücher's first wife, Galina Pavlovna, and his aviator brother, Pavel, perished in Gulag. His second wife, Glafira Lukinichna, survived to publish her memoirs in 1989.

Balkanization and Beneficiaries

Far Eastern administrative unity underlay institutions like the OKDVA and Dalkraikom as well as the power base of Gamarnik and Blücher. Stalin carved up Dalkrai to exorcise the specter of separatism. On 4 September 1938 the Far Eastern Front was divided into three separate armies, each directly subordinate to Defense Commissar Voroshilov.[45] On 20 October Dalkrai was dissolved and reconstituted as two administrative regions: Khabarovsk krai and Maritime (Primorsky) krai administered from Khabarovsk and Vladivostok, respectively (see Maps 9 and 10).[46] To staff positions vacated by arrests or created by reorganizations came a wave of starry-eyed Stalinists led by Nikolai Pegov.

In September 1938 Pegov, a thirty-three-year-old student and rising Party star at the Moscow Industrial Academy, was summoned to the Central Committee and informed that he had been appointed first secretary for the Far Eastern region and should immediately proceed to Khabarovsk after collecting 500 Communists from the Moscow Party organization. When he asked how he was expected to finish his studies, Pegov was told: "You'll defend [receive] your diploma by your work."[47] During the next few days, Pegov managed to recruit a few dozen Communists, including his brother. All were young and exhilarated by their new responsibilities. "Our whole life then," he wrote in 1982, "was illuminated by sunshine, joy, and happiness."[48]

Pegov's experience was replicated by thousands of komsomoltsy, soldiers, sailors, machinists, oil-well drillers, engineers, and geologists who flocked to the Far East in 1938 and 1939, drawn by patriotism, romance, and ambition. New arrivals inherited the empty homes of deported Chinese and Koreans, the offices and apartments of purged incumbents. For the idealistic and cynical alike, these were exciting times, memories of which would be cherished for decades. Nostalgically recalling her exultation at being appointed a secretary of the Dalkrai Komsomol in 1937, Valentina Khetagurova wrote fifty years later: "Oh, life just percolated in the Far East!"[49]

Party membership in the Far East also percolated. After declining since 1933, it leapt from 24,885 in 1938 to 56,776 in 1941.[50] By 1939 the Far East had the highest percentage of Party members in the population of any region in the USSR,[51] a circumstance attributable not only to the concentration of troops, sailors, frontier guards, and labor camp personnel but also to the massive influx of cadres from the Center.

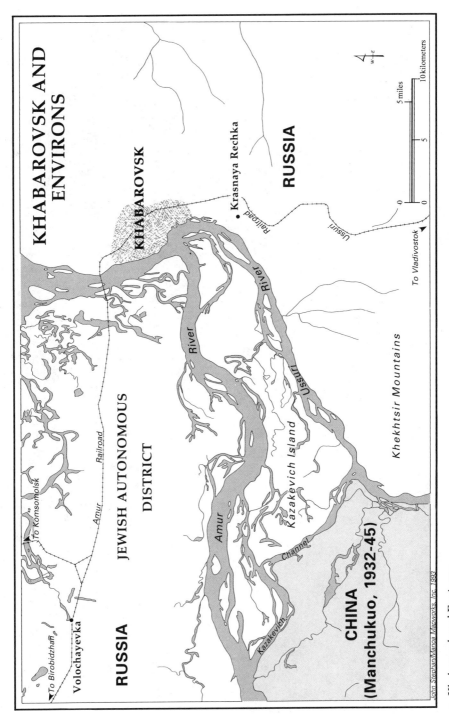

KHABAROVSK AND
ENVIRONS

KHABAROVSK

RUSSIA

• Krasnaya Rechka

Railroad

Ussuri

To Vladivostok ▶

River

River

Ussuri

Kazakevich Island

Khekhtsir Mountains

Channel

Kazakevich

Amur

JEWISH AUTONOMOUS

DISTRICT

Amur   Railroad

RUSSIA

Volochayevka •

▼*To Birobidzhan*

◀*To Komsomolsk*

CHINA
(Manchukuo, 1932-45)

0   5miles

0   5   10kilometers

N
W—E
S

John Stephan/Manoa Mapworks, Inc. 1993

9. Khabarovsk and Environs

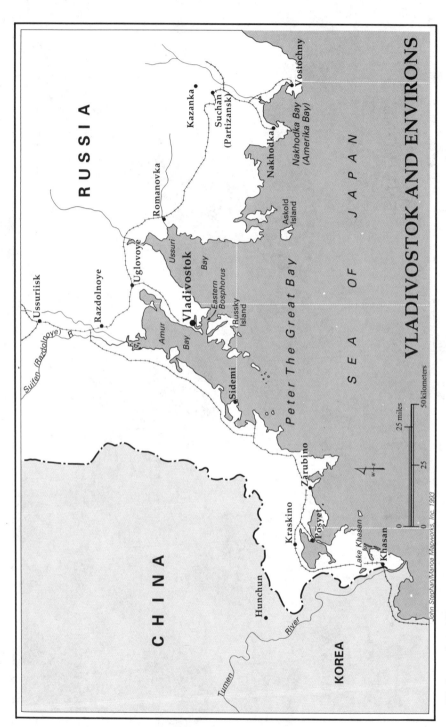

10. Vladivostok and Environs

Ideological perestroika in the Far East centered around a history of the Party popularly known as the *Short Course* and commonly ascribed to Stalin.[52] Fully 70 percent of Far Eastern Party members claimed to have read the *Short Course* during 1938–41.[53] It formed the core of the curriculum at Khabarovsk's Pedagogical Institute and Higher Party School, established in 1938 and 1939, respectively. By relieving readers of the burden of thought and of personal responsibility for collective acts, the *Short Course* promoted what Anastas Mikoyan hailed as the "Stalinist style of work."[54]

The Eighteenth Party Congress (March 1939), attended by thirty-nine Far Eastern beneficiaries of "cleansing",* celebrated the "Stalinist style of work." The freshly constituted Central Committee included Pegov and G. M. Shtern. Speeches by Far Easterners exuded exhilaration. Pegov praised the liquidation of "the Trotskyist-Bukharinite band [that] sought to give the Primorye to fascist employers."[55] Shtern thanked Comrade Stalin for ridding the Red Army of "black traitors of the motherland, foreign spies, Trotskyist-Bukharinite beasts" who had "crawled into responsible posts even in the Far Eastern Army, in contact with their Japanese and other foreign patrons. You and I destroyed this heap of filth — Tukhachevskys, Gamarniks, Uboreviches, and swine like them."[56] After the congress, Shtern told his wife that had it not been for the civil war, he would have become a historian. Had it not been for the mechanism that he had so faithfully served, Shtern might have become a witness to history. He was arrested in Moscow on the night of 7–8 June 1941, two weeks before the German invasion, and executed at Kuibyshev on 28 October.[57]

Costs

In the spring of 1939, Leningrad Party Secretary Andrei Zhdanov toured Khabarovsk, Vladivostok, and Nakhodka to take stock of the results of "cleansing." The Far East had met none of its Five-Year Plan targets.† Production indexes for industry, fisheries, and forestry were below 1935 levels. The construction of the Baikal-Amur Railroad had ground to a halt. Far Eastern agriculture suffered irreparable losses: repression of rural leaders

---

*For the names of the Far Eastern delegates, see Appendix I.

†Dalkrai targets for 1937 and actual levels reached (in parentheses): population, 2.8 million (2 million); cultivation, 2.3 million hectares (1 million); electric power, 400,000 kilowatts (150,000); steel, 500,000 tons (none); fish, 800,000 tons (350,000); oil, 800,000 tons (460,000); coal, 6.5 million tons (4.75 million). *Kyokutō Shiberiya yōran*, p. 9.

and specialists, compounded by the havoc wrought by forced collectivization and the expulsion of Chinese and Koreans, deprived the Far East of its most productive farmers.[58]

The precise magnitude of the human toll in the Far East during 1937–38 is unlikely ever to be known. According to Lyushkov, about 200,000 people were arrested (7,000 of them shot) or deported during his ten-month sojourn in Dalkrai (August 1937–June 1938).[59] These figures do not take into account deaths in NKVD-administered labor camps in the Northeast. Nor do they include the victims of his predecessors (Deribas, Balitsky) and successors (Mekhlis, Frinovsky, Gorbach, Goglidze, Gvishiani), who were active during the first half of 1937 and the last half of 1938, respectively. Assuming Lyushkov is close to the mark, roughly 8 percent of Dalkrai's 2,273,332 population (1937 census) was repressed, undoubtedly a higher percentage than for the USSR as a whole for the same period.[60]

The disproportionately high rate of repression in the Far East is suggested by Party statistics. Of 1,956 voting delegates to the Seventeenth Party Congress in 1934 from all parts of the USSR, 1,108 were arrested.[61] Of thirty-two Far Eastern delegates to the Seventeenth Party Congress, none appeared at the Eighteenth Party Congress in 1939 (see Appendix I). Of 139 candidate and full members of the Central Committee in 1934, ninety-eight were shot: all Far Eastern members and candidate members of the Central Committee in 1934 either were shot or committed suicide. Far Eastern party membership, 44,909 on 1 January 1933, fell to 27,730 by 1 January 1937 and to 24,885 at the beginning of 1938.[62] According to a Japanese source, more than one quarter of Far Eastern communists were purged during 1936–39.[63] Only four of the twenty-eight members of the Dalkraikom bureau in 1935 were alive in 1940.[64] All delegates to the Twelfth Far Eastern Party conference (May-June 1937) were eventually repressed.[65] No Far Eastern first secretary between 1923 and 1938 escaped the juggernaut. The fates of municipal and county Party secretaries remain to be illuminated, but as can be seen in Appendix F, district (obkom) turnover rates in 1937–38 were ominously high.

Repression gutted the armed forces, too. The Kolkhoz Corps as well as the OKDVA were abolished as incubators of subversion. According to Lyushkov, 1,200 officers and political commissars and 3,000 junior officers were arrested between July 1937 and May 1938.[66] In 1938 alone the OKDVA lost 40 percent of its regimental officers, 70 percent of its division and corps officers, and over 80 percent of its staff and department heads.[67]

How many of the roughly 30,000 chekists who perished in the Great Terror fell in the Far East has yet to be established.[68] During 1937–41, chekists destroyed each other in cycles reflecting personnel changes at the top. Yezhov and his entourage liquidated Yagoda men in 1937–38. Beria's mafia repeated the process with Yezhovians in 1939–41. The pace of collegial homicide slackened in 1939 as Sergei Goglidze and Mikhail Gvishiani consolidated their positions in Khabarovsk and Vladivostok. Trials of middle- and low-ranking torturers accused of "violations of socialist legality" produced mostly administrative reprimands and Party expulsions.[69] "Ethnographer with a pistol" Albert Lipsky received a five-year sentence that enabled him to sit out the Second World War in a Central Asian camp.[70]

Virtually all members of the Far Eastern cohort formed during and after the civil war were liquidated. The list included three of Blücher's associates during his leadership of the NRA in 1921–22, Lapin, Pokus, Postyshev; the partisan leaders Melnikov and Zverev; the Party leaders Trilisser, Shishlyannikov, Pshenitsyn, and Volsky; and Dalkraikom first secretaries Kubiak, Perepechko, and Lavrentiev.[71] Krasnoshchekov, the former Dalsovnarkom chairman and president of the Far Eastern Republic, was shot on 26 November 1937.[72] His fate was shared by such former FER officials as Minister of Foreign Affairs Yakov Yanson (who had survived tsarist and White prisons) and Chicagoan "Bill" Shatov.

Terror cut down thousands of nameless victims tagged as enemies of the people as a result of personal scores, quota-fulfilling zeal, and mistaken identities. Vladivostok old-timers recall how each night corpses were dumped into mass graves near Egersheld Cemetery.[73] A Far Eastern Katyn awaits excavation at Glukhaya Hill near the Ussuri Line.[74]

Destruction of the Far Eastern Intelligentsia

Although the names of metropolitan literary victims of the Terror are widely publicized, little is known about Far Eastern writers, editors, journalists, scholars, and poets who succumbed in the 1930s. Who has heard of Leonid Reshetov, the "Far Eastern Radek"? Or of Kharim Tsoi? Or of the six founding editors of the region's leading literary journal?* Intellectuals

---

*Namely, *Na rubezhe*'s editor-in-chief I. Shatsky, E. Brui, Vasily Kim, P. Kulygin, O. Tarkhanov (alias Erdberg), and I. Shabanov. Two of the founding editors, G. Petrov and N. Potapov, survived. Te Men Khi, head of *Na rubezhe*'s Korean section, was arrested in 1937 and shot on 11 May 1938.

who had sojourned in the Far East during the years of civil war and foreign intervention (1918–22) were marked as potential spies. Abstention from politics did not save the writer Sergei Tretyakov, who had co-edited a Vladivostok literary journal in 1920, from paying the supreme price for erstwhile cosmopolitanism in 1939.

An Englishman who had spent time in the Far East as a German POW wrote in 1919, "Everybody knows that if they [Bolsheviks] were returned to power in Vladivostok, not a single member of the Oriental Institute would be left alive."[75] Time turned this piece of reckless gossip into clairvoyance. Members of the Oriental Institute who had failed to emigrate, retire, or expire by 1937 had (although they did not yet know it) an excellent chance of not surviving the next year. For Japan specialists, the odds almost eliminated guesswork insofar as the stock of their trade constituted prima facie evidence of treason. A visit to Tokyo or Harbin, linguistic fluency, an encounter with Japanese journalists or diplomats in Vladivostok became grist for quota-fulfilling chekists. Had not Evgeny Spalvin succumbed to a twisted intestine in Harbin in 1933, he would have shared the fate of septuagenarian Dmitry Pozdneyev, rector of the Oriental Institute during the Russo-Japanese War, who was picked up and shot as a Japanese spy in October 1937. Though long dead, Spalvin and Arseniev were assigned leading roles in a lethal drama. NKVD scenarists groomed them posthumously as organizers of a Japanese spy ring in DVGU during the 1920s. Their "recruits," ten DVGU orientalists arrested on 5 November 1937, included Oriental Faculty head Vasily Voiloshnikov, Japan Department head Nikolai Ovidiev, Pacific Region Department head Konstantin Kharnsky, and DVGU librarian Zotik Matveyev. Seven months before his own defection to Japan, Dalkrai NKVD head Lyushkov dispatched Aleksandr Zherebtsov from Khabarovsk to "cleanse" DVGU by extracting confessions of espionage, wrecking, counterrevolutionary activity, and terror. Zherebtsov carried out his assignment to the letter. On 25 April 1938, nine Orientalists initialed their protocols, heard their verdicts from a troika, and were led to a basement where each received a bullet in the back of the skull. The tenth, Mikhail Vostrikov, had his death sentence commuted to twenty years. He perished in Kolyma six months later. Other DVGU faculties were also "cleansed," albeit with less thoroughness.[76]

Relatives of purged intellectuals were not spared. Wives were often sent to camps, and children placed in special institutions. Relatives thought twice about taking in orphans, for there were cases of families being imprisoned for sheltering children of "enemies of the people."[77] Pozdneyev's daughter Lyubov, a lecturer in Chinese at DVGU at the time of her father's arrest and execution, was picked up in 1939 and sent to a camp. Arseniev's widow Margarita Nikolaevna was arrested on 2 July 1937 and shot as a Japanese spy on 23 August 1938. Her seventeen-year-old daughter Natasha was arrested in 1939 on a morals charge, released, re-arrested in 1940 for "anti-Soviet" propaganda, and sentenced to ten years in a labor camp.[78]

"Cleansing" eliminated books and schools as well as people. Matveyev's manuscripts were thrown out on the street after his arrest.[79] Holdings of the Oriental Institute Library were dispersed or burned.[80] Almost all pre-1917 imprints were taken from the Primorye Regional Scientific Library in Vladivostok and torched, as was most of the Venyukov Collection at the Khabarovsk Regional Library.[81] Arseniev's personal archives suffered severe depredations.[82] "Cleansing" gutted higher education and science. In addition to pedagogical and agricultural institutes, all twelve Far Eastern Party schools ceased to exist in 1937.[83] In Vladivostok both DVGU and the Far Eastern Branch of the USSR Academy of Sciences closed in 1939.

Complicity and Memory

The machinery of repression caught up not only institutions — the NKVD, military tribunals, the Party, the press, the judicial and educational systems — but also the masses. "Cleansing" depended on the participation of thousands of people who acted as informants. Citizens in every walk of life publicly or secretly betrayed neighbors, colleagues, and relatives. DVGU faculty hoping to save their own departments wrote denunciations of colleagues. Researchers did the same in the Far Eastern Branch of the Academy of Sciences. Writers and poets behaved no differently. Semyon Bytovoi denounced his friend and fellow poet Elpidifor Titov for associating with Gamarnik.[84] There was no shortage of role models for such behavior. Newspapers bristled with letters and resolutions from factory and collective farm workers, miners, teachers, mariners, soldiers, writers, scientists, and explorers vilifying whoever had just been exposed as a "wrecker," "traitor," or "Trotskyist swine." Among prominent signatories were the "Far Eastern" writers Aleksandr Fadeyev and Pyotr Pavlenko, who enjoyed tremendous prestige and respect among the young. Even the venerable zaamurets Vladimir Komarov, who had trekked around Manchuria and Korea back in 1897 with Mikhail Yankovsky and who had once called himself a friend of Arseniev, added his name and prestige to the chorus as president of the USSR Academy of Sciences.[85] Motives varied from person to person and included patriotism, ambition, greed, envy, spite, and fear. Whatever the reason, few, if anyone, felt safe. Zealous informants could not count on immunity: those they denounced might well take revenge by implicating them as "co-conspirators." Exemplary behavior was no guarantee of innocence, for Stalin himself had said that "the true wrecker from time to time works well in order to win the trust of those around him so that he can continue his wrecking."[86]

Not a few Far Eastern victims of "Stalinism" had blood on their hands. "Honest" chekists done in by "violations of socialist legality" had in their day executed innocent people on trumped-up charges. Party secretaries and procurators had diligently run the machinery of repression before their own turn came in 1937–38. OKDVA officers such as Putna and Fedko had taken part in the brutal repression of sailors at Kronstadt in 1921. Even the bookish Zotik Matveyev had discreetly penned denunciations for the benefit of "competent authorities."

Of course some Far Easterners had the courage to be neither victims nor accomplices. One openly declared that rather than harm innocent people the authorities should shoot Kaganovich (Stalin's ruthless henchman died of natural causes on 25 July 1991 at the age of ninety-seven).[87] Scientists on Chukotka raised their hunting rifles when NKVD operatives showed up, and the chekists retired to fill their quotas elsewhere.[88] There were cases of resistance in rural areas and factories. Thousands got out of harm's way by losing themselves in larger cities or working in mines and logging camps where people did not inquire closely about antecedents.

With the opening of Party, Red Army, and KGB archives, historians will presumably reconstruct the "cleansing" of Dalkrai in greater detail and precision. But to plumb the depths of mass complicity, we shall have to wait for another Dostoyevsky to illuminate the frailty — and darkness — of the human heart.

23

« « » »

Kolyma

In Kolyma, winter lasts twelve months; the rest is
summer.   — Popular saying

Kolyma is a river, a mountain range, a region, and a metaphor. In Russia, the word conjures up contradictory images and emotions. What transpired in Kolyma under Soviet rule constitutes for some scintillating — and for others shameful — testimony to human capabilities.

Until 1917 the land between the Arctic Ocean and the Sea of Okhotsk was inhabited by aborigines and a handful of traders, convicts, and exiles. Although gold was discovered along the Kolyma River in 1910, little was done about it until 1926, when Stalin, intrigued by the economic impact of the Gold Rush on California, sent engineer-administrator Aleksandr Serebrovsky to survey mining techniques in the United States and invested him with broad powers to reorganize the gold industry.[1] Serebrovsky turned for help to geologists like Yury Bilibin who were surveying Kolyma (naming a lake there after the American writer Jack London). Expeditions led by Bilibin during 1926–29 revealed that the upper Kolyma River had plenty of gold, but getting it out would be neither easy nor cheap. Once extracted, gold would have to be hauled by trucks over mountains to the Okhotsk littoral for transshipment to Vladivostok.[2] Building a *trakt* across 350 miles of unopened territory in the permafrost zone became the first installment of a giant Stalinist construction project.

Dalstroi: The Berzin Years

Dalstroi, acronym for Far Eastern Construction Trust, was something of a hybrid creature when it was established on 13 November 1931 under

Eduard Berzin, a Latvian commander of Kremlin guards who, after crushing SR and British plots (real and imagined) in 1918, gained experience in handling forced laborers at an OGPU-run cellulose factory in the Urals.[3] Though Dalstroi was placed under the Council of Labor and Defense, its Party organization formed a component of Dalkraikom.[4]

Before leaving the Center, Berzin opened offices in Moscow, Leningrad, Odessa, Rostov, and Novosibirsk to recruit engineers, technicians, geologists, and supervisors. After signing contracts with various commissariats for provisions and laborers, he set out with a bevy of hand-picked cadres, landing at Nagayevo, the "Gateway to Kolyma," on 4 February 1932.[5]

Over 90 percent of the Dalstroi work force consisted of prisoners (the proportion dropped to roughly 80 percent in the late 1930s and 70 percent in the 1940s). In early 1932 OGPU Commissar Yagoda set up the Administration of Northeast Corrective Labor Camps (USVITL), colloquially called Sevvostlag, with headquarters in Srednikan, 300 miles north of Nagayevo. Sevvostlag was administratively subordinated to Dalstroi but operated by the OGPU's plenipotentiary to Dalkrai, Deribas. Berzin was allocated 16,000 prisoners in 1932; 9,928 reached Nagayevo alive. The number of arriving prisoners increased steadily: 27,390 in 1933, 32,304 in 1934, 44,601 in 1935, 62,703 in 1936, and 80,258 in 1937.[6]

Prisoners sent to Kolyma traveled like livestock. Crossing Siberia on "Stolypin cars," they were herded into transit camps at Krasnaya Rechka and Vtoraya Rechka (outside of Khabarovsk and Vladivostok respectively), then loaded into the holds of British- or American-built ships such as the *Sacco* and *Vanzetti* for the 1,700-mile voyage to Nagayevo.[7] The sea voyage was hazardous as well as unpleasant. In late 1933 the *Dzhurma* lodged in ice after passing through the Bering Strait. Over a thousand prisoners froze; the guards survived by eating them.[8] Two hundred miles from the entombed *Dzhurma*, 104 scientists and crewmen of the research vessel *Chelyuskin* were rescued by Soviet aviators as the world applauded and a Danish writer marveled, "I envy a country having such heroes, and I envy heroes having such a country."[9]

To accommodate incoming humans and outgoing gold, prisoners built jetties and breakwaters at Nagayevo and Vesyoly ("Cheerful"), where band music invariably accompanied arrivals and departures.[10] Dalstroi headquarters arose just inland at Magadan, which grew from a cluster of huts in 1932 into a town of 15,000 in 1936. From Magadan, the trakt led north to Seimchan, terminus of Kolyma River navigation and northern administrative center of Dalstroi. After OKDVA tank crews had cleared a path with tractors, prisoners lay a carpet of logs to form a roadbed on frozen soil. When the trakt was completed in 1936, what once took fifteen days to cover by reindeer could be traversed in as many hours by lorry.[11]

Berzin was vulnerable to flashes of decency. When Evenk herders fled to the tundra after his subordinates had tried to commandeer their reindeer, he prohibited confiscatory practices and offered aborigines access to housing, schools, and dispensaries.[12] He forbade the abuse of prisoners, gave them wholesome food, warm clothing, and a living wage, and allowed those with special skills to work as engineers, physicians, tailors, carpenters, and nurses. He rewarded diligence by paying bonuses and even reducing sentences. Under Berzin, one Kolyma survivor recalled, "we worked willingly and not from fear."[13] Enlightened rule paid off in gold output, which increased eightfold in the first two years, earning the Dalstroi chief an Order of Lenin in 1935.[14]

Distance insulated Dalstroi from the Center. In dealing with Moscow, Berzin put on a show of zeal, acknowledging directives, employing unwanted chekists (Leningrad NKVD operatives who knew too much about Kirov's murder), and extolling Stalin.[15] But he only went through the motions of carrying out the Party purge of 1933, the Party documents verification of 1935, and the vigilance campaign of 1936.[16] Moreover, he cooperated with the ill-starred Dalkrai leaders Deribas, Lavrentiev, and Krutov, who met with him in Magadan in 1936.[17]

Berzin's widow believed that Yezhov went for her husband after Stalin had remarked that it was time to "spill some Latvian blood,"[18] but it is more likely that the general-secretary targeted him as part of a larger prophylactic agenda. Yezhov moved to undermine Berzin in the summer of 1937 by sending NKVD Commissar Karp Pavlov to Magadan with a fresh contingent of chekists. Pavlov began arresting Dalstroi officials, but Berzin refused to be provoked. As his aides vanished one after another, the Dalstroi chief remained unruffled and deliberately took time out to entertain the touring comic Evgeny Petrov.[19]

In November 1937 Yezhov summoned Berzin to Moscow "for consultations." The NKVD Commissar evidently preferred not to risk arresting such a powerful satrap on his own turf. The Dalstroi chief had few illusions about what the summons meant, but, like so many of his peers, he walked fatalistically into the maws of the machine he had served. As a band played under the watchful eyes of Karp Pavlov, the Dalstroi chief boarded the *Feliks*

Dzerzhinsky and sailed out of Nagayevo for the last time. Taken into custody at a station outside of Moscow, Berzin was accused of conspiring to hand over the Northeast to Japan. Condemned by a troika after several months of confinement, Eduard Berzin was shot on 1 August 1938. After the fall of Yezhov a few months later, Stalin and his entourage found it advantageous to restore the reputations of a few recently murdered Communists, thereby distancing themselves from Yezhovian "excesses." Berzin fell into this category. His posthumous rehabilitation in 1939 was his final service to Stalin.[20]

Dalstroi under the NKVD

On 4 March 1938 Dalstroi was transferred from the Labor and Defense Council to the People's Commissariat of Internal Affairs and put under Karp Pavlov, assisted by S. N. Garanin, a Yezhov protégé who headed Sevvostlag.[21] With the acquisition of Dalstroi, the NKVD strengthened its involvement in the Far Eastern economy, an involvement that by 1940 embraced gold, platinum, and coal mines, logging camps, fisheries, and construction. Sevvostlag had a work force of over 250,000 men and women, exceeding the combined total of 200,000 laboring in Dal'lag (camps in the Khabarovsk region), Bamlag (camps for the Baikal-Amur railroad and Amur-Yakutsk road), Amurlag, and Burlag (Bureya Basin camps).[22] Arrivals leaped from 93,978 in 1938 to 163,475 in 1939.[23] Dalstroi's jurisdiction expanded as Sevvostlag sent prisoners to work the lead mines of Chukotka and cut roads through the Dzhugdzhur Mountains. By 1941 Dalstroi administered a million square miles between the Lena and the Pacific, a fourfold increase since 1932.[24]

Mortality rates more than kept pace with territorial expansion. High production quotas, the heavy influx of prisoners, and the Dalstroi-Sevvostlag staff's instrumental view of human life boded ill for longevity. Thousands died before reaching Nagayevo. Typhoid ravaged transit camps. Since hatches were routinely fastened shut as vessels passed through La Pérouse Strait between southern Sakhalin and Hokkaido, the *Indigirka*'s human cargo went down with the ship in 1939.[25]

In 1937, to relieve the bottleneck at Vladivostok's Vtoraya Rechka Transit Camp (where poet Osip Mandelshtam expired on 27 December 1938),[26] Moscow decided to build a new port in Amerika Bay. The village of Nakhodka (formerly Amerikanka) accordingly became the scene of "another beautiful Far Eastern construction project."[27] Upon completion of a rail spur from

Suchan in 1941, Nakhodka replaced Vladivostok as the principal departure point for Kolyma-bound prisoners.[28]

Humanity flowing into Kolyma mirrored domestic and international vicissitudes. Between 1937 and 1939 came Postyshev's widow and son, Tukhachevsky's three sisters, Béla Kun's widow, a Bulgarian Communist hero of the Reichstag fire trial, and *kharbintsy* (Harbiners) — repatriated CER employees who spoke jargon-free Russian and expired with effortless elegance.[29] The intelligentsia was well represented. Among the luminaries were Vasily Shukhayev, a former professor of painting,* and Vasily Kniazev, whose ballads Krupskaya had read aloud to a bedridden Lenin. Nina Gagen-Torn, anthropologist and student of Lev Shternberg and Vladimir Bogoraz, ended up there. Abram Khodorov, an eminent sinologist, landed the job of fetching reindeer fodder.[30] Evgeniya Ginzburg, a lecturer in journalism at Kazan, spent sixteen years in Kolyma for refusing to denounce a fellow teacher. The writer Varlam Shalamov arrived in 1937 and was due for release in 1943, but his term was extended for ten years after he called Nobel Prize laureate Ivan Bunin a "Russian classic."[31]

Hitler's and Stalin's division of Eastern Europe (August–September 1939) internationalized Kolyma's involuntary sojourners. About 10,000 deportees from eastern Poland arrived during 1940. The Winter War with Finland (1939–40) and annexation of the Baltic republics (1940) brought Finns, Estonians, Latvians, and Lithuanians. Rumanians and ethnic Hungarians followed in the wake of the Red Army's occupation of Bessarabia and northern Bukovina in 1940. Anti-Nazi Germans, Austrians, and Czechs trickled in, among them a moderately prominent German Communist. His sojourn turned out to be brief, for the NKVD handed him over to the Gestapo.[32]

Death and life both reaped a bountiful harvest in Kolyma under NKVD management. Of 10,000 Polish arrivals, 600 departed upright. None of the 3,000 Poles sent to Chukotka survived.[33] Sevvostlag executioners "neutralized" 40,000 enemies of the people, a quarter of them with bullets at the Serpantinka Camp, 375 miles west of Magadan.[34] Meanwhile, the "Athens of Okhotsk," as Magadan was called,[35] hummed with the purposeful energy of 50,000 inhabitants: chekists and their dependents, free settlers, and pris-

---

*Shuykhayev, a professor of painting at the Petrograd Academy of Arts (1914–20), had taken up residence in Paris and exhibited at galleries and museums in Europe, the United States, and Australia. He returned to the USSR in 1936 on a commission to paint a mural at the Lenin Library, only to be arrested with his wife as a spy the following year.

oners with marketable skills or connections. Magadan boasted a higher concentration of physicians, scholars, writers, poets, artists, and musicians than any metropolitan area east of the Urals, and its surgeons were reputedly better than those in Moscow or Leningrad. Under the auspices of Maglag's Cultural-Educational Department, enemies of the people played in the local symphony, produced and acted in Shavian dramas at the Magadan Musical Comedy Theater, and crafted toys for chekist tots.[36] Magadan was Kolyma's resort, a subarctic Sochi with its own privileged clientele.[37] In the municipal Park of Culture and Rest, dominated by an enormous statue of Stalin pointing north toward the gold mines, young couples strolled on long summer evenings or played tennis in white bucks.[38]

Thousands enthusiastically followed Stalin's outstretched arm. In Kolyma there was plenty of opportunity for ambitious, energetic, and idealistic youth. Niches in the interstices of Dalstroi and Sevvostlag offered the advantages of complicity in human engineering without imposing too much on the conscience. Decades later, not a few of these men and women looked back on their Kolyma days as the "brightest and most joyous" of their lives.[39] Twenty-four-year-old Nikolai Shilo arrived in Magadan in 1937 and launched a career by writing upbeat reports of forced laborers animatedly discussing elections to the Supreme Soviet. A rivulet named after Shilo still winds through a landscape of abandoned camps.[40]

As Beria's men "cleansed" Kolyma of Yezhovian incumbents in 1939, Dalstroi came under NKVD Commissar Ivan Nikishov and Sevvostlag was taken over by Sergei Goglidze, who had headed the NKVD in Khabarovsk.[41] Hitler's attack on the USSR put Nikishov and Goglidze in a difficult position, for they were expected to deliver more ore with less labor. As rolling stock was diverted to the front, the number of prisoners reaching Nagayevo fell from a peak of 176,685 in 1940 to 148,301 in 1941 and 126,044 in 1942.[42] Moreover, as if crushing men and minerals were not enough, Stalin entrusted his Kolyma chekists with a delicate assignment: to host the vice-president of the United States.

Innocents Abroad

Among Western visitors to the USSR between 1932 and 1944, few reached the Far East, for transcontinental travelers were routed through Transbaikalia and Manchuria, bypassing the Priamur and the Primorye. Those who set foot there saw mostly what they understood. Two visitors who passed through in 1940 were struck by the "typically American" quality of the region and its inhabitants. Kolyma, which they never approached, was a "land of the future" to which Poles "immigrated."[43]

Physical access did not necessarily remove the blinkers. An American who cruised the Northern Sea Route in 1935 observed that prisoners at the Kolyma estuary "looked exactly like free citizens," and some even "worked enthusiastically toward a bright future." On the happy assumption that the NKVD did not arrest people without cause, the visitor concluded that people were sent to Kolyma for a good reason.[44]

Although more accurate information was available in Washington,[45] the Soviet-American wartime alliance nourished credulity. Instead of mentioning awkward matters, books on Siberia and the Far East called attention to a "first-class highway" between Magadan and Kolyma, spoke of Blücher as if he were in fine form, and asserted that the difference between free settlers and "exiles" was that the latter looked "disgruntled and morose."[46] Yakutsk reminded Wendell L. Willkie, the presidential hopeful of 1940, of his hometown, Elwood, Indiana.[47]

The first official Soviet-American encounter in Kolyma possibly derived from President Roosevelt's suggestion to Stalin at Teheran in 1943 that they meet *à deux* in the North Pacific. The idea materialized in modified form. Each sent a deputy: Vice-President Henry A. Wallace and NKVD Commissar Sergei Goglidze. Goglidze prepared for the meeting as if his life depended on it, turning Magadan and Seimchan into Potemkin villages. Watchtowers came down, and stores were painted and stocked with provisions flown in from Moscow. Prisoners were removed from sight, their places in the mines taken by NKVD guards and office girls. Chekists were to form an ambulatory cocoon about the Wallace party, donning whatever identities were needed for the occasion.* Wallace prepared for the meeting by practicing Russian phrases and leaving substantive matters to three specialists in his party: the State Department's China specialist, John Carter Vincent; the deputy director of the USSR Branch of Foreign Economic Administration, John N. Hazard; and the director of Pacific Operations in the Office of War Information, Owen Lattimore.

---

*An American naval officer traveling to Vladivostok early in 1945 was approached at Krasnoyarsk by a brigadier general of the NKGB (security police, detached from NKVD in 1943), who boasted to him of having escorted the American vice-president the previous year. To prove it, he produced a photograph of Henry Wallace and himself in the uniform of a naval captain. George Roullard, Assistant Naval Attaché, Vladivostok to Office of Naval Intelligence, "Observations Made Along the Trans-Siberian RR, 20 Feb.–4 March 1945," 10 Mar. 1945. U.S. War Shipping Administration, Russian Area Shipping, RG 248, Box 52.

As soon as the Americans landed on Chukotka, NKVD operatives transferred them to a Soviet aircraft and flew them to Seimchan, where they were
warmly welcomed by Goglidze, whom Wallace took to be "the president of
the executive committee of Khabarovsk Territory" and "a close friend of
Stalin's."[48] Goglidze assured the vice-president that he would personally
accompany the guests during their sojourn in the USSR so as to be entirely
at their disposal. Grateful for this solicitude, Wallace recorded: "Goglidze is
a very fine man, very efficient, gentle and understanding with people."[49]

During his three-day sojourn in Kolyma, Wallace enjoyed himself im-
mensely, dining on caviar, pork, salmon, fresh fruit, vodka, wine, cham-
pagne, and mineral water flown in from Moscow. Briefed on the vice-
president's interest in agriculture, Goglidze arranged for him to inspect a
farm where greenhouse tomatoes, cucumbers, and melons were grown "for
the workers." At a tracer mine, Wallace found the "miners" well-paid,
"husky young men" who exuded enthusiasm and for some reason wore
U.S.-made rubber boots. Always ready to fraternize, the vice-president
played football with his escorts.[50]

Lattimore was also impressed by what he thought he saw. Noting that
Dalstroi, "a combination Hudson's Bay Company and TVA," operated "a
first-class orchestra and a good light-opera company," he concluded that
"high-grade entertainment just naturally seems to go with gold, and so does
high-powered executive ability," as exemplified by Nikishov and his wife
(*komendant* of Maglag), who had "a trained and sensitive interest in art and
music and also a deep sense of civic responsibility."[51] Many years later,
recalling his visit to Kolyma, Lattimore allowed that he was "totally igno-
rant about the actual situation."[52]

On his release from Kolyma, a Red Army officer signed an oath never to
talk about what he had seen and heard.[53] Silence, often masquerading as
optimism, outlived the camps. For fifty years, journalists, geologists, komsomoltsy, and aborigines rhapsodized about "Golden Kolyma," whose
mines "helped Yakuts, Eveny, Koryaks, and other peoples of the north to
understand the advantages of collective labor."[54] Banalities can be prescient.
After watching a film about Kolyma in 1936, Maksim Gorky predicted that
in fifty years "the extraordinary cultural work of chekists in the camps will
receive its deserved illumination in art and history."[55] And so it has.*

*One of the Kolyma mines was named after Gorky, whose surname was also Russian for
"bitter," prompting the sardonic pun, *maksim gorkaya epokha* ("maximum bitter epoch").

« « » »

War Without a Front

If Japan and the Soviet Union stay together, they will have
nothing to fear.   — Stalin (14 April 1941)

We have our own special account to settle with Japan. We
of the old generation waited forty years for this day.
                          — Stalin (2 September 1945)

War between Japan and the Soviet
Union, widely expected during
the 1930s, did not materialize. Until August 1945 the two neighbors observed a "strange neutrality" in which each allied with the other's enemies
and fought the other's allies. Far Easterners took scant comfort in this
anomaly. Memories of 1904–5 and 1918–22 haunted the older generation,
and the Kwantung Army threat from Manchukuo was on everyone's mind.
Everyone knew that Japan coveted northern Sakhalin and Kamchatka and
maybe even the Primorye. It would have surprised few had they known that
in 1938 South Manchurian Railway President Matsuoka Yōsuke privately
proposed to President Franklin Roosevelt that Japan and the United States
jointly purchase the Soviet Far East.[1]

Dalkrai faced the Japanese Empire along 3,000 miles of frontiers that
were ill-defined, aside from the 50th parallel dividing northern Sakhalin
from Karafuto. According to the treaties of 1858 and 1860, the Sino-
Russian river boundary ran along the main channel, but this "thalweg principle" fell victim to arbitrary initiatives. The tsarist regime treated the Chinese shoreline as the boundary and claimed possession of the entire river, as
did its successors. When, in 1919, a Chinese gunboat captain asked Ivan
Kalmykov for permission to sail up the Amur into the Sungari the ataman

retorted: "If you want to pass Khabarovsk, do it along the [river] bottom."[2] The Far Eastern Republic and Soviet government spoke more diplomatically but adhered to the same principle. The land boundary was problematic for different reasons. Wooden markers placed along the 370-mile frontier between Lake Khanka and the Tumen River in 1861 soon rotted, and most of the stone replacements had been removed by 1917, one to Khabarovsk where it was displayed at the Museum of Regional Studies.[3] Incidents multiplied after 1931, when the Kwantung Army faced the OKDVA from the Argun to the Tumen. To avoid escalation, the two armies established a border demarcation commission in 1935, but OKDVA delegates walked out a year later when Tokyo and Berlin signed the Anti-Comintern Pact.[4]

Just as the OKDVA gathered intelligence in Manchukuo, so did the Kwantung Army within Dalkrai. White Russian and Korean infiltrators sought out the disaffected and bribable. Japanese reconnaissance planes flew over Vladivostok, Khabarovsk, Komsomolsk, and Petropavlovsk on overcast days, cut their motors, and glided noiselessly under the cloud cover as Fairchild cameras snapped military facilities. With Finnish assistance, Japanese cryptographers deciphered local codes (one based on Stalin's *Short Course*), and other agents eavesdropped on telephone conversations via underground cables from Manchukuo.[5] Emboldened by the massive repression of Red Army commanders, the Kwantung Army in late June 1937 opened fire on an NKVD unit, sank a gunboat downstream from Blagoveshchensk, and infiltrated its agents more boldly. Dalkraikom Secretary Vareikis warned Stalin that Far Eastern borders were wide open.[6]

Repression interacted with border clashes during 1937–38 to foster a siege mentality in the Far East. All individually owned radio receivers were surrendered, registered, and kept under lock and key in factories and collective farms.[7] After the Lake Khasan incident (July-August 1938), during which Japanese troops had landed on Kazakevich Island in the shadow of Khabarovsk, the NKVD evacuated all residents living within two miles of the border and established a free fire zone. Thereafter, infiltration became suicidal, and the Kwantung Army lost almost all its agents.[8] But in catching genuine spies, the NKVD also destroyed genuine friends of the USSR.[9] Innocent citizens were chosen to serve as fodder for deadly quota-fulfilling ploys.*

---

*On 3 Jan. 1938, the celebrated actress Okada Yoshiko and her Communist lover, Sugimoto Ryōkichi, fled across the 50th parallel from Karafuto to Soviet Sakhalin and were arrested by the NKVD as spies. Sugimoto was tortured and shot in 1939. Okada spent four years in a camp

To prepare for an expected Japanese onslaught, Moscow invested heavily in the Far East in 1939 and 1940, allocating it 10 percent of total capital investment in the Third Five-Year Plan (1938–42). Strategic railroads were built to frontier strongpoints. Prisoners cut a 750-mile road through the taiga between the Trans-Siberian Line and Yakutsk. A secret tunnel was dug under the Amur at Khabarovsk, and a pipeline was laid under the Nevelskoi Strait to carry Sakhalin oil to Komsomolsk refineries. A "second Vladivostok" arose at Vanino-Sovetskaya Gavan on the Tatar Strait. Resettlement of collective farmers, industrial workers, and fishermen swelled the region's population from 2,273,000 in 1937 to 3,155,000 in 1940.[10]

When fighting broke out between Soviet and Japanese forces at Khalkhin Gol on the Mongolia-Manchukuo frontier in July 1939, the Far East went on a war footing. Japanese consulates were closed in Blagoveshchensk and Khabarovsk. Workers, collective farmers, and students underwent military training. But contrary to everyone's expectations, the war clouds evaporated in Northeast Asia as the storm broke over Europe.

Eurasian Conduit, 1939–41

The Hitler-Stalin Pact of August 1939 brought a breathing spell to the Far East by catalyzing a Soviet-Japanese détente. As Tokyo and Moscow drew back from the brink and settled outstanding border issues,* the Far East turned from a crucible into a conduit. Emissaries from the Third Reich passed through the Priamur and the Primorye, starting with Ernst Köstring, a Moscow-born, Russian-speaking military attaché. On the heels of Köstring came businessmen, journalists, and bureaucrats. The Reich's consulate-general in Vladivostok, closed since January 1938, reopened on 23 September 1940, when Georg Kühlborn returned to the Golden Horn from a stint in Manchukuo and took up residence at 20–22 Tigrovaya Street.[11]

---

and seven years in exile before taking up residence in Moscow, where she died in 1992. V. M. Drekov, Sakhalin NKVD chief, oversaw the execution of 40 Oroki and Nivkhi accused of being Japanese spies (the NKVD sent Nivkhi into Karafuto as agents). In the years 1938–41, the NKVD "recruited" 148 targeted Soviet citizens for assignments in Manchukuo, and sent them across a false frontier into the control zone on Kazakevich Island. There, chekists posing as White Russians recruited their unsuspecting captives (by torture if necessary) and sent them back across the "frontier" where they were arrested and shot as Japanese spies.

*A cease-fire was arranged at Khalkhin Gol, and Japan accepted a configuration of the Mongolian-Manchukuo frontier established by the Red Army victory. The joint demarcation of the Soviet-Manchukuo border resumed in the spring of 1940.

Germany derived both economic and military advantages from the Eurasian conduit. The "land bridge" enabled it to circumvent the British naval blockade and obtain strategically important rubber and wolfram from Indochina and to channel exports across the Pacific to the still neutral United States.[12] In the summer of 1940, a German commerce raider following in the wake of the icebreaker *Stalin* sailed from the Atlantic to the Pacific via the Northern Sea Route and sank 64,000 tons of British shipping.[13]

Washington as well as Berlin had an eye on Vladivostok. Although American commercial stakes in the Far East remained modest (wide-diameter steel pipe for the Sakhalin-Komsomolsk pipeline and handcuffs for the NKVD), the U.S. Navy saw a potential intelligence dividend accruing from a listening post less than 500 miles from Japan. In August 1940 the State Department notified Moscow that Soviet consulates on the West Coast would be closed if Vladivostok were not made available.[14] Moscow gave its consent, and on 15 January 1941 Angus Ward, a foreign service officer with experience in Russia and China, opened a temporary consular office in the Chelyuskin (formerly Versailles) Hotel.* In August, Ward was allocated a couple of rooms on 44 Dzerzhinsky Street. Insulated from local contacts by the NKVD, he had little to report beyond tetchy references to more commodious (double the floor space) German facilities.[15]

The Soviet-Japanese Neutrality Pact (13 April 1941) added verisimilitude to the illusion of Soviet-German-Japanese trilateralism. For two months, the "Eurasian bloc" (Germany, Russia, Japan) long touted by the Munich geopolitician Karl Haushofer seemed on the verge of becoming reality. In anticipation of a burgeoning transcontinental clientele, the South Manchurian Railway Company opened a travel bureau in Berlin on 2 May. Inhaling the atmosphere of Eurasian solidarity as he passed through Tokyo in June, Walter Duranty, the Pulitzer Prize–winning *New York Times* Moscow correspondent, asserted that Soviet-German or Soviet-Japanese hostilities were as likely as "frying snowballs."[16] But Hitler, whom Duranty misread as egregiously as he had misled others about Stalin, fried the Eurasian snowball with Operation Barbarossa.

---

*Canadian-born Ward (1893–1969) had served with the American Relief Mission in Russia in 1919–20, the U.S. consulate in Tianjin (1925–34), and the U.S. embassy in Moscow in 1934–40. Consul-general in Mukden during the civil war (1946–49), Ward remained at his post until detained by the Chinese Communists, earning him the sobriquet "last man out of Mukden."

The Great Patriotic War

Germany's invasion of the USSR, launched on 22 June 1941, revived the Japanese threat to the country's eastern flank. Preparing for the worst, army, Pacific Fleet, and NKVD units went on full alert. Blackouts darkened Khabarovsk, Blagoveshchensk, and Vladivostok. Civilians were mobilized to dig trenches and construct pillboxes around cities and towns. "Trackwalkers" patrolled the Amur and Ussuri lines looking for mines and infiltrators. Local elites sent their dependents to the interior. As German victories and hunger boosted defections to Manchukuo among army and border guard units, chekists dealt ruthlessly with defeatism.[17]

Geopolitical calculations rather than sentiment governed how foreign nationals were treated in the Far East. Reich Consul-General Kühlborn was escorted from Vladivostok to the Manchukuo border, but Korean friends of the USSR such as Kim Il-sung were interned.[18] Chinese diplomats were harassed, but Japanese were handled with kid gloves.[19] Haunted by the specter of a second front, Stalin walked on eggshells. On 15 October 1941, he summoned Far Eastern party and military leaders to his Kremlin office and ordered them not to do anything that might provoke hostilities. Even if Japan should attack, the Pacific Fleet was to withdraw northward, and land forces were to retreat into the taiga.[20]

Stalin overestimated Japanese capabilities. In June 1941 the Kwantung and Korean armies collectively had fourteen divisions (380,000 men) and 600 aircraft, compared with a Far East contingent of 700,000 men and 2,800 aircraft, buttressed by 2,700 tanks and armored cars.[21] The Kwantung Army built up to 700,000 troops for special maneuvers in August but adopted a defensive posture in October, when its commander forbade troops to fire even if Soviet forces entered a buffer zone on the Manchukuo side of the frontier.[22] American entry into the war against Japan and Germany and a Red Army victory outside Moscow in December precluded a Japanese strike north. Nonetheless, invasion rumors cropped up in the spring of 1942.[23] Japan was in fact unable to act in the summer of 1942 because of growing commitments in the South Pacific. By mid-1943 the Red Army had gone over to the offensive as the Kwantung Army continued to transfer units to Southeast Asia and the Pacific.

While girding itself against Japan, the Far East supported the struggle against Germany. Troop transfers to European Russia began four months before the German attack.[24] By the end of 1941, the equivalent of fourteen divisions had been moved from the Far East to the Moscow and Leningrad fronts.[25] To mislead Japanese intelligence, troops were withdrawn piecemeal from units that continued to exist on paper. All together the Far East provided 250,000 men to the western front between 1941 and 1944.[26]

As capital investment from the Center dropped to half the level of 1939, the Far East gave the rest of the country more fish, coal, timber, and steel.[27] This was done despite the fact that conscription depleted collective farms, factories, docks, and construction projects. Empty places were filled by the elderly, women, and students. The NKVD released "reliable" criminals from the camps for dock work and military duty.[28] Deprived of manpower and spare parts, agriculture suffered. Grain, potato, and rice production fell by over a third during the war,[29] leading to food shortages for people without access to the special rations given to Party, managerial, technical, military, and security personnel, trade union officials, and favored academics, writers, and journalists. Workers in war factories and shipyards received black bread, macaroni, porridge, and hot water at special dining halls.[30] Hunger bred resourcefulness. People collected berries and wild garlic from the Ussuri taiga, planted kitchen gardens, and, if they lived on the lower Amur or on Kamchatka, netted salmon. Widespread malnutrition would have been worse without the American Lend-Lease program.

Lend-Lease and Aviators

Congress passed the Lend-Lease Act on 11 March 1941, empowering President Franklin Roosevelt to provide goods and services to Great Britain and other nations whose defense he deemed vital to American security. Six days after Operation Barbarossa had transformed the Soviet Union from a partner into an adversary of the Third Reich, Ambassador Konstantin Oumansky submitted a list of desiderata to Washington, prompting Congress to approve extension of Lend-Lease assistance to the USSR.[31] Before the first convoys reached the USSR in November, the Soviet Far East merchant marine had been taking on oil at San Francisco and loading cargoes of lead and wool in Sydney and Napier.[32]

Wartime shipping routes followed northern (around Norway), southern (via Iran), and eastern (across the Pacific) trajectories to the USSR. Over half the USSR-bound Lend-Lease tonnage moved across the Pacific. Maneuvering between Soviet-Japanese neutrality and Japanese-American belligerency, U.S. "Liberty Ships" under Soviet registry and manned by

Soviet crews reached the Soviet Far Eastern ports via the La Pérouse, Tatar, or Tsushima straits or avoided the Japanese archipelago by unloading cargoes at Petropavlovsk or along the Northern Sea Route. Tokyo frowned on this traffic, especially when it passed through the Kurile Islands. The Imperial Navy detained 178 and sank nine Lend-Lease vessels between 1941 and 1944. When one foundered near Kunashir in 1943, half of the crew froze to death, and the survivors were interned as American spies. Avoiding the Kuriles incurred risks associated with navigation in combat zones. American submarines torpedoed four ships, including one carrying orphans to the United States.[33]

Liberty ships called at Vladivostok, Nakhodka, Sovetskaya Gavan, Nikolaevsk, Aleksandrovsk (Sakhalin), Nagayevo, Petropavlovsk, and Ambarchik. Cargoes were loaded onto trains or barges for transshipment. Lacking piers, cranes, and rolling stock, Vladivostok turned into a bottleneck as ships held at anchor in the Golden Horn waiting for berths, and pilferage depleted supplies stranded on shore. Matters improved somewhat after the summer of 1942, when Washington supplied giant cranes and flatcars and the NKVD tightened its supervision of stevedores, many of whom were convicts.[34] Low-bulk, high-value cargoes and important officials (Wallace, Gromyko, Molotov) passed through the Far East by air from Alaska to Uelkal, Seimchan, and Yakutsk. During 1943 and 1944 about 300 planes flown by Soviet and American crews covered the route monthly.[35]

Lend-Lease touched just about everybody in some way. Over 500 Soviet aviators and 15,000 Pacific Fleet sailors sojourned in Alaska and the Aleutians, the former at times bringing along wives and girlfriends.[36] Several thousand merchant seamen and 4,000 Red Army POWs liberated by Allied forces in France and Holland passed through Portland en route to Vladivostok and an uncertain fate.[37] The enterprising and the lucky bought black market American flour, sugar, and Spam. Almost everybody at one time or another hitched a ride in a Dodge or Studebaker.[38] In Kolyma, prisoners wielded Lend-Lease shovels, nibbled ethereally soft white bread (which according to camp wisdom evaporated before any reached the small intestine), and ingested glycerin ("American honey"), machine grease ("Lend-Lease butter"), and anti-freeze (fatally).[39]

The Far East's proximity to Japan attracted attention from amateur strategists as well as the Joint Chiefs of Staff. The November 1942 issue of the *National Geographic* carried an article predicting that "American bombers may soon be flying to Japan from the underground hangars of Vladivostok."[40] Like much wartime writing about the USSR, this scenario took no account of Stalin's deep-seated, multidirectional suspicions. Only on four occasions between 1942 and 1944 did Moscow allow the International Red Cross to send food and medicine through Nakhodka to Allied POWs in Japan. Fearing Japanese retribution and leery of internal repercussions, Stalin repeatedly deflected Washington's requests for air bases in Kamchatka and the Primorye.

Given Stalin's anxiousness not to provoke Tokyo, his reactions can be imagined when disabled U.S. planes headed for the Far East after flying missions against Japanese forces. Fully 291 American aviators landed in the Primorye and Kamchatka between 1942 and 1945, starting with the crew of a B-25 medium bomber at a military airport near Vladivostok on 18 April 1942. After interrogation and internment in Khabarovsk, the five men were transported to Central Asia and with NKVD connivance "escaped" to Iran. What started as an isolated incident grew into a pattern during 1944 as B-24s and B-25s operating over the Kuriles landed at Petropavlovsk and as B-29s on missions over Kyushu came down in the Primorye.[41] On orders from Moscow these uninvited guests were kept in strict isolation without the amenities accorded Henry Wallace. Aware from first-hand experience how well Soviet airmen fared in Alaska, interned American aviators had difficulty comprehending the logic of Lend-Lease, but they saw and probably understood more of Soviet reality than did the vice-president and his entourage.

"Short Purifying Storm"

As the strategic balance shifted in favor of the USSR in 1943, Stalin and his advisers prepared the diplomatic groundwork for war in Northeast Asia while taking advantage of Tokyo's illusions and complaisance.* Even as Molotov denounced the Neutrality Pact and Stalin himself publicly labeled Japan an "aggressor," Molotov privately assured Tokyo that the pact would remain in force until 1946, thereby holding out the hope of Soviet mediation in the Pacific War.[42] While anesthetizing Tokyo with the mirage of

---

*Detentions of Lend-Lease vessels by the Imperial Navy diminished in 1944 and ceased altogether in 1945. Until 1943 Japan continued to ship Malayan rubber to Vladivostok despite critical shortages at home, and in 1944 surrendered the oil and coal concessions on northern Sakhalin.

good offices, Stalin came out of the Big Three conference at Yalta in February 1945 with an endorsement of his price for a Soviet attack on Japan within three months of Germany's capitulation: joint management of the CER (sold to Manchukuo in 1935), lease of the naval base at Port Arthur, preeminence at the nominally "free" commercial port of Dairen, repossession of southern Sakhalin, and transfer of the Kurile Islands to the USSR.*

In tandem with metropolitan diplomacy, the Party conditioned Far Easterners for war with Japan. Hints started dropping as early as October 1944, when Moscow issued a postage stamp commemorating the partisan leader Sergei Lazo, murdered twenty-four years earlier with Japanese complicity. In closed meetings lecturers told factory workers and collective farmers that Japan had already broken the 1941 Neutrality Pact by plotting with Germany to attack the USSR. As a result, the announcement of Germany's surrender on 9 May aroused expectation as well as relief in the Far East.

Between May and July 1945, troops from East Prussia and Czechoslovakia poured into Transbaikalia, the Priamur, and the Primorye in preparation for a blitzkrieg campaign against Manchukuo, Korea, southern Sakhalin, and the Kurile Islands. By early August some 1,600,000 men, 5,000 aircraft, and 4,000 tanks were deployed from Mongolia to Kamchatka, poised to strike a million Japanese defenders.[43] Under the overall command of Marshal Aleksandr Vasilevsky, these forces were to come at the enemy from three sides: one group was to thrust into Manchuria from the west, a second was to cut into Manchuria and Korea from the Primorye, and the third was to cross the Amur into Manchuria from the Jewish Autonomous District and Blagoveshchensk. If all went well in Manchuria, army and naval units were to conduct landings on Karafuto, the Kurile Islands, and Hokkaido. Airborne troops and SMERSH[†] detachments stood by to parachute into Harbin, Dairen, and Pyongyang (Heijō).

Launched shortly after midnight on 9 August, the operation began successfully enough as the attackers overran Manchukuo's frontier defenses. But the Soviet troops soon encountered pockets of fierce resistance in the interior. They did not cross the 50th parallel of Sakhalin until the three days after Emperor Hirohito's 15 August broadcast announcing the end of the war, and an amphibious assault in the northern Kuriles foundered. Between

---

*According to Molotov, Stalin mused about getting Alaska too. Feliks Chuev, *Sto sorok besed s Molotovym* (Moscow: Terra, 1991), p. 100.

†Acronym for *smert shpionam* ("death to spies") used to designate Soviet military counterintelligence (1943–46).

28 August and 4 September, Soviet forces landed without resistance on Iturup, Kunashir, Shikotan, and the Habomai Islands.[44]

Preparing for any eventuality, Vladivostok and Khabarovsk authorities evacuated thousands to the interior in anticipation of air raids.[45] As if to justify these precautions, a lone Japanese aircraft appeared over Vladivostok on 18 August and dove vertically into Amur Bay, narrowly missing a tanker anchored at Pervaya Rechka.[46] Agitprop did its best to arouse suitable bellicosity. "May our hatred crush them!" headlined a Khabarovsk newspaper, which quoted a mother exhorting her sons: "Kill the Japanese bandits mercilessly! Remember what those two-legged beasts did to us. The time has finally come to get revenge."[47]

There was not much time to get revenge, as a Bikin mechanic discovered when, emulating a highly publicized Magadan couple, he handed over all his savings to the Party with a request to Comrade Stalin that he be allowed to buy a tank and kill "samurai."* The war ended the next day, and history does not record whether the Bikin patriot got a refund.[48]

Crowds gathering in Khabarovsk on 3 September to celebrate victory over Japan surpassed those of VE Day. Most people hoped that the end of the war in Asia would reunite families and allow a return to normal life after years of mobilization against internal and external enemies. Yet the "short purifying storm" did not clear the air for long,[49] for the United States filled the vacuum left by Imperial Japan, turning a Second World War backwater into a Cold War front.

---

*In 1943 Ivan and Aleksandra Boiko had cabled Comrade Stalin expressing patriotic readiness to buy a tank with their 50,000-ruble family savings and operate it themselves against the fascists. Comrade Stalin approved, and the Magadan couple reportedly wrought havoc among the enemy with a conjugal T-34, christened "Kolyma."

25

《 《 》 》

A Front Without War

Vladivostok offers experiences that Moscow never would:
hovels in which people live, the bad condition of the
streets, the primitive sewage disposal system and fitfully
functioning public services, and the prisoners marched
daily through the streets to and from work by soldiers
with fixed bayonets.   — O. Edmund Clubb (1945)

The Far East remained an armed camp for seven years after the Red Army withdrew from Manchuria in May 1946. With 400,000 troops, 40,000 sailors, and 50,000 chekists, every seventh inhabitant of the region was in uniform, deepening a regional military coloration that dated back to the nineteenth century. Demobilized troops swelled Party ranks from 65,260 in May 1945 to 148,446 in January 1951.[1] Once again, as under Blücher, a powerful military figure asserted himself vis-à-vis a regional Party representative. Maritime Region Party Secretary Pegov, riding high since the heady days of 1938, met his match in Far Eastern Supreme Commander Marshal Rodion Malinovsky.[2]

Balkanization resumed in 1947, when Sakhalin was detached from the Khabarovsk Region (krai) to form a new insular district embracing the Kurile Islands. In 1948 the Amur District (oblast) was created out of territory taken from the Chita District and Khabarovsk Region. Magadan and Kamchatka districts were carved out of the Khabarovsk Region in 1953 and 1956, respectively. Party and state organs in each district reported directly to Moscow.

Costs and Trophies

The Far East paid a heavy price in the war. About 15 percent of its inhabitants, excluding labor camp inmates, died in combat or from disease and malnutrition. Vladivostok lost 30,000 of its 208,000 residents, Khabarovsk 28,000 of 199,000.[3] Peace did not banish hunger, for only 325,000 tons of grain were harvested in 1945, compared with 507,000 tons in 1941.[4]

At a time when the Far East desperately needed outside help, it was not forthcoming. The Fourth Five-Year Plan (1946–50) diverted capital investment to war-ravaged Ukraine and Belorussia. Lend-Lease shipments halted upon Japan's surrender, and in contrast to the 1920s there were no infusions of foreign capital or technology.

Popular exhaustion slowed the pace of economic recovery. Malnutrition and lack of housing made people vulnerable to influenza and pneumonia. The worst-off had as recently as 1944 and possibly later lived in caves along the Amur embankment at Khabarovsk.[5] Although the police periodically deported "parasites" from Vladivostok, beggars lined the Leninskaya.[6] To be sure, not everyone was deprived. An unmarked store sold foodstuffs to American and Chinese diplomats,[7] and local elites enjoyed privileged access — calibrated by rank and connections — to scarce commodities.

Manchuria to some extent made up for the loss of Lend-Lease. Entire factories were dismantled and shipped to the USSR on railroads converted to accommodate Soviet rolling stock.[8] The innocuous-sounding Far East External Transport Agency cannibalized Japanese and White Russian enterprises.[9] Karafuto and Kurile settlements were stripped of everything from livestock to kitchenware.[10] Just about everyone trafficked in war trophies. Japanese watches, pens, stockings, paper fans, cosmetics, toothpaste, dolls, cigarettes, and chocolates turned up in state stores as well as on the black market. Among bureaucrats, Nippon Electric telephones enjoyed the status of desk icons.

While trophies eased commodity shortages, incoming settlers and prisoners helped jump-start the economy and populate newly acquired territories. To induce demobilized troops to stay on and to lure immigrants, authorities offered wage bonuses ranging from 20 percent in the Primorye to 100 percent in the Kuriles. Fanning embers of the Khetagurova movement, the Komsomol urged girls to head for the Northeast. Thousands did, although some wore out their welcome among permanent residents and released camp inmates by their arrogance and careerism.[11]

Prison labor was replenished by an influx of POWs (Germans, Hungarians, Italians, Rumanians, Japanese, and repatriated Red Army personnel), émigrés from Manchuria, deported nationalities (Crimean Tartars, Chechen-Ingush, Bessarabians, Volga Germans, Siberian Germans, German exiles, and German Jews), and women (consorts of Axis occupation troops, three daughters of Ataman Semyonov, mistresses of fallen communist officials, and "swallows" who had let down their chekist handlers).* The former consul-general in Vladivostok, George Kühlborn, was picked up in Manchuria and sent to a labor camp, from which he emerged in broken health in 1953. Forced repatriation claimed the lives of poet Arseny Nesmelov and Sidemi's last owner, Yury Yankovsky, who in 1924 had found what then looked like secure refuge in Manchuria and Korea, respectively. Arseniev's counterpart Nikolai Baikov was not touched, although this former tsarist officer had contributed articles to a Harbin Russian fascist newspaper. Yet a number of Manchurian-born White Russians who had never been to the USSR were charged with treason, among them Ataman Semyonov's son Mikhail.[12]

No region in the USSR had a higher concentration of penal labor between 1945 and 1953. Prisoners mined coal and cut forests, built ports, laid track, and dug a tunnel under the Tatar Strait. Prewar camp clusters such as Dal'lag, Maglag, Bamlag, Amurlag, and Burlag continued to thrive, while Sakhlag expanded into "liberated" southern Sakhalin.[13] Camps ringed Vladivostok and Khabarovsk, Vanino and Nakhodka, Blagoveshchensk and Nikolaevsk. In Kolyma penal labor for ordinary criminals came under the jurisdiction of the Ministry of Internal Affairs (MVD), while the Ministry of State Security (MGB) ran special camps for "enemies of the people." Far Easterners referred, without rancor, to men and women toiling under guard in their midst as "Vlasovites."†

Kolyma absorbed hundreds of thousands of "Vlasovites" after 1945. When Panteleimon Derevyanko succeeded Ivan Nikishov as head of Dalstroi in 1946, he followed his predecessor's footsteps by bestowing the privilege of survival, allowing selected inmates to exercise their talents as physicians, tailors, shoemakers, and actors. A dozen jazz musicians found their

---

Lastochki ("swallows") was slang for attractive young women assigned by the security organs to establish intimate relationships with targeted foreigners.
†Thomas J. Cory, Vladivostok, to Secretary of State, 20 Aug. 1946, State Dept. Decimal File, 861.48/8-2046. "Vlasovite" was a follower of Lt.-Gen. Andrei Andreevich Vlasov, who in German captivity (1942–45) led an anti-Stalin movement among Red Army POWs.

salvation in Eddie Rosner's Magadan Orchestra.[14] Prisoners designed and built dwellings for incoming free settlers, prompting the quip that under socialism houses sprang up in virgin taiga before pioneers arrived.[15]

Prison labor had its drawbacks, especially on the docks, where stevedores had access to ammonal, an explosive used to break up ice during arctic navigation. Ammonal contributed to a more equitable distribution of state supplies, judging from the unusual frequency of warehouse explosions. When the *Dalstroi* blew up at Nakhodka in July 1946, putting the harbor out of operation for weeks, rumors blamed (or credited) deportees from the Baltic for the fireworks.[16]

Japanese POWs

Among the various nationalities contributing to socialist construction under MVD auspices, the Japanese left a special imprint on the Far East. Of three million Japanese in areas occupied by the Red Army and Pacific Fleet in August 1945, over 600,000 or 20 percent were interned in the USSR. In addition, about half of the 400,000 Japanese and Korean residents of southern Sakhalin and the Kuriles were detained. Motives for these acts are still the subject of speculation. Some argue that Stalin was settling old scores. Others point to his frustration at being denied Hokkaido. Postwar labor shortages certainly played an important role. And had not Tokyo in its eagerness to engage Moscow as a mediator offered in July 1945 to supply laborers to the USSR?[17] Stalin "accepted" with a vengeance. Indeed, Soviet representatives on the Allied Council requested in 1946 that Japanese workers be sent to Sakhalin from Japan proper.[18]

After being organized into brigades, POWs were distributed among 200 MVD installations between the Black Sea and the Pacific. About 60 percent remained in the Far East around Khabarovsk, Nikolaevsk, Lake Khanka, Nakhodka, Magadan, Petropavlovsk, Birobidzhan, Tetyukhe, and Skorovodino. A special camp at Krasnaya Rechka outside of Khabarovsk accommodated 300 senior Kwantung Army officers and important civilian officials from Manchukuo, Korea, and Karafuto.[19]

Japanese labor figured prominently in Far Eastern "socialist construction" during 1946–49. About 50,000 Japanese POWs worked on BAM. Thousands more logged timber in the Stanovoi and Sikhote Alin ranges, mined coal in the Bureya Valley, and handled cargoes at Nagayevo, Sovetskaya Gavan, and Nakhodka. They repaired sidewalks and shoveled snow, constructed ammunition plants, and built naval yards. A hundred and fifty Japanese female typists, telephone operators, and nurses worked in Khabarovsk, Vladivostok, and Irkutsk. Japanese carpenters, masons, and electricians gave Khabarovsk a face-lift, building a municipal stadium, a prison, and the Higher Party School. Magadan's main thoroughfare, lined with POW-built structures, was dubbed "Japan Street."[20]

Re-education went hand in hand with labor. Upon arrival in the USSR, enlisted men were told that they had been "liberated" from "feudal" oppression. In time they were separated from their officers and mobilized into a "democratic movement." Inmates in each camp "spontaneously" established a "friendship society" to foster "progressive" attitudes. POW "democratic committees" set work norms, managed food distribution, promoted a Stakhanovite "Hiratsuka movement," and sat on "people's courts."[21] MVD specialists, assisted by POW collaborators, developed a curriculum around a Japanese translation of the *Short Course*. Vernacular newspapers in Yuzhno-Sakhalinsk and Khabarovsk diligently hammered home the message.* Meanwhile, broadcasts from Khabarovsk dwelt on the Soviet struggle for peace, the genius of Comrade Stalin, Japan's agony under American bayonets, and the good fortune of POWs in the USSR.[22]

An overwhelming majority of POWs went through the motions of collaboration by fulfilling work norms, attending lectures, signing petitions, and taking part in self-criticism sessions. A much smaller number served on the democratic committees and threw themselves into the Hiratsuka movement. Enthusiasts tended to be younger men with the psychological dexterity to replace the emperor with Stalin in the quicksilver hierarchy of their loyalties. Isolation promoted credulity. POWs had no access to independent sources of information, and such mail as did reach them starting at the end of 1946 was heavily censored.[23] Chekists had no qualms about using repatriation as leverage.[24]

POWs fraternized spontaneously and sometimes surreptitiously with ordinary Soviet citizens. The former were struck by the absence of racism, the latter by the presence of humor. Despite or perhaps because of the language barrier, Japanese men and Russian women were drawn to each other. To the unfeigned hilarity of women field workers, a passing column

---

Shin seimei ("New life") and *Nihon shimbun* ("Japan newspaper"), respectively. The latter was edited by Asahara Masaki and Lt.-Col. Ivan Ivanovich Kovalenko, chief of the Propaganda Section of the Khabarovsk kraikom. Kovalenko later headed the Japan Section of the International Department of the CPSU Central Committee until his retirement in 1988.

of prisoners might break into bawdy charades accompanied by unprintable but fetchingly accented Russian.[25] Pragmatism as well as hormones promoted intimacy, for pregnancy entitled one to increased rations and lighter work loads.[26] Because so few Russian men returned from the war, some POWs enjoyed an eligibility that exposed them to amatory assaults.[27] Relationships rarely resulted in matrimony, for Soviet women were forbidden to marry foreigners.

To anesthetize refractory impulses among POWs destined for internment in 1945, guards spread the rumor that all Japanese were being transported to the USSR for repatriation because Manchurian and Korean ports were closed.[28] Once in camps, internees were kept manageable by work norms, re-education, and malnutrition. Escapees who emerged alive from free-fire zones generally succumbed in the taiga.[29] Group resistance was strongest among officers. In 1947, forty of them extracted concessions from logging camp administrators by threatening to commit suicide.[30] In 1955 some 2,500 officers went on a hunger strike at Krasnaya Rechka for four months, until Moscow promised to investigate complaints.[31]

Most POWs were repatriated between 1947 and 1949. Brought to Nakhodka, they signed petitions expressing gratitude to Comrade Stalin and surrendered all printed materials before being allowed to board transports.[32] Although TASS announced in 1950 that all POWs had been repatriated, over 2,000 "war criminals" remained in detention serving sentences ranging from eight to twenty-five years.[33] After Tokyo and Moscow restored diplomatic relations in 1956, "war criminals" started trickling back to Japan; the last returned in 1958. Several hundred Japanese remained permanently domiciled in the USSR, joining approximately a thousand veterans of the 1939 Khalkhin Gol (Nomonhan) Incident.[34] Some stayed behind because they had taken Soviet citizenship and married or forfeited their "exitability" by joining the MVD. Others who did not choose or were not allowed to return home were conspicuous collaborators, such as the head of an indoctrination school for internees, Hakamada Mutsuo, nicknamed "Emperor of Siberia."* A few waited for revolution in Japan.[35]

Over 62,000 Japanese perished in Soviet labor camps between 1945 and 1956.[36] Death rates in the Far East varied. One Khabarovsk Camp lost 400 of 1,000 POWs between 1945 and 1947.[37] At the Birakan Camp in the Jewish Autonomous District, half of the 2,000 inmates did not survive.[38]

---

*Hakamada visited Japan as a Soviet journalist in 1976.

Japanese succumbed in large numbers along the BAM route, 3,200 at a single site.[39]

Forced labor had ambivalent repercussions. Japanese prisoners contributed five billion man-hours to the Soviet economy.[40] Some POWs formed attachments and returned as visitors,* but most carried within them a residue of bitter resentment. To the extent that memories have influenced people (one POW became prime minister),[41] the Soviet Far East lost more in goodwill than it gained in manpower.

A Cold War Front

Between 1945 and 1948 the Far East changed from a bridge between wartime allies into a front between Cold War adversaries. The United States posed a more complex challenge to the Soviet Far East than Imperial Japan had, for superpower rivalry invested regional frictions with global overtones. Civil war in China and war in Korea made Northeast Asia a vortex of international tensions. American forces, deployed from Alaska to Okinawa, probed Far Eastern perimeters. The nuclear threat, especially before 1949 when the United States monopolized atomic weapons, cast a pall over a region whose population centers lay within striking range of Japan-based B-29s.

Official attitudes toward Americans in the Far East began to cool in early September 1945, when the Pacific Fleet command learned that Truman had refused Stalin's request for an occupation zone in Hokkaido.[42] MVD surveillance and restrictions on consular staff in Vladivostok, more stringent than those in Moscow, led Consul-General O. Edmund Clubb in December 1945 to suggest semiannual rotation of personnel ("because of the barren social existence") and consideration of Khabarovsk as an alternate site.[43] U.S. Navy personnel in weather stations outside Khabarovsk and on Kamchatka were evacuated by January 1946.† After the departure of Assistant Naval Attaché George Roullard, the Vladivostok consulate-general closed its naval office in August 1946.[44] The arrest of Roullard's interpreter Irene Matusis in 1947 set the stage for the media to "expose" an American

---

*Notably Japan's leading historian of Siberia, Katō Kyūzō. For a wistful reference to his Siberian internment, see Katō, *Sibir'*, p. 3.

†March, "Yanks in Siberia," p. 340. Following an arrangement reached between Truman and Stalin at Potsdam, over 100 U.S. naval personnel had opened weather stations at Kniaz Volkonskoye and Petropavlovsk in early Sept. 1945.

"spy nest" in Vladivostok.[45] It was put about that Americans had smuggled lethal bacteria into Vladivostok on Lend-Lease ships as part of a plan to subdue the Soviet Far East.[46] Four days after the consulate-general shut its doors for the second time in twenty-five years, on 27 August 1948, the Ministry of Foreign Affairs informed Western governments that Soviet territory east of the Urals was henceforth off-limits to their citizens.[47] Siberia remained open to foreign Communists such as Mao Zedong in 1950 and Stalin Prize laureate Pablo Neruda in 1951.[48]

American electronic access to the Far East was not so easily blocked. The Voice of America started broadcasting Russian-language programs to the Primorye, the Priamur, and the Northeast from Honolulu in 1947.[49] Jazz, folk music, and Christmas carols carried by the U.S. armed forces network in Japan found their way into Kolyma camp loudspeakers.[50] Radio jamming began in the Far East several months earlier than in other parts of the USSR but covered only urban areas.[51]

As relations with the United States deteriorated, cooperation with China and North Korea strengthened. As soon as the People's Liberation Army gained the upper hand in Manchuria in 1948, trade with Communist areas hitherto conducted through dummy firms came into the open. The establishment of the Democratic People's Republic of Korea (May 1948) and the People's Republic of China (October 1949), together with the conclusion of Soviet-Korean and Sino-Soviet security treaties during 1948–50 created a new political framework for regional cooperation.[52]

With the outbreak of war in Korea on 25 June 1950, the Far East became a potential battle zone. U.S. spy flights over Chukotka, Kamchatka, and the Kuriles increased dramatically.[53] MiG-15 fighters produced at Komsomolsk were flown directly to Andong, Manchuria, from where Russian pilots took them into combat over North Korea.[54] On 8 October 1950 two F-80 Shooting Stars strafed Sukhaya Rechka military airfield, twenty miles west of Vladivostok.[55] Although the ground war receded when Chinese "volunteers" beat back the UN advance over the 38th parallel, an undeclared war raged in Far Eastern skies for three years. B-29s were shot down over the Tumen River in 1950 and the Kurile Islands in 1952. On 27 July 1953, ten hours before the Panmunjon cease-fire, four U.S. fighters attacked an Ilyushin-12 carrying military personnel from Port Arthur to Vladivostok. No survivors were found in the wreckage sixty-six miles north of the Yalu. When Washington did not respond to a strong diplomatic protest, Moscow ordered retaliation. Two days later MiGs destroyed a B-50 over Peter the Great Bay with the loss of sixteen crewmen.[56]

American intelligence-gathering in the Far East, inaugurated during the Intervention,* revived in 1946 under the aegis of the Supreme Commander of Allied Powers in Japan, General Douglas MacArthur. Using Japanese Army studies and personnel, MacArthur's staff prepared contingency plans for infiltrating agents into industrial enterprises.[57] The army and (from 1947) the Central Intelligence Agency sent Japanese into Sakhalin and the Kuriles, Chinese into the Primorye, and if Soviet sources are to be believed, Eskimos into Chukotka.[58] The U.S. Navy operated above and below the surface along the USSR's Pacific and arctic littorals. In July 1957 Moscow declared that all of Peter the Great Bay lay within Soviet territorial waters, but American submarines continued to gather intelligence within the bay. The inauguration of U-2 flights over the Far East in the late 1950s raised the possibility of American pilots finding themselves stranded there. A 1963 U.S. Air Force handbook on the Soviet Far East contained a passage in Russian for such a contingency: "I am an American and do not speak your language. I need food, shelter, and assistance. I will not harm you; I bear no malice toward your people. If you will help me, my government will reward you."[59]

On the Cultural Front

War and repression invigorated the Far Eastern cultural scene with metropolitan evacuees and exiles. The Leningrad State Theater relocated to Khabarovsk, the Moscow State Theater to Vladivostok. Security organs made their own contribution to this diaspora of talent. Osip Mandelshtam's exiled widow taught in Chita.[60] Evgeniya Ginzburg and Varlam Shalamov bore witness to life and death in Kolyma. The Comintern envoy to China (1923–27) and founding editor of *Moscow News* (1932), Mikhail Borodin, spent his final days outside of Yakutsk.[61]

The bureaucratization of regional culture resumed in 1946 as writers' unions sprouted in Vladivostok, Yuzhno-Sakhalinsk, Blagoveshchensk, Magadan, and Petropavlovsk. Member-authors trimmed their sails to ideo-

---

*During 1919 Col. William J. Donovan, subsequently founding director of the OSS and the CIA, collected intelligence between Vladivostok and Omsk.

logical winds from the Center. When Leningrad Party Secretary Andrei Zhdanov lambasted "rootless cosmopolitans" and proclaimed the "two camps" doctrine, Far Eastern ideological guardians echoed his words with a reverence second only to that accorded to Comrade Stalin. Without apparent irony, a Khabarovsk archivist rejoiced in 1949 that "Stalinist five-year plans" had made the Far East "even more impenetrable."[62] Zeal on the periphery won approbation at the Center. In 1949 *Pravda* congratulated the Khabarovsk literary journal *Dalny Vostok* for promoting "the growth of Communist consciousness in Soviet man."[63] Later that year at a conference of Far Eastern Writers in Khabarovsk, the delegates unanimously resolved to produce literary building blocks for Comrade Stalin on the Pacific.[64]

Far Eastern writers bursting into print after the war retained some vestiges of a youth suckled on the *Short Course*, chastened in some cases by experiences at the front. Shunning traitors such as Gamarnik and giving wide berth to non-persons such as Blücher, Dmitry Nagishkin cobbled a serviceable civil war hero out of Sergei Lazo, whose early death (1920) bleached the stain of his SR antecedents and attenuated his failure to recognize the genius of Comrade Stalin. By the late 1940s such a lapse could have unpleasant consequences, for hyperbolic claims about Comrade Stalin had congealed into historiographical canon.[65] Needless to say, the engineer of human souls figured prominently on construction sites, where Vasily Azhayev camouflaged prison labor on an oil pipeline, and Aleksandr Chakovsky ventriloquized vacuities in the mouths of enthusiasts turning Sakhalin into an "island of happiness."[66] Though Japanese still qualified as bogeys who trained wolves to eat unwary tots,[67] Americans took their place in the rogues' gallery of imperialists. Not only had Yanks orchestrated the Siberian intervention, they had engaged in an orgy of plunder, ripping off the corrugated roofs of Priamur houses and shipping them to the United States.[68] Nikolai Maksimov used the Bering Strait for a Zhdanovian "two camps" parable juxtaposing bright Chukotka and bleak Alaska.[69] Sergei Ivanov revealed how Douglas MacArthur and Herbert Hoover had plotted to invade the Soviet Far East in 1931.* The Red Army's Manchurian cam-

---

*Ivanov, *Amerikanskaia agressiia*, p. 70. MacArthur earned a niche in late Stalin-era demonology by monopolizing the occupation of Japan (Stalin's proposal of Marshal Vasilevsky as co-commander was rebuffed by Harry Truman) and by vigorously prosecuting the war in Korea (Inchon landings, advocacy of expanding hostilities north of the Yalu River). Former President Herbert Hoover made an ideal bogey, having crossed Siberia twice in 1909 as a mining

paign of August 1945 launched several literary careers. With *Eagles Over the Khingans* (1948), Georgy Markov patented formulas that carried him to the general-secretaryship of the Writers' Union. Vasily Efimenko earned himself a sinecure in the Soviet-Japanese Friendship Society (Khabarovsk branch) with an uplifting tale about a progressive kamikaze pilot.[70]

Quick to respond to the Party's "anti-cosmopolitan" campaign, Far Eastern authors suspended the laws of class struggle and rehabilitated Cossacks and tsarist officers as liberators of the Amur Valley, Sakhalin, and the Kuriles. Few cultivated the nationalist loam more sedulously than Nikolai Zadornov, who harvested novels celebrating Russian victories over Manchu aggressors, Japanese militarists, and American capitalists.* When Russian explorers show up in one Zadornovian parable, aborigines tell the reader: "We have been waiting for them for many years."[71] The search for Russian heroes led to a partial rehabilitation of Vladimir Arseniev, whose *Dersu Uzala* was republished in 1949.

Arseniev's alleged Great Russian chauvinism paled in comparison with the orchestration of aboriginal gratitude to Lenin, Stalin, the Great October Revolution, the Communist Party, and the Russian people. Yulia Shestakova, a Khabarovsk journalist, discovered and groomed "politically literate" natives as writers and spokesmen for their national groups. Typical was Jansi Kimonko, the first Udege Communist and organizer of the first Udege kolkhoz, who began his career hunting Whites during the civil war and ended it hunting game in 1949. Kimonko's stories, which the literary critic Ilya Lerman compared favorably with Rudyard Kipling's *Kim*, won him a niche in the Soviet literary firmament reserved for "little peoples."[72] Kimonko's Chukcha analogues credited Lenin with bringing Chukotka sunshine each morning and carved Stalin cameos out of mammoth bone.[73] Sycophancy at times bordered on parody, suggesting a possibility of authorial mischief: "For everything I've achieved, I'm indebted to the beloved Communist Party and to the Great Russian people. I'm the first Ulch to get a membership card to the USSR Writers' Union, and for this too, I'm obliged to my Russian friends."[74]

---

engineer representing the Russo-Asiatic Corporation, a partnership of Anglo-American investors and Russian aristocrats, officials, and entrepreneurs. Hoover's business associate and personal friend, Baron V. V. Meller-Zakomelsky, conveniently (if misleadingly) conjured up the butcher of the "Chita Republic" (1905–6).

*The Chita-born Stalin Prize laureate wrote in the 26 July 1945 issue of *Tikhookeanskaya zvezda* that the stone structures on the lower Amur at Tyr were of Russian rather than Chinese origin.

Anti-Semitic Coda

Birobidzhan's future looked bright in the first two years after the Second World War. Some 10,000 Jewish immigrants arrived from the Ukraine and Central Asia during 1946–48. Orphans from Rumania and Poland found new homes there. A Jewish cultural revival, generated in part by visiting intellectuals from metropolitan Russia, animated local educational, literary, and artistic life.[75] From abroad came gifts of food, clothing, typewriters, and more. A Birobidzhan street was lined with houses purchased in the Netherlands by American Jewish benefactors.[76]

The fragility of this promise became apparent in the last two months of 1948, when the central media warned that Zionism and American imperialism were targeting Birobidzhan. Such language stoked anti-Semitism in the Russian and Ukrainian population and prepared the ground for a series of official measures taken against Jews during 1949: denunciation by a Khabarovsk writers' commission of "cosmopolitan" and "bourgeois nationalist" elements in Birobidzhan publications; the closure of the Kaganovich Yiddish Theater, the Sholem Aleikhem Library, and the newspaper *Birobidzhaner shtern*; the arrest of eight Jewish leaders, including district Party secretary Aleksandr Bakhmutsky; and restrictions on the movements of all local Jews.[77]

These measures served as a dress rehearsal for the 1951–52 Moscow trial of the "Birobidzhan eight" on charges of espionage on behalf of the United States. Resurrecting the specter of a secessionist conspiracy used against Novograblenov in Kamchatka (1933), Berzin in the Northeast (1937), and Gamarnik in the Primorye (1937), the security organs painted a scenario of the accused plotting with Washington to detach Birobidzhan from the USSR. All were found guilty, but in a break with precedent, some survived their sentences.[78]

The anti-Semitic wave crested in the final weeks of Stalin's life. On 13 January 1953 newspapers announced the exposure of a conspiracy among Kremlin doctors to kill Party and government leaders. Many of the doctors listed had Jewish-sounding names. Amid a rising storm of orchestrated popular rage, Jewish leaders were approached by the MVD and instructed to write to Comrade Stalin asking that Jews be deported to the Far East for their own safety and as atonement for the criminal acts of the Kremlin doctors. Party organizations throughout the USSR were told to prepare for roundups, sparking rumors of a "final solution."[79] Dozens of prominent Far

Eastern Jews, including the director of the Khabarovsk Artillery School, were arrested as Zionists and American spies.[80] Thousands of others were ostracized in offices, factories, farms, and schools. The "doctors' plot" was officially denounced as a fabrication shortly after the announcement of Stalin's death on 5 March 1953, and the MVD ordered a halt to measures against Jews, but some officials on the periphery did not rush to comply.[81]

26

Khrushchevian Interlude

Come more often, so that our stores will always be as well
stocked as they are today.
— Vladivostok woman to Nikita Khrushchev (1959)

On 7 March 1953 someone broke Stalin's outstretched arm at the Magadan Park of Culture and Rest. Authorities cordoned the statue off and repaired the limb with carelessly mixed concrete that soon eroded, exposing a rusty iron strut. No one bothered to do anything until one night in 1956, when Comrade Stalin was quietly removed from the park.[1] The episode personifies developments in the Far East between 1953 and 1964: partial dismantlements, patchwork repairs, unceremonious disposals.

Partial Dismantlements

In October 1953, seven months after Stalin's death, three months after Beria's execution, and one month after Nikita Khrushchev's appointment as general-secretary, the Dalstroi Party committee convened at Magadan. The committee had been overseeing the preparation of a plan that lay out in bright colors Dalstroi operations from 1956 until 1970. Instead of celebrating a radiant future, however, the committee chided itself for neglecting health care in the gold mines. Thus did gentle self-criticism sound the death knell of an organ that had outlived its utility. Dalstroi lingered on as a ward of the Ministry of Nonferrous Metals and in 1957 was quietly abolished.[2]

Within two years of its birth on 3 December 1953, Magadan District lost over a quarter of its population as camp inmates poured from Kolyma. Ships, planes, and transit camps bulged with outward-bound humanity. But leaving Kolyma did not necessarily mean going home, as many discovered upon being designated "special settlers." Nor did it necessarily mean survival. Many of those emerging from the Butugychag uranium mine when it closed in 1955 carried lethal doses of radiation. Although authorities tried to put a bright aspect on matters by opening a resort called "Hot Springs" (*Goriachie kliuchi*) in 1955, the past clung to Kolyma. Children grew up amid rusting barbed wire and played with skulls plucked from eroded riverbanks.

As people came out of camps they tried to pick up the threads of their lives. None of the five Khudyakov brothers survived Stalin. Some of their children and grandchildren managed to resettle in the Primorye but not at the family farm.[3] Zotik Matveyev's daughter Tatiana, having lost father, uncle,* brother, and husband, returned to Vladivostok in 1958 after having worked in the arctic, Ukraine, and Kazakhstan. Arseniev's daughter Natasha, broken in health and spirit, lived for a while in Khabarovsk but unable to bear the painful reminders of her parents, moved to Blagoveshchensk.[4]

Meanwhile, quick to adapt to the new times, perspicacious chekists left the MVD/MGB in droves to find work in factories, the police, and the procuracy. Those with blood on their hands risked discovery by survivors emerging from the camps and so kept a low profile. Some remained proud of what they had done and resented the lack of public gratitude for their services to Party and motherland.[5]

Forced labor did not disappear with Stalin's demise. The Main Administration for Corrective Affairs in the Department of Internal Affairs continued to operate labor camps for juvenile delinquents, parasites, alcoholics, and addicts throughout the Far East. Punishments kept abreast of advances in science and technology. Prisoners served as guinea pigs for atomic explosions on Chukotka and cleaned the nozzles of nuclear submarines in the Primorye. At a KGB psychiatric hospital in Blagoveshchensk, physicians and nurses practiced what was euphemistically called forensic medicine on inmates.[6]

Destalinization

Personnel turnover picked up as Khrushchev consolidated his power, culminating in the defeat of the "anti-Party opposition" (Malenkov, Mo-

*Tatiana's uncle Venedikt Mart Matveyev, a poet, was like her father Zotik shot in 1938. Venedikt's son, Ivan Matveyev (1918–87), turned up in Germany during the Second World War, moved to the United States in 1950, and eventually taught Russian literature at the University of Pittsburgh. The younger Matveyev's verse, stories, translations, and memoirs appeared under the name Ivan Elagin.

lotov, Kaganovich) in 1957. Chekists were among the first to feel the consequences of political realignments at the Center. The fall of Beria doomed all
but one of his Far Eastern lieutenants. Goglidze was shot. Nikishov vanished. Gvishiani survived, probably thanks to family connections.[7] Pegov,
who had hitched his star to that of Malenkov, was put out to diplomatic
pasture as Khrushchev moved quickly to appoint members of his own
Ukrainian team as Far Eastern Party secretaries.[8]

Names changed not only on door plaques. The "most beloved leader of
all epochs and all peoples" began disappearing from Far Eastern nomenclature as early as 1954. In Kolyma the Magadan District Party committee
marked the first anniversary of Stalin's death by renaming the local paper,
Stalinsky tempy, *Seimchanskaya pravda*.[9] Vladivostok's army paper *Stalinsky
voin* ("Stalin Warrior") refurbished its masthead with an eighteenth-
century field marshal, becoming the *Suvorovsky natisk* ("Suvorov Attack").
"Stalinos," "Stalinsks," "Stalin districts," "Stalin Highway," and "Stalin privileges" went by the boards. The henchmen's turn came in 1957, when
"Molotovs," "Kaganoviches," and "Voroshilovs" vanished from factories,
collective farms, and settlements.

As some names disappeared, others reappeared. Gamarnik and Blücher
were rehabilitated on 7 October 1955 and 12 March 1956, respectively.
Deribas was also reinstated, and no one asked aloud how many lives this
chekist had snuffed out before his own turn came at the hands of his colleagues. Relatives of less elevated victims were notified after the Central
Committee had instructed local authorities to ask the KGB for the files of
candidates for rehabilitation.[10] In 1956, Tatiana Matveyeva was officially
informed that her father had died on 17 May 1939 (in fact he had been shot
on 25 April 1938) and received 7,005 rubles 48 kopeks (roughly $800) for
his unwarranted repression.[11] Not until 1959 did Arseniev's daughter Natasha learn the sentence received by her mother Margarita Nikolaevna in 1938
("ten years without right of correspondence") denoted execution. This
blow came as one of many that undermined Natasha's health and sent her to
the grave at the age of forty-nine in 1970. Meanwhile, Arseniev himself
became a Far Eastern icon. His remains were removed to a prestigious
cemetery, and status-conscious Communist functionaries were soon reserving adjacent plots so as to be assured of posthumous proximity to the
creator of *Dersu Uzala*. Distance spared Arseniev's most implacable enemy
the agony of having to witness this. Reinstated as an "honorable chekist,"
Albert Lipsky found a niche in an ethnographic museum at Abakan in the

Khakass Autonomous District of Krasnoyarsk Region, where he retired to live out his years as a pensioner.[12]

Four months after Khrushchev's secret speech denouncing Stalin at the Twentieth Party Congress in February 1956, the Central Committee issued a document on the "cult of personality," which was distributed for discussion in party cells, collective farms, factories, and schools throughout the USSR.[13] Instead of welcoming spiritual detoxification, many true believers felt betrayed, for as the late British curmudgeon Malcolm Muggeridge remarked, nothing enrages people more than to feel that they have been engaged in unprofitable adulation.[14] Nonetheless, the more agile beneficiaries of Stalinism quickly recovered and portrayed themselves retrospectively as victims. Lipsky confided to young audiences how he had suffered under the "cult of personality."[15] By heaping blame on Stalin and Beria, Lipsky and other Communists insulated themselves and the Party from the contagion of complicity. For their part, thousands of ordinary citizens who had made careers between 1929 and 1953 had little desire to reflect on their personal responsibility for human engineering gone awry.

Destalinization proved too much for Aleksandr Fadeyev, whose long bureaucratic career involved countless Faustian deals. As head of the Writers' Union from 1934 to 1953, Fadeyev did what was expected of him while trying to preserve his own self-respect. After Stalin's death, he found solace in alcohol. Khrushchev's denunciation of Stalin in February 1956 sent Fadeyev into a state of depression exacerbated by maneuvers against him within the Writers' Union Secretariat. Three months later, after composing an exculpatory letter to the Central Committee, he shot himself.[16]

What destroyed Fadeyev breathed a bit of life into education, science, and literature. The Far Eastern State University reopened after a seventeen-year hiatus. Aleksandr Zherebtsov, the NKVD operative who had handled the "cleansing" of DVGU orientalists in 1937–38, was summoned from honorable retirement and engaged as an expert witness for the Oriental Faculty's reconstitution.[17] Historians and memoirists resurrected Blücher, Gamarnik, and many others whose names had not appeared in print or who had been labeled "traitors" since 1937–38.[18] Vladimir Arseniev, quasi-rehabilitated in the late 1940s, was praised as a "scholar poet" by the well-known and respected writer Konstantin Paustovsky.[19] Kolyma burst into print in November 1962, when *Izvestiya*'s editor, Aleksei Adzhubei (Khrushchev's son-in-law), published a story by Chita writer-journalist Georgy Shelest a few days before *Novy mir* brought out Alexander Solzhenitsyn's

"One Day in the Life of Ivan Denisovich."[20] Far Eastern practitioners of socialist realism stayed away from camp themes and applauded in 1963 when Khrushchev harangued against liberal intellectuals.[21] In remote Magadan, where unorthodox impulses were tacitly (and provisionally) tolerated, some editors broke rank and published a Kolyma novel, albeit with a bowdlerized text.[22] But even Magadan mavericks stayed clear of Varlam Shalamov or Evgeniya Ginzburg, neither of whom lived to see their testimony published in the USSR.

Three prominent postwar writers started their literary careers in the Far East during the Khrushchev years. Evgeniya Ginzburg's son Vasily Aksyonov was sent to Magadan in 1949 to be reunited with his mother after the NKVD had taken her from him in 1937, when he was five. Far Eastern themes run through Aksyonov's early works, notably in "Oranges from Morocco" (1963), set amid a lemming-like stampede toward a citrus-filled freighter docked in Nakhodka. Pyotr Proskurin and Boris Mozhayev both made their literary debuts in the Far East during the 1950s.[23]

The Far East catalyzed fame but did not retain the famous. Not a single major author lingered there when given the chance to leave. Nesmelov emigrated. Mandelshtam, Ginzburg, and Shalamov sojourned involuntarily. Tretyakov, Fadeyev, Azhayev, Proskurin, Aksyonov, and Mozhayev found greater scope for their talents in the Center. By affording metropolitan opportunities for regional talent, destalinization did little to relieve the Far East's literary anemia.

The China Connection

During the 1950s the Sino-Soviet frontier recaptured some of its traditional porosity. Delegations of kolkhoz chairmen, trade unionists, komsomoltsy, scientists, and certified members of the "artistic intelligentsia" commuted between Blagoveshchensk and Heihe, Khabarovsk and Harbin, Vladivostok and Jilin. Museums, schools, and factories exhibited gifts from "Chinese friends." Local audiences flocked to Chinese circuses, and loudspeakers in parks and stadiums barked the familiar refrain ("Stalin and Mao are listening to us!") from the song "Moscow-Peking." Passengers waved fraternally when Chinese and Soviet steamers passed each other on "Friendship River" (the Amur). On weekends and holidays, an open-air bazaar on Kazakevich Island at the Amur-Ussuri junction was frequented by citizens of both countries. Fraternization ripened into marriages in a few cases, but its effects were more widely detectable in Sino-Russian pidgin.*

Inspired by various degrees of wishful thinking and opportunism, Far Eastern scriveners outdid themselves in sinophilic mush. A Pacific Fleet officer immortalized Mao in verse.[24] A Khabarovsk journalist wrote a popular novel about a Sino-Soviet uprising against Japanese rule in the Kurile Islands.[25] A colleague called the "Great Leap Forward" as "the greatest leap toward development of an economy in the history of humanity."[26]

The millennial mood nourished a variety of joint ventures. Binational commissions regulated Amur and Sungari river navigation and oversaw local barter arrangements. Engineers from local branches of the Soviet and Chinese academies of sciences sat down together and planned flood-control and hydroelectric dams along the Amur. Surveys were made for a canal linking the Ussuri to the Sea of Japan via Lake Khanka and the Suifen River.[27] In 1954, Khrushchev and Mao agreed that 200,000 Chinese would work seasonally in Siberia and the Far East.[28] Four years later Khrushchev reportedly suggested to Mao that they set up a joint Pacific naval command in Vladivostok.[29]

As fissures spread across the edifice of Sino-Soviet solidarity in the late 1950s, the Central Committee signaled regional Party committees well before activating the propaganda machine. Khabarovsk residents knew that something serious was amiss when they could no longer meet Chinese on Kazakevich Island and when Soviet advisers returned from China in 1960. Sensing opportunity, some composed texts downgrading Mao. The more clever kept metaphorically wet fingers aloft so as not to be caught unprepared by further shifts in the political wind.

Return to the Pacific

During the 1950s and early 1960s, the Soviet Union re-engaged with the Pacific Basin. Constrained by a weak infrastructure and red tape, the process developed unevenly, reflecting Khrushchev's own impulses and inconsistencies. Yet for all his gaucheries, Khrushchev was free of the paranoia that saw secessionist conspiracies lurking behind regional aspirations.

---

*Some residents of Khabarovsk still use the slang word *chifanit*, derived from the Chinese *chifan* ("to eat").

While the Pacific Fleet captured international attention, marine industries and transport made more significant breaks with tradition. For the first
time the Far Eastern fishing fleet moved into the open sea, and the Far
Eastern merchant marine came into its own, expanding operations to Indonesia, Vietnam, India, Pakistan, and Burma. By 1959 the Far Eastern
Steamship Company (FESCO), formed two years earlier by the merger of
Far Eastern merchant marine agencies, served thirty-nine ports in twenty-
four countries, including the United States and Canada. International cargoes, less than 10 percent of Far Eastern shipping in 1950, accounted for 44
percent in 1960.[30]

Japan energized the Far East's international economic activity after the
Soviet-Japanese Peace Declaration of 1956 and the commercial treaty of
1958. Sakhalin coal and Amur timber led Far Eastern exports while Japanese ships unloaded manufactures at Nakhodka. A 1963 coastal trade agreement providing for barter between enterprises in the Far East and firms in
prefectures along the Sea of Japan revived commercial patterns antedating
the 1930s.[31]

Khrushchev took the first steps toward making the Far East more accessible to the outside world. Over 2,000 Sakhalin Koreans and their Japanese
spouses were allowed to emigrate between 1957 and 1959.* Restrictions on
travel by foreigners were loosened in 1957 as Intourist opened offices in
Khabarovsk and Nakhodka. In 1961, as the jet age brought Khabarovsk
within nine hours of Moscow, FESCO inaugurated steamer service between Yokohama and Nakhodka. Within a couple of years, Khabarovsk and
Nakhodka were hosting 10,000 to 12,000 Western tourists annually and
servicing "friendship delegations" of athletes, trade unionists, scientists and
writers, touring musicians and actors, and data-gathering scholars and bureaucrats along with their KGB escorts en route to and from Japan. In 1964
central authorities endorsed the publication of guidebooks for Khabarovsk,
Sakhalin, and the Primorye in English and Japanese, suggesting that someone anticipated a wider *apertura*.

---

*About 100,000 Koreans were brought to Karafuto during the Second World War, most of
them as laborers in coal mines. Approximately 43,000 were still there at the end of the war.
Since Tokyo did not consider Koreans citizens, they were left in limbo during the years of
Japanese repatriation (1946–50). Most Sakhalin Koreans eventually took Soviet or North
Korean citizenship, but about 10 percent or just over 4,000 remained stateless and sought
admittance to Japan or repatriation to South Korea.

Khrushchev's Regional Imprint

Though the Far East never matched the virgin lands of Western Siberia and Kazakhstan in Khrushchev's priorities, it aroused his interest sufficiently to prompt visits in 1954 and again in 1959, something that no Russian or Soviet leader had ever undertaken. Curious about recently "liberated" territory, he visited southern Sakhalin, inaccessible even to Gamarnik and Blücher in their heyday. Addressing 50,000 at Vladivostok's Avangard Stadium on 6 October 1959, the general-secretary anticipated Gorbachevian perestroikists by nearly thirty years, reiterating what he had recently told a Los Angeles audience: that the Pacific Ocean unites the USSR and the USA.[32]

Khrushchev's reference to Pacific ties came in the context of his attempt after 1957 to decentralize the Soviet economy by reducing the number and power of ministries, abolishing machine tractor stations, and setting up regional economic councils. In theory each Far Eastern krai (Khabarovsk and Maritime) and oblast (Amur, Sakhalin, Magadan, Kamchatka) managed its own agriculture, industry, and construction. By leaving more decisions to local authorities, Khrushchev gave the Far East more administrative autonomy than it had enjoyed at any time since the 1920s. The Far Eastern Economic Planning Zone created in 1963 was designed to give regional coherence to separate programs of district economic councils. Attractive in theory, decentralization worked poorly in practice. Local managers lacked experience and were reluctant or unprepared to assume more responsibilities. The central bureaucracy resented encroachment on its prerogatives and eventually repossessed them. A few months after Khrushchev's ouster in October 1964, his successors Leonid Brezhnev and Aleksei Kosygin scrapped the regional councils and restored the power of central ministries.

Khrushchev left a mixed record. Dismantling the camps, opening the USSR to the outside world, engagement with the Pacific, and a partial rescue of the collective memory from Stalinist thralldom constituted real achievements. Although himself a major beneficiary of Stalinism, the earthy Ukrainian occasionally practiced what a later generation came to tout as glasnost. He was the first and only Soviet leader to publicly recognize the Birobidzhan experiment as a failure.[33] Moreover, he anticipated Gorbachev by urging Far Easterners to become more self-reliant.[34] For a quarter-century after his ouster, the name of Nikita Khrushchev vanished from

Soviet publications, but his efforts to give each family a separate apartment won him a place in colloquial speech: *khrushchevnik*, meaning a cubicle big enough in which to "sleep sitting and shit standing."

The New Nomenklatura

During the Khrushchevian interlude, the Central Committee installed a new generation of leaders in Far Eastern Party organizations. These were men who for the most part were born after 1917 and had joined the Party during or just after the Second World War. Yet though they were not direct beneficiaries of 1937–38, they did not have any qualms about using the Stalinist system to their own advantage. They were pragmatic men who cultivated patrons in Moscow and gradually built local networks through nepotism and patronage. Some held onto power for decades, running local political machines through the long "era of stagnation."

Members of the new Far Eastern nomenklatura shared career patterns, alternating central and provincial assignments. It was not uncommon for an upwardly mobile apparatchik to occupy a minor position in the Vladivostok municipal committee, spend a few years in the Jewish Autonomous District Party committee or in the Central Committee secretariat, and then settle into the Khabarovsk or Maritime Regional Party Committee. First secretaries of the Khabarovsk and Maritime kraikoms, ex officio on the Central Committee, were the most powerful men in the region.

Far Eastern Party secretaries held onto their posts when Khrushchev fell in the "Little October Revolution" of 1964. Unquestioning deference toward the Center combined with a highly developed instinct for self-preservation prolonged their careers but poorly equipped them to deal with creeping cynicism and apathy.

27

« « » »

The Era of Stagnation

We're building all over the country, but the pace is especially stirring here on the periphery.
— Leonid Brezhnev at Vladivostok (1966)

Few regions of the USSR were invested with more extravagant hopes than the Far East during the so-called era of stagnation (1964–85). "By the year 2000, the Far East will be one of the most advanced regions in the USSR" went one typical refrain.[1] "Siberia and the Far East have become a symbol of all that is new and progressive," went another.[2] Stagnation-era glitter gave way to glasnost gloom in the late 1980s, when readers were told that the Far East was the least-developed part of the country, had invariably failed to meet five-year plan targets, and accounted for a shrinking share of national output.[3] Both images oversimplified. In some ways the Far East did fall behind the rest of the Russian Republic. Yet transportation, education, and housing improved, and Far Easterners were given more opportunities to travel and participate in the economic and scientific life of the Pacific Basin. Naturally, some people benefited more than others.

The buildup of strategic rocket, army, navy, and KGB forces deepened the Far East's military ambience and detracted from badly needed investment in infrastructure. Troops stationed in the region increased from about 100,000 to 300,000. The Pacific Fleet metamorphosed from a coastal "lake flotilla" of 50,000 men and 200 ships to the largest and most powerful component of the Soviet Navy, with 150,000 men and 800 ships operating between Madagascar and California.[4] Widely perceived within the region as a response to pressures from the United States, China, and Japan, the Far Eastern military buildup pinched the civilian economy, crimped international contacts, and fed xenophobia.

The era of stagnation was the last hurrah of the Soviet Union's giant nature-taming projects. A canal was to link the Amur to the Sea of Japan that in turn was to be warmed by dams across the Tatar and La Pérouse straits. Another dam across the Bering Strait was to transform the arctic into a socialist realist Mediterranean.[5] The Baikal-Amur Railroad project was revived in 1974 amid predictions that it would, in the words of Yury Andropov, then head of the KGB, "solve social as well as economic problems."[6] BAM traversed the stagnation era like a comet, trailing a luminous shower of vendable exploits. Motivating people required more imagination than moving frozen earth. Aware of the limited appeal of Marx and Lenin and unable to resort to the methods of Stalin, authorities turned to Mammon. Bamovtsy, the shock troops of "mature socialism," pocketed four times the average wage, which may explain the subtext of their favorite slogan : "We made BAM; BAM made us!"[7] Though BAM was declared "completed" in 1984, it was still not fully operative in the next decade.

Efforts were made during the 1960s and 1970s to overcome the region's perennial energy deficit. Hydroelectric stations arose on the Zeya, Bureya, and Kolyma rivers. A geothermal plant was built on Kamchatka. The Far East's first nuclear power plant went into operation in 1976 at Bilibino on Chukotka permafrost. Three years later Andropov hailed the atomic wonder of Bilibino in the same breath as Chernobyl.[*]

Ongoing Pacific Engagement

Far Eastern engagement with the outside world gathered momentum under Brezhnev. The fishing fleet scoured every corner of the Pacific Basin, supplying half the country's marine products in 1985 compared with a third in 1960. FESCO became the largest freight carrier in the Pacific. Containers passing through Nakhodka and Vostochny accounted for 15 percent of all shipments between Japan and Europe in 1980.[8] Regular air service was inaugurated between Khabarovsk and Niigata in 1971.[†] The Far East reached a new high in its exports of timber, fish, and minerals and imports of industrial equipment, foodstuffs, and consumer goods. Japan replaced

[*]Yuri Andropov, *Izbrannye rechi i stat'i* (Moscow: Politizdat, 1983), p. 170. When Andropov gave this speech on 22 Feb. 1979, the KGB was aware of the design flaws that resulted in the disastrous meltdown at Chernobyl in 1986. In 1992 it was reported that the Bilibino plant was sinking into the ground because heat from the reactor had melted the permafrost. *RA Report*, 14 (Jan. 1993): 107.

[†]Attempts to establish civil air links between Vladivostok and Tokyo in 1921 and Anadyr and Juneau (Alaska) in 1934 foundered on technical, economic, and political obstacles.

China as the Far East's leading trade partner during the 1960s and by 1985 accounted for a third of the region's international commerce. Coastal trade was extended to Australia in 1978, and border trade opened with China in 1981. A Seattle firm worked out an arrangement with the Far Eastern Fisheries Administration in 1977 to harvest, process, and market fish products.[9]

With the establishment of the Far Eastern Science Center (DVNTs) at Vladivostok in 1970, science in the Far East regained a degree of administrative autonomy and international visibility. Headed at first by the geographer Andrei Kapitsa and from 1977 by Nikolai Shilo,* the Far Eastern Science Center participated in the world of learning within limits set by Moscow. Institute directors and department chiefs traveled abroad, after collecting visas and hard currency in Moscow, while research vessels afforded ordinary scientists a chance to see foreign ports and meet foreign colleagues. Vladivostok being closed, international gatherings convened in Khabarovsk or Nakhodka.[10]

Far Eastern tourism for Soviet citizens boomed during the Brezhnev years. Thousands of Muscovites, Leningraders, Ukrainians, and Belorussians took the waters at Shmakovka, sunned themselves on beaches along Peter the Great Bay, and gazed at Kurile and Kamchatka volcanoes. FESCO carried Soviet passengers from Vladivostok to South Pacific ports for which *putyovki* were in great demand.† To economize on hard currency and to facilitate surveillance, passengers slept aboard ship and shopped collectively.[11]

Foreign access to the Far East made less dramatic headway. Foreign tourists were funneled like containers through Nakhodka and Khabarovsk en route to and from Japan and Western Europe, but Vladivostok, Sakhalin, and the Northeast remained closed except for Soviet citizens with special passes and politically or economically useful foreigners such as Gulf Oil geologists and President Gerald Ford.[12]

The Politics of Dependence

During the Brezhnev-Andropov-Chernenko years, tensions with China and the United States made themselves felt in Far Eastern political life.

---

*The same Shilo who found Kolyma to be a land of opportunity in 1937, thanks in part to the heavy turnover of Dalstroi officials.
†A *putyovka* was a document issued by an enterprise's trade union committee entitling the bearer to join a tour or cruise, or to obtain accommodations at a resort or sanatorium.

Anti-"revisionist" propaganda during the Cultural Revolution, broadcast by Russian-language stations in China's northeastern provinces, rekindled vigilance campaigns redolent of the early 1950s. Moves by the United States and its friends to contain the USSR's expanding role in the Asia-Pacific region provided grist for purveyors of outrage at meetings and in the press. Chinese border "provocations" and American deployments enabled military, KGB, and Party elites to justify their privileges, as well as their powers, in the eyes of the region's inhabitants.

The Far East continued to be a victim of the metropolitan condescension that had so nettled Gamarnik four decades earlier.[13] A fin de siècle quip that sables ran around Vladivostok was reincarnated as "Do they have two-story buildings out there yet?" In high government and Party circles, it was fashionable to regard the Far East as a source of gold, game, and girls. No important political, social, or intellectual figure lived or even spent much time in the Far East. During an eighteen-year tenure as CPSU general-secretary, Brezhnev made whistle-stop visits in 1966 and 1978, but neither Andropov nor Chernenko set foot there. The All-Union heroine Khetagurova, disregarding her own advice to "come east," went west and settled in Riga. The "Far Eastern" novelist Nikolai Zadornov complained—from Riga—that metropolitan authors were not familiarizing themselves with the Far East.[14] Yury Rytkheu wrote about his native Chukotka from a comfortable apartment in Leningrad.[15] Evgeny Kozlovsky, a *vladivostokovets*, lived in Moscow and marketed his dissidence in Ann Arbor.[16]

The Far East could not compete with Western Siberia for influence in Moscow. Vladivostok and Khabarovsk had neither the connections nor the clout of Sverdlovsk (Ekaterinburg), particularly after huge oil and gas deposits were discovered in the Tyumen region in the 1960s.[17] Balkanization left the Far East divided against itself. Khabarovsk as always vied with Vladivostok for regional primacy. Sakhalin and Kamchatka competed with each other in the fishing industry. None of the six district Party organizations showed any inclination to work together.

Far Eastern Party leadership lived up to the era's nickname. First secretaries served for twelve years in Magadan, fifteen years in the Primorye and Kamchatka, eighteen years in Khabarovsk and Sakhalin, and twenty-one years in the Amur Party organizations. Entrenchment nurtured cronyism, high-handedness, and greed.[18] *Kormlenie* ("feeding," i.e. using one's office for personal gain) outgrew its individualist prerevolutionary antecedents and demonstrated collectivist qualities appropriate to the age of mature socialism. Brezhnevian *kormlenshchiki* coalesced into networks of Party apparatchiki, police and postal officials, procurators, labor union bureaucrats, heads of construction trusts, and members of the central nomenklatura who helped one another if expedient, advantageous, or necessary. Whenever circumstances required an image of probity, the press with a nod from the Party "exposed" a case of misconduct. In accord with a time-honored tradition, the culprit, if well connected or still useful, would be reassigned outside of the region.[19]

The Economics of Shortages

An unfavorable correlation of resources and space placed a perpetual strain on the Far Eastern economy. People and industry were located in the western part of the USSR; raw materials were concentrated in the east. A 1932 lamentation that the Far East was "richly endowed by Nature but poorly developed by man" held true fifty years later.[20]

In Moscow the Far East was commonly regarded as a white elephant because the region absorbed more investment than it yielded in raw materials. Worse, the Far East imported what it should have been exporting. With 30 percent of the USSR's timber reserves, it was chronically short of paper. Richly endowed with fossil fuels, it had an energy deficit. Despite the high priority accorded to agriculture in successive five-year plans, the Far East failed to achieve self-sufficiency in foodstuffs.[21] At the end of the 1960s, the region was importing two-thirds of its grain, over half of its meat, half of its milk and vegetables, a third of its eggs, and a fifth of its potatoes.[22] The sorry state of agriculture could not be blamed entirely on permafrost and flooding. Misused machinery destroyed a third of the soybean crop in 1971.[23] Roughly half of the potatoes, cabbages, cucumbers, and fish rotted each year while awaiting delivery. Once the breadbasket of the Far East, the Amur District in the early 1980s had one of the worst productivity rates in the USSR.[24]

Moscow bore no small responsibility for the Far East's poor performance, because central ministries wielded decisive leverage in the "east-west" struggle over development priorities and incrementally reduced the Far Eastern share of national investment.[25] By concentrating Far Eastern investment in extractive industries, central policies undercut the chances for balanced development, and the resulting neglect of social infrastructure (housing, roads, hospitals, schools) extracted a high cost in enormous labor turnover.[26] Despite wage bonuses, rapid promotion, and long vacations, only one in six new arrivals settled down. The proportion was even higher among engineers and managers, a third of whom departed annually.[27]

By 1985 the economic outlook for the Far East was not encouraging. National investment priorities were veering from the Pacific to Western Siberia. BAM brought no tangible upswing in trade and transport. The more accessible mineral deposits were being exhausted, and the mining industry faced the prospect of moving north where operations required heavy inputs of capital and technology that neither Japan nor the United States showed much of an inclination to provide.[28]

Regional transport could not keep up with demand. As the country's most distant and most heavily guarded periphery, the Far East formed the cul-de-sac of a 5,000-mile corridor leading to Moscow. With no highways across Siberia, the burden of carrying people and freight fell on railroads and aviation. Aeroflot coped lackadaisically with endemic aircraft and fuel shortages and an inadequate air traffic control system. Demand invariably exceeded the supply of seats, turning every traveler into a warrior. It came as a surprise to no one when, in 1983, a Vladivostok paper announced that passengers spent more time getting tickets than getting to their destinations.[29]

Despite shortages and isolation, life in the Far East had compensations. Most residents had gardens or dachas, where they grew their own flowers, cucumbers, and tomatoes. One did not have to go far to pick mushrooms and berries, a source of condiments and vitamins, respectively, during the long winter months. There were ample opportunities to hunt and fish, and poaching became something of an unofficial regional sport. State stores were well supplied with cabbages and potatoes and occasionally carrots, lemons, and bananas. When the salmon were running on Sakhalin and Kamchatka, red roe were practically given away by the bag. A variety of frozen fish and squid were sold in Vladivostok and Khabarovsk fish stores. Chicken and pork lard were nearly always available in Khabarovsk, as was boiled walrus on Chukotka. With connections, red meat could be had under the counter, and if one had the time to make a foraging trip to the right kolkhoz, a few well-directed bottles of schnapps would bring a cow or pig to the butcher block ahead of schedule.

Certain types of shortages were endemic to specific areas, as was eloquently testified to by press coverage of Kamchatka potato harvests and Sovetskaya Gavan apple orchards.[30] Even in Khabarovsk and Vladivostok, fresh fruits and vegetables were a rarity in winter, and dairy products grew scarce in summer because of spoilage or the diversion of available supplies to Young Pioneer camps. Outside the cities, it was hard to get clothes dry cleaned, shoes and appliances repaired, and photos developed. Housing shortages plagued the entire region. In Vladivostok people lived on ships anchored in the Golden Horn.[31] A worker could wait decades for an apartment.[32] Wage bonuses did not compensate for the high costs of living or the scarcity of housing, especially in the Northeast.[33] Of course the nomenklatura were insulated from these inconveniences by privileged access to special housing, foodstuffs, and medical care.

Public health in the Far East improved in some areas and deteriorated in others. Typhus, tuberculosis, and trachoma were brought under control, but tick-borne encephalitis periodically reached epidemic proportions in the summer taiga. The influx of young people gave the Far East a statistically low mortality rate, concealing the fact that life expectancy in the region fell below the USSR average by two years in the Priamur and the Primorye and by four in the Northeast.[34] Hospitals were built but lacked up-to-date equipment and drugs. Dental services were offered but for the most part only in urban areas. Apothecaries multiplied but chronically ran out of vitamins, so resourceful residents learned to use berries and medicinal plants. Municipalities built sewers and indoor plumbing but lacked potable water. The Amur, from which a fastidious New Yorker had once drunk without qualms,[35] turned into virulent sludge. Vladivostok poured raw sewage into Peter the Great Bay, as did Khabarovsk into the Amur. "Minerals" in Khabarovsk tap water required that pipes be unclogged each summer while people relied on street pumps. *Khabarovchane* wryly boasted that they led the country in kidney stones per capita, yet would-be patients thought twice before submitting themselves to surgery in local hospitals.

Far Easterners coped with fewer shortages and threats to health than their parents and grandparents had, to be sure. But the gains were overshadowed by rising expectations and nostalgia. Among youth, boredom begot political passivity and philistinism. Pensioners sat around courtyards on summer evenings and wistfully recalled how under Stalin people lived more cozily and could buy canned crab.

Compartmentalizing the Intellect

Far Easterners lived within a political culture that attached greater importance to appearances than to substance and that rewarded loyalty more than integrity. Once all the tiresome fuss about "cult of personality" was off the Party agenda, writers could resume celebrating the triumphs of partisans, border guards, and bamovtsy over White guards, Japanese militarists, Great Han chauvinists, American imperialists, and Mother Nature. Aging beneficiaries of Stalinism turned selective amnesia into a literary art form. Alexander Fadeyev was cast as a great writer, without a word about his functions in the mechanism of terror, his artistic and moral compromises, or his alcoholism and suicide.[36] Valentina Khetagurova settled down to the role of a mellow matron, basking in the gratitude of women who had taken her advice in 1937 and found fulfillment in the Far East.[37] As an octogenarian Klim Voroshilov was prepared to fondly recall Yan Gamarnik.[38] Nikolai Pegov, now in his seventies, wistfully reminisced how before June 1941 "our whole life was illuminated by sunshine, joy and happiness."[39] Semyon Bytovoi, molting the feathers of an NKVD informant, spread the plumage of a lyrical poet.

A new generation of Far Easterners learned how to compartmentalize the intellect and act out political charades. People indulged privately in black humor about Sergei Lazo ("Lazo bangs inside a tight stove") but no one publicly questioned his official status as the leading civil war martyr. There was no shortage of scientists, writers, teachers, factory workers, and collective farmers ready to sign letters and resolutions applauding the invasion of Czechoslovakia and Afghanistan or denouncing Ronald Reagan for the ill-fated Korean Airlines Flight 007.[40] Statements of solidarity by Far Easterners had special significance following Sino-Soviet clashes at Damansky Island on the Ussuri River in 1969 and during the campaign against Alexander Solzhenitsyn after *The Gulag Archipelago* was published in the West in 1974. Just as the Far East's proximity to China put its inhabitants on the front line in the struggle against Great Han chauvinism, so did its association with Kolyma (venue of "One Day in the Life of Ivan Denisovich") give Far Eastern voices special weight in "exposing" Solzhenitsyn's slanders. When prompted to join the chorus, most sang whether or not they had ever read *The Gulag Archipelago*. When asked about the controversial Nobel Prize laureate within official earshot, some found it politic to answer like the Kolyma-raised young mariner, who was quoted in 1974 as saying that Solzhenitsyn "is always defaming his country and people in his writings . . . so permit me not to consider him a true Russian writer."[41]

Aborigines selected for their "political literacy" during the 1940s and 1950s dispensed gratitude in return for flattering reviews, prizes, membership in the Writers' Union and on editorial boards, Moscow and Leningrad apartments, and foreign travel. Under titles such as *Story of Happiness* well-tutored "little peoples" ascribed their collective well-being to the Great October Revolution and to the "lofty humanism of our Party and government."[42] A few served on the historiographical front against bourgeois and Maoist falsifiers, providing serviceable testimony about Great Han chauvinists, Japanese exploiters, American plunderers, and Russian liberators.

The career of Yury Rytkheu illustrates how one politically conscious aborigine mastered the art of intellectual compartmentalization. Rytkheu left his native Chukotka at the age of fourteen in 1944 to work as a cook's helper in a construction camp, where he discovered the efficacy of well-aimed expressions of gratitude.[43] Deftly balancing creativity and accommodation, he progressed from the Anadyr Pedagogical Institute to Leningrad University, was taken into the USSR Writers' Union, and saw his first novel published in 1964 in the journal *Oktyabr*, then edited by Vsevolod Kochetov, a paragon of *partiinost*.[44] Although celebrated in a popular anecdote ("Rytkheu's not afraid to defend Solzhenitsyn, because the farther away they exile him the closer he gets to home"), he sang in tune with the Writers' Union. He once confided to an acquaintance how terrible conditions really were for aborigines in the Northeast. When the acquaintance asked him if he planned to write about it, Rytkheu reportedly replied: "Why? I know the kind of product they [the authorities] want."[45]

Genuine works of literature were written in the Far East during the Brezhnev years, but few appeared in print. The more interesting the writer, the more cautiously he or she was published. Sensitive people revealed themselves in verse rather than prose, and among Far Eastern poets of this period, few could match Magadan's Viktoriya Goldovskaya for evoking images of unmentionable shades of the Stalinist past.[46] Vladimir Vysotsky had a large and diverse following in the Far East, where he had once worked and about which he sang until death overtook him in 1980. His underground tapes were audible to anyone strolling around Khabarovsk on a summer evening in the 1970s and early 1980s.

Although Far Easterners had less access to forbidden literature than their counterparts in metropolitan Russia, well-connected residents acquired private stocks of Solzhenitsyn, Ginzburg, and Shalamov for prestige and perusal. *Samizdat* and *tamizdat* (Russian language works published abroad) circulated in larger cities. Thanks to informants, authorities had a fair idea of who partook in literary commerce.

Diversity and Deviancy

Although Russians formed over 85 percent of the Far East's population in 1979,* regional society was diverse and divided. Eighty-two nationalities were counted along the BAM route in 1984.[47] Two million Ukrainians inhabited the Priamur and Primorye.[48] Settlements with names like Astrakhanka, Kishinevka, Abo, Lifliansky, and Latviya reflected their Tatar, Moldavian, Finnish, Estonian, and Latvian antecedents.

Far Easterners had widely different attitudes about authority. Military officers and security personnel were pillars of conservatism. Merchant seamen, construction workers, and fishermen inherited some of the free spirit of Cossacks and the nonconformism of religious sectarians.† Camp survivors formed a gritty anti-chekist element in Magadan society.[49] Their successors who did time in penal institutions gravitated to Vladivostok, for the criminal code banned them from Moscow and Leningrad.[50]

Like the pre-Petrine Cossacks who distilled spirits from whortleberries, Far Easterners showed resourcefulness in supporting their drinking habits. Some started young, as a Khabarovsk kindergarten teacher discovered when she came across her flock behind a bush going through the motions of a drinking bout.[51] Keeping abreast of technology, Primorye-based fighter pilots slaked their thirst with hydraulic fluid.[52] Indulgence inevitably led to excesses, such as when an inebriated bulldozer driver demolished the house of a woman who had scolded him for nicking her picket fence.[53] Official measures to combat alcoholism (price hikes, fines, sobering-up cages, forced therapy) proved susceptible to the "illusion of stormy activity." Learning from Gogol's *Dead Souls*, Khabarovsk officials impressed Moscow with rehabilitation rates by recycling the same drunks.[54]

Far Eastern women made some economic gains. Divorce rates climbed from levels already above the national average (Magadan's was the highest in the USSR), suggesting lower levels of tolerance for alcoholism and domestic violence.[55] Unlike Khetagurovites, Brezhnev-era young women came to the Far East for wage bonuses, paid holidays, and access to "deficit" foodstuffs. They provided much of the "manpower" for the fishing indus-

---

*Russians accounted for 87% of Primorye and Khabarovsk regions, 89% of Amur District, 82% of Sakhalin District, 83% of Kamchatka District, 75% of Magadan oblast, and 51% of the Yakut Autonomous Republic. *Naselenie SSSR* (Moscow: Statistika, 1984), pp. 82, 90–94.
†During the 1970s a community of Pentecostalists moved from the Uzbek SSR to the area around Chuguyevka in the Sikhote Alin.

try. More than 15,000 went to sea each year, serving on floating canneries for months at a stretch. Women also captained FESCO freighters and staffed scientific laboratories on research vessels.[56] Day-care centers were built in cities, but not for the 62,000 children born along the BAM route between 1974 and 1984.[57]

Prostitution flourished in Vladivostok and Nakhodka, where merchant seamen, paid partly in hard currency, constituted a favored clientele. Each return of the fishing fleet triggered a migration from metropolitan Russia to Vladivostok, where prostitutes worked designated areas, tacitly tolerated by local authorities. In Nakhodka, visited by 30,000 foreign mariners annually, the trade attracted KGB involvement.[58]

Because society functioned through connections more than by laws, the distinction between enterprise and crime tended to blur. Poaching, practiced under the umbrella of hunting and fishing clubs, enriched the diets of family and friends while supplementing the incomes of underpaid gamekeepers. A scheme to divert shipments of Kamchatka red caviar from Moscow into local channels promoted cooperation between employees in the state railroads, fishing cooperatives, and research institutes.[59] Bookstore clerks honed their entrepreneurial skills by privately disposing of literature in high demand.[60] Greed, like idealism, could be taken to excess. In 1983 a former commander of the Pacific Fleet and his wife were bludgeoned to death in their apartment by a gang that wanted the admiral's fleet of decorations.[61]

Ethnic tensions officially did not exist in the Far East, for all Soviet nationalities were supposed to be suffused by what the Ukrainian poet Pavlo Tychina called "a feeling of a single family." This laudable sentiment does not seem to have been shared by all Far Easterners, let alone by members of Russian, Ukrainian, and Korean street gangs. One can safely assume that the eighty-two different nationalities thrown together at BAM construction sites devised some original combinations of ethnic animosity.

To deal with deviant behavior in the Far East, the Ministry of Internal Affairs in 1980 established a Higher School in Khabarovsk, and Party and Komsomol organizations held endless meetings in schools, factories, and collective farms to strengthen ideological discipline. During Andropov's brief intendancy (1982–84), *druzhiny* were mobilized to clamp down on adult truancy by spot-checking personal identification papers in stores during working hours. Such constabulary exercises achieved little beyond creating paperwork and promoting careers, for they addressed symptoms rather than causes of social malaise.

The natural as well as social environment deteriorated during the era of stagnation. Not in living memory had earth and forests, rivers, lakes, and coastal waters, fauna and flora been subjected to such despoliation. Scientists recognized the danger signs, but bureaucrats were slow to take action. Official insouciance took sustenance from an ideological conceit that defined environmental maladies as products of capitalism. In the words of the Vice-President of the USSR Academy of Sciences in 1972: "Ecological problems will not develop in the USSR, because under socialism there is unity of political and economic leadership."[62]

"Unity of political and economic leadership" delayed public awareness of the vulnerability of the Far East's biosphere to human intervention. During the 1970s fishermen noticed that salmon, once so plentiful that local peasants used roe as plaster, were disappearing.[63] In the early 1980s word spread that bulldozers and strip mining were destroying ancient forests. As awareness grew under glasnost, so did anger.

28

« « » »

Frontier Ethos

From Chukotka to Khasan's crest, we guard our land's
happiness.   — Song of Far Eastern border guards

In the early hours of 1 September 1983, a Sukhoi interceptor shot down a Korean Airlines' Boeing 747 over the Sea of Japan. All 269 passengers and crew perished. For reasons that are still unclear, KAL flight 007 had veered off course en route from Anchorage to Seoul and flew over Kamchatka and Sakhalin. Without having identified the intruder, authorities ordered it destroyed. Pilot Gennady Osipovich obeyed without hesitation, partly because of feelings instilled since childhood: "I knew that the plane had intruded across a frontier that should be under lock and key."[1] A Khabarovsk newspaper headline put the matter more succinctly: "Motherland Frontiers Are Sacred."[2]

Vasily Kliuchevsky's observation about the centrality of the frontier in Russian history held true in 1983, when two Soviet authors asserted: "The frontier is the pulse of the country."[3] Unlike the outwardly mobile rim of settlement of Kliuchevsky's Russia, however, the Soviet frontier connoted a fortified perimeter insulating "us" from "them." From the 1930s on, Soviet leaders cultivated a siege mentality in the Far East against external enemies of changing identity but of common purpose: to infiltrate the region "to harm our life in every way—to blow up bridges and factories, to poison wells, to kill people."[4] As a prism through which Far Easterners viewed the outside world, a frontier ethos shaped the region's social and intellectual life.

External Pressures — Internal Challenges

American "forward deployment" strategy meant sea and air probes along the USSR's Far Eastern periphery from bases in South Korea, Japan, Hawaii, and Alaska. As U.S.-led multinational naval exercises simulated strikes on Kamchatka, U.S. planes approached Soviet air perimeters and tested air defenses from the Primorye to Chukotka. For some these pressures acquired ominous overtones when taken in conjunction with American claims to parts of the Bering Sea and five islands in the East Siberian Sea.[5]

China could not be ignored by Far Easterners, most of whom lived within fifty miles of the border. Ambiguities about river boundaries transmuted into sources of friction as Sino-Soviet relations deteriorated in the 1960s. Both sides claimed Kazakevich (Heixiazi) Island, 116 square miles of low-lying land at the confluence of the Amur and the Ussuri.[6] Damansky (Zhenbao) on the Ussuri 110 miles south of Khabarovsk became the scene of armed clashes in 1969.[7] Behind disagreements over river boundaries loomed Beijing's demand that Moscow recognize the "unequal treaties" of Aigun and Beijing, thereby legitimizing China's claim that the Priamur and the Primorye lay within its "historical boundaries." Beijing also reminded Moscow about its lost access to the Sea of Japan, proposing in 1991 that the Tumen River corridor be restored to its rightful owner.[8]

Notwithstanding its defeat in 1945, Japan continued to be seen as a source of pressures, particularly in conjunction with China, the United States, and South Korea. Memories of the war of 1904–5, the Siberian Intervention, and the Kwantung Army were kept alive by high-tech poachers, incremental rearmament, and "Northern Territories" irredentism.* Worrisome signs of American, Chinese, Japanese, and South Korean collusion multiplied after the invasion of Afghanistan in 1979 amid international discussions about a "Pacific community" from which the USSR was conspicuously absent. The Tumen River boundary with North Korea reminded Far Easterners that even a short frontier with an officially fraternal neighbor could pose problems. Once emptying into Posyet Bay, the lower Tumen changed course and flowed into the Sea of Japan twenty-five miles south of

---

*"Northern Territories" in the broadest sense refers to Japanese territories occupied by Soviet forces in Aug.–Sept. 1945. As an irredentist slogan, the term means different things to different people: (1) Kunashir, Iturup, Shikotan, and the Habomai Group (claimed by the government), (2) the entire Kurile archipelago (claimed by some opposition parties); and (3) the Kurile archipelago and southern Sakhalin (claimed by right-wing groups and some former residents of Karafuto).

its old estuary. Beneath Moscow-Pyongyang negotiations about riparian encroachment flowed an undercurrent of Tumen irredentism.[9]

From the 1930s through the 1980s, authorities warned that the Far East was a prime target for infiltration, espionage, sabotage, and disinformation. In the words of a 1981 Primorye Party handbook: "Maritime Region residents, on the front line of the ideological struggle, are subject to the most powerful blows of bourgeois and revisionist propaganda. The proximity of the USA, Japan, and China requires that Party organizations display special vigilance in ideological-political work."[10] Indeed, the Far East was targeted by Russian-language broadcasts from China, North Korea, Japan, and the United States.[11] Hokkaido stations could easily be picked up on Sakhalin, as could Alaskan programs on Chukotka. About half a million foreigners came to the Far East between 1969 and 1985,[12] including North Korean and Vietnamese workers, tourists (Japanese, Americans, Australians, British, and Germans predominating), friendship delegations, and assorted bureaucrats. Businessmen, technical advisers, seamen, scientists, and pedagogues spent periods ranging from a few days to several months in Nakhodka, Khabarovsk, and Okha (northern Sakhalin) and along BAM construction sites. Each of these groups included people who spoke Russian, brought in "anti-Soviet" literature, dabbled in the black market, photographed restricted objects such as railroad stations and bridges, and established personal relationships with Soviet citizens. Illegal entrants posed a constant nuisance: errant pedestrians from Alaska on Big Diomede Island, an uninvited windsurfer on Sakhalin, Greenpeace anti-whaling activists on Chukotka.

Exfiltration caused as many headaches as infiltration. The Far East traditionally served as an escape valve for exiles, convicts, peasants, Cossacks, tsarist officers, religious sectarians, and chekists. In 1976 a pilot flew his MIG-25 from the Primorye to Hakodate.* Hijackers diverted local Aeroflot flights to China in 1973 and 1985. In the 1980s youths came from the Baltic republics to slip into China. To block such backdoor hemorrhaging, chekists watched inner as well as outer approaches to Far Eastern perimeters.

Border Control

According to the frontier law promulgated on 24 November 1982 ("On USSR State Frontiers"), Soviet borders were "inviolable," and illegal passage in or out of the country by land, sea, or air was subject to forcible

---

*Lt. Viktor Ivanovich Belenko made the flight on 6 Sept. 1976, leaving behind a wife and in-laws in the Magadan nomenklatura.

interdiction.[13] Unpublished administrative regulations gave authorities discretionary powers over frontier zones, which included the Primorye, Sakhalin, the Kurile Islands, the Okhotsk seaboard, Kamchatka, and Chukotka. Soviet citizens had to secure a special pass from the Ministry of Internal Affairs to enter the zone, and residents of the zone needed a special stamp in their internal passports to be readmitted.[14]

Authorities discouraged unauthorized contacts between foreigners and ordinary Soviet citizens by limiting the places and duration of sojourns, perlustrating correspondence, diaries, and address books, and requiring Soviet citizens to report conversations with foreigners. A law of 1 July 1984 criminalized any "unauthorized" accommodation and transport provided to foreigners.[15] Amid periodic calls for greater vigilance, Far Eastern branches of the All-Union Knowledge Society sponsored lectures to inoculate audiences against "ideological diversions."[16]

In 1957 the task of guarding state frontiers was entrusted to the KGB's Main Directorate for Border Troops, who numbered from 200,000 to 300,000. With over 40 percent of the USSR's frontiers (16,700 of 40,625 miles), the Far East probably accounted for no fewer than 40,000 border troops. The strongest component of the KGB maritime force patroled the Pacific littoral.[17]

Border security and intelligence were closely linked in the Far East. At KGB headquarters in Khabarovsk, Soviet Chinese were trained to infiltrate the People's Republic.[18] On the southern Kuriles and Sakhalin, chekists impounded Japanese trawlers and interrogated their crews, offering some of the fishermen access to Soviet waters in exchange for their cooperation in collecting data about the Self-Defense Forces in Hokkaido.[19] Border guards cooperated with customs at the "controlled access point" (kontrolno-propusknoi punkt or KPP) in Khabarovsk International Airport and the port of Nakhodka. While customs personnel checked passenger luggage for contraband and dutiable items, chekists scrutinized books and magazines for "information that could injure the country's political and economic interests, state security, public order, or the population's health or morals."[20]

Pogranichnik Profiles

"Professions are chosen; poets and pogranichniki are born," was more than just a KGB recruiting slogan.[21] Selected from among military and Komsomol personnel of unusual alertness, physical fitness, and ideological "hardness" (zakalka), border guards were trained at special schools in "frontier sciences": infiltration, stalking, martial arts, dog handling, map reading, electronic surveillance, and interrogation. Recruits who demonstrated exceptional promise might be sent to Alma Ata for advanced studies at the Feliks Edmundovich Dzerzhinsky Red-Bannered Higher Border Command Academy of the KGB.[22]

Pogranichniki assigned to the Far East usually served in a fifty-man outpost (*zastava*) responsible for guarding a zone ten to fifteen miles long and one to three miles wide. Patrols, mounted around the clock in shifts, were carried out on foot, horseback, motor vehicles, water craft, and helicopters. Particular attention was paid to a "control tracking strip" (*kontrolno sledovaya polosa* or KSP), a continuous belt of regularly plowed earth running parallel to the border and showing telltale signs of illegal entry or exit.

"The frontier doesn't like the weak," aptly described border duty in the Far East.[23] Climatic extremes, vexatious insects, utter isolation, and numbing routines punctuated by sudden danger were ideal ingredients for psychological stress. Comforts were few and rudimentary. A well-equipped field headquarters consisted of a dormitory, a club, a store, a bath, an electric power station, a bakery, and outhouses.[24]

Boredom taxed the ingenuity of officers, who knew all too well the dangers of inactivity. Pogranichniki on Big Diomede Island in the Bering Strait diverted themselves by corresponding with their "sister unit" on the westernmost extremity of Czechoslovakia, exchanging news about girlfriends and guard dogs.[25] Comrades in another outpost experienced a "joyous, uplifting mood" while listening on the wireless to a speech by Konstantin Chernenko.[26] Boredom eroded the pogranichnik's legendary immunity to human frailties. As early as 1937, it will be recalled, Far Eastern party secretary Vareikis warned Stalin that border guards were involved in contraband.[27] Smuggling picked up along Far Eastern frontiers with "inside" complicity under Khrushchev and persisted despite periods of international tension during the era of stagnation. Hemp plantations on both sides of the Sino-Soviet border in the southern Primorye constitute a prime arena of potential border guard enterprise in post-perestroika Russia.[28]

Whether in spite of or because of their access to foreign consumer goods, pogranichniki occupied a respected niche in Far Eastern society. In uniform, they were easily recognizable in green-topped service caps and green shoulder boards with the initials PV (*pogranichniye voiska*, — "frontier forces").[*]

---

[*]According to a chekist handbook, the color green was chosen because it exuded "the spring-like freshness of Russian fields and forests, the creativity of life." Quoted in *Granitsa*, p. 164.

Girls appraised them approvingly, and bus conductors reputedly refused to let them pay. Border guards were said to be cultured, linguistically talented, and even poetic (the father of all border guards, Dzerzhinsky, read Lermontov). Their mothers adjured them: "Guard our happiness more vigilantly!" Was it not thanks to their vigilance that honest Soviet citizens could sleep soundly?[29]

A Frontier Society

No observant traveler in the Far East between the 1960s and the 1980s would have missed the ubiquitous signs of a frontier society. Physical expressions of periodic vigilance campaigns met the eye at almost every turn. Towns, streets, collective farms, fish canneries, trawlers, and rail stations bore the names of border guards. The Posyet and Ussuri areas bristled with obelisks of pogranichnik heroes, including thirty-one chekists killed near Damansky Island in 1969.[30] Monuments honored KGB border guards and their earlier OGPU comrades who "fell defending Far Eastern frontiers in 1929."* Each Far Eastern city celebrated Border Guard Day (28 May) with parades and fireworks.[31]

For decades Far Easterners heard slogans such as "the frontier is guarded by all Soviet people" and "the frontier runs through people's hearts."[32] Mass involvement began in the 1930s, with vigilance campaigns and the mobilizing of "assistance brigades" of frontier zone residents to provide border guards with information, food, and shelter. In the 1960s the KGB upgraded these units into a "volunteer people's militia" that patroled the frontier zone, checked strangers' documents, and plowed the KSP. On Chukotka Eskimos were enlisted in the militia to patrol the coasts.[33]

Far Eastern youth was integrated into frontier defense by the Komsomol and the All-Union Volunteer Society for Assistance to the Army, Aviation, and Fleet (DOSAAF), which coordinated ties between the KGB and the Young Friends of Border Guards.[34] Young Friends were recruited largely in rural areas of the Russian Republic, where boys commonly saw border guards as role models and were as likely to say "border guard's honor" as "cross my heart" to underscore their sincerity.[35] Getting into the Young Friends was the dream of first graders at Amur district schools as late as

---

*A reference to the Special Far Eastern Army–OGPU strike into Manchuria to reassert Soviet rights on the Chinese Eastern Railroad.

1986.[36] DOSAAF arranged for pogranichniki to visit the classroom and guide school excursions to Lake Khasan, site of a Soviet-Japanese border conflict in 1938. At summer camps fourteen- and fifteen-year-old boys and girls accompanied patrols along the KSP, frolicked with guard puppies, and learned the ABCs of tracking infiltrators.[37] The Komsomol carried on after a Young Friend entered pubescence. Throughout the Far East local Komsomol organizations periodically held send-off festivities for members joining the border guard and maintained ties with designated border guard units through the practice of *shefstvo*.[*]

Far Eastern children had a number of border guard heroes, the most beloved being Alla Ivanovna, an OKDVA nurse, the Florence Nightingale of Lake Khasan; Ivan Trubitsyn, an OGPU polymath who taught Chukchi how to play the harmonica; and Nikita Karatsupa, who in thirty years liquidated 129 "spies and saboteurs" along the Primorye frontier, for which he was awarded the title "Hero of the Soviet Union."[38] Karatsupa and his German shepherd Ingush became domesticated folk heroes in the 1970s. *Karatsupa* enjoyed currency as juvenile slang for stalker, and Ingush was adopted as a guard dog title in the Democratic Republic of Vietnam.[39]

The frontier permeated Far Eastern society through literature, music, films, place-names, monuments, and rituals. Nikolai Zadornov occasionally left his Riga apartment to inspire young men in Far Eastern border posts with stirring tales of their forefathers.[40] Not enough writers followed Zadornov's example, so KGB First Deputy Chairman (until his death in 1982) Semyon Tsvigun organized a conference in Moscow in December 1978 under the rubric "Literature, Art, and the Security of the Motherland's Sacred Frontiers." In a keynote address entitled "Artist and Frontier," Tsvigun declared it the duty of every Soviet "ideological worker" (writer) to heighten popular awareness of the chekists defending USSR state borders.[41]

Tsvigun's clarion call elicited a palpable response. A Georgian poet, Nodar Dumbadze, composed an ode to the fragrance of a freshly plowed KSP.[42] Composers came up with a collection of border guard songs.[43] Far Eastern aspirants for a border guard literature prize instituted by the KGB in 1979 took up the pen and wrote earnestly about catching poachers.[44] After the destruction of KAL 007, the Khabarovsk Publishing House

---

[*]Regularized help given by one institution to another, officially as evidence of "Communist consciousness."

brought out a novel about interdicting air intruders, piquantly titled *Birds Fly Without a Compass*.[45]

Over the years frontier demonology adjusted to changing political requirements. Following the 1969 clashes on the Ussuri, Chinese border guards were described as having eyes with "an evil squint like German fascists."[46] From the late 1970s, Americans vied with Great Han chauvinists for primacy as Agitprop's border bogeys. The Bering Strait served as a metaphorical divide between socialist triumphs and capitalist crises. Chukotka aborigines "commanded the heights of literature and electronics"; their Alaskan cousins endured "oppression, discrimination, and genocide."[47] Small wonder that when a greenhorn pogranichnik on Big Diomede asked an experienced colleague why Tuesday in Chukotka was Monday in Alaska, the latter patiently explained: "Because America is a yesterday country."[48]

« « » »

Conclusion
Stormy Activity in a Time of Troubles

Sooner or later a Far Eastern Republic will be established.
— Oleg Rumyantsev (1991)

We would like it to be our window opened widely on the
East. — Mikhail Gorbachev (1986)

There is nothing petty about the Russian mind when it
comes to the gap between the scale of conception and the
amount of achievement.
— William Alexander Gerhardie (1931)

The impact of perestroika and the collapse of the USSR on Russia's eastern periphery eludes precise measurement, for distinguishing substantive change from the "illusion of stormy activity" (regional vernacular for the Gerhardian gap) is an imprecise exercise even under less tumultuous conditions and with more hindsight. The Gorbachev era (1985–91) bequeathed a welter of contradictions. Democratically elected "reformers" took on the attributes of their predecessors, while entrenched elites camouflaged their power and privilege with new labels. Robber baron capitalism flourished as the breakdown of old controls opened breathtaking opportunities for self-enrichment. Freedom unfettered the criminal as well as the artistic imagination. Glasnost liberated and polarized public discourse. Not since the 1930s had the Far East been subjected to such heavy doses of hope and malaise.

Gorbachev's emergence as general-secretary in 1985 had little impact on Far Eastern Party committees. Three years later, four of seven regional secretaries remained in place. When mass demonstrations forced a not unusually corrupt Sakhalin party secretary to resign in May 1988, Moscow merely replaced him with another apparatchik from the Central Committee.[1] Old networks, resilient as ever, held their own.

Entrenched elites got their first real scare in the March 1989 elections, when six of the seven regional Party secretaries, all Gorbachevian appointees, failed to win seats in the Congress of People's Deputies. The commanders of the Far Eastern Military District and Pacific Fleet were also rejected at the polls.* Most of the visible beneficiaries of populist anger were political amateurs — collective farm chairmen, factory managers, teachers, and journalists — supported by ad hoc citizen organizations appealing to voters on environmental, housing, and consumer issues. Emblematic of the new species of people's deputy was Evdokiya Gayer, a Vladivostok ethnographer of Nanai nationality, who took her campaign to army bases and outpolled the commander of the Far Eastern Military District.[2]

The electoral repudiation of Communists in 1989 prompted some comrades to look for new vehicles for career advancement. When they felt it would be safe to do so, some turned in their Party cards and recast themselves as democrats. Others dabbled in cooperatives, joint ventures, and the peace industry, marketing themselves as facilitators. One Khabarovsk apparatchik opened a restaurant with a Japanese partner. Another founded an Institute of Friendship and Cooperation to expedite overseas junkets.[3] Analogous institutional acrobatics followed the abortive Moscow coup (August 1991), Boris Yeltsin's ban on the Communist Party, and the dissolution of the USSR. Established in 1939 as a monument to Stalin and housed in a structure built by Japanese POWs, the Khabarovsk Higher Party School reinvented itself as the Institute of International Business.

Perspicacity yielded dividends in the form of privilege as well as dollars. "Businessmen" started going to the head of lines, a right once reserved for veterans of the Great Patriotic War and Western tourists.

Gorbachev evoked mostly negative feelings on the Pacific periphery during his six years in office. His admonitory calls for self-reliance rang hollow amid his pleas for economic aid from the West. By attempting to revitalize a morally compromised and economically sclerotic system, the father of perestroika managed at once to infuriate conservatives, disillusion democrats,

*Lt-Gen. Viktor Novozhilov and Adm. Gennady Khvatov, respectively. Gorbachev had promoted Novozhilov's three predecessors, Ivan Tretyak, Dmitry Yazov, and Mikhail Moiseyev, to high positions in Moscow.

and amuse cynics. There was general agreement across the political spectrum that the "mineral-water secretary" excelled as a windbag and prestidigitator.*

The Moscow coup changed appearances more than substance. Dock workers, air traffic controllers, and one submarine commander immediately denounced the putsch, but regional elites sat on the fence until it was clear who had won at the Center. The regional Party nomenklatura and half of the officers in the Far Eastern Military District sympathized with the short-lived Emergency Committee.[4] When the coup had manifestly collapsed before the defiance of crowds around Boris Yeltsin at the White House, Far Eastern apparatchiki and other bureaucrats suddenly found their voices and denounced what they had been prepared to welcome. Most held onto their posts, including the Primorye KGB chief, whose pro-coup actions prompted complaints by subordinates. An investigation concluded that the senior chekist had broken no law, so he remained in place while the whistle-blowers were retired.[5]

Local cynics called the Far East a post-Soviet "Communist preserve,"[6] yet the region defied any simple characterization. Each city had a distinctive political dynamic deriving from geography, economics, and tradition. Khabarovsk retained its traditionally conservative complexion. With a literally and figuratively floating population, Vladivostok took the lead in removing Lenin statues and opening AIDS clinics. Blagoveshchensk, Yuzhno-Sakhalinsk, and Petropavlovsk became barometers for relations with China, Japan, and the United States, respectively. Gold shaped Magadan's politics; northern exposure and high wages accentuated its demographic instability.[7]

Boris Yeltsin's grass-roots popularity in the Far East oscillated as he moved to assert control over the periphery and crushed parliamentary opposition in October 1993. During his Far Eastern tour of 1992, local audiences loved his harangues ("This place is a dump!" "Do you seriously live here?" "Places like this make me ashamed to be Russian!").[8] Proliferating presidential appointments in each district, explicitly tagged with expectations of loyalty, gave off a bracing (or repellent as they case may be) authoritarian ambience. The insensitivity of some Moscow functionaries to Far Eastern sensibilities also tarnished Yeltsin's image on the periphery. Foreign Office spokesmen in particular aroused suspicions that the president was crafting his own deal with Tokyo to exchange the southern Kuriles for

Mineralny sekretar ("Mineral-water secretary"), play of words referring to Gorbachev's anti-alcohol campaign.

Japanese largesse. Hostility to Yeltsin found vociferous expression in Far Eastern branches of the National Salvation Front. Regional councils carried more obstructionist clout, threatening to withhold tax revenues. By dissolving the Front and moving against regional councils in October 1993, Yeltsin made a bold attempt to reimpose central controls.

Katastroika

Perestroika exacerbated symptoms of "apoplexy at the Center and anemia at the extremities."[9] To compensate for its diminishing ability to subsidize the periphery, the Center came up with ever sunnier scenarios. In 1987 Moscow unveiled a blueprint for regional development to the year 2000, by which time the Far East was, by great leaps in industrial production, to have achieved self-sufficiency in energy and basic foodstuffs while housing every family in a separate apartment or detached dwelling.[10] The scheme was quietly shelved in 1989, the victim of a budgetary deficit. Nonetheless, in 1991 and 1992 Moscow announced another set of mega-plans for the Far East, which promptly shared the fate of their predecessors. By 1993 the region was an economic basket case. Thanks to readily exploitable resources, Sakhalin and Kamchatka fared somewhat better than Khabarovsk and the Primorye, but gold-rich Magadan staggered as thousands of workers abandoned the Northeast.[11]

Releasing energies redolent of America's Gilded Age, privatization turned the Far East into a Wild West. After lurking on the fringe for decades, hustlers, speculators, and black-marketeers occupied center stage, their ranks swelled by "honest" entrepreneurs who had discovered, often at no small expense, that business could not be conducted without recourse to bribes. Cooperatives proliferated in the form of restaurants, haberdasheries, hotels, and fish farms. Commercial banks and stock exchanges sprouted in Vladivostok and Khabarovsk. When the Soviet airline Aeroflot was dismantled, stray pieces coalesced into ad hoc carriers such as Magadan's short-lived "Cyclone Air." As defense plants converted to civilian production, Komsomolsk submarine yards retooled to produce fishing trawlers and yachts for Japanese customers. Military aircraft transported caviar from Sakhalin to metropolitan markets. Pacific Fleet sailors opened a "Magic Burger" clone of MacDonalds in Vladivostok. With an eye for tourists, Magadan craftsmen refashioned Kolyma skulls into ashtrays, bangles, and motorcycle ornaments.[12]

Major beneficiaries of privatization were ex-Communist officials and managers of state enterprises. Retaining control of ships, factories, and mines, they hired themselves as "consultants" and stonewalled municipalities, claiming "detachable" assets such as vacation homes and sanatoria. Some acquired personal caches of foreign currency through exports of fish, timber, and minerals and imports of used cars in league with cosmopolitan tribes of mafiosi. There was talk, but little proof, of hard currency accounts in Japan and Hong Kong. Even chekists were hard put not to engage in remunerative sidelines. Border guards were offered deals by contrabandists to transform "frontier under lock and key" from a slogan into a logo.

The collapse of the USSR had an uneven demographic impact on the eastern periphery. Tens of thousands of Ukrainians, Belorussians, Georgians, Armenians, and Central Asians on work contracts in the Northeast returned to newly independent republics. About 167,000 left the Magadan District in 1992 alone, turning some settlements into ghost towns. Conversely, Russian women flocked to the Far East in search of employment, as their Khetagurovite grandmothers had come in search of romance over a half-century earlier. While the Northeast hemorrhaged, thousands bought apartments and farms in the Khabarovsk Region, in the Amur District, and on Sakhalin.[13]

No economic reform in the Far East garnered more international publicity than a capitalist experiment launched by Valentin Fyodorov, the "Napoleon of Sakhalin" from his election in 1990 until his dismissal by Yeltsin in 1993. Taking advantage of his bailiwick's insularity and proximity to Japan, Governor Fyodorov, an economist by training, promoted locally managed private enterprise and foreign investment. Haggling with central ministries, he retained a larger percentage of fish hauls than had his predecessors and distributed parcels of state lands to private farmers. Going beyond Adam Smith (whose portrait hung above his desk), Fyodorov came up with the idea of marketing indigence, offering the West a chance to donate cash, securities, and technology to his Sakhalin Fund.[14] Learning quickly, local security organs set up their own fund and solicited contributions for down-and-out chekists.[15]

Fyodorov's appropriative sallies lent urgency to the question of who owned Far Eastern resources. Although Yeltsin ceded control of the land and continental shelf to regional authorities late in 1991, he steadfastly asserted Moscow's jurisdiction over Far Eastern exports. Fyodorov defiantly made his own arrangements with foreign firms to develop Sakhalin's offshore oil and gas deposits, whereupon Yeltsin removed him from office in April 1993. The larger issue, however, remained unsettled.[16]

The decline of central subsidies and domestic trade sent the Far East into an economic free fall starting in the autumn of 1991. Acute fuel shortages crippled utilities, curtailed services, and cut off supplies to outlying areas. Power shutdowns in Khabarovsk forced the army to set up field kitchens for residents. Kurile Islanders relied upon border guards to deliver food and medicine by helicopter. Throughout the region enterprises and institutes retrenched or closed. Unemployment hit women particularly hard. Malnutrition hospitalized hundreds and claimed the lives of four Pacific Fleet sailors. Yet most Far Easterners showed their proverbial resilience when it came to food, growing and pickling produce from their dachas. Poaching, long an unofficial sport, helped fill the protein gap.[17]

Glasnost

Glasnost came to the Far East belatedly, finding full expression only in 1990, when raucously independent newspapers appeared in Yuzhno-Sakhalinsk, Magadan, Petropavlovsk, Vladivostok, and Khabarovsk. Ecology provided the opening wedge as scientists and journalists sounded a clarion heard only faintly since the zaamurtsy fell silent in the 1920s. Readers learned that the Amur was dying, that Yuzhno-Sakhalinsk had the most polluted air in the country, that radioactive fall-out blanketed the arctic, and that Peter the Great Bay had been exposed to dangerous levels of radiation from military mishaps.[18] Consciousness catalyzed resistance. "Greens" organized a "save the Amur" movement, blocked geothermal drilling on Kamchatka, publicized the location of atomic waste dumps, and prevented port calls of nuclear-powered ships. Giant "Nature-taming" construction projects fell into disrepute. Routinely hailed as the "project of the century" in 1984, BAM was widely denounced as a monument to waste in 1989. Journalists switched from covering labor feats to uncovering labor camps.[19]

Glasnost caught professional historians unawares. Unwilling to jettison ideological baggage as long as the durability of "new thinking" remained uncertain, research institute staff and professors repeated stagnation-era shibboleths. In Khabarovsk they continued to denounce "class enemies" and to exalt socialist construction in Kolyma.[20] In Vladivostok they continued to compose dithyrambs to victories over American imperialists and Japanese militarists under the supervision of Andrei Krushanov, who in

1987 after a long and loyal apprenticeship was elected Academician of the USSR Academy of Sciences.

Magadan broke rank with Krushanovians in 1988 when a local journal's publication of Varlam Shalamov's *Kolyma Tales* unleashed a torrent of pent-up testimony.[21] Sakhalin followed Magadan's lead in 1989, when local archivists and museum staff, including former Krushanov students, founded a history journal that probed hitherto taboo topics and implicitly chided orthodox colleagues in Vladivostok.[22] In contrast glasnost made a gingerly début in Khabarovsk where a local journal asked in carefully chosen words whether collectivization had been an unmitigated blessing.[23]

Glasnost brought out Vladivostok's reserves of business acumen. After printing one of three volumes, a publisher decided that it would be more profitable to resell rights to Solzhenitsyn's *Gulag Archipelago* outside the region. Two history buffs took advantage of a popular taste for nostalgia and marketed tinted images of zaamurtsy.[24] Drawing on another tradition, a journalist proposed that Russia's window on the Pacific develop a Japan-oriented sex industry.[25] Sometime trawler captain Amir Khisamutdinov took over the presidency of the Society for Study of the Amur Region.[26] To finance a protracted struggle with bureaucrats over downtown real estate, he leased some of the Society's premises to a fast-food restaurant.*

Glasnost prepared the way for Far Easterners to come to terms with their past. Memorials to the victims of Stalinism arose in each city. Chita chekists chivalrously offered to cover costs.[27] Services were held to commemorate those who had perished in Kolyma goldfields, in Sikhote Alin forests, and along the BAM route. Newspapers in Magadan, Khabarovsk, and Vladivostok published rosters of local victims.[28] Families looking for lost relatives at times found that NKVD case files might constitute the only proof of a person's erstwhile existence.[29] Compilers of an encyclopedia of the Far East set out to resurrect people, organizations, and events consigned to oblivion since the 1920s.

One unlamented casualty of glasnost was native sycophancy, a symptom of starry-eyed opportunism that had infested Far Eastern literature since the 1920s. A half-dozen troubadours of aboriginal gratitude had made careers out of serviceable paeans to Lenin, Stalin, and the Communist Party for

---

*The Society for Study of the Amur Region declared its independence from the USSR Geographical Society in 1991 and, claiming ownership of its property, which was nationalized in 1924, took possession of a building housing the presidium of the Far Eastern Branch of the Academy of Sciences.

saving their peoples from extinction and giving them a higher culture — proletarian internationalism.[30] Revelations about disease, arctic radiation, alcoholism, suicide, and death transformed these privileged panegyrists into protean ingrates struggling to salvage their reputations. Grigory Khodzher declared that life for Amur natives under Stalin might not have been so luminous after all, but this belated discovery did not keep him on the editorial board of the leading Far Eastern journal.[31] Yury Rytkheu did better by retroactively switching his mother's ethnicity from Chukcha to Inuit, thereby securing himself the co-chairmanship of the Siberian-Alaska Cultural Exchange.[32] Vladimir Sangi, veteran Communist and USSR Writers' Union stalwart, launched a new career as the founder of a Nivkh Autonomous Republic on Sakhalin.[33]

Economics undercut glasnost's potential to nourish serious literature. Beset by the daily struggle to survive, most people had neither time nor desire to read anything that taxed their intellect or pricked their conscience. Coping with the present took precedence over confronting the past. Deprived of state subsidies, editors and publishers struggled with soaring costs and shrinking supplies. Academics wrote for money while administrators tried to parlay phatic mush into overseas junkets. Serious history, imaginative literature, and poetry could not compete with marketable pulp.

Glasnost did little to sustain, let alone inspire, scientists whose research suddenly required generous inputs of hard currency and foreign travel. The ambitious cultivated Western contacts with renewed perspicacity, trolling for invitations, grants, and fellowships. Those who could, emigrated. The director of a fleetingly glamorous Vladivostok institute wrote from Japan: "I recommend to everyone: whoever has the chance, leave! There will not be any science in this country for a long time."[34]

Social Fragmentation

During Russia's recent "Time of Troubles," multidirectional grievances tested the imperturbability said to lie at the heart of the Far Easterner's character.[35] Political uncertainty and economic woes put additional strains on ethnic, generational, and conjugal relationships. Transients from closed defense plants and labor camps helped Vladivostok consolidate its position as the national suicide and crime capital, where disputes over bazaar franchises might be settled by a hand grenade. Labor discipline deteriorated in each sector. Longshoremen, miners, and teachers acquired the strike habit.

Managers and clerks contented themselves with truancy. Consumers discharged their pent-up frustrations in sudden and unpredictable eruptions of mayhem. Passengers hijacked a plane in Yuzhno-Sakhalinsk and blocked a runway in Magadan. Thousands of thirsty imbibers rioted in Chita.[36] Social tensions, compounded by defeat in Afghanistan and the downsizing of the army and navy, could not but undermine morale. In Vladivostok admirals warned that the Pacific Fleet might not survive. In Khabarovsk army officers formed a strike committee to demand pay raises and housing. One took more active steps and flew to Moscow intending to introduce Yeltsin to a cluster bomb.[37]

Far Easterners divided on how to deal with the wreckage of Communism. Some felt that the moral wounds of mass complicity could never heal. Others insisted that such wounds did not exist. Some shut out the present and idealized the tsarist, Stalinist, and Brezhnevian past. Bibulous comrades nostalgically recalled the late Party General-Secretary Yury Andropov, during whose brief intendancy no-frills vodka could be had cheaply at state stores.*

National aspirations asserted themselves in the Far East but not as virulently as in the Caucasus or Central Asia. One delegate to the Supreme Soviet talked of making Birobidzhan "genuinely Jewish."[38] A national council of ethnic Koreans called for an autonomous enclave around Posyet.[39] Descendants of Amur and Ussuri Cossacks claimed ancestral lands along the Amur, Ussuri, and Tumen rivers.[40] Chukchi, Koryak, and Nanai activists formed the International League of Small Peoples and demanded that large tracts of taiga be set aside for exclusive aboriginal use. Russians, 85 percent of the region's inhabitants, rediscovered their roots. Capacity crowds flocked to Orthodox churches. Prerevolutionary street names reappeared: Svetlanskaya in Vladivostok, Muravievo-Amurskaya in Khabarovsk. Muraviev's ashes were brought from Paris to Vladivostok and buried with pomp along the Golden Horn. The governor-general's statue, recast from original molds, was unveiled on its original pedestal overlooking the Amur at Khabarovsk. Rehabilitation extended to White leaders in the civil war. In Irkutsk, some entrepreneurs declared their intention to raise a monument to Admiral Kolchak.[41] Cossacks held a mass for Ataman Semyonov in Chita.[42] For the time being, Kalmykov and Ungern-Shternberg remained beyond the pale.

---

* Seasoned imbibers held that the no-frills brand "Vodka" introduced in 1983 was an acronym for *Vot Ona Dobrota Kommunista Andropova* ("Here's the goodness of Communist Andropov").

Regionalism or Localism?

Republican, district, and local authorities vied between (and among) themselves to shape the Far East in the post-Soviet era. For the first time since the 1920s, one could openly talk about regional interests diverging from those of the Center. It became fashionable to fault Moscow for pocketing Far Eastern revenue, for stunting Far Eastern development, and for circumscribing Far Eastern contacts with Asia-Pacific neighbors. A once supinely accepted Center-periphery relationship came to be openly referred to as colonial. Less than four years after Gorbachev's 1986 Far Eastern tour, a Khabarovsk newspaper headlined: "The Center betrayed us—let's save ourselves."[43] Magadan rebuffed ministerial involvement in commemorating the victims of Stalin. Kamchatkans protested when told that marijuana, diamonds, gold, and hard currency confiscated by local customs would be turned over to central authorities. Fyodorov showed up in Tokyo during Gorbachev's visit in April 1991 and upbraided the president for neglecting Russia's eastern periphery. These pronouncements and incidents led some observers to predict that a full-fledged separatist movement was only a matter of time.[44] Yet although they claimed the prerogatives of autonomy, Far Eastern regionalists showed little readiness to relinquish the perquisites of dependence (food and fuel deliveries, subsidies from the Center).

The regionalist persuasion entertained several models for emulation, among them California, British Columbia, and the Far Eastern Republic (FER). The FER attracted particular interest as a historical entity with which Far Easterners could identify. Its aficionados hailed Aleksandr Krasnoshchekov, sometime FER president, as a champion of independence and democracy. They reprinted the FER constitution, celebrated the FER's 70th anniversary, published the newspaper *Far Eastern Republic*, and founded a Far Eastern Republic Freedom Party.[45] Regional organizations sprouted: a Far Eastern Association of Supreme Soviet delegates, a Far Eastern Economic Association, a Far Eastern News Agency, a Far Eastern Airline, and, at least on paper, a Far Eastern Academy of Sciences.[46]

In practice the idea of regional autonomy served as a multi-purpose political instrument. When, in 1991, Yeltsin said that he wanted a quick solution of the Northern Territories problem, Governor Fyodorov, sensing that Yuzhno-Sakhalinsk might be squeezed out of a deal involving Japanese largesse, declared that the Far East should form a separate republic if Moscow bartered away Russia's patrimony.[47] The Russian General Staff raised the same bogey a year later as a means to extract more allocations from the national treasury.[48] The Far Eastern Association and the Primorye Territorial Council (strongholds of unreconstructed bureaucrats) made noises about a Far Eastern Republic in order to acquire a greater say in economic decisions and to upgrade the region's status within the Russian Federation.[49]

Theatrics notwithstanding, Far Eastern regionalism faced formidable obstacles from above and from below. Moscow continued to lease fishing rights to foreigners and collected most of the hard currency earnings. While promising Far Eastern leaders more autonomy if they supported him against his opponents in the Parliament, the president instructed his personal representatives to counter centrifugal proclivities. Although the Russian military showed symptoms of regionalization in 1993, senior army, naval, and security organ officers in the Far East did not support a separatist initiative. Localism inhibited the formulation of common strategies toward the Center as district leaders followed their own agendas. Khabarovsk showed no sign of putting aside its perennial rivalry with Vladivostok.[50] The Jewish Autonomous District declared its autonomy from Khabarovsk Region, as did the Chukotsk and Koryak national areas from the Magadan and Kamchatka districts, respectively. Divisiveness fragmented Vladivostok, where two groups came up with rival plans for long-term development.[51]

At the grass-roots level, talk of regional autonomy went beyond theatrics. Some communities felt impelled to look after their own interests rather than wait for metropolitan or district bureaucrats to act on their behalf. Having suffered years of neglect while watching marine resources exploited for the benefit of outsiders, Kurile Islanders grew suspicious of bureaucrats in general and began monitoring presidential, parliamentary, and gubernatorial maneuvers. But the habit of dependence was hard to kick. When Moscow indicated that it would send only prepaid fuel to the Kuriles, a county official requested — and received — a loan from Japan.[52]

Outpost or Window?

Long called an outpost, the Far East is now referred to as a window. The semantic watershed runs through 1986, when Mikhail Gorbachev paused at Vladivostok to proclaim a "new" era of engagement with Asia and the Pacific. Gorbachevian rhetoric inspired visions of the Far East as a model for a brave new world.[53] The dissolution of the USSR did not depress demand for Far Eastern happy outcomes thanks to a robust Western market for bracing scenarios of post–Cold War Northeast Asia. Researchers produced scenarios for resolving the Northern Territories problem and for turning the Tumen River delta into a "future Hong Kong."[54]

Extravagant hopes for the Far East have a long and cosmopolitan pedigree. For over a hundred years, Americans periodically promoted trans-Bering rail networks and touted the Priamur as a new California. A Chinese traveler affirmed in 1885 that Vladivostok would become a northern Shanghai.[55] To Korean farmers the Primorye shimmered as a Promised Land. In 1909 a tsarist official predicted that 100 million Russians would live on the Pacific in A.D. 2000.[56] Five decades and several radiant futures after the October Revolution, a Tokyo entrepreneur called for the establishment of a Russo-Japanese Magadan Republic that would reify the internationalist ideal while thriving on sex and gold.[57]

Experience conditioned Far Easterners to be skeptical about their region's potential, but few were prepared for the economic blows that buffeted it during the late 1980s and early 1990s. Anyone who stood in breadlines, contemplated empty store shelves, saw inflation eat up savings, and went for days without heat or water might have wondered, as the amurets Mikhail Venyukov had a century earlier: "Why hasn't the Priamur developed as quickly and sumptuously as California, New Zealand, South Australia, or even Canada?"[58] A few optimists counted on privatization and engagement with Asia-Pacific markets to revitalize the regional economy. In their view the breakup of the USSR was a cloud with a silver lining, for by curtailing access to the Baltic and Black seas it increased the Far East's significance as Russia's unobstructed access to the Pacific and the world's most dynamic market economies. But to engage with the Pacific, the Far East had to become truly accessible.

Harbingers of Far Eastern internationalization surfaced during the mid-1980s, when upbeat rhetoric and upgraded itineraries adumbrated Moscow's shift from defensiveness to clubbability. The "Pacific Community," denounced as a "threat to peace" as late as 1985,[59] suddenly acquired respectability in Soviet discourse. Winsome apparatchiki showed up in Tokyo, Honolulu, Seattle, Bangkok, Singapore, and Canberra as applicants for complimentary membership in distinctly unsocialist organizations. Ministries, agencies, and institutes spawned "Pacific" departments, divisions, and sections capped by a Soviet ("Russian" since 1992) National

Committee for Asia-Pacific Economic Cooperation. Peeved at being under-represented, Far Eastern authorities set up their own local equivalents.[60]

After Moscow abolished closed frontier zones in 1989, foreigners flocked to the Far East in numbers not seen since the Siberian Intervention (if one overlooks the involuntary sojourns of Japanese and Europeans in the decade after the Second World War). Chinese fanned out from dozens of newly opened entry points (40 in the Primorye alone). Japanese, Korean, American, and Taiwanese businessmen reconnoitered the entrepreneurial terrain between Vladivostok and Chukotka. Journalists poked around Kolyma and descended on the Kuriles. Baha'i evangelists proselytized on Sakhalin. Big game hunters hired army helicopters for airborne safaris over the Sikhote Alin Range, using techniques pioneered a half century earlier by kulak-hunting chekists.

Officially opened on 1 January 1992, Vladivostok personified the Far East's quirky accessibility. Washington, Tokyo, Seoul, Canberra, and New Delhi established consulates, whose staffs found themselves in erratic communication with the outside world. Journalists, diplomats, academics, businessmen, mariners, students, Peace Corps volunteers, Fulbright lecturers, missionaries, and tourists played musical chairs with scarce accommodations. To increase the supply of hotel rooms, Canadian entrepreneurs assembled some modules outside the city and christened the results "Vlad Motor Inn."[61] Nonetheless, for all the hoopla, Gorbachev's "window on the Pacific" remained a *fortochka*.*

To cope with shortages of manpower, capital, and technology, Moscow opened the Far East to laborers, engineers, businessmen, and the Peace Corps. Chinese joined the ranks of North Korean and Vietnamese seasonal workers in forests and factories, on construction sites and farms. Japanese, Korean, North American, European, and Australian firms set up offices and retail outlets in district centers.[62] A Soviet émigré returned with an American passport and proclaimed that the region's business with Pacific Asia had surpassed that with Moscow.[63]

As entry points multiplied to accommodate various forms of traffic, the Far East regained some of its erstwhile porosity. Posyet joined Vladivostok as an open port. New roads supplemented rail lines connecting China and the Primorye. Engineers drafted plans for a highway bridge across the Amur joining Heihe and Blagoveshchensk. As river steamers resumed ser-

*In many Russian houses and apartments, a hinged frame within the pane of a window, designed to admit fresh air in winter without opening the window.

vice between Khabarovsk and Harbin, the Sungari and Amur again linked Northeastern China with Japan. Flights proliferated from Khabarovsk, Vladivostok, Yuzhno-Sakhalinsk, and Magadan to Harbin, Seoul, Beijing, Nagoya, Niigata, Hakodate, Anchorage, and San Francisco. Inspired by a "friendship flight" between Alaska and Chukotka in 1988, visionaries rediscovered what had animated imaginations a century earlier: a Bering Strait tunnel.[64]

As getting into the Far East became easier, so did getting out. In principle Russian citizens with enough hard currency could leave unless they had unsettled accounts with criminal justice, creditors, or former spouses. Consulates and Foreign Ministry offices in Khabarovsk and Vladivostok streamlined exit procedures. Visa-free travel made a début as Chukotka Inuits visited relatives in Alaska, Amur District residents shopped in Heihe, and Kurile Islanders went sightseeing in Tokyo.[65] Sakhalin Koreans got to see their motherland after a half-century of enforced separation.[66] An unknown but significant number of Jews left Birobidzhan for Israel and the United States.[67] These and other signs of outward mobility suggested that the Far East was reverting from a mattress into a springboard.

Mechanisms engaging the Far East with the rest of the world diversified. By 1993 there were over 1,000 joint ventures with Chinese, Japanese, Korean, North American, European, and Australian partners involving restaurants, department stores, hotels, boutiques, computers, sturgeon hatcheries, sausage plants, and Dutch windmills. Amur timber, Yakutia coal, and Sakhalin offshore oil and natural gas came under international development. Special economic zones for foreign investment, talked about since 1987, showed signs of materializing in Nakhodka, Sakhalin, Blagoveshchensk, and Magadan. Planners proposed a "Greater Vladivostok" stretching from Posyet to Nakhodka. Yeltsin announced late in 1992 the creation of a Kurile special economic zone. Most ambitious of all the envisioned enclaves was the Tumen Free Economic Zone, embracing contiguous parts of Russia, North Korea, and China and involving the participation of Japan, South Korea, and Mongolia. Promoters of this project predicted that the Tumen River would become a "northern Silk Road."[68]

Until the early 1990s Japan continued to be the Far East's most important international partner, accounting in 1991 for 50 percent of joint ventures, 60 percent of regional exports, and on Sakhalin 70 percent of foreign commerce.[69] But when perestroika and the demise of the USSR failed to break an impasse over Tokyo's claims to the southern Kurile Islands, trade stagnated except for imports of used cars and exports of guns and crabs.

China overtook Japan as the Far East's leading economic partner in 1992. Granted latitude by Moscow and Beijing, provincial authorities set up "border economic cooperation zones" around Heihe, Suifenhe, and Hunchun. Paced by myriad local barter arrangements and brisk vodka imports, regional trade surpassed its metropolitan (Beijing-Moscow) counterpart. Thousands of merchants and workers poured into the Priamur and the Primorye, bringing along enough dependents to require the establishment of a school for Chinese children in Khabarovsk. In a twist to history that would have brought a sardonic smile to the face of Sergei Witte, Beijing made a bid to build a railroad across Russian territory to the port of Zarubino, restoring "Manchuria's" access to the Sea of Japan. Chinese also revived schemes for Amur flood control. For its part Moscow removed a vestigial irritant by acknowledging Chinese sovereignty over Damansky Island, the scene of clashes in 1969. After Yeltsin's visit to Beijing in 1992, a Hong Kong newspaper reported that the Russian president had hinted he was ready to negotiate about the status of Kazakevich Island within sight of Khabarovsk.[70]

The normalizing of Moscow-Seoul relations in 1990 lent impetus to a South Korean economic presence in the Far East. Bilateral trade expanded briskly with the opening of Vladivostok and Pusan. Seoul firms built a casino in Vladivostok, distributed Bibles in Khabarovsk, retailed electric billies in Blagoveshchensk, and imported reindeer horns from Chukotka.[71] Some observers entertained the notion that the Korean connection would, by reducing the Far East's reliance on Japanese capital and technology, rescue regional development from the Northern Territories problem.

Upbeat prognoses aside, the internationalization of the Far East continued to face stubborn obstacles: infrastructural weaknesses, inflation, regulatory and legal confusion, managerial inexperience, crime, corruption, and political uncertainty. Heady expectations not uncommon among foreign entrepreneurs evaporated as joint ventures went sour. Northern Territories placebos proffered by Yeltsin and Fyodorov neither satisfied irredentists nor reassured creditors in Japan.* Post-Tiananmen wariness in Beijing about the anti-Communist "Russian virus" constrained the range of interactions in areas of contiguity. An unpredictable Stalinist regime in Pyongyang threw a cloud over Russian-Korean relations and the projected Tumen Free Economic Zone.

---

*Yeltsin called for conclusion of a peace treaty, turning the southern Kuriles into a free enterprise zone, demilitarizing the region, and leaving a final solution to future generations. Fyodorov proposed making the Sakhalin District and Hokkaido a free enterprise zone.

It would be a mistake to assume that Far Easterners welcomed all aspects of engagement with Asia and the Pacific. Russian national sensibilities flared up when dollar-wielding wiseacres referred to the Far East as America's fifty-first state. Patriotism as well as environmentalism fed opposition to special economic zones and joint ventures. The revelation that Pyongyang security organs had been operating timber camps on Russian soil shocked Far Easterners. Conservatives, environmentalists, and Udege activists joined in opposing a South Korean joint venture to cut trees at Svetlaya, a former Gulag camp in the Sikhote Alin. Local authorities balked when Seoul proposed to build an industrial park near Nakhodka and populate it with Koreans relocated from Central Asia. Signs of resentment at Chinese penetration multiplied amid accusations of shoddy goods and unfair trade practices. Tokyo's reluctance to invest did not dissipate anxieties about the Far East becoming a Russian Manchukuo.[72]

For those who took more readily to foreign goods than to foreigners, xenophobia assumed protean guises. AIDS was grafted onto the bogey of American imperialism. A Yellow Peril recrudesced in the form of Chinese peddlers, Japanese fishermen, Korean loggers, and Vietnamese workers. Amid calls for re-enlisting Amur and Ussuri Cossacks and restoring tight border controls, Sakhalin Cossacks expressed their readiness to settle on and defend Shikotan.[73] "Frontiers Are Forever," proclaimed the reformed Party newspaper.[74] "We would rather let the land go to waste than allow foreigners in," declared one Far Easterner, echoing Governor-General Unterberger's alleged preference for a Russian desert to a Korean paradise.[75]

Suspended between continent and ocean, between Europe and Asia, the Far East in 1993 was a congeries of localities groping for a common purpose. Dependent on Moscow, vulnerable to shock waves from Korea and China, and neither able or willing to rely upon Japan or the United States, the Far East faced a problematic future, irrespective of the outcome of Russia's Time of Troubles. Should "Asia-first" views prevail at the Center, the Far East could again become a laboratory for metropolitan experiments. Should Russia come apart, the Far East could affiliate with an autonomous Siberia, stand alone, or fragment, posing dilemmas — and temptations — for neighboring states.

In the meantime, the Far East moved toward engagement with Pacific Asia but not necessarily in ways that headlines or pundits predicted. Rhetoric outpaced reality on the periphery no less than in Moscow. From the moment of its christening as "Ruler of the East" in 1860, Vladivostok personified the Gerhardian gap between the scale of conception and the degree of achievement. Sailors of the Imperial Navy transferred from the Black Sea Fleet came up with "Vladivostopol" to convey a meridional ambience, knowing full well that a Crimean cachet could not keep the Golden Horn from freezing over in winter. Two decades ago the bard Vladimir Vysotsky grated "Vladivostok is open now" when he and his audiences knew that it was as closed as ever. Vladivostok did eventually open, thanks to the collapse of the USSR. The Golden Horn did stop freezing over, thanks to effluents. In the spirit of such precedents, the Far East may yet live up to a venerable sobriquet "Amur California," assuming that Russia can afford more radiant futures.

《 《　　》 》
Reference Matter

Administrative Chronology of the Far East

1632   Yakutsk *voevodstvo* ("military office") created

1652   Nerchinsk voevodstvo created

1665   Albazin voevodstvo created

1697   Kamchatka voevodstvo created

1708   Voevodstvo system abolished. Siberian administration established at Tobolsk.

1719   Irkutsk Province created

1732   Okhotsk Administration created

1775   Yakutsk District (*oblast*) created

1803   Siberian Governor-Generalship created

1822   Eastern Siberia Governor-Generalship established at Irkutsk. Incorporated Okhotsk Administration and Yakutsk District.

1851   Kamchatka District established (22 Jan.)

1855   Treaty of Shimoda (7 Feb.). Russo-Japanese frontier in Kuriles drawn between Iturup and Urup islands. Sakhalin remained unpartitioned.

1856   Creation of Maritime District or Primorskaya oblast (26 Nov.). Administered from Nikolaevsk-na-Amure. Made up of lower Amur, Sakhalin, central and northern Kurile Islands, Kamchatka, and Chukotka.

1858   Treaty of Aigun (28 May). China recognized Russian acquisition of Amur left bank. Amur right bank below Ussuri junction designated a joint possession.
        Creation of Amur District (20 Dec.). Administered from Blagoveshchensk.

1860   Treaty of Beijing (14 Nov.). China ratified Treaty of Aigun and recognized Russian acquisition of the Primorye.

1875   Treaty of St. Petersburg (7 May). Russia acquired full possession of Sakhalin and ceded to Japan the central and northern Kuriles (Urup to Alaid islands).

1880   Maritime District administrative center moved to Khabarovka. Office of Vladivostok Military Governor created.

1884   Establishment of Priamur Governor-Generalship with headquarters at Khabarovka (28 June). Included Maritime, Amur, Sakhalin, and Transbaikal districts.

1888   Office of Vladivostok Military Governor abolished

1889   Anadyr District created

1898   Defense of Chinese Eastern Railroad strip across Manchuria assumed by Priamur governor-general (Aug.)

1903   Creation of Viceroyalty of the Far East administered from Port Arthur and including Kwantung Territory Leasehold and Priamur Governor-Generalship (12 Aug.)

1905   Viceroyalty of the Far East abolished (1 July)
Kwantung Territory Leasehold, southern spur of Chinese Eastern Railroad (Changchun to Port Arthur), and southern Sakhalin ceded to Japan (5 Sept.)

1906   Transbaikal District transferred from Priamur Governor-Generalship to Irkutsk Governor-Generalship

1909   Kamchatka District detached from Maritime District
Sakhalin District created (30 June)

1910   Priamur Governor-Generalship divided into civilian, military administrations

1914   Udsk uezd (incl. Nikolaevsk-na-Amure) added to Sakhalin District (Feb.)

1917   Priamur Governor-Generalship ceased to exist (16 Mar.)
Committees of public safety formed in Vladivostok and Khabarovsk (16 Mar.)
Vladivostok and Khabarovsk soviets formed (17 Mar.)
Dalsovnarkom established in Khabarovsk (25 Dec.)

1918   Peter Derber moves headquarters of Provisional Government of Autonomous Siberia to Vladivostok (Apr.)
Soviet rule overthrown in Vladivostok (29 June)
Ataman Kalmykov regime established in Khabarovsk (5 Sept.)

Dalsovnarkom dissolved (17 Sept.)

Semyonov's Buryat Mongol Autonomous Republic established at Chita

Omsk government assumed power in Vladivostok (Oct.)

Admiral Kolchak appointed head of state at Omsk (18 Nov.)

1919   Kolchak and his government evacuated Omsk (10–12 Nov.)

Kolchak designated Semyonov as supreme commander in the Far East (23 Dec.)

1920   General S. N. Rozanov (Kolchak representative) overthrown and Zemstvo Government established in Vladivostok (31 Jan.)

Soviet rule proclaimed in Blagoveshchensk (6 Feb.)

Zemstvo Government established in Khabarovsk (16 Feb.)

Triapitsyn regime established in Nikolaevsk (29 Feb.)

Provisional Government of Pribaikalia proclaimed at Verkhneudinsk (7 Mar.)

Soviet rule established in Khabarovsk (11 Mar.)

Far Eastern Republic founded at Verkhneudinsk (6 Apr.)

Likhoidov-Plyusnin government established in Khabarovsk (6 Apr.)

Buryat Mongol Autonomous Republic moved from Chita to Dauriya (July)

Likhoidov-Plyusnin government dissolved in Khabarovsk (Oct.)

Buryat Mongol Autonomous Republic dissolved (Nov.)

Antonov government formed in Vladivostok (11 Dec.)

1921   Merkulov government formed in Vladivostok (21 May)

1922   Yakut Autonomous Socialist Republic established (22 Apr.)

Russian "estates general" convened in Vladivostok (9 June)

Dalrevkom established (16 Nov.)

Far Eastern Republic incorporated into Soviet Russia (18 Nov.)

Far Eastern Province (Dalnevostochnaya Guberniya) established at Chita (20 Nov.). Made up of Pribaikal, Zabaikal, Amur, Priamur, Primorye, Kamchatka, North Sakhalin districts, and the Chinese Eastern Railroad zone.

1923   Far Eastern Province renamed Far Eastern District (oblast) (1 Jan.)

Far Eastern District administration moved to Khabarovsk (13 Dec.)

Soviet rule established around Okhotsk littoral and on Kamchatka

1924   Soviet rule established on Chukotka and Wrangel Island (Aug.)

1926   Far Eastern District renamed Far Eastern Region (Dalkrai) (4 Jan.). Embraced Chita, Sretensk, Amur, Priamur, Primorye, Kamchatka, North Sakhalin districts (okrugs), and Chinese Eastern Railroad zone.

1930   Chita and Sretensk districts detached from Dalkrai
Birobidzhan, Okhotsk-Evenk, Koryak, and Chukotsk autonomous districts created (20 Aug.)

1931   Dalstroi established (13 Nov.)

1932   Primorye, Amur, Sakhalin, Kamchatka districts (oblasts) created within Dalkrai

1933   Ussuri District created with administrative center at Ussuriisk

1934   Jewish Autonomous District created (7 May)
Zeya District detached from Amur District

1935   Chinese Eastern Railroad sold to Manchukuo. CER zone removed from Dalkrai (23 Mar.).

1937   Zeya District dissolved and reabsorbed into Amur District

1938   Dalstroi placed under NKVD (4 Mar.)
Dalkrai divided into Khabarovsk and Maritime regions (20 Oct.)

1939   Kolyma District (okrug) formed within Khabarovsk Region
Ussuri District (oblast) formed within Maritime Region

1941   Dalstroi expanded to embrace Lena and Aldan basins, Kamchatka, Chukotka, and Sakhalin

1943   Ussuri District dissolved

1945   Port of Vanino placed under Dalstroi administration
Occupation of southern Sakhalin and Kurile Islands (18 Aug.–4 Sept.)

1946   South Sakhalin District created within Khabarovsk Region (2 Feb.)

1947   Sakhalin District formed from Sakhalin and Kurile Islands and detached from Khabarovsk Region (2 Jan.)

1948   Amur District detached from Khabarovsk Region (2 Aug.)

1953   Magadan District organized as part of Khabarovsk Region (2 Dec.) and detached from Khabarovsk Region (3 Dec.)

1956   Kamchatka District detached from Khabarovsk Region (23 Jan.)

1957   Dalstroi dissolved

1963   Soviet Far East Economic Planning Region created. Embraced
        Khabarovsk and Maritime regions, Amur, Sakhalin, Kamchatka,
        and Magadan districts, and Yakut ASSR.

1990   Jewish, Koryak, and Chukotsk autonomous districts declared
        themselves autonomous republics
        Yakut ASSR declared itself Yakut-Sakha ASSR

1991   District (oblast) and region (krai) executive committees
        superseded by territorial councils. President Yeltsin appointed
        representatives to each Far Eastern region and district.
        Yakut-Sakha ASSR renamed Republic of Sakha (Yakutia)

Population of the Far East

PART I: *The Far East Population, 1860–1993*

Year	Number	Year	Number
1860	70,000	1937	2,273,000
1880	140,000	1939	2,562,000
1900	430,000	1959	4,347,000
1911	855,000	1970	5,116,000
1917	875,000	1979	5,980,000
1923	1,087,600	1989	6,860,000
1926	1,281,000	1993	ca. 7,000,000

SOURCES: Derber and Sher; *Dal'sovnarkom*; *Dal'revkom*; *Sel'skoe khoziaistvo*; Rybakovskii; *Vsesoiuznaia perepis' naseleniia 1937 g.* (Moscow: Institut Istorii, AN SSSR, 1991); *SUPAR Report*, 12 (Jan. 1992); *Dal'nii Vostok Rossii*; Rodgers; *Chislennost' estestvennoe dvizheniie i migratsiia* (Moscow: Goskomstat, 1991).

NOTE: Excludes Yakutia, Transbaikalia, and prisoners.

PART II: *The Far East Population by District, 1991–92*

District	Year	Number
Maritime Region	1992	2,313,500
Sakhalin District	1991	718,100
Khabarovsk Region	1991	1,838,000
Magadan District	1991	546,400
Amur District	1992	1,075,200
Kamchatka District	1991	478,700
Republic of Sakha (Yakutia)	1991	1,121,300

SOURCES: Same as for Part I.

NOTE: Includes Yakutia, but excludes Transbaikalia and prisoners.

« « APPENDIX C » »

Senior Russian Officials in the Far East, 1822–1922

Governor-Generals of Eastern Siberia		Priamur Governor-Generals[a]		Military Governors of the Primorye		Presidents of the Far Eastern Republic	
1822–33	A. S. Lavinsky	1884–93	A. N. Korf	1856–65	P. V. Kazakevich	6 Apr.–Nov. 1920	A. M. Krasnoshchekov
1833–34	N. S. Sulima	1893–98	S. M. Dukhovskoi	1865–71	I. V. Furugelm	Nov. 1920–Apr. 1921	B. Z. Shumyatsky
1834–37	S. B. Bronevsky	1898–1902	N. I. Grodekov	1871–75	A. E. Kraun	May–Dec. 1921	P. M. Nikiforov
1837–47	V. Ya. Rupert	1903	D. I. Subbotich	1875–80	G. F. Erdman	Dec. 1921–Nov. 1922	N. M. Matveev
1847–61	N. N. Muraviev	1903–4	N. P. Linevich	1880–81	M. P. Tikhmenev	14–16 Nov. 1922	P. A. Kobozev
1861–71	M. S. Korsakov	1904–6	R. A. Khreshchatitsky	1881–88	I. G. Baranov		
1871–73	N. P. Sinelnikov	1906–10	P. F. Unterberger	1888–97	P. F. Unterberger	Commanders of the People's Revolutionary Army (NRA)	
1874–80	P. A. Frederiks	1910–11	N. N. Martos (acting)	1897–99	D. I. Subbotich		
1880–85	D. G. Anuchin	1911–17	N. L. Gondatti[a]	1899–1903	N. M. Chichagov	Mar. 1920–Apr. 1921	G. Kh. Eikhe
				1903–5	A. M. Kolyubakin	Apr.–May 1921	S. A. Burov
				1905–10	V. E. Flug	May–June 1921	A. Ya. Lapin
				1910–11	I. N. Svechin	June 1921–July 1922	V. K. Blücher
				1911–14	M. M. Manakin	July–Aug. 1922	K. A. Avksentevsky
				1914–16	A. D. Stashevsky	Aug.–Nov. 1922	I. P. Uborevich
				1916–17	V. A. Tolmachev		

SOURCES: Unterberger, *Primorskaia oblast'* and *Priamurskii krai*; Zosima Vostokov, in *Priamurskie vedomosti*, 17 Apr. 1992, p. 2; Hata Ikuhiko, ed., *Sekai shokoku no seido soshiki jinji, 1847–1987* (Tokyo: Tokyo University Press, 1988); Personal communications from Vladimir Khokhlov, 12 July and 22 Aug. 1992, 30 May 1993; *Vestnik DVR*.

NOTE: The post of Viceroy of the Far East was created briefly and held by one man, E. I. Alekseyev, from Aug. 1903 to July 1905.

[a] From 1910, heads of the civil administration are listed only. The military administration was headed by Generals P. A. Lechitsky (1910–14) and A. Nishchenkov (1914–17).

« « A P P E N D I X   D » »

Biographical Notes

Aksyonov, Vasily Pavlovich (b. 1932). Born in Kazan. Son of Evgeniya Ginzburg. Joined mother in Kolyma (1949) after twelve-year separation. Stories and novels published in USSR from 1959. Forced to emigrate for editing unofficial almanac *Metropol* (1980). Settled in U.S.

Albers, Gustav (1838–1911). Hamburg merchant. Met Gustav Kunst in Shanghai and established firm Kunst & Albers in Vladivostok (1864). Son Vincent Alfred (1877–1960) made partner in firm (1910).

Aleksei Aleksandrovich, Grand Duke (1850–1908). Brother of Alexander III, uncle of Nicholas II. Visited Vladivostok on frigate *Svetlanka*, accompanied by Admiral Posyet (1873). General-admiral and Navy minister (1882). Relieved of post after Battle of Tsushima (1905).

Alekseyevsky, Aleksandr Nikolaevich (1878–?). Right SR. Graduated from St. Petersburg Seminary (1903). Taught in Blagoveshchensk (1903–5). Imprisoned for revolutionary activity, escaped, and emigrated to Western Europe (1907). Returned to Blagoveshchensk, elected head of municipal duma and deputy to Constituent Assembly (1917). Arrested by Red Guards and imprisoned (Mar.–Sept. 1918). Headed Blagoveshchensk government (Sept.–Nov. 1918). Led Amur zemstvo administration until deported by Kolchak authorities (1918–19). Emigrated.

Amfiteatrov, Aleksandr Valentinovich (1862–1938). Writer. Co-edited St. Petersburg newspaper *Rossiya* with Vlas Doroshevich (1899). Exiled to Minusinsk for publishing a satire of the imperial family (1902). Author of *Sibirskie etiudy* (1904). Emigrated to Paris (1905), returned to Russia (1916), re-emigrated (1920). Died in Levanto, Italy.

Aronshtam, Lazar Naumovich (1896–1937). Joined RSDRP (1915). OKDVA political commissar (1933–37). Central Control Commission (1934–37). CC VKP(b) (1934–37). Dismissed Mar. 1937. Arrested May 1937. Shot Dec. 1937.

Arseniev, Vladimir Klavdievich (1872–1930). Military officer, ethnographer, explorer, writer, *zaamurets*. Came to Far East in 1900. Led expeditions to Sikhote Alin (1906–10). Director Khabarovsk Museum of Regional Studies (1910–18, 1924–

26). Expedition around Okhotsk littoral (1922). Lecturer at DVGU (1926–30). Works include *Dersu Uzala* (1921; German trans. 1924, English trans. 1941).

Aseyev, Nikolai Nikolaevich (1889–1963). Writer, poet. Friend and collaborator of Vladimir Mayakovsky. Lived in Vladivostok (1917–21). Co-founder with Nikolai Chuzhak and Sergei Tretyakov of futurist group *Tvorchestvo* (1920). Work on Mayakovsky awarded Stalin Prize (1941).

Azhayev, Vasily Nikolaevich (1915–68). Writer. Sakhalin-based novel *Far from Moscow* (1948) awarded Stalin Prize (1949).

Baikov, Nikolai Apollonovich (1872–1958). Imperial Army officer, ethnographer, naturalist, explorer, zaamurets. CER frontier guard unit (1901). Explored taiga of Eastern Manchuria (1902–16). Served on First World War front (1914–17). Moved to Harbin (1922). Established Society for Study of Manchurian Region (1923). Emigrated to Australia (1956).

Bakunin, Mikhail Aleksandrovich (1814–76). Revolutionary. Publicist. Philosopher of populism and anarchism. Born into aristocratic family. Associated with Herzen, Marx, Engels, Proudhon, Turgenev while traveling in Western Europe. Took part in uprising in Dresden (1849). Arrested in Saxony and handed over to Russian authorities (1851). Exiled to Siberia and settled in Irkutsk near his cousin, Governor-General of Eastern Siberia N. N. Muraviev (1857). Escaped via Japan to the United States (1861). Lived in England, Italy, and Switzerland.

Balmont, Konstantin Dmitrievich (1867–1942). Symbolist poet. Born into an aristocratic family. Expelled from Moscow Univ. for participating in student movement. Began publishing verse (1890). Visited Vladivostok en route to and from Japan (1916). Emigrated (1921). Died outside of Paris.

Berzin, Eduard Petrovich (1893–1938). Commander, Latvian Rifles guarding Kremlin (1918). Secretary to Cheka head Feliks Dzerzhinsky (1919–26). Traveled in Germany (1929). Built cellulose combine at Visher in Urals (1920–31). Head of Dalstroi (1931–37). Arrested on 19 Dec. 1937. Shot on 1 August 1938.

Berzin, Yan Karlovich [real name: *Kiuzis Peteris*] (1889–1938). Head Fourth Bureau, Red Army Intelligence (1924–35, beginning of 1937). Sent to Dalkrai to inspect OKDVA (1935). Adviser to Republican Army in Spain under alias "Grishin" (1936–37). Arrested 1937. Shot 1938.

Bichurin, Nikita Yakovlevich (1777–1853). Chuvash, orientalist, traveler. Led Russian Orthodox Mission in Beijing (1807–21). Wrote historical and linguistic studies of China, Mongolia. Organized first Russian school of Chinese language at Kiakhta.

Bishop, Isabella Bird (1832–1904). English traveler, lecturer, writer. Wrote accounts of Hawaii (1875), Japan (1880), China (1899), Korea (1898), and the Primorye (1898). First woman to be elected Fellow of the Royal Geographical Society (1892).

Blücher, Vasily Konstantinovich (1889 or 1890–1938). Army commander. Born into a peasant family near Yaroslavl. Worked in metal factory. Served as noncommissioned officer at front (1914–16). Joined RSDRP (1916). Red Guard commissar, Samara, Chelyabinsk (1917–18). Commander 51st Sharpshooter Division, Eastern and Southwestern fronts (1918–20). Commander NRA (1921–22). Head Soviet military mission to China (1924–27). Commander OKDVA (1929–38). Candidate Member CC VKP(b) (1934–38). Marshal of the Soviet Union (1935). Arrested 22 Oct. 1938. Died 9 Nov.

Bogoraz, Vladimir Germanovich (1865–1936). Revolutionary, ethnographer. Narodnik. Arrested in St. Petersburg (1886). Exiled to Yakutia (1889–98). Conducted research on natives of Kolyma and Chukotka as member of Sibiryakov Expedition (1894–96) and Jesup North Pacific Expedition (1900–1901). Wrote stories about Northeast under pseudonyms N. A. Tan and V. G. Tan. Professor of ethnography, Petrograd (later Leningrad) University (1921). Composed writing for languages of "small peoples" of the North.

Bryner, Yulius Ivanovich [*Jules Johann Brüner*] (1849–1920). Born in Mörikin, near Zurich. Worked as silk merchant in Shanghai in 1870s, then for a British firm in Yokohama. Traveled through Korea to the Primorye (1880). Settled in Vladivostok, founded an import-export business, and invested in timber, lead, and coal. Sons Leonid, Boris, and Felix carried on the business until the late 1920s. Grandsons Paul and Alexander maintained operations in China until 1962. American actor Yul Brynner (1920–85), a grandson, added an "n" to the surname.

Burliuk, David Davidovich (1882–1967). Artist, poet. Champion of futurism, cubism. Friend of Vladimir Mayakovsky, Sergei Tretyakov, Nikolai Aseyev, and Nikolai Chuzhak. Participated in *Tvorchestvo* group in Vladivostok (1920). Emigrated to Japan (1920). Moved to United States (1922).

Busse, Fyodor Fyodorovich (1838–96). Official, ethnographer, archaeologist, historian, zaamurets. Cousin of N. V. Busse. Studied at St. Petersburg Univ. (1855–61). On staff of governor-general of Eastern Siberia, military governor of the Primorye (1862–83). Member Imperial Russian Geographical Society (1871–96). First chairman Society for Study of the Amur Region (1884–88). Director South Ussuri Resettlement Office (1883–93). Left Far East (1894).

Busse, Nikolai Vasilevich [*Vilgelmovich*] (1828–66). Cousin of F. F. Busse. Imperial Army officer, amurets. First commander on Sakhalin (1853–55). Chief of staff to N. N. Muraviev (1856–58). Military governor Amur District (1858–66).

Bytovoi, Semyon Mikhailovich (1909–85). Born in Belorussia. Came to Far East (1933). Correspondent of *Tikhookeanskaya zvezda* (1933–45). Author of novels, short stories, poems, memoirs of Aleksandr Fadeyev.

Chekhov, Anton Pavlovich (1860–1904). Writer, playwright. Spent several months in Far East descending Shilka and Amur from Sretensk to Nikolaevsk, studying the penal colony of Sakhalin, returning via Vladivostok (June–October 1890). *Ostrov Sakhalin* [The Island of Sakhalin] (1895) was his longest work of prose.

Chernin, Mikhail Yakovlevich (d. 1938). Born in Ukraine. Procurator for Dalkrai (1934–37). Arrested 1937. Shot 28 May 1938.

Chumak, Andrei Konstantinovich (1878–1919). Joined RSDRP (1903). Emigrated to United States (1905). Returned to Russia (1917). Party work on CER (1917). Chairman Nikolsk soviet (1918). Railroad commissar for Ussuri front (1918). Party underground in Blagoveshchensk (1918–19). Shot by Kalmykov troops 26 Mar. 1919.

Chuzhak, Nikolai Fyodorovich [real name: *Nasimovich*] (1876–1937). Editor, writer, critic. Joined RSDRP (1908). Exiled to Siberia (1909–17). Wrote books on Siberian literature (1916–26). Co-founder with Sergei Tretyakov of futurist group *Tvorchestvo* (1920). Edited Vladivostok newspapers *Krasnoye znamya* (1917), *Dalnevostochny telegraf* (1918–21), and *Dalnevostochny put* (1921–22). Returned to Moscow (1922). Criticized Vladimir Mayakovsky. Editor All-Russian Society of Political Exiles (1926–32).

Cochrane, John Dundas (1780–1825). Naval officer, traveler. Served in Royal Navy (1790–1814). Embarked from London on pedestrian journey around the world (1821). Reached Kamchatka via Dieppe, Paris, Berlin, St. Petersburg, Tobolsk, Irkutsk, and Yakutsk (1823). Abandoned walk across North America and returned to England (1824). Died in Valencia, Colombia (now Venezuela).

Czekanowski, Alexander (1833–76). Polish nationalist, geologist. Exiled to Transbaikalia for participation in 1863 uprising. Studied geology of lower Tunguska River, discovering deposits of coal and graphite.

Czerski, Iwan (1845–92). Polish nationalist, geologist. Exiled to Transbaikalia for participation in 1863 uprising. Produced first geological map of Lake Baikal (1886). Took part in geological expedition to Kolyma (1891–92).

Dattan, Adolf Vasilevich (1849–1924). Born in Thuringia. Came to Vladivostok and joined firm of Gustav Kunst and Gustav Albers (1871). Took Russian citizenship (1884). Became partner of Kunst & Albers (1886). Formed partnership with Alfred Albers (1910). Arrested as German agent (1914). Settled in Tomsk (1916). Succeeded as partner in Kunst & Albers by son Georg von Dattan (1924).

Delvig, M. E. [real name: *Efraim*] (d. 1938). Born in Latvia. Emigrated to U.S. Bolshevik activist in Vladivostok (1917), Blagoveshchensk (1918). Chairman underground Party committee in Vladivostok under alias "Shubin" (Dec. 1918–Jan. 1920). Organized uprising against Kolchak plenipotentiary in Vladivostok (Jan. 1920). Political commissar NRA (1920–22). Member Dalbiuro (1920–22).

Denbigh, George Phillips (1840–1916). Businessman, zaamurets. Born in Scotland. Came to Vladivostok via Japan in 1880s. Took Russian citizenship. Married a Japanese. Formed partnership with Yakov Semyonov (Denbigh & Semyonov). Benefactor of Oriental Institute. Died in Honolulu.

Derber, Pyotr Yakovlevich (1888–1929). Siberian regionalist. Born in Odessa. Right

SR in Extraordinary Siberian Regionalist Congress, Tomsk (Dec. 1917). Before Siberian Regional Duma dissolved by Tomsk soviet, secretly elected head of a Siberian "government" (26 Jan. 1918). Fled to Harbin (Feb.). Established headquarters in Vladivostok (Apr.). Proclaimed self head of the Provisional Government of Autonomous Siberia (4 July). Unseated by Pyotr Vologodsky, representative of Omsk government (Sept.). Ceased political activities when Siberian Regional Duma dissolved itself (10 Nov.). Wrote about Japanese emigration for Moscow journal *Novy Vostok* (1924). Advocated economic integration of Soviet Far East into Pacific region (1927).

Derevyanko, Anatoly Panteleevich (b. 1943). Archaeologist, ethnographer, historian. Born in Kosmo-Demianovka, Amur District. Son of NKVD-MVD official. Graduated Blagoveshchensk Pedagogical Institute (1963). Joined CPSU (1970). Awarded Lenin Komsomol Prize (1972). Secretary CC Komsomol (1979–81). Secretary Novosibirsk District Party Committee (1981–82). Director Institute of History, Philology, and Philosophy, Novosibirsk (1981–91). Rector Novosibirsk University (1982–83). Academician, USSR Academy of Sciences (1987–91), Russian Academy of Sciences (1992–).

Deribas, Terenty Dmitrievich (1883–1938). Born in Odessa. Joined RSDRP (1903). Exiled for participation in 1905 Revolution. Party work in Orenburg (1917). Joined Cheka (1920). Interrogated prisoners from Kronstadt uprising (1921). Suppressed peasant uprisings in Tambov and Voronezh provinces (1921–22). OGPU/NKVD plenipotentiary to Far East (1929–37). Candidate member CC VKP(b) (1934). NKVD commissar of first rank (1935). Arrested 12 Aug. 1937. Shot 27 July 1938.

Dieterichs [Diterikhs], Mikhail Konstantinovich (1874–1937). Imperial and White army officer. Graduated General Staff Academy (1900). Division commander, Salonika front (1916–June 1917). Quartermaster, Russian Army (Aug.–Nov. 1917). Commander and chief of staff, Czech Legion (1918). Led investigation of murder of Nicholas II and his family (1918–21). Commander, Kolchak army (1919). Headed White government in Vladivostok (June–Oct. 1922). Evacuated to Japan. Settled in Shanghai. Headed Far Eastern Association of Russian Military Union (1923–37).

Doroshevich, Vlas Mikhailovich (1864–1922). Journalist, publicist, critic. Visited Sakhalin in 1897–98. Co-edited St. Petersburg newspaper *Rossiya* with Aleksandr Amfiteatrov (1899). Author of *Sakhalin* (1903).

Dukhovskoi, Sergei Mikhailovich (1838–1901). Imperial Army officer. Priamur governor-general (1893–98). Oversaw establishment of Priamur Branch of Imperial Russian Geographical Society (1894).

Dybowski, Benedykt Ivanovich (1833–1930). Polish zoologist. Graduated Dorpat (Tartu) Univ. and appointed professor of zoology at Warsaw Univ. Exiled to Siberia for participation in 1863 uprising. Studied fauna of Transbaikalia under auspices of Imperial Russian Geographical Society. Descended Amur, wintering in Blagoveshchensk (1873). Worked on Kamchatka (1878–82). Professor at Lwow Univ. (1883–1906).

Eikhe, Genrikh Khristoforovich (1893–1968). Military commander, historian. Served on Ural front (1919–20). Commander NRA (Mar. 1920–Apr. 1921). Wrote on civil war in Siberia. Not a relative of Robert Indrikovich Eikhe (1890–1940), secretary of West Siberian Party Committee (1929–37).

Emelyanov, Ivan Panteleevich (1860–1915). Narodnik. Sentenced to death, commuted to life of convict labor for involvement in assassination of Alexander II (1881). Allowed to settle in Khabarovsk (1899). Edited liberal newspaper, *Priamurye* (1908–11).

Fadeyev, Aleksandr Aleksandrovich (1901–56). Writer, literary bureaucrat. Came with family to Far East (1908). Attended rural school in Chuguyevka (1908–12). Enrolled in Vladivostok Commercial School (1912–19). Joined RKP(b) (1918) and entered underground under pseudonym "Bulyga." Sent by Party as commissar in Suchan partisan group (1919). Attended 10th Party Congress (1921). Participated in assaults on Kronstadt (1921) and Spassk (1922). Official in Russian Association of Proletarian Writers (1926–32). Deputy secretary (1934–39), secretary (1939–44), general-secretary (1946–54) USSR Writers' Union. Shot himself at his dacha on 13 May 1956.

Fedko, Ivan Fyodorovich (1897–1939). Born in Ukraine. Served with Gamarnik and then Blücher in Urals (1919–22). Commander Primorye OKDVA (1934–38). Deputy commissar of defense (1938). Arrested Oct. 1938. Shot 26 Feb. 1939.

Flegontov, Aleksei Kandievich (1888–1943). Cossack, partisan, chekist. Joined RSDRP (1917). Red Guard commander Khabarovsk soviet (1918). Partisan leader Transbaikalia (1919) and the Primorye (1921–22). NRA division commander (1920–21). Worked in Far Eastern Customs Administration (1923). Commander OGPU border guards (1924–27). Killed while organizing partisan units in Belorussia (Mar. 1943).

Frinovsky, Mikhail Petrovich (d. 1939). Head NKVD Border Troops (1924–37). Deputy Commissar NKVD (1937–38). Led NKVD mission to Far East (June–Oct. 1938). Navy Commissar (Dec. 1938–Mar. 1939). Arrest and shot Mar. 1939.

Fukushima Yasumasa (1852–1919). Japanese Army officer. Surveyed Korea and China (1882–83), India (1886). Military attaché Berlin (1887–92). Made solo equestrian journey from Berlin to Vladivostok (Feb. 1892–June 1893). Chief of staff Japanese Army in Korea (1904–5). Commander Kwantung Army (1912–14).

Gamarnik, Yan [Akel] Borisovich (1894–1937). Born in Ukraine. Joined RSDRP (1916). Kiev revkom (1917). Commissar Southern Army (1919–20). Chairman Odessa gubkom (1919), Kiev gubkom (1920–23), Primorye gubispolkom

(1923–24), Dalrevkom (1924–26), Dalkraiispolkom (1926–28). First secretary Dalkraikom (1927–28). CC VKP(b) (1927–37). First secretary Belorussian VKP(b) (1928–29). Head Army Political Administration (1929–37). Deputy Defense Commissar (1930–37). Politburo plenipotentiary to Far East (1931–37). Committed suicide or murdered 31 May 1937.

Gerasimov, Luka Evdokimovich (d. 1918). First chairman of Dalsovnarkom (1917). Chairman Khabarovsk RSDRP(b) committee and Khabarovsk soviet (1917–18). Captured and shot on orders of Ivan Kalmykov.

Gerhardi (e), William Alexander (1895–1977). Anglo-Russian writer. Born and educated in St. Petersburg. Served as adviser to British military mission to Russia (1917–20). Lived in Vladivostok (1918–20). Studied at Worcester College, Oxford (1920–24). Achieved celebrity status with novel set in Vladivostok, *Futility* (1922). Added "e" to surname (1967).

Ginzburg, Evgeniya Solomonovna (1906–77). Writer, historian. Arrested while instructor of history at Kazan Univ. (1937). Spent 730 days in solitary confinement before being sent to Kolyma (1939). Released from camp, settled in Magadan (1947). Sent back to camp (1951). Rehabilitated (1956). Author of two books on Kolyma. Mother of writer Vasily Aksyonov.

Golovnin, Vasily Mikhailovich (1776–1831). Naval officer. Led circumglobal expeditions (1807–9, 1817–19). Seized by Japanese on Iturup in Kurile Islands and held at Hakodate (1811–13). Author of *Memoirs of a Captivity in Japan* (1816; English trans. 1824).

Goncharov, Ivan Aleksandrovich (1812–91). Writer. Secretary to Vice Admiral Efimy Putiatin during part of his expedition to Japan (1852–54). Author of notes about Japan serialized in *Morskoi sbornik* (1855–57) and published as *Fregat Pallada* (1884). Author of classic novel *Oblomov* (1859).

Gondatti, Nikolai Lvovich (1860–1946). Born into peasant family and adopted by wealthy merchant. Studied at Moscow Imperial Univ. (1881–85). Traveled in Siberia, France, Austro-Hungary, Italy, Turkestan, North and South America, Ceylon, New Zealand, China, Japan (1885–92). Professor of ethnography, Moscow Univ. (1889–91). Governor Anadyr District (1893–97). Director South Ussuri Resettlement Office (1899–1902). Executive assistant to Irkutsk governor-general (1902–5). Governor of Tobolsk (1905–8) and Tomsk (1908–9). Led Amur Expedition (1909–10). Priamur governor-general (1911–17). Lectured Helsinki Univ. (1918). Settled in Harbin (1918). Chief CER Science and Land Department (1918–25). Chairman Society of Russian Orientalists (1922–27). Director Harbin Homeowner Union (1926–31).

Graves, William Sidney (1865–1940). Army officer. Secretary, U.S. Army General Staff (1911–12, 1914–18). Commander American Expeditionary Force in Siberia (1918–20), Panama Canal Zone (1926–28). Retired as major general (1928). Author of *America's Siberian Adventure* (1931, Russian ed. 1932).

Grebenshchikov, Aleksandr Vasilevich (1880–1941). Orientalist, zaamurets. Born in Kazan. Student in Chinese-Manchu department, Oriental Institute, Vladivostok (1902–7). Professor of Chinese and Manchu (1911–20). Studied in Manchuria (1908, 1909, 1912, 1914, 1915, 1917, 1921). Professor DVGU (1920–31). No works published after 1929.

Greener, Richard T. (1844–1922). Jurist, diplomat, educator. First African-American graduate of Harvard College (1869). Professor of Metaphysics and Logic, South Carolina Univ. (1872–77). Dean Howard Univ. Law School (1879–80). U.S. consul-general Vladivostok (1898–1902).

Grigorenko, Pyotr Grigorevich (1907–87). Army officer, memoirist, human rights activist. Staff officer in Far East (1939–43). Computer Department head Frunze Military Academy (1958–61). Fired and transferred to Far East after calling for democratization at Moscow Party meeting and writing an open letter to Nikita Khrushchev (1961). Arrested Khabarovsk (1964). Joined human rights movement (1965). Spent four years in mental hospitals. Allowed to emigrate to Canada, stripped of Soviet citizenship (1977).

Grodekov, Nikolai Ivanovich (1843–1913). Imperial Army officer. Served in Caucasus, Turkestan. Author of *Through Afghanistan* (1879). Adjutant to Priamur Governor-General S. M. Dukhovskoi (1893–98). Council chairman, Priamur Branch of Imperial Russian Geographical Society (1894–1902). Benefactor of Nikolaevsk Library and Khabarovsk Museum. Priamur governor-general (1898–1902).

Horvath [Khorvat], Dmitry Leonidovich (1858–1937). Military engineer. Manager of Ussuri Railroad (1895–97). Managing Director CER (1903–20) and governor of the CER railway zone (1903–18). "Temporary Ruler" of Russia (July 1918). "High Plenipotentiary" of Admiral Kolchak in Far East (Sept. 1918–Jan. 1920). Retired to Beiping (1924).

Ishimitsu Makio (1867–1942). Japanese undercover agent in Siberia. Served as army lieutenant in Sino-Japanese War (1894–95). As army captain, entered Vladivostok in civilian clothes under alias Kikuchi Shōzō (1899). Resided in Khabarovsk (1899–1901). Returned to Siberia on intelligence mission (1917).

Kalmykov, Ivan Pavlovich (1890–1920). Cossack leader. Born in Grodekovo. Decorated for bravery in First World War. Deputy ataman (1917), ataman (1918) Ussuri Cossacks. Headed Japanese-supported regime in Khabarovsk (5 Sept. 1918–12 Feb. 1920). Fled to Manchuria, arrested by Chinese authorities, and taken to Jilin (1920). Shot in July while being taken under escort to Beiping.

Kalmykov, Mikhail Vasilevich (1888–1937). Served under Blücher in Urals (1918–19). Adjutant to Blücher (1930–32). Commander OKDVA Kolkhoz Corps (1932–37). Arrested May 1937. Shot 27 Dec.

Kawakami Toshihiko (1861–1935). Japanese diplomat. Commercial agent in Vladivostok (1900–1904, 1905–7). Interpreted for Marshal Nogi Maresuke at Port

Arthur (1905). Consul Harbin (1907–12). Consul-general Moscow (1912–13). Managing director South Manchurian Railroad Co. (1913–20). Led negotiations on normalizing Soviet-Japanese relations (1920–23). President North Sakhalin Coal Co. (1926–29). President, Russo-Japanese Fisheries Co. (1929–35).

Kazakevich, Pyotr Vasilevich (1814–87). Naval officer, amurets. Participated in Muraviev's Amur expeditions (1854–58). First governor Maritime District (Primorskaya oblast) (1856–65). Opened first school for Gilyak children (1859).

Kennan, George (1845–1924). American journalist. Surveyed Kamchatka and Anadyrsk region for Western Union Co. (1865–67) and Siberian penal system for *Century* magazine (1885–86). Author of *Tent Life in Siberia* (1870) and *Siberia and the Exile System* (1891). Denounced Bolsheviks after October Revolution.

Khakanian, Grigory Davidovich (1896–1939). Served with Blücher in Urals, Siberia (1919–20). OKDVA liaison with Dalkraikom (1929–37). OKDVA political commissar (1937). Arrested 1938. Shot 26 Feb. 1939.

Kharnsky, Konstantin [Karl] Andreevich (1884–1937). Born in Lithuania. Son of Imperial Army officer. Entered Cadet Corps (1895). Graduated Mikhailovskoye Artillery Academy (1904). Assigned to Vladivostok (1911). Studied in Japan (1912). Graduated from Oriental Institute (1914). Served on front (1914–16). Assigned as intelligence officer to Priamur governor-general (1916). Joined SR military unit (1917). Member Khabarovsk soviet, Dalsovnarkom (1918). Publicist in Vladivostok (1918–20). Intelligence officer for Vladivostok Zemstvo government (1920). Joined RKP(b) (20 Apr. 1920). Represented Soviet telegraph agency in Beiping (1920–21). First secretary Soviet embassy Beiping (1921–22). Head Dalbiuro publications section (1922–23). Dalbiuro representative DVGU (1923–25). Head DVGU Department of Economics and Politics of Pacific Basin Countries (1927–37). Arrested 7 July 1937. Shot 25 Apr. 1938.

Khetagurova, Valentina Semyonovna (1914–). To Far East from Leningrad as komsomolka (1932). Married OKDVA officer Georgy Ivanovich Khetagurov, commander of Soviet forces in Baltic republics (1958–71, d. 1975). Exhorted young women to come to Far East (1937). Deputy Supreme Soviet (1937–46). Living in Riga (1990).

Khodorov, Abram Evseevich (1886–1949). Sinologist, historian. Born in Odessa. Worked in China (1919–22). Lectured at Military Academy (1924–36). Arrested (1936). In Kolyma (1937–44). Rearrested (1948). Died in prison 12 Aug. 1949.

Kholshchevnikov, Ivan Vasilevich (1852–1928). Imperial army officer. Brother-in-law of General A. F. Rediger, minister of war (1905–9). Military governor of Transbaikalia (1903–6). Under house arrest during rule of Chita soviet (11 Dec. 1905–24 Jan. 1906). Court-martialed and imprisoned. Died in Sevastopol.

Khudyakov family. Pioneers in the Primorye. Family founders Leonty (1836–1913) and Ekaterina (1847–1912). Sons Fyodor (1866–1926), Pavel (1868–1950), Yustin (1870–1939), Aleksandr (1871–1951), Afanasy (1874–1943), grandson Sergei (b. 1911). Settled on land near Razdolnoye (1881). Forcibly resettled to upper Zeya River (1930).

Kim, Afanasy Arsentievich (d. 1938). Soviet-Korean political leader. Introduced to Lenin (1921). Secretary Posyet raikom VKP(b) (1930–35). Delegate to 17th Party Congress (1934). Expelled from Party 1935. Arrested 1936. Accused of plotting with Kwantung Army to lead uprising in Posyet District. Shot 25 May 1938.

Kim [*Stankevich*], *Aleksandra Petrovna* (1885–1918). Born in southern Primorye. Joined RSDRP (1902). Married Polish immigrant and lived in Harbin. Remarried Korean (1910). Bolshevik organizer among Korean, Chinese, Hungarian workers in Urals (1914–16). Secretary Khabarovsk RKP(b) committee and commissar for foreign affairs Khabarovsk soviet (1917–18). Captured after fleeing Khabarovsk and executed on Kalymkov's orders.

Kobozev, Pyotr Alekseevich (1878–1941). RSDRP organizer in Latvia. Chairman FER Council of Ministers (1922). Secretary Dalbiuro (1922–25). Chairman Dalrevkom (1922–24), Far East Section, Gosplan (1924–30).

Kolchak, Aleksandr Vasilevich (1873–1920). Naval officer, White leader. Graduated from Naval Academy (1894). Came to Vladivostok on cruiser *Riurik* (1895). Served in Pacific Fleet (1895–99). Member Baron Toll expedition to Arctic (1900–1902). At Port Arthur (1904–5). Gold medalist, Imperial Russian Geographical Society (1906). Navy general staff (1907–9). Conducted hydrological research around Bering Strait (1910). Commander Black Sea Fleet (1916). Sent by Provisional Government to U.S. (July 1917). To Japan (Nov. 1917) and Harbin (Apr. 1918). Joined Omsk government (Sept. 1918). After military coup in Omsk (18 Nov.), declared "Supreme Ruler of Russia." Handed over by Czechs to "Political Center" in Irkutsk 17 Jan. 1920. Shot on Lenin's instructions 7 Feb.

Komarov, Pyotr Stepanovich (1911–49). Poet, editor. Born in Novgorod Province. Moved to Amur District with family (1918). Wrote for Far Eastern Komsomol and Party newspapers (1929–39). Editor *Na rubezhe* (1939–41). Khabarovsk office of TASS (1941–45). Secretary Khabarovsk Branch Writers' Union (1943–46). Editor *Dalny Vostok* (1946–49).

Komarov, Vladimir Leontievich (1869–1945). Botanist, administrator. Surveyed flora of Manchuria, Mongolia, Priamur, Korea (1896–1917). Academician Russian Academy of Sciences (1920). Vice-president (1930–36), director Far Eastern Branch (1932–36), and president USSR Academy of Sciences (1936–45).

Korf, Andrei Nikolaevich (1831–98). Baron, Imperial Army cavalry general. Favorite of Alexander III. Priamur governor-general (1884–93). Ataman Amur and Ussuri Cossacks (1887–93). Promoted development of Priamur while opposing expansion into Korea, Manchuria.

Korolenko, Vladimir Galaktionovich (1853–1921). Writer and political radical. Exiled to Siberia for refusing to take oath of loyalty to tsar (1879–85). Wrote stories about life in Yakutia (1881–84). Eventually settled in Nizhni Novgorod and achieved a reputation through novels as a master of style. Opposed Bolshevik regime after October Revolution.

Korsakov, Mikhail Semyonovich (1826–71). Cousin of N. N. Muraviev. Took part in Amur expeditions (1854–58). Governor-general of Eastern Siberia (1861–71).

Krasnoshchekov [alias *Tobelson, Tobinson*], *Aleksandr Mikhailovich* (1880–1937). Born in Kiev. Worked with Trotsky (1898). Emigrated to United States (1905). Industrial Workers of the World organizer in Chicago. Graduated Chicago Univ. (1912). Headed Chicago Workers' Institute (1913). Returned to Russia (1917). Chairman Nikolsk soviet (1917). Chairman Dalsovnarkom (1918). Jailed in Irkutsk (1919). Chairman RKP(b) committee in Irkutsk (Jan. 1920). President and foreign minister FER (Apr.–Nov. 1920). Deputy commissar of finance Russian Republic (1921–22). Chairman Industrial Bank USSR (1922–24). Tried for embezzlement (1924). Director, New Fiber Institute, Moscow (1934–37). Arrested 16 July 1937. Shot 26 Nov.

Kropotkin, Pyotr Alekseevich (1842–1921). Prince, revolutionary, theorist of anarchism, geographer, geologist, historian, sociologist. Corps of Pages (1862). As officer for special assignments under Governor-General of Eastern Siberia Korsakov, traveled around the Far East and Manchuria (1862–67). Resigned from state service and moved to St. Petersburg, where he attempted to radicalize urban workers. Arrested in 1874. Escaped abroad in 1876. Lived in Switzerland, France, and England. Returned to Russia in 1917.

Krushanov, Andrei Ivanovich (1921–91). Party functionary, historian. Joined VKP(b) (1944). Graduated Vladivostok Pedagogical Institute (1949). Taught at Mikhailovsk Middle School, Primorye (1949–55). Department head, then Director Institute of History, Archaeology, and Ethnography of Peoples of the Far East, Vladivostok (1958–71, 1971–91). Corresponding Member (1970), Academician (1987) USSR Academy of Sciences.

Krutov, Grigory Maksimovich (1892–1938). Supporter of Trotsky (1924–27). Chairman Dalkraiispolkom (1932–37). Member of Dalkraikom (1932–37). Delegate to 16th and 17th (1930, 1934) Party conferences. Arrested 4 June 1937. Shot Apr. 1938.

Kruzenshtern, Ivan Fyodorovich (1770–1846). Naval officer. Led circumglobal expedition (1803–6). Honorary member Russian Academy of Sciences (1806). Admiral (1842). Co-founder Imperial Russian Geographical Society (1845).

Kubiak, Nikolai Afanasievich (1881–1937). Joined RSDRP (1898). Member Petrograd soviet (1917). Active in "workers' opposition" (1920–22). First secretary Dalbiuro (1922–25). First secretary Dalkraikom (1926–27). Member CC VKP(b) (1923–34). Arrested and shot in 1937.

Kühlborn, Georg Gottfried Christian (1888–1969). Trained in Russian and Chinese at Berlin Univ. (1909–14). POW in Japan (1914–19). Consul in Vladivostok (1923–24), Mukden (1924–38), Xinjing (1938–39, 1941–45). Consul-general, Vladivostok (1940–41). Interned in USSR (1945–53).

Kukel, Vladimir Andreevich (1885–1938). Grandson of navigator Gennady Nevelskoi and of Boleslav Kukel (Polish exile and adjutant of Governor-General N. N. Muraviev). Served in Pacific Squadron (1908–17). Second secretary Soviet embassy Afghanistan (1921–28). Entered OGPU (1928). Purchased submarines in Italy for Pacific Fleet (1933–34). Commander NKVD maritime frontier forces in Dalkrai (1934–36). Arrested in 1937. Shot 18 Sept. 1938.

Kulygin, Pyotr Gavrilovich (1906–38). Writer. Correspondent *Tikhookeanskaya zvezda* (1930–37). Editor *Na rubezhe* (1933–37). Delegate to 1st Congress of USSR Writers' Union (1934). Collaborated with E. I. Titov on play about Sergei Lazo (1936). Arrested 1937. Shot 7 Aug. 1938.

Kunst, Gustav (1836–1905). Hamburg merchant. Met Gustav Albers in Shanghai. Established firm Kunst & Albers in Vladivostok (1864).

Kurnatovsky, Viktor Konstantinovich (1868–1912). Social Democrat activist. With Lenin in Sheshenskoye exile (1898–99). Worked with Stalin in Tiflis (1900). Arrested and exiled in Yakutsk (1901). Led Chita RSDRP committee (1905–6). Sentenced to life of hard labor, escaped from Verkhneudinsk hospital to Japan (1906). Worked in Australia (1907–10). Died in Paris.

Kurteyev, Konstantin Konstantinovich (1853–1928). Journalist, publicist. Born in Odessa. Narodnik. Implicated in assassination of Alexander II and condemned to hard labor in Kara mines (1881). Allowed to live in Chita as exile (1887). Brought to Khabarovsk to work as economist for Priamur Governor-General P. F. Unterberger (1908). Edited in succession *Priamurye* and *Priamurskie vedomosti* (1911–17). Moved to Vladivostok (1917). Lecturer at DVGU (1923).

Kyuner, Nikolai Vasilevich (1877–1955). Orientalist. Born in Tiflis. Graduated from St. Petersburg Univ. (1900). Studied in Japan, China, and Korea (1900–1902, 1909, 1912, 1913, 1915). Lecturer Oriental Institute, Vladivostok (1902–25), Leningrad Univ. (1925–55). Research associate Institute of Ethnography (1934–55).

Lapin [*Lapinysh*], *Albert Yanovich* (1899–1937). Joined RSDRP (1917). Red Guards staff Moscow (1917). Political commissar 5th Army (1918–20). Deputy commander NRA (1921–22). Member Soviet military mission to China (1924–27). OKDVA chief of staff (1929–34), corps commander (1934–35). Far Eastern Air Force chief (1935–37). Arrested in Kislovodsk, interrogated in Moscow, and committed suicide in Khabarovsk prison 21 Sept. 1937.

Larin, Ivan Emelyanovich (1890–?) Activist in Northeast. SR. Switched allegiance to RSDRP during 1917. Sent by Vladivostok soviet to Petropavlovsk to establish Soviet rule in Kamchatka (1917). Member, Kamchatka District soviet (1917–

22). Fled Petropavlovsk to avoid White diehards (1922). Deputy chairman Kamchatka revkom and Kamchatka District soviet (1923–31). Left Kamchatka (1931). Worked in Ural and Krasnoyarsk forest preserves. Living near Moscow as pensioner in 1979.

Lattimore, Owen (1900–89). Orientalist. Born in Washington, D.C. Educated in England and Switzerland. Journalist Shanghai and Beiping (1920–26). Traveled in Manchuria and Mongolia (1929–35). Professor, Johns Hopkins Univ. (1938–63). Political adviser to Chiang Kai-shek (1941–42). Deputy director of Pacific Operations, U.S. Office of War Information (1942–44). Director of Chinese Studies, Leeds Univ. (1963–75). Spent last years in Paris. Died in Providence, Rhode Island.

Laufer, Berthold (1874–1934). Anthropologist, orientalist. Born in Germany. Emigrated to United States (1898). Studied aborigines on Sakhalin and along lower Amur (1898–99). In China (1901–4, 1908–10, 1923). Curator of Anthropology, Field Museum of Natural History, Chicago (1915–34). Committed suicide.

Lavrentiev [Kartvelishvili], Lavrenty Yosifovich (1890–1938). Joined RSDRP (1910). Kiev Party committee (1917–18). Political commissar 12th Army (1919). Party work in Odessa (1919–30). Candidate member CC VKP(b) (1930–34). First secretary Dalkraikom (1933–15 Jan. 1937). Transferred to Sevastopol, Tbilisi. Shot 22 Aug. 1938.

Lazo, Sergei Georgievich (1894–1920). Born in Bessarabia. Attended St. Petersburg Technical Institute and Moscow Univ. Graduated Alekseyev Infantry School (1916). Red Guard commander and chairman soldiers' section of Krasnoyarsk soviet (1917). Left SR, switching to RSDRP (late 1917). Member Tsentrosibir (1918). Commander Primorye partisan units (1919). Prepared Vladivostok uprising of Jan. 1920. Arrested by Japanese 4–5 Apr. 1920. Killed by Whites at Muraviev (now Lazo) station of Ussuri Line 28 May.

Lebedev, Evgeny Vladimirovich (1897–1938). Party underground in Verkhneudinsk (1919–20). Delegate FER Constituent Assembly (1921–22). Headed Primorye police (1923–26). Chairman Sakhalin and Blagoveshchensk revkoms and executive committees (1927–35). Worked in Dalkraikom (1935–37). Deputy chairman Dalkraiispolkom (May–June 1937). Arrested June 1937. Shot 9 Apr. 1938.

Lebedeva, Anna Nikitichna (1900–1938). Wife of E. V. Lebedev. Party underground in Verkhneudinsk (1919–20). Fought at Volochayevka (1922). Chairman Ussuriisk revkom (1923–26). Procurator on Sakhalin (1927–31). Arrested in 1937. Shot 27 May 1938.

Lemberg, Lev Vladimirovich (d. 1937). Born in Ukraine. Red Army commissar Ukraine (1918–20). Head Far Eastern Railroad Administration (1933–37). Committed suicide 1 Apr. 1937.

Levandovsky, Mikhail Karlovich (1890–1938). Commander on Turkestan front (1920). OKDVA corps commander (1935–38). Shot.

Likhoidov, Konstantin Tikhonovich (dates unknown). Conservative political leader. Headed White government in Khabarovsk (Apr.–Nov. 1920). Chairman Popular Assembly Vladivostok (1921–22) under Merkulov and Dieterichs governments. Emigrated to Harbin.

Lipsky, Albert Nikolaevich [alias *Grigory Dmitrievich Kurenkov*] (1894–1973). Ethnographer, chekist. Born in Mogilyovsk Province. Graduated St. Petersburg Univ. (1914). Participated in expeditions to Altai, Mongolia (1914–16). Admitted to Priamur Branch, Russian Geographical Society on recommendations of V. K. Arseniev (1918). Started denigrating Arseniev's work (1919). Offered services to Cheka (1920). Director Khabarovsk Museum of Regional Studies (1920–21). FER Minister of Nationalities (1921–22). Took part in GPU mop-up operations along Okhotsk seaboard (1923). Lecturer in ethnography DVGU (1923–24). Charged Arseniev with selling artifacts to U.S. (1923). Plenipotentiary for aboriginal affairs, Nikolaevsk-na-Amure (1924–38). Appointed secretary of Indigenous Peoples Department of journal *Etnografiia* (1925). Took part in OGPU punitive operations in Chumikan district (1931). Arrested (1938). Released from labor camp and settled in Abakan, 170 miles southwest of Krasnoyarsk (1943). Worked in Abakan Museum. Rehabilitated as "honorary chekist."

Lopatin, Ivan Alekseevich (1888–1970). Ethnographer, zaamurets. Born in Olochi on Transbaikalian-Manchurian frontier. Attended technical school in Khabarovsk (1901–8), Kazan Univ. (1908–12). Taught at women's academy in Khabarovsk (1912–17). Studied Goldy (Nanai) on lower Amur (1913–19). Director Khabarovsk Museum of Regional Studies (1919–20). Lecturer in ethnography and archaeology DVGU (1920–23), Chita People's Education Inst. (1923–25). Emigrated to Harbin (1925). Moved to Canada (1926). M.A., British Columbia Univ. (1929). Ph.D., Univ. Southern California (1935). Assistant to full professor, USC (1935–1970).

Luks, Karl Yanovich (1888–1932). Latvian. Joined Latvian Social Democratic Party (1904). Took part in uprising in Liepau (1905). Arrested and exiled to Transbaikalia (1911–17). Studied Buryat Mongols (1917–18). Partisan leader in Transbaikalia (1918–19). NRA commander Transbaikalian front (1920). FER Minister of Nationalities (1921–22). Rector, Pedagogical Institute for Peoples of the North (1925–32). Director Khabarovsk Museum of Regional Studies (1926–28). Died on expedition to Kolyma, reportedly in an accident.

Lyushkov, Genrikh Samoilovich (1900–1945). Chekist. Born in Odessa. Political commissar southern front (1919–20). Joined Cheka (1920). Handled investigation of Grigory Zinoviev (1935). Headed a secret political department within NKVD (1936). Awarded Order of Lenin (1937). Chief NKVD in Far East (July 1937–June 1938). Fled to Manchukuo (12–13 June 1938). Intelligence consultant, Army General Staff, Tokyo (1938–45). Shot 20 Aug. 1945 by Special Services officer Takeoka Yutaka in Dairen after refusing to commit suicide.

Maak, Richard Karlovich (1825–86). Explorer, ethnographer, amurets. Lived and taught in Irkutsk. Explored Amur (1855–56) and Ussuri (1859–60). Accounts of the expeditions published by the Imperial Russian Geographical Society in 1859 and 1861, respectively.

Makarov, Stepan Osipovich (1848 or 1849–1904). Naval officer, oceanographer. Led research expeditions around the Pacific (1886–89, 1894–96) and Arctic (1899–1901). Member Society for Study of the Amur Region. Co-founder Museum of the Primorye Branch, Imperial Russian Geographical Society, Vladivostok (1890). Commander Pacific Squadron (1904). Went down with flagship *Petropavlovsk* on 13 Apr. 1904.

Mamiya Rinzō (1780–1844). Japanese explorer, cartographer. Dispatched by Tokugawa shogunate to ascertain the Chinese and Russian presence along the northern frontier (1800). Surveyed the western coast of Sakhalin and confirmed Sakhalin's insularity (1808). Traveled up Amur River and met with Manchu officials at trading post of Deren (1809). Maps based on Mamiya's surveys were smuggled out of Japan by Philipp Franz von Siebold in 1829 and shown to Ivan Krusenshtern in 1834.

Matveyev [*"Amursky"*], *Nikolai Petrovich* (1866–1941). Historian, poet, editor, publisher, zaamurets. Born in Hakodate. Son of physician. Worked in Vladivostok shipyards. Published stories, poems, travel guides about the Primorye. Secretary Society for Study of the Amur Region (1898–99). Editor Vladivostok paper *Dalekii krai* (1906). Imprisoned six months for receiving seditious literature (1906). Wrote history of Vladivostok (1910). Member Vladivostok duma. Chairman Gogol Public Library. Emigrated to Japan (1919). Wrote mostly children's stories thereafter. Died 10 Feb. 1941 in Kobe.

Matveyev, Zotik Nikolaevich (1889–1938). Librarian, orientalist, historian. Born in Vladivostok. Son of N. P. Matveyev. Graduated from Vladivostok gymnasium and joined RSDRP. Inclined toward Menshevik faction (1908–17). Expelled from St. Petersburg Polytechnical Institute (1911). Attended Oriental Institute (1912–16). Imperial Army (1916–17). Vladivostok Telegraph Office (1917–20). Union of Cooperatives (1920–21). Educational adviser, Merkulov government (1921–22). Lecturer DVGU and director DVGU Library (1923–31). Director Library of Far Eastern Branch, USSR Academy of Sciences (1932–37). Arrested 5 Nov. 1937. Shot 25 Apr. 1938.

Mekhlis, Lev Zakharovich (1889–1953). Party official, Red Army commissar. Joined RKP(b) (1918). Institute of Red Professors (1927–30). Editor *Pravda* (1930–37). Head Red Army Political Administration (1937–44). Conducted purge in Far East (June–Oct. 1938). Member CC VKP(b) (1939–53). Deputy Defense Commissar (1941–42). High Command representative to Crimean front until removed for incompetence (May 1942). Buried in Kremlin Wall.

Meller-Zakomelsky, Aleksandr Nikolaevich (1844–after 1923). Imperial Army officer.

Suppressed Sevastopol uprising (1905). Commanded armored train moving from Moscow to Chita, restoring order along railroad (1906). Governor Baltic Province (1907). Emigrated (1917). Living in Paris in 1923.

Melnikov, Boris Nikolaevich (1896–1937). Joined RSDRP (1916). Red Guard commander Irkutsk (1917). Fought on Daurian front (1918–19). Member military soviet of Vladivostok Zemstvo Government (1920). Chairman FER administration in Khabarovsk and member Amur RKP(b) committee (1920–21). NRA political commissar Eastern front (1921–22). Consul general Harbin (1929–31). Chargé d'affaires Tokyo (1931). Far Eastern representative VKP(b) Foreign Section (1935). Arrested 1936. Shot.

Mezis, Avgust Ivanovich (1894–1937). Latvian. Joined RSDRP (1912). Political commissar Siberian Military District (1928–30). OKDVA political commissar (1930–33). Arrested May 1937. Shot.

Molchanov, Viktorin Mikhailovich (1886–1974). Born in Kazan Province. Educated Yelabuga gymnasium. Joined Imperial Army (1905). Stationed in Razdolnoye (1908–13). Served at front (1914–18). Escaped from German captivity (Apr. 1918). Returned to Yelabuga and organized peasant self-defense forces to resist Bolshevik grain collectors (1918). Brought Yelabugans and Ural peasants into Izhevsk Workers' Brigade fighting against Bolsheviks (1919). Retreated with Yelabugans across Siberia to Transbaikalia, Manchuria, and Primorye (1919–20). Led *belopovstantsy* "March on Moscow" (1921–22). Defeated by Blücher at Volochayevka (Feb. 1922). Took part in defense of southern Primorye (June–Oct. 1922). Sought refuge in China (Oct. 1922). Moved to California (1923). Settled in Petaluma, north of San Francisco.

Muraviev ["*Amursky*"], *Nikolai Nikolaevich* (1809–81). Army officer, administrator, diplomat, amurets. Governor-general of Eastern Siberia (1847–61). Sent expeditions to Amur estuary (1849–50), Sakhalin (1853), down Amur (1854–58), along Primorye coast (1859–60). Concluded Treaty of Aigun (1858). Emigrated to France (1862). Died in Paris, buried in Montmartre. Ashes brought to Vladivostok (1991).

Nansen, Fridtjof (1861–1930). Norwegian explorer, oceanographer, statesman, humanitarian. Led series of expeditions to the Arctic (1888–96), North Atlantic (1910–14). First Norwegian minister to Great Britain (1906–8). Traveled from mouth of Ob River to Transbaikalia, Manchuria, and the Far East, visiting Vladivostok and Khabarovsk (1913). On behalf of League of Nations, worked for repatriation of (among others) Austro-Hungarian POWs from Siberia (1920–22). Directed International Red Cross famine-relief efforts in Russia (1921–23). Awarded Nobel Peace Prize (1922). Admired Vladimir Arseniev, whom he predeceased by four months.

Neibut, Arnold Yakovlevich (1889–1919). Latvian. Joined RSDRP (1905). Emigrated to United States (1912). Joined Socialist Party of America (1912). Returned to Russia (1917). Chairman Vladivostok soviet (1917). Editor *Krasnoye znamya* (1917–18). Moved to Western Siberia (1918). Shot by Kolchak forces in Omsk on 8 Feb. 1919.

Nesmelov [real name: *Mitropolsky*], *Arseny Ivanovich* (1889–1945). Poet. Published first verse in Moscow (1915). Officer in Imperial and Kolchak armies (1915–19). Lived in Vladivostok (1920–24). Fled to Manchuria with assistance of Vladimir Arseniev (1924). Settled in Harbin, publishing verse. Arrested by Soviet security organs and died in Grodekovo transit prison.

Nevelskoi, Gennady Ivanovich (1813–76). Naval officer, explorer, amurets. Confirmed Sakhalin's insularity (1849). Established Russian settlements on lower Amur (1850). Participant Amur expeditions (1854–58). Invested unsuccessfully in Amur Company (1858). Admiral (1874).

Nikiforov, Pyotr Mikhailovich (1882–1974). Joined RSDRP (1904). Party activist in Baltic Fleet (1904–5). Death penalty for murder of postman commuted to twenty years of hard labor (1910). Deputy chairman Vladivostok soviet and RSDRP(b) committee (1917). Chairman Primorye workers' control council (1918). Member Dalbiuro (1920–22). Chairman FER Council of Ministers (1921–22). Minister to Mongolia (1925–27).

Ōba, Kakō (1872–1924). Journalist. Studied Russian with writer Futabatei Shimei (1891). Lived in Vladivostok (1896–99). Interpreter, Japanese Army Staff (1902, 1904–5). Arrested for bringing revolutionary literature into Vladivostok (1906). In Russia (incl. Siberia) as correspondent for Mainichi (1908), Asahi (1914–17), Yomiuri (1921) newspapers. Imprisoned by Cheka (1921–24). Shot as a spy in Siberia while en route to Japan (1924).

Okladnikov, Aleksei Pavlovich (1908–81). Archaeologist, ethnographer, historian. Born in Irkutsk Province. Joined VKP(b) (1946). Awarded Stalin Prize (1950). Director Institute of History, Philology, and Philosophy, Novosibirsk (1966–81). Academician USSR Academy of Sciences (1968). Awarded Lenin Prize (1973). Awarded title "Hero of Socialist Labor" (1978).

Orzhikh, Boris Dmitrievich (1864–after 1934). Revolutionary, editor, writer. People's Will activist. Exiled to Sakhalin (1888). Moved to Vladivostok (1898). Emigrated to Japan (1905) and edited newspaper *Volya* ("Will"). Author of popular revolutionary poems and songs.

Ossendowski, Antoni Ferdynand (1878–1945). Chemist, author. Graduated from St. Petersburg Univ. Studied in Paris. Senior lecturer Tomsk Polytechnic Institute (1901). Academic secretary Society for Study of the Amur Region (1901–3). Technical adviser to Count Witte (1903–5) and Russian Navy (1903–5, 1907–16). Leader of CER strike committee, Harbin (1905). Arrested and imprisoned in Harbin (1906–7). Awarded gold medal by Society for Study of the Amur Region (1907). Professor of chemistry St. Petersburg Polytechnic (1908–17). Published articles in Petrograd press accusing Kunst & Albers director Adolf Dattan of being German agent (1914). Professor of chemistry Omsk University and economic adviser to Admiral Kolchak (1918–19). Served under Baron R. F. Ungern-Sternberg (1921). Wrote prolifically and unreliably on Siberia, Mongolia, and Manchuria. Died, possibly murdered, on his estate outside Warsaw 3 Jan. 1945.

Ōta Kakumin (1866–1944). Buddhist priest. Entered Jōdō Shinshū temple in Nagasaki as an acolyte (1877). Studied Russian with Araki Sadao (future army minister and proponent of "active" northern strategy) at Tokyo School of Foreign Languages (1902). To Vladivostok Honganji Mission (1904). Accompanied Japanese Army in Manchuria, meeting with Marshal Nogi Maresuke in 1905. Reopened Vladivostok Mission (1906). Greeted Marshal Nogi in Vladivostok (1911). Left Vladivostok after mission closed (1931). Died in Mongolia.

Ovidiev, Nikolai Petrovich (1891–1938). Japanologist. Graduated from Oriental Institute, Vladivostok (1918). Headed Japanese Language Department Oriental Faculty DVGU (1930–37). Arrested 20 Sept. 1937. Shot 25 Apr. 1938.

Panov, Viktor Ananevich (1854–1922). Naval officer, journalist, newspaper editor, publicist. Editor of newspapers *Vladivostok* (1885–92) and (with wife) *Dalny Vostok* (1892–1922). Member Vladivostok duma (1898–1902).

Parfyonov, Pyotr Semyonovich (1894–1937). Author, composer, revolutionary. Born Ufa District. Joined RSDRP (1917). Party underground and intelligence assignments in Far East (1918–21). Composed "Partisan Anthem" in honor of friend Sergei Lazo (1920). CC VKP(b) envoy to Far East (1925–27). Author of books on civil war in Far East (1922–31). Deputy director Gosplan (1927–29). Arrested 1935. Shot. Dispute with Sergei Alymov over authorship of "Partisan Hymn" decided in favor of Parfyonov after latter's posthumous rehabilitation (1962).

Pashkovsky, Konstantin Kazimirovich (1891–1937). Close associate of V. K. Blücher. OKDVA division commander (1930–32) and corps commander (1932–37). Arrested May 1937. Shot Dec.

Pegov, Nikolai Mikhailovich (1905–91). Joined VKP(b) (1930). First secretary Dalkraikom (Sept.–Oct. 1938), Primorsky kraikom (1938–47). In CC VKP(b) Secretariat (1947–56, 1975–82). Ambassador to Iran (1956–64), Algeria (1964–67), India (1967–73). Deputy minister of foreign affairs (1973–75). Member, Party CC (1939–86).

Pepeliaev, Anatoly Nikolaevich (1892–1938). Imperial Army officer, White commander. Born in Tomsk. Younger brother of last prime minister of Omsk regime, Viktor, who was shot with Admiral Kolchak in Irkutsk (7 Feb. 1920). Served at front during First World War, attaining rank of lieutenant-colonel. As commander of Kolchak army unit, captured Perm (1918). Enjoyed popularity among Siberian regionalists. Emigrated to Harbin (1920). Organized Siberian "Druzhina" and led assault on Yakutsk from the Okhotsk seabord (1922–23). Captured at Ayan (June 1923). Death sentence commuted to ten years' imprisonment after he publicly urged followers to surrender on 18 July 1923. Assumed to have been killed during the Great Terror.

Perepechko, Ivan Nikolaevich (1897–1943). Party secretary. Chairman Odessa trade unions' soviet (1919). Supported "Workers' Opposition" (1920–22). Political commissar Eastern front (1920). Chairman Belorussian trade union organization (1925–28). First secretary Dalkraikom (1928–31). Arrested on personal orders of Stalin and died in Kansk prison 30 Jan. 1943.

Perfiliev, Vasily Vlasevich (1865–1914). Military doctor, administrator. Director Nikolaevsk Library, Khabarovsk (1894–1902). Governor Kamchatka (1909–1912). Rival of N. L. Gondatti.

Pilsudski, Bronislaw Osipovich (1866–1918). Polish nationalist, ethnographer. Born in Vilna Province. Brother of Polish military leader and statesman Josef Pilsudski (1867–1935). Sentenced to fifteen years penal servitude on charge of conspiring to assassinate Alexander III (1887). Exiled to Sakhalin (1888) where he began ethnographic research. Published by Priamur Branch of the Imperial Russian Geographical Society (1898). Moved to Vladivostok and worked in museum of Society for Study of the Amur Region (1899). Returned to Sakhalin under auspices of Academy of Sciences (1902). To Austrian Poland via Japan and the United States (1905). Lived in Cracow, Vienna. Committed suicide in Paris.

Plyusnin, Aleksandr Vasilevich (1864–1921). Khabarovsk merchant and municipal leader. Inherited family business in 1909. Elected head municipal duma (1914). Opposed Social Democrats in Committee of Public Security (1917). Active in K. T. Likhoidov regime (1920). Moved to Vladivostok (1920).

Plyusnin, Andrei Fyodorovich (1826–1880). Born in Transbaikalia. Part Buryat. Influenced by Decembrist ideas as a young man. Founder of family businesses in newly established military post of Khabarovka (1858).

Podstavin, Grigory Vladimirovich (1875–1924). Orientalist, zaamurets. Graduated St. Petersburg Univ. (1894). Studied in Korea (1899–1900). Head Korean Section, director Oriental Institute, Vladivostok (1900–1919, 1919–20). Rector DVGU (1920–22). Emigrated to Harbin (1923).

Pokus, Yan Zakharovich (1894–1940?). Commander NRA division Eastern front (1921–22). Commander Priamur Red Army units (1922–29) and Primorye OKDVA (1930–31). Arrested 1937. Cause and date of death uncertain.

Postyshev, Pavel Petrovich (1887–1939). Joined RSDRP (1906). Arrested (1907). Exiled to Irkutsk (1910). Deputy chairman Irkutsk soviet (1917). Tsentrosibir representative to Dalrevkom (1918). Partisan leader (1919). CC RKP(b) representative in Khabarovsk and candidate member Dalbiuro (1920). Political commissar NRA Eastern front (1921–22). Chairman Pribaikal revkom (1923). In Party CC Secretariat (1924–34). First secretary VKP(b), Ukraine (1934–38).

Candidate member CC VKP(b) (1925–27), member (1927–38). Candidate member, Politburo (1934–38). Shot 26 Feb. 1939.

Posyet, Konstantin Nikolaevich (1819–99). A Finn. Member Putiatin expeditions to Primorye coast and Japan (1852–55). Led naval squadron to Vladivostok with Grand Duke Aleksei Aleksandrovich (1873). Minister of communications (1874–88). Advocated development of Far East.

Potanin, Grigory Nikolaevich (1835–1920). Explorer, folklorist, publicist, champion of Siberian autonomy. Born in Akmolinsk Province. Son of Cossack officer. Educated at Cadet Corps, Omsk, St. Petersburg Univ. Secretary statistical committee, Tomsk (1865). Arrested with Nikolai Yadrintsev for "Siberian separatism" (1865). In prison and exile (1865–73). Participated in expeditions to Tuva, Mongolia, China, Tibet (1876–99). Elected president of Provisional Regional Council by Extraordinary Siberian Regionalist Congress, Tomsk (Dec. 1917). Inactive after Tomsk soviet dissolved Congress in Feb. 1918.

Pozdneyev, Aleksei Matveevich (1851–1920). Brother of D. M. Pozdneyev. Mongolist. Professor of Oriental studies, St. Petersburg Univ. (1884–99). Rector Oriental Institute, Vladivostok (1899–1903). Returned to St. Petersburg Univ.

Pozdneyev, Dmitry Matveevich (1865–1937). Brother of A. M. Pozdneyev. Orientalist, zaamurets. Graduated from Kiev Theological Seminary (1889). Lecturer St. Petersburg Univ. (1893–94). Employed by Imperial Chinese Customs (1898–1903). Professor and (from 1904) rector Oriental Institute, Vladivostok (1903–6). Manager Japan branch, Russo-Asiatic Bank (1906–10). Lecturer Prakticheskaya Vostochnaya Akademiya, St. Petersburg/Petrograd (1910–17), Frunze Military Academy and Petrograd/Leningrad Univ. (1918–37). Arrested 1 Oct. 1937 as a Japanese spy. Shot 20 Oct.

Przhevalsky, Nikolai Mikhailovich (1839–88). Army officer, explorer, ethnographer. Traveled around Ussuri region (1867–69) and Central Asia, Mongolia, China, Tibet (1870–85). Wrote and published prolifically.

Pshenitsyn, Konstantin Fyodorovich (1892–1938). Born in Ukraine. Joined RSDRP in Irkutsk (1917). Party-partisan liaison work in Priamur (1918–20). Dalbiuro representative to FER and Primorye partisan groups (1920–22). Headed military department Primorye revolutionary staff (1920–22). Deputy chairman Primorye revkom (1922–24). In Party CC Secretariat (1925–32). First secretary Primorye obkom (1933–35). Second secretary Sverdlovsk gorkom (1935–36). Arrested 23 May 1937. Shot.

Putna, Vitovt Kazimirovich (1893–1937). Joined RSDRP (1917). Red Army commander in Eastern (Urals) and Polish fronts (1919–20). Military attaché Tokyo (1928), Berlin (1930–31). Commander Primorye OKDVA (1931–34). Deputy commander OKDVA (1934–35). Arrested in Aug. 1936. Shot 11 June 1937.

Raikhman, Elizar Grigorevich (d. 1938). Far Eastern representative of Gosplan and deputy chairman Dalkraiispolkom (1932–37). Chairman Khabarovsk gorkom (1935–37). Arrested in 1937. Shot 3 June 1938.

Rayev, Grigory Fyodorovich (1885–1923). Emigrated to United States. Joined Socialist Party of America in Chicago (1911). Returned to Russia (1917). RSDRP organizer in Vladivostok (1917–19). Sent to Sverdlov Communist Univ. Moscow (1920).

Rennenkampf, Pavel Karlovich (1854–1918). Imperial Army officer. Commanded Transbaikalian cavalry division in Manchuria (1904–5). Commanded armored train moving from Harbin to Chita, restoring order along Trans-Siberian Railroad (1906). Commanded one of two armies in disastrous offensive into East Prussia (Aug. 1914). Governor of St. Petersburg (1915). Commanded Northern front (1916). Captured and shot by Bolsheviks at Taganrog.

Rimsky-Korsakov, Voin Andreevich (1822–71). Naval officer, explorer, amurets. Surveyed Sakhalin (1853–56). Headed Imperial Naval Academy (1861–71). Died in Pisa, Italy. Older brother of composer Nikolai (1844–1908).

Rudakov, Apollinary Vasilevich (1871–1949). Sinologist. Born near Baku. Graduated from Oriental Faculty, St. Petersburg Univ. (1896). Lecturer, professor of Chinese, Oriental Institute, Vladivostok (1899–20). Institute director (1906–April 1917). Professor of Chinese, DVGU (1920–39). Called for re-establishment of Oriental Institute in Vladivostok paper *Krasnoye znamya* (1 May 1946).

Rusanov, Aleksandr Nikolaevich (1881–1936). Graduated St. Petersburg University. Taught at Khabarovsk Technical School. Director of Grodekov Museum (1909–10). SR delegate to 4th Duma (1912). Commissar of the Far East, Provisional Government (Mar.–Nov. 1917). Cabinet member Provisional Government of Autonomous Siberia (1918). Emigrated to Shanghai (1921). Founder, principal of Shanghai Realschule (1921–36).

Ryutin, Martemyan Nikitich (1890–1938). Chairman Harbin soviet (1917). Commander Irkutsk Military District (1918). Chairman Irkutsk gubkom (1920–21). Secretary Dagestan obkom (1924–26) and Moscow Krasnopresnensky District (1926–32). Assistant editor *Krasnaya zvezda* (1929–30). Expelled from Party and given ten-year sentence for preparing a document blaming Stalin for the economic crisis and for anti-Leninist policies (1932). Shot.

Sangursky, Mikhail Vladimirovich (1894–1937). Joined RKP(b) (1919). Served in Red Army on Eastern front (1919–20). Chief of staff OKDVA and member, Dalkraikom (1930–37). Arrested Apr. 1937. Shot Dec.

Schmidt, Pyotr Petrovich (1869–1938). Sinologist, folklorist, zaamurets. Born in Latvia. Attended gymnasium in Riga. Studied at Oriental Faculty, St. Petersburg Univ. (1892–96), and in China (1896–1900). Professor of Russian, Beijing Univ. (1900). Professor of Chinese and Manchu, Oriental Institute, Vladivostok (1903–20). Professor of Chinese, Riga Univ. (1921–38).

Semyonov, Grigory Mikhailovich (1890–1946). Transbaikalian Cossack of Buryat

Mongol descent. Imperial Russian Army officer. Served on Austro-German front (1914–17). Military commissar of Transbaikalia (1917). With Japanese support proclaimed himself "Ataman," led Special Manchurian Detachment into Transbaikalia (1918). Proclaimed Buryat Autonomous Republic in Chita (1919). Retreated into Manchuria (1920). To United States via Canada (1921). Deported following hearing in U.S. Senate (1922). Lived in Dairen (1922–45). Flown by Soviet security forces to Moscow (Aug. 1945). Tried by Military Tribunal 26–29 Aug. 1946. Hanged 30 Aug.

Semyonov, Yakov Lazarevich (d. 1913). Businessman. Settled in Vladivostok (1861). Became "seaweed king" by exporting Posyet Bay tangle to Shanghai. Formed partnership with G. P. Denbigh (ca. 1881).

Serebrovsky, Aleksandr Pavlovich (1884–1938). Industrial manager. Participated in 1905 Revolution. Lived in emigration, graduating from Brussels Technical School. Administered oil (1920–26) and gold (1926–36) industries. Deputy Commissar of Heavy Industry (1931–37). Arrested 26 Sept. 1937. Shot.

Seryshev, Stepan Mikhailovich (1889–1928). Red Guard commander Irkutsk (1917). Commissar in Transbaikalia and Amur District (1918). Imprisoned by Kolchak forces (1918–20). Coordinated partisans and NRA units in Khabarovsk and Amur districts (1920–21). Commander FER Eastern front (1921–22). Military attaché in Japan (1926–27).

Sewaki Hitosa (1823–78). Japanese diplomat, journalist. Commercial agent in Vladivostok (1876–78). Co-founder of *Yomiuri shimbun.*

Shalamov, Varlam Tikhonovich (1907–82). Writer, poet. Arrested and released while a law student at Moscow Univ. (1929). Published poems (1932–37). Rearrested and sent to Kolyma (1937). Allowed to enroll in course for medics (ca. 1948). Left Kolyma for European Russia (1953). Settled in Moscow (1956). Published in USSR from 1957. *Kolyma Tales* circulated in samizdat from 1966.

Shatov, Vladimir Sergeevich ["Bill"] (1887–1938). Anarcho-syndicalist, disciple of Peter Kropotkin, Party activist in Far East. Born in Kiev. Emigrated to United States and settled in Chicago (1906). Active in Industrial Workers of the World. Returned to Russia (1917). Railroad defense commissar in Petrograd (1918). FER minister of war (1921) and transport (1922). Directed construction of Turk-Sib Railroad (1927–30). Deputy people's commissar of transport in charge of railroad construction (1932–36). Arrested in 1937. Shot.

Shelest, Georgy [pseud. of *Georgy Ivanovich Malykh*] (1903–1965). Journalist, writer. Born in Tomsk. Fought in civil war. Wrote stories about civil war in Siberia (1924–36). Arrested and sent to Kolyma (1937–54). Spent last years in Chita.

Shishlyannikov, Rafail Abramovich (1898–1937). Joined RKP (1920). Party-partisan liaison in Primorye (1920–22), Primorye revkom (1922–23). Chairman northern Sakhalin revkom (1925–26). Arrested in 1937. Shot.

Shtern, Grigory Mikhailovich [*Isaakovich*] (1900–41). Born in Ukraine. Joined

RSDRP (1917). Commissar Southern front (1919–22), Turkistan front (1922–24). CHON commander Central Asia (1924). Commissar in Minsk (1924–26). Studied Chinese at Frunze Military Academy (1926–29). Commissariat of Defense (1929–36). Commander 7th Samara Division (1936–37). Advisor in Spain (1937–38). Commander OKDVA, First Far Eastern Army of Far Eastern front (1938–39), 8th Army in war against Finland (1939–40), Far Eastern front (1940–41); USSR Air Defense (1941). Arrested 7–8 June and shot 28 Oct. 1941.

Shternberg, Lev Yakovich (1861–1927). Narodnik, ethnographer. Exiled to Sakhalin (1889–98). Studied local ethnography. Returned to Sakhalin in 1910 and 1926. Worked in Anthropological and Ethnographic Museum, Petrograd. Arrested, then released on intercession of Maksim Gorky (1921). Corresponding Member, Russian (from 1925 USSR) Academy of Sciences (1924). Major work on Ainu and Gilyaks published in Khabarovsk in 1933.

Shumyatsky, Boris Zakharovich (1886–1938). Party activist, journalist, diplomat. Born in Verkhneudinsk. Joined RSDRP (1903). Party work in Krasnoyarsk, Verkheneudinsk, Harbin (1904–6). Active in Vladivostok uprising (1907). Lived in South America. Arrested on return to Russia (1913). Exiled in Turukhansk with Stalin (1914). Served in Imperial Army (1915–17). Chairman Sibbiuro (1917). Chairman Tsentrosibir (1917–18). Secretary Dalbiuro (1920–21). FER minister of foreign affairs under alias "Andrei Chervonny" (1920). Chairman FER Council of Ministers and plenipotentiary of People's Ministry of Foreign Affairs to Siberia and Mongolia (1920–21). Member 5th Army military revolutionary soviet (1921–22). Headed Far Eastern Bureau of Comintern, Irkutsk (1920–22). Ambassador to Persia (1923–26). Rector Communist University of Toilers of the East (1926–28). Editor *Sibirskaia pravda* (1917). Chief editor *Sibirskaia sovetskaia entsiklopediia* (1930–36). Chairman, Committee on Cinematography (1930–36). Awarded Order of Lenin (1935). Arrested in 1937. Shot.

Shumyatsky, Fyodor Vasilevich (1887–1937). Joined RSDRP (1904). Member Vladivostok soviet executive committee and Tsentrosibir (1917). Partisan organizer in Primorye (1919–21). Party work in Primorye (1922–23). Arrested in 1937. Shot.

Shver, Aleksandr Vladimirovich (1898–1938). Born in Odessa. Close to Party functionary Yosif Vareikis from 1921. Edited a variety of newspapers, from *Sibirskie izvestiia* and *Stalingradskaya pravda* to *Tikhookeanskaya zvezda* (1937). Arrested 1937. Shot 14 Apr. 1938.

Sibirtsev, Vsevolod Mikhailovich (1893–1920). Revolutionary. Grandson of Decembrist. Son of teacher at Vladivostok Commercial School. Cousin of Aleksandr Fadeyev. Joined RSDRP (1917). Secretary Vladivostok soviet (Mar.–June 1918). Party work in Primorye (1918–20). Member Military Council of Zemstvo Government (Jan.–Apr. 1920). Arrested by Japanese on 4–5 April and murdered by Whites together with Sergei Lazo on 28 May.

Sieroszewski, Waclaw Leopoldovich (1858–1945). Polish ethnographer, writer. Arrested and exiled to Yakutia for involvement in socialist movement (1878–93). Began ethnographic studies in 1884 and published a book of stories about Yakutia in 1895. Participated in Siberian expedition of Imperial Russian Geographical Society (1900). Moved to Paris (1906). Returned to Poland (1918). President Polish Academy of Literature (1933–39).

Silnitsky, Anton Petrovich (1853–1912). Historian, publicist of the Russian Far East. Worked in Priamur governor-general's office (1884–93). Governor Kamchatka (1903–5). Editor *Priamurskie vedomosti* (1894–1903, 1905–8) and *Priamurye* (1908–11).

Skvirsky, Boris Evseevich (1887–1941). FER deputy minister of foreign affairs (1921–22). Led FER mission to the United States (1921–22). In United States (1933–36). Ambassador to Afghanistan (1936–37). Arrested 1937. Died in prison.

Slinkin, Ilya Vasilevich (1899–1938). Schoolteacher, partisan, Party activist. Worked in Primorye teachers' union (1917–18). Partisan organizer Olga district of Primorye (1919–20). Joined RKP(b) (1920). Delegate FER Constituent Assembly (1921–22). Chairman Primorye revkom (1922). First secretary Khabarovsk obkom (1930–37). Arrested 1937. Shot 26 Mar. 1938.

Spalvin, Evgeny Genrikhovich (1872–ca. 1933). Japanologist, zaamurets. Born in Riga. Graduated from Oriental Faculty, St. Petersburg Univ. (1899). Studied in Japan (1899–1901). Director Japan Department, Oriental Institute (1905–22). Married Elizaveta Aleksandrovna, Institute librarian and widow of colleague, Maeda Kiyotsugu (1921). Acting rector DVGU (1922–23). Secretary USSR embassy, Tokyo (1925–31). Adviser CER (1932–33). Died in Harbin of intestinal disorder.

Strod, Ivan [*Yan*] *Yakovlevich* (1894–1938). Partisan, historian in Yakutia. Born in Vitebsk Province. Served on front in First World War. Partisan leader in Yakutia (1918). Captured and imprisoned at Olyokminsk by Kolchak authorities (1919). Commanded NRA cavalry unit (1920–22) and operations against A. N. Pepeliaev's assault on Yakutsk (1922–23). Joined VKP(b) (1927). Worked in Yakutsk branch of Society for Assistance to Defense, Aviation, and Chemical Construction. Arrested in 1937. Shot.

Sukhanov, Aleksandr Vasilevich (1864–1921). Tsarist official in Priamur Governor-Generalship. Governor South Ussuri District. Acting governor Maritime District. Friend of Mikhail Yankovsky. Father of Konstantin Sukhanov.

Sukhanov, Konstantin Aleksandrovich (1894–1918). Party activist. Son of South Ussuri District Governor Aleksandr Sukhanov. Studied at St. Petersburg Univ. (1912–16). Joined RSDRP (1913). Sent by Party to Vladivostok (1916). Member Vladivostok RSDRP committee (1917). Chairman Vladivostok soviet (Nov. 1917). Arrested by Czechs on 29 June 1918 and shot 17 Nov. in transit to prison.

Surovkin, Viktor Pavlovich [alias *Viktor Kin*] (1903–37). Party activist, writer. Began work in Far East in 1921 as Komsomol organizer in Blagoveshchensk, Svobodny, Vladivostok. Published novel on his experiences in 1928. Arrested in 1937. Shot.

Svetlanin, Andrei Vasilevich [real name: *Nikolai Nikitich Likhachev*] (1905–65). Journalist. Born in Ryazan Province. Joined Komsomol (1920). Attended Ryazan Party School (1926–28). Joined VKP(b) and edited newspaper in Krasnodar (1929–32). Assigned to OKDVA Kolkhoz Corps newspaper in Birobidzhan (1932). Worked on OKDVA paper *Trevoga* in Khabarovsk and edited divisional paper in Blagoveshchensk (1934–38). Worked for military newspaper *Na strazhe* (1939–41). Captured with A. A. Vlasov by Germans and collaborated (1942–44). Fled Königsberg under pseudonym "A. S. Frolov" and taken to England by British Intelligence (1945). Started publishing about "Far Eastern conspiracy" in émigré journal *Grani* (1949). Died in Frankfurt-am-Main.

Tanygin, Pavel Mikhailovich (d. 1938). Head Dalkraikom transport division (1932–34). Secretary Primorye obkom (1934–37). Arrested in 1937. Shot in Vladivostok 6 June 1938.

Tarkhanov-Razumov, Oskar Sergeevich (1901–38). Writer, orientalist, intelligence officer with multiple aliases: Oskar Erdberg, O. Erman, O. Taub, O. Tanin, Karrio, Yan Chulai, Yotawari. Born in Odessa. Joined RSDRP (1917). Worked in Party underground Odessa (1918–19). Carried out missions in Germany and Czechoslovakia for Comintern International as a protégé of Grigory Zinoviev (1919–22). Komsomol secretary (1922–24). In China with Mikhail Borodin (1925–27). Expelled from Party as "activist of Trotskyist opposition" (1927). Readmitted after denouncing opposition (1929). Trained in military intelligence (1929–30). Studied Chinese agrarian problems and taught at Institute of Red Professors (1930–32). OKDVA intelligence officer (1932–34). Member editorial board *Na rubezhe* (1933–34). Diplomatic appointment in Mongolia (1935–37). Recalled and shot.

Tevlyanto (1905–59). Chukcha official and Party activist. Interpreter and instructor in Anadyr revkom (1926–29). Chairman, Chukotka District executive committee (1934–47). Joined Party (1937). Delegate to Supreme Soviet.

Titov, Elpidifor Innokentievich (1896–1938). Ethnographer, writer. Educated at Irkutsk Univ. (1919–23). Ethnographic expeditions (1923–25). Worked with Vladimir Arseniev in Vladivostok (1925). Lived in Harbin (1927–32). Expelled from Party (1933). Reinstated (1935). Head foreign section, *Tikhookeanskaya zvezda* (1935–37). Secretary *Na rubezhe* (1933–37). Arrested 5 Aug. 1937 as Japanese spy. Shot 14 Jan. 1938.

Tretyakov, Sergei Mikhailovich (1892–1939). Writer, poet, dramatist. Graduated Moscow Univ. (1915). Lived in Vladivostok, where he published a book of poems and co-founded the futurist group *Tvorchestvo* with N. N. Aseyev (1920). Lectured on literature in China (1924). Subsequently collaborated with film director Sergei Eizenshtein, theatrical producer Vsevolod Meyerhold. Arrested. Died in captivity.

Trilisser, Meier Abramovich (1883–1938). Joined RSDRP in Odessa (1901). Worked in Party underground in Urals, Finland. Arrested (1907). Exiled to Irkutsk (1914). Crushed uprising of cadets in Irkutsk (Dec. 1917). Tsentrosibir envoy to Blagoveshchensk (1918). Party secretary in Amur region (1919–21). Member Dalbiuro (1920). Joined Cheka (1920). Headed GPU/OGPU Foreign Department (1921–26). Deputy head OGPU (1926–30). Soviet Control Commission plenipotentiary to Dalkrai (1934–35). Member Comintern Executive Committee (1935–36). Arrested in 1937. Shot.

Uborevich, Ieronym Petrovich (1896–1937). Joined RSDRP (1917). NRA commander and FER war minister (1922). Commander 5th Army Khabarovsk (1922–24). Commander Belorussian Military District (1931–37). Candidate member CC VKP(b) (1930–37). Arrested 29 May 1937. Shot on 11 June.

Ukhtomsky, Esper Esperovich (1861–1921). Prince. Proponent of Russia's historic mission in Asia. Accompanied tsarevich on Asian tour (1890–91). Published widely on Russia's mission in Asia. Protégé of Sergei Witte (1892–1903). Chairman Russo-Chinese Bank (1896–1903). Fell silent after Portsmouth Conference (1905). Thought to have died in Soviet Russia.

Ungern-Sternberg, Baron Roman Fyodorovich von (1886–1921). White officer. Dismissed from Imperial Army and exiled to Tomsk (1916). At request of Provisional Government organized Buryat Mongol regiment (1917). Served under G. M. Semyonov (1918–20). Led Asiatic Cavalry Division into Mongolia and drove Chinese from Urga (Feb. 1921). Invaded Transbaikalia, defeated by NRA. Captured in Mongolia. Tried and executed in Novonikolaevsk 15 Sept. 1921.

Unterberger, Pavel Fyodorovich (1842–1921). Army officer. Military governor of Primorskaya oblast (1888–97). Priamur governor-general (1905–10). Published studies of Primorye (1900), Priamur (1912). Delegate Imperial Duma (1910–17). Member Imperial Russian Geographical Society. Emigrated to France (1918). Died in Paris.

Vareikis, Yosif Mikhailovich (1894–1938). Joined RSDRP (1913). Member CC VKP(b) (1930–37). First secretary Dalkrai (15 Jan.–3 Oct. 1937). Arrested 9 Oct. 1937. Shot 29 July 1938.

Venyukov, Mikhail Ivanovich (1832–1901). Military officer, geographer, ethnographer, amurets. Came to Irkutsk and joined Amur expedition (1857). Explored Ussuri region (1858). Served in Central Asia (1859–60). Caucasus (1861–63), Poland (1863–67). Traveled in China and Japan (1869–71). Secretary Imperial Russian Geographical Society (1874). Moved to Paris (1877) and wrote for émigré press. Bequeathed personal book collection to Nikolaevsk Library, Khabarovsk.

Vilensky-Sibiryakov, Vladimir Dmitrievich (1888–1937?). Party activist, writer. Born in

Tomsk. Joined RSDRP in 1903. Party work in Tomsk (1905). Arrested and exiled to Nerchinsk (1908). Moved to Yakutsk (1912). Chairman Yakutsk soviet (1917). Party work in Irkutsk, Moscow (1918–19). Member Tsentrosibir (1918). Plenipotentiary of Russian Republic's ministry of foreign affairs to FER (1920). Commissar Frunze Military Academy (1925). Expelled from Party for supporting Trotsky (1927). Readmitted (1930). Founded journal *Severnaya Aziya*. Edited journal *Etnografiya*. Co-founder of Society for the Study of Urals, Siberia, and Far East. Wrote books about China, Japan, Mongolia, revolutionary movement in Siberia. Arrested in 1936. Thought to have perished next year in custody.

Vizel, Yakov Savelevich (1900–1937). Chekist. Born in Zhitomir. Member Jewish Social Democratic Party. Joined Cheka (1919). Headed Primorye NKVD (1934–37). Committed suicide Aug. 1937.

Voiloshniikov, Vasily Aleksandrovich (1897–1938). Transbaikal Cossack. Served in Red Army, NRA (1918–22). Member Soviet military mission to China (1925–27). Graduated from Oriental Institute, Vladivostok (1928). Dean Oriental Faculty, DVGU (1932–37). Arrested 5 Nov. 1937. Shot 25 Apr. 1938.

Volkenshtein, Lyudmila Aleksandrovna (1857–1906). Revolutionary. Narodnik. Sentenced to death for attempted assassination of the governor of Kharkhov (1884). Commuted to fifteen years of hard labor. To Sakhalin (1897), accompanied by husband Aleksandr Aleksandrovich (1851–1925), a physician. Moved to Vladivostok (1902). Contributed to newspaper *Amurskii krai*. Shot while leading a demonstration 23 Jan. 1906.

Volsky, Mikhail Petrovich (1897–1938). Military leader, chekist. Red Guard and partisan organizer in Primorye (1918–20). Dalbiuro representative in Suchan (1920–22). Delegate FER Constituent Assembly (1921–22). Liaison between NRA and Primorye partisans (1922). Liquidated White resistance in the Northeast (1922–26). Chairman Kamchatka revkom (1923–25). Chairman Amur District soviet (1926–27). Member Dalkraiispolkom (1927–37). Head Far Eastern Forestry Trust (1929–31). Chairman Vladivostok soviet (1931–36). Member Dalkraikom and deputy chairman Dalkraiispolkom (1936–37). Acting chairman, Dalkraiispolkom (1937). Arrested in 1937. Shot 3 June 1938.

Vostretsov, Stepan Sergeevich (1883–1932). Military commander. Joined RSDRP (1905). Menshevik until 1918. Decorated with three St. George crosses for bravery in Imperial Army (1914–16). Red Army commander on Volga, Eastern fronts (1919–20). Commanded Cheka troops in Siberia (1921), "shock group" at Spassk (1922), Okhotsk-Ayan expedition against A. N. Pepeliaev (1922–23), and First Pacific Division (1924–29). Shot himself.

Vysotsky, Vladimir Semyonovich (1938–80). Actor, poet, bard. Periodically in Far East during 1960s. Associated with Taganka Theater, Moscow (1964–80).

Wallace, Henry Agard (1888–1965). Agriculturalist, politician, editor. Scion of prominent Louisiana family. U.S. Sec. of Agriculture (1933–40). Vice-President (1941–45). Led mission to Siberia, China (June–July 1944). Secretary of Commerce (1945–46). Urged friendship with USSR, opposed Marshall Plan. Ran unsuccessfully for president of U.S. as Progressive Party candidate (1948). Criticized U.S. involvement in Korean War (1950).

Williams, Albert Rhys (1883–1962). Born in Greenwich, Ohio, son of Congregationalist minister. Graduated Hartford Theological Seminary (1907). Minister Maverick Congregational Church, Boston (1907–14). To Russia as correspondent for New York *Evening Post* (1917). Participated in storming of Winter Palace (7 Nov.). Worked with John Reed in Bureau of Revolutionary Propaganda Commissarit of Foreign Affairs (1917–18). Joined International Legion of Anglo-American Communists in Red Army (Feb. 1918). In Vladivostok (June–July 1918). Addressed Vladivostok soviet. Wrote sympathetically on Lenin, October Revolution, Stalin. Decorated by Soviet regime (1958). Died in Ossining, New York.

Witte, Sergei Yulievich (1849–1915). Statesman. Minister of communications (1892). Minister of finance (1892–1903). Promoted railroad construction and penetration of Manchuria (1895–1903). President, council of ministers (1903–5). Negotiated Treaty of Portsmouth (1905). Author of October Manifesto issued by Nicholas II (30 Oct. 1905). First constitutional Russian premier (Nov. 1905–May 1906). Member council of the empire (1906–15).

Wrangel, Ferdinand Petrovich (1796 or 1797–1870). Baron, naval officer, navigator. Led expeditions along the arctic coast of Siberia (1820–24), around the world (1825–27). Administrator of Russian settlements in North America (1829–35). Co-founder of Imperial Russian Geographical Society (1845). Minister of the navy (1855–57).

Yadrintsev, Nikolai Mikhailovich (1842–94). Ethnographer, traveler, publicist, champion of Siberian autonomy. Born in Omsk. Educated at Tomsk gymnasium, St. Petersburg Univ. Arrested in Omsk with Grigory Potanin for "Siberian separatism" (1865). While in prison and exile conducted research on Siberian penal system (1865–73). Published *Siberia as a Colony* (1882). On expeditions to Altai (1886), Mongolia (1889).

Yankovsky, Mikhail Yanovich (1842–1912). Farmer, zoologist, philanthropist, zaamurets. Arrested after the 1863 Polish uprising and sentenced to hard labor. Exiled to Far East (1870). Mined gold on Askold Island. Settled at Sidemi on Amur Bay (1879). Farmed, cultivated ginseng, raised horses and deer. Hosted officials, merchants, and intellectuals at Sidemi. Eloped with young woman to Sochi (1910).

Yankovsky, Yury Mikhailovich (1879–1956). Son of M. Ya. Yankovsky. Inherited estate at Sidemi (1912). Escaped with family to Ch'ongjin, Korea (1924). Built hunting lodge (Novina) in mountains above Chu'ul Hot Springs, favorite vacation place for Russian émigrés from China and Japan (1926–40). Arrested by Soviet security organs and sent to a labor camp in Taishet, where he died in May a few weeks before his scheduled release. His son Mikhail, a veteran of the Second World War and of Stalin's camps, is a writer in Vladivostok.

Yanson, Yakov Davidovich (1886–1938). Revolutionary, Party activist, historian. Born in Latvia. Joined RSDRP (1904). Took part in uprising in Riga (1905). Arrested and exiled to Eastern Siberia (1908–17). Chairman Irkutsk soviet (1917–18). Arrested and imprisoned by Kolchak forces (1918–19). Chairman Irkutsk revkom (1920). FER foreign affairs minister (1921–22). Member Dalbiuro (1921–25). First Soviet trade representative to U.S. (1922). Commercial attaché Tokyo (1926–27). Edited works on history of Party, civil war in Siberia, and Far East (1925–32). Director Academia Press and Comintern publishing department (1935–37). Shot.

Yaroslavsky, Emelyan Mikhailovich [real name: *Minei Izrailevich Gubelman*] (1878–1943). Party activist. Born in Chita. Joined RSDRP (1898). Organized and served on Chita RSDRP committee (1901–4). Member Moscow RSDRP committee (1905–6). Arrested and exiled to Nerchinsk (1907). Settled in Yakutsk (1915). Chairman Yakutsk soviet (1917). Member Moscow revkom and political commissar Moscow military district (1917–18). Member Sibbiuro (1920–21). Secretary Central Control Commission (1923–34) and Party Control Commission (1934–39). Published two Party histories (1926, 1933). Head League of Militant Atheists (1935). Member CC VKP(b) (1921–23, 1939–43). Academician USSR Academy of Sciences (1939).

Yokhelson, Vladimir [in West known as *Waldemar Jochelson*] (1856–1937). Ethnographer. Born in Vilnius. Narodnik. Fled to Switzerland to escape arrest. Arrested on return to Russia and sentenced to ten years' exile in Yakutia (1898–99). Studied local ethnography. Results of research published by Imperial Russian Geographical Society. Took part in Sibiryakov Expedition (1894–96), Jesup North Pacific Expedition (1900–1901), expedition to Chukotka (1908). Member Asiatic Museum, St. Petersburg/Petrograd, and associate curator Institute of Ethnography (1912–22). Arrested, then released on intercession of Maksim Gorky (1921). Emigrated to France (1922). Moved to United States (1924). Worked in American Museum of National History and Carnegie Institute, Washington, D.C.

Zapadny [*Kesselman*], *Semyon Izrailevich* (1899–1938). Chekist. Joined RSDRP (1917). Assistant to Dalkrai NKVD plenipotentiary T. D. Deribas (1934–37). Arrested 8 Aug. 1937. Shot 3 June 1938.

Zavalishin, Dmitry Irinarkhovich (1804–92). Writer. Member of M. P. Lazarev circumglobal expedition (1822–24). Condemned to hard labor for life for involvement in the Decembrist uprising (1825). Worked in the Nerchinsk mines (1827–39). Allowed to settle in Chita (1839). Wrote prolifically and caustically on the Amur question in general and on N. N. Muraviev in particular.

Zavoiko, Vasily Stepanovich (1810–98). Naval officer, amurets. Seconded to Russian-American Co. (1840). Commandant Ayan (1846–49). Military governor Kamchatka (1849–55). Repulsed Anglo-French assault on Petropavlovsk (1854). Admiral (1874). Statue in Vladivostok erected in 1908 and replaced during the 1930s by statue of Sergei Lazo.

Zhukov, Yury [Georgy Aleksandrovich] (1908–). Journalist, Party functionary. Toured Dalkrai (1938). Wrote books on Soviet Far East and Japan (1938–45). Editorial board *Pravda* (1946–87). Deputy chairman (1962–82), chairman (1982–87) Soviet Committee for the Defense of Peace.

Communist Party Membership in the Far East, 1907–86

Year	Number	Year	Number
1907	200	1938	24,885
1917 (Nov.)	3,000	1939	67,480
1920 (Apr.)	4,000	1941	56,776
1920 (Nov.)	9,500	1942	44,000
1922	12,000	1943	45,000
1923	10,313	1945 (May)	65,260
1925	17,000	1946	77,000
1926	18,500	1951	148,446
1928	20,000	1961	210,000
1929	27,000	1970	350,000
1932	37,200	1976	390,980
1933	44,909	1980	415,340
1937	27,730	1986	448,700

SOURCES: *Ocherki istorii Dal'nevostochnykh organizatsii KPSS. 1900–1937, 1938–87*; Riabov and Shtein, *Ocherki istorii russkogo Dal'nego Vostoka*; *Dal'revkom*; *Istoriia Sibiri*; *Kyokutō Shiberiya yōran*; Unpelev, *Sotsialisticheskaia industrializatsiia*; *Sotsial'no-ekonomicheskoe razvitie dal'nevostochnoi derevni: Sovetskii period.*

   NOTE: All figures are for 1 Jan. unless otherwise noted. Rounded figures are presumably estimates.

Far Eastern Party Secretaries, 1922–91

PART I: *Far Eastern Regional Secretaries*

1922–27	N. A. Kubiak	1933–37	L. Yo. Lavrentiev
1927–28	Ya. B. Gamarnik	1937	Yo. M. Vareikis
1928–31	I. N. Perepechko	1937–38	G. M. Statsevich
1931–33	S. A. Bergavinov	1938	S. M. Sobolev

PART II: *District Secretaries*

Khabarovsk oblast
(krai from 1938)

1922–30	—
1930–37	I. V. Slinkin
1938–40	V. A. Donskoi
1940–45	G. A. Borkov
1945–49	R. K. Nazarov
1949–53	A. P. Efimov
1953–55	A. B. Aristov
1955–57	M. M. Stakhursky
1957–70	A. P. Shitikov
1970–88	A. K. Cherny
1988–90	V. S. Pasternak
1990–91	S. A. Makarov

Sakhalin oblast

1930–34	N. I. Ivanov
1934–37	P. M. Ulyansky
1938	F. V. Bespalko
1939–40	G. I. Shatalin
1940–43	A. M. Spiridonov
1943–45	I. D. Chizhov
1945–51	D. N. Melnik
1951–60	P. F. Cheplakov
1960–78	P. A. Leonov
1978–88	P. I. Tretyakov
1988–89	V. S. Bondarchuk
1989–91	V. N. Zhigailo

Magadan oblast

1954–58	T. I. Ababkov
1958–68	P. Ya. Afanasiev

Magadan oblast
(cont'd)

1968–78	S. A. Shaidurov
1978–86	N. I. Malkov
1986–89	A. D. Bogdanov
1989–91	V. V Svekolkin

Primorsk (Maritime) oblast
(krai from 1938)

1922–34	—
1934–37	P. M. Tanygin
1938–47	N. M. Pegov
1947–52	N. N. Organov
1952–55	D. N. Melnik
1955–56	N. N. Shatalin
1956–59	T. F. Shtykov
1959–69	V. E. Chernyshev
1969–84	V. P. Lomakin
1984–89	D. N. Gagarov
1989–90	A. A. Volyntsev
1990–91	A. S. Golovizin

Amur oblast

1920	M. A. Trilisser
1920–21	S. G. Cheremnykh
1921	A. I. Kazakova
1921	M. I. Taishin
1921–22	M. V. Titov
1922–23	V. O. Kornitsky
1923–25	M. L. Granovsky
1925–27	Ya. A. Popok
1927–28	A. N. Nevolin

PART II: *District Secretaries*

Amur oblast (cont'd)		Kamchatka oblast (cont.)	
1928–30	E. I. Nakaryakov	1938–39	V. I. Kuteinikov
1930–33	I. K. Mikhalko	1939–42	G. F. Aksyonov
1933	V. A. Verny	1942–44	S. A. Vasin
1933–37	V. S. Ivanov	1944–48	I. F. Petrov
1937	K. K. Kosokin	1948–49	I. I. Grachev
1938	S. A. Makagonov	1949–52	T. G. Kalinnikov
1938–40	V. M. Istomin	1952–56	P. N. Soloviev
1940–42	N. A. Gornov	1956–71	M. A. Orlov
1942–43	S. S. Rumyantsev	1971–86	D. I. Kachin
1943–48	A. M. Spiridonov	1986–89	P. I. Reznikov
1948	N. V. Mayorov	1989–90	P. P. Zinoviev
1948–52	F. R. Vasilyev	1990–91	V. Ya. Abayev
1952–55	A. I. Sobenin		
1955–57	S. A. Ignatov	Jewish Autonomous oblast	
1957–64	P. I. Morozov	1934–35	Gurevich
1964–85	S. S. Avramenko	1935–37	M. P. Khavkin
1985–90	L. V. Sharin	1937	A. B. Ryskin
1990–91	V. N. Shilov	1937	G. N. Sukharev
		1937–38	Ya. A. Levin
Kamchatka oblast		1939–41	I. F. Nikishov
1922–23	V. M. Kruchina	1946–49	A. Bakhmutsky
1923–26	D. S. Buzin	1952–55	A. P. Shitikov
1926–28	N. I. Kuznetsov	1959–62	A. K. Cherny
1928–30	N. D. Zykin	1962–70	G. E. Podgaev
1930–31	D. T. Yakushin	1970–87	L. B. Shapiro
1931–34	I. I. Samsonov	1987–90	B. L. Korsunsky
1934–37	V. A. Orlov	1990–91	A. V. Kapeistov
1937–38	D. I. Nikonov		

SOURCES: *Khronika Magadanskoi partiinoi organizatsii, 1923–1986*; *Ocherki istorii Dal'nevostochnykh organizatsii KPSS, 1900–1937, 1938–87*; *Ocherk istorii Khabarovskoi kraevoi organizatsii KPSS*; *Partiinye organizatsii sovetskogo Severa*; *Organizatsiia KPSS Evreiskoi Avtonomnoi oblasti, 1934–1985*; *Primorskaia kraevaia organizatsiia KPSS*; *SUPAR Report*.

Commissars of State Security in the Far East, 1922–53

1922–29	L. N. Belsky	shot or died in camp 1939
1929–37	T. D. Deribas	shot in 1938
1934–37	S. I. Zapadny	shot in 1938
1931–37	E. P. Berzin	shot in 1938
1937	V. A. Balitsky	shot in 1937
1934–37	Ya. S. Vizel	suicide in 1937
1937–38	G. S. Lyushkov	shot in 1945
1938	G. M. Osinin	shot in 1938
1938	M. P. Frinovsky	shot in 1939
1938	G. F. Gorbach	shot in 1939
1938–45	I. F. Nikishov	fate uncertain
1939–53	S. A. Goglidze	shot in 1953
1938–47	M. M. Gvishiani	alive in 1953

SOURCES: Conquest, *Inside Stalin's Secret Police*; Japan, Naikaku chōsakyoku, "Sorenpō jijō"; Khisamutdinov, *Russian Far East*; Nikolaev, "Tseny istiny" and "Vystrely v spinu"; Suturin, *Delo kraevogo masshtaba*.

« « A P P E N D I X H » »

Far Eastern Military Commanders, 1929–93

Far Eastern Army Commanders		Commanders of the Pacific Fleet	
1929–38	V. K. Blücher	1932–37	M. V. Viktorov
1938–40	G. M. Shtern, First Far Eastern Army	1937–38	G. P. Kireyev
1938–40	I. S. Konev, Second Far Eastern Army	1938–39	N. G. Kusnetsov
1940–41	G. M. Shtern, Far Eastern Front	1939–47	I. S. Yumashev
1941–43	Yo. R. Apanasenko	1947–50	A. S. Frolov (5th fleet)
1943–45	M. A. Purkayev	1947–51	I. I. Baikov (7th fleet)
1945	A. M. Vasilevsky	1951–53	G. N. Kholostyakov (7th fleet)
1945–56	R. Ya. Malinovsky	1951–56	Yu. A. Panteleyev (5th fleet to 1953)
1956–61	V. A. Penkovsky	1956–58	V. A. Chekurov
1961–63	Ya. G. Kreizer	1958–62	V. A. Fokin
1963–67	I. G. Pavlovsky	1962–69	N. N. Amelko
1967–69	O. A. Losik	1969–74	N. I. Smirnov
1969–72	V. F. Tolubko	1974–79	V. P. Maslov
1972–76	V. I. Petrov	1979–81	E. N. Spiridonov
1976–84	I. M. Tretyak	1981–87	V. V. Sidorov
1984–87	D. T. Yazov	1987–93	G. A. Khvatov
1987–89	M. A. Moiseyev	1993–94	G. N. Gurinov
1989–92	V. I. Novozhilov	1994–	I. Khmelov
1992–	V. Chechevatov		

SOURCE: *Krasnoznamennyi dal'nevostochnyi*; *Krasnoznamennyi Tikhookeanskii flot*; *SUPAR Report*; *RA Report*.
NOTE: From 1947 to 1953, the Pacific Fleet was divided into the 5th and 7th fleets.

« « A P P E N D I X   I » »

Far Eastern Delegates
to the 17th and 18th Party Congresses

17th (1934)	18th (1939)
N. M. Antselovich, L. N. Aronshtam,[†] E. P. Berzin, V. K. Blücher,[†] P. A. Bondar, Ya. G. Bravin, T. D. Deribas,[†] D. T. Fesenko, Ya. B. Gamarnik,[*] N. I. Ivanov, E. B. Kaplan, A. A. Kim, M. M. Kim, I. N. Kobychev, P. T. Kondruk, I. M. Kopp, A. K. Kopiev, G. M. Krutov, G. G. Kukolev, L. Yo. Lavrentiev, I. S. Maltsev, N. A. Myakinin, A. I. Osipov, S. I. Ovchinnikov, K. F. Pshenitsyn, A. N. Sennov, V. Ya. Shilkin, I. V. Slinkin, A. M. Surovtsev, P. M. Tanygin, P. M. Ulyanovsky, I. A. Vasiliev	I. K. Biryukov, S. A. Chernykh, V. A. Donskoi,[*] A. I. Gulyaev, K. S. Gumeryuk, M. M. Gvishiani,[†] V. S. Ibragimov, N. A. Istomin, V. M. Istomin, I. S. Konev, A. A. Kudryatsev, I. I. Kuznetsov, N. G. Kuznetsov, P. I. Laukhin, N. P. Lebedev, I. G. Litvinenko, R. K. Nazarov, I. F. Nikishov, F. S. Oktyabrsky, N. M. Pegov,[*] V. M. Pegov, G. G. Petrov, Yu. K. Prikhodov, A. A. Romanenko, P. V. Rychago, D. I. Savelev, F. A. Semenovsky, S. I. Shabalin, G. I. Shatalin, I. A. Shmelev, G. M. Shtern,[*] P. S. Shulga, I. A. Skoptsev, A. P. Sokolov, I. N. Terentiev, A. V. Timofeyev, A. V. Tushunov, A. G. Vologin, M. S. Zloi

SOURCE: USSR, KPSS, *XVII s"ezd VKP(b)*; *XVIII s"ezd VKP(b)*.
  * Indicates Central Committee member.
  † Indicates candidate member.

Far Eastern Governors and Territorial Council Chairmen, 1991–

District/ region	Governors	Council chairmen
Khabarovsk	Viktor Ishaev (1991–)	Igor Tsvetkov (1991–)
Maritime	Vladimir Kuznetsov (1991–93) Evgeny Nazdratenko (1993–)	Dmitry Grigorovich (1991–)
Amur	Albert Krivchenko (1991–93) Anatoly Surat (1993) Vladimir Polivanov (1993–)	Anatoly Belonogov (1991–)
Sakhalin	Valentin Fyodorov (1991–93) Evgeny Krasnoyarov (1993–)	Anatoly Aksyonov (1991–)
Kamchatka	Vladimir Biryukov (1991–)	Pyotr Permyak (1991–)
Magadan	Viktor Mikhailov (1991–)	Vyacheslav Kobets (1991–93) Vyacheslav Goncharov (1993–)

SOURCE: *RA Report*; *Kto est' kto v Primor'e*; *Russian Far East Update*.

Glossary of Place-Names

Place-names are barometers of cultural and political change. Far Eastern nomenclature has a cosmopolitan ring, featuring words of Tungusic, Mongol, Paleosiberian, Russian, Ukrainian, Chinese, Japanese, Korean, British, French, Dutch, Finnish, and American origin. Most place-names have changed once or twice during the past 130 years. Ussuriisk was called Voroshilov before 1957, Nikolsk-Ussuriisk before 1935, Nikolskoye before 1898, and Shuangchengzi before 1861.

Asian and Western place-names were replaced by Russian and then Soviet ones; if current trends persist, we will again see Russian ones. In the 19th century what the Chinese called Haishenwei and the British called Port May became Zolotoi Rog ("Golden Horn"), the harbor of Vladivostok. Vladivostok's Pekinskaya ("Peking Street") now bears the name of former Pacific Fleet Commander Admiral Fokin. Koreiskaya ("Korea Street") is now called Pogranichnaya ("Border Street"). The change, let it be noted, was meant to commemorate the guards, not to indicate the street's onetime demarcation of the city's red light district.

Soviet authorities manipulated regional toponymy to expunge evidence of historical associations with China and Japan. During 1945–47 nearly all Japanese place-names of southern Sakhalin and the Kurile Islands vanished as these territories were incorporated into the USSR. In 1973 Chinese names in the Amur, Khabarovsk, and Maritime (Primorye) regions were replaced by Russian names.

Tsarist officials have outlasted their Soviet successors in toponymical durability. Posyet, Anuchin, Korf, Muraviev-Amursky, Kazakevich, Korsakov, and Grodekov still figure in Far Eastern geographical nomenclature. Stalin, Voroshilov, Mikoyan, Molotov, Kaganovich, and Kuibyshev have been removed from Far Eastern towns, streets, factories, and collective farms.

The table on the following pages gives Far Eastern place-names appearing in the text. Where ascertainable, dates are appended. For a detailed list of Chinese place-names in the Soviet Far East, see *Sulian diming cidian*; Solov'ev, *Slovar' kitaiskikh toponimov*; and Forsyth, "Chinese Place-Names." Glossaries of Russian and Japanese names on Sakhalin and the Kurile Islands can be found in S. D. Galtsev-Beziuk, *Toponimicheskii slovar' Sakhalinskoi Oblasti* (Iuzhno-Sakhalinsk, 1992). For place-names in the Northeast, see Leont'ev and Novikova, *Toponimicheskii slovar' Severo-*

Vostoka SSSR, and for the Primorye, see A. I. Gruzdev, *Istoricheskie nazvaniia pamiatniki kul'tury* (Vladivostok, 1992).

The following abbreviations are used for regions: Amur = Amur District; Chita = Chita District; JAD = Jewish Autonomous District; Kam = Kamchatka District; Khab = Khabarovsk Region; Mag = Magadan District; Prim = Primorsk (Maritime) Region; and Sakh = Sakhalin District.

Name	Alternate name(s)	Region
Albazin (est. 1654)	Yaksa (pre-1654)	Amur
Albert Peninsula (1856)	Muraviev-Amursky Pen. (1860)	Prim
Aleksandrovsk (1926–35)	Bochkarevo (1902–26); Kuibyshevka (1935–57); Belogorsk (1957)	Amur
Alekseyevsk (1905–23)	Svobodny (1923)	Amur
Amerika Bay (1859–1972)	Hornet Bay (1856); Nakhodka Bay (1972)	Prim
Amerikanka (ca. 1865–1939)	Nakhodka (1939)	Prim
Amur River	Heilongjiang	
Amur Bay (1859)	Guerin Bay (1856)	Prim
Amursk (1958)	Padali (pre-1958)	Khab
Anadyr (1930)	Novo-Mariinsk (1889–1930)	Mag
Aniele Bay (1852)	Posyet Bay (1854); Novogorodsky Bay (1859)	Prim
Antonovka River (1973)	Fudzin River (pre-1973)	Prim
Ariadnoye	Chenwaisa	Prim
Arseniev (1930)	Semyonovka (ca. 1880–1930)	Prim
Artyomovka River (1973)	Maihe (pre-1973)	Prim
Avvakum River (1857)	Gilbert River (1856)	Prim
Barabash (from ca. 1890)	Menggujie	Prim
Belogorsk (1957)	Bochkarevo (1902–26); Aleksandrovsk (1926–35); Kuibyshevka (1935–57)	Amur
Big Diomede Island	Ratmanov Island	Mag
Birobidzhan (1931)	Tikhonkaya (ca. 1880–1931)	JAD
Blagoveshchensk (1858)	Huanghetun (pre-1854); Ust Zeisk (1854–58)	Amur
Bliukherovo (1935–39)	Mikhailovo-Semyonovskoye (1890–1935); Leninskoye (1939)	JAD
Bochkarevo (1902–26)	Aleksandrovsk (1926–35); Kuibyshevka (1935–57); Belogorsk (1957)	Amur
Boli (from ca. 15th c.)	Khabarovka (1858–93); Khabarovsk (1893)	Khab
Bolshaya Ussurka (1973)	Iman River (pre-1973)	Prim
Bureya River	Niuman River	Khab
Chenwaisa	Ariadnoye	Prim
Cheremshany (1973)	Sinancha (pre-1973)	Prim
Chernyshevsk (1957)	Im. Kaganovicha (1935–57)	Chita

Name	Alternate name(s)	Region
Dairen (1905–45)	Dalny (1898–1905), Dalian	(China)
Dalnegorsk (1973)	Tetyukhe (pre-1973)	Prim
Dalnerechensk (1973)	Iman (pre-1973)	Prim
Dalny (1898–1905)	Dairen (1905–45); Dalian	(China)
Eastern Bosphorus	Hamelin Strait	Prim
Fudzin River (pre-1973)	Antonovka (1973)	Prim
Gamov, Cape (1854)	Cape Hugon (1852)	Prim
Gilbert River (1856)	Avvakum River (1857)	Prim
Gondatti (ca. 1913–50)	Shimanovsk (1950)	Amur
Grodekovo (1900–1957)	Pogranichnyi (1957)	Prim
Guerin Bay (1856)	Amur Bay (1859)	Prim
Gurskoye (1973)	Khungari (pre-1973)	Khab
Haishenwei (ca. 1700)	Port May (1856);	Prim
	Vladivostok and Zolotoi Rog (1859)	
Hamelin Strait	Eastern Bosphorus	Prim
Heilongjiang	Amur River	
Heixiazi Dao	Kazakevich Island	Khab
Hornet Bay (1856)	Amerika Bay (ca. 1859–1972);	Prim
	Nakhodka Bay (1972)	
Huanghe	Jingqilihe; Zeya River	Amur
Hugon, Cape (1852)	Cape Gamov (1854)	Prim
Ilistaya (1973)	Lefu River (pre-1973)	Prim
Iman (pre-1973)	Dalnerechensk (1973)	Prim
Iman River (pre-1973)	Bolshaya Ussurka (1973)	Prim
Im. Kaganovicha (1935–57)	Chernyshevsk (1957)	Chita
Im. Mikoyana (1939–60)	Oktyabrsky (1960)	Kam
Im. Poliny Osipenko (1939)	Kerbi (pre-1939)	Khab
Imperatorskaya Gavan (1859–1922)	Sovetskaya Gavan (1922)	Prim
In (pre-1935)	Smidovich (1935)	JAD
Jingqilihe	Huanghe; Zeya River	Amur
Kamappu (ca. 1750–1945)	Yuzhno-Kurilsk (1945)	Sakh
Karafuto	Sakhalin (from ca. 1750);	Sakh
	Southern Sakhalin (1905–45)	
Kazakevich Island	Heixiazi Dao	Khab
Kerbi (pre-1939)	Im. Poliny Osipenko (1939)	Khab
Khabarovka (1858–93)	Boli (from ca. 15th c.);	Khab
	Khabarovsk (1893)	
Khabarovsk (1893)	Boli (from ca. 15th c.);	Khab
	Khabarovka (1858–93)	
Kholmsk (1945)	Maoka (1905–45);	Sakh
	Mauka (1870–1905)	
Khungari (pre-1973)	Gurskoye (1973)	Khab
Komissarovka River (1973)	Xinduzhe (pre-1973)	Prim
Komsomolsk-na-Amure (1932)	Permskoye (1898–1932)	Khab
Konstantinovsk (1853–1944)	Vanino (1944)	Prim
Korsakov (1875–1905, from 1945)	Muravievsky Post (1853–75);	Sakh
	Otomari (1905–45)	
Korsakovka (1880)	Qiufeng (pre-1880)	Prim
Kraskino (1938)	Yanqiu (pre-1862);	Prim
	Novokievskoye (1862–1938)	
Kruzenshtern Island	Little Diomede Island	(USA)

Name	Alternate name(s)	Region
Kuibyshevka (1935–57)	Bochkarevo (1902–26); Aleksandrovsk (1926–35); Belogorsk (1957)	Amur
Kurilsk (1945)	Shana (ca. 1750–1945)	Sakh
Kuyedao	Karafuto; Sakhalin	Sakh
Lazo (1923)	Muraviev-Amursky (ca. 1890–1923)	Prim
Lazo (1949)	Vangou (pre-1949)	Prim
Lefu River (pre-1973)	Ilistaya (1973)	Prim
Leninskoye (1939)	Bliukherovo (1935–39); Mikhailovo-Semyonovskoye (1890–1935)	JAD
Lifudzin (pre-1973)	Rudny (1973)	Prim
Little Diomede Island	Kruzenshtern Island	(USA)
Maihe (pre-1973)	Artyomovka River (1973)	Prim
Malinovka River (1973)	Waku River (pre-1973)	Prim
Manzovka (pre-1973)	Sibirtsevo (1973)	Prim
Maoka (1905–45)	Mauka (1870–1905); Kholmsk (1945)	Sakh
Mauka (1870–1905)	Maoka (1905–45); Kholmsk (1945)	Sakh
Melgunovka River (1973)	Mo River (pre-1973)	Prim
Menggujie	Barabash (from ca. 1890)	Prim
Mikhailovo-Semyonovskoye (1890–1935)	Bliukherovo (1935–39); Leninskoye (1939)	JAD
Mo River (pre-1973)	Melgunovka River (1973)	Prim
Mucheng (pre-1858)	Troitskoye (1858)	Khab
Mukhomornoye (1956)	Stalino (1935–56)	Mag
Muraviev-Amursky (ca. 1890–1923)	Lazo (1923)	Prim
Muraviev-Amursky Peninsula (1860)	Albert Peninsula (1856)	Prim
Muravievsky Post (1853–75)	Korsakov (1875–1905, from 1945); Otomari (1905–45)	Sakh
Nagibovo (1956)	Stalinsk (1935–56)	JAD
Nakhodka (1939)	Amerikanka (ca. 1865–1939)	Prim
Nakhodka Bay (1972)	Amerika Bay (1859–1972); Hornet Bay (1856)	Prim
Napoleon Bay (1856)	Ussuri Bay (1859)	Prim
Nevelskoi Strait	Mamiya Strait	Sakh
Nikolaevsk (1856–1926)	Nikolaevsk-na-Amure (1926); Nikolaevsky Post (1850–56)	Khab
Nikolsk-Ussuriisk (1898–1935)	Shuangchengzi (12th c.–1861); Nikolskoye (1861–98); Voroshilov (1935–57); Ussuriisk (1957)	Prim
Niuman River	Bureya River	Khab
Norogorodsky Bay (1859)	Aniele Bay (1852); Posyet Bay (1854)	Prim
Novik Bay (1859)	Port Dundas (1856)	Prim
Novogorodsky Post (1859–65)	Posyet (1865)	Prim
Novokievskoye (1862–1938)	Kraskino (1938); Yanqiu (pre-1862)	Prim
Novo-Mariinsk (1889–1930)	Anadyr (1930)	Mag

Name	Alternate name(s)	Region
Oktyabrskoye (1956)	Stalinsk (1935–1956)	Khab
Oktyabrsky (1960)	Im. Mikoyana (1939–60)	Kam
Olga/St. Olga (1857)	Port Seymour (1856)	Prim
Otomari (1905–45)	Muravievsky Post (1853–75); Korsakov (1875–1905, from 1945)	Sakh
Padali (pre-1958)	Amursk (1958)	Khab
Partizansk (1973)	Suchan (pre-1973)	Prim
Partizanskaya River (1973)	Suchan River (pre-1973)	Prim
Permskoye (1898–1932)	Komsomolsk-na-Amure (1932)	Khab
Peter the Great Bay (1859)	Victoria Bay (1856)	Prim
Pogranichnaya (1901–47)	Suifenhe, Heilongjiang (1947)	(China)
Pogranichny (1957)	Grodekovo (1900–1957)	Prim
Port Arthur	Lüshun, Ryojun (1905–45)	(China)
Port Dundas (1856)	Novik Bay (1859)	Prim
Port May (1856)	Haishenwei (ca. 1700); Vladivostok and Zolotoi Rog (1859)	Prim
Port Seymour (1856)	Olga/St. Olga (1857)	Prim
Posyet (1865)	Novogorodsky Post (1859–65)	Prim
Posyet Bay (1854)	Aniele Bay (1852); Novogorodsky Bay (1859)	Prim
Qiufeng (pre-1880)	Korsakovka (ca. 1880)	Prim
Ratmanov Island	Big Diomede Island	Mag
Razdolnaya River (1973)	Suifen River (pre-1973)	Prim
Rudnaya Pristan (1973)	Tetyukhe Pristan (ca. 1864–1973)	Prim
Rudny (1973)	Lifudzin (pre-1973)	Prim
Sakhalin	Karafuto; Kuyedao	Sakh
Semyonovka (ca. 1880–1930)	Arseniev (1930)	Prim
Severny Suchan (ca. 1874–1973)	Uglekamensk (1973)	Prim
Severo-Kurilsk (1945)	Kashiwabara (1875–1945)	Sakh
Shimanovsk (1950)	Gondatti (ca. 1913–50)	Amur
Shuangchengzi (12th c.–1861)	Nikolskoye (1861–98); Nikolsk-Ussuriisk (1898–1935); Voroshilov (1935–57); Ussuriisk (1957)	Prim
Sibirtsevo (1973)	Manzovka (pre-1973)	Prim
Sinancha (pre-1973)	Cheremshany (1973)	Prim
Smidovich (1935)	In (pre-1935)	JAD
Sovetskaya Gavan (1922)	Imperatorskaya Gavan (1859–1922)	Prim
Stalino (1935–56)	Mukhomornoye (1956)	Mag
Stalinsk (1935–56)	Nagibovo (1956)	JAD
Stalinsk (1935–56)	Oktyabrskoye (1956)	Khab
Suchan (pre-1973)	Partizansk (1973)	Prim
Suchan River (pre-1973)	Partizanskaya River (1973)	Prim
Suifen River (pre-1973)	Razdolnaya River (1973)	Prim
Suifenhe, Heilongjiang (1947)	Pogranichnaya (1901–47)	(China)
Svobodny (1923)	Alekseyevsk (ca. 1905–23)	Amur
Tetyukhe (pre-1973)	Dalnegorsk (1973)	Prim
Tetyukhe Pristan (ca. 1864–1973)	Rudnaya Pristan (1973)	Prim
Tikhonkaya (ca. 1880–1931)	Birobidzhan (1931)	JAD
Toyohara (1905–45)	Vladimirovka (1875–1905); Yuzhno-Sakhalinsk (1945)	Sakh

Name	Alternate name(s)	Region
Troitskoye (1858)	Mucheng (pre-1858)	Khab
Uglekamensk (1973)	Severny Suchan (ca. 1874–1973)	Prim
Ulan Ude (1935)	Verkhneudinsk (1666–1935)	
Ussuri Bay (1859)	Napoleon Bay (1856)	Prim
Ussuriisk (1957)	Shuangchengzi (12th c.–1861); Nikolskoye (1861–98); Nikolsk-Ussuriisk (1898–1935); Voroshilov (1935–57)	Prim
Ust Zeisk (1854–58)	Huanghetun (pre-1854); Blagoveshchensk (1858)	Amur
Vangou (pre-1949)	Lazo (1949)	Prim
Vanino (1944)	Konstantinovsk (1853–1944)	Prim
Verkhneudinsk (1666–1935)	Ulan Ude (1935)	
Victoria Bay (1856)	Peter the Great Bay (1859)	Prim
Vladivostok and Zolotoi Rog (1859)	Haishenwei (ca. 1700); Port May (1856)	Prim
Voroshilov (1935–57)	Shuangchengzi (12th c.–1861); Nikolskoye (1861–98); Nikolsk-Ussuriisk (1898–1935); Ussuriisk (1957)	Prim
Waku River (pre-1973)	Malinovka River (1973)	Prim
Xinduzhe River (pre-1973)	Komissarovka River (1973)	Prim
Yaksa (pre-1654)	Albazin (1654)	Amur
Yanqiu (pre-1862)	Novokievskoye (1862–1938); Kraskino (1938)	Prim
Yuzhno-Kurilsk (1945)	Kamappu (ca. 1750–1945)	Sakh
Yuzhno-Sakhalinsk (1945)	Vladimirovka (1875–1905); Toyohara (1905–45)	Sakh
Zeya River	Jingqilihe; Huanghe	Amur

« « » »

Notes

For complete authors' names, titles, and publishing data on sources cited in short form in the Notes, see the Select Bibliography. The following abbreviations are used in the Notes:

DVO (1)   *Ocherki istorii Dal'nevostochnykh organizatsii KPSS (1900–1937)*
DVO (2)   *Ocherki istorii Dal'nevostochnykh organizatsii KPSS (1938–1987)*
ES   *Entsiklopedicheskii slovar' (1890–1907)*
FRUS   *Foreign Relations of the United States*
GVVI   *Grazhdanskaia voina i voennaia interventsiia v SSSR*
HA   Hoover Institution Archives, Stanford, California
IDV   *Istoriia Dal'nego Vostoka SSSR*
LC   Library of Congress, Washington, D.C.
MERSH   *Modern Encyclopedia of Russian and Soviet History*
SSE   *Sibirskaia sovetskaia entsiklopediia*
VOV   *Velikaia Otechestvennaia voina 1941–1945: Entsiklopediia*

1 «» Geography and Prehistory

Epigraph. Vladimir Vysotskii, "Dal'nii Vostok," *Nerv* (Moscow: Sovremennik, 1981), pp. 167–68.

1. For a thoughtful discussion, see Bassin, "Russia," pp. 1–17.
2. Kruber, *Aziatskaia Rossiia*, p. 545.
3. Gaunt, p. 206.

4. "Wild Amur Tigers Menace Soviet Far East Again," *Japan Times,* 26 Mar. 1986. *Russian Far East Update*, 3, no. 3 (Mar. 1993): 9.

5. Bassin, "Russian Mississippi?"; Kropotkin, *Memoirs*, p. 155.

6. TASS, 4 Sept. 1987.

7. IDV, 1: 14.

8. Okladnikov and Derevianko, pp. 46–47; Chard, p. 4; *Ocherki istorii Chukotki*, p. 20; Dikov, *Novye arkheologicheskie pamiatniki*, p. 2.

9. Okladnikov, *Soviet Far East*, pp. 25, 27, 32; Okladnikov and Derevianko, pp. 5, 48, 50, 58; Derevianko, p. 24. IDV, 1:15–26; For a summary of archaeological work in the Far East from 1863 until 1985, see Brodianskii.

10. *Istoriia Sibiri*, l (1968): 136–40; IDV, 1: 67–76; Vasil'evskii, *Drevnie kul'tury*.

11. Kiuner, p. 217; McCune, p. 165; Kim Kyeoung-choon, "Tumankang haryu," pp. 167–70; E. V. Shavkunov in Tikhomirov, p. 152; E. V. Shavkunov in *Materialy po arkheologii*, p. 108; Okladnikov, *Soviet Far East*, pp. 148, 151, 157, 168.

2 «» The Chinese Millennium

Epigraph. Xiboliya wenti lunzhan, title page. Li Ji (1896–1979) was the director of the Institute of History and Philology of the Academia Sinica, Taibei, from 1955 to 1972.

1. Kiuner, p. 218.

2. Okladnikov, *Soviet Far East*, pp. 163–65, 170; Okladnikov and Derevianko, pp. 308–26; N. I. Riabov and Shtein, p. 9; Kiuner, p. 218; Wada, pp. 457–58. *Sha E qin Hua shi*, 1: 10.

3. Xue Hong, p. 179; Researchers at Northeast Normal University have reportedly discovered evidence that Alaskan aborigines sent envoys to Emperor Taizhong in 640. Xinhua, 3 Oct. 1991.

4. Viktor Panov, p. 7.

5. Pozdneev, 2: 13–15; *Kōjien*, ed. Shimmura Izuru (Tokyo: Iwanami, 1955), p. 1968.

6. *Dongbei lidai jiangyu shi*, p. 125; Herrmann, p. 36.

7. Okladnikov, *Soviet Far East*, pp. 10, 254; IDV, 1: 232–36.

8. Okladnikov, *Soviet Far East*, pp. 10, 254; *Ocherki istorii sovetskogo Primor'ia*, pp. 15–16; V. E. Medvedev, *Srednevekovye pamiatniki*, p. 25.

9. *Sha E qin Hua shi*, 1: 19; *Dongbei lidai jiangyu shi*, p. 173.

10. IDV, 1: 239.

11. Hora, *Karafutoshi kenkyū*, pp. 99, 120–121; Wada, pp. 465–66.

12. Tao Yuanzhen, p. 133; *Sha E qin Hua shi*, 1: 36–55; *Dongbei lidai jiangyu shi*, pp. 266–77; Hora, *Karafutoshi kenkyū*, p. 104.

13. For photographs of the inscription taken in 1919, see Torii, frontispiece.

14. P. Popov, pp. 12–20; Torii, pp. 146–52, 390–92.

15. Okladnikov, *Soviet Far East*, p. 5; Torii, pp. 146–52.

16. Laufer, p. 4.

17. Vinogradov, p. 125.

18. Viktor Panov, pp. 5–37.

19. Arsenjew, *Russen und Chinesen*; Zotik Matveev, "Istoriia," p. 341.

20. Arsenjew, *Russen und Chinesen*, plate opposite p. 41. The tortoise came from outside Nikolsk (today, Ussuriisk) where it had adorned a mill owned by Otto Lindholm, a Swedish-American from San Francisco. Sverdlov, pp. 102–9.

21. Okladnikov, *Soviet Far East*, p. 20.

22. Ibid., pp. 5, 7.

23. V. G. Shchebenkov and E. V. Shavkunov in Tikhomirov, pp. 156, 211–12.

24. N. I. Riabov and Shtein, p. 12; *Vladivostok, 1860–1960*, p. 13; *Ocherki istorii sovetskogo Primor'ia*, p. 17.

25. *Asahi shimbun*, 14 July 1964.

26. *Zhongguo lidai jiangyu xingshi shi tu*, p. 70.

27. Statement of the Ministry of Foreign Affairs in *Peking Review*, no. 41 (10 Oct. 1969): 8–15.

28. Zhao Chizi, "Xianbi wenti," in *Xiboliya wenti lunzhan*, pp. 28–36.

29. "China Says That Relics Back Claim," *New York Times*, 25 July 1977. See also *Dongbei lidai jiangyu shi*, p. 323; and *Sha E qin Hua shi*, 1: 7.

30. *Sha E qin Hua shi*.

31. *Dongbei lidai jiangyu shi*, p. 254.

32. The term employed by S. L. Tikhvinsky, sinologist, chekist, academician, and former chief of the History Department of the USSR Academy of Sciences. See *Pravda*, 2 Sept. 1964, 1 June 1985.

33. Okladnikov, "Novoe v arkheologii Dal'nego Vostoka;" Vasil'evskii, *Arkheologiia Amuro-Sakhalinskogo regiona*.

34. Alekseev and Melikhov, p. 58; *Istoriia severo-vostochnogo Kitaia*, pp. 27–108.

35. Kabuzan, *Dal'nevostochnyi krai*, p. 3.

36. For a partial list of changes, see Appendix K.

37. The Suifen River is anachronistically called Razdolnaya in Biankin, *V dal'nevestochnykh moriakh*, p. 17.

38. IDV, 1: chaps. 3 and 4.

3 «» Russian Entrée

Epigraph. Klipel in *Granitsa: Dokumental'no*, p. 6.

1. For a review of interpretations, see Basil Dmytryshyn, "Russian Expansion to the Pacific, 1580–1700: A Historiographical Review," *Siberica*, 1, no. 1 (Summer 1990): 4–37; Lantzeff and Pierce, pp. 81–140; chapters by David N. Collins, J. L. Black, and James Forsyth in Wood, ed., *History of Siberia*, pp. 36–91.

2. Dmytryshyn, "Russian Expansion," p. 17; Lantzeff, pp. 155–61; N. I. Riabov and Shtein, pp. 21–22.

3. Lantzeff, pp. 13, 47–53, 201–2.

4. Ibid., pp. 36, 37, 39–40; Tokarev, p. 49; F. G. Safronov, *Russkie na severo-vostoke Azii*, pp. 16, 49.

5. N. I. Riabov and Shtein, p. 20; V. Senin, "Sibirskoe vziatie," *Pravda*, 21 Sept. 1981.

6. Janhunen, pp. 73, 75, 76.

7. According to Tokarev, p. 40, "this tale in general accurately conveys a major event in the history of the Yakut people."

8. Ibid., pp. 51, 59.

9. Ibid., p. 59; Lantzeff and Pierce, p. 139.

10. Tokarev, pp. 63, 76, 105; Lantzeff, p. 106.

11. Tokarev, p. 105.

12. Fisher, *Russian Fur Trade*, pp. 71–79; Lantzeff, p. 100.

13. Tokarev, p. 67.

14. Ibid., p. 73; Lantzeff, p. 103; Armstrong, *Russian Settlement*, p. 117.

15. Gapanovich, 1: 53, 176; Lantzeff, pp. 93, 144–46.

16. Lantzeff, pp. 70, 90; N. I. Riabov and Shtein, p. 22; Epifanov, pp. 76, 77.

17. Tokarev, p. 108; *Ocherki istorii Chukotki*, pp. 75, 88; Gibson, *Feeding the Russian Fur Trade*, pp. 11, 14.

18. Gapanovich, 1: 38.

19. Ibid., p. 54.

20. Ibid., pp. 52, 55, 57; *Ocherki istorii Chukotki*, p. 91.

21. Tokarev, pp. 61, 107; Lantzeff, p. 99; Gapanovich, 1: 50, 152.

22. Lantzeff, pp. 96–97; Tokarev, pp. 116–19.

23. F .G. Safronov, *Russkie na Severo-Vostoke Azii*, pp. 130, 241, 245.

24. Fisher, *Russian Fur Trade*, pp. 80–84; Lantzeff, pp. 19, 32.

25. Tokarev, p. 73.

26. Lantzeff, pp. 83–84.

27. Lantzeff, p. 80n.

28. Tokarev, p. 130; Slezkine, "From Savages to Citizens," p. 55.

29. Nesterov, pp. 88–89; Tokarev, p. 130; Lantzeff, p. 101.

30. Gapanovich, 1: 54, 67, 105, 178.

31. F. G. Safronov, *Russkie na Severo-Vostoke Azii*, p. 215; Zenzinov, *Road*, p. 29; Armstrong, *Russian Settlement*, p. 96.

4 «» Amur Setback

Epigraph. Russians on the Amur, p. 25.

1. Kabuzan, *Dal'nevostochnyi krai*, p. 34; Aleksandrov (1984), pp. 6, 17; N. I. Riabov and Shtein, pp. 15–16.

2. Lee, *Manchurian Frontier*, pp. 3, 19, 53–54; *Sha E qin Hua shi*, 1: 55–70.

3. Lantzeff, p. 78; Gibson, *Feeding the Russian Fur Trade*, p. 223.

4. Kabanov, p. 11.

5. Lantzeff, p. 80.

6. Ibid., p. 108. A school text states that Poyarkov "gave them [Amur natives] Russian citizenship." *Tvoi rodnoi krai*, p. 14.

7. Grum-Grzhimailo, p. 9. Mindful of current territorial questions, some Soviet historians have Poyarkov reporting that the Amur peoples were independent. Sergeev, p. 18; Aleksandrov (1984), p. 23; Nikitin, p. 182; *Istoriia Sibiri*, 2: 53. According to Mark Bassin, Poyarkov was ordered to explore Dauria by Tsar Mikhail Fyodorovich. Bassin, "Expansion and Colonialism," p. 12.

8. Grum-Grzhimailo, p. 11.

9. Bakhrushin, pp. 22, 97–98; Aleksandrov, *Rossiia na dal'nevostochnykh rubezhakh* (1969), p. 10.

10. Mancall, p. 162.

11. *Ocherki istorii sovetskogo Primor'ia*, p. 18; Sergeev, p. 19. Chinese accounts treat the 1658 encounters as a "war of resistance" against Russian "invaders." *Sha E qin Hua shi*, 1: 122–27; Xu Jingxue, *Eguo zhengfu*, p. 155. A Soviet sinologist maintained in 1985 that Manchus launched an aggressive campaign against peaceful Russian pioneers as the first step toward invading Siberia and "world conquest." Tikhvinsky, *Chapters*, p. 9.

12. Kabuzan, *Dal'nevostochnyi krai*, p. 35; N. I. Riabov and Shtein, pp. 44–45.

13. Gapanovich, 1: 56.

14. *Sha E qin Hua shi*, 1: 135.

15. Ibid., 1: 165, gives the figure 3,000. Kabanov, p. 18, says 15,000.

16. Mancall, p. 134; *Sha E qin Hua shi*, 1: 130, 166–68; Prokhorov, p. 51; Kabanov, p. 19; Aleksandrov (1984), pp. 155–74; Besprozvannykh, pp. 47–51.

17. This account of the negotiations at Nerchinsk is based primarily on Prokhorov, pp. 65–79; Miasnikov, pp. 207–51; and Besprozvannykh, pp. 51–57. For primary documents, see *Russko-kitaiskie otnosheniia v XVII veke*.

18. Prokhorov, p. 53.

19. For details, see Bassin, "Expansion and Colonialism."

20. Lobanov-Rostovsky, *Russia and Asia*, p. 62.

21. In 1847 Alexander Balasoglo wrote that "had Russians known Latin, [they] wouldn't have lost the Amur." Quoted in Bassin, "A Russian Mississippi?," p. 84. Golovin knew Latin according to Aleksandrov (1984), p. 253. Moreover, a Jesuit adviser in 1677 secretly provided a Muscovite envoy in Beijing with Manchu strategic plans for the Amur. Mancall, p. 100.

22. Prokhorov, p. 83; *Istoriia severo-vostochnogo Kitaia*, pp. 181–82; Epifanov, p. 70; Miasnikov, pp. 257, 264.

23. *Sha E qin Hua shi*, 1: 216–18.

24. Besprozvannykh, p. 57, Prokhorov, pp. 65, 85, and Kabanov, p. 23, argue

that the Chinese considered the Amur a tributary of the Sungari. Chinese maps show the Heilongjiang (Amur) flowing as far as its junction with the Sungari, where it becomes the Huntongjiang (lit. "joined river"). Cao Tingjie, p. 4; *Zhong E guanxi shiliao*, 1: foldout map opposite p. 2.

25. Kabuzan, *Dal'nevostochnyi krai*, pp. 3, 39; Polevoi, *Pervootkryvateli Sakhalina*, pp. 68–69.

26. Melikhov, p. 195.

27. Daniel Defoe, *Robinson Crusoe* (London: Dent, 1945), p. 402.

28. Lerman, *Po serdtsu blizkie druz'ia*, p. 4.

5 «» Pacific Window

Epigraph. Bering to Admiral Osterman, 23 June (O.S.) 1737, in *Russkaia tikhookeanskaia epopeia*, p. 187.

1. F. G. Safronov, *Russkie na Severo-Vostoke Azii*, pp. 25–27; Tokarev, p. 107.

2. F. G. Safronov, *Russkie na Severo-Vostoke Azii*, p. 101.

3. Until recently, the First Kamchatka Expedition was commonly believed to have derived from Peter's search for a northern sea route to China, Japan, and the East Indies in general, and for a strait between Asia and America in particular. Dezhnev's report of his passage around the "Big Nose" (Chukotka) in 1648 languished in the Yakutsk archives until discovered by G. F. Müller in 1736 and was presumably unknown to Peter. Fisher, *Bering's Voyages*, argues that Peter's real objective was to follow the Kamchatka coast to America. In *Bering's First Expedition*, Carol Urness concludes that the expedition aimed neither to discover the strait (whose existence was already known in Russia) nor to find a route to America but to survey Siberia's northeastern littoral. For a historiographical overview of the issue, see Bolkhovitinov, *Rossiia otkryvaet*, pp. 10–15.

4. Lensen, *Russian Push*, pp. 47–57.

5. Georg Wilhelm Steller, *Journal of a Voyage with Bering, 1741–1742*, ed. O. W. Frost (Stanford, Calif.: Stanford University Press, 1988); Stepan P. Krasheninnikov, *Explorations of Kamchatka, 1735–1741*, tr. E.A.P. Crownhart-Vaughan (Portland: Oregon Historical Society, 1972).

6. Miller, *Istoriia Sibiri*.

7. F. G. Safronov, *Russkie na Severo-Vostoke Azii*, pp. 130, 241, 245; Gibson, *Feeding the Russian Fur Trade*, pp. 162–84.

8. Maier, p. 235.

9. Tokarev, p. 107; F. G. Safronov, *Russkie na Severo-Vostoke Azii*, pp. 25–27, 32, 37; Zhikarev, p. 5; Dmytryshyn, "Administrative Apparatus."

10. Makarova, pp. 182–87.

11. John Ledyard visited Kamchatka in 1779 and later tried to interest Thomas Jefferson in North Pacific commerce. Bolkhovitinov, *Beginnings*, pp. 153–54. For details on Ledyard, see Watrous.

12. Glynn Barratt, lecture at the University of Hawaii, 7 July 1981.

13. *Russkaia tikhookeanskaia epopeia*, p. 370.

14. Chekhov, *Journey to Sakhalin*, pp. 232, 236; *A. P. Chekhov: sobranie sochinenii* (Moscow: Gosizdat, 1963), 10: 236; Kantorovich, p. 9; Fainberg, pp. 97–101; Iurii Zhukov, *Russkie i Iaponiia* (Moscow: Politizdat, 1945), pp. 54–78.

15. Cochrane, p. 324; N. N. Bolkhovitinov, "Vydvizhenie i proval proektov P. Dobella, 1812–1821," in *Amerikanskii ezhegodnik 1976* (Moscow: Nauka, 1976), pp. 264–82.

16. Richard A. Pierce, *Russia's Hawaiian Adventure* (Berkeley: University of California Press, 1965); N. N. Bolkhovitinov, "Avantiura Doktora Sheffera na Gavaiiakh," *Novaia i noveishaia istoriia*, 1972, no. 1: 121–37.

17. *Ocherki istorii Chukotki*, p. 111.

18. For a succint analysis of the Russian-American Company as an economic enterprise and instrument of imperial expansion, see Gibson, "Tsarist Russia."

19. Raeff, p. 4.

20. *Istoriia Sibiri*, 2: 453; SSE, 4: 309–10.

21. *Istoriia Sibiri*, 2: 458; Poppe, pp. 141–42.

22. Irkutsk Historical Museum deputy director Oleg Bychkov, lecture at the University of Hawaii, 16 Apr. 1992.

23. Gapanovich, 1: 60; Iasman, pp. 212–13. In *Feeding the Russian Fur Trade*, p. 212, Gibson indicates that a horticulturalist was sent from the Moscow Agricultural School to Kamchatka in 1828 to instruct natives in the cultivation of grain and vegetables.

24. Bassin, "Russian Mississippi?," p. 68.

6 «» Return to the Amur

Epigraph. Lobanov-Rostovsky, *Russia and Asia*, p. 147.

1. Okladnikov and Derevianko, p. 418; *Ocherki istorii sovetskogo Primor'ia*, p. 19; Kabuzan, *Dal'nevostochnyi krai*, p. 39; N. I. Riabov and Shtein, p. 108.

2. *Dongbei lidai jiangyu shi*, pp. 303–12.

3. Lee, *Manchurian Frontier*, pp. 43–44; *Sha E qin Hua shi*, 2: 12.

4. Hora, *Mamiya*, pp. 161–67. For the explorer's own account see Mamiya.

5. Murov, pp. 2–4; Lee, *Manchurian Frontier*, p. 90.

6. *Sha E qin Hua shi*, 2: 21, 57; Murov, p. 3; Kolarz, *Peoples*, p. 43; Lee, *Manchurian Frontier*, pp. 47, 89.

7. Besprozvannykh, p. 182; *Sha E qin Hua shi*, 2: 34.

8. Notably by Gerhard Friedrich Müller (1705–83), scientist, historian, and member of the Second Kamchatka Expedition. Black, p. 134.

9. Cochrane, p. 353.

10. Aleksandrov (1984), p. 234.

11. Bassin, "Russian Mississippi?," pp. 56, 92; Bassin, "Inventing Siberia," pp. 775–79.

12. Alekseev, *Amurskaia ekspeditsiia*, p. 10.

13. Ibid., p. 14; Bassin, "Russian Mississippi?," pp. 75–77. For details of the expedition, see Middendorf, *Puteshestvie*.

14. Alekseev, *Amurskaia ekspeditsiia*, p. 12.

15. Bassin, "Russian Mississippi?," p. 264.

16. Alekseev, *Amurskaia ekspeditsiia*, p. 15n.

17. Quoted in Bassin, "Russian Mississippi?," p. 126.

18. According to Mark Bassin, Nevelskoi rather than Muraviev took the initiative in moving toward the Amur in 1849–50. Muraviev, oriented toward the Pacific, gave priority to Petropavlovsk until the mid-1850s. Personal communication, 4 Nov. 1991.

19. Quoted in Bassin, "Russian Mississippi?," p. 142.

20. Alekseev, *Amurskaia ekspeditsiia*, pp. 52–56; Russia, *Aziatskaia Rossiia*, 1: 517–19; N. I. Riabov and Shtein, p. 91.

21. For details, see George A. Lensen, *Russia's Japan Expedition, 1852–1855* (Gainesville: Univ. of Florida Press, 1955). For surveys along the lower Amur and Tatar Strait, see Boshniak, "Ekspeditsiia."

22. Alekseev, *Amurskaia ekspeditsiia*, p. 89; Alekseev and Melikhov, "Otkrytie i osvoenie," p. 71; Sergeev, p. 58.

23. Sergeev, pp. 35, 45, 47.

24. Alekseev, *Amurskaia ekspeditsiia*, p. 139.

25. Russian documents about the defense of Petropavlovsk are collected in *Zashchitniki otechestva*. For an account based on British Admiralty archives, see Stephan, "Crimean War," pp. 261–68.

26. Quested, *Expansion of Russia*, p. 55.

27. Bassin, "Russian Mississippi?," p. 160; F. G. Safronov, *Russkie na severo-vostoke Azii*, p. 47; N. I. Riabov and Shtein, p. 102; Alekseev, *Amurskaia ekspeditsiia*, pp. 17n, 179.

28. Quested, *Expansion of Russia*, pp. 148–53; Prokhorov, pp. 98–120; *Sha E qin Hua shi*, 2: 125–43. For a map of the sixty-four Chinese villages, see Wang Hualong, opposite p. 30.

29. Russia, *Aziatskaia Rossiia*, 1: 519.

30. Masuda, p. 98; Quested, *Expansion of Russia*, p. 151.

31. Masuda, pp. 99–100; Alekseev, *Amurskaia ekspeditsiia*, p. 17.

32. Khisamutdinov, *Terra incognita*, p. 61.

33. Several officials connected with the Aigun treaty were dismissed for gross negligence. Masuda, pp. 99–100; Quested, *Expansion of Russia*, p. 179.

34. For the treaty text, see Prokhorov, pp. 255–58.

35. Masuda, pp. 104–7; Alekseev, *Kak nachinalsia Vladivostok*, p. 179.

36. "Russia's Successes in the Far East," in *Karl Marx–Frederick Engels: Collected Works* (Moscow: Progress, 1980), 16: 83.

37. A. I. Krushanov in Alekseev, *Kak nachinalsia Vladivostok*, p. 4; Kabuzan, *Dal'nevostochnyi krai*, p. 49.

7 «» Toward a Far Eastern Viceroyalty

Epigraph. Ukhtomsky quoted in Rudolf Martin, *The Future of Russia* (London: Smith, Elder, 1906), p. 36.

1. SSE, 3: 604–5.

2. Bassin, "Russian Mississippi?," p. 264; SSE, 2: 44.

3. Semyonov, *Siberia*, p. 278.

4. Alekseev, *Khoziaika Zaliva Schast'ia*, pp. 184, 190, 201; SSE, 1: 31.

5. Olga Poutiatine, *War and Revolution*, ed. George A. Lensen (Tallahassee, Fla.: Diplomatic Press, 1971), p. 7.

6. Alekseev, *Utro Sovetskoi Gavani*, pp. 240–41.

7. Malozemoff, *Russian Far Eastern Policy*, p. 15; Marks, pp. 13, 53–54.

8. "Amurskoe delo," pp. 99–100. The observer is identified as "V. I."

9. Hoetzsch, p. 139.

10. IDV, 2: 230.

11. Vinogradov, pp. 145, 147; Chernysheva, *Khabarovsk, 1858–1983*, pp. 17–71; Morozov, p. 22.

12. Bodisco, *Iz zhizni Khabarovska*, p. 16; Enomoto, p. 227.

13. Malozemoff, *Russian Far Eastern Policy*, pp. 16–17, 21; "Pervye shagi russkogo imperializma," pp. 55–61.

14. Malozemoff, *Russian Far Eastern Policy*, p. 23; Cao Tingjie, pp. 5, 8.

15. Russia, *Aziatskaia Rossiia*, 2: 517.

16. Vostrikov and Vostokov, p. 61.

17. For the administrative dynamics underlying the Trans-Siberian Line, see Marks, pp. 57–114.

18. "Pervye shagi russkogo imperializma," pp. 83–93; *Russko-iaponskaia voina*, 1: 171; Geyer, p. 191. On Dukhovskoi's complaints of being "overlooked," see Wolff, pp. 98–99.

19. Lensen, *Russo-Chinese War*, p. 278. On massacres of Chinese in villages around Blagoveshchensk, see Mo Yongming, ed. *Sha E qin Hua shi*, p. 294.

20. On interministerial rivalry in Manchuria, see Geyer, p. 190; Wolff, pp. 106–11.

21. Witte, *Memoirs of Count Witte*, pp. 277, 282–83, 303–4, 348–49, 365–66, 368–69; "Pervye shagi russkogo imperializma," pp. 118–19; Kuropatkin, *Russian Army*, 1: 160–66, 190–93; White, *Diplomacy*, pp. 48–75.

22. Kuropatkin, *Russian Army*, 1: 171. I. G., "Ocherki," p. 165.

23. Geyer, p. 209.

24. White, *Diplomacy*, pp. 72–73; Malozemoff, *Russian Far Eastern Policy*, p. 224; Geyer, pp. 212–13; Shindialov, p. 12. For feelings of a large number of ranking Russian officers in the Far East toward Alekseyev, see Weale, *Manchu*, p. 552.

25. IDV, 2: 228.

26. Russia, *Dal'nii Vostok*, 3: 107.

27. Kharkov University Professor Migulin, cited in Geyer, p. 227.

8 «» Patterns of Settlement

Epigraph. Chekhov quoted in Vostrikov, p. 13.

1. Russia, *Aziatskaia Rossiia*, 1: 70; Rybakovskii, p. 71; White, *Siberian Intervention*, p. 45.

2. Knox, pp. 194–95.

3. Kropotkin, *Memoirs*, p. 186; Sergeev, p. 93.

4. Bassin, "Russian Mississippi?," p. 279; Malozemoff, *Russian Far Eastern Policy*, p. 2.

5. Murov, pp. 149–51; Volgin, p. 139; Sergeev, p. 36; *Nashi dalekiia okrainy*, p. 25.

6. Sergeev, p. 80; *Iz istorii revoliutsionnogo dvizheniia*, pp. 135–36.

7. Sergeev, pp. 62, 74; Kabuzan, *Dal'nevostochnyi krai*, p. 117; N. I. Riabov and Shtein, pp. 124–25; Shindialov, p. 15; MERSH, 41: 137.

8. Sergeev, pp. 83–85, 92–111; Shindialov, p. 13; *Iz istoriia revoliutsionnogo dvizheniia*, p. 44.

9. N. I. Riabov and Shtein, p. 110.

10. Ibid., p. 112; Kabuzan, *Dal'nevostochnyi krai*, p. 60.

11. *Ocherki istorii sovetskogo Primor'ia*, p. 24.

12. Aleksandrovskaia, p. 33; Biankin, p. 184; Kabuzan, *Dal'nevostochnyi krai*, p. 88; Rekk-Lebedev, pp. 10–11.

13. Kabuzan, *Dal'nevostochnyi krai*, pp. 62, 74–76; Sergeev, p. 66; N. I. Riabov and Shtein, pp. 108, 110–12; Bassin, "Russian Mississippi?," p. 276; Alekseev and Morozov, "Ekonomicheskoe razvitie Dal'nego Vostoka," p. 38.

14. Khisamutdinov, *Terra incognita*, pp. 236, 242–44; Khudiakov, "Avtobiografiia."

15. Alekseev, *Kak nachinalsia Vladivostok*, p. 201.

16. Biankin, pp. 186–90; Katō, *Shiberia ki*, p. 34; *Vladivostok: Gorod u okeana*, p. 53; Malozemoff, *Russian Far Eastern Policy*, pp. 13, 34.

17. Anosov, p. 6; Kabuzan, *Dal'nevostochnyi krai*, p. 96.

18. Kabuzan, *Dal'nevostochnyi krai*, pp. 123–24; Russia, *Aziatskaia Rossiia*, 1: 69.

19. Derber and Sher, *Ocherki zhizni*, p. 30; Gerasimov, *Patrioty Dal'nego Vostoka*, p. 99; N. I. Riabov and Shtein, p. 123; Rybakovskii, p. 68.

20. Svit, p. 3; Nesterov, p. 93; Biankin, pp. 185, 232.

21. Kabuzan, *Dal'nevostochnyi krai*, p. 97; N. I. Riabov and Shtein, pp. 120, 122; *Ocherki istorii sovetskogo Primor'ia*, pp. 25–26.

22. *Iz istorii revoliutsionnogo dvizheniia*, p. 134.

23. Kabuzan, *Dal'nevostochnyi krai*, pp. 137–40, 190; N. I. Riabov and Shtein, pp. 154–56.

24. Kabuzan, *Dal'nevostochnyi krai*, p. 135.

25. Ibid., pp. 127, 154; Derber and Sher, *Ocherki zhizni*, p. 90.

26. Shindialov, p. 14; *Nashi dalekiia okrainy*, p. 15.

27. Murov, pp. 98–100, 113; *Vol'naia Sibir'*, 1927, no. 1: 166; *Ocherki istorii sovetskogo Primor'ia*, p. 26; *Iz istorii revoliutsionnogo dvizheniia*, p. 141; Raikhman, *Economic Development*, p. 30; *Narody sovetskogo Dal'nego Vostoka*, p. 64.

28. *Iz istorii revoliutsionnogo dvizheniia*, pp. 45, 139–40; N. I. Riabov and Shtein, p. 166. For a general treatment of "class struggle," see IDV, 2: 283–88.

29. Derber and Sher, *Ocherki zhizni*, p. 68.

30. Ibid., p. 15.

31. Russia, *Aziatskaia Rossiia*, 1: 51.

32. *Obzor russkoi periodicheskoi pechati*, 3: 31.

33. Armstrong, *Russian Settlement*, pp. 92, 196.

34. Russia, *Pereselenie na Dal'nii Vostok*, p. 11; Balalaeva, p. 3; Fedor Danilenko, p. 13; Kabuzan, *Dal'nevostochnyi krai*, p. 88; Malozemoff, *Russian Far Eastern Policy*, p. 10.

35. SSE, 3: 731–32; Kabuzan, *Dal'nevostochnyi krai*, p. 58.

36. Kropotkin, *Memoirs*, p. 216.

37. Balalaeva, p. 4.

38. Ibid., p. 4; Miagkoff, *Aux bords du Pacifique*, p. 13; Karpenko, p. 19.

39. Zenzinov, *Road*, p. 12.

40. Kolpenskii, pp. 16–19.

41. Eliseev, p. 5.

42. Khisamutdinov, "Vladimir Arsen'ev."

43. Latyshev, "Pis'ma Bronislava Pilsudskogo," pp. 168, 171.

44. "Sidemi: K otkrytiiu pamiatnika M.I. Iankovskomu" (Vladivostok: Krasnoe znamia, 1991). Yul subsequently added an "n" to his name so that it would not be pronounced with a long "i" as in "brine." Personal communication from Cyril Bryner, 9 Sept. 1987.

45. SSE, 4: 851–52; Vostrikov and Vostokov, pp. 120–22; Khisamutdinov, *Russian Far East*, p. 41.

9 «» East Asian Communities

Epigraph. Unterberger quoted in SSE, 2: 236.

1. Solov'ev, *Kitaiskoe otkhodnichestvo*, pp. 34–43.

2. Khisamutdinov, "Vladimir Arsen'ev"; ES, 69: 29; Arsenjew, *Russen und Chinesen*, p. 56.

3. Solov'ev, *Kitaiskoe otkhodnichestvo*, pp. 10–33; Siegelbaum, pp. 308–10; Merkulov, pp. 9–10; Kabuzan, *Dal'nevostochnyi krai*, p. 157; Lee, *Manchurian Frontier*, pp. 107–9; Wang Hualong, pp. 30–32.

4. *Hui fang* elders commemorated the spot with a monument that still stood in 1956. Udovenko, p. 43n. See also Raikhman, *Economic Development*, p. 48.

5. Murov, p. 88.

6. Russia, *Pereselenie na Dal'nii Vostok*, p. 54.

7. Gaunt, pp. 206–7; Katō, *Shiberia ki*, pp. 54–55. A Frenchman traveling down the Amur in 1991 made the same observation. Philippe Pons, "Sans visa," *Le Monde*, 19 Oct. 1991.

8. Arsenjew, *Russen und Chinesen*, p. 133. See also Buiakov, "Narkobiznes," p. 64.

9. Cao Tingjie, p. 8.

10. Arsenjew, *Russen und Chinesen*, pp. 125–27; Chikhachev, p. 562n.

11. Murov, pp. 25–26; Katō, *Shiberia ki*, p. 117; Shreider, p. 17.

12. *Guide to the Great Siberian Railway*, p. 444; Chernysheva, *Khabarovsk, 1858–1983*, p. 66; Vinogradov, p. 145; ES, 72: 946; Russia, *Aziatskaia Rossiia: Atlas*, map 60. Cao Tingjie, p. 4; Fraser, p. 191.

13. Siegelbaum, p. 312; SSE, 2: 1109.

14. V. P. Shmotin, "Mining Industry in the Priamur Region," *Russkii Dal'nii Vostok*, 2 (Nov. 1920): 17. Siegelbaum, p. 325, gives more dramatic figures: 20% in 1906 to 82.7% in 1910.

15. Siegelbaum, pp. 312, 316; Malozemoff, *Russian Far Eastern Policy*, p. 190; Denisov, p. 12.

16. Miagkoff, *Aux bords du Pacifique*, pp. 16–17; Gaunt, p. 218.

17. Siegelbaum, p. 316; N. I. Riabov and Shtein, p. 130.

18. Murov, pp. 20–21; See also ES, 12: 625–26.

19. Khisamutdinov, "Vladimir Arsen'ev"; Shkurkin, p. 70n.

20. "Amurskaia Kaliforniia"; Malozemoff, *Russian Far Eastern Policy*, pp. 11–12, 23; Siegelbaum, p. 315.

21. Murov, p. 101; Beveridge, p. 13.

22. Murov, pp. 16–17, 46–52; Gaunt, p. 158.

23. Gaunt, p. 184. See also SSE, 2: 687.

24. Hyun, 1: 743–45; Ravenstein, *Russians on the Amur*, p. 231.

25. Anosov, p. 9; James, p. 353; Yamauchi, p. 74; Kolarz, *Peoples*, p. 33.

26. Anosov, pp. 6, 27; Arsenjew, *Russen und Chinesen*, p. 23; Murov, p. 37; Kabuzan, *Kak zaselialsia Dal'nii Vostok*, p. 188; SSE, 2: 949; Kim Syn Khva, *Ocherki*, p. 42; Ginsburgs, "Citizenship," p. 4; Wada Haruki in Suh, *Koreans*, p. 30.

27. Ginsburgs, "Citizenship," pp. 2–3; Anosov, pp. 9–10.

28. Russia, *Pereselenie na Dal'nii Vostok*, p. 12.

29. Kabuzan, *Dal'nevostochnyi krai*, pp. 85, 94–95; SSE, 2: 949.

30. Murov, pp. 35, 44.

31. Shin Chey in Suh, *Koreans*, p. 64.

32. Denisov, p. 22.

33. Murov, p. 35; Anosov, p. 12.

34. N. G. Garin-Mikhailovskii, *Sobranie sochinenii*, (Moscow: Goskhudozhizdat, 1958), 5:121.

35. Hara Teruyuki in Suh, *Koreans*, pp. 3–4; *V toi kipuchei bor'be*, p. 43. The following Korean newspapers were published in Vladivostok: *Haejo sinmun* (1908), *Taedong kongbo* (1908–10), and *Kwonop sinmun* (1912–14). Personal communication from Ban Byung-yool, 13 Sept. 1990.

36. Ochiai Tadashi, *Hoppō ryōdo* (Tokyo: Taka shobō, 1971), pp. 14–15; Ōkuma Ryō'ichi, *Hoppō ryōdo mondai no rekishiteki haikei* (Tokyo: Nanpō dōhō engokai, 1964), p. 330.

37. Ishizuka, p. 2.

38. The 4,000 figure is based on Vaskevich, Table IV. See also Valliant, p. 185; Katō, *Shiberia ki*, pp. 94–95; Russia, *Aziatskaia Rossiia*, 1: 80; and Kolarz, *Peoples*, p. 51.

39. Vaskevich, pp. 5–7; Katō, *Shiberia ki*, pp. 84–85; Kuzuu, 1: 591; Irie, 2: 432.

40. Ishimitsu, pp. 234–36; Katō, *Shiberia ki*, pp. 122–26; *Urajio nippō* 9, 11 Dec. 1917; Kondō, p. 31; Vaskevich, pp. 3, 8.

41. Hirano Ken'ichirō, quoted in *The Japan Times*, 24 June 1970.

42. Vaskevich, p. 4. The preponderance of women in the Japanese community continued into the next century. Irie, 2: 433.

43. Kondō, pp. 45, 76, 79–80, 87–90, 126; Kuzuu, 1: 593–95; Valliant, pp. 188–89.

44. Kuzuu, 1: 569–71, 593–95, 598–604; Katō, *Shiberia ki*, pp. 87–93, 143; Irie, 2: 431; Ōta, "Romantic Experience"; Ishimitsu, pp. 10, 68, 75–76.

45. Raikhman, *Economic Development*, pp. 18, 34; Alekseev, *Utro Sovetskoi Gavani*, p. 247; Ishizuka, pp. 2–4; Hara, *Shiberia shuppei*, pp. 4–6.

46. Filimonov, *Belopovstantsy*, p. 14.   47. Beveridge, pp. 128–29.

48. Gerrare, pp. 221–22.   49. Katō, *Shiberia ki*, p. 99.

50. *Obzor russkoi periodicheskoi pechati*, 4: 28–29.

51. Anosov, p. 10; Arsenjew, *Russen und Chinesen*, pp. 178–82; Kabuzan, *Dal'nevostochnyi krai*, p. 133; Siegelbaum, p. 311. Malozemoff, *Russian Far Eastern Policy*, p. 25.

52. Diary of former War Minister A. N. Kuropatkin, 30 Jan. (O.S.) 1906, *Krasnyi arkhiv*, 8 (1925): 84; Timofeev, p. 20.

53. Unterberger, *Priamurskii krai*, p. 419.

54. Anosov, p. 11, as quoted by Wada Haruki in Suh, *Koreans*, p. 29.

55. Anosov, p. 15, as quoted by Wada Haruki in ibid., pp. 30–31.

56. *Sibirskie voprosy*, 1911, no. 17: 27.

57. Denisov, p. 23.

58. Consul-general John F. Jewell, Vladivostok, to Secretary of State, 20 Apr. 1912. U.S., State Dept. decimal file 861a.55, M316, roll 175.

59. *Sibirskie voprosy*, 1911, no. 17: 27–28.

60. N. A. Popov, pp. 12, 17; Siegelbaum, pp. 323–24.

10 «» International Emporium

Epigraph. Olan'on, p. 248.

1. Saul, pp. 410–17.

2. Golder, "Russian-American Relations," p. 475.

3. Vysheslavtsev, pp. 272–76.

4. Saul, p. 419.

5. Consular files of Hawaiian Kingdom representatives in Russia, Hawaii State Archives, Honolulu; Knox, p. 119.

6. Vysheslavtsev, p. 271; L'vovich, p. 11; "I. Ya. Churin & Co.," *Manchuria*, 7, no. 9 (1 Sept. 1941): 323. IDV, 2: 264–65.

7. In 1900 the population of Vladivostok and Khabarovsk was 35,000 and 15,000 respectively. Beveridge, p. 230; Udovenko, p. 75; Vostrikov and Vostokov, p. 30; N. I. Riabov and Shtein, p. 127; Russia, *Pereselenie na Dal'nii Vostok*, p. 12; Kruber, *Aziatskaia Rossiia*, p. 538.

8. Vinogradov, p. 148; ES, 72: 946; Enomoto, pp. 223–36.

9. Queen, pp. 170, 201–2; Vanderlip, pp. 11–12; Olan'on, p. 249; Chikhachev, p. 552.

10. Gaunt, p. 174; Chernysheva, *Khabarovsk: 1858–1983*, p. 165.

11. Vaskevich, p. 2; Alekseev, *Kak nachinalsia Vladivostok*, pp. 134–59, 194; Khisamutdinov, *Terra incognita*, p. 104.

12. "Amurskoe delo," pp. 99–100; Malozemoff, *Russian Far Eastern Policy*, p. 8.

13. Amir Khisamutdinov, *Russian Far East*, p. 139. See also Khisamutdinov, *Terra incognita*, p. 214; Murov, pp. 8–9; Denisov, p. 34; Nikolai Matveev, p. 86; and Shkurkin, p. 36.

14. Great Britain, War Office, *Shores of the Northwest Pacific*, pp. 22–23.

15. Cao Tingjie, p. 8.

16. Ibid., p. 8; Chikhachev, p. 562; Biankin, pp. 14, 121; Great Britain, War Office, *Shores of the Northwest Pacific*, pp. 22, 25; Denisov, pp. 36–37, 43–44, 56; Zakharov et al., 3rd. ed., p. 72; Katō, *Shiberia ki*, p. 33; Malozemoff, *Russian Far Eastern Policy*, pp. 5–6; Nikolai Matveev, p. 150.

17. Sieveking, "Hamburgische Firma," pp. 268–99; Germany, Weltwirtschafts-archiv, Hamburg, "Kunst und Albers," pp. 4–17; SSE, 2: 1122; Olan'on, p. 249; Miagkoff, *Aux bords du Pacifique*, pp. 27–28, 33–34; Meakin, p. 245.

18. Personal communications from Cyril Bryner, 9 and 13 Sept. 1987; Malozemoff, *Russian Far Eastern Policy*, p. 177. For political and diplomatic maneuvers surrounding the Bryner concession, see White, *Diplomacy*, pp. 32–45.

19. A. F. Bonch-Osmolovskii in *Primor'e*, p. 304.

20. Merkulov, p. 9; Beveridge, p. 250; Vinogradov, pp. 123, 127; Gaunt, p. 159. For a guide to Vladivostok in 1909, see Bogdanov, *Putevoditel'*.

21. Gapanovich, 1: 131.

22. Shklovsky, *In Far North-east Siberia*, pp. 5–6, 8; SSE, 1: 364.

23. Swenson, p. 22.

24. Kennan, *Tent Life*, pp. 81–82, 104, 329–30.

25. Knox, p. 53.

26. Vanderlip, p. 64.

27. Miagkoff, *Aux bords du Pacifique*, p. 20.

28. Knox, p. 91.

29. Amfiteatrov, p. 349; Gapanovich, 2: 135–37.

30. Sverdlov, p. 96; *Ocherki istorii Chukotki*, p. 123; Gapanovich, 1: 131.

31. Malozemoff, *Russian Far Eastern Policy*, p. 4; Slezkine, "Russia's Small Peoples," pp. 215–30.

32. Cited in Parry, "Yankee Whalers," p. 36.

33. *Ocherki istorii Chukotki*, pp. 125–27; Vostrikov and Vostokov, pp. 87–94.

34. Vanderlip, p. 70; Parry, "Washington B. Vanderlip."

35. *Seattle Times*, 27 Jan. 1919; Korsakov, pp. 9–10, 25; Dikov, *Istoriia Chukotki*, p. 124. For a detailed first-hand account, see "Materialy po istorii Chukotskogo predpriatiia, 1900–1923," Mexico City, 1939, in Korzukhin Papers, Manuscripts Division, DL.

36. Gapanovich, 1: 71, 149, 135, 154; Korsakov, pp. 12–13; *Russkii Dal'nii Vostok*, 4 (Jan. 1921): 20.

37. Henry Adams to Henry Cabot Lodge, 4 Aug. 1891, in *Letters of Henry Adams (1858–1891)*, ed. W. C. Ford (Boston: Houghton Mifflin, 1930), 1: 511.

38. Enoch Emery to Ethan Allen Hitchcock, U.S. ambassador, St. Petersburg, cited in Queen, p. 101.

39. As noted by Amur steamship passengers Brodovich and Hoffmann (not further identified) in Kruber, *Aziatskaia Rossiia*, p. 540.

40. Richard T. Greener, "American Interests and Opportunities in Siberia," U. S. Dept. of Commerce, Bureau of Statistics, *Monthly Consular Reports*, 276 (Sept. 1903): 35. For McCormick and Deere advertising, see H. Norman, *All the Russias* (New York: Heinemann, 1902), p. 154. On corrugated roofs, Udovenko, p. 56. On *amerikanki*, see *Slovar' russkikh govorov Priamur'ia* (Moscow: Nauka, 1983), p. 13.

41. Derber and Sher, *Ocherki zhizni*, p. 237; Vostrikov and Vostokov, p. 251.

42. Malozemoff, *Russian Far Eastern Policy*, pp. 193–94; Olan'on, p. 248; Queen, p. 108. According to Weale (*Manchu*, p. 56), Khabarovsk was to a large extent dependent on food shipped down the Sungari.

43. Nikolai Matveev in *Priroda i liudi Dal'nego Vostoka*, no. 5 (Feb. 1906), n. p. I am grateful to Pat Polansky for bringing this item to my attention.

44. Viktor Panov, *Dal'nevostochnoe polozhenie*, p. 75; Merkulov, pp. 2, 29–38; Timofeev, p. 7; SSE, 4: 430–33; Unterberger, *Priamurskii krai*, p. 183; Korsakov, p. 17; Masuda, pp. 90–91; *Istoriia severo-vostochnogo Kitaia*, p. 296.

45. A. A. Panov, p. 16.

11 «» Stirrings of a Regional Consciousness

Epigraph. Cao Tingjie, "Xiboli dongpian jiyao," p. 8.

1. Maksim Kovalevsky, editor of *Vestnik Evropy*. Kovalevskii, p. 437.

2. Lantzeff, p. 33.

3. Bassin, "Russian Mississippi?," p. 191, n. 43; N. I. Riabov and Shtein, p. 116.

4. Semyonov, p. 278; Wolff, p. 125.

5. Raeff, p. 53.

6. Pereira, pp. 112–15; Dotsenko, *Struggle*, p. 3; *Sibirskie voprosy*, 1911, no. 17: 25; Stephen Watrous, "The Regionalist Conception of Siberia," in Diment and Slezkine, pp. 113–32. For a more detailed discussion, see Stephen Digby Watrous, "Russia's Land of the Future: Regionalism and the Awakening of Siberia, 1819–1894," Ph.D. diss., University of Washington, 1970.

7. Price, p. vii.

8. Quoted in Dotsenko, *Struggle*, p. 4.

9. Serebrennikov, "Siberian Autonomous Movement," p. 405.

10. Khisamutdinov, *Russian Far East*, p. 39n.

11. Lishchinskii, pp. 156–60; Bishop, pp. 254–61.

12. Vostrikov and Vostokov, pp. 55–62, 69–70; ES, 31: 354, 36: 946; SSE, 1: 786–87; Malozemoff, *Russian Far Eastern Policy*, p. 25.

13. Khisamutdinov, *Russian Far East*, p. 44.

14. Fraser, p. 192. On looting see also Witte, *Memoirs of Count Witte*, p. 108.

15. Latyshev, "Pis'ma Bronislava Pilsudskogo," pp. 173–74. The Sakhalin-Amur Oil Syndicate ran out of funds before it could sink any wells. For details, see Stephan, *Sakhalin*, pp. 93–94.

16. Viktor Panov, *Dal'nevostochnoe polozhenie*, p. 47.

17. Russia, *Aziatskaia Rossiia*, 1: 265–66.

18. D. S. Buzin-Bich in *Revoliutsiia na Dal'nem Vostoke*, p. 12.

19. *Khabarovskii Kadetskii Korpus*, pp. 49, 61; ES, 36: 946.

20. *Spravochnaia knizhka*; Grigortsevich, "Iz istorii otechestvennogo vostokove-

deniia"; Richard T. Greener, "Education Notes"; U.S. Consul Lester Maynard, Vladivostok, to Sec. State, 3 July 1909, U.S. State Dept. Archives, M862, roll 1096, item 20872.

21. *Spravochnaia knizhka*, pp. iii–vi.

22. Suggesting that it could be picked up at odd moments, the orientalist Berthold Laufer called Manchu a "breakfast language." Hartmut Walravens in "Russian Contributions to Manchu Studies," lecture at University of Hawaii, 15 May 1991; SSE, 1: 551.

23. Ligin, p. 96.

24. Grigortsevich, "Iz istorii otechestvennogo vostokovedeniia," p. 132.

25. Ibid., p. 133; *Spravochnaia knizhka*, pp. ii, ix, x. SSE, 4: 381–82.

26. Smirnov, pp. 2–4; *Testimony of Kolchak*, pp. 10–13; Amir Khisamutdinov in *Krasnoe znamia*, 5 Apr. 1989.

27. Khisamutdinov, "Vladimir Arsen'ev"; Zhernakov, p. 7.

28. Vostrikov and Vostokov, p. 114; Tarasova, *Vladimir Klavdievich Arsen'ev*, p. 218; Khisamutdinov, "Vladimir Arsen'ev"; Khisamutdinov, *Russian Far East*, pp. 83–84.

29. Tarasova, *Vladimir Klavdievich Arsen'ev*, pp. 40, 50–51; Khisamutdinov, "Vladimir Arsen'ev."

30. Khisamutdinov, *Terra incognita*, pp. 305–8; Khisamutdinov, "Vladimir Arsen'ev"; Vostrikov, pp. 74–75; Tarasova, *Vladimir Klavdievich Arsen'ev*, pp. 21, 107–8, 111, 136–37.

31. *Vestnik Azii* (1909–27); SSE, 1: 468; Walravens, *Rudakov*, p. 3.

32. Katō, *Shiberia ki*, p. 50; Grigortsevich, "Iz istorii otechestvennogo vostokovedeniia," p. 132.

12 «» Rumblings

Epigraph. Iz istorii revoliutsionnogo dvizheniia, p. 41.

1. N. I. Riabov and Shtein, p. 127.

2. Zotik Matveev, "Istoriia," p. 352.

3. Serebrennikov, "Siberian Autonomous Movement," p. 403.

4. *Ocherki istorii sovetskogo Primor'ia*, p. 32; Gubel'man, pp. 20–22; Kolykhalova, pp. 5, 24; Shindialov, pp. 21–22; *Iz istorii revoliutsionnogo dvizheniia*, pp. 14–17, 50.

5. Vetoshkin, p. 252; *Revoliutsionnoe dvizhenie*, p. 16. For deployments of Russian troops in Manchuria and the Priamur at this time, see Weale, *Truce*, p. 418.

6. *The Memoirs of Marshal Mannerheim*, tr. Count Eric Lewenhaupt (London: Cassell, 1953), pp. 21–22. For a general description of the uprisings, see Bushnell, pp. 86–89.

7. Quested, *"Matey" Imperialists?*, pp. 149–52; *Revoliutsionnoe dvizhenie*, pp. 91–94.

8. Chernysheva, *Khabarovsk, 1858–1983*, pp. 92–95; Shindialov, pp. 51–52; N. I. Riabov and Shtein, pp. 147–49; *Iz istorii revoliutsionnogo dvizheniia*, pp. 49, 54–56.

9. *Iz istorii revoliutsionnogo dvizheniia*, pp. 84–90.

10. Accounts differ about how the violence started. One source calls it spontaneous (*Ocherki istorii sovetskogo Primor'ia*, pp. 38–40). Another blames a local commander who refused to allow his troops to attend public lectures (IDV, 2: 343). Yet another attributes the riots to hooliganism (Nikolai Matveev, p. 284). Finally, there is the suggestion that the riot began when soldiers beat up Chinese tradesmen (Bushnell, p. 91). For casualty statistics, see Ascher, p. 270.

11. *Iz istorii revoliutsionnogo dvizheniia*, pp. 68–69; *Ocherki istorii sovetskogo Primor'ia*, p. 41; *Istoriia Sibiri*, 3: 277; IDV, 2: 344.

12. My description of the events of 23–27 January 1906 is based on: *Istoriia Sibiri*, 3: 287; *Iz istorii revoliutsionnogo dvizheniia*, pp. 71–74; *Revoliutsionnoe dvizhenie*, pp. 167–84; and IDV, 2: 345–47.

13. *Istoriia Sibiri*, 3: 287; *Iz istorii revoliutsionnogo dvizheniia*, pp. 74, 112; *Ocherki istorii sovetskogo Primor'ia*, p. 44.

14. *Istoriia Sibiri*, 3: 282–83; Striuchenko, *Pechat' Dal'nego Vostoka*, pp. 125–27. Serebrennikov, "Siberian Autonomous Movement," p. 406; Krivtsov, p. 152.

15. *Revoliutsionnoe dvizhenie*, pp. 38–73; *Iz istorii revoliutsionnogo dvizheniia*, pp. 26–31; Vetoshkin, pp. 128–62; *Istoriia Sibiri*, 3: 284; *Bol'sheviki*, p. 106; Bushnell, pp. 88–89; Vladimir Khokhlov, personal communication, 30 May 1993.

16. *Iz istorii revoliutsionnogo dvizheniia*, p. 39; Bushnell, p. 119.

17. SSE, 2: 1131–1132; *Leninskaia gvardiia*, pp. 62–63; *Iz istorii revoliutsionnogo dvizheniia*, p. 39.

18. *Zotik Nikolaevich Matveev*, pp. 2, 25; Levitskii, p. 11; Khisamutdinov, *Terra incognita*, pp. 230–31.

19. Vetoshkin, p. 252; *Ocherki istorii sovetskogo Primor'ia*, p. 45; *Iz istorii revoliutsionnogo dvizheniia*, pp. 75–77.

20. *Iz istorii revoliutsionnogo dvizheniia*, pp. 79–82; *Bol'sheviki*, pp. 112–15.

21. *Bol'sheviki*, p. 115. White, *Siberian Intervention*, p. 35. S. A. Garfield, founder of the Vladivostok newspaper *Dalekaia okraina* ("Distant periphery"), also authored a book of verse on the Russo-Japanese War. S. A. Garfil'd, *Russo-iaponskaia voina: Poema na sovremennie motivy* (Vladivostok, 1907). Copy deposited in the Library of the Society for Study of the Amur Region, Vladivostok.

22. For details, see Vetoshkin, pp. 163–206; *Ocherki istorii sovetskogo Primor'ia*, pp. 46–49; *Iz istorii revoliutsionnogo dvizheniia*, pp. 82, 125; and IDV, 2: 351.

23. Vetoshkin, pp. 221–52, 265, 271; *Ocherki istorii sovetskogo Primor'ia*, p. 49; IDV, 2: 352–53.

24. Udovenko, p. 71. Morley, "Russian Revolution," p. 452.

25. SSE, 1: 517.

26. Gubel'man, pp. 34–35; Levitskii, pp. 27–28, 34.

27. Interview with the late Peter Balakshin, 6 Dec. 1986; Balakshin, "Man from Primorye," p. 14; Chernysheva, *Khabarovsk, 1858–1958*, p. 47; IDV, 2: 420; Nikolai Matveev, pp. 297–99.

28. Fridtjof Nansen, *Through Siberia: The Land of the Future* (London: Heinemann, 1914), pp. 346–49.

29. Azadovskii and D'iakonova, pp. 34, 68–69, 73n.

30. Khisamutdinov, "Vladimir Arsen'ev;" *Vestnik Azii*, 1916, nos. 38–39: 50–76.

13 «» Revolution

Epigraph. Klipel in *Granitsa*, p. 15.

1. Gapanovich, 1: 74.

2. Unterberger, *Priamurskii krai*, pp. 399–400; Fedor Danilenko, p. 54.

3. GVVI (1983): 287–88; SSE, 2: 950; Anosov, p. 19; Hara in Suh, *Koreans*, p. 6; Morley, "Russian Revolution," pp. 450–54.

4. Dotsenko, *Struggles*, pp. 5–6; Svetachev, pp. 13, 19, 66.

5. Snow, p. 28; Nikiforov, p. 4; Svetachev, p. 19; Parfenov, *Uroki proshlogo*, p. 17; *Sel'skoe khoziaistvo*, p. 6.

6. V. Golionko, "Partiia i sovety v Khabarovske za period 1917–1918 gg.," *Dal'istpart*, 3: 8; *Dal'sovnarkom*, p. 8; Nikiforov, p. 5; Snow, pp. 50, 84, 88.

7. Fedor Danilenko, p. 75; Coleman, pp. 67–68.

8. Fedor Danilenko, pp. 75, 78.

9. Ibid., pp. 76–77; Coleman, pp. 57–59, 64–65.

10. *Dal'istpart*, 3: 8, 11.

11. Nikiforov, pp. 4, 6–7; *Dal'sovnarkom*, pp. 8, 340–41; *Leninskaia gvardiia*, pp. 482–83; Avdeeva and Chechulina, p. 40; Iakimov, *Geroicheskie gody*, p. 380.

12. Karpenko, p. 24.

13. *Dal'sovnarkom*, p. 341.

14. Krasnoshchekova, pp. 138–40; MERSH, 18: 42–46; Mukhachev, "Prezident respubliki," pp. 136–38; *Leninskaia gvardiia*, pp. 79, 133, 489; Iakimov, *Geroicheskie gody*, pp. 372, 379; Lerman, *Po serdtsu blizkie druz'ia*, p. 7; Montandon, p. 123; Norton, pp. 171–73, 184–86; GVVI (1983), p. 661.

15. Nikiforov, pp. 6–8, 10–12, 17; *Ocherki istorii sovetskogo Primor'ia*, pp. 63–65; *Leninskaia gvardiia*, p. 78; Gubel'man, p. 40.

16. *Dal'istpart*, 1: 142–43; Nikiforov, pp. 13–14; *V toi kipuchei bor'be*, p. 8.

17. Nikiforov, pp. 15–17; *Ocherki istorii sovetskogo Primor'ia*, p. 65.

18. Nikiforov, pp. 17–19; Gubel'man, pp. 44–45; Matveeva, *Poslantsy partii*, p. 8; *Ocherki istorii sovetskogo Primor'ia*, p. 66; *Dal'sovnarkom*, pp. 8–9. *V toi kipuchei bor'be*, p. 10.

19. *Revkomy Severo-Vostoka SSSR*, p. 230; Gubel'man, pp. 67–69; Parfenov, *Uroki proshlogo*, p. 17; Zhikharev, p. 12; Khisamutdinov, "Vladimir Arsen'ev."

20. White, *Siberian Intervention*, p. 79; Quested, *"Matey" Imperialists?*, pp. 309–24; Gubel'man, pp. 51–55; Nikiforov, p. 24; *Ocherki istorii sovetskogo Primor'ia*, pp. 68–69; *Istoriia Sibiri*, 4: 44.

21. *Dal'istpart*, 3: 21; *Dal'sovnarkom*, p. 11; *Partiinye organizatsii Sibiri*, p. 46; Nikiforov, pp. 24–26; N. I. Riabov and Shtein, pp. 52–53, 90–91, 182–83.

22. *Dal'sovnarkom*, pp. 3, 11, 19; Chernysheva, *Khabarovsk, 1858–1983*, p. 111; MERSH, 18: 42.

23. Nikiforov, pp. 29, 32, 28; Chernysheva, *Khabarovsk, 1858–1983*, p. 113; Avdeeva and Chechulina, p. 15; *V toi kipuchei bor'be*, p. 52.

24. *Za sovetskuiu vlast' v Iakutii*, pp. 16–23, 89; Tokarev, pp. 164, 221–22.

25. Gapanovich, 1: 74.

26. Zhikharev, pp. 10–27; *Sovety Severo-Vostoka SSSR (1928–1940)*, p. 274.

27. Zhikharev, pp. 27–32; *Ocherki istorii Chukotki*, pp. 149–51. For Krushanovian treatment of these events, see Mukhachev, *Stanovlenie sovetskoi vlasti*, pp. 90–130, and Dikov, *Istoriia Chukotki*, pp. 138–46. For a Siberian regionalist's perspective of these events, see Purin, "V dni revoliutsii."

14 «» Civil War

Epigraph. Kalmykov quoted in *Dal'istpart*, 1: 44.

1. *Dal'sovnarkom*, p. 27; Parfenov, *Uroki proshlogo*, p. 20; MERSH, 18: 43.

2. Karpenko, p. 29; Nikiforov, p. 46; Chernysheva, *Khabarovsk, 1858–1983*, pp. 112–13; *Dal'sovnarkom*, p. 13.

3. *K desiatiletiiu interventsii*, p. 118; Parfenov, *Uroki proshlogo*, p. 20; Nikiforov, pp. 42, 63; Svetachev, p. 70. On army grain purchases before 1917, personal communication from Nikolai Aleksandrovich Bilim, 31 July 1989.

4. *Partiinye organizatsii Sibiri*, p. 46.

5. Anosov, p. 20; Nikiforov, p. 44; Gubel'man, p. 81; *Dal'istpart*, 3: 21; FRUS, 1918, Russia, 2: 152.

6. GVVI (1983), p. 534; Iakimov, *Dal'nevostochnyi avangard*, p. 6; Nikiforov, p. 48; Gubel'man, p. 76; "Bulletin Number 3," Foreign Information Section, Omsk Gov't., 31 Oct. 1918, in Ackerman Papers, LC.

7. *Dal'sovnarkom*, p. 13; Nikiforov, pp. 24, 26; Morley, "Russian Revolution," p. 468; Karpenko, p. 29; Shishkin, pp. 14–17.

8. Materials on Blagoveshchensk in Varska and Shapiro collections, HA; Gubel'man, pp. 77–80; Hara, *Shiberia shuppei*, pp. 194–201; *Amurskaia oblast'*, pp. 131–32.

9. "Ravich" Report, in Varska Collection, HA.

10. Ibid.; Nikiforov, p. 39; Karpenko, p. 31.

11. "Ravich" Report (1938), in Varska Collection, HA; Blagoveshchensk accounts in Shapiro Collection, HA.

12. GVVI (1983), p. 235.

13. Ibid., pp. 88, 314; Girchenko, pp. 2–7.

14. SSE, 1: 517–18; Khramtsova, "Sozdanie," p. 6; Girchenko, pp. 11, 30–31.

15. "Memoirs," p. 6, in Shapiro Collection, HA.

16. GVVI (1987), p. 93. For his own version, see Albert Rhys Williams, *Through the Russian Revolution* (New York: Boni and Liveright, 1921).

17. FRUS, 1918, Russia, 2: 235. According to Hara, *Shiberia shuppei*, p. 348, 194 Red Guards died in combat.

18. For developments in Siberian regionalism at this juncture, see Pereira, "Regional Consciousness"; Pereira, "Democratic Counterrevolution"; Dotsenko, *Struggle*, pp. 20–24.

15 «» Intervention

Epigraph. Kharnskii, *Iaponiia v proshlom i nastoiashchem* (Vladivostok: Knizhnoe delo, 1926), pp. 214–15.

1. John Caldwell, U.S. consul-general Vladivostok, to Sec. State, 5 July 1918, in FRUS, 1918, Russia, 2: 261.

2. V. Sonin in *Dal'nevostochnaia panorama*, 1992, no. 1: 48–52. See also Mel'chin, *Razgrom*, p. 20; Gulyga, pp. 12–22; Gulyga and Geronimus, p. 2; Gubel'man, pp. 50, 74; Grigortsevich, *Amerikanskaia interventsiia*, p. 96; Samoilov, p. 278; Svetachev, pp. 8–9, 22, 59, 166; Before the Cold War Japanese territorial appetites were highlighted in the works of Parfenov, Vilenskii, Shumiatskii, Karpenko, Borisov, and Reikhberg, as well as in the Comintern tract *Iaponiia na russkom Dal'nem Vostoke*.

3. Katō, *Shiberia ki*, p. 102; White, *Siberian Intervention*, pp. 182–83; SSE, 2: 236; Hara, *Shiberia shuppei*, pp. 5–24. A Japanese-language newspaper *Urajio nippō*, began publication in Vladivostok on 20 December 1917.

4. Morley, *Japanese Thrust*, p. 219; Katō, *Shiberia ki*, p. 103; Hara, *Shiberia shuppei*, p. 217.

5. Such allegations appear in Mel'chin, *Razgrom*, p. 14; Gulyga, pp. 10, 13; Nikiforov, pp. 41, 52; Svetachev, p. 20; Grigortsevich, *Amerikanskaia interventsiia*, p. 22; Gubel'man, p. 81; Sonin, *Stanovlenie*, pp. 68–71.

6. Notably the newspaper *Dalekaia okraina*, according to *Deistviia Iaponii*, p. 1. See also Faulstich, 2: 16, in Hoover Library; FRUS, 1918, Russia, 2: 352; White, *Siberian Intervention*, pp. 194–95.

7. Faulstich, 2: 1, in Hoover Library.

8. Hayashi, p. 24; White, *Siberian Intervention*, p. 254.

9. Assertions that Americans took part in combat during the Czech-Japanese advance are contradicted by *Dal'istpart*, 1: 146–48; "Diary of a Russian Wolfhound," in Barrett Collection, HA; Faulstich, 2: 61, in Hoover Library; Charles Morrow interview, *Stars and Stripes*, 23 Aug. 1973; and FRUS, 1918, Russia, 2: 340–48.

10. *Dal'sovnarkom*, p. 25; FRUS, 1918, Russia, 2: 292; Grigortsevich, *Amerikanskaia interventsiia*, p. 52.

11. GVVI (1983), pp. 213, 524; Avdeeva and Chechulina, p. 42; Babichev, p. 152; Khramtsova, "Sozdanie," pp. 6–7; Khramtsova, "Internatsional'nye formirovaniia," p. 94; Lerman, *Po serdtsu blizkie druz'ia*, p. 11; *V toi kipuchei bor'be*, pp. 7, 49, 52; *Ekho partizanskikh sopok*, pp. 10, 29.

12. Nikiforov, p. 65; *Dal'istpart*, 1: 147; Gubel'man, p. 105.

13. *Dal'istpart*, 3: 39–40; *Dal'sovnarkom*, p. 25.

14. *Dal'istpart*, 3: 39–42; Kindall, pp. 18–19; Anosov, p. 21; *V toi kipuchei bor'be*, p. 55.

15. *Dal'sovnarkom*, pp. 25–26; Shishkin, pp. 34–39.

16. Gubel'man, p. 108; Girchenko, p. 28; Khramtsova, "Internatsional'nye formirovaniia," p. 93; Mankhart, *Zapiski internatsionalista*, p. 30.

17. *Delovaia Sibir'*. For a list of serials published in Vladivostok at this time, see Zotik Matveev, "Periodicheskaia pechat'."

18. Elesh, pp. 59–60; Smith, p. 63; Zotik Matveev, "Istoriia," p. 375; "Diary of a Russian Wolfhound," in Barrett Collection, HA.

19. *Kratkaia literaturnaia entsiklopediia*, 7: 431, 613; 8: 555–56; *Literaturnaia Sibir'*, 1: 285–90; Burliuk, p. 47.

20. *Vestnik Azii*, 1924, no. 52: 2–3. Until 1939, the university was usually referred to as the State Far Eastern University (GDU), but Far Eastern State University (DVGU) was also used. For examples of the latter, see Obshchestvo Vostokovedov pri DVGU, *Informatsionyi biulleten'*, 1930, no. 1. DVGU has been employed exclusively since the university reopened in 1956.

21. Kindall, p. 26; Montandon, p. 15; Diary, 1919, in Johnson Collection, HA.

22. Elesh, pp. 45–46.

23. Photograph of picnic, with captions, in Grace Bungey Collection, HA.

24. Vladimir Kuperman, "Kovcheg detei," *Dal'nii Vostok*, 1989, no. 1: 122–31.

25. "Diary of a Russian Wolfhound," p. 7, in Barrett Collection, HA; Faulstich, 2: 29, in Hoover Library.

26. Kondō, pp. 124–56. Harrison, p. 94.

27. Kindall, p. 216; "Diary of a Russian Wolfhound," p. 9, in Barrett Collection, HA; Elesh, pp. 59–60.

28. Diary, 1919, in Johnson Collection, HA.

29. Wenyon, pp. 77–78; Great Britain, War Office. *Shores of the Northwest Pacific*, p. 25.

30. Memoirs, pp. 4–6, in Yeaton Collection, HA; "Diary of a Russian Wolfhound," p. 10, in Barrett Collection, HA.

31. Kindall, pp. 198, 200, 229; "Diary of a Russian Wolfhound," pp. 7, 24, in Barrett Collection, HA.

32. Graves, pp. 86, 90.

33. Faulstich, 2: 71, in Hoover Library (Morrow quote); "Diary of a Russian

Wolfhound," p. 27, in Barrett Collection, HA; Kindall, pp. 198–200, 219, 249–50; *Deportation of Grigorii Semenov*, pp. 32–33.

34. Shurygin, p. 92; Elesh, p. 41; Iakushevskii, p. 115. Ivanov, p. 125, asserts, without documentation, that Americans actively assisted Kalmykov in his repressive measures.

35. Iakushevskii, pp. 112–18; Il'iukhov and Titov, p. 113; Shurygin, p. 90.

36. Joseph Freeman, *An American Testament* (New York: Farrar, Rinehart, 1936), pp. 355–64.

37. Gubel'man, p. 177; Iakimov, *Geroicheskie gody*, p. 353; Muchik, p. 198; Hara, *Shiberia shuppei*, pp. 570–71; Georgiev.

38. Dal'istpart, 3: 126.

39. Il'iukhov and Titov, p. 142; *Ekho*, 6 July 1919. English transcript of *Partizanskoe dvizhenie v Sibiri* (Moscow: Gosizdat, 1925), p. 3 in Varneck Collection, HA; Gubel'man, p. 117; N. A. Avdeeva in *Sel'skoe khoziaistvo*, p. 7.

40. *Japanese Intervention in the Russian Far East*, pp. 18–19. See also N. A. Popov, p. 137; Babichev, pp. 148–52, 158; Gubel'man, pp. 182–87; Kim, *Koreiskie internatsionalitsy*; Hara Teruyuki in Suh, *Koreans*, pp. 10–14; A. A. Beliaev, "Uchastie nanaitsev v bor'be za vlast' Sovetov," in *Dal'nii Vostok za 40 let sovetskoi vlasti*, pp. 172–83; and *Partiinye organizatsii sovetskogo severa*, p. 11.

41. Babichev, p. 157; Anosov, pp. 21–23.

42. Interview with the late Paul Dotsenko, Stanford, Calif., 29 Oct. 1986; "Polozhenie v Primorskoi oblasti," *Ekho*, 6 July 1919; N. A. Avdeeva in *Sel'skoe khoziaistvo*, p. 37.

43. Smith, p. 11; *Ocherki istorii sovetskogo Primor'ia*, pp. 81–82.

44. Il'iukhov and Titov, pp. 112–16; Il'iukhov and Samusenko, p. 117; "Suchanskaia dolina v gody grazhdanskoi voiny," *Krasnyi arkhiv* (1938), p. 43; Gulyga and Geronimus, pp. 73–76; G. F. Kennan "Soviet Historiography," p. 303; Nikiforov, pp. 85–86.

45. Il'iukhov and Titov, p. 131; Il'iukhov and Samusenko, p. 177. A Soviet source characterized the attack as an "annihilation" of Americans. Grigortsevich, *Amerikanskaia interventsiia*, p. 59.

46. Il'iukhov and Titov, pp. 129, 139. The 1962 edition of Il'iukhov's memoirs (Il'iukhov and Samusenko) upgrades Lazo to the status of a Bolshevik hero and concludes that the Suchan operation was a great success. Specific discrepancies between the first and second editions include the number of partisan dead (13 in 1928, 2 in 1962); how the Americans behaved ("retreated taking their dead and wounded with them," 1928 p. 133; "ran away," 1962, p. 123); and how Lazo's adjutant Yakov Popov died (killed by Whites on 13 June 1919, 1928, p. 141; killed by Americans in revenge for Romanovka, 1962, p. 144).

47. Graves, p. 91. The following information on Kalmykov's victims is drawn from Montandon, pp. 38, 96; and White, *Siberian Intervention*, p. 267.

48. Grigortsevich, *Amerikanskaia interventsiia*, p. 44–45; Gulyga and Geroni-

mus, p. 79; Gulyga, p. 15; Gusarevich and Seoev, p. 18; Sonin, *Velikii Oktiabr'*, p. 76; N. Larionova, "Pogovorim ob okkupantakh," *Pravda*, 9 Jan. 1987; Avdeeva and Chechulina, p. 17; Mel'chin, *Razgrom*, p. 21; Gubel'man, p. 143; Ivanov, pp. 120–35.

49. U.S. Congress, 66th Congress, 1st Session, *Congressional Record* (Washington: Government Printing Office, 1919), p. 4901; G. F. Kennan, "Soviet Historiography," p. 304.

50. Mankhart, *Zapiski internatsionalista*, p. 32; *Dal'istpart*, 1: 51; Gubel'man, p. 129; Nikiforov, pp. 81–83; Sugimori and Fujimoto, pp. 287–91; Hara, *Shiberia shuppei*, pp. 475–78.

51. "Diary of a Russian Wolfhound," p. 22, in Barrett Collection, HA.

52. Elesh, p. 70; Svetachev, p. 205; Grigortsevich, *Amerikanskaia interventsiia*, p. 63; Smith, pp. 14–15.

53. Boldyrev, *Direktoriia*, p. 305.

54. The Kalmykov material in the text and the accompanying footnote is based on Montandon, p. 95; Elesh, p. 81; and MERSH, 41: 139.

55. Gutman, p. 178; *Khabarovskii Kadetskii Korpus*, pp. 85–86.

56. Nikiforov, pp. 114–15; Avdeeva and Chechulina, p. 39; Grigortsevich, *Amerikanskaia interventsiia*, pp. 65, 74.

57. "Diary of a Russian Wolfhound," p. 28, in Barrett Collection, HA.

58. Kindall, p. 250.

16 «» The Far Eastern Republic

Epigraph. Skvirsky quoted in *Far Eastern Republic, Siberia, and Japan*, p. 1. Skvirsky was then the republic's deputy minister of foreign affairs.

1. Debo, pp. 398–99.

2. A. M. Krasnoshchekov, "Dal'nevostochnaia Respublika," 14 Nov. 1920, reproduced in *Region*, Dec. 1990, p. 2; Nikiforov, p. 175.

3. Papin, p. 132; interview with Paul Dotsenko, Stanford, Calif., 14 Oct. 1986; Svetachev, p. 240; Elesh, pp. 109–18; Grigortsevich, *Amerikanskaia interventsiia*, p. 95; Kaplin, p. 62.

4. Norton, p. 136.

5. Borisov, p. 25; Iakimov, *Dal'nii Vostok*, pp. 12–13; Grigortsevich, *Amerikanskaia interventsiia*, p. 86.

6. Hayashi, pp. 26–27; Iakimov, *Dal'nii Vostok*, p. 12.

7. The following reconstruction of events in Nikolaevsk is based upon Aussem; Buzin-Bich; Dneprovskii; Emel'ianov; and Ovchinnikov, "Memoirs of the Red Partisan Movement," pp. 304–72; Ech; Gutman; Ishizuka; Hara, *Shiberia shuppei*, pp. 518–25, 536–44; *Nihon gaikōshi jiten*, pp. 637–38; and *Shuppei shi*, 2: 400–401.

8. Hayashi, p. 27.

9. Grigortsevich, *Amerikanskaia interventsiia*, pp. 76–77; Borisov, pp. 34–35;

White, *Siberian Intervention*, p. 364. The following account of Lazo's death is taken from the memoirs of M. I. Gubelman in *Taezhnye pokhody*, p. 188; Elesh, p. 89; and Iakimov, *Dal'nii Vostok*, p. 8.

10. Papin, p. 142; Elesh, pp. 96–97; *Krasnyi ostrov*, p. 342; Smith, p. 44.

11. An official history of the Far Eastern party organization published in 1923–24 described Triapitsyn's men as "representatives of the Red Army" and noted that "all peaceful Japanese citizens including women and children were destroyed." *Dal'istpart*, 1: 119; 2: 137–38. An encyclopedia published in 1929–32 noted that "Triapitsyn shot all Japanese prisoners" and practiced "unnecessary and thoughtless cruelty." SSE, 2: 301; 3: 764. But after the 1950s, Soviet historians made no reference to the presence or death of Japanese women and children in Nikolaevsk, instead inflating the size of the Japanese garrison. Papin, p. 133; Gubel'man, pp. 118n, 208; Elesh, p. 111; Nikiforov, pp. 121–24.

12. Sentiments aroused by the incident are graphically expressed in Mizoguchi. Some Soviet historians alleged that the Japanese and Triapitsyn plotted the incident together. Borisov, p. 28; Avdeeva and Chechulina, p. 48.

13. Elesh, pp. 100–101.

14. Ibid., pp. 87–88; Smith, p. 54; Chernysheva, *Khabarovsk, 1858–1983*, pp. 54, 124, 132.

15. Smith, pp. 24–26; Papin, pp. 131–36; Nikiforov, pp. 118–20; Gubel'man, p. 176; Elesh, pp. 81–83; Iakimov, *Dal'nii Vostok*, p. 3; Svetachev, p. 215; Avdeeva and Chechulina, p. 49.

16. Smith, p. 49; MERSH, 8: 160; Papin, pp. 140, 166; Elesh, p. 109; Iakimov, *Dal'nii Vostok*, pp. 12–13; *Krasnyi ostrov*, p. 349.

17. White, *Siberian Intervention*, p. 371; Parfenov, *Na soglashatelskikh frontakh*; Smith, pp. 60–61.

18. Hayashi, p. 27; Iakimov, *Dal'nii Vostok*, p. 46; Papin, pp. 155, 174; Debo, pp. 382–84.

19. Hayashi, p. 28; Shumiatskii, pp. 32–33; Iakimov, *Dal'nii Vostok*, p. 51.

20. Smith, p. 71; Avdeeva and Chechulina, p. 49; Nikiforov, p. 153.

21. For the text of the 30 Dec. 1920 treaty, see Far Eastern Republic Collection, HA. See also *K desiatiletiiu interventsii*, p. 124.

22. Smith, pp. 71–78.

23. Shumiatskii, p. 34; Smith, pp. 96–100; *Ocherki istorii sovetskogo Primor'ia*, p. 86.

24. Smith, p. 119; *K desiatiletiiu interventsii*, p. 93.

25. Igor' Kobzev, "S krasnym flagom protiv krasnykh," *Ogonek*, 1990, no. 30: 9–12; Filimonov, *Belopovstantsy*, 1: 60–62; *Pervopokhodnik*, 22 (Dec. 1974): 46–50; Boldyrev, *Direktoriia*, p. 406.

26. Smith, pp. 128–30; White, *Siberian Intervention*, p. 390; Grigortsevich, *Amerikanskaia interventsiia*, pp. 147–49, 194–96.

27. Ianguzov, *Zabven'ia net*, p. 135.

28. Iakimov, *Dal'nii Vostok*, pp. 31, 37. Partisans refusing to disband or subordinate themselves to the NRA were liquidated. Nikiforov, p. 179.

29. Filimonov, *Belopovstantsy*, 2: 13.

30. Boldyrev, *Direktoriia*, p. 458.

31. Blücher to Molchanov, 23 Feb. 1922, in V. K. Bliukher, pp. 88–90.

32. *Vestnik DVR*, 3 (July 1922): 17; Vainshtein; Vasil'chenko; Avdeeva, *Dal'nevostochnaia narodnaia respublika*, p. 46; V. N. Fomin in *Iz istorii Dal'nevostochnoi respubliki*, pp. 92–103; Khisamutdinov, *Russian Far East*, p. 104. For details of GPO, see Sonin, *Stanovlenie*, pp. 218–26; and *Shchit i mech Priamur'ia*, pp. 21–31.

33. Until the 1930s the U.S. role in Japan's withdrawal was acknowledged in some Soviet accounts. See, for example, Speransky in *K desiatiletiiu interventsii*, p. 94; Parfenov, *Na soglashatelskikh frontakh*, p. 208.

34. Smith, pp. 148–49, 151, 153–55; *Khabarovskii Kadetskii Korpus*, p. 95; Hayashi, p. 30.

35. Yamauchi, *Urajio to Enkaishū*, p. 398; Iakimov, *Dal'nii Vostok*, p. 87.

36. Filimonov, *Konets belogo Primor'ia*, p. 316; Smith, p. 162; Hayashi, p. 30.

37. Elesh, pp. 201–202; Iakimov, *Dal'nii Vostok*, p. 97.

38. Smith, pp. 164–65; Memoirs, 2: 4. in Stark Collection, HA.

39. P. P. Petrov, p. 235; GVVI (1983), p. 70; *Shchit i mech*, p. 48; Smith, pp. 164–65; Khisamutdinov, *Russian Far East*, p. 104.

40. Filimonov, *Konets belogo Primor'ia*, pp. 355–57, 362.

41. *Pervopokhodnik*, 22 (Dec. 1974): 46.

17 «» Anomalous Enclave

Epigraph. V. I. Lenin, *Collected Works*, 4th ed. (Moscow: Progress, 1966): 33: 437.

1. Gapanovich, 1: 136.

2. Zakharov et al. (1981), p. 99.

3. Mukhachev, *Sovety Severo-Vostoka SSSR*, p. 7; *Revkomy Severo-Vostoka SSSR*, pp. 3, 10, 15; *Dal'revkom*, pp. 10–11, 215.

4. *Revkomy Severo-Vostoka SSSR*, pp. 27, 229; *Dal'revkom*, p. 84; *Leninskaia gvardiia*, pp. 487, 350; Iakimov, *Geroicheskie gody*, pp. 364, 380; Iakimov, *Dal'nii Vostok*, p. 99.

5. Gapanovich, 1: 76–77; *Ocherki istorii Chukotki*, pp. 150–54; Zhikharev, pp. 27–36, 42–46, 48, 60–63, 70–72.

6. *Revkomy Severo-Vostoka SSSR*, p. 5; *Ocherki istorii Chukotki*, pp. 160–64; Zhikharev, pp. 85, 108; Gapanovich, 1: 78–79; *Granitsa*, p. 5; Swenson, p. 155.

7. GVVI (1987), p. 697; Tokarev, p. 228.

8. Vishnevskii, pp. 18–19; SSE, 4: 8; Ianguzov, *Ot Volgi do Tikhogo*, pp. 150–65.

9. MERSH, 27: 171; GVVI (1987), p. 697; Tokarev, pp. 232–33; G. Grachev, "Iakutskii pokhod," pp. 39–40; Vishnevskii, p. 191; *Revkomy Severo-Vostoka SSSR*, pp. 5, 54–55.

10. GVVI (1987), p. 531; Fetisov, p. 93; Pashkov, *Za krai rodnoi*, pp. 26–28.

11. Kornilov, "From Siberia to Finland," pp. 105–7; *Dal'nevostochnyi pograni-chnyi*, pp. 43–44.

12. Soviet historians differed about the identity of those from whom Wrangel was liberated: "Anglo-Americans," *Revkomy Severo-Vostoka SSSR*, p. 9; "Americans," Grigortsevich, *Amerikanskaia interventsiia*, p. 194, *Dal'nevostochnyi pogranichnyi*, p. 40; "English," Biankin, p. 77, *Voprosy istorii partiinykh organizatsii*, p. 51; "Anglo-Canadians," *Ocherki istorii Chukotki*, p. 177. For Stefansson's view of these events, see his *Adventure of Wrangell Island*.

13. Pashkov, *Za krai rodnoi*, p. 25.

14. Derber and Sher, *Ocherki zhizni*, p. 213; Pashkov, "Deiatel'nost' kommuni-sticheskoi partii," p. 13.

15. *Pogranichnye voiska SSSR, 1918–1928*, pp. 800–801; *Dal'revkom*, p. 246; *Dal'ne-vostochnyi pogranichnyi*, p. 46. *Shchit i mech Priamur'ia*, pp. 39–40.

16. *Sorempō nenkan, 1943–1944*, pp. 1051–1056 (text of USSR State Frontier Law of 7 Sept. 1923); Pashkov, *Za krai rodnoi* , pp. 10, 12, 13; *Dal'nevostochnyi pograni-chnyi*, pp. 23–30.

17. *Pogranichnye voiska SSSR, 1918–1928*, p. 803.

18. *Dal'nevostochnyi pogranichnyi*, p. 31. See also *Revkomy Severo-Vostoka SSSR*, pp. 102–3.

19. *Revkomy Severo-Vostoka SSSR*, pp. 5, 23–24, 34–35, 76; *Granitsa na zamke*, pp. 85–86; *Pogranichnye voiska SSSR, 1918–1928*, p. 803.

20. Lapin, pp. 19, 28–29; Galkin, pp. 199–214.

21. Raikhman, *Economic Development*, p. 31; *Dal'revkom*, p. 13.

22. Udovenko, p. 71.

23. SSE, 2: 304; Gubel'man, p. 120.

24. Kandidov, pp. 14–15, 18–43, 60; Il'iukhov and Titov, pp. 153–55; White, *Siberian Intervention*, pp. 294–95.

25. Krivtsov, p. 129; Arsenjew, *Russen und Chinesen*, p. 58; *Voprosy istorii par-tiinykh organizatsii*, p. 13; *Vol'naia Sibir'*, 1927, no. 1: 68; Boldyrev, "Iaponiia," p. 192; Yamauchi, *Urajio to Enkaishū*, pp. 100–101; Gapanovich, 1: 179; Fetisov, p. 37; Raikhman, *Economic Development*, p. 19; Rybakovskii, p. 78. Information on Wagner and Kühlborn, courtesy of Dr. Maria Keipart, German Foreign Ministry Archives, Bonn. For details on Japanese fisheries, see Sukhovii, pp. 69–81.

26. Tselishchev, pp. 49–51. See also SSE, 1: 720; Kolarz, *Peoples*, p. 45; and *Dal'revkom*, p. 250.

27. *Organizatsionno-khoziaistvennaia deiatel'nost'*, pp. 3–21; *Voprosy istorii partii-nykh organizatsii*, p. 11; *Revkomy Severo-Vostoka SSSR*, pp. 141–43; SSE, 1: 767; Tseli-shchev, p. 111; Smith, p. 165; Paul Dotsenko, interview, Stanford, Calif., 14 Oct. 1986.

28. Derber and Sher, *Ocherki zhizni*, pp. 13, 34–35, 55–56, 61, 72–73, 135–36, 275, 294.

29. Arkhipov, p. 167.

30. *Ian Gamarnik*, pp. 32, 94; *Dal'revkom*, p. 247; *Ves' Dal'nii Vostok*.

31. Kostikov, p. 29.

32. Koltsov, p. 87.

33. C. K. Cumming and Walter W. Pettit, eds., *Russian-American Relations, March 1917–March 1920: Documents and Papers* (New York: Harcourt Brace, 1920), p. 211.

34. *The Far Eastern Republic, Siberia, and Japan*, p. 2; A. A. Yazikov, FER delegation head, to Herbert Hoover, 15 Dec. 1921, in Far Eastern Republic Collection, HA; G. S. Saradzhan in *Deiatel'nost' kommunisticheskoi partii*, pp. 75–77.

35. Parry, "Washington B. Vanderlip"; Shishkov, pp. 232–33.

36. Speech delivered at a meeting of secretaries of the Moscow Party organization, 26 Nov. 1920. *V. I. Lenin: Sochineniia*, ed. N. I. Bukharin et al. (Moscow: Gosizdat, 1931), 25: 502. The full text of this speech, including the remark alluded to, was not reprinted in subsequent editions of Lenin's collected works.

37. Koltsov, p. 87; Elesh, p. 106; Raikhman, *Economic Development*, p. 14; Kostikov, p. 34; *Dal'revkom*, p. 252.

38. Fithian, pp. 205–22; Stephan, *Sakhalin*, pp. 101–3.

39. Swenson, pp. 154–55, 172–266. Swenson nonetheless recrudesced as a bête noire in postwar Soviet sources. See, for example, *Revkomy Severo-Vostoka SSSR*, pp. 8, 76, 86, 94–96; *Ian Gamarnik*, p. 95; Pashkov, *Za rodnoi krai*, p. 51; Elesh, p. 206; Raikhman, *Economic Developments*, p. 19; Ianguzov, *Ian Gamarnik*, p. 30.

40. Kostikov, pp. 29–36; Koltsov, pp. 89–90.

41. Veniukov, p. 17.

42. Khudiakov, "Avtobiografiia"; Personal communication, Nikolai Bilim, 31 July 1989. *Sotsial'no-ekonomicheskoe razvitie dal'nevostochnoi derevni*, pp. 3, 4, 32; *Dal'sovnarkom*, p. 7; *Ocherki istorii sovetskogo Primor'ia*, p. 95; Kozhevin, p. 134.

43. *Sel'skoe khoziaistvo*, pp. 29–30; Mikhail Kuznetsov, p. 233; *Ocherki istorii sovetskogo Primor'ia*, p. 92; *Partiinye organizatsii Sibiri*, pp. 142–43.

44. Sanachev, "Krest'ianskoe," pp. 177, 180, asserts that "no less than a thousand" peasants were killed, of whom only eight were bona fide kulaks. See also Flerov, *Dal'nii Vostok*, pp. 399n, 409, 422–23; and Chausov, "Dal'nevostochnoe krest'ianstvo," p. 53.

45. *Vol'naia Sibir'*, 1927, no. 1: 168; Brianskii, pp. 58–59; *Priamur'e moe*, p. 307.

46. Kandidov, pp. 25–26; *Leninskaia gvardiia*, pp. 449, 481.

47. USSR, KPSS, Dal'kraikom, p. 81; SSE, 2: 951; Mikhail Kuznetsov, pp. 198, 209, 210.

48. Lopatin moved from Vladivostok to Chita in 1923 (*Novyi Dal'nii Vostok*, 12–13 [10 Aug. 1923]: 170) prior to emigrating to Harbin in 1925.

49. Nesmelov, "Odinochestvo," *Invalid*, 4 Sept. 1922.

50. Khisamutdinov, *Russian Far East*, p. 87; *Vestnik Azii*, 1924, no. 52: 1–8; Walravens, *Rudakov*, pp. 26–27.

51. Mark Gayn, *Journey from the East* (New York: Knopf, 1944), p. 104.

52. Mikhail Kuznetsov, pp. 93–96, 100–111, 119. See also SSE, 1: 767; MERSH, 11: 56–58; *Dal'revkom*, p. 128; Amir Khisamutdinov in *Krasnoe znamia*, 19 June 1993.

53. Khisamutdinov, *Terra incognita*, pp. 309–13; Matveeva, pp. 103–6; SSE, 3: 332; *V toi kipuchei bor'be*, pp. 387–95; *Revkomy Severo-Vostoka SSSR*, p. 234; Mikhail Kuznetsov, pp. 129–30. On first DVGU Oriental Faculty graduate, see *Sibirskie ogni*, 1928, no. 3: 246.

54. Conversation with Amir Khisamutdinov, Honolulu, 21 June 1992.

55. Khisamutdinov, *Terra incognita*, p. 322; Khisamutdinov, "Vladimir Arsen'ev."

56. Slezkine, "Fall of Soviet Ethnography," p. 477.

57. Khisamutdinov, *Terra incognita*, pp. 324–25.

58. Khisamutdinov, "Vladimir Arsen'ev." According to Titov's daughter, he was a "confirmed Communist." Quoted in Suturin, *Delo kraevogo masshtaba*, p. 104.

59. Khisamutdinov, *Terra incognita*, p. 314; Khisamutdinov, *Russian Far East*, pp. 84–85.

60. Torii, p. 135.

61. For details, see Khisamutdinov, *Terra incognita*, pp. 313–14; Khisamutdinov, "Vladimir Arsen'ev."

62. A. N. Lipskii, *'Goldy' I. A. Lopatina: Kriticheskii obzor chasti knigi* (Vladivostok: Gosudarst. Dal'nevostoch. Univ., 1925). Sponsored by Dalrevkom, Lipsky's work carried an intimidating cachet of political correctness.

63. Tarasova, "Pis'ma," p. 76.

64. Material on Arseniev in this paragraph was taken from Zasel'skii, 1: 153; Tarasova, *Vladimir Klavdievich Arsen'ev*, pp. 24–25, 31, 164–65, 183n, 262–64, 275, 320; and the following works by Khisamutdinov, "Vladimir Arsen'ev;" *Terra incognita*, pp. 323–29; and *Russian Far East*, pp. 87–90.

65. For a photo of Yankovsky and his guests at Novina, see *Rubezh* [Harbin], 29 (13 July 1935): 10. For Russian émigré community in Korea, see Clark ms. For Comintern in Vladivostok, see report of U.S. consul, Harbin, 14 Oct. 1930, appended to "Bolshevik" File no. 19086–106, doc. 18868, Insular Bureau, War Dept., NARS, RG 350 (126).

66. Glushchenko, pp. 179–81; *Dal'nevostochnoe morskoe parokhodstvo*, pp. 559–60; Kolarz, *Peoples*, p. 46; For a photo of White Russian children waving banners hailing the Japanese Empire, see *Japan in Pictures* 6, no. 6 (June 1938): 9.

67. USSR, KPSS, *XV s"ezd*, 2: 1552; SSE, 2: 950–51; A. Suturin in *Priamurskie vedomosti*, 12 Feb. 1991; Wada Haruki in Suh, *Koreans*, p. 38; USSR, KPSS, Dal'kraikom, p. 410.

18 «» The Far Eastern Cohort

Epigraph. Gamarnik quoted by E. M. Borisov in Ianguzov, *Ian Gamarnik*, p. 27.

1. Jerry F. Hough and Merle Fainsod, *How the Soviet Union Is Governed* (Cam-

bridge, Mass.: Harvard Univ. Press, 1979), p. 88; Schapiro, p. xiii; Getty, p. 6.

2. Krivtsov, p. 153; *Leninskaia gvardiia*, p. 350.

3. *Voprosy istorii partiinykh organizatsii*, p. 12.

4. For a list of oppositionists expelled at the Party Congress, see USSR, KPSS, *XV s″ezd*, 2: 1397. For biographical information on Tarkhanov, see Volobuev and Chernyi, p. 213. For information on Smilga, see MERSH, 36: 26.

5. At the Congress, E. M. Yaroslavsky ridiculed an oppositionist banner unfurled during a 7 Nov. parade in Spassk. USSR, KPSS, *XV s″ezd*, 1: 542.

6. Lemeshko, pp. 130–31; DVO (1), p. 206.

7. Elesh, p. 99; Lemeshko, pp. 131–32.

8. Lemeshko, p. 143; See also Mikhail Kuznetsov, p. 182; and DVO (1), pp. 204–5.

9. Avdeeva and Chechulina, p. 51. At the 11th Party Congress in 1922, Dalbiuro secretary A. B. Buiko announced without apology that Far Eastern party secretaries had not held a regional conference to elect delegates to the Moscow congress. USSR, KPSS, *XI s″ezd*, p. 368.

10. Iakimov, *Geroicheskie gody*, pp. 354–58, 372, 380; *Dal'revkom*, p. 84; *Leninskaia gvardiia*, pp. 487, 502, 505; *Revkomy Severo-Vostoka SSSR*, pp. 27, 59, 229, 231, 278; Leonov *Ocherki istorii*, p. 65; Gubel'man, pp. 137–38.

11. *Ian Gamarnik*, p. 93.

12. Ibid., pp. 99, 104; Ianguzov, *Ian Gamarnik*, pp. 34, 36, 41, 44, 58; Salekhov, p. 47; MERSH, 12: 74.

13. Schapiro, pp. 256, 262; Rigby, *Political Elites*, pp. 61–62.

14. Salekhov, p. 48; *Dal'revkom*, p. 17; *Leninskaia gvardiia*, p. 390; Samoilov, p. 242.

15. Recollection of M. B. Kuzenits in Ianguzov, *Ian Gamarnik*, p. 50; See also *V toi kipuchei bor'be*, p. 281; DVO (1), p. 344; *Ocherk istorii Khabarovskoi kraevoi organizatsii KPSS*, p. 475; *Dal'revkom*, p. 17; Salekhov, p. 53; *Voprosy istorii partiinykh organizatsii*, p. 14; Iakimov, *Geroicheskie gody*, p. 358; Iakimov, *Dal'nevostochnyi avangard*, pp. 67, 95; *Nichi-Ro nenkan*, p. 559; and *Kyokutō Soren yōran*, p. 4.

16. Work on a Far Eastern encyclopedia, directed by V. Ya. Volynsky, head of the Dalkraikom Publication Department and a former political exile in Yakutia, was inaugurated in 1928 with the plan of publishing four volumes in 1931. During the next two years, an editorial staff of 150 and 566 contributors (including émigré Vladimir Yokhelson) prepared 10,187 entries. A prospectus was published in 1930, but the encyclopedia itself never appeared. *Entsiklopediia Dal'nevostochnogo kraia*. On the 1924 Far Eastern Olympiad in Khabarovsk, see *Tikhookeanskaia zvezda*, 5 Oct. 1991.

17. Gamarnik in *Na novom puti*, pp. 11–15; *Voprosy istorii partiinykh organizatsii*, p. 24; *Dal'revkom*, pp. 233–34, 253; Ianguzov, *Ian Gamarnik*, pp. 29–30, 35; Tarasova, *Vladimir Klavdievich Arsen'ev*, p. 309; Salekhov, p. 50.

18. *Dal'revkom*, pp. 234, 254; Ianguzov, *Ian Gamarnik*, p. 12; Chudesov, p. 72; Salekhov, p. 50; SSE, 1: 914.

19. *Nisso bōeki handobukku*, p. 216; *Stanovlenie sovetsko-kitaiskikh otnoshenii*, p. 99; Raikhman, *Economic Development*, p. 31; *Dal'revkom*, p. 256; Ianguzov, *Ian Gamarnik*, p. 58; Lamin, *Kliuchi k dvum okeanam*, p. 106. For an overview of the Far Eastern economy in 1926, see *Proizvoditel'nye sily Dal'nego Vostoka*.

20. Krivtsov, p. 142; Mikhail Kuznetsov, pp. 16–77; Bensman, *Kul'turnoe stroitel'stvo*, pp. 6–8; Raikhman, *Economic Development*, p. 41. For an account of these efforts on northern Sakhalin, see Grant, pp. 86–91.

21. *Voprosy istorii Dal'nego Vostoka*, 3: 129.

22. For more about the Komitet Sodeistviia Narodnostiam Severnykh Okrain, see Zhikharev, p. 129; *Ocherki istorii Chukotki*, p. 172; *Leninskaia gvardiia*, p. 391; Mikhail Kuznetsov, p. 112; and Slezkine, "Russia's Small Peoples," pp. 278–99.

23. *Revkomy Severo-Vostoka SSSR*, pp. 103–4; *Dal'revkom*, pp. 183–85; *Partiinye organizatsii sovetskogo severa*, pp. 30–32; Mikhail Kuznetsov, p. 236; *Ocherki istorii Chukotki*, pp. 184–90; *Spravochnik po DV kraiu na 1927 god*, p. 86; Grant, p. 100.

24. Gamarnik quoted in *Na rubezhe* (Khabarovsk), 1934, no. 2: 39; *Revkomy Severo-Vostoka SSSR*, pp. 128–29.

25. On the persistence of disease, see G. Petrov, *Ukrepim sovety DVK*, p. 112. On intellectual semi-literacy, see Ilya Ehrenburg, *Memoirs: 1921–1941* (New York: World, 1964), p. 226.

26. Slezkine, "Fall of Soviet Ethnography," p. 483.

27. Lapin, *Tikhookeanskii dnevnik*, pp. 19, 27. See also Krivtsov, p. 149; Gapanovich, 1: 111.

28. USSR, KPSS, *XV s"ezd*, p. 5.

29. Salekhov, pp. 57, 66; Ianguzov, *Ian Gamarnik*, pp. 55, 61.

19 «» Red-Bannered Satraps

Epigraph. Chiang Kai-shek, *Soviet Russia in China* (New York: Farrar, Straus, 1957), p. 51, a translation of Jiang Zhongzheng, *Su E zai Zhongguo* (Taibei: Zhongyang wenwu gongying she, 1957).

1. IDV, 2:230.

2. John Erickson, personal communication, 14 Mar. 1986.

3. G. Bliukher, 1990, no. 1: 8.

4. Iakimov, *Dal'nevostochnyi avangard*, p. 76; *Krasnoznamennyi Dal'nevostochnyi* (1971), p. 112.

5. *Pravda*, 11 Nov. 1936.

6. *Krasnoznamennyi Dal'nevostochnyi* (1971), p. 113; Ianguzov, *Osobaia Krasnoznamennaia*, p. 25.

7. Ianguzov, *Zabven'ia net*, p. 258; Kondrat'ev, p. 254; Ianguzov, *Osobaia Kras-*

noznamennaia, pp. 36, 41, 226; *Krasnoznamennyi Dal'nevostochnyi* (1979), p. 94; Mantetsu, Harbin jimusho, "Kyokutō chihō chūō tō kikan no soshiki," p. 21, in LC.

8. Kartunova, pp. 12–13; Ianguzov, *Ian Gamarnik*, p. 19.

9. Erickson, *Soviet High Command*, p. 241; Erickson, "Military and Strategic Factors," p. 177; Ianguzov, *Osobaia Krasnoznamennaia*, pp. 29–30; *Soren kyokutō sōran*, p. 429; "Soviet Russia in the Orient," Olferieff Collection, HA.

10. Hayashi, pp. 39–42; Erickson, *Soviet High Command*, p. 244; *Krasnoznamennyi Dal'nevostochnyi* (1971), p. 115; *Krasnoznamennyi Dal'nevostochnyi* (1979), p. 87.

11. Kondrat'ev, p. 269.

12. Ibid., pp. 271–73; Kartunova, p. 12.

13. G. Bliukher, 1989, no. 4: 81, 85.

14. USSR, KPSS, Dal'kraikom, p. 71.

15. *Krasnoznamennyi Dal'nevostochnyi* (1979), p. 95.

16. Coox, *Nomonhan*, 1: 76–78; Mackintosh, p. 173.

17. This figure includes 30,000 border guards. "Territorials" redeployed from Western Siberia and the Volga were turned into cadre troops in the Far East. Ianguzov, *Osobaia Krasnoznamennaia*, p. 157; Hayashi, p. 76; *Soren kyokutō sōran*, p. 360; Coox, "L'Affaire Lyushkov," pp. 414, 419.

18. *Sel'skoe khoziaistvo*, p. 68. See also Rybakovskii, p. 79.

19. *Sel'skoe khoziaistvo*, pp. 77–78; *Voprosy istorii Dal'nego Vostoka*, 3: 186–87; *Kyokutō Soren yōran*, pp. 94–95; Rybakovskii, p. 82.

20. Ianguzov, *Ian Gamarnik*, pp. 33, 36; *Voprosy istorii Dal'nego Vostoka*, 3: 190; *Deiatel'nost' kommunisticheskoi partii*, p. 85.

21. Ianguzov, *Osobaia Krasnoznamennaia*, p. 109; *Deiatel'nost' kommunisticheskoi partii*, p. 86; *Krestianstvo Dal'nego Vostoka*, p. 78; Chausov, "Istoriografiia sploshnoi kollektivizatsii," p. 85.

22. Ianguzov, *Osobaia Krasnoznamennaia*, pp. 111–12, 227; Ianguzov, *Zabven'ia net*, pp. 62, 232; Ianguzov, *Sozvezdie polkovodtsev*, p. 359; *Krasnoznamennyi Dal'nevostochnyi* (1971), pp. 127–28; *Krasnoznamennyi Dal'nevostochnyi* (1979), pp. 99–100.

23. Zakharov et al. (1981), p. 87; Vorob'ev, p. 7.

24. Ianguzov, *Ian Gamarnik*, pp. 18–19; Vorob'ev, pp. 7–8, 10–12; Zakharov et al. (1981), pp. 100–102, 125, 127; Biankin, pp. 132–62; *Dal'nevostochnoe morskoe parokhodstvo*, p. 141; *Soren kyokutō sōran*, p. 430; Hayashi, p. 82.

25. Zakharov, et al. (1981), p. 111. The Pacific Fleet was officially established by Defense Commissar Voroshilov on 11 January 1935. Vorob'ev, p. 12.

26. Viktorov quoted in Kolarz, *Peoples*, p. 7n, citing *Pravda*, 29 Mar. 1937.

27. Yamauchi, *Urajio to Enkaishū*, p. 317.

28. J. V. Stalin, *Works* (Moscow: Foreign Languages Publishing House, 1955): 13: 307; Kunert, *General Ljuschkows Geheimbericht*, p. 33.

29. This description is based on a journal kept by Admiral Yarnell, Department

of the Navy, Naval Historical Center, Operational Archives Branch, Personal Papers of Admiral Harry Erwin Yarnell, Series 1, Box 2; Mantetsu, Hokuman keizai chōsajo, "Kyokutō Soren jūyō jikō kishi (1937)," in Orientalia Division, LC. No mention of this visit is made in the official history of the Soviet Pacific Fleet. Zakharov et al. (1966 and 1981). After the advent of glasnost, the visit was described by Andrei Kalachinskii, "Amerikanskaia eskadra v sovetskom Zolotom Roge," *Vechernii Vladivostok*, 29 Apr. 1990; and Aleksandr Gruzdev, "Togda, 53 goda nazad," *Dal'nevostochnyi uchenyi*, no. 32 (Sept. 1990): 6.

30. Albrecht, p. 373; Rapoport and Alexeev, p. 291; Hayashi, p. 84.

31. Recollection of Gamarnik's personal secretary, I. M. Rachkov, in Ianguzov, *Ian Gamarnik*, p. 54. See also Salekhov, p. 12; *Ian Gamarnik*, pp. 32, 68; and Dubinina, "Protivostoianie."

32. Recollections of Gamarnik's daughter, Viktoriya Kochneva, in *Ian Gamarnik*, p. 186. According to Gamarnik's secretary, the Gamarnik-Blücher relationship was close "until the end of their days." I. M. Rachkov in Ianguzov, *Ian Gamarnik*, p. 54.

33. *Ian Gamarnik*, p. 68; Ianguzov, *Ian Gamarnik*, p. 9.

34. Pashkov, *Za krai rodnoi*, p. 98; Hayashi, pp. 54–55, 59, 61–62, 101, 105; *Granitsa*, p. 105; Salekhov, p. 67.

35. According to V. Kulikov, chairman of the Khabarovsk branch of "Memorial" (a society commemorating the victims of Stalinism), no less than 100,000 prisoners took part in the construction of Komsomolsk during the 1930s. *Priamurskie vedomosti*, 26 Oct. 1991. See also Khisamutdinov, *Russian Far East*, p. 109; Pismanik, pp. 67, 92; Ianguzov, *Zabven'ia net*, p. 236; Ianguzov, *Ian Gamarnik*, pp. 4, 18, 58; Kondrat'ev, p. 277; and *Krasnoznamennyi Dal'nevostochnyi* (1979), p. 101; *Komsomol'sk-na-Amure*, p. 19.

36. N. Potapov, "Zheny pogranichnikov," *Pravda*, 20 May 1937.

20 «» Building Socialism on the Pacific

Epigraph. G. Petrov in *Na rubezhe*, 1939, no. 1: 3.

1. DVO (1), p. 310; Raikhman, *Economic Development*, p. 3; *Voprosy istorii partiinykh organizatsii*, p. 24; *Voprosy ekonomiki Dal'nego Vostoka*, pp. 72–74; *Nichi-Ro nenkan*, p. 561.

2. *Voprosy ekonomiki Dal'nego Vostoka*, p. 73.

3. *Sotsial'no-ekonomicheskoe razvitie dal'nevostochnoi derevni: Sovetskii period*, pp. 15–16, 18; *Dal'revkom*, p. 262; Ianguzov, *Ian Gamarnik*, p. 36; Voishnis, "Bol'sheviki Dal'nego Vostoka," pp. 211–12.

4. Tucker, p. 408. For the role of Western Siberian grain collections in Stalin's termination of NEP, see Hughes.

5. Voishnis, "Bol'sheviki Dal'nego Vostoka," p. 212; Tibekin, pp. 80–81.

6. Voishnis, "Bol'sheviki Dal'nego Vostoka," pp. 213, 214, 219; *Voprosy istorii partiinykh organizatsii*, pp. 17–18; Khudiakov, "Avtobiografiia."

7. Mantetsu. Keizai chōsa kai, "Dassō gyomin no kataru Soren saikin no jitsujō," p. 2, in LC.

8. The Central Committee's order is based on *Voprosy istorii partiinykh organizatsii*, p. 18; *Partiinye organizatsii sovetskogo severa*, p. 70; *Ocherki istorii Chukotki*, p. 181; Chausov, "Istoriografiia sploshnoi kollektivizatsii," p. 84. On peasant uprisings, see Pismanik, pp. 75–78; and Popov Papers, in Bakhmeteff Archive.

9. *Tikhookeanskaia zvezda*, 25 Mar., 4 May 1990; Suturin, *Delo kraevogo masshtaba*, pp. 8–10; *Krest'ianstvo Dal'nego Vostoka*, p. 77.

10. Khisamutdinov, "Kleveta seksota," p. 10; Khisamutdinov, *Russian Far East*, p. 85; Pismanik, p. 71.

11. Petrov, *Soviet Gold*, p. 373; *Krest'ianstvo Dal'nego Vostoka*, p. 79.

12. Wollenberg, p. 212; Krivitsky, *I Was Stalin's Agent*, pp. 244–45.

13. Wada Haruki in Suh, *Koreans*, p. 40.

14. Lavrov, pp. 213–14; Fukuda, p. 45; Nakamura; Grigorenko, *Memoirs*, pp. 47–48.

15. Mantetsu. "Dassō gyomin," p. 1, as cited in n. 7 above.

16. Khudiakov, "Avtobiografiia"; Khisamutdinov, *Russian Far East*, p. 56.

17. The material in this section is drawn from Kolarz, *Peoples*, p. 45; Abramsky, "Birobidzhan Project," pp. 68–69; Emiot, p. 4; Arnovitz, pp. 129–33; *Encyclopedia Judaica*, p. 1046; Solomon M. Schwartz, *The Jews in the Soviet Union* (Syracuse: Syracuse University Press, 1951), pp. 174–94; Nora Levin, pp. 282–311; and Pinkus, pp. 71–76.

18. SSE, 4: 83; *Encyclopedia Judaica*, pp. 1045–1046; Nora Levin, p. 292. For a useful survey of the region in 1928, see *Birsko-Bidzhanskii raion DVK*.

19. *Encyclopedia Judaica*, p. 1046; Abramsky, "Birobidzhan Project," p. 71; Emiot, p. 4.

20. *Encyclopedia Judaica*, p. 1047; *Zemlia*, pp. 77, 88, 125; Emiot, p. xiv.

21. Samarin and Antonovich, p. 35; Emiot, p. xiii.

22. Armstrong, *Northern Sea Route*, pp. 15, 25; *Ocherki istorii Chukotki*, p. 198.

23. Vladimir Danilenko, pp. 31–35.

24. For a detailed account of the CER sale, see George A. Lensen, *The Damned Inheritance* (Tallahassee, Fla.: Diplomatic Press, 1974), pp. 291–334.

25. *Volk und Reich*, 10 (Oct. 1942): 599; *National Geographic*, 82, no. 5 (Nov. 1942): 607. See also Lamin, *Kliuchi k dvum okeanam*, pp. 139–40; and Chudesov, p. 73.

26. For background, see Sheila Fitzpatrick, ed. *Cultural Revolution in Russia, 1928–1931* (Bloomington: Indiana Univ. Press, 1978).

27. USSR, KPSS, Dal'kraikom, p. 327.

28. Voishnis, "Iz istorii formirovaniia sovetskoi intelligentsii," pp. 53, 91; Mikhail Kuznetsov, p. 91; Bensman, *Kul'turn'oe stroitel'stvo*, p. 40; DVO (1), p. 346.

29. Slezkine, "From Savages to Citizens," pp. 60–75.

30. Beliaev, pp. 145–47; *Istoriia Sibiri*, 4: 424–25; Chernysheva, *Khabarovsk: 1858–1983*, p. 186; Lerman, *Po serdtsu blizkie druz'ia*, p. 59.

31. Beliaev, p. 147. See also Lerman, *Po serdtsu blizkie druz'ia*, pp. 39–40, 43, 45; Alenkina, p. 43; and *Aleksandr Fadeev*, p. 136.

32. Nikolai Yadrintsev, quoted in Chikhachev, p. 560.

33. USSR, KPSS, *XVII s"ezd*, p. 630.

34. *Granitsa*, p. 183.

35. Testimony of NKVD Commissar Gennadii Lyushkov in Kunert, *General Ljuschkows Geheimbericht*, p. 29.

36. Coox, *Nomonhan*, 1: 100.

37. Pavlenko, *Na Vostoke*; Fraerman; Semen Bytovoi, *Granitsa: stikhi* (Khabarovsk: Dal'giz, 1936); Nikolai Rogal, *U granitsy* (Khabarovsk: Dal'giz, 1939); Anatoly Gai, *U rubezha* (Khabarovsk: Dal'giz, 1937). *U berega Amura* ("On the banks of the Amur") by Matvei Blanter.

38. Tselishchev, p. 9.

39. Dubinina, *Dal'nevostochnitsy v bor'be*, p. 102.

40. Hazard, p. 66; Golovkin, p. 136; Dubinina, *Dal'nevostochnitsy v bor'be*, pp. 111–12; DVO (1), p. 322; Mantetsu, Hokuman keizai chōsajo, "Kyokutō Soren jūyō jikō 1937," *Hokkei Soren shiryō*, 134 (1938): 20.

41. Tucker, p. 483.

42. *Na rubezhe*, 1937, no. 5: 56–58.

43. Ibid., pp. 42–43.

21 «» Center vs. Periphery

1. *SSSR i Iaponiia*, p. 37.

2. Albrecht, p. 373.

3. *Krest'ianstvo Dal'nego Vostoka*, pp. 81–82; DVO (1), pp. 323, 347; *Dal'nevostochnoe morskoe parokhodstvo*, p. 154; Pashkov, *Za krai rodnoi*, p. 97.

4. Voishnis "Bol'sheviki Dal'nego Vostoka," pp. 215–16.

5. *Soren kyokutō sōran*, p. 429; USSR, KPSS, *XI s"ezd*, p. 289.

6. Voishnis, "Bol'sheviki Dal'nego Vostoka," pp. 219, 220, 223; Unpelev, *Sotsialisticheskaia industrializatsiia*, pp. 70, 80, 100–101; Kolarz, *Peoples*, p. 5; U.S., Army Dept., "Interrogation of General Liushkov," frame 0978.

7. USSR, KPSS, Dal'kraikom, pp. 69, 401.

8. Ibid., pp. 65, 69; Voishnis, "Bol'sheviki Dal'nego Vostoka," pp. 219, 222, 223, 225; DVO (1), p. 345.

9. Unpelev, *Sotsialisticheskaia industrializatsiia*, pp. 99–100, 105.

10. Voishnis, "Bol'sheviki Dal'nego Vostoka," pp. 221, 227; DVO (1), p. 101; *Partiinye organizatsii sovetskogo severa*, p. 73.

11. Pashkov, *Za krai rodnoi*, p. 124; DVO (1), pp. 302–3.

12. Mantetsu, Harbin jimusho, "Soren no tō oyobi seifu kansa kikan," pp. 41–44, in Orientalia Division, LC.

13. Ianguzov, *Zabven'ia net*, p. 252.

14. *Krest'ianstvo Dal'nego Vostoka*, p. 76.

15. Khisamutdinov, *Russian Far East*, pp. 53, 90; Khisamutdinov, *Terra incognita*, pp. 330–31; N. N. Khanchuk in *Vestnik DVO AN SSSR*, 6 (1990): 132. For more on Novograblenov, see Kharitanovskii.

16. USSR, KPSS, *XVII s"ezd*, pp. 14, 235, 587.

17. Medvedev, *Let History Judge* (1972), pp. 166–67; Medvedev, *Let History Judge* (1989), pp. 349, 676. On Afanasy Kim, see *Belaia kniga*, p. 21; and Wada Haruki in Suh, *Koreans*, p. 47.

18. *Tikhookeanskaya zvezda*, 25 Sept. 1989; Medvedev, *Let History Judge* (1972), p. 170.

19. *Na rubezhe*, 1936, no. 4: 4; Dubinina, "Tragediia lichnosti," p. 133.

20. Dubinina, "Tragediia lichnosti," p. 128; Suturin, *Delo kraevogo masshtaba*, p. 217; *Belaia kniga*, p. 21.

21. Mantetsu, Harbin jimusho, "Kyokutō chihō chūō tō kikan no soshiki," p. 21, in Orientalia Division, LC; *Krasnaia zvezda*, 4 June 1988.

22. Ianguzov, *Ian Gamarnik*, pp. 19–20, 158–59; *Krasnoznamennyi Dal'nevostochnyi* (1979), p. 103.

23. G. Bliukher, 1990, no. 1: 79.

24. *Pravda*, 11 Nov. 1936.

25. Wollenberg, p. 215; Erickson, *Soviet High Command*, p. 466; *Ian Gamarnik*, p. 32.

26. U.S., Army Dept., "Interrogation of General Liushkov," frames 0977–78.

27. Mikhail Kuznetsov, p. 168; Suturin, "Delo kraevogo masshtaba," 25 Mar; Lappo, p. 102; Khisamutdinov, *Russian Far East*, p. 110.

28. "O nedostatkakh partiinoi raboty," in Stalin, *Sochineniia*, 1 (14): 200.

29. "Interrogation of General Liushkov," frames 0979–0980. Aronshtam was OKDVA political commissar, Sangursky chief of staff, and Lapin commander of the Far East Air Force.

30. Suturin, "Delo kraevogo masshtaba," 26 Mar; Nikolaev, "Tsena istiny," 25 Sept.

31. *Pravda*, 23, 28 Apr. 1937.

32. Krivitsky, *I Was Stalin's Agent*, p. 254; Volkogonov, 1, part 2: 263.

33. U.S., Army Dept., "Interrogation of General Liushkov," frames 0976, 0979; *Krasnaia zvezda*, 4 June, 13 Aug. 1988; Rapoport and Alexeev, p. 245; Erickson, *Soviet High Command*, p. 460; G. Bliukher, 1990, no. 1: 79.

34. G. Bliukher, 1990, no. 1: 79.

35. For various versions of Gamarnik's death, see Volkogonov, 1, part 2: 264; Salekhov, p. 79; Colton, p. 138; MERSH: 12: 76; and Yamauchi Hōsuke, "Sekigun

hasshōgun inbō jiken to sono eikyō," in Naikaku chōsakyoku. Chōsashitsu, "Sorempō jijō," 24 (5 Oct 1937), in LC.

36. *Krasnaia zvezda*, 6 June 1937; Volkogonov, 1, part 2: 264.

37. *Izvestiia TsK KPSS*, 1989, no. 4: 52–53.

38. Ianguzov, *Zabven'ia net*, p. 293.

39. "Soviet Russia in the Orient," p. 17, in Olferieff Collection, HA; Ante Ciliga, *The Russian Enigma* (London: Ink Links, 1979), p. 294.

40. Mantetsu, Keizai chōsa kai, "Dassō gyomin no kataru Soren saikin no jitsujō," pp. 28–29, in LC.

41. Japan, Naikaku chōsakyoku, "Sorempō jijō," 14 (15 July 1937): 1, and Yamauchi, "Sekigun hasshōgun inbō jiken to sono eikyō" in "Sorempō jijō," 25 (5 Oct. 1937), in LC; Wollenberg, pp. 210–11, 241–42; Walter Duranty, *The Kremlin and the People* (New York: Reynal & Hitchcock, 1941), p. 62; Isaac Deutscher, *Stalin: A Political Biography* (London: Oxford Univ. Press, 1949), p. 379.

42. For biographical information, see N. Tarasova, "Andrei Vasil'evich Svetlanin," *Grani*, 1966, no. 61: 82–97.

43. Svetlanin published this scenario in installments in the émigré journal *Posev*. Posev Publishers (Frankfurt-am-Main) brought out Svetlanin's book, *Dal'nevostochnyi zagovor* ("Far Eastern conspiracy"), in 1953.

44. Khrushchev, p. 35. For hints of Gamarnik's involvement in an anti-Stalinist plot, see Alexander Orlov, *The Secret History of Stalin's Crimes* (New York: Random House, 1953), pp. 237, 239.

45. A. N. Rollin, "Chekistskaia fantastika" (n.d.), in Nicolaevsky Collection, HA; Robert C. Tucker, "Problems of Interpretation," *Slavic Review*, 42, no. 1 (Spring 1983): 80. John Erickson characterizes Svetlanin's book as "black propaganda" for distribution among Soviet troops stationed in East Germany. Personal communications, 14 Mar. 1986, 4 Sept. 1987.

46. Rapoport and Alexeev, p. 291.

47. Catherine Andreyev, *Vlasov and the Russian Liberation Movement* (Cambridge: Cambridge Univ. Press, 1987), p. 167; Getty, p. 267; Grover C. Furr, "New Light on Old Stories about Marshal Tukhachevskii: Some Documents Reconsidered." *Russian History/Histoire Russe* 13, nos. 2–3 (summer–fall 1986): 305–6.

48. Goble, "Ukrainians in the Soviet Far East"; Svit, *Ukrainskii Dal'nii Vostok. Ukraina* (Shanghai: Dal'nevostochnye ukrainskie natsionalisty, 1937).

49. Aleksei Khorov in *Krasnaia zvezda*, 13 Aug. 1988.

22 «» "Cleansing" Dalkrai

Epigraph. Khetagurova, "Veriu v derzost' molodykh," p. 127.

1. *Na rubezhe*, 1936, no. 4: 6.

2. Dubinina, "Tragediia lichnosti," p. 130.

3. Japan, Naikaku chōsakyoku, "Soren kyokutō no saikin no jōsei," in "Sorempō jijō," 13 (10 July 1937): 16–37, in Orientalia Division, LC.

4. Kolarz, *Peoples*, pp. 5–6; Suturin, *Delo kraevogo masshtaba*, pp. 14, 122; Medvedev, *Let History Judge* (1989), p. 453; Coox, *Nomonhan*, 1: 113.

5. Dubinina, "Tragediia lichnosti," p. 129; Suturin, "Delo kraevogo masshtaba," 26 Mar; "Soren kyokutō no saikin no jōsei," p. 37, as cited in n. 3, above.

6. For an examination of this process in a district Party committee, see Weinberg, "Birobidzhan in 1937."

7. *Pravda*, 13, 14, 28 June 1937.

8. U.S., Army Dept., "The Interrogation of General Liushkov," frame 0976; Coox, "L'Affaire Lyushkov," p. 416.

9. Mantetsu, Hokuman keizai chōsajo, "Kyokutō Soren jūyō jikō, 1937," p. 10 in Orientalia Division, LC; Suturin, "Delo kraevogo masshtaba," 26 Mar.; A. Suturin in *Tikhookeanskaia zvezda*, 4 May 1990; S. Nikolaev, "Tsena istiny," 26 Sept.; USSR, KPSS, *XXII s"ezd*, 2: 404.

10. S. Nikolaev, "Tsena istiny," 25 Sept.

11. *Izvestiia TsK KPSS*, 1989, no. 12: 88.

12. Erickson, *Soviet High Command*, p. 468; Hayashi, pp. 106–9.

13. Coox, "L'Affaire Lyushkov," pp. 407–8; Conquest, *Inside Stalin's Secret Police*, p. 24.

14. U.S., Army Dept., "The Interrogation of General Liushkov," frames 0976–77. Kunert, *General Ljuschkows Geheimbericht*, pp. 21–22, also describes Stalin's instructions, citing a protocol of the Lyushkov interrogation deposited in the Public Record Office, London.

15. Documents showing Far Eastern quotas in 1937 were described by Maj.-Gen. V. G. Provotorov of the Main Military Procurator's Office in an interview in *Sovetskaia kul'tura*, 25 Feb. 1989, p. 8, translated in *Foreign Broadcasts Information Service*, USSR, 89–046 (10 Mar. 1989), p. 81. See also "Kyokutō Soren jūyō jikō," pp. 13–14, 16, as cited in no. 9, above.

16. Kostanov, *Istoriia bez 'belykh piaten'*; *Za rabochee delo*, p. 46; *Organizatsiia KPSS Evreiskoi Avtonomnoi oblasti*, p. 29; Suturin, "Delo kraevogo masshtaba," 4 Apr.

17. Suturin, *Delo kraevogo masshtaba*, p. 39.

18. A. Suturin, "Kharbintsy," *Tikhookeanskaia zvezda*, 4 May 1990.

19. Suturin, *Delo kraevogo masshtaba*, pp. 40–41, 158.

20. Suturin, "Delo kraevogo masshtaba," 26 Mar., 30 Mar.

21. *Izvestiia TsK KPSS*, 1989, no. 12: 89, 105; Dubinina, "Tragediia lichnosti," p. 132; Suturin, "Delo kraevogo masshtaba," 27 Mar.

22. Amir Khisamutdinov brought to my attention in May 1992 the notion of a Vareikis team, partly brought from Voronezh and partly recruited after his arrival in Khabarovsk. Khisamutdinov, ms. "Komanda Vareikisa."

23. Khisamutdinov, *Russian Far East*, p. 119.

24. Boldyrev, "Iaponiia," pp. 193–94. On the Stalin Club in the Korean section (*slobodka*) of Vladivostok, see *Ves' Vladivostok: Spravochnik na 1935/36* g., p. 53.

25. SSE, 2: 950; G. Petrov, *Ukrepim sovety DVK*, p. 97; *Vladivostok*, 22 May 1991.

26. Suturin,*Delo kraevogo masshtaba*, pp. 190–91. *Belaia kniga*, p. 22.

27. A. M. Nair, *An Indian Freedom Fighter in Japan* (New Delhi: Vikas, 1985), pp. 141–46.

28. *Belaia kniga*, pp. 68, 82. Hundreds of Koreans in northern Sakhalin were also subjected to forced relocation. Grant, pp. 128–29.

29. Coox, "L'Affaire Lyushkov," p. 416; *Kyokutō Shiberiya yōran*, p. 345; Khisamutdinov, *Russian Far East*, p. 121.

30. Suturin, *Delo kraevogo masshtaba*, p. 188. *Belaia kniga*, p. 21.

31. Amir Khisamutdinov, "Repression of Soviet Koreans," lecture at University of Hawaii, 23 Apr. 1992; Kunert, *General Ljuschkows Geheimbericht*, p. 39.

32. *Pravda*, 15 Dec. 1937; Kolarz, *Peoples*, p. 7.

33. *Pravda*, 24 Feb. 1938; Ianguzov, *Zabven'ia net*, p. 287.

34. "Marshal Bliukher," *Novyi mir*, 1938, no. 2: 211–23.

35. Kunert, *General Ljuschkows Geheimbericht*, p. 29; Colton, p. 144; Conquest, *Inside Stalin's Secret Police*, p. 90; G. Bliukher, 1990, no. 1: 80.

36. A file in the KGB archives suggests indirectly that Lyushkov may have expected to be accused of complicity in the recent suicide of the chief of the NKVD administration in the Primorye, Yakov Vizel, who swallowed arsenic concealed in a bar of soap in his cell. USSR, NKVD, Upravlenie NKVD po Dal'nevostochnomu kraiu, Arkhivno-sledstvennoe delo no. 980947, "Spravka," p. 1. For general background, see Coox, "L'Affaire Lyushkov," pp. 405–10; and Nishino, *Nazo no bōmeisha*.

37. "Prikaz narodnogo komissara oborony Soiuza SSR no. 0040," *Voenno-istoricheskii zhurnal*, 1990, no. 1: 86; Coox, "L'Affaire Lyushkov," p. 419; Hayashi, p. 120.

38. For details of these operations, see Coox, *Anatomy of a Small War*, pp. 128–86. For an excellent map of the lower Tumen, see *Nihon gaikōshi chizu*, map no. 25.

39. G. Bliukher, 1990, no. 1: 81; Ianguzov, *Zabven'ia net*, pp. 313–20; Ianguzov, *Ian Gamarnik*, p. 97; Volkogonov, 1, part 2: 272–73.

40. Kondrat'ev, p. 289; V. Vial'tsev, "Istoriia menia opravdaet," *Tikhookeanskaia zvezda*, 12 Oct. 1988; Ianguzov, *Zabven'ia net*, p. 326.

41. "Prikaz narodnogo komissara oborony Soiuza SSR no. 0040," *Voenno-istoricheskii zhurnal*, 1990, no. 1: 84–85; Kondrat'ev, p. 289.

42. Ianguzov, *Zabven'ia net*, pp. 328–29; Suturin, *Delo kraevogo masshtaba*, p. 38.

43. Zhukov, *Granitsa*, came out on 15 July 1938. Zhukov, *Kak my bili iapontsev*, is the revised version appearing in October, incorporating a description of the Lake Khasan incident and eliminating all references to Marshal Blücher.

44. Chiang Kai-shek, *Soviet Russia in China* (New York: Farrar, Straus, 1957), pp. 51–52.

45. Hayashi, pp. 135–37; Ianguzov, *Ian Gamarnik*, p. 112; Rapoport and Alexeev, pp. 387–88.

46. DVO (2), pp. 10, 33; *Ocherk istorii Khabarovskoi kraevoi organizatsii*, p. 478.

47. Pegov, p. 7.

48. Ibid., p. 104.

49. Khetagurova, p. 132.

50. *Sotsial'no-ekonomicheskoe razvitie dal'nevostochnoi derevni: Sovetskii period*, p. 40; DVO (2), pp. 35, 176.

51. Rigby, *Communist Party Membership*, p. 503; *Nichi-Ro nenkan 1942*, p. 560; *Kyokutō Shiberiya yōran*, p. 88.

52. *Istoriia vsesoiuznoi kommunisticheskoi partii (Bol'shevikov): Kratkii kurs* (Moscow: Gospolitizdat, 1938).

53. Ogurtsova, p. 62.

54. *Dvadtsat' let VChK-OGPU-NKVD*, p. 37.

55. *XVIII s"ezd*, pp. 225–26.

56. *Pravda*, 16 Mar. 1939. Shtern's speech, without the last sentence quoted above, appears in *XVIII s"ezd*, pp. 231–36.

57. *Krasnaia zvezda*, 6 Aug. 1988; Ianguzov, *Ian Gamarnik*, p. 133.

58. Naikaku chōsakyoku, "Shukusei kōsaku no shinten to sono eikyō," p. 2, in Orientalia Division, LC; *Kyokutō Shiberiya yōran*, p. 9; Bol'bukh, pp. 70–71; Lamin, *Kliuchi k dvum okeanam*, p. 145.

59. Hayashi, pp. 116–17.

60. Citing Party and KGB archives, J. Arch Getty notes 2,500,000 arrests and 681,692 executions in the USSR during 1937–38. *American Historical Review*, 98, no. 4 (Oct. 1993), p. 1022.

61. Khrushchev, pp. 17, 18.

62. *Istoriia Sibiri*, 4: 395; *Sotsial'no-ekonomicheskoe razvitie dal'nevostochnoi derevni: Sovetskii period*, p. 40; Mantetsu, Hokuman keizai chōsajo, "Kyōsantō no gekigen" (15 July 1938), in Orientalia Division, LC.

63. *Kyokutō Shiberiya yōran*, p. 79.

64. Mantetsu, Harbin jimusho, "Kyokutō chihō chūō tō kikan no soshiki," 23 Apr. 1935, in Orientalia Division, LC.

65. Dubinina, "Tragediia lichnosti," p. 135.

66. U.S., Army Dept., "The Interrogation of General Liushkov," frame 0982.

67. Erickson, *Soviet High Command*, p. 493. *Dal'nii Vostok*, 1988, no. 7: 143, puts losses at half the regimental and virtually all divisional and corps commanders.

68. See S. Nikolaev, "Vystrely v spinu."

69. Suturin, *Delo kraevogo masshtaba*, p. 260.

70. Khisamutdinov, "Kleveta seksota A. N. Lipskogo."

71. Conquest, *Inside Stalin's Secret Police*, pp. 54–55, 76, 90, 99, 136; Medvedev, *Let History Judge* (1972), pp. 189, 219, 243; Medvedev, *Let History Judge* (1989), p. 388; Dubinina, "Protivostoianie," pp. 138–40.

72. Krasnoshchekova, p. 149; Mukhachev, "Prezident respubliki," p. 136. Probably the last American to see Krasnoshchekov alive (aside from his immediate family) met him in Moscow at the Commissariat of Agriculture on 28 Jan. 1937 and concluded that he was a "wrecker." John Sutton, "Wreckers in High Places," *New Masses* 27, no. 9 (24 May 1938): 8.

73. Khisamutdinov, "Zotik," *Krasnoe znamia*, 2 Nov. 1989.

74. Lev Razgon, "The Executioner's Song," *Moscow News*, 48 (1988). Robert Conquest estimates that about 50,000 were shot at Glukhaya Hill in 1937–38. Personal communication, 24 Sept. 1990.

75. Hereward Thimbleby Price, *Boche and Bolshevik: Experiences of an Englishman in the German Army and in Russian Prisons* (London: John Murray, 1919), p. 241.

76. USSR, Upravlenie NKVD po dal'nevostochnomu kraiu, Primorskoe oblastnoe upravlenie, Delo no. 14040 Kontr-revoliutsionnoi shpionsko-vreditel'skoi organizatsii sushchestvovavshei v DV Gosudarstvennom Universitete, vkhodivshei v sostav pravo-trotskistskogo zagovora na Dal'nem Vostoke. Donskoi, "Tragicheskie dni," p. 3. Vladimir Donskoi is a retired KGB officer living in Vladivostok.

77. Suturin, *Delo kraevogo masshtaba*, p. 107.

78. Khisamutdinov, *Terra incognita*, p. 332; Khisamutdinov, "Natasha," *Krasnoe znamia*, 19 Jan. 1990.

79. A. Khisamutdinov in *Zotik Matveev*, p. 42.

80. Khisamutdinov, "Zotik," *Krasnoe znamia*, 2 Nov. 1989.

81. Of 48,000 volumes in the Gogol Library in 1923, about 100 were extant in 1989. Khisamutdinov, *Mir biblioteki*, p. 53. On the destruction of Venyukov Collection, see Khisamutdinov, *Russian Far East*, p.60.

82. Tarasova, *Vladimir Klavdievich Arsen'ev*, pp. 72–73, 306; Tatiana Matveeva, interviewed by Afanasii Serdiuk in *Dal'nevostochnyi uchenyi*, 50 (14–20 Dec. 1989).

83. Voishnis, "Iz istorii formirovaniia sovetskoi intelligentsii," pp. 90, 105–10.

84. The text of Bytovoi's denunciation of Titov is reproduced in Suturin, *Delo kraevogo masshtaba*, pp. 101–2.

85. *Izvestiia*, 12 June 1937; *Literaturnaia gazeta*, 15 June 1937; *Pravda*, 12 June 1937.

86. Quoted in *Shpiony i diversanty za rabotoi* (Moscow: Gosizdat, 1937), p. 13.

87. Suturin, "Delo kraevogo masshtaba," 25 Mar.

88. Raisa Berg, *Sukhovei* (New York: Chalidze, 1983), p. 161.

23 «» Kolyma

1. John D. Littlepage, *In Search of Soviet Gold* (New York: Harcourt, Brace, 1938), pp. 26–27.

2. Ustiev, pp. 235, 237; Zhikharev, p. 148; Alexander Tropkin, "Chukotka," *Soviet Life*, Dec. 1986, p. 23.

3. *Magadan: Putevoditel'-spravochnik*, pp. 175–77. Confusion surrounding the name Berzin has led some authors to identify the head of Dalstroi as "Reingold Berzin" (Dallin and Nicolaevsky, pp. 116, 131) or "Yan Berzin" (S. V. Utechin, *Everyman's Concise Encyclopedia of Russia* [New York: Dutton, 1961]. p. 62). Reingold Yosifovich Berzin (1888–1939), a Red Army commissar, was never in the Far East. Yan Karlovich Berzin [pseudonym for Kiuzis Peteris] (1889–1938), chief of Red Army Intelligence (1924–35, 1937), visited Dalkrai in 1935.

4. *Partiinye organizatsii sovetskogo severa*, p. 95; *Ocherki istorii Chukotki*, p. 222; Zhikharev, pp. 159, 161; *Voprosy istorii partiinykh organizatsii*, p. 53.

5. Zhikharev, pp. 159–61; Fetisov, p. 173; Petrov, *Soviet Gold*, pp. 172, 179; Smolina, p. 197.

6. "Pokazateli po trudu." This OGPU-NKVD file in the Magadan Archives was published in 1992 by the curator of the Magadan Historical Museum, Aleksandr Kozlov.

7. Conquest, *Kolyma*, p. 19; Lipper, p. 76; Dallin and Nicolaevsky, pp. 124–26, 137; Nikolaevskii, "Dal'stroi: Sovetskaia katorga," p. 256; Raikhman, *Economic Development*, p. 28; Rudnev, p. 103.

8. Conquest, *Kolyma*, p. 26; Lipper, p. 94; Dallin and Nicolaevsky, pp. 128–29.

9. Sungorkin, p. 37.

10. Golovkin, p. 138; Smolina, p. 206.

11. Zhikharev, p. 164; Dallin and Nicolaevsky, p. 124; Fetisov, p. 174; Raikhman, *Economic Development*, p. 23.

12. Zhikharev, p. 162; Petrov, *Soviet Gold*, pp. 399–400; Raikhman, *Economic Development*, p. 24.

13. Petrov, *Soviet Gold*, p. 172; See also Conquest, *Kolyma*, pp. 44–45; and Medvedev, *Let History Judge* (1972), p. 279.

14. Zhikharev, p. 181; Fetisov, p. 173.

15. See, for example, Eduard Berzin, "Zolotaia Kolyma" *Pravda*, 11 Nov. 1936.

16. Zhikharev, pp. 189, 205; Mantetsu, Hokuman keizai chōsajo, "Chūmoku subeki Ohōtsuku kai hokugan no kensetsu," in Orientalia Division, LC.

17. Kozlov, p. 125; *Sovety Severo-Vostoka SSSR (1928–1940)*, p. 176.

18. Smolina, p. 208.

19. Kozlov, p. 127; Golovkin, pp. 134–38.

20. Smolina, pp. 207, 217; Zhikarev, pp. 209–10; Kozlov, p. 128; Dallin and Nicolaevsky, p. 131.

21. Conquest, *Kolyma*, pp. 40–41; Conquest, *Inside Stalin's Secret Police*, pp. 31, 180; Zhikharev, p. 209; Kozlov, pp. 128–30; *Ocherki istorii Chukotki*, p. 222.

22. According to "Pokazateli po trudu," OGPU-NKVD files, 356,000 prisoners were brought to Sevvostlag between 1932 and 1942.

23. "Pokazateli po trudu."

24. Zhikharev, p. 161; Dallin and Nicolaevsky, pp. 140–41; *Ocherki istorii Chukotki*, p. 222; Grusha, *25 let Dal'stroia*, p. 3.

25. For a detailed study of this incident, see Hara, *Indeigiruka-go no higeki*, esp. pp. 4–32, 274–305.

26. *Iunost'*, 8 (1988): 34; *Vladivostok*, 14 Nov. 1990.

27. F. Vinogradov, "Bukhta Nakhodka," *Pravda*, 30 May 1937.

28. Lipper, p. 288; Gorbatov, pp. 125, 135; Pegov, p. 51; After the completion of the Komsomolsk-Sovetskaya Gavan railroad in 1943, Vanino supplemented Nakhodka in this function.

29. Lesniak, p. 174; Glushchenko, p. 178; *Voenno-istoricheskii zhurnal*, 1989, no. 3: 97; Lipper, p. 17. The Reichstag trial co-star was Vasily Tanev. *Biographical Dictionary*, p. 459.

30. On Kniazev, see *Pamiat' Kolymy*, p. 57. On Shukayav and Gagen-Torn, see Andreeva, pp. 143–53. On Khodorov, see Ines Rubin, "Approach to Factual Material in Recent Soviet Biographical and Bibliographical Publications," Research Paper no. 41 (Jerusalem: Soviet and East European Research Centre, Univ. of Jerusalem, 1981), pp. 29, 31.

31. *Na severe dal'nem*, 1988, no. 2: 5–6; John Glad in Shalamov, *Kolyma Tales*, p. 12. See also Leona Toker, "Varlam Shalamov's Kolyma," in Diment and Slezkine, pp. 151–69.

32. Lipper, p. 94.

33. Dallin and Nicolaevsky, p. 141; Conquest, *Kolyma*, p. 219.

34. Andreeva, p. 148.

35. *Sovietland*, 1939, no. 4: 10.

36. Dallin and Nicolaevsky, pp. 133–34; Nikolaevskii, "Dal'stroi: Sovetskaia katorga," p. 257; Zhikarev, p. 174; Samarin and Antonovich, p. 25; *Sorempō nenkan, 1943–1944*, p. 778; U.S. Office of Strategic Services, RG 226, North Pacific Russian Shipping, 1942–1945, "Northeastern Siberia," p. 3.

37. Gorbatov, p. 128.

38. Dagor.

39. *Sovety Severo-Vostoka SSSR (1928–1940)*, p. 243.

40. *Sovetskaya Kolyma*, 16 May 1938, in ibid., p. 229; *Ocherki istorii Chukotki*, p. 23.

41. Conquest, *Inside Stalin's Secret Police*, pp. 18, 70–71, 178, 465. See also Rapoport and Alexeev, pp. 244, 414.

42. "Pokazateli po trudu."

43. Davies and Steiger, pp. xi–xiii, 15, 280.

44. Gruber, pp. 140, 142–44.

45. "The Economy of the Kolyma Valley," report of O. Edmund Clubb, U.S. consul-general in Vladivostok, 6 November 1944. U.S. State Dept. Archives, RG 59, 861.50/11–644.

46. Mandel, p. 8; Rhodes, pp. 43–44, 65–66; Lengyel, p. 323.

47. Wendell L. Willkie, "One World," in *Prefaces to Peace* (New York: Simon & Schuster, 1943), p. 72.

48. Wallace, *Price of Vision*, p. 337.

49. Wallace, *Soviet Asia Mission*, p. 32. See also Lattimore, "New Road to Asia," p. 657; and Hazard, p. 67.

50. Mazuruk, p. 22; Conquest, *Kolyma*, pp. 205–10; David Sherl, "Alaska-Chukotka Front." *Soviet Life*, Dec. 1986, p. 50; Wallace, *Price of Vision*, pp. 336–38.

51. Lattimore, "New Road to Asia," p. 657.

52. Lattimore, *China Memoirs*, p. 179.

53. Gorbatov, p. 137.

54. Zhikharev, p. 182.

55. *Maksim Gorkii: Sobranie sochinenii v 30 tomakh*, 27: 509 quoted in Geller and Nekrich, 1: 291. See also Smolina, p. 216; Solomon, p. 104; and Lipper, p. 169.

24 «» War Without a Front

Epigraphs. Stalin's remark to Matsuoka Yōsuke, as quoted by Matsuoka's secretary Hasegawa Shin'ichi in *Nippu jiji*, 28 Apr. 1941; Stalin's 1945 statement in Stalin, *Sochineniia*, 2 (15): 213–14.

1. Hallett Abend, *Pacific Charter* (New York: Doubleday, 1943), p. 249.

2. *Zhong E guanxi shiliao*, 2: 784–85.

3. Masuda, pp. 106, 113–16, 122.

4. Hayashi, pp. 45, 100, 105; *Dal'nevostochnyi pogranichnyi*, p. 86.

5. Inaba Chiharu in Akashi, *Rakka ryūsui: Colonel Akashi's Report*, p. 84; Olavi K. Fält in ibid., p. 195; "Japanese Intelligence on Soviet Intentions — Annex I" (28 Feb. 1950), MacArthur Archives, RG 6, box 99, folio 4, pp. 8–9, 11 (hereafter "Japanese Intelligence — Annex I"); *Pogranichnye voiska SSSR, 1929–1938*, p. 553; *Pravda*, 21 May 1937.

6. Vareikis to Stalin, 8 Sept. 1937, quoted in Suturin, *Delo kraevogo masshtaba*, p. 51.

7. Thomas J. Cory, "Radio Audience of the Soviet Far East," Vladivostok consulate-general, 8 Jan. 1947, U.S., State Dept., main decimal file 861.76/1–847.

8. "Japanese Intelligence — Annex I," pp. 1, 3, 9, 11 (see n. 5 above). For Japanese infiltrators on Kazakevich Island, see Chugunov, *Na strazhe*, p. 242.

9. Valentin Riabov, "Delo no. 537," *Ogonek*, 1989, no. 15: 10–12 (Okada Yoshiko); *Literaturnye novosti*, 1993, no. 49, p. 10; and *Izvestiia TsK KPSS*, 1989, no. 11: 49–51 (targeted victims); Grant, ms, p. 115 (Drekov); *Dos'e*, 1 (Sept. 1990): 2 (on infiltrating Nivkhi into Karafuto).

10. *Voprosy ekonomiki Dal'nego Vostoka*, p. 73; *Ogonek*, 1989, no. 38: 5; A. Ishchenko in *Tikhookeanskaia zvezda*, 29 July 1990; *Dal'nevostochnyi uchenyi*, 40 (1988): 3.

11. Angus Ward, Vladivostok, to Sec. State, 4 Feb. 1941, U.S., State Dept, main decimal file 125.9771/58.62; FRUS, 1940, 3: 338–39.

12. I. G. Farben files, U.S. National Archives, microfilm T-82, roll 77, frames 0235473, 0235483. I thank Robert Fahs for bringing this material to my attention.

13. Armstrong, *Northern Sea Route*, p. 48; Gerhard L. Weinberg, *Germany and the Soviet Union, 1939–1941* (Leiden: E. J. Brill, 1954), pp. 78–84.

14. FRUS, 1940, 3: 338–39.

15. FRUS, 1940, 3: 463; FRUS, 1942, 3: 458; Angus Ward, Vladivostok, to Sec. State, 4, 8, 13 Feb. 1941, U.S., State Dept., RG 59, 125.9771 and 125.9771/58.

16. Quoted in *Pictorial Orient*, 9, no. 6 (15 June 1941): 199.

17. Japanese accounts claim 262 troops (including 10 officers) defected to Manchukuo and Karafuto between June 1941 and June 1942. Hayashi, pp. 214, 216–17; *Nichi-Ro nenkan, 1942*, p. 1072; Coox, *Nomonhan*, 2: 1045.

18. *Nichi-Ro nenkan, 1942*, p. 1069; Suh, *Koreans*, pp. 103–4.

19. FRUS, 1942, 3: 456; Angus Ward to Sec. State, 10 Oct. 1942, U.S., State Dept., RG 59, 702.9361/12.

20. Pegov, p. 112; Stephan, ed. *USSR*, pp. 33–36.

21. "Japanese Intelligence — Annex I," p. 2, as cited in n. 5, above; Coox, *Nomonhan*, 2: 1036.

22. Coox, *Nomonhan*, 2: 1052, 1054.

23. UK, FO 371, 31834/31835, file 858, contains invasion prognoses by G. F. Hudson, Foreign Research and Press Service, Balliol College, Oxford, to J. C. Sterndale Bennett, Far East Dept. FO, 23 Feb. 1942; French Ambassador Tokyo to Min. For. Affairs, Vichy, 19 Mar. 1942; and Edward F. L. Wood, Earl of Halifax, British ambassador, Washington, to FO, 20 Mar 1942 (citing authority of Stanley Hornbeck, State Dept. Division of Far Eastern Affairs). Savin, "Sryv planov," upgrades these rumors into Japanese operational plans.

24. Coox, *Nomonhan*, 2: 1035. The American military attaché noted troop trains from the Far East passing through Moscow en route to Belorussia on 18 June 1941. "Memoirs, 1919–1953," in Yeaton Collection, HA.

25. Grigorenko, *Memoirs*, p. 133; Coox, *Nomonhan*, 2: 1052.

26. Hayashi, p. 220; *Soren kyokutō sōran*, p. 433; Geller and Nekrich, 2: 166; Erickson, "Military and Strategic Factors," p. 181; VOV, p. 229.

27. VOV, pp. 229–30; *Voprosy ekonomiki Dal'nego Vostoka*, p. 73.

28. Grigorenko, *Memoirs*, pp. 132–33.

29. VOV, p. 230; Anichkov, p. 146.

30. Angus Ward, Vladivostok, to Sec. State, 12 Feb, 1942, U.S., State Dept., RG 59, 861.5018/60.

31. "USSR Lend-Lease Program (20 Sept. 1945)," pp. 2, 6, in Yeaton Collection, HA.

32. *Dal'nevostochnoe morskoe parokhodstvo*, pp. 562, 564; *Sorempō nenkan, 1943–1944*, p. 887.

33. "Soviet Far Eastern Shipping Operations," in U.S., War Shipping Administration, RG 248, box 52; "Lend-Lease Routes," in U.S., Office of Strategic Services, RG 226, Report 62006 (6 Mar. 1944), box 719; Angus Ward, Vladivostok, to

Sec. State, 25 June 1943, U.S., State Dept., main decimal file 861.00/12016; *Krasnaia zvezda*, 26 Oct. 1982; Rudnev, pp. 192–225, 237; Kolotov.

34. Pegov, pp. 174, 177–78; "Soviet Concern with Vladivostok," British Naval Intelligence Report, 2 July 1943, UK, FO 371/37006/N3987, File 1544; U.S., Office of Strategic Services, RG 226, OSS report 69684 (6 May 1944), box 810; "USSR Lend-Lease Program," pp. 54–55, in Yeaton Collection, HA; O. Edmund Clubb, Vladivostok, to Sec. State, 20 Oct. 1944, U.S., State Dept., RG 59, 861.50/10–2044.

35. *Khronika Magadanskoi partiinoi organizatsii*, pp. 69, 74; "USSR Lend-Lease Program," pp. 54–55, in Yeaton Collection, HA.

36. Edward Pinkowski, "Soviet Trainees in the USA in World War II," *Russian Review*, 5, no. 1 (Autumn 1945): 15–16.

37. "Passenger File, " in U.S., War Shipping Administration, RG 248, box 51.

38. FRUS, 1942, 3: 458; FRUS, 1943, 3: 761; Angus Ward to Secretary of State, 17 May 1943, U.S., State Dept., main decimal file, 861.00/12–16.

39. Shalamov, *Kolyma Tales*, pp. 173–75, 184; Lipper, p. 244.

40. Willard Price, "Japan Faces Russia in Manchuria," *National Geographic*, 82, no. 5 (Nov. 1942): 603.

41. Hays, pp. 3, 28–54, 121–30, 196; Lensen, *Strange Neutrality*, pp. 255, 257.

42. Lensen, *Strange Neutrality*, pp. 128–29.

43. *Voenno-istoricheskii zhurnal*, 1965, no. 8: 64–73; *Manshū ni okeru tai-So sen*, p. 20.

44. An official Soviet account of the August campaign is given in Malinovskii, ed., *Final*. Japanese accounts of the Manchurian and southern Sakhalin fighting are given in *Manshū ni okeru tai-So sen* and Kaneko, respectively. Operations in the Kurile Islands are dealt with in Stephan, *Kuril Islands*, pp. 151–70. For a discussion of Soviet historiography of these campaigns, see Stephan, ed., *USSR and Defeat of Imperial Japan*.

45. O. Edmund Clubb, Vladivostok, to Sec. State, 10 Aug. 1945, U.S., State Dept., RG 59, 740.0011 P.W./8–1045; DVO (2), p. 108.

46. Pegov, pp. 209–10.

47. *Khabarovskaia kraevaia partiinaia organizatsiia*, pp. 274–75, 278–79.

48. *Tikhookeanskaia zvezda*, 14 Aug. 1945, cited in *Khabarovskaia kraevaia partiinaia organizatsiia*, p. 283. On the Boikos of Kolyma, see Gerasimov, *Patrioty Dal'nego Vostoka*, p. 141; Fetisov, pp. 189–90; and Verin.

49. "Short purifying storm" (*korotkaia ochistitel'naia groza*) is used in *Pobeda na Dal'nem Vostoke*, p. 5, and evokes the famous phrase "short victorious war" incorrectly attributed to Interior Minister Vyacheslav Pleve (Plehwe) by his rival Sergei Witte on the eve of war with Japan in 1904. See Sidney Harcave's note in *Memoirs of Count Witte*, p. 781.

25 «» A Front Without War

Epigraph. O. Edmund Clubb to Sec. State, 18 Dec. 1945, U.S., State Dept. main decimal file, 125.977/12–1845.

1. DVO (2), pp. 99, 100, 176.

2. Pegov, p. 216; Thomas J. Cory, "Leading Personalities of the Maritime Province" (31 Jan. 1947), U.S., State Dept. main decimal file 111.20A/1–3147.

3. Pegov, pp. 45, 116; Chernysheva, *Khabarovsk: 1858–1983*, p. 198.

4. VOV, p. 230; Anichkov, p. 360; Tibekin, pp. 120–22; Udovenko, p. 123.

5. Personal communication from an American aviator interned in Khabarovsk during 1944, Lt.-Col. Edwin Morrison, 17 May 1985.

6. Lauterbach, pp. 39–40; Thomas J. Cory, Vladivostok, to Sec. State, 10 Jan. 1947, U.S., State Dept., RG 59, 861.4016/1-1047.

7. Oscar C. Holder, "Notes on Vladivostok" (25 July 1948), U.S., State Dept. main decimal file, 861.00/7-2548.

8. Slavinskii, p. 42; Beloff, *Soviet Policy*, pp. 37–39; Levine, pp. 49, 63, 68–69. *Stanovlenie sovetsko-kitaiskikh otnoshenii*, p. 102, portrays the removal of industrial equipment to the USSR as a measure designed to revitalize the Manchurian economy.

9. Slavinskii, p. 45; Hayashi, p. 311.

10. Capt. Clifford J. McGregor, report to Office of Naval Intelligence, 8 Feb. 1946, U.S., War Shipping Administration RG 248, Soviet Far Eastern Shipping Operations, box 52.

11. Lipper, p. 161; Gerasimov, *Patrioty Dal'nego Vostoka*, p. 103.

12. Conversations in Khabarovsk with former Harbin resident Georgy Derzhavin, February–March 1984. Mikhail Semyonov, born in Manchuria in 1922, was seized in Harbin and removed to Khabarovsk to be judged by a military tribunal. He was later shot. *Sibirskaia gazeta*, 26 Aug. 1993. For other cases, see Nikolaevskii, "Dal'stroi: Sovetskaia katorga," pp. 256–57; Solomon, pp. 87, 127; and Suzanne Rosenberg, *A Soviet Odyssey* (Toronto: Oxford University Press, 1988), pp. 158, 169, 182.

13. *Chitaia 'Ostrov Sakhalin'*, 2: 90–101; Ponomarev pp. 140–46; Galina Dudarets in *Germes* 17 (1–15 July 1990): 5. For a list of Far Eastern labor camps in 1946, see Dallin and Nicolaevsky, pp. 69–71.

14. *Moscow News*, 1989, no. 15: 16.

15. Solomon, pp. 170–71.

16. Vladivostok consulate-general to Sec. State, 29 July, 20 Aug., 9 Sept., and 29 Oct. 1946, U.S., State Dept. main decimal file, 800.2026 and 861.48.

17. This offer is mentioned by Hosaka Masayasu in *Bungei shunjū* 65, no. 7 (May 1987), p. 280.

18. Nimmo, p. 85. See also Hayashi, p. 295; *Bungei shunjū* 60, no. 11 (Sept. 1982): p. 234; Wakatsuki, 1: 1, 19; and "Shiberia horyo shūyōsho," p. 29.

19. Nimmo, p. 80; Kinoshita, pp. 1, 32–33, 57, 245; Wakatsuki, 1: 12–13, 18.

20. *Hokkaido shimbun*, 20 Mar. 1989; Holder, "Notes" (see no. 7); Katō, *Shiberia ki*, pp. 169–71; Nimmo, p. 58; "Shiberia horyo shūyōsho," p. 84; "Interrogation Reports," pp. 32–37, in MacArthur Archives.

21. Miura, p. 229; *Bungei shunjū* 60, no. 11 (Sept. 1982): 260.

22. Kimura, pp. 49–51; Miura, pp. 229, 232; Kinoshita, p. 33; "Interrogation Reports," in MacArthur Archives, p. 50.

23. Wakatsuki, 1: 68.

24. Kinoshita, p. 20.

25. Miura, p. 45.

26. Wakatsuki, 1: 70–71; *Bungei shunjū* 60, no. 11 (Sept. 1982): 51–52.

27. Kinoshita, p. 28.

28. Katō, *Shiberia ki*, p. 22; Wakatsuki, 1: 11–12.

29. *Dal'nevostochnyi pogranichnyi*, p. 214; "Shiberia horyo shūyōsho," p. 26.

30. Solzhenitsyn, *Sobranie sochinenii*, 6: 284.

31. Kinoshita, pp. 101–8; *Bungei shunjū* 60, no. 11 (Sept. 1982): 39–40.

32. "Shiberia horyo shūyōsho," p. 81.

33. These included the last commander of the Kwantung Army, the commander of Unit No. 731, and ten other officers tried in Khabarovsk in 1949 on charges of waging bacteriological warfare. VOV, p. 766; *Bungei shunjū* 65, no. 5 (May 1987): 279.

34. Only 204 of the more than 3,000 Kwantung Army troops and airmen captured during the Khalkhin Gol Incident were repatriated. Coox, *Nomonhan*, 2: 929, 949, 951; Wakatsuki, 2: 435.

35. Wakatsuki, 2: 432–35.

36. Aleksei Kirichenko in *Japan Times*, 22 June 1990, 22 Jan. 1991.

37. "Interrogation Reports," in MacArthur Archives, p. 26.

38. Wakatsuki, 2: 429.

39. *Daily Yomiuri*, 27 Feb. 1991; "Bamu tetsudō shi no rōdō genba," *Asahi shimbun*, evening ed., 9 May 1991; "Shiberia horyo shūyōsho," p. 83.

40. Nimmo, p. 59.

41. Uno Sōsuke (b. 1922), prime minister in 1989. For his reminiscences about life in a Primorye camp, see Uno, *Damoi, Tokyo*.

42. O. Edmund Clubb, Vladivostok, to Sec. State, 15 Sept. 1945. U.S., State Dept. main decimal file, 740.00119 P.W./9–1545.

43. O. Edmund Clubb, Vladivostok, to Sec. State, 7 Dec. 1945, in FRUS, 5:1170; O. Edmund Clubb to Sec. State, 18 Dec. 1945, U.S., State Dept. main decimal file, 125.977/12–1845.

44. Vladivostok consulate-general to Sec. State, 27 Aug. 1946, U.S., State Dept. Archives, RG 59, 125.9771/8-2746.

45. Oscar Holder, "Notes" (see no. 7); Annabelle Bucar, *The Truth About American Diplomats* (Moscow: Litgazeta, 1949), p. 21.

46. Ivanov, p. 199.

47. FRUS, 1948, 4: 1051, 1053n.

48. Lerman, *Po serdtsu blizkie druz'ia*, p. 47.

49. Vladivostok consulate-general to Sec. State, 1 Dec. 1947, U.S., State Dept., RG 59, 811.42700(R)12-147.

50. Solomon, p. 141.

51. Kolarz, *Peoples*, p. 12; Grigorenko, *Memoirs*, p. 431.

52. *Stanovlenie sovetsko-kitaiskikh otnoshenii*, pp. 102–4; Slavinskii, pp. 44–46.

53. *Pogranichnye voiska SSSR, 1945–1950*, p. 661.

54. I am grateful to James Carter for bringing this to my attention. Professor Kathryn Weathersby's research in Russian archives during 1993 promises to throw new light on Soviet policies toward Korea at this time.

55. Correspondence between commander, Far East Air Force, Tokyo, and chief of staff, U.S. Air Force, Washington, 10–12 Oct. 1950, in MacArthur Archives, RG 9, Box 6.

56. *New York Times*, 30–31 July, 1 Aug., 12 Aug. 1953.

57. See "Terrain Studies," "Use Elements of Japan's Anti-Soviet Intelligence Experience," and "Japanese Intelligence — Annex II" (28 Feb. 1950), in MacArthur Archives, RG 6, box 94, folio 2, and box 99, folio 4.

58. *Pogranichnye voiska SSSR, 1945–1950*, p. 602; *Dal'nevostochnyi pogranichnyi*, p. 203; Korsakov, p. 4; *Granitsa*, p. 314.

59. U.S. Air Force Dept., *Intelligence Activities*, p. 72.

60. Carl R. Proffer, *The Widows of Russia* (Ann Arbor, Mich.: Ardis, 1987), p. 59.

61. MERSH, 5: 140–46.

62. Vera Chernysheva in *Dal'revkom*, p. 24.

63. Yurii Lukin, "Zhiznennye temy," *Pravda*, 13 Feb. 1949.

64. Agishev, pp. 7–8; Alenkina, pp. 16–17.

65. Kondrashev. Intimations of this can be detected in a 1935 publication that identified Lenin's famous 7 Apr. 1918 telegram to the Vladivostok soviet warning about the Japanese as "Comrade Lenin Telegram to Vladivostok Soviet with Corrections in Title by Comrade Stalin." The "corrections" consisted of a change of address. *Taezhnye pokhody* (1935 ed.), p. 7.

66. Vasilii Azhaev, *Daleko ot Moskvy* (1947), Stalin Prize, 1949; Aleksandr Chakovskii, *U nas uzhe utro* (1949), Stalin Prize, 1950.

67. Anatolii Vakhov, *Dvoe v taige* (Vladivostok: Primizdat, 1946), p. 67.

68. Ivanov, p. 144. The Americans must have overlooked the Amur District, where surveyors in the 1950s were struck by the ubiquity of corrugated roofs not found in other parts of the USSR. Udovenko, p. 56.

69. Nikolai Maksimov, *Poiski schast'ia* (Moscow: Profizdat, 1952).

70. Conversation with Vasily Efimenko, Khabarovsk, 20 Apr. 1970.

71. Nikolai Zadornov, *Dalekii krai* (Leningrad: Gosizdat, 1950), p. 375.

72. Lerman, *Po serdtsu blizkie druz'ia*, p. 77; Zaitseva, pp. 64–65; Khodzher et al., p. 172; Pismanik, pp. 80, 87; *Kratkaia literaturnaia entsiklopediia*, 3: 515.

73. Gerasimov, *Patrioty Dal'nego Vostoka*, p. 71; *Sever: almanakh* (Magadan: Dalstroi, 1946), p. 31.

74. Aleksei Valdiu, quoted in Khodzher et al., p. 113.

75. Solomon, pp. 99–100. See also Emiot, pp. xvi, 6; Abramsky, "Birobidzhan Project," p. 73; *Encyclopedia Judaica*, 4: 1048; Nora Levin, p. 491; and Benjamin Pinkus, *The Jews of the Soviet Union* (Cambridge: Cambridge Univ. Press, 1988), p. 193.

76. Emiot, p. 8.

77. Ibid., pp. 9, 13, 34; Abramsky, "Birobidzhan Project," p. 73; Nora Levin, p. 509; *Encyclopedia Judaica*, 4: 1048–1049.

78. Nora Levin, pp. 535–41.

79. Ya. Rapoport, "Vospominaniia o dele vrachei," *Druzhba narodov*, 1988, no. 4: 225; Lidiia Shatunovskaia, *Zhizn' v Kremle* (New York: Chalidze, 1982), p. 335.

80. Solomon, p. 219.

81. Rachlin and Rachlin, p. 187; Stajner, p. 357.

26 «» Khrushchevian Interlude

Epigraph. Pravda, 8 Oct. 1959.

1. Lesniak, pp. 193–94.

2. Udovenko, p. 238; *Khronika Magadanskoi partiinoi organizatsii*, p. 133; *Voprosy istorii partiinykh organizatsii Dal'nego Vostoka*, p. 54; Levikov et al., p. 57; Grusha, p. 3.

3. Khudiakov, "Avtobiografiia."

4. Amir Khisamutdinov, "Natasha," *Krasnoe znamia*, 19 Jan. 1990.

5. Suturin, *Delo kraevogo masshtaba*, p. 244; Donskoi, "Tragicheskie dni," p. 4n.

6. Shinkarev, pp. 101–3; *SUPAR Report*, 12 (Jan. 1992): 149; Shifrin, pp. 30, 35, 275–76, 285; Grigorenko, *Memoirs*, pp. 320, 407.

7. In 1948 Gvishiani protected the future premier, Aleksei Kosygin, during the "Leningrad case," because his son Dzhermen had married Kosygin's daughter. As a member of the Politburo, Kosygin was in a position to return the favor in 1953. Conquest, *Inside Stalin's Secret Police*, p. 156.

8. For background on Khrushchev's personnel changes, see Rigby, *Political Elites*, p. 154.

9. *Khronika Magadanskoi partiinoi organizatsii*, p. 136.

10. Stephen Kotkin, "An Interview with Dmitrii Iurasov," *Russian Review* 51, no. 2 (Apr. 1992): 252.

11. Khisamutdinov in *Zotik Matveev*, p. 42; Donskoi, "Tragicheskie dni," p. 6.

12. Khisamutdinov, *Russian Far East*, p. 86.

13. *Dal'nii Vostok za 40 let sovetskoi vlasti*, p. 475.

14. *The Most of Malcolm Muggeridge* (New York: Simon and Schuster, 1966), p. 72.

15. Khisamutdinov, "Kleveta seksota A. N. Lipskogo."

16. "O predsmertnom pis'me A.A. Fadeeva," *Izvestiia TsK SSSR*, 1990, no. 10: 146–55. For an insightful portrait of Fadeyev, see Kornei Chukovskii, "Iz dnevnika, 1955–1969," *Znamia*, 1992, no. 12: 145.

17. Donskoi, "Tragicheskie dni," p. 4n.

18. See Grigortsevich; Shishkin; Gubel'man; Nikiforov; Salekhov; and Kondrat'ev.

19. Tarasova, *Vladimir Klavdievich Arsen'ev*, p. 40.

20. Shelest's story, "Rough Diamond," was carried in the 7 Nov. issue of *Izvestiia*. See Alexander Solzhenitsyn, *The Oak and the Calf, A Memoir*, trans. Harry Willetts (New York: Harper Colophon, 1981), p. 44. See also Shelest, "Kolymskie zapisi."

21. *Ocherki istorii sovetskogo Primor'ia*, p. 212.

22. Viktor Semenovich Viatkin, *Chelovek rozhdaetsia dvazhdy* (Magadan: MKI, 1964).

23. Agishev, p. 167; Vol'fgang Kazak, *Entsiklopedicheskii slovar' russkoi literatury s 1917 goda* (London: Overseas Publications Interchange, 1988), pp. 29–31; *Kratkaia Literaturnaia Entsiklopediia*, 4: 913; David C. Gillespie, "History, Politics, and the Russian Peasant: Boris Mozhaev and the Collectivization of Agriculture," *Slavonic and East European Review*, 67, no. 2 (Apr. 1989): 183–84.

24. Vladimir Turkin, *Moskva-Pekin: stikhi* (Vladivostok: Primizdat, 1951).

25. Aleksandr Grachev, *Padenie*.

26. Klopov, p. 78.

27. Slavinskii, pp. 76, 91, 92–96; Chernysheva, *Khabarovsk: 1858–1983*, pp. 91–92; *Dal'nii Vostok za 40 let sovetskoi vlasti*, p. 477.

28. *Khrushchev Remembers: The Last Testament*, tr. and ed. Strobe Talbott (Boston: Little, Brown, 1974), pp. 249–50. The idea of importing 200,000 Chinese to work in Siberia was first broached by Soviet economists in the 1920s. See SSE, 4: 354.

29. Raymond Garthoff, ed., *Sino-Soviet Military Relations* (New York: Praeger,

1966) p. 88; O. Edmund Clubb, *China and Russia: The "Great Game"* (New York: Columbia University Press, 1971), p. 429.

30. *Dal'nevostochnoe morskoe parokhodstvo*, pp. 302–3, 310; *Vladivostok, 1860–1960*, p. 125.

31. *Dal'nevostochnoe morskoe parokhodstvo*, pp. 303, 310, 323; *Nisso bōeki hand-obukku*, pp. 216–18, 223, 462.

32. *Vladivostok, 1860–1960*, pp. 7, 100–101; Slavinskii, p. 88.

33. Khrushchev interview, *Le Figaro* 9 Apr. 1958, cited in *Encyclopedia Judaica*, 4: 1049.

34. *Ocherki istorii sovetskogo Primor'ia*, p. 215; Khabarovskaia kraevaia biblioteka, *Kalendar' 1964*, p. 24.

27 «» The Era of Stagnation

Epigraph. Pravda, 20 May 1966.

1. Pushkar', *Zdes' nachinaetsia Rossiia*, p. 297.

2. N. N. Akin'shin and Yu. P. Alimov, *Krai, ustremlennyi v budushchee* (Moscow: Mysl', 1984), p. 4.

3. Kalachinskii, p. 147; *Priamurskie vedomosti*, 21 Feb. 1991.

4. Da Cunha, "Maritime Border Guard," p. 1567; Zakharov et al. (1966), p. 252.

5. *Yomiuri shimbun*, 30 Nov. 1969; Aganbegian and Ibragimova, pp. 231, 233; Tepliakov, p. 19; Paderin, *Rediscovered Country*, pp. 186–87; Kirby, p. 32.

6. Yurii Andropov, *Izbrannye rechi i stat'i* (Moscow: Politizdat, 1983), p. 110.

7. *Pravda*, 30 Sept. 1984.

8. Mote, p. 305; Victor Mote in Robert G. Jensen, Theodore Shabad, and Arthur W. Wright, eds. *Soviet Natural Resources in the World Economy* (Chicago: University of Chicago Press, 1983), p. 135; Bartkova, p. 42.

9. Michael Bradshaw in Rodgers, p. 264; Dienes, "Economic and Strategic Position," p. 153; Dienes, "Soviet-Japanese Economic Relations," p. 517; North, p. 214.

10. For details of Brezhnev-era science in the Far East, see Pushkar', *Tikhookean-skii forpost nauki*.

11. A. Pushkar', "Zdravnitsy u Tikhogo okeana," *Izvestiia*, 2 Mar. 1984; *Izvestiia*, 28 Jan. 1972.

12. Vladimir Safronov, *Litsom k litsu*, p. 28; *Izvestiia*, 21 Mar. 1973.

13. *Ian Gamarnik*, p. 94; Voishnis, "Bol'sheviki Dal'nego Vostoka," p. 220.

14. *Sovetskaia kul'tura*, 15 Mar. 1988.

15. Boris Khazanov, "Proza poeta," *Grani*, 137 (1985): 300–301. For more sympathetic treatment, see Adele Barker, "The Divided Self: Yuri Rytkheu and Contemporary Chukchi Literature," in Diment and Slezkine, pp. 215–26.

16. Evgeny Kozlovsky in *Katalog* (Ann Arbor, Mich.: Ardis, 1982), p. 105.

17. Dienes, "Economic and Strategic Position," pp. 150, 172; Dienes, "Soviet-Japanese Economic Relations," p. 522.

18. DVO (2), pp. 271, 293, 301–2, 377.

19. On the reassignment of discredited Siberian and Far Eastern officials in the 1860s and 1940s, see Kropotkin, *Memoirs*, pp. 172–73; and Rigby, *Political Elites*, p. 119, respectively.

20. Shatskii, p. 4.

21. For exhortations on attaining food self-sufficiency between 1928 and 1961, see Unpelev, p. 73; and USSR, KPSS, *XXII s″ezd*, 2: 65.

22. Dibb, pp. 151–52.   23. *Izvestiia*, 4 Apr. 1972.

24. DVO (2), p. 294.   25. Schiffer, pp. 124–85.

26. Dienes, "Economic and Strategic Position," pp. 167–69; *Izvestiia*, 7 Apr. 1989.

27. Mote, p. 304; Tepliakov, p. 21; DVO (2), p. 294.

28. For a discussion of these problems, see Leslie Dienes in Rodgers, pp. 269–301.

29. *Krasnoe znamia*, 22 Oct. 1983. For a discussion of transport in the Far East, see Robert N. North in Rodgers, pp. 185–224.

30. *Pravda*, 14 Aug. 1984; *Dal'nii Vostok*, 1968, no. 2: 191.

31. Tepliakov, p. 31.

32. *Pravda*, 1 Aug. 1986; *Izvestiia*, 7 Aug. 1986.

33. Ann Helgeson in Rodgers, p. 71.

34. Rybakovskii, p. 166.

35. Knox, p. 231.

36. See the collection of articles on the 80th anniversary of Fadeyev's birth in *Tikhookeanskaia zvezda*, 24 Dec. 1981. See also Chernaia, "Dal'nevostochnaia tema."

37. *Marsh molodosti*, p. 35.

38. *Ian Gamarnik*, p. 125, citing a 1967 interview.

39. Pegov, p. 104.

40. For an example of this genre, see the letter of Vadim Konstantinovich Zausaev, deputy director of the Khabarovsk Institute for Economic Research, on Washington's KAL "provocation." *Tikhookeanskaia zvezda*, 10 Sept. 1983.

41. Amir Khisamutdinov, as quoted in Lev Nikolaevich Kniazev, *Korabli idut na San Frantsisko* (Vladivostok: Dal'nevostochnoe knizh. izdat., 1974), p. 98.

42. Aleksei Val'diu, in Khodzher et al., p. 143. See also *Skazanie o schast'e*. Sycophancy found expression in ethnography as well as literature. See for example Balitskii, *Malye narody* and Boiko, *Sotsial'noe razvitie*. Vitaly Balitsky, former professor of the MVD Police Academy in Khabarovsk, asserted in *Voprosy istorii partiinykh organizatsii*, p. 97, that aborigines underwent a "painless transition" to socialism thanks to the Party.

43. Rytkheu confided this to Boris Khazanov. See Khazanov, "Proza poeta," *Grani*, 1985, no. 137: 300–301.

44. Ibid.; Zaitseva, pp. 85–86.

45. Khazanov, "Proza poeta," as cited in no. 43, p. 301.

46. "Vetka stlanika," *Na severe dal'nem*, 1982, no. 1: 72.

47. *Pravda*, 9 Dec. 1984.

48. Goble, ms., p. 1.

49. Georgii N. Mikhailov, Magadan District, to Elizabeth Neuffer, *New York Times*, 29 June 1987.

50. Shelley, p. 120.

51. *Khabarovskaia nedelia*, 18 Feb. 1984.

52. John Barron, *MiG Pilot* (New York: Readers Digest, 1980), p. 81.

53. *Soviet Analyst*, 9. no. 11 (28 May 1980).

54. *Izvestiia*, 4 Feb. 1984.

55. *Naselenie SSSR, 1973* (Moscow: Statistika, 1973), pp. 167–69; *Tikhookeanskaia zvezda*, 8 June 1983; *Magadanu — 50 let*, p. 5.

56. Conversations with FESCO crew (1–3 Sept. 1966, 16–24 Apr. 1970, 12, 14 July 1972, 15–17 Aug. 1981; with crew of *Ochakov* (21–22 Sept. 1970); scientists aboard *Dmitry Mendeleev* (18–19 Mar. 1971, 15 Sept. 1972, 29 Sept.–2 Oct. 1981); and Far Eastern fishing fleet worker Lyubov Sheichenko (8–10 May 1983).

57. Aganbegian and Ibragimova, p. 168; *Pravda*, 9 Dec. 1984.

58. Mark Popovskii, "Sovetskaia prostitutka: professiia kotoroi net," *Grani*, 1984, no. 132: 145–56; Vladimir Safronov, *Litsom k litsu*, p. 37.

59. L. Kapeliushnyi, "Ikra s dushkom," *Izvestiia*, 19 Oct. 1983.

60. *Literaturnaia gazeta*, 26 (29 June 1983): 15.

61. The sought-after medals belonged to Georgy Kholostyakov, commander of the 7th (Pacific) Fleet (1951–53). *Izvestiia*, 25 July 1984.

62. Mikhail Millionshchikov, quoted in the *New York Times*, 30 Mar. 1972.

63. Alla Epsteyn, "Is the Amur River Dying?," *Soviet Observer*, 9 Dec. 1988; "Nuzhno li 'pokoriat' reki?," *Dal'nii Vostok*, 1989, no. 4: 119–35.

28 «» Frontier Ethos

Epigraph. My berezhem svoiu granitsu, p. 20.

1. Gennadii Osipovich, "Gigantskii dzhambo sbil ia," *Molodoi dal'nevostochnik*, June–July 1991.

2. *Tikhookeanskaia zvezda*, 10 Sept. 1983.

3. Kots and Shmakov, p. 47. On Kliuchevsky: Treadgold, "Russian Expansion," p. 148.

4. Karatsupa, p. 6.

5. The islands of Wrangel, Herald, Bennett, Henrietta, and Jeannette total 2,819

square miles. On 5 Oct. 1991 the Russian Foreign Ministry concluded a boundary treaty with the United States delimiting claims in the Bering Sea.

6. Although the main Amur-Ussuri channels separate Kazakevich from the USSR, Soviet authorities claimed that the international frontier ran along the Kazakevich (Fuyuan) Channel. Moscow closed this channel to Chinese shipping from 1967 to 1977 in retaliation for Chinese claims to the area. Kazakevich is occupied by Russian Army and border guard units.

7. Shifting currents transformed the Damansky-Zhenbao area (one square mile) from a peninsula to an island 300 feet from the Chinese shore and 1,200 feet from the Soviet shore. KGB border guards began to patrol it after the invasion of Czechoslovakia in Aug. 1968 and were ambushed by units of the People's Liberation Army. China retained possession.

8. *Asahi shimbun*, 7 Dec. 1991, cited in *SUPAR Report*, 12 (Jan. 1992): 35.

9. Kim Kyeoung-choon, "Tumankang haryu," pp. 206–7. A Tumen border treaty was ratified on 27 Nov. 1991. *SUPAR Report*, 12 (Jan. 1992): 65–66.

10. Vladimir Safronov, *Litsom k litsu*, p. 6.

11. Vladimir Stepanov, *Ideologicheski*, p. 45.

12. Penzin, p. 124.

13. For the full text, see *Pravda*, 26 Nov. 1982. The law went into effect on 1 Mar. 1983. *Chasovye sovetskikh granits*, p. 316.

14. *Ogonek*, 1987, no. 40: 4–5.

15. *Japan Times*, 15 June 1984.

16. Examples of "vigilance literature" include: Vladimir Safronov, *Litsom k litsu*, p. 18; D. A. Volkogonov, *Psikhologicheskaia voina* (Moscow: Voenizdat, 1983); Viktor Volkov, *Ne stynet nenavist' k vragu* (Moscow: Voenizdat, 1984); Iurii Kornilov and Boris Chekhonin, *Gubernantka iz TsRU* (Moscow: Sovetskaia Rossiia, 1984); Vladimir Stepanov, *Ideologicheski*.

17. da Cunha, "Maritime Border Guard," pp. 1563–65.

18. Aleksei Myagkov, *Inside the KGB* (New York: Ballantine, 1981), pp. 35–36.

19. Stephan, *Kuril Islands*, pp. 191–92; *Japan Times*, 1 Nov. 1988.

20. Art. 28, 1982 Law on USSR State Frontiers.

21. Kots and Shmakov, p. 47; *Dzerzhintsy*, p. 148.

22. *Dzerzhintsy*, pp. 3, 8; *Marsh molodosti*, pp. 82–83.

23. Quoted in *Vechernii Vladivostok*, 28 May 1990.

24. Official regulations specify the distance of outhouse from other installations: 75 meters except in extreme northern latitudes.

25. *Pravda*, 21 Sept. 1984. For some piquant passages on fraternal ties between Soviet and Czech border guards, see *Chasovie sovetskikh granits*, p. 215.

26. *Krasnaia zvezda*, 5 Mar. 1984.

27. Vareikis to Stalin, 8 Sept. 1937, quoted in Suturin, *Delo kraevogo masshtaba*, p. 51.

28. "Narkobiznes v pogranich'e," *Vostok Rossii* 3, no. 25 (Jan. 1992): 12.

29. *Granitsa*, p. 203; *Dzerzhintsy*, pp. 147, 154; *Zemlia, na kotoroi ia schastliv*, p. 25; *Literaturnaia gazeta*, 7 Oct. 1981.

30. *Organizatsiia KPSS Evreiskoi Avtonomnoi oblasti*, p. 113; *Granitsa*, pp. 444–61.

31. *Dal'nevostochnyi pogranichnyi*, p. 240; *Sovetskaia kul'tura*, 20 Aug. 1987; Pashkov and Nikiforov, p. 71.

32. *Granitsa na zamke*, p. 221; *Pogranichnaia zastava*, pp. 128–29; *Stoiat na Amure russkie sela*, p. 12.

33. *Pravda*, 21 Sept. 1984.

34. *Dal'nevostochnoe uskorenie*, pp. 8, 10, 30–60; *Voprosy partiinoi raboty*, pp. 237–38.

35. *Dzerzhintsy*, pp. 143, 157; K. P. Rotov, "What Do Soviet Children Want to Be?," *Sovietland*, 1938, no. 2 (Feb.): 22.

36. *Stoiat na Amure russkie sela*, p. 4.

37. *Dal'nevostochnoe uskorenie*, pp. 28, 31, 34, 40, 50; *Priamurskie vedomosti*, 1 Feb. 1991.

38. *Sovetskii entsiklopedicheskii slovar'* (Moscow: Sovetskaia entsiklopediia, 1983), p. 544; Pashkov, *Za krai rodnoi*, p. 123; Pashkov and Nikiforov, p. 60; *Kalendar' voina 1984* (Moscow: Voenizdat, 1983), p. 174; *Dal'nevostochnyi pogranichnyi*, pp. 82–83.

39. Karatsupa, p. 46; *Dzerzhintsy*, p. 153.

40. Vyacheslav Sukhnev in *Dal'nii Vostok*, 1989, no. 11: 137; *Dal'nevostochnyi pogranichnyi*, p. 279.

41. Tsvigun, p. 2; *Dal'nevostochnyi pogranichnyi*, p. 249.

42. Quoted in *Pogranichnaia zastava*, p. 299.

43. *My berezhem svoiu granitsu*, p. 38.

44. Valerii Andreev; *Granitsa*, pp. 302–11; *Dal'nii Vostok*, 1988, no. 2: 8; *Chasovye sovetskikh granits*, p. 315.

45. Aleksandr Mishkin, *Ptitsy letaiut bez kompasa* (Khabarovsk: Khab. knizh. izdat., 1984).

46. *Dzerzhintsy*, p. 3; *Granitsa*, pp. 319–24; and Tsvigun, p. 2.

47. *Granitsa*, p. 313; Zibarev and Chistiakova, p. 102.

48. *Granitsa*, p. 313; *Voprosy istorii partiinykh organizatsii*, p. 5; and Bartkova, p. 4.

Conclusion: Stormy Activity in a Time of Troubles

Epigraphs. Gorbachev, *New Stage*, p. 37; Rumyantsev, then head of the Constitutional Commission, RSFSR Supreme Soviet, quoted in *Vladivostok*, 30 Nov. 1991; and William Alexander Gerhardie, *Memoirs of a Polyglot* (New York: Knopf, 1931), p. 102.

1. For a detailed description of Sakhalin's "perestroika from below," see Saktaganov.

2. Conversations with Evdokiya Gayer, 9–10 July 1990; *Izvestiia*, 7 Apr. 1989; *Report on the USSR*, 3, no. 32 (9 Aug. 1991): 29.

3. When a South Korean patron cut off funds in 1992, Viktor Smoliak dropped the word "Friendship" and reorganized the institute into a joint stock company (*Priamurskie vedomosti*, 29 Apr. 1992). His Party background buried by several layers of semantic sediment, Smoliak was identified by an American journalist as "a joint-venture businessman and former economist who heads the Amur Business Club." Richard Read in *The Oregonian*, 24 Mar. 1992.

4. Interview with Far Eastern Military Commander, Viktor Novozhilov, *Le Monde*, 5 Sept. 1991.

5. Khisamutdinov, *Russian Far East*, p. 158.

6. *Vladivostok*, 30 Nov. 1991.

7. *Vostok Rossii* 3, no. 25 (Jan. 1992): 5; *Priamurskie vedomosti*, 25 Aug. 1992.

8. Quoted in Grant, ms, p. 39.

9. Phrase of an unnamed Indian politician, quoted in the [London] *Times Literary Supplement*, 29 May 1992, p. 10.

10. DVO (2), pp. 446–47; Tepliakov, p. 156.

11. "Zhiznennyi uroven' padaet," *Krasnoe znamia*, 27 Apr. 1993; "Economic Life of the Russian Far East," *ITL Bulletin* (Informational Technology Lab, Vladivostok), 23–29 May 1993. For a sober overview of the impact of economic reforms on region, see Minakir, *Ekonomicheskaia reforma*.

12. *Anchorage Daily News*, 5 July 1992; *Priamurskie vedomosti*, 14 Feb. 1991; *SUPAR Report*, 13 (July 1992): 124.

13. *RA Report*, 14 (Jan. 1993): 69, 126; *Russian Far East Update*, 3, no. 2 (Feb. 1993): 3.

14. *SUPAR Report*, 10 (Jan. 1991): 163; Fedorov, p. 2.

15. *Svobodnyi Sakhalin*, 22 Feb. 1992.

16. *Russian Far East Update*, 3, no. 3 (Mar. 1993): 10.

17. *Priamurskie vedomosti*, 26 Oct. 1991; *Hokkaido shimbun*, 25 Nov. 1991; *Russian Far East Update*, 2, no. 6 (June 1992): 5.

18. *Ogonek*, 1990, no. 39: 22–23; *Sostoianie prirodnoi sredy v SSSR v 1988 godu* (Moscow: n.p., 1989), cited in *Report on the USSR* 2, no. 9 (2 Mar. 1990): 8; *Russian Far East*, June–July 1992, p. 35; *Hokkaido shimbun*, 16 Apr. 1992.

19. O. Zhuravina in *Dal'nii Vostok*, 1989, no. 3: 52; *Ogonek*, 1989, no. 26: 1; *SUPAR Report*, 7 (July 1989): 75, 88; *Region* (Apr. 1990): 4; *Komsomolskaia pravda*, 21 Feb. 1989; *Report on the USSR*, 2, no. 30 (27 July 1990): 36; *Priamurskie vedomosti*, 19 Feb. 1991.

20. P. Kh. Chausov in *Formirovanie i razvitie rabochego klassa*, pp. 72–73; Viktor Smoliak, *Dal'nii Vostok*, 1987, no. 8: 156.

21. *Na severe dal'nem*, 1988, no. 2: 3–76.

22. *Kraevedcheskii biulleten'*, published quarterly from 1990 under the editorship of Mikhail Vysokov, assisted by Vladislav Latyshev (director of the Sakhalin Regional Museum), Aleksandr Kostanov (Sakhalin Regional Archives), Valery Shubin, Olga Shubina, and Marina Ishchenko.

23. I. Litvinenko "Zakrytyi perelom," *Dal'nii Vostok*, 1988, no. 6: 139–54.

24. *Rubezh*, published in Harbin (1927–45) and revived in Vladivostok in 1992 as *Rubezh: Tikhookeanskii al'manakh* under the editorship of Aleksandr Kolesov and Boris Dyachenko.

25. Anatolii Lialiakin, *Vostok Rossii*, 1991, no. 19: 1. Andrei Kalachinsky, chairman of the DVGU Journalism Department, expressed respect for Lialiakin as a journalist. *Utro Rossii*, 25 Nov. 1992.

26. See Khisamutdinov, *Russian Far East*, pp. 164–67; Amir Khisamutdinov, *U Admiral'skoi pristani* (Vladivostok: Obshchestvo izucheniia Amurskogo kraia, 1993).

27. *Radio Liberty Research Bulletin*, 29 Aug. 1988, p. 4; Suturin, "Ogon' po svoim," p. 18. A memorial to Osip Mandelshtam was dedicated in Vladivostok. *Vladivostok*, 14 Nov. 1990.

28. "Nazoem vsekh poimenno," *Utro Rossii*, 31 July 1992; *Priamurskie vedomosti*, 20 Oct. 1990; 4, 20 Jan. 1991; 28 Feb. 1991; *Reklamnaia gazeta*, 26 Sept. 1989.

29. *Tikhookeanskaia zvezda*, 7 Dec. 1990.

30. Examples include *Skazanie o schast'e*; *Porodnilis' na Amure* (Khabarovsk: Khab. knizh. izdat., 1982); and V. Zibarev and N. Chistiakova, *S pomoshch'iu pobedivshego proletariata: O pomoshchi sovetskogo gosudarstva v preodolenii otstalosti malykh narodnostei Dal'nego Vostoka pri perekhode k sotsializmu* (Magadan: Magadan. knizh. izdat., 1982).

31. Khodzher's perestroikist novel, *Veshchun* (Prophet), was serialized in *Dal'nii Vostok*, 1989, nos. 8–12, during which its author was dropped from the editorial board.

32. *Radio Liberty Research Bulletin*, 8 Mar. 1988, p. 3.

33. *Russian Far East Update*, 3, no. 4 (Apr. 1993): 10.

34. Rafik Aliev, former Director of the Center of Asia-Pacific Research. *Dal'nevostochnyi uchenyi*, 14 Jan. 1993, p. 4.

35. Sungorkin, p. 14.

36. *Vostok Rossii*, 1991, no. 20 (Dec.): 3.

37. *RA Report*, 14 (Jan. 1993): 128.

38. Leonard Shkolnik to Peter Gumbel in *Wall Street Journal*, 18 July 1989. Jews constituted 4 percent of Birobidzhan's population in 1989. *Komsomolskaia pravda*, 12 July 1990.

39. *SUPAR Report*, 12 (Jan. 1992): 155; *Russian Far East Update*, 2, no. 7 (July 1992): 3.

40. *Tikhookeanskaia zvezda*, 7 Dec. 1990; *SUPAR Report*, 12 (Jan. 1992): 152.

41. *Tikhookeanskaia zvezda*, 26 Oct. 1991.

42. *Sibirskaia gazeta*, 9 Sept. 1993.

43. *Region* (Dec. 1990), p. 1.

44. Vladimir Yakubovsky in *Japan Times*, 25 Nov. 1992. David Hooson, Professor of Geography at the University of California, foresaw the emergence of an independent Siberian–Far Eastern polity by the year A.D. 2000. Conference on Soviet-Japanese Relations, University of California, Berkeley, 21 Sept. 1991.

45. *Region* (Dec. 1990), p. 1; *Krasnoe znamia*, 11 Sept. 1990; *Krasnaia zvezda*, 22 Sept. 1990; *Vechernii Vladivostok*, 19 May 1990; *Dal'nevostochnaia Respublika*, published in Vladivostok starting in 1990.

46. *Priamurskie vedomosti*, 20 Feb. 1991; Boris Lvovich Reznik in *Izvestiia*, 8 Feb. 1990, p. 2; *SUPAR Report*, 10 (Jan. 1991): 160.

47. *Primorskie vedomosti*, 24 Oct. 1991.

48. *RA Report*, 14 (Jan. 1993): 45.

49. *SUPAR Report*, 12 (Jan. 1992), 55, 57, 60, 143; 13 (July 1992): 31, 74, 87; "Uzhe ne krai, eshche ne respublika," *Sibirskaia gazeta*, 29 (July 1993): 5.

50. *Vladivostok*, 6 Oct. 1992.

51. *SUPAR Report*, 10 (Jan. 1991): 12–13.

52. *Japan Times*, 22 June 1993; *Russian Far East Update*, 3, no. 6 (June 1993): 1, 12. See also *Vostok Rossii*, 1991, no. 11 (Oct.): 2; Vladimir Larchenkov in *Gipoteza*, 1991, no. 11: 2; *Svobodnyi Sakhalin*, 2 Sept. 1991; *Sovetskii Sakhalin*, 2 Oct. 1991; *Molodaia gvardiia* (Yuzhno-Sakhalinsk ed.), 1 Oct. 1991; and *SUPAR Report*, 12 (Jan. 1992): 58.

53. Jerry Sullivan and Elisa Miller, "How a Soviet Pacific Rim Strategy Could Help World Peace," *The Weekly* (Seattle), 20–26 Jan. 1988; Wada Haruki, "A Model for a New World," *Japan Times*, 4 Sept. 1990.

54. Damon Darlin, "Booming Free-Trade Zone in Far East is Goal of Huge Tumen River Project," *Wall Street Journal*, 10 June 1992; "Trilateral Project" at the John F. Kennedy School of Government, Harvard University; "Plan issued to end island row," *Japan Times*, 30 Sept. 1992. For more sober appraisals, see Dienes, "Economic and Strategic Position"; and Xu, ed., *Sulian dongbu*, p. 436.

55. Cao, "Xiboli dongpian jiyao," p. 8.

56. Kuropatkin, *Russian Army*, 1: 71.

57. Fujita, pp. 218–24.

58. Veniukov, p. 75.

59. N. Tripolsky, "Plans to Set Up a 'Pacific Community': A Fresh Threat to Peace," *Far Eastern Affairs*, 1985, no. 2: 112.

60. For criticism of Moscow's domination of the Russian National Committee, see *Priamurskie vedomosti*, 25 Aug. 1992. For local equivalents, see *Russian Far East Update*, 3, no. 3 (Mar. 1993): 10.

61. *Wall Street Journal*, 1 Feb. 1993; *Japan Times*, 23 Nov. 1992; *RA Report*, 14 (Jan. 1993): 68; *Russian Far East Update*, 3, no. 3 (Mar. 1993): 8.

62. The growing number of foreign firms prompted Russian entrepreneurs such as Vladivostok-based Information Technology Lab to publish English-language directories such as *Business Nakhodka* (1992), *Business Sakhalin* (1992), and *Amur Territory: Business Directory* (1993). Useful as a general reference work is *Pocket Handbook of the Russian Far East*, ed. Elisa Miller and Alexander Karp. (Seattle: Russian Far East Update, 1994). See also *The Russian Far East: An Economic Handbook*, ed. Pavel A. Minakir (Armonk, N.Y.: M.E. Sharpe, 1994).

63. *RA Report*, 14 (Jan. 1993): 85; *Russian Far East*, June 1992, p. 3.

64. *RA Report*, 14 (Jan. 1993): 108–16.

65. *Hokkaido shimbun*, 22 Apr. 1992. *Japan Times*, 25 May 1993.

66. For background on Sakhalin Koreans, see Onuma Yasuaki, *Saharin kimin* (Tokyo: Chūō kōronsha, 1992).

67. *Priamurskie vedomosti*, 28 Feb. 1991.

68. *Russian Far East Update*, 3, no. 1(Jan. 1993): 3; *RA Report*, 14 (Jan. 1993): 79.

69. *SUPAR Report*, 13 (July 1992): 91.

70. Reported in the Hong Kong newspaper *Shijie ribao*, 18 Dec. 1992.

71. *Priamurskie vedomosti*, 22 Feb. 1991; *SUPAR Report*, 12 (Jan. 1992): 157.

72. Material from this paragraph has been drawn from *Russian Far East Update*, 3, no. 3 (Mar. 1993): 6; 3, no. 4 (Apr. 1993): 1, 10; 3, no. 5 (May 1993): 8; *SUPAR Report*, 11 (July 1991): 97; 12 (Jan. 1992): 66.

73. *Russian Far East Update*, 3, no. 8 (Aug. 1993): 10.

74. *Krasnoe znamia*, 27 May 1993.

75. Milan Hauner, "Does the Soviet Far East Have a Future?," *Report on the USSR* 1, no. 9 (3 Mar. 1989): 7. See also *Region*, 4 (Apr. 1990): 3; *SUPAR Report*, 10 (Jan. 1991): 89, 171; *RA Report*, 14 (Jan. 1993): 65, 137.

«« «« »» »»

Select Bibliography

The Select Bibliography contains sources cited in the notes as well as materials deemed useful for the study of Far Eastern history. For additional bibiliographical information, see David N. Collins, *Siberia and the Soviet Far East: World Bibliographical Series*, vol. 127 (Oxford: Clio Press, 1991); Vasilii A. Grachev, *Obzor istochnikov po istorii Priamur'ia i Okhotsko-Kamchatskogo kraia.* (Vladivostok: DVGU, 1927); *Istoriia Dal'nego Vostoka SSSR: Bibliograficheskii ukazatel'* (Vladivostok: IIAENDV, 1980); *Istoriia dal'nevostochnoi derevni (1861–1975 gg.): Ukazatel' literatury i istochnikov* (Vladivostok: DVNTs AN SSSR, 1979); *Istoriia Vladivostoka, 1860–1959 gg.: Kratkaia bibliografiia*; T. I. Iakovleva, comp. (Vladivostok: Dal'nevostochnyi filial, SO AN SSSR, 1959); Robert J. Kerner, *Northeastern Asia: A Selected Bibliography*, 2 vols. (Berkeley: Univ. of California Press, 1939); Iakov Gertselevich Khaninson, *Istoriia, sostoianie i zadachi bibliografii Sibiri i Dal'nego Vostoka* (Novosibirsk: Gosudarstvennaia publichnaia nauchnaia tekhnologicheskaia biblioteka SO AN SSSR, 1970); A. N. Lebedeva, G. A. Ozerova, and L. S. Pankratova, comp., *Ukazatel' bibliograficheskikh posobii po Sibiri i Dal'nemu Vostoku, XIX v.–1968* (Novosibirsk: Gosudarstvennaia publichnaia nauchno-tekhnicheskaia biblioteka, 1975) with annual updates; Zotik Nikolaevich Matveev, *Chto chitat' o Dal'nevostochnoi oblasti* (Vladivostok: Knizh. delo, 1925); Patricia Polansky, "Resources for Current Research on Siberia and the Soviet Far East: A Bibliographic Profile," in Rodger Swearingen, ed., *Siberia and the Soviet Far East* (Stanford, Calif.: Hoover Institution Press, 1987), pp. 273–89; and Patricia Polansky, "Siberian and Far Eastern Publishing in Late Imperial Russia," *Pacifica*, 1, no. 2 (Sept. 1989): 77–100. Far Eastern archives (1844–1939), moved from Vladivostok to Tomsk in 1940–42, are discussed by Aleksandr Gruzdev, "Ot kogo berezhem? O sud'be Dal'nevostochnogo arkhiva," *Problemy Dal'nego Vostoka*, 1990, no. 1: 180–86. Current works on the Far East are listed in *RA [Russia in Asia] Report*, published in January and July by the Center for Russia in Asia, Univ. of Hawaii.

I. Unpublished Sources

Bakhmeteff Archive, Columbia Univ.. Klavdii I. Popov Papers.

Balakshin, Peter [Petrovich]. "Man from Primorye." Unpublished manuscript. Berkeley, Calif. 1989. Univ. of Hawaii Library.

Bassin, Mark. "A Russian Mississippi? A Political-Geographical Inquiry into the Vision of Russia on the Pacific, 1840–1865." Ph.D. diss., Univ. of California at Berkeley, 1983.

Clark, Donald N. "Vanished Exiles: The Prewar Russian Community in Korea and Its Fate." Paper delivered at the 1st Pacific Basin International Conference on Korean Studies, Honolulu, 27 July–2 Aug. 1992.

Donskoi, Vladimir Konstantinovich. "Tragicheskie dni Zotika Matveeva." Vladivostok, 19 May 1993. Signed, dated typescript in Univ. of Hawaii Library.

Germany. Weltwirtschafts-archiv, Hamburg. Firmen archiv. "Kunst & Albers: Aus der Geschichte eines Handelshauses im Fernen Osten, 1864–1914." Unsigned typescript, Oct. 1939.

Goble, Paul A. "Ukrainians in the Soviet Far East: Background Notes and Current Developments." Unpublished manuscript. Washington, n.d. [1988].

Grant, Bruce. "Memory and Forgetting Among the Nivkhi of Sakhalin Island." Ph.D. diss. Univ. of Texas, 1993.

Hoover Institution Archives, Stanford, California
    William S. Barrett Collection
    Grace Bungey Collection
    Far Eastern Republic Collection
    William H. Johnson Collection
    Boris Nicolaevsky Collection
    Theo. Olferieff Collection
    M. L. Shapiro Collection
    Rodney Searle Sprigg Collection
    Yurii Karlovich Stark Memoirs
    Elena Varnek Collection
    A. S. Varska [Ravich] Collection
    Ivan D. Yeaton Collection
Hoover Institution Library, Stanford, California
    Edith M. Faulstich, "The Siberian Sojourn," 2 vols. typescript (1972–77).

Khisamutdinov, Amir Aleksandrovich. Unpublished manuscripts.
"Kleveta seksota A. N. Lipskogo." Apr. 1992. Author's collection.
"Vladimir Arsen'ev." Apr. 1992. Univ. of Hawaii Library.
Khudiakov, Sergei Afanas'evich. "Avtobiografiia." Unpublished manuscript dated 5
July 1990. Author's collection.
Library of Congress, Washington, D.C.
Manuscripts Division
Carl W. Ackerman Papers
Ivan Alekseevich Korzukhin Papers
Roland Sletor Morris Papers
Orientalia Division, Japan Section
Mantetsu [South Manchurian Railway Company]. Reports from the Keizai
chōsakai [Economic survey society], Harubin jimusho [Harbin Office];
and Hokuman keizai chōsajo North Manchurian Economic Research Of-
fice].
Naikaku chōsakyoku. Chōsashitsu [Cabinet research office, research room].
"Sorempō jijō" [Conditions in the USSR]. 24 vols. 1936–37. Uncata-
loged "B Collection," Washington Documents Center.
MacArthur Memorial Archives. Norfolk, Virginia.
"Interrogation Reports: Soviet Use and Treatment of Japanese Prisoners of War"
(interviews with repatriated POWs, 1947–50). RG 6, box 15, folio 4.
Materials relating to Japanese intelligence operations in the Soviet Far East,
1931–45, RG 6, box 99, folio 4.
"Terrain Studies — Soviet Far East," Papers of Charles A. Willoughby
Queen, George Sherman. "The United States and the Material Advance of Russia,
1881–1906." Ph.D. diss., Illinois Univ., 1941.
Slezkine, Yuri. "Russia's Small Peoples: The Policies and Attitudes towards the
Native Northerners," Ph.D. diss., Univ. of Texas, 1989.
United Kingdom, Foreign Office Archives. FO 371/31834–35. Public Records Of-
fice, London.
United States (all documents are in the National Archives unless otherwise noted)
Department of the Army. "Interrogation of General Liushkov" (reel 4) and
other materials in U.S. Military Intelligence Reports: The Soviet Union,
1919–1941, microfilmed by Univ. Publications of America, Frederick Mary-
land, 1984.
Department of State. RG 59 and State Department Main Decimal File. Consular
Reports, Vladivostok, 1898–1923, 1940–48.
Department of the Navy. Operational Archives Branch. Naval Historical Center.
Washington, D.C.
Chief of Naval Operations, Telegrams between Washington, Moscow, Vladi-
vostok. Aug.–Dec. 1945.

Personal Papers of Admiral Harry Erwin Yarnell. Series 1, Box 2. Log and Other Materials Relating a Visit to Vladivostok, 28 July–1 Aug. 1937.

Office of Strategic Services. RG 226 East European Section. North Pacific Russian Shipping, 1942–1945.

War Department. RG 350. Bureau of Insular Affairs. File on Bolsheviks, 1918–39. no. 28342.

War Shipping Administration. RG 248. Records of Russian Area Shipping.

USSR, NKVD, Upravlenie NKVD po Dal'nevostochnomu kraiu, Central KGB Archives, Omsk.

Delo no. 14040 Kontr-revoliutsionnoi shpionsko-vreditel'skoi organizatsii sushchestvovavshei v DV Gosudarstvennom Universitete, vkhodivshei v sostav pravo-trotskistskogo zagovora na Dal'nem Vostoke. 1938.

Delo no. 980847 na Liushkova G. S. "Spravka" Aug. 1938.

Valliant, Robert Britton. "Japan and the Trans-Siberian Railroad, 1885–1905." Ph.D. diss., Univ. of Hawaii, 1974.

Watrous, Stephen Digby. "Russia's Land of the Future: Regionalism and the Awakening of Siberia, 1819–1894." Ph.D. diss., Univ. of Washington, 1970.

Wolff, David. "To the Harbin Station: City Building in Russian Manchuria, 1898–1914." Ph.D. diss., Univ. of California at Berkeley, 1991.

II. Far Eastern Newspapers

Ainu (Yuzhno-Sakhalinsk), 1990–

Amurskaia kooperatsiia (Blagoveshchensk), 1918–19

Amurskaia pravda (Blagoveshchensk), 1918–

Boevaia vakhta (Vladivostok), 1936–

Dalekaia okraina (Vladivostok), 1907–17

Dal'nevostochnaia Respublika (Vladivostok), 1990–

Dal'nevostochnyi moriak (Vladivostok), ca. 1937–

Dal'nevostochnyi uchenyi (Vladivostok), 1974–

Dal'nii Vostok (Vladivostok), 1892–1922

Dal'nii Vostok (Khabarovsk), 1946–

Del-in: Pacific Business Herald (Vladivostok), 1990–

Delovaia Sibir'-Business Siberia (Vladivostok), 1918–20

Demokraticheskii vestnik (Vladivostok), 1991–

Dialog (Petropavlovsk-Kamchatskii), 1990–

Dos'e (Yuzhno-Sakhalinsk), 1990–

Ekho: gazeta bezpartiinaia demokraticheskaia (Vladivostok), 1919–20

Germes (Yuzhno-Sakhalinsk), 1990–91

Gipoteza (Khabarovsk), 1990–

Invalid (Vladivostok), 1922. Ed. V. M. Mal'kov.

Izvestiia Vostochnogo Instituta (Vladivostok), 1899–1917
Kamchatskii komsomolets (Petropavlovsk-Kamchatskii), 1989–
Khabarovskaia nedelia (Khabarovsk), 1973–
Kraevedcheskii biulleten' (Yuzhno-Sakhalinsk), 1990–
Krasnoe znamia (Vladivostok), 1917–
Leninets (Vladivostok), 1988–
Magadanskaia pravda, 1954–
Molodoi dal'nevostochnik (Khabarovsk), 1989–
Na rubezhe (Khabarovsk), 1933–37, 1939–41
Na rubezhe (Yuzhno-Kurilsk), 1991–
Na severe dal'nem (Magadan), 1955–
Nihon shimbun (Khabarovsk), 1945–48
Novyi Dal'nii Vostok (Vladivostok), 1923–36
Pogranichnik severo-vostoka (Magadan), 1945–
Priamur'e (Khabarovsk), 1906–17
Priamurskie vedomosti (Khabarovsk), 1894–1917, 1991–
Put' Il'icha (Petropavlovsk), 1941– . (*Znamia Stalina* to 1954)
Region: Dal'nevostochnye novosti (Khabarovsk), 1990–
Reklamnaia gazeta (Magadan), 1989–
Respublika (Khabarovsk), 1992–
Rossiia i ATR (Vladivostok), 1992–
Rubezh (Harbin), 1923–40
Rubezh (Vladivostok), 1992–
Russkaia armiia (Vladivostok), 1921–22
Russkii Dal'nii Vostok (Tokyo and Vladivostok), 1920–21
Sakhalin News (Yuzhno-Sakhalinsk), 1993–
Shin seimei (Yuzhno-Sakhalinsk), 1945–48
Sovetskii Sakhalin (Yuzhno-Sakhalinsk), 1925–
Svobodnyi Sakhalin (Yuzhno-Sakhalinsk), 1990–
Territoriia (Magadan), 1991–
Tikhii okean (Vladivostok), 1992–
Tikhookeanskaia zvezda (Khabarovsk), 1920–
Tikhookeanskii komsomolets (Vladivostok), 1920–92
Tikhookeanskii kur'er (Vladivostok), 1993–
Urajio nippō (Vladivostok), 1917–23
Utro Rossii (Vladivostok), 1990–
Vechernii Vladivostok, 1989–90
Velikii okean (Vladivostok), 1917–22
Vestnik Azii (Harbin), 1909–27
Vestnik DVO AN SSSR (Vladivostok), 1932–39, 1990–
Vestnik DVR (Chita), 1920–22

Vladivostok, 1883–1906
Vladivostok, 1990–
Vladivostok News, 1993–
Vostok Rossii (Magadan) 1991–93

III. Published Sources in East Asian Languages

Cao Tingjie. "Xiboli dongpian jiyao" [Record of eastern Siberia], 1885. In *Liaohai congshu* [Distant seas series], 26: 1–48. Taibei: Yiwen yinshuguan, 1971.

Dongbei lidai jiangyu shi [History of the northeastern frontier regions through dynastic periods]. Comp. Zhang Boquan et al. Jilin: Jilin renmin chubanshe, 1981.

Enomoto Takeaki. *Shiberia nikki* [Siberia diary]. Ed. Hirose Hikota. Tokyo: Tōchō shoin, 1943.

Fujita Sadao. *Shiberia no yoake* [Siberian dawn]. Tokyo: Keizai bungei sha, 1971.

Fukuda Shinsei. *Hokuman no Roshiyajin buraku* [Russian settlements of northern Manchuria]. Tokyo: Tama shobō, 1942.

Hara Teruyuki. *Indeigiruka-go no higeki: 1930 nendai no Roshia kyokutō* [The *Indigirka* tragedy: Russian Far East in the 1930s]. Tokyo: Chikuma shobō, 1993.

———. *Shiberia shuppei: kakumei to kanshō, 1917–1922* [The Siberian expedition: revolution and intervention, 1917–22]. Tokyo: Chikuma shobō, 1989.

Hayashi Saburō. *Kantōgun to kyokutō Sorengun* [The Kwantung Army and Far Eastern Soviet Army]. Tokyo: Fūyō shobō, 1974.

Hiratake Denzō. *Shin Tōa no kensetsu: Soren, Shina, Manshū, hokuyō mondai* [Construction of new East Asia: Soviet Union, China, Manchuria, and north Pacific problems]. Tokyo: Keibundō, 1939.

Hora Tomio. *Karafutoshi kenkyū* [Studies in Sakhalin history]. Tokyo: Shinkisha, 1956.

———. *Mamiya Rinzō* [Biography of Mamiya Rinzō]. Tokyo: Yoshikawa kōbunkan, 1960.

Hosoya Chihiro. *Shiberia shuppei no shiteki kenkyū* [Historical research on the Siberian expedition]. Tokyo: Yūhikaku, 1955.

Hyun Kyoo-whan. *Han'guk yuiminsa* [History of Korean emigrants and wanderers]. 2 vols. Seoul: Omungak, 1976.

Irie Toraji. *Hōjin kaigai hatten shi* [History of Japanese overseas expansion]. 2 vols. Tokyo: Hara shobō, 1981 [1942].

Ishimitsu Makio. *Kōya no hana* [Wild flower]. Tokyo: Chūō kōron sha, 1978.

Ishizuka Keiji. *Amūru no sasayaki* [Amur whispers]. Hakodate: Senkensha, 1972.

Kaneko Toshio. *Karafuto 1945 nen natsu: Karafuto shūsen kiroku* [Karafuto 1945 summer: Record of the end of the war in Karafuto]. Tokyo: Kōdansha, 1972.

Katō Kyūzō. *Shiberia ki* [Siberian record]. Tokyo: Shio shuppansha, 1980.

Kim Kyeoung-choon. "Tumankang haryu ui Korea irredenta ye taeha ilko" [A consideration of Korean irredenta on the Tumen River]. *Paeksan hakpo*, 30–31 (Mar. 1985): 167–214.

Kimura Kei'ichi. *Mosukuwa, Nihon, Habarofusuku* [Moscow, Japan, Khabarovsk]. Sapporo: Kawasaki shoten, 1949.

Kinoshita Hideaki. *Yokuryū seikatsu jū'ichinen* [Eleven years in detention]. Tokyo: Kankosha, 1957.

Kondō Kan'ichi. *Shiberia supai nikki* [Diary of a spy in Siberia]. Tokyo: Chūō shoin, 1974.

Kuzuu Yoshihisa. *Tō-A senkaku shishi kiden* [Biographical notes on pioneer patriots of East Asia]. 3 vols. Tokyo: Kokuryūkai, 1933–35.

Kyokutō Shiberiya yōran [Eastern Siberia handbook]. Dairen: Mantetsu chōsabu, 1941.

Kyokutō Soren yōran [Soviet Far East handbook]. Harbin: Mantetsu chōsabu, 1939.

Liu Minsheng and Meng Xianzhang. *Shiqi shiji Sha E qinlüe Heilongjiang liuyu biannian shi* [Chronological history of tsarist Russia's encroachment in the Heilongjiang River basin during the seventeenth century]. Beijing: Zhonghua shuju, 1989.

Mamiya Rinzō. *Tōdatsu kikō* [Travels through eastern Tatar]. Ed. Shimada Yoshi. Dairen: Mantetsu, 1938.

Manshū ni okeru tai-So sen [War against the USSR in Manchukuo]. Ed. Bōeichō, Bōeikenshūjo, Senshishitsu. Tokyo, 1986.

Masuda Tadao. *Manshū kokkyō mondai* [Manchurian border problems]. Tokyo: Chūō kōronsha, 1941.

Miura Yō. *Shiberiya yokuryūki* [A record of Siberian internment]. Tokyo: Chikuma shobō, 1984.

Mizoguchi Hakuyō. *Kokujokuki* [Record of national insult]. Tokyo: Nippon hyōronsha, 1920.

Mo Yongming, ed. *Sha E qin Hua shi* [History of tsarist aggression against China]. Shanghai: Renmin chubanshe, 1986.

Nakamura Yoshikazu. "Manshū no Roshia kyūkyōtotachi" [Russian Old Believers in Manchuria]. In *Kyōdō kenkyū Roshia to Nihon* [Joint research on Russia and Japan], pp. 170–83. Tokyo: Hitotsubashi Univ. Sociology Department, 1990.

Nichi-Ro nenkan, 1942 [Russo-Japanese yearbook, 1942]. Tokyo: Oa tsūshinsha, 1942.

Nihon gaikōshi chizu [Atlas of the history of Japanese foreign relations]. Tokyo: Kajima kenkyūjo, 1974.

Nihon gaikōshi jiten [Dictionary of Japanese diplomatic history]. Tokyo: Ōkurashō, 1979.

Nishino Tatsukichi. *Nazo no bōmeisha Ryushikofu* [Lyushkov, the enigmatic exile]. Tokyo: San'ichi shobō, 1979.

Nisso bōeki handobukku [Soviet-Japanese trade handbook]. Tokyo: Soren Tō'ō bōeki kai, 1983.

Okazaki Yūshirō. *Manshū yori mitaru Tōa Soren* [Eastern USSR seen from Manchuria]. Shinkyō [Xinjing]: Manshū jijō annaisho, 1942.

Qing dai Zhong E quanxi dangan shiliao xuanbian [Selected archival materials from Sino-Russian relations in the Qing period]. 3 vols. Beijing: Zhonghua shuju, 1979–81.

Sha E qin Hua shi [History of tsarist aggression against China]. Ed. Yu Shengwu. 3 vols. Beijing: Renmin chubanshe, 1978–81.

"Shiberia horyo shūyōsho" [Siberian prison camps], *Asahi gurafu*, 17 Mar. 1989: 20–45, 81–84.

"Shiberia kyōsei shūyōjo" [Forced detention centers in Siberia]. *Bungei shunjū*, 60, no. 11 (Sept. 1982). Special issue.

Shuppei shi [History of the Siberian expedition]. Comp. Imperial Japanese Army Chief of Staff. 3 vols. Tokyo: Shinjidaisha, 1972 [1941].

Sorempō nenkan, 1943–1944 [USSR yearbook, 1943–44]. Tokyo: Sorempō tsūshinsha, 1943.

Soren kankei kikan sōmokuroku [General catalogue of Soviet-related organs]. Dairen: Mantetsu chōsabu, 1938.

Soren kyokutō sōran [Soviet Far East handbook]. Ed. Shimamura Shirō, Kimura Hiroshi, Aida Tatsuo. Tokyo: Enterprise, 1987.

Sugimori Kōji, and Fujimoto Wakio. *Nichi-Ro Ni-So kankei 200 nen shi* [200 years of Russo-Japanese and Soviet-Japanese relations]. Tokyo: Shinjidaisha, 1983.

Sulian diming cidian: Xiboliya yu Yuandong [Dictionary of Soviet place-names: Siberia and the Far East]. Ed. Zhang Huanhai. Harbin: Heilongjiang remin chubanshe, 1984.

Takeoka Yutaka. "Watashi ga Lyushukofu o utta!" [I shot Lyushkov!]. *Bungei shunjū*, 56, no. 8 (Aug. 1978): 348–55.

Tao Yuanzhen. "Kuyedao de falü diwei" [Sakhalin's legal position]. In *Zhongguo jindaishi luncong* [Modern China history series], 2d series, 7: 133–36. Taibei: Taiwan zhengzhong shuju, 1969.

Torii Ryūzō. *Kokuryūkō to kita Karafuto* [Amur River and northern Sakhalin]. Tokyo: Seikatsu bunka kenkyūkai, 1943.

Uno Sōsuke. *Damoi, Tokyo* [Home, to Tokyo]. Tokyo: Katsushiro shobō, 1948.

Wada Sei. "Shina no kisai ni arawaretaru Kokuryūkō karyu iki no genjumin" [Aborigines of the lower Amur appearing in Chinese sources]. In *Tōa shi ronsō* [Discourses on East Asian history], pp. 454–506. Tokyo: Seikatsusha, 1942.

Wakatsuki Yasuo. *Shiberia horyo shūyōsho* [Detention centers for Siberian POWs]. 2 vols. Tokyo: Saimaru, 1979.

Wang Hualong. *E di qin Hua dizhi* [Topographical records of Russian aggression against China]. Taibei: Zhongyang wenwu gongyingshe, 1954.

Wang Sheng and Cao Min. *E di qin Hua celüe zhi yanjiu* [Research on the tactics of Russian aggression against China]. Taibei: Liming wenhua shiye gonsi, 1977.

Xiboliya wenti lunzhan [Discourses on Siberian problems]. Ed. Chen Jiying. Taibei, 1972.

Xu Jingxue. *Eguo zhengfu Xiboliya jilue* [The Russian conquest of Siberia: A short record]. Harbin: Heilongjiang chubanshe, 1984.

——, ed. *Sulian dongbu diqu kaifa de huigu yu zhanwang* [The past and future development of eastern areas of the USSR]. Changchun: Donbei shifan daxue chubanshe, 1987.

Xue Hong. "Kuyedao zai lishishang de jiuzhu wenti" [The problem of sovereignty over Sakhalin in the light of history]. *Lishi yanjiu*, 5 (1981): 178–92.

Yamauchi Hōsuke. *Shibiriya hishi* [Secret history of Siberia]. Tokyo: Nippon hyōronsha, 1923.

——. *Urajio to Enkaishū* [Vladivostok and the Maritime Region]. Tokyo: Nippon denshin tsūshinsha, 1943.

Zhong E guanxi shiliao: Dongbei bianfang [Historical materials on Russo-Chinese relations: Northeast frontier defense]. Ed. Deng Ruyan. Part 4, 2 vols. Taibei: Zhongyang yanjiuyuan, Jindaishi yanjiusuo, 1960.

Zhongguo lidai jiangyu xingshi shi tu [Historical map of China's dynastic frontiers]. Ed. Yang Dejun. Taibei: Zhongguo shengming xian, 1964.

IV. Published Sources in Russian

Note: The following abbreviations are used for publishers in this section: AN, Akademiia nauk; DVGU, Dal'nevostochnyi gosudarstvennyi universitet; DVKI, Dal'nevostochnoe knizhnoe izdatel'stvo; DVNTs, Dal'nevostochnyi nauchnyi tsentr; DVO, Dal'nevostochnoe otdelenie; IIAENDV, Institut istorii, arkheologii i etnografii narodov Dal'nego Vostoka; KKI, Khabarovskoe knizhnoe izdatel'stvo; MKI, Magadanskoe knizhnoe izdatel'stvo; RAN, Rossiiskaia akademiia nauk; SO, Sibirskoe otdelenie.

A. K. "Novye priemy bor'by s kitaitsami v Priamur'e." *Sibirskie voprosy*, 1911, no. 17: 27–28.

Aganbegian, Abel Gezevich, and Zamira Mirzovna Ibragimova. *Sibir' na rubezhe vekov*. Moscow: Sovetskaia Rossiia, 1984.

Agishev, Rustam Konstantinovich. *Sovetskii Dal'nii Vostok v khudozhestvennoi literature*. Khabarovsk: KKI, 1957.

Akkuratov, Valentin Ivanovich. *Led i pepel*. Moscow: Sovremennik, 1984.

Akshinskii, Vasilii Semenovich. *Kuril'skii desant*. Petropavlovsk-Kamchatskii: DVKI, 1984.

Aleksandr Fadeev. Ed. A. S. Bushmin. Moscow: Prosveshchenie, 1964.

Aleksandrov, Vadim Aleksandrovich. *Rossiia na dal'nevostochnykh rubezhakh (vtoraia polovina XVII v.)*. Moscow: Nauka, 1969. Rev. ed. Khabarovsk: KKI, 1984.

Aleksandrovskaia, Larisa Vital'evna. *Opyt pervogo morskogo pereseleniia v iuzhno-ussuriiskii krai v 60-x godax XIX veka*. Vladivostok: DVGU, 1990.

Alekseev, Aleksandr Ivanovich. *Amurskaia ekspeditsiia 1849–1855 gg*. Moscow: Mysl', 1974.

———. *Kak nachinalsia Vladivostok*. Vladivostok: DVKI, 1985.

———. *Khoziaika Zaliva Schast'ia*. Khabarovsk: KKI, 1981.

———. *Osvoenie russkimi liud'mi Dal'nego Vostoka i Russkoi Ameriki*. Moscow: Nauka, 1982.

———. *Utro Sovetskoi Gavani*. Khabarovsk: KKI, 1984.

Alekseev, A. I., and G. V. Melikhov. "Otkrytie i pervonachal'noe osvoenie russkimi liud'mi Priamur'ia i Primor'ia." *Voprosy istorii*, 1984, no. 3 (Mar.): 57–71.

Alekseev, A. I., and B. N. Morozov. "Ekonomicheskoe razvitie Dal'nego Vostoka vo vtoroi polovine XIX veka." *Voprosy istorii*, 1981, no. 5 (May): 37–47.

———. *Osvoenie russkogo Dal'nego Vostoka, konets XIX v.–1917 g*. Moscow: Nauka, 1989.

Alenkina, Evgeniia Mikhailovna. *Pisateli Dal'nego Vostoka: Bibliograficheskii spravo-chnik*. Khabarovsk: KKI, 1973.

Amfiteatrov, Aleksandr Valentinovich. *Sibirskie etiudy*. St. Petersburg: Obshchestv. pol'za, 1904.

Amur: reka podvigov. Ed. N. K. Kiriukhin. Khabarovsk: KKI, 1983.

"Amurskaia Kaliforniia." *Sibirskii sbornik*, 1886, no. 1: 138–68.

Amurskaia oblast': Opyt entsiklopedicheskogo slovaria. Blagoveshchensk: Amurskoe ot-delenie KKI, 1989.

"Amurskoe delo i vliianie ego na Vostochnuiu Sibir' i gosudarstvo." *Russkaia starina*, 32 (Sept. 1881): 75–100.

Andreev, G. "Svobodnaia tribuna: K polemike o zagovore Tukhachevskogo." *Posev*, 32 (6 Aug. 1950): 10–11.

Andreev, Valerii Stepanovich. *Kuril'skii dnevnik*. Moscow: Molodaia gvardiia, 1981.

Andreeva, Lidiia. "Posleslovie k avtoportretu khudozhnika." *Na severe dal'nem*, 1988, no. 2: 142–54.

Anichkov, Viktor Tikhonovich. *Kolkhoznoe krest'ianstvo Sibiri i Dal'nego Vostoka — frontu, 1941–1945 gg*. Barnaul: Altaiskoe knizh. izdat., 1966.

Anosov, Semen Davidovich. *Koreitsy v Ussuriiskom krae*. Khabarovsk: Knizhnoe delo, 1928.

Arkhipov, N. B. *SSSR po raionam: Dal'nevostochnaia oblast'*. Moscow: Gosizdat, 1926.

Arkheologiia i etnografiia narodov Dal'nego Vostoka. Vladivostok: IIAENDV, 1984.

Arsen'evskie chteniia, 6. Ussuriisk: Gospedinstitut, 1992.

Aussem, Otto Khristianovich. "Nikolaevskaia-na-Amure Kommuna 1920 g." *Pro-letarskaia revoliutsiia*, 1924, no. 5: 36–61.

Avdeeva, Nina Aleksandrovna. *Dal'nevostochnaia narodnaia respublika*. Khabarovsk: KKI, 1957.

Avdeeva, Nina Aleksandrovna, and Galina Stepanovna Chechulina. *Piat' let geroicheskoi bor'by*. Blagoveshchensk: KKI, 1972.

Azadovskii, Konstantin Markovich, and Elena Mikhailovna D'iakonova. *Bal'mont i Iaponiia*. Moscow: Nauka, 1992.

Aziatskaia Rossiia. See Russia. Glavnoe upravlenie zemleustroistva i zemledeliia.

Babichev, I. "Uchastie kitaiskikh i koreiskikh trudiashchikhsia v bor'be protiv interventov i belogvardeitsev na sovetskom Dal'nem Vostoke." In *Dal'nii Vostok za 40 let sovetskoi vlast'*, pp. 148–71. Komsomolsk-na-Amure: Gosizdat, 1958.

Bagrov, Viktor Nikolaevich. *Pobeda na ostrovakh*. Iuzhno-Sakhalinsk: DVKI, 1985.

Baikalo-Amurskaia magistral': Ukazatel' literatury, 1925–1974. Novosibirsk: SO AN SSSR, 1986.

Bakhrushin, Sergei Vladimirovich. *Kazaki na Amure*. Leningrad: Brokgauz-Efron, 1925.

Balakshin, Petr [Petrovich]. *Final v Kitae: Vozniknovenie, razvitie i ischeznovenie Beloi Emigratsii na Dal'nem Vostoke*. 2 vols. San Francisco: Sirius, 1958–59.

Balalaeva, N. M. "O popytke pereseleniia zemledel'cheskogo naseleniia Amurskoi oblasti na Kamchatku v 1911–1912 godakh." In *Voprosy istorii Dal'nego Vostoka*, vol. 3, pp. 3–9. Khabarovsk: Khabpedinstitut, 1973.

Balitskii, Vitalii Grigor'evich. *Malye narody Dal'nego Vostoka v Velikoi Otechestvennoi voine*. Vladivostok: DVGU, 1985.

Barsukov, Ivan Platonovich. *Graf Nikolai Nikolaevich Murav'ev-Amurskii po ego pis'mam, ofitsial'nym dokumentam, razskazam sovremennikov i pechatnym istochnikam*. 2 vols. Moscow: Sinodal'naia, 1891.

Bartkova, Ida Il'inichna. *Rasselenie na Tikhookeanskom poberezh'e*. Vladivostok: DVGU, 1983.

Belaia kniga o deportatsii koreiskogo naseleniia Rossii v 30–40x godakh: Kniga pervaia. Ed. Li U Khe [Vladimir Fedorovich Li]. Moscow: Interprax, 1992.

Beliaev, B. "A. A. Fadeev: Redaktor zhurnala *Na rubezhe*." *Dal'nii Vostok*, 1968, no. 4 (Apr.): 145–48.

Belikova, Larisa Iosifovna. *Bor'ba bol'shevikov za ustanovlenie i uprochenie sovetskoi vlasti v Primor'e (1917–1918 gg.)*. Vladivostok: Primizdat, 1957.

Belousov, Ivan Emel'ianovich. *Golosa ostrovnogo kraia*. Iuzhno-Sakhalinsk: DVKI, 1977.

Bensman, Esfir' Grigor'evna. *Kul'turnoe stroitel'stvo v Khabarovskom krae*. Khabarovsk: KKI, 1965.

Berezkin, A. *SShA: Aktivnyi organizator i uchastnik voennoi interventsii protiv Sovetskoi Rossii (1918–1920 gg.)*. Moscow: Gospolitizdat, 1952.

Besprozvannykh, Evgenii Leonidovich. *Priamur'e v sisteme russko-kitaiskikh otnoshenii XVII–seredina XIX v*. Moscow: Nauka, 1983.

Biankin, Valentin Petrovich. *V dal'nevostochnykh moriakh*. Vladivostok: DVKI, 1981.

Bibliograficheskii slovar' sovetskikh vostokovedov. Comp. Sofiia Davidovna Miliband. Moscow: Nauka, 1977.

Birsko-Bidzhanskii raion DVK. Moscow: Komzet, 1928.

Bliukher, Glafira [Lukinichna Bezverkhova]. "Vospominaniia o lichnom." *Voenno-istoricheskii zhurnal,* 1989, no. 3: 92–96; no. 4 : 79–87; no. 5: 88–95; 1990, no. 1: 79–83.

Bliukher, Vasilii Konstantinovich. *Stat'i i rechi.* Moscow: Voenizdat, 1963.

Bodisko, A. M. *Iz zhizni Khabarovska.* Khabarovsk: Khabarovskoe gorodskoe obshchestvennoe samoupravlenie, 1913.

Bogdanov, D. *Putevoditel' po Vladivostoku i promysly Primorskoi oblasti, Kamchatki i Sakhalina.* Vladivostok: Ekspress, 1909.

Boiko, Vladimir Ivanovich. *Sotsial'noe razvitie narodov nizhnego Amura.* Novosibirsk: Nauka, 1977.

Bok Zi Kou. *Sakhalinskie koreitsy: Problemy i perspektivy.* Iuzhno-Sakhalinsk: Sakhalinskii oblastnoi kraevedcheskii muzei, 1989.

Bol'bukh, A. V. "Razvitie stakhanovskogo dvizheniia v promyshlennosti Dal'nevostochnogo kraia v 1936–1937 gg." In *Iz istorii rabochego klassa Dal'nego Vostoka,* pp. 65–71. Vladivostok: DVGU, 1971.

Boldyrev, Vasilii Georgievich. *Direktoriia, Kolchak, interventy.* Intro. V. D. Vegman. Novonikolaevsk: Sibkraiizdat, 1925.

———. "Iaponiia i Sovetskii D. Vostok." *Sibirskie ogni,* 1925, no. 1: 187–94.

Bolkhovitinov, Nikolai Nikolaevich. *Rossiia otkryvaet Ameriku, 1732–1799.* Moscow: Mezhdunarodnye otnosheniia, 1991.

Bol'shaia sovetskaia entsiklopediia. 1st ed., 65 vols. Moscow: Ogiz, 1926–31. 2d ed., 51 vols. Moscow: Bol'shaia sovetskaia entsiklopediia, 1949–58. 3d ed., 30 vols. Moscow: Sovetskaia entsiklopediia, 1970–78.

Bol'sheviki v bor'be za organizatsiiu revoliutsionnogo dvizheniia v Sibiri i na Dal'nem Vostoke (1903–1917 gg.). Tomsk: Izdat. Tomskogo univ., 1980.

Bondarenko, E. "O sud'be direktora Internatsional'nogo kluba moriakov vo Vladivostoke." *Problemy Dal'nego Vostoka,* 1990, no. 5: 141–47.

Bondarenko, Oleg. *Neizvestnye Kurily.* Moscow: VTI-Deita Press, 1992.

Bor'ba za sovety na Dal'nem Vostoke. Moscow: Voenizdat, 1932.

Borisov, S. P. *Bor'ba za sovetskii Dal'nii Vostok.* Moscow: Voenizdat, 1940.

Boshniak, Nikolai Konstantinovich. "Ekspeditsiia v Priamurskom krae." *Morskoi sbornik,* 2 parts, 38 (Dec. 1858):179–94; 39 (Jan. 1859): 111–31.

Braslavets, Konstantin Makarovich. *Istoriia v nazvaniiakh na karte Sakhalinskoi oblasti.* Iuzhno-Sakhalinsk: DVKI, 1983.

Brianskii, A. M. *Ekonomicheskoe rassloenie dal'nevostochnoi derevni.* Khabarovsk: Dal'nevostoch. oblastnoe statisticheskoe upravlenie, 1925.

Brodianskii, David Lazarevich. *Vvedenie v dal'nevostochnuiu arkheologiiu.* Vladivostok: DVGU, 1987.

Buiakov, Aleksei Mikhailovich. "Narkobiznes v Primor'e i na Dal'nem Vostoke Rossii." *Zapiski Obshchestva izucheniia Amurskogo kraia*, 1992, no. 28: 61–69.

Burliuk, David. "Literatura i khudozhestvo v Sibiri i na Dal'nem Vostoke (1919–1922 gg)." In *Novaia russkaia kniga*, pp. 44–48. Berlin: Ladyzhnikova, 1922.

Buturlinov, V. F. et al. *O sovetsko-kitaiskoi granitse*. Moscow: Voenizdat, 1982.

Buzin-Bich, D. S. "Partisansko-povstancheskoe dvizhenie v nizoviakh reki Amura, 1919–1920 gg.," *Revoliutsiia na Dal'nem Vostoke*, 1: 5–23. Moscow-Petrograd: Istpart, 1923.

Bytovoi, Semen Mikhailovich. *Desiat' tysiach let*. Leningrad: Sovetskii pisatel', 1953.

Chasovye sovetskikh granits; Kratkii ocherk pogranichnykh voisk SSSR. Comp. V. S. Ivanov et al. Moscow: Politizdat, 1983.

Chausov, P. Kh. "Dal'nevostochnoe krest'ianstvo v period vosstanovleniia narodnogo khoziastva (1923–1926 gg.). In *Problemy agrarnoi istorii Dal'nego Vostoka*, pp. 43–55. Khabarovsk: Khab. gospedinstitut, 1979.

———. "Istoriografiia sploshnoi kollektivizatsii na Dal'nem Vostoke SSSR." In *Sel'skoe khoziastvo i krest'ianstvo Dal'nego Vostoka SSSR v period stroitel'stva sotsializma i kommunizma*, pp. 81–94. Khabarovsk: Khabpedinstitut, 1984.

Cherevko, Kirill Evgen'evich. "Maoistskie pritiazaniia bez Mao." *Morskoi sbornik*, 1980, no. 8: 90–93.

Chernaia, G. "Dal'nevostochnaia tema v sovetskoi literature." *Dal'nii Vostok*, 1971, no. 10: 142–43.

Chernyi, Aleksei Klement'evich. *Krai sversheni i muzhestva*. Moscow: Sovetskaia Rossiia, 1982.

Chernysheva, Vera Ivanovna. *Iz istorii revoliutsionnogo dvizheniia na Dal'nem Vostoke v 1905–1907 godakh*. Khabarovsk: KKI, 1955.

———. *Khabarovsk*. Khabarovsk: KKI, 1958.

———. *Khabarovsk, 1858–1983: Ocherk istorii*. Khabarovsk: KKI, 1983.

———. *Khabarovsk: prezhde i teper'*. Khabarovsk: KKI, 1971.

———, ed. *Dal'revkom: Sbornik materialov*. Khabarovsk: Dal'gosizdat, 1949.

Chesalin, Vasilii Vasil'evich. *Zdes' nachinalas' istoriia*. Iuzhno-Sakhalinsk: Iuzhno-Sakh. knizh. izdat., 1987.

Chikhachev, Platon. "Kaliforniia i Ussuriiskii krai." *Vestnik Evropy*, 25, no. 6 (June 1890): 545–68.

Chitaia 'Ostrov Sakhalin'. 2 vols. Iuzhno-Sakhalinsk: Sakhalinskii oblastnoi kraevedcheskii muzei, 1990.

Chudesov, V. V. "Iz istorii stroitel'stva Baikalo-Amurskoi zheleznodorozhnoi magistrali." In *Istoriia promyshlennogo razvitiia sovetskogo Dal'nego Vostok*, pp. 72–79. Vladivostok: IIAENDV, 1979.

Chugunov, Aleksandr Ivanovich. *Na strazhe sovetskikh rubezhei*. Moscow: Voenizdat, 1981.

Dal'istpart: Sbornik materialov po istorii revoliutsionnogo dvizheniia na Dal'nem Vostoke. Ed. Dal'biuro TsK RKP. 3 vols. Chita-Vladivostok: Knizhnoe delo, 1923–25.

Dal'nevostochnoe morskoe parokhodstvo. Comp. Iu. I. Ostrovskii. Vladivostok: DVKI, 1980.

Dal'nevostochnoe uskorenie: Sbornik. Ed. Stanislav Veniaminovich Tiro. Moscow: DOSAAF [Vsesoiuznoe dobrovol'noe obshchestvo sodeistviia armii, aviatsii i flotu] SSSR, 1984.

Dal'nevostochnyi pogranichnyi: Ocherk istorii krasnoznamennogo dal'nevostochnogo pogranichnogo okruga. Ed. V. I. Stus. Khabarovsk: KKI, 1983.

Dal'nii Vostok Rossii: Ekonomicheskii ezhegodnik. Khabarovsk: Institut ekonomicheskikh issledovanii, RAN, 1991.

Dal'nii Vostok za 40 let sovetskoi vlasti. Ed. V. A. Shvarev. Komsomolsk-na-Amure: Dal'nevostochnyi filial, SO AN SSSR, 1958.

Dal'revkom: Pervyi etap mirnogo sovetskogo stroitel'stva na Dal'nem Vostoke, 1922–1926 gg.: Sbornik dokumentov. Ed. N. I. Riabov. Khabarovsk: KKI, 1957.

Dal'sovnarkom 1917–1918 gg.: Sbornik dokumentov i materialov. Ed. G. P. Kolbin and V. S. Flerov. Khabarovsk: KKI, 1969.

Danilenko, Fedor Fedotovich. *Priamurskii krai: Ocherk*. Harbin: Zaitsev, 1935.

Danilenko, Vladimir Fedorovich. *Kryl'ia Dal'nego Vostoka*. Khabarovsk: KKI, 1979.

Deiatel'nost' kommunisticheskoi partii Sovetskogo Soiuza po razvitiiu proizvoditel'nykh sil i ukrepleniiu oboronosposobnosti Dal'nego Vostoka (1917–1976 gg.). Vladivostok: DVGU, 1976.

Deistviia Iaponii v Priamurskom krae. Vladivostok: Svobodnaia Rossiia, 1921.

Demin, Lev Mikhailovich. *Sakhalinskie zapiski*. Moscow: Sovetskaia Rossiia, 1983.

Denisov, V. I. *Rossiia na Dal'nem Vostoke*. St. Petersburg: Iu. Ia. Riman, 1913.

Derber, Petr Iakovlevich, and M. L. Sher. *Ocherki khoziaistvennoi zhizni Dal'nego Vostoka*. Moscow-Leningrad: Gosizdat., 1927.

Derevianko, Anatolii Panteleevich. *Paleolit Dal'nego Vostoka i Korei*. Novosibirsk: Nauka, 1983.

D'iachenko, Boris Alekseevich, ed. *Staryi Vladivostok*. Vladivostok: Utro Rossii, 1992.

Dikov, Nikolai Nikolaevich. *Istoriia Chukotki s drevneishikh vremen do nashikh dnei*. Moscow: Mysl', 1989.

———. *Novye arkheologicheskie pamiatniki severa Dal'nego Vostoka*. Magadan: DVNTs AN SSSR, 1979.

Divin, Vasilii Afanas'evich. *Russkie moreplavaniia na Tikhom okeane v XVIII veke*. Moscow: Mysl', 1971.

Dneprovskii, Stepan Petrovich. *Po dolinam i po vzgor'iam*. Khabarovsk: KKI, 1956.

Dokumenty oprovergaiut: Protiv fal'sifikatsii istorii russko-kitaiskikh otnoshenii. Ed. S. L. Tikhvinskii. Moscow: Mysl', 1982.

Dubinina, Nina Ivanovna. *Dal'nevostochnitsy v bor'be i trude: Istoricheskii ocherk 1917–1941*. Khabarovsk: KKI, 1982.

——. "Protivostoianie." *Dal'nii Vostok*, 1989, no. 8: 132–40.

——. "Tragediia lichnosti." *Dal'nii Vostok*, 1989, no. 7: 128–35.

——. *Ty pozovi, Dal'nii Vostok! Khetagurovskoe dvizhenie devushek-patriotok 1937–1939 gody*. Khabarovsk: KKI, 1987.

Dvadtsat' let VChK-OGPU-NKVD. Moscow: Ogiz, 1938.

Dzerzhintsy. Comp. A. Sadiukov. Alma Ata: Izdat. Kazakhstan, 1975.

Ech', V. *Ischeznuvshii gorod: Tragediia Nikolaevska-na-Amure*. Vladivostok: Iosif Korot, 1920.

Ekho partizanskikh sopok: Grazhdanskaia voina na territorii khabarovskogo kraia v vospominaniiakh uchastnikov i zametkakh istorikov-kraevedov. Comp. E. M. Zolotykh. Khabarovsk: KKI, 1973.

Ekspansiia Iaponii na Dal'nem Vostoke. Ed. A. I. Krushanov. Vladivostok: IIAENDV, 1990.

Elesh, Viacheslav Mikhailovich. *Na beregakh Volgi i Tikhogo okeana*. Moscow: Sovetskaia Rossiia, 1970.

Eliseev, Aleksandr Vasil'evich. *V taige*. St. Petersburg: Soikin, 1891.

Emel'ianov, Konstantin Aleksandrovich. *Liudi v adu*. Shanghai: Dal'nevostochnoe vremia, [ca. 1940].

Entsiklopedicheskii slovar'. 86 vols. St. Petersburg: Brokgauz-Efron, 1890–1907.

Entsiklopediia Dal'nevostochnogo kraia: Prospekt, slovnik. Khabarovsk: Knizhnoe delo, 1930.

Epifanov, P. P. "K istorii osvoeniia Sibiri i Dal'nego Vostoka v XVII veke." *Istoriia SSSR*, 1981, no. 4 : 70–84.

Fainberg, Esfir' Iakovlevna. *Russko-iaponskie otnosheniia v 1697–1875 gg*. Moscow: Izdat. vostoch. lit., 1960.

Fedin, S. I. "Zhizn' i deiatel'nost' Vladimira Klavdievicha Arsen'eva." In *Strany i narody Vostoka*, vol. 20, pp. 21–47. Moscow: Nauka, 1979.

Fedorov, Valentin. "Sakhalin i rynok." *Dal'nii Vostok*, 1991, no. 1: 120–28.

Fetisov, Anatolii Pavlovich. *Razbuzhennye prostory: Stranitsy istorii Okhotskogo poberezh'ia*. Khabarovsk: KKI, 1982.

Filimonov, Boris Borisovich. *Belopovstantsy: Khabarovskii pokhod zimy 1921–1922 godov*. 2 vols. Shanghai: Tip. izdat. slovo, 1932–33.

——. *Konets belogo Primor'ia*. Rockville, Md.: Victor Kamkin, 1971.

Flerov, Vasilii Sergeevich. *Dal'nii Vostok v period vosstanovleniia narodnogo khoziaistva*. Tomsk: Izdat. Tomskogo univ., 1973.

——. *Stroitel'stvo sovetskoi vlasti i bor'ba s inostrannoi ekspansiei na Kamchatke (1922–1926)*. Tomsk: Knizh. izdat., 1964.

Formirovanie i razvitie rabochego klass i krest'ianstva na sovetskom Dal'nem Vostoke. Ed. P. Kh. Chausov. Khabarovsk: Khab. gospedinstitut, 1988.

Fraerman, Ruvim Isaevich. *Povesti o Dal'nem Vostoke*. Moscow: Sovetskii pisatel', 1938.

Galkin, N. *V zemle polunochnogo solntsa*. Moscow: Molodaia gvardiia, 1929.

Gapanovich, Ivan Ivanovich. *Rossiia v Severo-Vostochnoi Azii*. 2 vols. Beiping: Tip. pekinskoi russkoi missii, 1933–34.

Garusov, Ivan Sergeevich. *Razgrom belogvardeishchiny v Okhotsko-Kamchatskom krae*. Magadan: MKI, 1963.

Geller, Mikhail and Aleksandr Nekrich. *Utopiia u vlasti*. 2 vols. London: Overseas Publications Interchange, 1982.

Georgiev, Iu. V. "Iaponskie internatsionalisty v Sibiri." In *Iaponiia: Ezhegodnik 1987*, pp. 242–54. Moscow: Nauka, 1989.

Gerasimov, S. K. *Patrioty Dal'nego Vostoka*. Moscow: Pishchepromizdat, 1946.

———. *U Tikhogo okeana*. Moscow: Molodaia gvardiia, 1949.

Girchenko, Vladimir Petrovich. *Revoliutsionnaia deiatel'nost' inostrannykh internatsionalistov voenno-plennykh v Vostochnoi Sibiri*. Verkhneudinsk: Burgosizdat, 1933.

Glushchenko, Ideia Iosifovna. *Rabochii klass sovetskogo Dal'nego Vostoka v perekhodnyi k sotsializmu period (1922–1937 gg.)*. Vladivostok: DVGU, 1986.

Golovkin, E. "Evgenii Petrov na Dal'nem Vostoke." *Dal'nii Vostok*, 1989, no. 2: 134–38.

Gorbatov, Aleksandr Vasil'evich. "Gody i voiny." *Novyi mir*, 1964, no. 4: 99–138.

Grachev, Aleksandr Matveevich. *Padenie Tisima-retto*. Khabarovsk: KKI, 1957.

Grachev, G. "Iakutskii pokhod gen. Pepeliaeva." *Vol'naia Sibir'*, 1929, no. 5: 23–40.

Granitsa: Dokumental'no-khudozhestvennoe povestvovanie o dal'nevostochnoi granitse. Ed. L. S. Ovechkin. Khabarovsk: KKI, 1976.

Granitsa na zamke. Ed. V. Taborko and M. Lavrik. Moscow: Molodaia gvardiia, 1969.

Grave, V. V. *Kitaitsy, koreitsy i iapontsy v Priamur'e: Trudy Amurskoi ekspeditsii*. St. Petersburg: V. F. Kirshbaum, 1912.

Grazhdanskaia voina i voennaia interventsiia v SSSR: Entsiklopediia. Moscow: Sovetskaia entsiklopediia, 1983. Rev. ed., 1987.

Grigortsevich, Stanislav Siliverstovich. *Amerikanskaia i iaponskaia interventsiia na sovetskom Dal'nem Vostoke i ee razgrom (1918–1922)*. Moscow: Gospolitizdat, 1957.

———. "Iz istorii otechestvennogo vostokovedeniia: Vladivostokskii Vostochnyi institut v 1899–1916 gg." *Sovetskoe vostokovedenie*, 1957, no. 4: 131–40.

Grum-Grzhimailo, Grigorii Efimovich. *Opisanie Amurskoi oblasti*. St. Petersburg: S. M. Nikolaev, 1894.

Grusha, M. V. *25 let Dal'stroia*. Magadan: Dal'stroi, 1956.

Gubel'man, Moisei Izrailevich. *Bor'ba za sovetskii Dal'nii Vostok, 1918–1922*. Moscow: Voenizdat, 1958.

Gulyga, A. V. *SShA: Organizator i aktivnyi uchastnik antisovetskoi interventsii v 1918–1920 godakh*. Moscow: Znanie, 1952.

Gulyga, A. V., and A. Geronimus. *Krakh antisovetskoi interventsii SShA (1918–1920 gg.)*. Moscow: Gosizdat, 1952.

Gurvich, I. S., ed. *Narody Dal'nego Vostoka SSSR v XVII–XX vv.* Moscow: Nauka, 1985.

Gusarevich, Stanislav Dmitrievich, and Vladimir Borisovich Seoev. *Na strazhe dal'nevostochnykh rubezhei*. Moscow: Voenizdat, 1982.

Gutman, I. Ia. [Anatolii Gan]. *Gibel' Nikolaevska-na-Amure*. Berlin: Ekonomist, 1924.

I. G. "Ocherki sovetskogo Dal'nego Vostoka." *Vol'naia Sibir'*, 1927, no. 1: 165–76.

Iadrintsev, Nikolai Mikhailovich. *Sibir' kak koloniia*. St. Petersburg: I. M. Sibiriakov, 1892.

Iakimov, Aristarkh Tikhonovich. *Dal'nevostochnyi avangard*. Vladivostok: DVKI, 1977.

———. *Dal'nii Vostok v ogne bor'by s interventami i belogvardeitsami (1920–1922)*. Moscow: Nauka, 1979.

———. *Geroicheskie gody bor'by i pobed*. Moscow: Nauka, 1968.

———. *Grazhdanskaia voina na Dal'nem Vostoke (1918–1922): Vospominaniia veteranov*. Moscow: Nauka, 1973.

Iakushev, I. A. "Ocherki oblastnogo dvizheniia v Sibiri." *Vol'naia Sibir'*, 3 parts, 1928, no. 3: 9–27; 1929, no. 5: 59–68; 1929, nos. 6–7: 88–103.

Iakushevskii, Anatolii Stepanovich. *Propagandistskaia rabota Bol'shevikov sredi voisk interventov v 1918–1920 gg*. Moscow: Nauka, 1974.

Ian Gamarnik: Vospominaniia druzei i soratnikov. Moscow: Voenizdat, 1978.

Ianguzov, Zakir Sharifovich. "Istoriografiia istorii sovetskikh vooruzhennykh sil na Dal'nem Vostoke (1929–1941 gg.)." In *Metodologiia issledovanii i istoriografiia Dal'nego Vostoka*, pp. 165–69. Iuzhno-Sakhalinsk: DVKI, 1975.

——— *Osobaia Krasnoznamennaia Dal'nevostochnaia Armiia na strazhe mira i bezopasnosti SSSR (1929–1938 gg.)*. Blagoveshchensk: Blag. knizh. izdat., 1970.

———. *Ot Volgi do Tikhogo*. Vladivostok: DVKI, 1988.

———. *Zabven'ia net: Stranitsy zhizni i polkovodcheskoi deiatel'nosti Marshala Sovetskogo Soiuza V.K. Bliukhera*. Khabarovsk: KKI, 1990.

———, ed. *Ian Gamarnik — Komandarm Shtern*. Vladivostok: DVKI, 1985.

———, ed. *Sozvezdie polkovodtsev*. Vol. 2. Khabarovsk: KKI, 1982.

Iasman, Z. D. "Nachalo russkogo zemledeliia na Kamchatke." *Voprosy istorii*, 1975, no. 10: 209–13.

Iaponiia na russkom Dal'nem Vostoke. Moscow: Dal'nevostochnyi otdel Kominterna, 1922.

Il'iukhov, Nikolai Kirillovich, and Ivan Petrovich Samusenko. *Partizanskoe dvizhenie v Primor'e (1918–1922 gg.)*. Moscow: Voenizdat, 1962.

Il'iukhov, N., and M. Titov. *Partizanskoe dvizhenie v Primor'e (1918–1920 gg.)*. Leningrad: Priboi, 1928.

Istoriia Dal'nego Vostoka SSSR. 2 vols. Vladivostok: IIAENDV, 1989–91.

Istoriia Sakhalinskoi oblasti. Comp. N. I. Kolesnikov and V. L. Poliakov. Iuzhno-Sakhalinsk: DVKI, 1981.

Istoriia Severo-Vostochnogo Kitaia XVII–XX vekov. 2 vols. Vladivostok: DVKI, 1987–89.

Istoriia Sibiri s drevneishikh vremen do nashikh dnei. 5 vols. Leningrad: Nauka, 1968–69.

Istoriografiia istorii rabochego klassa Dal'nego Vostoka SSSR. Vladivostok: IIAENDV, 1984.

Ivanov, Sergei Alekseevich. *Amerikanskaia agressiia na sovetskom Dal'nem Vostoke*. Vladivostok: Primizdat, 1952.

Iz istorii Dal'nevostochnoi respubliki. Vladivostok: IIAENDV, 1992.

Iz istorii Grazhdanskoi voiny i interventsii na Dal'nem Vostoke. Khabarovsk: Khab. gospedinstitut, 1978.

Iz istorii interventsii i Grazhdanskoi voiny v Sibiri i na Dal'nem Vostoke (1917–1922 gg.). Ed. Iu. I. Korablev and V. I. Shishkin. Novosibirsk: Nauka, 1985.

Iz istorii revoliutsionnogo dvizheniia na Dal'nem Vostoke v gody pervoi russkoi revoliutsii. Vladivostok: Primorskoe knizh. izdat., 1956.

K desiatiletiiu interventsii. Comp. Obshchestvo sodeistviia zhertvam interventsii. Moscow: Gosizdat, 1929.

Kabanov, Petr Ivanovich. *Amurskii vopros*. Blagoveshchensk: Amurskoe knizh. izdat., 1959.

Kabuzan, Vladimir Maksimovich. *Dal'nevostochnyi krai v XVII–nachale XX vv. (1640–1917): Istoriko-demograficheskii ocherk*. Moscow: Nauka, 1985.

———. *Kak zaselialsia Dal'nii Vostok*. Khabarovsk: KKI, 1976.

———. "Zaselenie Sibiri i Dal'nego Vostoka v kontse XVII–nachale XX vv. (1795–1917)." *Istoriia SSSR*, 1979, no. 3: 22–38.

Kalachinskii, Andrei Vladimirovich. "Liubov' k pravde i strannosti liubvi." *Dal'nii Vostok*, 1988, no. 9: 141–47.

Kandidov, Boris. *Iaponskaia interventsiia v Sibiri i tserkov'*. Moscow: Ogiz, 1932.

Kandyba, Vitalii Il'ich. *Istoriia stanovleniia i razvitiia khudozhestvennoi zhizni Dal'nego Vostoka (1858–1938)*. Vladivostok: DVGU, 1985.

Kantorovich, Vladimir Iakovlevich. *Sakhalinskie tetradi*. Moscow: Sovetskii pisatel', 1965.

Kaplin, Sergei Savvateevich. *Bol'sheviki na Dal'nem Vostoke, 1918–1922*. Moscow: Gospolitizdat, 1960.

Karatsupa, Nikita Fedorovich. *Zhizn' moia: granitsa*. Khabarovsk: KKI, 1983.

Karpenko, Z. *Grazhdanskaia voina v dal'nevostochnom krae, 1918–1922*. Khabarovsk: Dal'partizdat, 1934.

Kartunova, Anastasiia Ivanovna. *V. K. Bliukher v Kitae, 1924–1927*. Moscow: Nauka, 1979.

Kato Kiudzo. *Sibir' v serdtse iapontsa*. Novosibirsk: Nauka, 1992.

Khabarovsk: Geograficheskii atlas. Moscow: Glavnoe upravlenie geodezii i kartografii pri Sovete Ministrov SSSR, 1989.

Khabarovskaia kraevaia partiinaia organizatsiia v period Velikoi Otechestvennoi voiny (1941–1945 gody): Sbornik dokumentov i materialov. Khabarovsk: KKI, 1964.

Khabarovskii Grafa Murav'eva-Amurskogo Kadetskii Korpus (1888–1978). San Francisco: Globus, 1978.

Khabarovskii krai, 1917–1977. Comp. A. K. Chernyi, I. M. Tret'iak, V. S. Pasternak, V. G. Balitskii, and N. M. Rogal'. Khabarovsk: KKI, 1977.

Kharitanovskii, A. A. "Vydaiushchiisia naturalist Kamchatki." *Voprosy geografii Kamchatki*, 1963, no. 1: 41–58.

Khetagurova, Valentina Semenovna. "Veriu v derzost' molodykh." *Dal'nii Vostok*, 1987, no. 2: 127–33.

Khisamutdinov, Amir Aleksandrovich. *Mir biblioteki*. Vladivostok: DVKI, 1990.

———. *Terra incognita*. Vladivostok: DVGU, 1989.

———. *Vladivostok": Etiudy k istorii starogo goroda*. Vladivostok: DVGU, 1994.

——— [under pseud. A. Dinov]. "Zotik." *Krasnoe znamia*, 2 Nov. 1989.

Khodzher, Grigorii, Aleksei Val'diu, and Chuner Taksami. *Porodnilis' na Amure*. Khabarovsk: KKI, 1982.

Khramtsova, N. A. "Internatsional'nye formirovaniia na Dal'nem Vostoke." In *Voprosy istorii Dal'nego Vostoka*, vol. 4, pp. 91–97. Khabarovsk: Khab. gospedinstitut, 1974.

———. "Sozdanie i deiatel'nost' organizatsii kommunistov-internatsionalistov (1918–1922 gg.). In *Iz istorii Grazhdanskoi voiny i interventsii na Dal'nem Vostoke*, pp. 3–13. Khabarovsk: Khab. gospedinstitut, 1978.

Khrestomatiia po istorii Dal'nego Vostoka. Ed. N. K. Kiriukhin. Vladivostok: DVKI, 1983.

Khronika Magadanskoi partiinoi organizatsii, 1923–1986. Ed. V. I. Sorokin. Magadan: MKI, 1987.

Khronika osvoeniia Rossiei Dal'nego Vostoka i Tikhogo okeana, 1639–1989. Comp. A. I. Gruzdev. Vladivostok: Primorskii filial geograficheskogo obshchestva SSSR, 1989.

Khrushchev, N. S. *Doklad na zakrytom zasedanii XX s"ezda KPSS*. Moscow: Gospolitizdat, 1959.

Kim, Matvei Timofeevich. *Koreiskie internatsionality v bor'be za vlast' sovetov na Dal'nem Vostoke (1918–1933)*. Moscow: Nauka, 1979.

Kim Sen Suk et al. *Nam zhizn' dana*. Iuzhno-Sakhalinsk: DVKI, 1989.

Kim Syn Khva. *Ocherki po istorii sovetskikh koreitsev*. Alma Ata: Nauka, 1965.

Kiuner, Nikolai Vasil'evich. *Kitaiskie izvestiia o narodakh Iuzhnoi Sibiri, Tsentral'noi Azii i Dal'nego Vostoka*. Moscow: Izdat. vostoch. lit., 1961.

Klopov, Sergei Vasil'evich. *Amur: Reka druzhby*. Khabarovsk: KKI, 1959.

Kolotov, Nikolai Alekseevich. *Okean v ogne: moriaki transportnogo flota Dal'nego Vostoka v Velikoi Otechestvennoi voine 1941–1945*. Vladivostok: DVKI, 1972.

Kolpenskii, V. *Iakutskaia ssylka i delo romanovtsev*. Peterburg: Gosizdat, 1920.

Koltsov, V. V. "Ispol'zovanie inostrannogo kapitala dlia razvitiia proizvoditel'nykh sil Dal'nego Vostoka v perekhodnyi period." In *Istoriia promyshlennogo razvitiia sovetskogo Dal'nego Vostoka*, pp. 86–90. Vladivostok: IIAENDV, 1979.

Kolykhalova, Tamara Fominichna. *Sotsial-demokraticheskie organizatsii Dal'nego Vostoka nakanune pervoi russkoi revoliutsii (1903–1907)*. Tomsk: Izdat. Tomskogo univ., 1982.

Komanovskii, Boris Leont'evich. *Puti razvitiia literatur narodov krainego severa i Dal'nego Vostoka SSSR*. Magadan: MKI, 1977.

Komsomol'sk-na-Amure: Gorod muzhestva, truda i geroizma. Ed. V. M. Krysin. Khabarovsk: KKI, 1982.

Kondrashev, Ivan Filippovich. *Lenin i Stalin: Vdokhnoviteli i organizatory razgroma inostrannoi voennoi interventsii i vnutrennei kontrrevoliutsii (1918–1920 gg.)*. Moscow: Znanie, 1953.

Kondrat'ev, Nikolai Dmitrievich. *Marshal Bliukher*. Moscow: Voenizdat, 1965.

Koptelov, A. "M. Gorkii i Sibir'." *Sibirskie ogni*, 1937, no. 3: 89.

Korsakov, E. *Amerikanskaia ekspansiia na Severo-Vostoke Rossii v nachale XX veka*. Khabarovsk: Khab. vysshaia partiinaia shkola, 1968.

Kostanov, Aleksandr Ivanovich. "Iz istorii Sakhalinskikh arkhivov." In *Chitaia 'Ostrov Sakhalin'*, 2: 4–15. Iuzhno-Sakhalinsk: Sakhalinskii oblastnoi kraevedcheskii muzei, 1990.

———, ed. *Istoriia bez 'belykh piaten'*. Iuzhno-Sakhalinsk: Ispolkom sakhalinskogo oblastnogo soveta narodnykh deputatov, 1989.

Kostikov, G. I. "Ispol'zovanie gosudarstvennogo kapitalizma v sozdanii sotsialisticheskoi ekonomiki na Dal'nem Vostoke." In *Deiatel'nost' kommunisticheskoi partii Sovetskogo Soiuza po razvitiiu proizvoditel'nykh sil i ukrepleniiu oboronosposobnosti Dal'nego Vostoka (1917–1976 gg.)*, pp. 29–36. Vladivostok: DVGU, 1976.

Kots, Igor' Aleksandrovich, and Iurii Dmitrievich Shmakov. *Slushaem tebia, granitsa*. Khabarovsk: KKI, 1983.

Kovalevskii, Maksim. "Porto Franko vo Vladivostoke." *Vestnik Evropy*, 255 (Jan. 1909): 423–37.

Kozhevin, Vladimir Efimovich. *Partizanskie tropy geroev*. Ulan-Ude: Buriatskoe knizh. izdat., 1986.

Kozlov, Aleksandr. "Dolg i chest'." *Dal'nii Vostok*, 1988, no. 10: 121–30.

Kozovskii, Iurii Mikhailovich. *Molodost' Kropotkina*. Khabarovsk: KKI, 1983.

Krasnoshchekova, Luella Aleksandrovna. "Iz vospominanii ob otse i sem'e." *Dal'nii Vostok*, 1990, no. 4: 138–49.

Krasnov, Evgenii Vasil'evich, ed. *Vek zamyslov i svershenii*. Vladivostok: DVKI, 1987.

Krasnoznamennyi Dal'nevostochnyi: Istoriia Krasnoznamennogo Dal'nevostochnogo voennogo okruga. Moscow: Voenizdat, 1971. Rev. ed. Khabarovsk: KKI, 1979.

Krasnyi ostrov: Vospominaniia, ocherki, dokumenty o bor'be za vlast' sovetov na Amure, 1918–1922. Ed. I. I. Mints. Khabarovsk: KKI, 1967.

Kratkaia literaturnaia entsiklopediia. 9 vols. Moscow: Sovetskaia entsiklopediia, 1962–78.

Krest'ianstvo Dal'nego Vostoka SSSR (XIX–XX vv.). Vladivostok: IIAENDV, 1979.

Krivshenko, Sergei Filippovich. *Bereg otechestva: Literaturno-kriticheskie stat'i i ocherki o tvorchestve pisatelei-dal'nevostochnikov.* Vladivostok: DVKI, 1978.

———. *Dorogami zemleprokhodtsev.* Khabarovsk: KKI, 1984.

———. *Geroika osvoeniia i sotsialisticheskogo preobrazovaniia Dal'nego Vostoka v russkoi i sovetskoi literature.* Vladivostok: DVGU, 1985.

Krivtsov. S. S., ed. *Dal'nevostochnyi krai.* Moscow: Moskovskii rabochii, 1929.

Kruber, Aleksandr Aleksandrovich. *Aziatskaia Rossiia: Geograficheskii sbornik.* Moscow: I. N. Kushnerev, 1903.

Krushanov, Andrei Ivanovich. *Imperialisticheskaia interventsiia na sovetskom Dal'nem Vostoke (1918–1922 gg.).* Vladivostok: IIAENDV, 1988.

———. "Ob organizatsii istoricheskikh issledovanii na Dal'nem Vostoke." *Voprosy istorii,* 1975, no. 8: 20–30.

———. *Pobeda sovetskoi vlasti na Dal'nem Vostoke i v Zabaikal'e (1917–aprel' 1918).* Vladivostok: DVKI, 1983.

Kto est' kto v Primorskom krae. Vladivostok: Information Technology Lab, 1993.

Kulakova, Irina Filippovna. *Primorskaia kraevaia partiinaia organizatsiia v period mezhdu XX i XXII s''ezdami KPSS (1956–1961 gg.).* Vladivostok: IIAENDV, 1975.

Kul'turnoe stroitel'stvo na Dal'nem Vostoke SSSR. Khabarovsk: Khab. gospedinstitut, 1980.

Kuzin, Anatolii. *Dal'nevostochnye Koreitsy.* Iuzhno-Sakhalinsk: DVKI, 1993.

Kuznetsov, Mikhail Sergeevich. *Bor'ba partiinykh organizatsii Dal'nego Vostoka za stanovlenie sovetskoi kul'tury, 1922–1927 gg.* Tomsk: Izdat. Tomskogo univ., 1978.

Kuznetsov, V. S. "Iz istorii vzaimootnoshenii Kitaia s chzhurchzheniami v XVI–nachale XVII v." In *Materialy po istorii Dal'nego Vostoka*, pp. 143–55. Vladivostok: IIAENDV, 1973.

Lamin, Vladimir Aleksandrovich. *Kliuchi k dvum okeanam.* Khabarovsk: KKI, 1981.

Lapin, Boris. *Tikhookeanskii dnevnik.* Moscow: Federatsiia, 1929.

Lappo, D. D. "Stranitsy zhizni i deiatel'nosti I. M. Vareikisa." *Voprosy istorii KPSS,* 1963, no. 11: 100–105.

Latyshev, Vladislav Mikhailovich. "Pis'ma Bronislava Pilsudskogo na Dal'nii Vostok." *Vestnik Dal'nevostochnogo otdeleniia RAN,* 1992, nos. 1–2: 164–78.

Lavrov, Ivan Aleksandrovich. *V strane eksperimentov.* Harbin: Zaitsev, 1934.

[Lazo]. *Sergei Lazo: Vospominaniia i dokumenty.* Comp. A. P. Shurygin, A. S. Lazo, and G. E. Reikhberg. Moscow: Politizdat, 1974.

Lemeshko, P. M. "Deiatel'nost' dal'nevostochnykh partiinykh organizatsii po ideino-politicheskomu vospitaniiu kommunistov v 1924–1925 gg." In *Voprosy istorii Dal'nego Vostoka*, vol. 4, pp. 129–45. Khabarovsk: Khab. gospedinstitut, 1974.

Leninskaia gvardiia na Dal'nem Vostoke. Ed. G. S. Chechulina. Khabarovsk: KKI, 1970.

Leonov, Pavel Artemovich. *Oblast' na ostrovakh.* Iuzhno-Sakhalinsk: DVKI, 1979.

——. *Ocherki istorii Sakhalinskoi organizatsii KPSS*. Iuzhno-Sakhalinsk: DVKI, 1975.

Leont'ev, V. V. and K. A. Novikova. *Toponimicheskii slovar' Severo-Vostoka SSSR*. Magadan: MKI, 1989.

Lerman, Il'ia Naumovich. *Po serdtsu blizkie druz'ia*. Khabarovsk: KKI, 1980.

Lesniak, B. N. "U vkhoda v proshloe." *Na severe dal'nem*, 1988, no. 2: 155–95.

Levikov, Aleksandr Il'ich, et al. *Kolyma i kolimchane*. Moscow: Sovetskaia Rossiia, 1971.

Levitskii, Vladimir Leonidovich. *Konstantin Sukhanov*. Vladivostok: Primizdat, 1956.

Ligin, Iurii. *Na Dal'nem Vostoke*. Moscow: Zadruga, 1913.

Lishchinskii, Boris Davidovich. "Puteshestvie s Chekhovym." *Dal'nii Vostok*, 1990, no. 7: 156–60.

Litvinenko, Igor'. "Zakrytyi perelom." *Dal'nii Vostok*, 1988, no. 6: 139–54.

Lomakin, Viktor Pavlovich. *Primor'e: vchera, segodnia, zavtra*. Moscow: Politizdat, 1981.

L'vovich, V. *Po Dal'nemu Vostoku*. Moscow: M. V. Kliukin, 1905.

Maak, Richard Karlovich. *Puteshestvie na Amur*. St. Petersburg: Imper. Russ. Geog. Obshchestvo, 1859.

——. *Puteshestvie po doline reki Ussuri*. 2 vols. St. Petersburg: Imper. Russ. Geog. Obshchestvo, 1861.

Magadan: Putevoditel'-spravochnik. Magadan: MKI, 1989.

Magadanu — 50 let: Statisticheskii sbornik. Magadan: MKI, 1989.

Makarov, Gavriil Georgievich. *Severo-Vostok RSFSR v 1918–1921 gg*. Yakutsk: Yakutskoe knizh. izdat., 1988.

Makarova, Raisa Vsevolodovna. *Russkie na Tikhom okeane vo vtoroi polovine XVIII v*. Moscow: Nauka, 1968. English trans. 1975.

Malinovskii, Rodion Iakovlevich, ed. *Final: Istoriko-memuarnyi ocherk o razgrome imperialisticheskoi Iaponii v 1945 gg*. Moscow: Nauka, 1966.

Mankhart, Gans. *Zapiski internatsionalista*. Blagoveshchensk: Amurskoe otdel. KKI, 1969.

Marsh molodosti: K 60-letiiu Khabarovskoi kraevoi organizatsii VLKSM. Khabarovsk: KKI, 1981.

Materialy po arkheologii Dal'nego Vostoka SSSR. Vladivostok: IIAENDV, 1981.

Materialy po istorii Dal'nego Vostoka. Vladivostok: IIAENDV, 1973.

Matveev, Nikolai Petrovich. *Kratkii ocherk istorii g. Vladivostoka*. Vladivostok: Ussuri, 1990 [1910].

Matveev, Zotik Nikolaevich. "Istoriia Dal'nevostochnogo kraia." *Zapiski Vladivostokskogo otdela gosudarstvennogo russkogo geograficheskogo obshchestva*, 20, no. 2 (1929): 341–76.

——. "Periodicheskaia pechat' na DV v period revoliutsii." *Izvestiia Primorskogo gubernskogo arkhivnogo biuro*, 3, no. 1 (1923): 43–64.

Matveeva, Tat'iana Zotikovna. "Bibliograf Dal'nevostochnogo kraia Z. N. Matveev (1889–1939)." In *Nauchnye biblioteki Sibiri i Dal'nego Vostoka*, vol. 2, pp. 103–19. Novosibirsk, 1972.

———. *Poslantsy partii na Dal'nem Vostoke.* Vladivostok: DVGU, 1972.

Mazuruk, Ilya. "Vozdushnaia trassa Aliaska-Sibir'." *Na severe dal'nem*, 1983, no. 1: 16–26.

Medvedev, Vitalii Egorovich. *Srednevekovye pamiatniki ostrova Ussuriiskogo.* Novosibirsk: Nauka, 1982.

Mel'chin, A. I. *Amerikanskaia interventsiia na sovetskom Dal'nem Vostoke v 1918–1920.* Moscow: Voenizdat, 1951.

———. *Razgrom amerikano-iaponskikh interventov na sovetskom Dal'nem Vostoke v 1920–1922 godakh.* Moscow: Znanie, 1953.

Melikhov, Georgii Vasil'evich. *Man'chzhury na Severo-Vostoke, XVII v.* Moscow: Nauka, 1974.

Merkulov, Spiridon Dionisievich. *Porto-franko i kolonizatsiia Priamurskago kraia russkim naseleniem.* St. Petersburg: Iu. A. Mansfeld, 1908.

Miasnikov, Vladimir Stepanovich. *Imperiia Tsin i russkoe gosudarstvo v XVII veke.* Moscow: Nauka, 1980.

Middendorf, Aleksandr von. *Puteshestvie na sever i vostok Sibiri.* 2 vols. St. Petersburg: Imper. Akad. nauk, 1860–77.

Miller [Müller], G. F. *Istoriia Sibiri.* 2 vols. Moscow: AN SSSR, 1937–41.

Minakir, Pavel Aleksandrovich, ed. *Ekonomicheskaia reforma na Dal'nem Vostoke.* Khabarovsk: Institut ekon. issled., 1993.

Morozov, Pavel Leont'evich. *Khabarovsk: kratkaia spravochnaia kniga.* Khabarovsk: KKI, 1980.

Muchik, G. A. *Dvadtsat' let partiinoi raboty v Sibiri i na Dal'nem Vostoke.* Moscow: Izdat. politkatorzhan, 1935.

Mukhachev, Boris Ivanovich. "Prezident respubliki." *Dal'nii Vostok*, 1990, no. 4: 136–38.

——— *Sovety Severo-Vostoka SSSR v period sotsialisticheskoi rekonstruktsii narodnogo khoziaistva (1926–1936 gg.).* Magadan: MKI, 1987.

———. *Stanovlenie sovetskoi vlasti i bor'ba s inostrannoi ekspansiei na Severo-Vostoke SSSR.* Novosibirsk: Nauka, 1975.

Müller, G. F., *see* Miller, G. F.

Murov, G. T. *Liudi i nravy Dal'nego Vostoka.* Tomsk: Tipograf. P. I. Makushina, 1901.

My berezhem svoiu granitsu: Pesni o voinakh-pogranichnikakh. Moscow: Sovetskii kompozitor, 1981.

Na novom puti: Zhizn' i khoziaistvo Dal'ne-Vostochnoi oblasti v 1923–1924 godu. Vladivostok: Knizhnoe delo, 1925.

Narody sovetskogo Dal'nego Vostoka v dooktiabrskii period istorii SSSR. Vladivostok: Dal'nevostoch. filial SO AN SSSR, 1968.

Nashi dalekiia okrainy. Moscow: Pechatnoe delo, 1912.

Naumov, Igor' Vladimirovich. *Grazhdanskaia voina na Dal'nem Vostoke v sovetskoi istoriografii serediny 1950–serediny 1980-e godov*. Irkutsk: Izdat. Irkutskogo universiteta, 1991.

Nazimok, Vasilii Nikitich. *Bor'ba sovetov protiv burzhuaznykh organov samoupravleniia na Dal'nem Vostoke*. Tomsk: Izdat. Tomskogo univ., 1968.

Nesterov, Fedor Fedorovich. *Sviaz' vremen*. Moscow: Molodaia gvardiia, 1984.

Nikiforov, Petr Mikhailovich. *Zapiski prem'era DVR*. Moscow: Politizdat, 1974.

Nikitin, N. I. "Ekspeditsiia Poiarkova na Amur." *Voprosy istorii*, 1981, no. 9: 180–82.

Nikolaev, S. [pseud.] "Tsena istiny." *Tikhookeanskaia zvezda*, 7 parts, 24–30 Sept. 1989.

——. "Vystrely v spinu," *Dal'nii Vostok*, 2 parts, 1991, no. 2: 136–43; no. 3: 132–44.

Nikolaev, Sergei Nikolaevich. *Pamiatniki i pamiatnye mesta v Primor'e*. Vladivostok: Primorskoe knizh. izdat., 1958.

Nikolaevskii, Boris. "Dal'stroi: Sovetskaia katorga v Kolymskom krae." *Sotsialisticheskii vestnik*. 21–22 (10 Dec. 1945): 256–57.

Obzor russkoi periodicheskoi pechati: Sibir' i Dal'nii Vostok. 4 vols. St. Petersburg: Gos. Tipograf., 1908.

Ocherk istorii Khabarovskoi kraevoi organizatsii KPSS (1900–1978 gody). Ed. A. K. Chernyi. Khabarovsk: KKI, 1979.

Ocherki istorii Chukotki s drevneishikh vremen do nashikh dnei. Ed. N. N. Dikov. Novosibirsk: Nauka, 1974.

Ocherki istorii Dal'nevostochnykh organizatsii KPSS (1900–1937). Ed. N. A. Gogolev. Khabarovsk: KKI, 1982.

Ocherki istorii Dal'nevostochnykh organizatsii KPSS (1938–1987). Ed. G. S. Khokhliuk. Khabarovsk: KKI, 1987.

Ocherki istorii Kamchatskoi oblastnoi partiinoi organizatsii, 1917–1985. Ed. S. V. Zakharov. Petropavlovsk: DVKI, 1986.

Ocherki istorii sovetskogo Primor'ia. Vladivostok: Primorskoe knizh. izdat., 1963.

Ogurtsova, M. E. "Deiatel'nost' partiinykh organizatsii Dal'nego Vostoka po perestroike ideologicheskoi raboty (1938–1941)." In *Iz istorii revoliutsionnogo dvizheniia, deiatel'nosti partiinykh i komsomol'skikh organizatsii Dal'nego Vostoka*, pp. 57–76. Vladivostok: DVKI, 1973.

Okladnikov, Aleksei Pavlovich. "Novoe v arkheologii Dal'nego Vostoka." *Problemy Dal'nego Vostoka*, 1972, no. 3: 97–117.

Okladnikov, A. P., and A. P. Derevianko. *Dalekoe proshlie Primor'ia i Priamur'ia*. Vladivostok: DVKI, 1973.

Olan'on, Kliment. *Sibir' i eia ekonomicheskaia budushchnost'*. St. Petersburg: Prosveshchenie, 1902.

Opyt sotsiologicheskikh issledovanii na Dal'nem Vostoke. Vladivostok: DVNTs AN SSSR, 1974.

Organizatsiia KPSS Evreiskoi Avtonomnoi oblasti, 1934–1985: Khronika. Khabarovsk: KKI, 1986.

Organizatsionno-khoziaistvennaia deiatel'nost' mestnykh sovetov na Dal'nem Vostoke (1922–1985 gg). Vladivostok: DVNTs AN SSSR, 1986.

Paichadze, Sergei Antonovich. *Kniga Dal'nego Vostoka.* Khabarovsk: KKI, 1983.

———. *Knizhnoe delo na Dal'nem Vostoke: Dooktiabr'skii period.* Novosibirsk: Gos. publich. nauch. tekh. biblioteka SO AN SSSR, 1991.

Pamiat' Kolymy: Vospominaniia, pis'ma, fotodokumenty o godakh repressii. Comp. L. V. Andreeva and V. A. Rezinovskaia. Magadan: MKI, 1990.

Pamiatniki istorii i kul'tury Primorskogo kraia. Ed. A. I. Krushanov. Vladivostok: DVKI, 1982.

Panov, A. A. *Griadushchee mongol'skoe igo.* St. Petersburg: Pirozhkov, 1906.

Panov, Viktor Anan'evich. *Amerikanskie podlozhnie dokumenty.* Vladivostok: Yosif Korot, 1918.

———. *Dal'nevostochnoe polozhenie: Ocherk Priamur'ia.* Vladivostok: Elektro-tip. gaz. "Dal'nii Vostok," 1912.

Papin, Leonid Mikhailovich. *Krakh kolchakovshchiny i obrazovanie Dal'nevostochnoi Respubliki.* Moscow: Moskovskii gosudarstvennyi universitet, 1957.

Parfenov, Petr Semenovich. *Na soglashatel'skikh frontakh.* Moscow: Moskovskii rabochii, 1927.

———. *Uroki proshlogo: Grazhdanskaia voina v Sibiri.* Harbin: "Pravda," 1921.

Partiinye organizatsii Sibiri i Dal'nego Vostoka v period Oktiabr'skoi revoliutsii i Grazhdanskoi voiny (1917–1922 gg.). Novosibirsk: Novosibirskii gosudarstvennyi universitet, 1978.

Partiinye organizatsii sovetskogo Severa. Ed. V. A. Zibarev. Tomsk: Izdat. Tomskogo univ., 1980.

Pashkov, Aleksandr Mikhailovich. "Deiatel'nost' kommunisticheskoi partii po obespecheniiu bezopasnosti dal'nevostochnykh granits SSSR (1922–1941 gg.)." In *Deiatel'nost' kommunisticheskoi partii Sovetskogo Soiuza po razvitiiu proizvoditel'nykh sil i ukrepleniiu oboronosposobnosti Dal'nego Vostoka (1917–1976 gg.),* pp. 13–16. Vladivostok: DVGU, 1976.

———. *Za krai rodnoi — Dal'nevostochnyi.* Iuzhno-Sakhalinsk: DVKI, 1985.

Pashkov, Aleksandr Mikhailovich, and A. A. Nikiforov. *Estafeta muzhestva.* Iuzhno-Sakhalinsk: Iuzhno-Sakhalinsk. knizh. izdat., 1988.

Paustovskii, Konstantin. "Marshal Bliukher." *Novyi mir,* 1988, no. 2: 211–23.

Pavlenko, Petr Andreevich. *Na Vostoke.* Moscow: Gosizdat. khudozhlit, 1937.

Pecheritsa, Vladimir Fedorovich. *Podgotovka i vospitanie partiinykh kadrov na Dal'nem Vostoke.* Vladivostok: DVNTs AN SSSR, 1985.

Pegov, Nikolai Mikhailovich. *Dalekoe-blizkoe: Vospominaniia.* Moscow: Politizdat, 1982.

Penzin, Ilya Dmitrievich. *Khabarovskii krai.* Khabarovsk: KKI, 1988.

"Pervye shagi russkogo imperializma na Dal'nem Vostoke (1888–1903 gg.)." *Krasnyi arkhiv*, 3, 1932, no. 52: 34–124.

Petrov, G. E., ed. *Ukrepim sovety DVK*. Khabarovsk: Dal'giza, 1934.

Petrov, P. P. *Ot' Volgi do Tikhogo okeana v riadakh belykh*. Riga: Didkovskii, 1930.

Pisateli Dal'nego Vostoka: Biobibliograﬁcheskii spravochnik. Khabarovsk: KKI, 1989.

Pismanik, M. [Moisei L'vovich Pis'mannik]. *Komissar gosudarstvennoi bezopasnosti*. Tashkent: Esh gvardiia, 1981.

Pobeda na Dal'nem Vostoke. Khabarovsk: KKI, 1985.

Poedinok na granitse. Alma Ata: Izdat. Kazakhstan, 1966.

Pogranichnaia zastava. Ed. G. M. Ignatkovich and V. A. Mel'nichuk. Moscow: Politizdat, 1980.

Pogranichnye voiska SSSR, 1918–1928: Sbornik dokumentov i materialov. Moscow: Nauka, 1973.

Pogranichnye voiska SSSR, 1929–1938: Sbornik dokumentov i materialov. Moscow: Nauka, 1972.

Pogranichnye voiska SSSR, 1939–1941: Sbornik dokumentov i materialov. Moscow: Nauka, 1970.

Pogranichnye voiska SSSR, 1941: Sbornik dokumentov i materialov. Moscow: Nauka, 1976.

Pogranichnye voiska SSSR, 1942–1945: Sbornik dokumentov i materialov. Moscow: Nauka, 1976.

Pogranichnye voiska SSSR, 1945–1950: Sbornik dokumentov i materialov. Moscow: Nauka, 1975.

Pogranichnyi dozor. Moscow: DOSAAF [Vsesoiuznoe dobrovol'noe obshchestvo sodeistviia armii, aviatsii i flotu], 1973.

"Pokazateli po trudu, 1932–1942." *Magadanskaia pravda*, 26 Mar. 1992.

Polevoi, Boris Petrovich. *Pervootkryvateli Kuril'skikh ostrovov*. Iuzhno-Sakhalinsk: DVKI, 1982.

——. *Pervootkryvaterli Sakhalina*. Iuzhno-Sakhalinsk: Sakh. knizh. izdat., 1959.

Ponomarev, Sergei. "Sakhalinskii tonnel'." *Problemy Dal'nego Vostoka*, 1990, no. 9: 140–46.

Popov, Nikita Aleksandrovich. *Oni s nami srazhalis' za vlast' sovetov: Kitaiskie dobrovol'tsy na frontakh Grazhdanskoi voiny v Rossii (1918–1922)*. Leningrad: Lenizdat, 1959.

Popov, P. "O Tyrskikh pamiatnikakh." *Zapiski Vostochnogo otdela Russkogo arkheologicheskogo obshchestva*, 16, no. 1 (1906): 12–20.

Pozdneev, Dmitrii Matveevich. *Materialy po istorii severnoi Iaponii i eia otnoshenii k materiku Azii i Rossii*. 2 vols. Tokyo-Yokohama: Zh. Gliuk', 1909.

Priamur'e: Fakty, tsifry, nabliudeniia. Moscow: Obshchezemskaia organizatsiia, 1909.

Priamur'e moe. Blagoveshchensk: KKI, 1990.

Primor'e: Ego priroda i khoziaistvo. Ed. A. Krishtofovich. Vladivostok: Gosizdat, 1923.

Primorskaia kraevaia organizatsiia KPSS v period razvitiia i sovershenstvovaniia sotsial-isticheskogo obshchestva (60–80-e gody). Vladivostok: DVKI, 1987.

Primorskii krai. Ed. A. I. Krushanov. Vladivostok: DVKI, 1981.

Problemy agrarnoi istorii Dal'nego Vostoka. Khabarovsk: Khab. gospedinstitut, 1979.

Problemy istorii Dal'nego Vostoka SSSR (XVII–XX vv.) v otechestvennoi literature. Ed. A. I. Krushanov. Vladivostok: IIAENDV, 1986.

Proizvoditel'nye sily Dal'nego Vostoka. Khabarovsk: Dal'nevostoch. kraevaia planovaia komissiia, 1927.

Prokhorov, Aleksandr Aleksandrovich. *K voprosu o sovetsko-kitaiskoi granitse*. Moscow: Mezhdunarodnye otnosheniia, 1975.

Przheval'skii, Nikolai Mikhailovich. *Puteshestvie v Ussuriiskom krae, 1867–1869*. Moscow: Izdat. geog. lit., 1947.

Purin, A. A. "V dni revoliutsii v Okhotsko-Kamchatskom i Chukotsko-Anadyr-skom krae." *Vol'naia Sibir'*, 2 parts, 1927, no. 2: 61–92; 1928, no. 3: 61–83.

Pushkar', Arnol'd Ignat'evich. *Tikhookeanskii forpost nauki*. Khabarovsk: KKI, 1979. Rev. ed. 1982.

———. *Zdes' nachinaetsia Rossiia*. Moscow: Sovetskaia Rossiia, 1977.

Raiony Dal'nevostochnogo kraia: Khabarovsk: Knizhnoe delo, 1931.

Ravich, A. [A. S. Varsa]. "Krovavye dni na Amure." *Russkoe obozrenie*, 5 Mar. 1938.

Reikhberg, Grigorii Evgen'evich. *Razgrom iaponskoi interventsii na Dal'nem Vostoke*. Moscow: Gosizdat, 1940.

Rekk-Lebedev, Anatolii. *Dal'nevostochnaia Lifliandiia: Estontsy na Ussuriiskoi zemle*. Tallinn: Eesti raamat, 1989.

"Repressirovannoe vostokovedenie: Vostokovedy, podvergshiesia repressiiam v 20–50-e gody." *Narody Azii i Afriki*, 2 parts, 1990, no. 4: 113–25; no. 5: 96–106.

Revkomy Severo-Vostoka SSSR (1922–1928 gg.): Sbornik dokumentov i materialov. Ed. V. S. Flerov. Magadan: MKI, 1973.

Revoliutsiia na Dal'nem Vostoke. Vol. 1. Moscow-Petrograd: Istpart, 1923.

Revoliutsionnoe dvizhenie na Dal'nem Vostoke. Ed. Dal'nevostochnaia komissiia po organizatsii iubileia 20–letiia 1905 g. i Istpartotdel Dal'biuro TsK RKP(b). Vladivostok: Knizhnoe delo, 1925.

Riabov, Nikolai Ivanovich. *Ocherki po istorii Dal'nego Vostoka (17–19 vv.)*. Khabarovsk: Dal'giz, 1939.

Riabov, Nikolai Ivanovich, and Moisei Grigor'evich Shtein. *Ocherki istorii russkogo Dal'nego Vostoka (XVII–nachalo XX veka)*. Khabarovsk: KKI, 1958.

Riabov, Nikolai Pavlovich. *Ulitsy Khabarovska rasskazyvaiut*. Khabarovsk: KKI, 1977.

Romanov, Boris Aleksandrovich. *Ocherki diplomaticheskoi istorii russko-iaponskoi voiny, 1895–1907*. Moscow: Izdat. AN SSSR, 1947.

——. *Rossiia v Man'chzhurii (1892–1906)*. Leningrad: Izdanie Leningradskogo Vostochnogo Instituta, 1928.

Rossiiskaia Federatsiia: Dal'nii Vostok. Ed. A. B. Margolin. Moscow: Mysl', 1971.

Rudnev, Georgii Alekseevich. *Kursy, prolozhennye pod ognem*. Vladivostok: DVKI, 1983.

Russia. *Aziatskaia Rossiia*. Comp. Glavnoe upravlenie zemleustroistva i zemledeliia. Pereselencheskoe upravlenie. 3 vols. + atlas. St. Petersburg: A. F. Marks, 1914.

——. *Dal'nii Vostok*. Comp. Armiia, Glavnoe upravlenie General'nogo shtaba. 9 vols. St. Petersburg: A. Benke, 1911.

——. *Pereselenie na Dal'nii Vostok v 1906 g*. St. Petersburg: F. Vaisberg, 1906.

Russkaia tikhookeanskaia epopeia. Ed. V. A. Divin. Khabarovsk: KKI, 1979.

Russko-iaponskaia voina, 1904–1905 gg. Ed. Voenno-istoricheskaia komissiia. 9 vols. St. Petersburg: Suvorkin 1910.

Russko-kitaiskie otnosheniia v XVII veke. Ed. N. F. Demidova and V. S. Miasnikov. 2 vols. Moscow: Nauka, 1969–72.

Rybakovskii, Leonid Leonidovich. *Naselenie Dal'nego Vostoka za 150 let*. Moscow: Nauka, 1990.

Safronov, Fedot Grigor'evich. *Russkie na severo-vostoke Azii v XVII–seredine XIX v*. Moscow: Nauka, 1978.

——. *Tikhookeanskie okna Rossii*. Khabarovsk: KKI, 1988.

Safronov, Vladimir Dmitrievich. *Litsom k litsu s ideologicheskim protivnikom*. Moscow: Politizdat, 1981.

Saktaganov, Sergei. "Vosem' dnei, kotorye potriasli Sakhalin." In *Sakhalin: Literaturno-khudozhestvennyi sbornik*, pp. 7–35. Iuzhno-Sakhalinsk: Sakhalinskoe otdelenie, DVKI, 1989.

Salekhov, Nikolai Ivanovich. *Ian Borisovich Gamarnik*. Moscow: Politizdat, 1964.

Samarin, G., and V. Antonovich. *Dal'nii Vostok zhdet pereselentsev*. Moscow: Sel'khozgiz, 1940.

Samoilov, Aleksandr Danilovich. *Na strazhe zavoevanii Oktiabria: Krakh kontrrevoliutsii na Dal'nem Vostoke*. Moscow: Mysl', 1986.

Samsonov, Nikolai Ivanovich. *40 let sovetskoi vlasti na Dal'nem Vostoke*. Khabarovsk: KKI, 1957.

Sanachev, I. D. "Krest'ianskoe vosstanie na Amure: Kulatskii miatezh ili shag otchaianiia?" *Vestnik DVO*, 1992, nos. 3–4: 170–80.

Savin, A. S. "Sryv planov agressii Iaponii protiv SSSR v 1942–1943 gg." *Voenno-istoricheskii zhurnal*, 1983, no. 1: 48–56.

Sel'skoe khoziaistvo i krest'ianstvo Dal'nego Vostoka SSSR v period stroitel'stva sotsializma i kommunizma. Khabarovsk: Khab. gospedinstitut, 1984.

Sem, L. I., Iu. A. Sem, and L. E. Fetisova, ed. *Kul'tura narodov Dal'nego Vostoka SSSR (XIX–XX vv.)*. Vladivostok: IIAENDV, 1978.

Sergeev, Oleg Igorevich. *Kazachestvo na russkom Dal'nem Vostoke v XVII–XIX vv*. Moscow: Nauka, 1983.

S"ezdy sovetov Amurskoi oblasti, 1918–1936: Sbornik dokumentov i materialov. Blagovesh-chensk: Amurskoe otdelenie KKI, 1987.

Shalamov, Varlam. *Kolymskie rasskazy*. Paris: YMCA Press, 1982.

Shatskii, I. *Pokhod DVK vo vtoruiu piatiletku*. Khabarovsk: Dal'giz, 1932.

Shchit i mech. Vladivostok: DVKI, 1978.

Shchit i mech Priamur'ia. Blagoveshchensk: Amurskoe otdel. KKI, 1988.

Shelest, Georgii Ivanovich. "Kolymskie zapisi." *Znamia*, 1964, no. 9.

Shereshevskii, Boris Mikhailovich. *V bitvakh za Dal'nii Vostok (1920–1922 gg.)*. Novo-sibirsk: Nauka, 1974.

Shindialov, Nikolai Antonovich. *Pervaia russkaia revoliutsiia na Amure*. Blagovesh-chensk: Amurskoe otdel. KKI, 1985.

Shinkarev, Leonid. "Zona." *Dal'nii Vostok*, 1989, no. 8: 101–15.

Shishkin, Sergei Nikolaevich. *Grazhdanskaia voina na Dal'nem Vostoke, 1918–1922 gg*. Moscow: Voenizdat, 1957.

Shishkov, Valerii Aleksandrovich. *Sovetskoe gosudarstvo i strany Zapada v 1917–1923 gg*. Leningrad: Nauka, 1969.

Shkurkin, Pavel Vasil'evich. *Igroki*. Harbin: Abramovich, 1926.

Shpiony i diversanty za rabotoi. Moscow: Gosizdat, 1937.

Shreider, D. I. *Nash Dal'nii Vostok*. St. Petersburg: A. F. Devriena, 1897.

Shternberg, Lev Iakovlevich. *Giliaki, orochi, gol'dy, negidal'tsy, ainy*. Khabarovsk: Dal'giz, 1933.

Shumiatskii, Boris Zakharovich, ed. *Bor'ba za russkii Dal'nii Vostok*. Irkutsk: VSVO [Vostoch. Sibir. voennyi okrug], 1922.

Shurygin, A. "Revoliutsionnoe dvizhenie v interventskikh voiskakh na Dal'nem Vostoke (1918–1922 gg.)." *Na rubezhe*, 1934, no. 2: 84–98.

Sibirskaia sovetskaia entsiklopediia. 3 vols. Eds. A. A. Anson and B. Z. Shumiatskii. Novosibirsk: Sibirskoe kraevoe izdat., 1929–32.

Sibirskaia sovetskaia entsiklopediia. vol. 4. Eds. A. A. Anson, M. M. Basov, and B. Z. Shumiatskii. Intro. Edward Kasinec and Robert H. Davis, Jr. New York: Norman Ross, 1992 [1936]

Sibirskie ogni [Novosibirsk], 1922–

Skazanie o schast'e: V. I. Lenin v poezii narodov sovetskogo krainego severa. Ed. M. G. Voskoboinikov. Leningrad: Sovetskii pisatel', 1970.

Sladkovskii, Mikhail Iosifovich. "Pervyi tsentr vostokovedeniia na Dal'nem Vostoke." *Problemy Dal'nego Vostoka*, 1979, no. 4: 143–52.

Slavinskii, Boris Nikolaevich. *Vneshniaia politika SSSR na Dal'nem Vostoke, 1945–1986*. Moscow: Mezhdunarodnye otnosheniia, 1988.

Slovar' russkikh govorov Priamur'ia. Moscow: Nauka, 1983.

Smirnov, Mikhail Ivanovich. *Admiral Aleksandr Vasil'evich Kolchak*. Paris: Voenno-morskii soiuz, 1930.

Smolina, Tamara Pavlovna. "Sud'ba Berzinykh." *Na severe dal'nem*, 1988, no. 2: 196–221.

Solov'ev, Fedor Vladimirovich. *Kitaiskoe otkhodnichestvo na Dal'nem Vostoke Rossii v epokhu kapitalizma (1861–1917 gg.)*. Moscow: Nauka, 1989.

——. *Slovar' kitaiskikh toponimov na territorii sovetskogo Dal'nego Vostoka*. Vladivostok: IIAENDV, 1975.

Solzhenitsyn, Aleksandr. *Sobranie sochinenii*. 7 vols. Paris: YMCA Press, 1980.

Sonin, Viktor Vladimirovich. *Stanovlenie Dal'nevostochnoi respubliki, 1920–1922*. Vladivostok: DVGU, 1990.

——. *Velikii Oktiabr' i stanovlenie sovetskoi gosudarstvennosti na Dal'nem Vostoke (1917–1922)*. Vladivostok: DVGU, 1987.

Sotsialisticheskoe stroitel'stvo na Dal'nem Vostoke SSSR. Khabarovsk: Khab. gosped-institut, 1981.

Sotsial'no-ekonomicheskoe razvitie dal'nevostochnoi derevni: Dorevoliutsionnyi period. Vladivostok: IIAENDV, 1982.

Sotsial'no-ekonomicheskoe razvitie dal'nevostochnoi derevni: Sovetskii period. Vladivostok: IIAENDV, 1984.

Sotsial'no-kul'turnoe razvitie Dal'nego Vostoka SSSR. Vladivostok: IIAENDV, 1986.

Sovetskii entsiklopedicheskii slovar'. Moscow: Sovetskaia entsiklopediia, 1983, 1989.

Sovety Severo-Vostoka SSSR (1928–1940): Sbornik dokumentov i materialov. Magadan: MKI, 1979.

Sovety Severo-Vostoka SSSR (1941–1961): Sbornik dokumentov i materialov. Magadan: MKI, 1982.

Spravochnaia knizhka po Vostochnomu institutu. Vladivostok: Tip. Vostoch. instituta, 1909.

Spravochnik po DV kraiu na 1927 god. Eds. I. P. Voronchanin and A. L. Shpaer. Khabarovsk: Tikhookeanskaia zvezda, 1927.

SSSR i Iaponiia. Ed. I. A. Latyshev. Moscow: Nauka, 1987.

Stalin, I. V. *Sochineniia*. 2 vols. (14, 15). Stanford, Calif.: Hoover Institution Press, 1967.

Stanovlenie sovetsko-kitaiskikh otnoshenii (1917–1950 gg.). Vladivostok: IIAENDV, 1987.

Stepanov, A. I. *Russkii bereg*. Vladivostok: DVKI, 1976.

Stepanov, Vladimir Il'ich. *Ideologicheski obespechit'*. Khabarovsk: KKI, 1983.

Stoiat na Amure russkie sela. Khabarovsk: KKI, 1986.

Striuchenko, Ivan Grigor'evich. *Ideino-politicheskaia bor'ba bol'shevikov Dal'nego Vostoka protiv burzhuazii i melkoburzhuaznykh partii za massy v 1917 godu*. Vladivostok: DVKI, 1985.

——. *Pechat' Dal'nego Vostoka nakanune i v gody pervoi russkoi revoliutsii (1895–1907)*. Vladivostok: DVKI, 1982.

"Suchanskaia dolina vo gody grazhdanskoi voiny." *Krasnyi arkhiv*, 6, 1938, no. 91: 16–88.

Sukhovii, S. F., comp. *Sovetskii Dal'nii Vostok*. Chita-Vladivostok: Knizhnoe delo, 1923.

Sungorkin, Vladimir Nikolaevich. *Dal'nii Vostok*. Moscow: Planeta, 1989.

Sushkov, Boris Aleksandrovich. *Dal'nevostochnye moria i ikh poberezh'ia*. Vladivostok: Primorskoe knizh. izdat., 1958.

Suturin, Aleksandr Stepanovich. "Delo kraevogo masshtaba." *Tikhookeanskaia zvezda*, 11 parts, 25–30 Mar., 4–8 Apr. 1989.

———. *Delo kraevogo masshtaba: O zhertvakh stalinskogo bezzakoniia na Dal'nem Vostoke*. Khabarovsk: KKI, 1991.

———. "Kharbintsy." *Tikhookeanskaia zvezda*, 4 May 1990.

———. "Ogon' po svoim." *Bloknot agitatora*, 1989, no. 24: 18–27.

Sverdlov, N. V. "Kitoboinyi promysel Rossii na Tikhom okeane (XIX–nach. XX vv.)." In *Sotsial'no-ekonomicheskie problemy vseobshchei istorii*, pp. 90–133. Khabarovsk: Khab. gospedinstitut, 1979.

Svetachev, Mikhail Ivanovich. *Imperialisticheskaia interventsiia v Sibiri i na Dal'nem Vostoke (1918–1922 gg.)*. Novosibirsk: Nauka, 1983.

Svetlanin, Andrei Vasil'evich [Nikolai Nikitich Likhachev]. *Dal'nevostochnyi zagovor*. Frankfurt-am-Main: Posev, 1953.

Svit, I. V. *Ukrainskii Dal'nii Vostok*. Harbin: UVS, 1934.

Taezhnye pokhody: Sbornik epizodov iz istorii Grazhdanskoi voiny na Dal'nem Vostoke. Ed. Maksim Gorkii, Pavel Postyshev, and Isaak Mints. Moscow: Gosizdat, 1935. Rev. G. S. Chechulina and N. A. Avdeeva. Khabarovsk: KKI, 1972.

Taksami, Chuner Mikhailovich. *Osnovnye problemy etnografii i istorii nivkhov*. Leningrad: Nauka, 1975.

Talantsev, Vladimir Ivanovich. *Analiz razvitiia bytovogo obsluzhivaniia regiona*. Moscow: Legpishchprom, 1981.

Tarasova, Anna Ivanovna. "Pis'ma L. Ia. Shternberga k V. K. Arsen'evu." In *Strany i narody Vostoka*, 20: 57–80. Moscow: Nauka, 1979.

——— [A. I. Vasina]. *Vladimir Klavdievich Arsen'ev*. Moscow: Nauka, 1985.

Tepliakov, Iurii Nikolaevich. *Bereg Rossii*. Moscow: Politizdat, 1987.

Tibekin, Aleksandr Romanovich. *Organizatsiia i ekonomika sel'skogo khoziaistva Dal'nevostochnogo ekonomicheskogo raiona (1858–1985 gg.)*. Khabarovsk: KKI, 1989.

Tikhomirov, Mikhail Nikolaevich, ed. *Sbornik statei po istorii Dal'nego Vostoka*. Moscow: AN SSSR, 1958.

Timofeev, P. *Porto-franko na Dal'nem Vostoke i rossiiskii kosmopolitizm*. Moscow: I. D. Sytin, 1908.

Tokarev, Sergei Aleksandrovich. *Ocherk istorii iakutskogo naroda*. Moscow: Gosizdat, 1940.

Trofimov, I. P. "Rabochie zolotodobyvaiushchei promyshlennosti Dal'nego Vostoka v 1860–1917 gg." In *Narody sovetskogo Dal'nego Vostoka v dooktiabrskii period istorii SSSR*, pp. 38–48. Vladivostok: AN SSSR, 1968.

Tselishchev, M. I., ed. *Materialy po raionirovaniiu Dal'nego Vostoka*. Khabarovsk: Dal'plankom, 1925.

Tsvigun, Semen Kuz'mich. "Khudozhnik i granitsa." *Literaturnaia gazeta*, 17 Jan. 1979.

Tvoi rodnoi krai. Comp. A. E. Tikhonova. Khabarovsk: KKI, 1982.

Udovenko, Vitalii Grigor'evich. *Dal'nii Vostok*. Moscow: Gosizdat, 1957.

Unpelev, Georgii Aleksandrovich. *Sotsialisticheskaia industrializatsiia Dal'nego Vostoka*. Vladivostok: DVKI, 1972.

——. *Zavershenie sotsialisticheskoi rekonstruktsii promyshlennosti Dal'nego Vostoka (1933–1937 gg.)*. Vladivostok: DVGU, 1975.

Unterberger, Pavel Fedorovich. *Priamurskii krai, 1906–1910 gg*. St. Petersburg: V. F. Kirshbaum, 1912.

——. *Primorskaia oblast', 1856–1898 gg*. St. Petersburg: V. F. Kirshbaum, 1900.

USSR, KPSS. *XI s"ezd RKP(b): Stenograficheskii otchet*. Moscow: Gospolitizdat, 1961.

——, —. *XV s"ezd VKP(b): Stenograficheskii otchet*. Moscow: Gospolitizdat, 1962.

——, —. *XVI s"ezd VKP(b): Stenograficheskii otchet*. Moscow: Gosizdat, 1930.

——, —. *XVII s"ezd VKP(b): Stenograficheskii otchet*. Moscow: Partizdat, 1934.

——, —. *XVIII s"ezd VKP(b): Stenograficheskii otchet*. Moscow: Gospolitizdat, 1939.

——, —. *XXII s"ezd KPSS: Stenograficheskii otchet*. Moscow: Gospolitizdat, 1962.

——, —. *Shestnadtsataia konferentsiia VKP(b): Stenograficheskii otchet*. Moscow: Gospolitizdat, 1962.

——, —. Dal'kraikom. *Deviataia Dal'nevostochnaia kraevaia partiinaia konferentsiia: Stenograficheskii otchet*. Khabarovsk: Dal'kraikom VKP(b), 1929.

Ustiev, Evgenii Konstantinovich. *U istokov zolotoi reki*. Khabarovsk: KKI, 1985.

V toi kipuchei bor'be: Zamechatel'nye dal'nevostochniki. Ed. G. S. Chechulina. Khabarovsk: KKI, 1980.

Vainshtein, I. A. "Iz istorii CHON Dal'nego Vostoka (1923–1924 gg.)." In *Voprosy istorii Dal'nego Vostoka*, vol. 4, pp. 109–28. Khabarovsk: Khab. gospedinstitut, 1974.

Vasil'chenko, El'vira Aleksandrovna. *Partiinoe rukovodstvo deiatel'nost'iu chekistskikh organov po bor'be s kontrrevoliutsiei na Dal'nem Vostoke (1920–1922)*. Vladivostok: DVGU, 1984.

Vasil'ev, Viacheslav. "Zemlia neotkrytaia: Iz istorii literaturnogo osvoeniia Kamchatki." *Dal'nii Vostok*, 1990, no. 10: 151–58.

Vasil'evskii, Ruslan Sergeevich. *Arkheologiia Amuro-Sakhalinskogo regiona*. Vladivostok: DVNTs, 1979.

——. *Drevnie kul'tury Tikhookeanskogo severa*. Novosibirsk: Nauka, 1973.

Vaskevich, Pavel Georgievich. "Ocherk byta iapontsev v Priamurskom krae." *Izvestiia Vostochnogo Instituta*, 15, 1906, no. 1: 1–31.

Velikaia Otechestvennaia voina 1941–1945: Entsiklopediia. Moscow: Sovetskaia entsiklopediia, 1985.

Veniukov, Mikhail Ivanovich. *Puteshestviia po Priamur'iu, Kitaiu i Iaponii*. Khabarovsk: KKI, 1970.

Verin, L. "Zolotaia Kolyma i Chukotka v surovye gody Velikoi Otechestvennoi voiny (1941–1945)." In *Deiatel'nost' kommunisticheskoi partii Sovetskogo Soiuza po razvitiiu proizvoditel'nykh sil i ukrepleniiu oboronosposobnosti Dal'nego Vostoka (1917–1976 gg.)*, pp. 131–33. Vladivostok: DVGU, 1976.

Ves' Dal'nii Vostok: Spravochnik. Khabarovsk: Dal'kta, 1925.

Ves' Kharbin. Harbin: KVZhD [Kitaisko-vostochnaia zheleznaia doroga], 1926.

Ves' Vladivostok: Spravochnik na 1935/36 g. Vladivostok: Primorsk. oblast. spravoch. infor. kontory, 1936.

Vetoshkin, Mikhail Kuz'mich. *Bol'sheviki Dal'nego Vostoka v pervoi russkoi revoliutsii*. Moscow: Gospolitizdat, 1956.

Vilenskii, Vladimir Dmitrievich [Sibiriakov]. *Rossiia na Dal'nem Vostoke*. Moscow: VVRS, 1923.

Vinogradov, A. *V dal'nikh kraiakh*. Moscow: I. N. Kushnerev, 1901.

Vishnevskii, E. K. *Argonavty beloi mechty*. Harbin: n.p., 1933.

Vladivostok, 1860–1960. Vladivostok: Primorskoe knizh. izdat., 1960.

Vladivostok: Gorod u okeana. Moscow: Planeta, 1980.

Vladivostok: Shtrikhi k portretu. Vladivostok: DVKI, 1985.

Voennyi entsiklopedicheskii slovar'. 2d ed. Moscow: Voenizdat, 1986.

Voishnis, Vatslav Eduardovich. "Bol'sheviki Dal'nego Vostoka v bor'be s pravym uklonom v VKP(b) (1928–1930 gg.)." In *Voprosy istorii Dal'nego Vostoka*, pp. 209–39. Khabarovsk: Khab. gospedinstitut, 1975.

———. "Iz istorii formirovaniia sovetskoi intelligentsii na Dal'nem Vostoke (1933–1937 gg.)." In *Kul'turnoe stroitel'stvo na Dal'nem Vostoke SSSR*, pp. 50–111. Khabarovsk: Khab. gospedinstitut, 1980.

Volgin, F. *Amur*. St. Petersburg: Soikin, 1896.

Volkogonov, Dmitrii Antonovich. *Triumf i tragediia: Politicheskii portret I. V. Stalina*. 2 vols. 4 parts. Moscow: Novosti, 1989.

Volobuev, O. V., and V. M. Chernyi. "Oskar Sergeevich Tarkhanov." *Narody Azii i Afriki*, 1971, no. 6: 211–14.

Voprosy ekonomiki Dal'nego Vostoka. Blagoveshchensk: Amur. knizh. izdat., 1958.

Voprosy istorii Dal'nego Vostoka. 3 vols. Khabarovsk: Khab. gospedinstitut, 1973–75.

Voprosy istorii partiinykh organizatsii Dal'nego Vostoka. Khabarovsk: Vysshaia Partiinaia Shkola, 1968.

Voprosy istorii sovetskogo Dal'nego Vostoka. Vladivostok: SO AN SSSR, 1963.

Voprosy partiinoi raboty: Iz opyta organizatsii KPSS Dal'nego Vostoka. Blagoveshchensk: Vysshaia Partiinaia Shkola, 1970.

Vorob'ev, Valentin Petrovich. *Vperedi atakuiushchikh*. Moscow: Politizdat, 1983.

Voronov, A., and V. Bogdanov. *Byt' bditel'nym, strogo khranit' voennuiu i gosudarstvennuiu tainu*. Khabarovsk: Dal'giz, 1946.

Vorontsov, V., and A. Muradian. "Rossiiskii Dal'nii Vostok: Dal'nevostochnyi regionalizm." *Problemy Dal'nego Vostoka*, 1991, no. 6: 21–27.

Vostrikov, Leonid Aleksandrovich. *I privesti v izvestnost' krai*. Khabarovsk: KKI, 1989.

Vostrikov, Leonid Aleksandrovich, and Zosima Vasil'evich Vostokov. *Khabarovsk i khabarovchane*. Khabarovsk: KKI, 1991.

Vysheslavtsev, Aleksei Vladimirovich. *Ocherki perom i karandashom iz krugosvetnogo plavaniia v 1857, 1858 i 1860 godakh*. St. Petersburg: M. O. Vol'f, 1867.

Za rabochee delo. Iuzhno-Sakhalinsk: DVKI, 1987.

Za sovetskuiu vlast' v Iakutii: Vospominaniia. Iakutsk: Iakutsk. knizh. izdat., 1967.

Zaitseva, S. *Pisateli malykh narodov Dal'nego Vostoka: Bibliograficheskii spravochnik*. Khabarovsk: KKI, 1966.

Zakharov, S. E. et al. *Krasnoznamennyi Tikhookeanskii flot*. Moscow: Voenizdat, 1966. Rev. ed. Moscow: Voenizdat, 1981.

Zasel'skii, Vladimir Ilych. "*Vestnik DVO* Obraztsa 1932–1939 gg." *Vestnik DVO AN SSSR*, 2 parts, 1990, no. 1: 151–55; no. 2: 150–55.

Zashchitniki Otechestva: Geroicheskaia oborona Petropavlovska-Kamchatskogo v 1854 godu: Sbornik ofitsial'nykh dokumentov, vospominanii, statei i pisem. Ed. B. P. Polevoi. Petropavlovsk: Dal'nevostoch. knizh. izdat., 1989.

Zdor, D. A. "Bol'shevistskaia pechat' Dal'nego Vostoka v bor'be za ob"edinenie literaturnykh sil kraia (1925–1932 gg.)." In *Materialy po istorii Dal'nego Vostoka*, pp. 204–7. Vladivostok: IIAENDV, 1974.

Zemlia, na kotoroi ia schastliv: Evreiskoi avtonomnoi oblasti-50 let. Khabarovsk: KKI, 1984.

Zhernakov, V. N. *Nikolai Apollonovich Baikov*. Melbourne: Melbourne Univ., 1968.

Zhikharev, Nikolai Aleksandrovich. *Ocherki istorii Severo-Vostoka RSFSR, 1917–1953*. Magadan: MKI, 1961.

Zhukov, Iurii [Georgii Aleksandrovich]. *Granitsa*. Moscow: Khudozhlit, 1938.
———. *Kak my bili iaponskikh samuraev*. Moscow: Molodaia gvardiia, 1938.

Zibarev, V., and N. Chistiakova. *S pomoshch'iu pobedivshego proletariata: O pomoshchi sovetskogo gosudarstva v preodolenii otstalosti malykh narodnostei Dal'nego Vostoka pri perekhode k sotsializmu*. Magadan: MKI, 1982.

Zotik Nikolaevich Matveev: K 100-letiiu co dnia rozhdeniia. Vladivostok: Primorskaia Kraevaia Biblioteka im. A. M. Gor'kogo, 1990.

V. Published Sources in Western Languages

Abramsky, Chimen. "The Birobidzhan Project, 1927–1959." In Lionel Kochan, ed., *The Jews in the Soviet Union Since 1917*, pp. 62–75. New York: Oxford Univ. Press, 1970.

Akashi Motojirō. *Rakka ryūsui: Colonel Akashi's Report on His Secret Cooperation with the Russian Revolutionary Parties during the Russo-Japanese War*. Tr. Inaba Chiharu. Ed. Olavi K. Fält and Antti Kujala. Helsinki: Societas Historica Finlandiae, 1988.

Albrecht, Karl I. *Der verratene Sozialismus, zehn Jahre als hoher Staatsbeamter in der Sowjetunion*. Berlin-Leipzig: Nibelungen, 1939.

Amur Territory: Business Directory. Vladivostok: Information Technology Lab, 1993.

Armstrong, Terence E. *The Northern Sea Route*. Cambridge: Cambridge Univ. Press, 1952.

———. *Russian Settlement in the North*. Cambridge: Cambridge Univ. Press, 1965.

Arnovitz, Banton. "Zion in Siberia." *Survey*, 29, no. 3 (Aug. 1985): 129–52.

Arsenjew [Arseniev], Wladimir K. *Russen und Chinesen in Ostsibirien*. Berlin: August Scherl, 1926. Translation of *Kitaitsy v Ussuriiskom krae: Ocherki istorichesko-etnograficheskii*. Khabarovsk: Tip. Kantseliarii Priamurskogo general'-gubernatora, 1914.

Arseniev, Vladimir Klavdievich. *Dersu the Trapper*. Tr. Malcolm Burr. New York: E. P. Dutton, 1941.

Ascher, Abraham. *The Revolution of 1905*. Stanford, Calif.: Stanford Univ. Press, 1988.

Bassin, Mark. "Expansion and Colonialism on the Eastern Frontier: Views of Siberia and the Far East in Pre-Petrine Russia." *Journal of Historical Geography*, 14, no. 1 (1988): 3–21.

———. "Inventing Siberia: Visions of the Russian East in the Early Nineteenth Century." *American Historical Review*, 96, no. 3 (June 1991): 763–94.

———. "Russia Between Europe and Asia: The Ideological Construction of Geography." *Slavic Review*, 50, no. 1 (Spring 1991): 1–17.

———. "The Russian Geographical Society, the 'Amur Epoch,' and the Great Siberian Expedition 1855–1863." *Annals of the Association of American Geographers*, 73, no. 2 (1983): 240–56.

Beloff, Max. *Soviet Policy in the Far East, 1944–1951*. London: Oxford Univ. Press, 1953.

Beveridge, Albert J. *The Russian Advance*. New York: Harper, 1904.

Biographical Dictionary of the Comintern. Ed. Branko Lazitch, in collaboration with Milorad M. Drachkovitch. Stanford, Calif.: Hoover Institution Press, 1986.

Bishop, Mrs. [Isabella L. Bird]. *Korea and Her Neighbors*. London: John Murray, 1898.

Black, J. L. *G. F. Müller and the Imperial Russian Academy*. Kingston and Montreal: McGill-Queen's Univ. Press, 1986.

Bobrick, Benson. *East of the Sun: The Epic Conquest and Tragic History of Siberia*. New York: Poseidon Press, 1992.

Bolkhovitinov, Nikolai N. *The Beginnings of Russian-American Relations, 1775–1815*. Tr. Elena Levin. Cambridge, Mass.: Harvard Univ. Press, 1975.

Bushnell, John. *Mutiny Amid Repression: Russian Soldiers in the Revolution of 1905–1906*. Bloomington: Univ. of Indiana Press, 1985.

Business Nakhodka: Reference Book. Vladivostok: International Technology Lab, 1992.

Business Sakhalin: Reference Book. Vladivostok: International Technology Lab, 1992.

Chard, Chester S. *Northeast Asia in Prehistory*. Madison: Univ. of Wisconsin Press, 1974.

Chekhov, Anton. *A Journey to Sakhalin*. Tr. Brian Reeve. Cambridge, U.K.: Ian Faulkner Publishing, 1993.

China, Ministry of Foreign Affairs. "Refutation of the Soviet Government's Statement of June 13, 1969." *Peking Review*, 41 (10 Oct. 1969): 8–15.

Cochrane, Capt. John Dundas. *A Pedestrian Journey Through Russia and Siberian Tartary to the Frontiers of China, the Frozen Sea and Kamtchatka*. Edinburgh: Constable, 1829.

Coleman, Frederic. *Japan Moves North*. London: Cassell, 1918.

Collins, Perry McDonough. *A Voyage Down the Amoor with a Land Journey Through Siberia and Incidental Notices of Manchooria, Kamschatka and Japan*. New York: Appleton, 1860.

Colton, Timothy J. *Commissars, Commanders, and Civilian Authority: The Structure of Soviet Military Politics*. Cambridge, Mass.: Harvard Univ. Press, 1979.

Conolly, Violet. *Siberia Today and Tomorrow*. New York: Taplinger, 1975.

Conquest, Robert. *The Great Terror*. New York: Macmillan, 1968.

——. *The Great Terror: A Reassessment*. New York: Oxford Univ. Press, 1990.

——. *Inside Stalin's Secret Police: NKVD Politics, 1936–39*. Stanford, Calif.: Hoover Institution Press, 1985.

——. *Kolyma: The Arctic Death Camps*. New York: Viking, 1978.

Coox, Alvin D. "L'Affaire Lyushkov: Anatomy of a Defector." *Soviet Studies*, 19, no. 3 (Jan. 1968): 405–20.

——. *The Anatomy of a Small War: The Soviet-Japanese Struggle for Changkufeng/Khasan, 1938*. Westport, Conn.: Greenwood, 1977.

——. *Nomonhan: Japan Against Russia, 1939*. 2 vols. Stanford, Calif.: Stanford Univ. Press, 1985.

Da Cunha, Derek. "The Maritime Border Guard of the KGB." *International Defense Review*, 12 (Dec. 1988): 1563–1567.

Dagor, K. "Magadan." *Sovietland*, no. 4 (Apr. 1939): 33.

Dallin, Alexander. *Black Box: KAL 007 and the Superpowers*. Berkeley: Univ. of California Press, 1985.

Dallin, David J. *The Rise of Russia in Asia*. New Haven, Conn.: Yale Univ. Press, 1949.

——. *Soviet Russia and the Far East*. New Haven, Conn.: Yale Univ. Press, 1948.

Dallin, David J., and Boris I. Nicolaevsky. *Forced Labor in Soviet Russia*. New Haven, Conn.: Yale Univ. Press, 1947.

Davies, Raymond Arthur, and Andrew J. Steiger. *Soviet Asia: Democracy's First Line of Defense*. New York: Dial, 1942.

Deane, John R. *The Strange Alliance*. New York: Viking, 1947.

Debo, Richard K. *Survival and Consolidation: The Foreign Policy of Soviet Russia, 1918–1921*. Montreal: McGill-Queen's Univ. Press, 1992.

The Deportation of Grigorii Semenov. Hong Kong: Beamur, 1972.

De Sabir, C. *Le Fleuve Amoûr: Histoire Geographie, Ethnographie*. Paris: Kugelman, 1861.

Dibb, Paul. *Siberia and the Pacific*. New York: Praeger, 1972.

Dienes, Leslie. "Economic and Strategic Position of the Soviet Far East." *Soviet Economy*, 1, no. 2 (Apr.–June 1985): 146–76.

———. "Soviet-Japanese Economic Relations: Are They Beginning to Fade?" *Soviet Geography*: 26, no. 7 (Sept. 1985): 509–25.

Diment, Galya, and Yuri Slezkine, eds. *Between Heaven and Hell: The Myth of Siberia in Russian Culture*. New York: St. Martin's Press, 1993.

Dmytryshyn, Basil. "The Administrative Apparatus of the Russian Colony in Siberia and Northern Asia, 1581–1700." In Alan Wood, ed. *The History of Siberia*, pp. 17–36. London: Routledge, 1991.

Dmytryshyn, Basil, E. A. P. Crownhart-Vaughan, and Thomas Vaughan, eds. *Russia's Conquest of Siberia: A Documentary Record, 1558–1700*. Portland: Oregon Historical Society, 1985.

———. *The Russian American Colonies, 1798–1867: A Documentary Record*. Portland: Oregon Historical Society, 1989.

———. *Russian Penetration of the North Pacific Ocean, 1700–1799. A Documentary Record*. Portland: Oregon Historical Society, 1988.

Dotsenko, Paul. *The Struggle for a Democracy in Siberia, 1917–1920*. Stanford, Calif.: Hoover Institution Press, 1983.

Emiot, Israel. *The Birobidzhan Affair*. Philadelphia: Jewish Publication Society of America, 1981.

Encyclopedia Judaica. Vol. 4. Jerusalem: Keter, 1971.

Erickson, John. "Military and Strategic Factors." In Alan Wood, ed., *Siberia: Problems and Prospects for Regional Development*, pp. 171–92. London: Croom Helm, 1987.

———. *The Soviet High Command: A Military-Political History, 1918–1941*. London: St. Martin's Press, 1962.

The Far Eastern Republic, Siberia, and Japan. New York: Foreign Policy Association, 1922.

Findlay, John, and Dorothy Findlay. "Letters from Vladivostok, 1918–1923." *Slavonic and East European Review*, 45, no. 105 (July 1967): 497–530.

Fisher, Raymond H. *Bering's Voyages: Whither and Why*. Seattle: Univ. of Washington Press, 1977.

———. *The Russian Fur Trade, 1550–1700*. Berkeley: Univ. of California Press, 1943.

Fithian, Floyd J. "Dollars Without the Flag: The Case of Sinclair and Sakhalin Oil." *Pacific Historical Review*, 39, no. 2 (May 1970): 205–22.

Forsyth, James. "Chinese Place-Names in the Russian Far East." In W. Ritchie, ed., *Essays for Professor R. E. H. Mellor*, pp. 133–39. Aberdeen, Scotland: Univ. of Aberdeen Press, 1986.

——. *A History of the Peoples of Siberia*. Cambridge: Cambridge Univ. Press, 1992.

Fraser, John Foster. *The Real Siberia*. London: Cassell, 1902.

FRUS, *see* United States, Dept. of State.

Garrett, Wilber, and Steve Raymer. "Air Bridge to Siberia." *National Geographic Magazine*, 174, no. 4 (Oct. 1988): 504–9.

Gaunt, Mary. *A Broken Journey*. Philadelphia: Lippincott, 1918.

Gayn, Mark. *Journey from the East*. New York: Knopf, 1944.

Gerrare, Wirt [William Oliver Greener]. *Greater Russia*. London: Heinemann, 1904.

Getty, J. Arch. *Origins of the Great Purges*. Cambridge: Cambridge Univ. Press, 1985.

Geyer, Dietrich. *Russian Imperialism: The Interaction of Domestic and Foreign Policy, 1860–1914*. New York: Berg, 1987.

Gibson, James R. *Feeding the Russian Fur Trade*. Madison: Univ. of Wisconsin Press, 1969.

——. *Imperial Russia in Frontier America*. New York: Oxford Univ. Press, 1976.

——. "Tsarist Russia in Colonial America: Critical Constraints." In Alan Wood, ed. *The History of Siberia*, pp. 92–116. London: Routledge, 1991.

Ginsburgs, George. "The Citizenship Status of Koreans in Pre-Revolutionary Russia and the Early Years of the Soviet Regime." *Korean Affairs*, 5, no. 2 (July 1975): 1–19.

Ginzburg, Evgeniia. *Journey into the Whirlwind*. Tr. Paul Stevenson and Max Hayward. New York: Harcourt Brace Jovanovich, 1975.

——. *Within the Whirlwind*. Tr. Ian Boland. New York: Harcourt Brace Jovanovich, 1981.

Gold Resources and the Gold Mining Industry of the Far Eastern Republic. Washington, D.C.: Special Delegation of the Far Eastern Republic to the United States of America, 1922.

Golder, F. A. "Russian-American Relations During the Crimean War." *American Historical Review*, 31, no. 2 (Jan. 1926): 462–76.

——. *Russian Expansion on the Pacific, 1641–1850*. Cleveland: Arthur H. Clark, 1914.

Gorbachev, Mikhail. *A New Stage in the Development of the Soviet Far East*. Moscow: Novosti, 1986.

Graves, William S. *America's Siberian Adventure*. New York: Peter Smith, 1941 [1931].

Great Britain, Naval Staff, Intelligence Department. *A Handbook of Siberia and Arctic Russia*. London: H.M. Stationery Office, 1918.

———, War Office, Intelligence Division. *The Shores of the Northwest Pacific*. London: H.M. Stationery Office, 1878.

Greener, Richard T. "Education Notes from Siberia." In *Annual Reports of the Department of Interior, 1899–1900*, vol. 2, pp. 1427–31. Washington, D.C.: Government Printing Office, 1901.

Grigorenko, Pyotr Grigor'evich. *Memoirs*. Tr. Thomas P. Whitney. New York: Norton, 1982.

Gruber, Ruth. *I Went to the Soviet Arctic*. New York: Viking Press, 1944.

Guide to the Great Siberian Railway. Ed. A. I. Dmitriev-Mamonov and A. F. Zdziarski. St. Petersburg: Artistic Printing Society, 1971 [1900].

Harrison, J. *Peace or War East of Baikal?* Yokohama: Kelly and Walsh, 1910.

Harrison, Marguerite E. *Red Bear or Yellow Dragon?* New York: Doran, 1924.

Hasegawa, Tsuyoshi, Jonathan Haslam, and Andrew C. Kuchins, ed. *Russia and Japan: An Unresolved Dilemma Between Distant Neighbors*. Berkeley: International and Area Studies, Univ. of California, 1993.

Haslam, Jonathan. *The Soviet Union and the Threat from the East, 1933–1941*. London: Macmillan, 1992.

Hauner, Milan. *What Is Asia to Us?* Boston: Unwin Hyman, 1990.

Hays, Otis. *Home from Siberia*. College Station: Texas A&M Univ. Press, 1990.

Hazard, John N. *Recollections of a Pioneering Sovietologist*. New York: Oceana, 1984.

Heller, Otto. *Die rote Fahne am Pazifik: Zehn Jahre Sowjetmacht im Fernen Osten*. Moscow: Verlagsgenossenschaft Ausländischer Arbeiter in der UdSSR, 1933.

Herrmann, Albert. *An Historical Atlas of China*. Chicago: Aldine, 1966 [1935].

Hoetzsch, Otto. *Russland in Asien*. Stuttgart: Deutsche Verlags-Anstalt, 1966.

Hughes, James. *Stalin, Siberia, and the Crisis of the New Economic Policy*. Cambridge: Cambridge Univ. Press, 1991.

James, Henry Evan Murchison. *The Long White Mountain or a Journey in Manchuria*. London: Longmans, 1888.

Janhunen, Juha. "The Tungus Peoples and the Conquest of Siberia." In *Kungl. Vitterhets Historie och Antikvitets, Akademiens Konferenser*, vol. 12, pp. 73–77. Stockholm, 1985.

Japanese Intervention in the Russian Far East. Washington, D.C.: Special Delegation of the Far Eastern Republic to the United States of America, 1922.

Jochelson, Waldemar [Vladimir Yokhelson]. *Peoples of Asiatic Russia*. New York: American Museum of Natural History, 1928.

Kabuzan, V. M. "The Settlement of Siberia and the Far East from the Late 18th to the Early 20th Century (1795–1917)." *Soviet Geography*, 32, no. 9 (Nov. 1991): 616–32.

Kennan, George. *Siberia and the Exile System*. 2 vols. London: Osgood, McIlvaine, 1891.

———. *Tent Life in Siberia*. New York: G. P. Putnam, 1870.

Kennan, George F. "Soviet Historiography and America's Role in the Intervention." In John Keep and Liliana Brisby, eds., *Contemporary History in the Soviet Mirror*, pp. 286–305. New York: Praeger, 1964.

Kerner, Robert J. *The Urge to the Sea*. Berkeley: Univ. of California Press, 1942.

Khisamutdinov, Amir. *The Russian Far East: Historical Essays*. Honolulu, n.p., 1993.

Kindall, Sylvian G. *American Soldiers in Siberia*. New York: Richard R. Smith, 1945.

Kirby, E. Stuart. *The Soviet Far East*. London: Macmillan, 1971.

Knox, Thomas W. *Overland Through Asia: Pictures of Siberian, Chinese, and Tartar Life*. Hartford, Conn.: American Publishing Co., 1870.

Kolarz, Walter. *The Peoples of the Soviet Far East*. New York: Archon, 1969 [1954].

Kornilov, Mikhail. "From Siberia to Finland." *Journal de la Société Finno-Ougrienne*, 82 (1989): 101–21.

Krasheninnikov, Stepan Petrovich. *Explorations of Kamchatka*. Tr. E. A. P. Crownhart-Vaughan. Portland: Oregon Historical Society, 1972.

Krivitsky, W. G. *I Was Stalin's Agent*. London: Hamish Hamilton, 1939.

Kropotkin, P. *Memoirs of a Revolutionist*. New York: Horizon, 1968.

Kunert, Dirk. *General Ljuschkows Geheimbericht über die Stalinische Fernostpolitik 1937/38*. Bern, Switzerland: Heraus. vom Schweizerischen Ost-Institut, n.d. [ca. 1980].

Kuropatkin, General [Aleksei Nikolaevich]. *The Russian Army and the Japanese War*. Trans. A. B. Lindsay. 2 vols. New York: Dutton, 1909.

Landgraf, Dieter. *Amur, Ussuri, Sachalin*. Neuried, Germany: Hieronymus, 1989.

Lantzeff, George V. *Siberia in the Seventeenth Century: A Study of Colonial Administration*. Berkeley: Univ. of California Press, 1943.

Lantzeff, George V., and Richard A. Pierce. *Eastward to Empire: Exploration and Conquest on the Russian Open Frontier to 1750*. Montreal: McGill-Queens Univ. Press, 1973.

Lattimore, Owen. *China Memoirs*. Comp. Fujiko Isono. Tokyo: Univ. of Tokyo Press, 1990.

———. "New Road to Asia." *National Geographic Magazine* 86, no. 6 (Dec. 1944): 641–76.

Laufer, Berthold. "The Decorative Art of Amur Tribes." *Memoirs of the American Museum of Natural History*, 7 (Jan. 1902): 1–86.

Lauterbach, Richard E. *Through Russia's Back Door*. New York: Harper, 1946.

Lee, Chong-Sik. *Revolutionary Struggle in Manchuria: Chinese Communism and Soviet Interest*. Berkeley: Univ. of California Press, 1983.

Lee, Robert H. G. *The Manchurian Frontier in Ch'ing History*. Cambridge, Mass.: Harvard Univ. Press, 1970.

Lengyel, Emil. *Siberia*. Garden City, N.Y.: Garden City, 1943.

Lensen, George Alexander. *The Russian Push Toward Japan: Russo-Japanese Relations, 1697–1875*. Princeton, N.J.: Princeton Univ. Press, 1959.

——. *The Russo-Chinese War*. Tallahassee, Fla.: Diplomatic Press, 1967.

——. *The Strange Neutrality: Soviet-Japanese Relations During the Second World War, 1941–1945*. Tallahassee, Fla.: Diplomatic Press, 1972.

Léon, Max. *A Frenchman Discovers the Soviet Far East*. Moscow: Foreign Languages Publishing House, 1961.

Leong, Sow-Theng. *Sino-Soviet Relations, 1917–1926*. Honolulu: Univ. of Hawaii Press, 1976.

Levin, M. G. *Ethnic Origins of the Peoples of Northeastern Asia*. Ed. Henry N. Michael. Toronto: Univ. of Toronto Press, 1963.

Levin, Nora. *The Jews in the Soviet Union Since 1917*. New York: SUNY Press, 1988.

Levine, Steven I. *Anvil of Victory: The Communist Revolution in Manchuria, 1945–1948*. New York: Columbia Univ. Press, 1987.

Lipper, Elinor. *Eleven Years in Soviet Prison Camps*. Chicago: Regnery, 1951.

Lobanov-Rostovsky, Andrei. *Russia and Asia*. New York: Macmillan 1933.

Lvavi, Jacob. *The Jewish Colonization in Birobidzhan*. Jerusalem: Historical Society of Israel, 1965.

McCune, Evelyn and Shannon McCune. "The Tumen River Corridor." *Far Eastern Survey*, 14, no. 12 (20 June 1945): 164–166.

Mackintosh, J. M. "The Soviet Army in the Far East, 1922–1955." In B. H. Liddell Hart, ed., *The Soviet Army*, pp. 172–81. London: Weidenfeld and Nicolson, 1956.

Maier, Lothar. "Gerhard Friedrich Müller's Memorandum on Russian Relations with China and the Reconquest of the Amur." *Slavonic and East European Review*, 59, no. 2 (Apr. 1981): 219–40.

Malozemoff, Andrew. *Russian Far Eastern Policy, 1881–1904*. Berkeley: Univ. of California Press, 1958.

Mancall, Mark. *Russia and China: Their Diplomatic Relations to 1728*. Cambridge, Mass.: Harvard Univ. Press, 1971.

Mandel, William. *The Soviet Far East and Central Asia*. New York: Institute of Pacific Relations, 1944.

March, G. Patrick. "Yanks in Siberia: U.S. Navy Weather Stations in Soviet East Asia, 1945." *Pacific Historical Review*, 57, no. 3 (Aug. 1988): 327–42.

Marks, Steven G. *Road to Power: The Trans-Siberian Railroad and the Colonization of Asian Russia, 1850–1917*. Ithaca, N.Y.: Cornell Univ. Press, 1991.

Meakin, Annette M. B. *A Ribbon of Iron*. Westminster, Eng.: Constable, 1901.

Medvedev, Roy A. *Let History Judge: The Origins and Consequences of Stalinism*. Tr. Colleen Taylor. New York: Knopf, 1972. Rev. enlarged ed. tr. George Shriver. New York: Columbia Univ. Press, 1989.

Miagkoff, Efim Dmitrievich. *Aux bords du Pacifique*. Lausanne: Miagkoff, 1916.

Mihalisko, Kathleen. "SOS for Native Peoples of Soviet North." *Report on the USSR*, 1, no. 5 (3 Feb. 1989): 3–6.

Modern Encyclopedia of Russian and Soviet History. 55 vols. Gulf Breeze, Fla.: Academic International, 1976–93.

Montandon, George. *Deux ans chez Koltchak et chez les Bolcheviques.* Paris: Alcan, 1923.

Morley, James William. *The Japanese Thrust into Siberia.* New York: Columbia Univ. Press, 1957.

———. "The Russian Revolution in the Amur Basin." *American Slavic and East European Review,* 16, no. 4 (Dec. 1957): 450–72.

Mote, Victor L. "Containerization and the Trans-Siberian Land Bridge." *Geographical Review,* 74, no. 3 (July 1984): 304–13.

Nimmo, William F. *Behind a Curtain of Silence: Japanese in Soviet Custody, 1945–1956.* Westport, Conn.: Greenwood, 1988.

North, Robert N. "The Soviet Far East." *Pacific Affairs,* 51, no. 2 (Summer 1978): 195–215.

Norton, Henry Kittredge. *The Far Eastern Republic of Siberia.* New York: John Day, 1927.

Okladnikov, Aleksei Pavlovich. *The Soviet Far East in Antiquity.* Tr. and ed. Henry N. Michael. Toronto: Univ. of Toronto Press, 1965.

Ossipenko, Paulina [Polina Denisovna Osipenko]. *The Soviet Far East.* Moscow: Foreign Languages Publishing House, 1939.

Ota Kakumin, "Romantic Experience of a Japanese Buddhist Priest in Siberia." *Young East,* 1, no. 10 (Mar. 1926): 328–30.

Ovchinnikov, Anton Zakharovich. "Memoirs of the Red Partisan Movement in the Russian Far East, 1918–1920." In Elena Varneck and H. H. Fisher, eds., *The Testimony of Kolchak and Other Siberian Materials,* pp. 265–372.

Paderin, G. *Rediscovered Country.* Moscow: Foreign Languages Publishing House, n.d. [1966].

Parry, Albert [Osipovich]. "Washington B. Vanderlip, the 'Khan of Kamchatka.'" *Pacific Historical Review,* 17, no. 3 (Aug. 1948): 311–30.

———. "Yankee Whalers in Siberia." *Russian Review,* 5, no. 2 (Spring 1946): 36–49.

Pavlenko, Petr Andreevich. *Red Planes Fly East.* Tr. Stephen Garry. New York: International Publishers, 1938.

Pereira, N. G. O. "The 'Democratic Counterrevolution' of 1918 in Siberia." *Nationalities Papers,* 16, no. 1 (Spring 1988): 91–93.

———. "Regional Consciousness in Siberia Before and After October 1917." *Canadian Slavonic Papers,* 30, no. 1 (Mar. 1988): 113–33.

Petrov, Vladimir. *Soviet Gold.* Tr. Mirra Ginsburg. New York: Farrar, Straus, 1949.

Pinkus, Benjamin. *The Jews of the Soviet Union.* Cambridge: Cambridge Univ. Press, 1988.

Poppe, Nicholaus. "The Economic and Cultural Development of Siberia." In Erwin Oberländer, ed., *Russia Enters the Twentieth Century, 1894–1917,* pp. 138–51. London: Temple Smith, 1971.

Price, M. Philips. *Siberia*. London: Methuen, 1912.

Quested, R. K. I. *The Expansion of Russia in East Asia, 1857–1860*. Kuala Lumpur: Univ. of Malaya Press, 1968.

——. *"Matey" Imperialists? The Tsarist Russians in Manchuria, 1895–1917*. Hong Kong: Univ. of Hong Kong Press, 1982.

RA [Russia in Asia] Report. Honolulu: Center for Russia in Asia, 1993–

Rachlin, Rachel, and Israel Rachlin. *Sixteen Years in Siberia*. Tr. Birgitte M. de Weille. Tuscaloosa: Univ. of Alabama Press, 1988.

Raeff, Marc. *Siberia and the Reforms of 1822*. Seattle: Univ. of Washington Press, 1956.

Raikhman, E. [Elizar Grigor'evich]. *The Economic Development of the Soviet Far East*. New York: American Russian Institute, 1936.

Rapoport, Vitaly, and Yuri Alexeev. *High Treason: Essays on the History of the Red Army, 1918–1938*. Ed. Vladimir G. Treml and Bruce Adams. Durham, N.C.: Duke Univ. Press, 1985.

Ravenstein, E. G. *The Russians on the Amur: Its Discovery, Conquest, and Colonization*. London: Trubner, 1861.

Rhodes, H. Winston. *Russia: The Coming Power in the Pacific*. Wellington, N.Z.: Progressive Publishing Society, 1944.

Riasanovsky, Nicholas V. "Asia Through Russian Eyes." In Wayne S. Vucinich, ed., *Russia and Asia*, pp. 3–29. Stanford, Calif.: Hoover Institution Press, 1972.

Rigby, T. H. *Communist Party Membership in the USSR, 1917–1967*. Princeton, N.J.: Princeton Univ. Press, 1968.

——. *Political Elites in the USSR: Central Leaders and Local Cadres from Lenin to Gorbachev*. Aldershot, Eng.: Edward Elgar, 1990.

Rodgers, Allan, ed. *The Soviet Far East: Geographical Perspectives on Development*. London: Routledge, 1990.

Russian Far East. Anchorage, 1992–93.

Russian Far East Update [*Soviet Far East Update* until 1992] Seattle, 1991–

Ryzhkov, A. *Soviet Far East: A Tour of Sakhalin*. Moscow: Progress, 1966.

Saul, Norman. "An American's Siberian Dream." *Russian Review*, 37, no. 4 (Oct. 1978): 405–20.

Schapiro, Leonard. *The Communist Party of the Soviet Union*. New York: Random House, 1971.

Schiffer, Jonathan R. *Soviet Regional Economic Policy: The East-West Debate over Pacific Siberian Development*. New York: St. Martin's Press, 1989.

Semyonov, Yuri. *Siberia: Its Conquest and Development*. Tr. J. R. Foster. Baltimore, Md.: Helicon Press, 1963.

Serapinin, A. "Prospects of Commercial Aviation in the Far East." *The Russian Far East: Economic Monthly*, 2 (Nov. 1920): 54–56.

Serebrennikov, I. I. "The Siberian Autonomous Movement and Its Future." *Pacific Historical Review*, 3, no. 4 (Dec. 1934): 400–415.

Shabad, Theodore, and Victor L. Mote. *Gateway to Siberian Resources (the BAM)*. New York: John Wiley, 1977.

Shalamov, Varlam. *Kolyma Tales*. Tr. John Glad. New York: Norton, 1980.

Shelley, Louise. "The Geography of Soviet Criminality." *American Sociological Review*, 45 (Feb. 1980): 111–22.

Shifrin, Avraham. *The First Guidebook to Prisons and Concentration Camps of the Soviet Union*. Seewis, Switzerland: Stephanus Verlags, 1980.

Shklovsky, I. W. *In Far North-east Siberia*. Tr. L. Edwards and Z. Shklovsky. London: Macmillan, 1916.

Siegelbaum, Lewis H. "Another 'Yellow Peril': Chinese Migrants in the Russian Far East and the Russian Reaction Before 1917." *Modern Asian Studies*, 12, no. 2 (Apr. 1978): 307–30.

Sieveking, Heinrich. "Die Hamburgische Firma Kunst & Albers in Wladiwostok, 1864–1914." *Vierteljahrschrift für Sozial- und Wirtschaftsgeschichte*, no. 34 (1941): 268–99.

Slezkine, Yuri. "The Fall of Soviet Ethnography, 1928–38." *Current Anthropology*, 32, no. 4 (Aug.–Oct. 1991): 476–84.

———. "From Savages to Citizens: The Cultural Revolution in the Soviet Far North, 1928–1938." *Slavic Review*, 51, no. 1 (Spring 1992): 52–76.

Smith, Canfield F. *Vladivostok under Red and White Rule*. Seattle: Univ. of Washington Press, 1975.

Snow, Russell E. *The Bolsheviks in Siberia, 1917–1918*. Rutherford, N. J.: Fairleigh Dickinson Univ. Press, 1977.

Solomon, Michael. *Magadan*. Princeton, N.J.: Auerbach, 1971.

Solzhenitsyn, Alexander I. *One Day in the Life of Ivan Denisovich*. New York: E. P. Dutton, 1963.

The Soviet Far East: Questions and Answers. Moscow: Novosti, 1985.

Soviet Far East Update. Seattle, 1991.

Spiess, Kurt. *Periphere Sowjetwirtschaft: Das Beispiel Russisch-Fernost, 1897–1970*. Zurich: Atlantis, 1980.

Stajner, Karlo. *Seven Thousand Days in Siberia*. New York: Farrar, Straus & Giroux, 1988.

Stefansson, Vilhjalmur. *The Adventure of Wrangell Island*. New York: Macmillan, 1925.

Stepanov, A. *Soviet Far East: A Tour of Khabarovsk Territory*. Moscow: Progress, 1966.

Stephan, John J. "The Crimean War in the Far East." *Modern Asian Studies*, 3, no. 3 (July 1969): 257–77.

———. "Far Eastern Conspiracies? Russian Spectres of Separatism on the Pacific." *Australian Slavonic and East European Studies*, 4, nos. 1–2 (1990): 135–52.

———. *The Kuril Islands: Russo-Japanese Frontier in the Pacific*. Oxford: Clarendon Press, 1974.

———. *The Russian Fascists: Tragedy and Farce in Exile, 1925–1945*. New York: Harper and Row, 1978.

———. *Sakhalin: A History*. Oxford: Clarendon Press, 1971.

———, ed. *USSR and the Defeat of Imperial Japan. Soviet Studies in History*, 24, no. 3 (Winter 1985–86).

Stephan, John J., and V. P. Chichkanov, ed. *Soviet-American Horizons on the Pacific*. Honolulu: Univ. of Hawaii Press, 1986.

Strod, Ivan Iakovlevich. *Civil War in the Taiga*. London: Modern Books, 1932.

Suh Dae-sook, ed. *Koreans in the Soviet Union*. Honolulu: Center for Korean Studies, 1987.

SUPAR Report, Honolulu: Center for Soviet Union in the Pacific and Asia Region, 1986–92.

Swearingen, Rodger, ed. *Siberia and the Soviet Far East*. Stanford, Calif.: Hoover Institution Press, 1987.

Swenson, Olaf. *Northwest of the World: Forty Years of Trading and Hunting in Northern Siberia*. New York: Dodd, Mead, 1944.

The Testimony of Kolchak and Other Siberian Materials. Ed. Elena Varneck and H. H. Fisher. Stanford, Calif.: Stanford Univ. Press, 1935.

Thiel, Erich. *The Soviet Far East*. Tr. Annelie and Ralph M. Rockwood. New York: Praeger, 1957.

Tikhvinsky, S. L., ed. *Chapters from the History of Russo-Chinese Relations: 17th–19th Centuries*. Moscow: Progress, 1985.

Tkachev, V., and S. Nikolayev. *Soviet Far East: A Tour of Primorye Territory*. Moscow: Progress, 1966.

Treadgold, Donald W. *The Great Siberian Migration*. Princeton, N.J.: Princeton Univ. Press, 1957.

———. "Russian Expansion in the Light of Turner's Study of the American Frontier." *Agricultural History*, 26, no. 4 (Oct. 1952): 147–52.

Tronson, J. M. *Personal Narrative of a Voyage to Japan, Kamtschatka, Siberia, Tartary, and Various Parts of the Coast of China in HMS Barracouta*. London: Smith Elder, 1859.

Tucker, Robert C. *Stalin as Revolutionary, 1879–1929*. New York: Norton, 1973.

Tupper, Harmon. *To the Great Ocean*. Boston: Little, Brown, 1965.

United States, Department of the Air Force. *Intelligence Activities: Characteristics of the Far East USSR*. Washington, D.C.: Government Printing Office, 1963.

———, Department of State. *Foreign Relations of the United States*. Washington, D.C.: Government Printing Office. Various volumes from 1896 on.

———, Hydrographic Office. *Sailing Directions for the East Coast of Siberia*. Washington, D.C.: Government Printing Office, 1947.

———, War Department, Office of the Chief of Staff. *Siberia and Eastern Russia*. 5 vols. Washington, D.C.: Government Printing Office, 1918.

Urness, Carol. *Bering's First Expedition*. New York: Garland, 1987.

Vanderlip, W. B. *In Search of a Siberian Klondike*. New York: Century, 1903.

Wallace, Henry A. *The Price of Vision: The Diary of Henry A. Wallace*. Ed. John Morton Blum. Boston: Houghton Mifflin, 1973.

——. *Soviet Asia Mission*. New York: Reynal and Hitchcock, 1946.

Walravens, Hartmut. *Ivan A. Lopatin: Erforscher der tungusischen Amurstaemme*. Hamburg: Bell, 1982.

——. *Peter Schmidt: Ostasianwissenschaftler, Linguist und Folklorist*. Hamburg: Bell, 1982.

——. *Zwei wenig bekannte russische Ostasienwissenschaftler: A. V. Rudakov und A. V. Grebenscikov*. Hamburg: Bell, 1983.

Watrous, Stephen D., ed. *John Ledyard's Journey Through Russia and Siberia, 1787–1788*. Madison: Univ. of Wisconsin Press, 1966.

Weale, B. L. Putnam [Bertram Lenox Simpsom]. *Manchu and Muscovite*. London: Macmillan, 1904.

——. *The Truce in the East and Its Aftermath*. London: Macmillan, 1907.

Weinberg, Robert. "Purge and Politics in the Periphery: Birobidzhan in 1937." *Slavic Review*, 52, no. 1 (Spring 1993): 13–27.

Wenyon, Charles. *Across Siberia*. London: C. H. Kelly, 1896.

White, John Albert. *The Diplomacy of the Russo-Japanese War*. Princeton, N.J.: Princeton Univ. Press, 1964.

——. *The Siberian Intervention*. Princeton, N.J.: Princeton Univ. Press, 1950.

Whiting, Allen S. *Siberian Development and East Asia: Threat or Promise?* Stanford, Calif.: Stanford Univ. Press, 1981.

[Witte, Sergei]. *The Memoirs of Count Witte*. Tr. and ed. Sidney Harcave. Armonk, N.Y.: M. E. Sharpe, 1990.

Wollenberg, Erich. *The Red Army*. London: Secker and Warburg, 1938.

Wood, Alan, ed. *The History of Siberia From Russian Conquest to Revolution*. London: Routledge, 1991.

——, ed. *Siberia: Problems and Prospects for Regional Development*. London: Croom Helm, 1987.

Young, John. *The Research Activities of the South Manchurian Railway Company, 1907–1945*. New York: East Asian Institute, Columbia Univ., 1966.

Zenzinov, Vladimir Mikhailovich. *The Road to Oblivion*. New York: McBride, 1931.

« « » »

Index

In this index an "f" after a number indicates a separate reference on the next page, and an "ff" indicates separate references on the next two pages. A continuous discussion over two or more pages is indicate by a span of page numbers, e.g., "pp. 57–58." *Passim* is used for a cluster of references in close but not consecutive sequence.

Library of Congress Cataloging-in-Publication Data

Stephan, John J.
The Russian Far East : a history / John J. Stephan.
p. cm.
Includes bibliographical references and index.
ISBN 0-8047-2311-7 (cl.) : ISBN 0-8047-2701-5 (pbk.)
1. Russian Far East (Russia) — History. I. Title.
DK771.D3S74   1994
950 — dc20   93-42011   CIP